THE IMPERIAL ACHIEVEMENT

*   *   *

The
Imperial
Achievement

The Rise and Transformation
of the British Empire

JOHN BOWLE

LITTLE, BROWN AND COMPANY · BOSTON · TORONTO

FIRST AMERICAN EDITION

T 07/75

Maps by Cartographic Enterprises

LIBRARY OF CONGRESS CATALOGING IN PUBLICATION DATA

Bowle, John.
  The imperial achievement.

  Includes bibliographical references and index.
  1. Great Britain—Colonies—History.
2. Great Britain—History—Modern period, 1485–
I. Title.   3-2-76
DA16.B63 1975   909′.09′71241   75-8594
ISBN 0-316-10409-4

CONTENTS

BOOK III

BOOK IV

BOOK V

LIST OF ILLUSTRATIONS

Between pages 244 *and* 245

Between pages 404 *and* 405

MAPS

PREFACE

Now that the British, having lost an Empire, are seeking a new role on the continent of Europe, they may take a more dispassionate view of their imperial past. The Jingoism of Edwardian England, the doubts, hostility and even the shame of some, the paternalism and defensive regret of others apparent since the Second World War, may now give place to a calmer assessment. Obviously it is important to make this new assessment, for even if British imperial history has come to an end, it cannot be consigned to oblivion. The British will hardly achieve a clearer sense of confidence and purpose within the European community on the basis of a collective amnesia.

Continental Europeans, too, now that the British are within their gates, naturally want to know what the islanders are like; nor can they understand them without some knowledge of their imperial as well as their insular history. Moreover, for better or worse, the history of the British, as of the other European Empires, has set the scene for new relationships between Europe and the former colonial world. Indeed, Asians and Africans themselves will need to take a new and cooler look at Europe; and as the first intoxication of independence recedes, they, too, may be able to form a picture of 'colonialism' and 'imperialism' and of their pre-colonial past free from the distortion which has mirrored the old attitudes of the former 'colonizers'.

An attempt to restore the balance of British imperial history may thus be timely; and not least also for the peoples of predominantly British stock who have formed separate nations in Canada, Australia and New Zealand. Most Americans, too, whatever their descent, are increasingly conscious of their past, being now far too realistic to believe that 'history is bunk'. And that past is rooted in British Colonial America.

Naturally, so long as history is studied anywhere, the attention and imagination of men will be caught by the rise and transformation of the greatest sea-borne Empire in world history, and by the vast and powerful Anglo-Saxon civilizations which have derived from it.

Yet just as this need for a calm judgment has arisen—in the island itself, in continental Europe, in the Commonwealth, old and new, and in the United States—there has been a curious denigration of imperial history by the British themselves: not among academic historians but among the popularizers and in the mass media.[1] The reasons for this distortion will later be considered; in general insular class resentments have been extrapolated into the history of the Empire and Commonwealth and, like adolescents out to shock their parents, those concerned have written off the world-historical achievement as an aspect of an 'establishment' all the more resented because it remains pragmatic, tenacious, adaptable and representative. Whether such versions of imperial and Commonwealth history now fashionable stand up to the facts here set out, I leave the reader to decide.

These travesties, of course, do not reflect academic knowledge; but though there is a wealth of authoritative books that fairly assess the real achievements of the British Empire and Commonwealth, many are too massive and detailed and concerned with particular areas for general reading, while few depict it as a whole and relate it to world history. In popular history, on the other hand, the balance is being restored: as in James Morris' *Pax Britannica* and Alan Moorehead's *The White Nile* and *The Fatal Impact*.

I have therefore attempted to provide a general survey of the whole field; an interpretation of the rise and transformation of the Empire and Commonwealth in the light of the modern world and the way it is going. The book forms a sequel to my *The English Experience*, and I hope rounds it off and completes it, for new facets of the British character come out in the experience of empire.

In writing this work I have incurred so many obligations to academic friends that I hope that they will accept a general and grateful

---

[1] As, for example, in a recent television series on the British Empire, which depicted Canadian history without Lord Durham; the British *Raj* in India mainly in terms of blowing 'mutineers' from guns, and with hardly any treatment of the great works which created the modern infrastructure of the sub-continent, or of the fact that the British were the first rulers to bring peace over it since Asoka. Australian history was covered without mentioning McArthur, who founded the wool industry, and without adequate description of the feats of Australian explorers—all was convicts, misery and the Eureka stockade. Yet the settings were magnificent and often little known: the colonial architecture of the West Indies, the superb scenery of the Great Lakes of Africa, the historical monuments of India, Muslim and Hindu.

acknowledgment. Sir Edgar Williams, Warden of Rhodes House, has very kindly read the proofs and saved me from various errors and inaccuracies. Professor R. E. Robinson, Beit Professor of the History of the British Commonwealth at Oxford, has read much of this book and given shrewd advice, and Mr Felix Markham has made valuable criticisms. I am particularly grateful to my publisher, Mr David Farrer, for his help over the detail and structure of the final revision, and to Mr Fredric Warburg and Mr Maurice Temple-Smith who first suggested the project. Mr J. Q. Davies of H.M. Diplomatic Service has advised me on aspects of economic history and on the correct spelling of some Muscovite names and places, and The Hon. Lady Betjeman on some recondite aspects of Indian civilization. I have also to acknowledge various permissions kindly accorded for quotations cited in this book.

Mrs Barbara Phillips has typed and re-typed the script with undaunted competence; to her and to others concerned in the production I record my thanks.

John Bowle
Oxford 1973

INTRODUCTION

Sir Mortimer Wheeler once observed that the history of the Roman Empire could be regarded as 'a rather ponderous cautionary tale in somewhat questionable taste'. Today the history of the British Empire is widely considered, if not a cautionary tale, at least one of a colossal and even reprehensible exploitation. Far from being proud of the greatest sea-borne empire in world history, of having founded great nations of European stock in other continents, of having often set standards of fair dealing and justice over ancient civilizations and barbaric peoples accustomed to regimes of arbitrary and capricious power, many of the post-imperial British feel a retrospective guilt. Yet, to an objective historian, imperialism is a normal aspect of the human condition; in its context, no more reprehensible than other manifestations of power in all their variety and disguises. Moreover, as empires go, the British has been relatively humane. It was the spontaneous creation of a maritime trading people, made with little encouragement from governments and generally in spite of them. Though the Indian and colonial Empires were created mainly by the upper classes and their dependents, the colonies of settlement were largely a creation of the people. For the British Empire was not, like the Roman or Spanish hegemonies, a deliberate political imperialism until its forced and over-extended defensive climax in the late nineteenth and early twentieth centuries.

Further, as well as extending the range of ordered government, of the rule of law and of competent administration, the Empire brought with it the knowledge of modern scientific method, technology and medicine. And, although its cultural enterprise has often been limited, it has sometimes mitigated the impact of modern industry on undeveloped societies, so that they have suffered less than the Europeans who pioneered the Industrial Revolution. Moreover, if it has declined, it has not fallen; it has never, like the Roman Empire, been overrun; and of set policy it has launched a whole progeny of nation states within a New Commonwealth. In spite of difficult beginnings, they promise a rich variety of civilization.

The British Empire at its climax was much larger than anything created by the Romans, the Persians, the Mughals, the Spaniards in the Americas or even by the Chinese; and its influence went much deeper than the only other empire of comparable size—that of the medieval Mongols, who ruled from southern China to western Russia. Whatever the fate of Great Britain, whether it is to be merged into a European Union or to subside into a social democracy comparable with Holland or Scandinavia, the British, who first launched the Industrial Revolution, with its worldwide consequences, also determined the political development of North America and Australasia. They briefly united and pacified the Indian sub-continent and, more extensively than any other Europeans, brought the ancient civilizations of Asia, the illiterate if sometimes highly organized societies of black Africa and the palaeolithic and neolithic peoples of Australasia and the Pacific in touch with the civilization of the West. This achievement, along with the outstanding contribution of British writers, scientists and inventors, is now secure: considering the relatively small population and even smaller territory out of which it has all sprung, the impact has been astonishing. For, as the Roman Empire, whatever its glaring defects, determined the political and cultural future of eastern and western Europe, or as the Persian and Chinese that of the Middle and Far East, or the Iberian that of Central and South America, so the British Empire, its language and culture have had an even wider influence on peoples far stranger to the British than the barbarians of northern and central Europe, and the Berbers, Syrians and Egyptians had been to Rome, or than the peoples of Outer Mongolia or central or southeast Asia had been to the Chinese.

Extending over a quarter of the globe, across the whole sweep of Canada to the Pacific and at one time including the entire east coast of North America from Florida to Labrador, as well as the most valuable of the West Indies, the British Empire also comprised vast territories in Australasia of which no previous architects of empire, Roman, Persian, Chinese, Indian or Iberian, had even been aware. The strategic base in India made the British the greatest power in Asia, from the Red Sea and the Persian Gulf to Singapore, Malaya, Sarawak and North Borneo to Hong Kong and the China Sea. Add to this the domination of South and much of West Africa, of East Africa, the Sudan and of Egypt, as well as a string of naval bases across the world which kept the whole enormous concern together and sustained the Victorian *Pax Britannica*, and here is a world-historic event: the climax of an extraordinary west European maritime enterprise of which the long-term consequences are only now becoming apparent.

When, in the fifteenth century, the Portuguese had felt their way down the West Coast of Africa, rounded the Cape and outflanked the huge landpowers of China, India and central and western Asia (whence the Grand Turk was even then threatening Central Europe itself), and when Columbus had discovered the Americas, a new phase of world history had begun. The European peoples, long confined to the far west of the Eurasian continent, and since the decline of Rome greatly inferior in wealth, culture, population and technology to the great civilizations of Asia, now reached out across the oceans to make an extraordinary come-back. The sea-borne empires of the Portuguese, the Spaniards, the Dutch and the French, like the continental expansion of the Russians to the Pacific, were all to have their historic impact; but the British Empire was the last, the most far-flung and most important of all the western European oceanic dominations.

As such, it may now be considered in an impartial perspective. Not, as often hitherto, mainly from the British point of view in narratives clogged with the minutiae of administration and politics, or stuffy with the ambience of 'Land of Hope and Glory', but from the receiving end as well. As, for example, it appeared to the ancient civilizations so much affected by this brief but decisive incursion, or as it seemed to the technologically primitive peoples of the colonial Empire, who have now been better understood through anthropology and environmental studies. Nor need the Victorian and Edwardian obsession with administrative problems, natural to those who had to deal with them, any longer eclipse the extraordinary feats of exploration which opened up vast underdeveloped and underpopulated areas and changed the economic and demographic pattern of the world. Moreover, these exploits and their significance can now be better appreciated through the current revolution in geographical studies. Maps of the Empire and Commonwealth are often still presented on Mercator's misleading projection, which dwarfs the Indian subcontinent and tropical Africa and grossly magnifies northern Europe and the Canadian Arctic. But with the new sense of geopolitics, pioneered by Mackinder in England but first acted on in Germany, the permanent physical and climatic facts can be scientifically portrayed. Modern cartographers now depict the structural realities behind commerce, settlement and conquest; the strategic passes, the island bases of communication and supply, the areas of tropical, deciduous or coniferous forest, of rice, cereals, fruit crops, pasture and fisheries, as well as the mineral and oil resources and weight of population.

In the light of this advance, as in that of social and environmental studies, political history written in terms of imperialist pride or post-colonial resentment is on its way out. The Roman Empire is no longer assessed either as it appeared to Trajan, Marcus Aurelius, Diocletian and Constantine, or to Vercingetorix, Boudicca or Shapur I; the British Empire need no longer be considered as it appeared to Chatham, Disraeli, Cecil Rhodes and Kitchener, or to the leaders of the American Revolution, to President Kruger or the Mahdi.

Anti-colonialist nationalism now seems a natural reaction against an often self-righteous, strident and philistine latter-day imperialism: an aspect of the European nationalism that coincided with the final phases of British satiety, defensiveness and decline. Today, after the transformation of empire, as the nations still within the New Commonwealth find their feet, they can afford to sort out the lasting cultural, administrative and economic advantages from the debris of political and social humiliation and its sequel. The present contrast between the rise of a cosmopolitan civilization in terms of science, communications, technology, medicine, agriculture and the conservation of the environment, and the now belated widespread and originally European cult of the nation-state, already being super-seded in Europe itself, is all too familiar. But the first trend will probably predominate, for economic and social facts tell. Both racial arrogance and racial self-assertion, like current doctrines of inevitable class conflict inherited from the nineteenth century, may gradually subside, as part of an adaptation to an environment transformed by modern applied science and technology, so that both imperialist and anti-imperialist views of the British Empire will be superseded. For we are here concerned with a world-historic creative influence; similar, on an even greater scale, to that of Graeco-Roman civilization on Europe, of Persian culture on the Muslim world, of Indian civilization on Indonesia, of the Chinese on the Far East, of the Iberians on Central and South America and of the Russians in central Asia.

An impartial view, in the light of world history, may even promote better understanding between the developed and underdeveloped countries in the Commonwealth and outside it. Such a view, along with a study of British character which the development of empire reveals, I have endeavoured to present.

BOOK I

Reconnaissance and Early Settlement

1497–1660

CHAPTER 1

The Island Base

The phase of reconnaissance and tenacious if limited settlement, the prelude to the first or Old Colonial British Empire, an empire always more of commercial than political intent, lasted for about a hundred and fifty years. It covers the early Tudor ventures to the Levant, Muscovy and Persia, Hawkins' slave-trading voyages to West Africa and the Caribbean; the Elizabethan reconnaissance and the Jacobean and Caroline plantations in North America, and the early exploration of the sub-Arctic. On the other side of the world, it comprises the establishment of the East India Company's warehouses at Surat, Madras, and at Hooghli in Bengal, and it concludes with the momentous Navigation Acts of 1650–1 and 1657. The formidable Republican Government then gave British and colonial shipping the monopoly of the Atlantic trade, launched the Western Design against the Spanish Empire in the Caribbean and seized Jamaica. It first put the power of the state behind a mercantilist policy of commerce and colonization, a policy reaffirmed by the Acts of Trade of the Restoration Government and extended to the whole Empire by 1696, when a Board of Trade and Plantations was established.

The English came late to oceanic enterprise. As early as 1420, only five years after Agincourt, the Portuguese navigator Zarco had discovered Madeira, and by the 'fifties their ships were sweltering off West Africa in search of gold, ivory and slaves; by 1472 they were off the mouth of the Congo, and by 1487, two years after the Tudor takeover in England, they had rounded the Cape. By the turn of the century they had discovered Brazil and, a generation later, they were colonizing it; by 1510, a year after Henry VIII's accession, they had established themselves at Bombay, Goa and Calicut and were penetrating to Malaya and Indonesia. By 1516 they were at Macao near Canton, and by 1542 trading armaments to the eager Japanese—

exploits commemorated by the elaborate Manueline architecture of Belem and Batalha.

Spanish enterprise had been equally swift and much more thorough. In the great Cathedral at Seville the monument to Columbus recalls an even greater ambition, as two kings and two queens, the sway of their robes caught in bronze, bear him on 'the enterprise of the Indies'—which became the conquest of Central and South America. For, by 1519–20, Cortés had subjugated the rich and elaborate Aztec civilization in Mexico; and by 1530–3 Pizarro had seized the highly organized mountain empire of the Incas in Peru; while in 1520–1 a Spanish expedition under the Portuguese Magellan had navigated the Pacific and its survivors had returned round the world. Moreover, the Spaniards had soon penetrated to Florida, and by 1542, when the Portuguese had reached Japan, they were even on the Ohio, trading horses with the Amerindians and so transforming their economy.

A *fait accompli* thus confronted the northern Europeans, French, English and Dutch. And it had been given a sort of legality by a Spanish Borgia Pope, when Alexander VI, anxious to avoid a Catholic and inter-Iberian conflict, with the haziest notion of what his award implied, had divided the world, by a line running 370 miles out in the Atlantic from the Cape Verde Islands, into two spheres of influence—Portuguese to the east and Spanish to the west—bounded by another line through the western Pacific which would assign the Philippine islands to Spain. This award, embodied in 1494 in the Treaty of Tordesillas, established a monopoly long resented and soon challenged by the French, the British and the Dutch.

The French had been the first to defy the monopoly. They had unsuccessfully challenged the Portuguese in Brazil and the Spaniards in Florida, and their corsairs out of La Rochelle already harassed the Caribbean. But it was in the north that they made a much more important initiative which was to lead to vast and brilliant if superficial explorations of the vast interior of North America. By 1534–6 Jacques Cartier of St Malo was prospecting the St Lawrence up to the site of what would be Montreal and beginning the fur-trade in 'New France', now Canada. But neither the *coureurs des bois*, penetrating vast solitudes, nor the Breton fishermen on the foggy cod-banks off Newfoundland, would be the pioneers of substantial settlement. For although their exploration would be far-flung, it was long before they obtained much support from governments, concerned with the perennial Valois–Habsburg European power struggle and with wars of religion at home.

II

This was the prospect that confronted the British when they emerged from their late-medieval preoccupations in their own island and in France, and the Dutch when they emerged from their struggle with Alva's pikemen and siege trains in the Netherlands as a first-class naval power, able to compete with all comers and to dominate the Far East and the trade of the Caribbean. For the English it was a daunting, though for some an exciting, prospect: and in the long run they were to surpass all their rivals.

After the defeat of the attempted French invasion of 1546, and of the much more formidable menace of the Armada of 1588 and its attempted sequel, the English alone had an invulnerable because an insular base. They had the population, the rudimentary capital resources and the freedom from centralized bureaucratic control which enabled them to exploit the most advantageous position of any Western power. They commanded the sea routes to the Baltic and round the North Cape to Muscovy, and the exits from the North Sea round Scotland and through the Straits of Dover; and they had long traded with Gascony, the Iberian peninsula, the Mediterranean countries and the Levant. Now, with oceanic prospects opening up, they could exploit the sea routes of the Atlantic, westward to the Americas and the Pacific; south and eastward round Africa to India and the Far East. From being a provincial island, a second-rate power off a continent whose peoples had looked to the Mediterranean since their civilization had begun, and greatly inferior in wealth and manpower to the militarized Continental states, this compact and vigorous nation, whose peoples blended Iberian and Celtic with Teutonic, Scandinavian and Norman stocks, and who were already by the fifteenth century becoming more sea-minded, now began their tentative ascent to sea-borne empire.

The advantages of geography were combined with a social order which had long been flexible and in which economic interests had long had an unmedieval priority. For all their chivalric panache, the English raids into France had been elaborately organized business ventures for loot and ransom, and under Edward III they had paid off. The English aristocracy had long been much less exclusive than the *noblesse* of France or the *hochgeboren* military caste in the Germanies, and they had married into gentry and mercantile families, some of whom had themselves attained nobility and even the honour of execution. Nor were younger sons, who did not, as on most of the Continent, inherit their father's title, forbidden by social custom, as in France or Spain, to go into trade. London was far the largest city in the country, at once capital and seaport, and its wealth and political life had produced a rich mercantile interest which the parvenu Tudor dynasty knew how to manage. Moreover, the political development of England had long made commercial as well as landed interests powerful; even at the end of the fourteenth century Richard II had been deposed and subsequently murdered, mainly for attacking tenure and property.

The dynastic conflicts of the Plantagenets had been sanguinary and notorious abroad—what could one expect of such a barbarous people, wondered the French, plundered by the English armies? Out of six monarchs, within just over a century and a half, three had been murdered in prison, while Richard III, the last Plantagenet, had died in battle. But government itself had been successful; a relatively strong administration in a manageable area, where only the Welsh and Scottish marches remained centres of disaffection, had established an effective conciliar government, without standing armies or cumbrous bureaucracy. Already, by 1327, on the accession of Edward III, there had been a parliamentary monarchy, conducted, indeed, by an aristocratic Council, but including the regular representatives of the counties and boroughs, consulted on a variety of business and authorized to present a wide range of petitions. The eclipse of the monarchy and the terrorizing of Parliaments in the mid-fifteenth century had been due to a chance of personality—the minority and incompetence of Henry VI—not to any deep-rooted weakness in the administration. The rehabilitation of kingship by Edward IV and the first Tudor had been possible because tried old institutions were to hand. The early Tudors had not founded a 'new monarchy' in collaboration with a supposed 'rising bourgeoisie', but restored, extended and adapted a long-established medieval instrument of government. The Tudor peace, their great achievement, had been made in association with the wide range of pressure groups representing the interests of aristocrats, gentry and merchants. And they were backed by a rudimentary public opinion within a politically conscious minority with a sharp eye for the main chance, to which the first Tudor had appealed by the novel device of printed proclamations stressing his determination to enforce law and order.

This Tudor establishment had included the more adaptable of the old nobility, most of whom had not, as is often believed, been killed off in the so-called Wars of the Roses; as well as new men who had risen through service to the Crown by the law, sheep farming, cloth manufacturing and commerce. And if, by the later years of Henry VIII, a roaring inflation had set in, so that by the end of the century the cost of living had quadrupled and many who could not adapt themselves had been ruined, it had at least shaken up the whole society and provided new openings for those with the capital, nerve and luck to profit by them.

Among these men the big sheep-masters and clothiers had long been pre-eminent. Anglo-Saxon textiles had been famous, and during the high Middle Ages by far the greatest English export had been raw wool; then gradually cloth had superseded it. As the late-medieval churches, stained glass and guildhalls still testify, a wealthy and ramified industry had grown up, already conspicuous in the countryside as described by Henry VIII's antiquary Leland.

Yet a specialized economy is precarious; and the cloth-trade had long been at the mercy of a Continental market fluctuating through political crises and war. When, therefore, the new oceanic prospects opened up, it was not only the adventurous seamen or the fortune-hunters who scanned the horizon, but, economically more important, the solid men of business who wanted 'vent of cloth'. This desire and the collaboration to attain it are early and plainly expressed in the highly significant narrative of '*The Newe Navigation and Discoverie of the Kingdome of Moscovia, by the North East* ... enterprised by Sir Hugh Willoughbie, Knight, and performed by Richard Chancellor, Pilot', in 1553 in the reign of Edward VI. 'At that time', it begins, when 'our Merchants perceived the commodities and wares of England to bee in small request with the countrys and people about us, and nere unto us ... and the price thereof abated ... certain grave citizens of London, and men of great wisdome, and careful for the good of their country began to thinke with themselves, howe this mischiefe might be remedied.' And seeing the wealth obtained by the 'Spaniards and Portingales' through their discoveries, they resolved themselves 'upon a new and strange navigation'. So they fitted out three ships 'for the search and discoverie of the Northern parts of the world, to open the way and passage to newe and unknowen kingdoms'. They formed a company to raise £6,000 in shares of £25 apiece to buy three ships 'newly built and trimmed ... very strong and [with] well seasoned planks for the building'.[1]

Their venture was a success. Court and City had combined to back the traditional objective of 'vent of cloth' though they had also aimed at the spice-trade with the Far East. Thus the sheep of the Cotswolds, Wessex, East Anglia and the Yorkshire dales were still as much behind the Tudor reconnaissance as they had been behind the

[1] Richard Hakluyt, *Voyages and Documents*, selected with an introduction and glossary by Janet Hampden, Oxford, 1958, pp. 39–40.

medieval wealth that made it possible; and if the Northern Renaissance lit up men's minds to wider ambitions, the ancient cloth-trade still provided the main driving force, though spectacular plunder could and would be had from the more desperate and romantic sort of adventures in wider fields.

The sale of textiles seemed most likely in northern territories. It was believed that a Northeast passage existed to China and the Far East through the ice-bound seas of the Siberian coast. Experts had maintained, wrote one merchant to Elizabeth I, that no one could survive the tropic heat: the same kind of people now argued that no one could survive the Arctic cold. The first had been proved wrong: why not the second? It was likely, too, that there would be a market in Muscovy, if a way could be found round Scandinavia to by-pass the eastern Baltic where the trade was blocked by the Lithuanians and Poles. And beyond Muscovy lay Persia; beyond that India and the Far East. So in the 1550s, the normal British trade east to the Baltic was supplemented by a new venture far to the northeast.

Here, as in the Levant, the enterprise of independent capitalists was backed by government; and by the end of the century a far more ambitious project was launched, the most important of these expeditions to Asia. Following contacts with India and the Far East, the English followed in the wake of the Portuguese round the Cape. In 1600 the East India Company was founded—its main objectives in the spice islands of the East Indies; for the Company only concentrated on India when the Dutch had forestalled them in their original aim. Such was the thrust to the east: north into Muscovy, south round the Cape. The long-term result was the British *raj* in India, the strategic eastern foundation of empire in Asia and Australasia.

Westward, in the Atlantic, the main interest had first been directed to Africa. By 1530 the original William Hawkins of Plymouth had reached what is now Liberia, in quest, like the Portuguese, of pepper, ivory and gold; he had then proceeded to Brazil whence he had shipped a cargo of Brazil-wood—the source of a rare, expensive dye. He had also brought back a Brazilian *cacique*, who caused some sensation at the court of Henry VIII; no one, even in that bedizened circle, had thought of inserting a ruby in their lower lip. And Hawkins' voyages were the prelude to the slave-trade exploited by his sons, William and John, the latter, on a more official level, becoming Treasurer of the Navy and the principal expert who prepared it to face the Armada.

Bristol merchants always had a hand in the West African trade, but they had also been interested in North America. In 1497 the elder Cabot had sailed to find the inhospitable shores of the 'New

Found Land', and by the 'twenties West-Country fishermen were exploiting the cod banks and returning with their repellent but sustaining catch, the 'stockfish' for which there was always a market in Lent, and out of which the Portuguese and Spaniards, if not the English, made an appetizing dish—the still popular *bacalao*.

In more intellectual circles among the Erasmian humanists, America had now become the fashion; and a party of London lawyers (of all people) had even gone over to take a look: the first English tourists to the new world. Only a few survived. And the crew, who had signed on under another, wisely refused to obey their amateur sea-captain, though he had been John Rastell, brother-in-law of the impeccable Sir Thomas More. They set him ashore at Cork and returned to London; so the ingenious man wrote a brisk poem all about North America, though he had never set eyes on it.

It was not until late in the sixteenth century that the English pressed further with their exploration of the North Atlantic, though the hope of a Northwest Passage to the Far East had always held their minds. In the meantime, West Africa, Brazil, the Caribbean all looked more inviting. Hawkins and his son both believed that the traditional anti-French understanding with Spain could cover access for British merchants and slavers to the Spanish-American Empire; it was only in the 'sixties and 'seventies that Drake and the English corsairs systematically broke into the Spanish sphere of influence and that this objective combined with a vast oceanic reconnaissance of the 'South Sea', when Drake reached California and circumnavigated the world. This exploit was to lead to claims on the East Indies—had he not made a treaty with the Sultan of Ternate? —and to visions of a great continent in the south—for did not the earth need to be balanced by a land mass in that area, *terra incognita Australis*? The full Tudor reconnaissance was thus swift and fabulous; but it did not lead to settlement. Newfoundland was early annexed and Baffin Land and Davis's Strait explored; the coasts of North Carolina and Virginia were prospected, but there was no lasting colonization. Raleigh was more interested in Ireland and in Guiana in South America with its promise of access to *El Dorado*, the Golden King. It would not be until Jacobean times that the foundation of the American Empire would be laid in major plantations of settlement. The main effort of colonization would then shift from Ireland to Virginia and New England, where in the long run the results would be even more decisive for the world than the British ascendancy in India and the East. For the British, however, India and the West Indies were long considered far more important and had greater effects on politics in the island itself.

III

Such, by the mid-sixteenth century, was the insular background to this far-ranging reconnaissance; first to the east through the White Sea into Muscovy and Persia, then round the Cape to India and the Far East; then south to the Gold Coast and across to the Caribbean; then due west across the North Atlantic to Newfoundland and Arctic Canada, to Bermuda, Virginia and New England. None of it would have been successful had not the Tudor governments secured the base from which it could develop. They had prevented internal disruption fomented by their enemies abroad, and they were themselves sea-minded and built up a navy capable of defending the island.

Henry VII had been a shrewd man of business. He understood the importance of sea power both for commerce and diplomacy, and had built two first-rate ships at his dockyard at Portsmouth. Henry VIII had thus inherited a nucleus for a regular navy which he trebled within five years of his accession. Moreover, he established the main dockyards at Deptford and Woolwich in the Thames estuary and saw to it that the pilots of these difficult approaches were organized in what became the Corporation of Trinity House, charged with the general furtherance of navigation, and still extant. He also created the Navy Board and his officials thoroughly surveyed the coast. His castles for its defence were strategically placed, from Newcastle upon Tyne, round East Anglia and Kent to the Solent and the West Country, where many of them, as at Portland and St Mawes, can still be seen. Moreover, he was alive to new ideas, and had ships constructed no longer to grapple and board, but to stand away from the enemy and sink him with broadsides of heavy guns, the foundation of the ship-smashing tactics that were later to dominate naval war.

The ships of Henry VIII's time were clumsy and difficult to manoeuvre, but in 1546 they beat off the French invasion at Portsmouth, and the strategy and tactics which they foreshadowed were adopted in Elizabethan times. Henry VIII is often regarded as having been blind to the possibilities of Atlantic exploration; but given his situation he had to keep his eyes on the dangerous affairs of Europe. If he was interested in the fleet only as an instrument of diplomatic blackmail and defence against the French and imperial powers which outclassed his own, he was the founder of the Royal Navy.

His grasp of realities was inherited by his son and his advisers. Edward VI was not, as he is often represented, a priggish Calvinist *dévot*, but precociously concerned with naval and economic problems. For his age, he had singular grasp of the commercial possibilities of his realm in relation to the Continent, and it is not surprising that it was during his brief reign with the ascendancy of the Duke of Northumberland (a more businesslike adventurer than the King's uncle, the Protector Somerset, whom he had ousted) that the first English expedition set out for Muscovy for reasons already described. But by 1553 the boy was already shut up in the stifling rooms in which Tudor invalids were confined: too ill to see the flourish with which the expedition set out, as the ships moved down-river past Greenwich, well appointed and well armed, and the courtiers ran out on the lawns and the Privy Councillors looked out of the windows to watch them pass, bound for the open sea and the far north and Muscovy for the Court of the young Tsar Ivan Vasilievich—Ivan *Groznyi*, to be known in the West as the 'Terrible', but to the Russians as the 'Thunderbolt', and already the conqueror of Kazan.

IV

The venture was a landmark in economic enterprise, the first officially sponsored attempt to break out to the northeast. It would be followed during the next half century by the immense and radiating late Tudor reconnaissance.

The Elizabethans, following the break away from the old limitations under Edward VI and Mary I, improvised a global strategy; and Drake's crossing of the Pacific foreshadowed the voyages of Anson and Cook, when the Elizabethan strategy in the South Sea was again taken up. Their objectives were now not only 'vent of cloth', but gold and silver, spices and slaves; a short cut, east or west, to Cathay, and straight plunder.

Thus, less than a century after the courtiers at Greenwich had watched the ships moving down-river for the unknown north, the English horizons would be worldwide. A network of trade eastward to Muscovy and Persia, to India and the East Indies, south to West Africa and west to the plantations in the Caribbean and North America, now linked the early Stuart and Republican English with all the known continents.

Once a formidable military and naval power ruled Great Britain, this network could be drawn tight into a mercantilist sea-borne empire. And that power, which would in part realize Elizabethan ambitions, would be brought to bear in the mid-seventeenth century when the Commonwealth and Protectorate governments emerged out of the Civil Wars. Their Navigation Acts of 1650 and '51, confirmed and extended in 1657, would be the first step in this consolidation and be followed up after the Restoration and the revolution of 1688.

So England would catch up with and surpass her long-established rivals and create the first, Old Colonial, Empire. When, in 1644, Milton declared that God 'decreeing to begin some new and great period', revealed himself 'first to His Englishmen', he voiced most contemporary English opinion. 'Whether God or some other high authority was responsible,' writes Dr Hill, with a nice irony, 'England was undoubtedly first on the road to the modern world.'[2]

[2] Christopher Hill, *God's Englishmen: Oliver Cromwell and the English Revolution*, London, 1970, p. 167.

CHAPTER 2

The Muscovy Company, Persia and the East Indies

The City merchants behind the Muscovy enterprise had been as ignorant of the 'route northward within the Mare Glacial' as of the prospects in the Arctic. They had even interrogated 'two Tartarians, which were in the King's Stables', who proved 'able to answer nothing to the purpose: being in deede more acquainted (as one of them merrily and openly said) to toss potts, than to learn the states and disposition of people'. The expedition sailed in total ignorance of its course or landfall.

But its consequences were momentous. Willoughby's ship perished with all hands; but Chancellor's rounded the North Cape, observed the midnight sun 'upon the huge and mightie sea', and fetched up in 'a certain great bay'—in fact the White Sea, near modern Arkhangelsk.[1] They did not even know they were in Muscovy until some terrified fishermen refused to trade with foreigners without leave from the Tsar. Messengers to Moscow were delayed; local officials obstructive. But by the early autumn the mission had arrived. After traversing enormous forests haunted by 'Buffes [bison] Beares and Black Wolves, and another kind of beast unknowen to us called the Rossomaka'—the Muscovites hunted the Buffes on horseback, 'but their Beares afoot with wooden forks'—the envoys were well received. Since the fall of Byzantium the Grand Princes of Moscow had combined being Tsagan, or White Khan in Tatar style, their crown not the open diadem of the West but a pointed bejewelled and fur-lined central Asian cap, with the claim to be Tsar (Caesar). Ivan was now Samodyerzhets (Autocrat), with a service nobility and bureaucracy behind him, and ambitions for conquest both south to the steppe and west to the Baltic. He needed not merely textiles, but armaments, mercenaries, technicians.

[1] Hakluyt, *op. cit.* p. 44.

And these the contending Poles, Lithuanians and Swedes who now dominated the Baltic were determined to deny him. In 1547, the year of Henry VIII's death and the fourteenth year of Ivan's reign, a hundred and twenty-four experts hired by the Tsar had been turned back at Lübeck. Chancellor's mission was doubly welcome and his report was comprehensive and favourable. The Muscovite realm appeared barbaric, but its trade potential was immense. At Novgorod there were much flax and hemp, useful for shipping, and a great wealth of furs—martens and foxes, beavers, minivers, ermines and the 'precious sables of Colmagro'—as well as walrus ivory 'of which they make great account, as we do of elephant's teeth'.

The mission held the trump card in diplomacy—a common interest in negotiation. In spite of the eighteen-foot-thick walls of the 'inexpugnable' Kremlin, the golden 'pots' five foot high, the silver casks for the Tsar's own potations, the furs and brocades, and the hundred and forty servitors in cloth of gold, they refused to be 'dasht out of countenance by the Tsar's majesty' and greeted him firmly 'after the manner of England', an English gambit to be repeated in many contexts over the centuries. And when, in 1561, the first mission was followed by a larger one under that remarkable man Anthony Jenkinson, already experienced in North Africa and the Near East, the English again stood on protocol: Jenkinson refused to present Elizabeth I's letter to anyone but the Tsar himself, and even threatened to leave Moscow. And his tactics paid off: in 1562 he was proceeding down the Volga to Persia, commissioned to further the Tsar's interests as well as his own, on the first English trade mission by that route to central Asia.

Already by 1567 Anglo-Muscovite trade was provoking alarm in Poland, where Sigismund August prohibited it through Danzig and warned Elizabeth I of the consequences. 'The more the Muscovite power will grow,' he wrote, 'the more dangerous will it become not only to us but to the whole of Christianity ... One supplies them with munitions of war, with arms the use of which they did not know, and what appears most dangerous to us, one procures to them adroit engineers ... These engineers would easily construct even in this barbarous country all the machines needed for war and so far unknown to that people. One must therefore apprehend lest these works are not carried out for the ruin of the Christian states before one expects it.' And after the Russians had taken Narva on the Dwina, he would warn the Queen: 'We know the Muscovite, enemy to all liberty under the heavens, daily to grow mightier by the increase of such things as be brought to the Narva, while not only wares but also weapons heertofore unknowen to him, and artificers and arts be brought unto him; by means whereof he maketh himself strong to vanquish others.'[2]

These warnings went unheeded. Despite Sigismund August, in 1568 Elizabth I sent the first English embassy to the Kremlin: her ambassador, Thomas Randolf, already experienced in Scotland. And the negotiations succeeded. After months of comfortable isolation, in February 1559 the English were suddenly invited to a gargantuan feast. Four days later the ambassador was summoned at midnight to the Kremlin and closeted with the Tsar. The English obtained most of the privileges they had come for; the release of certain English merchants in custody, the punishment of other, competing, adventurers; the right to exploit valuable iron mines; and, subject to a fixed taxation, freedom to trade with Persia.[3] But they had also to fend off an embarrassing *démarche*. Ivan, now committed to his notorious terror and to the hard Livonian war for access to the Baltic, wanted a political alliance. Should either monarch, he proposed, be turned out of their country, he or she might be given asylum in the other's. And Ivan—who would surpass Henry VIII by marrying seven times—proposed marrying one of the Queen's relations. The proposal was not well received by Elizabeth I. 'The Queen,' the ambassador told the Tsar, with diplomatic tact, 'thinks that Jenkinson might have misconstrued the words of the emperor, for that she hath no manner of doubt of the continuance of her peaceable government ... and knows nothing contrary in the state of the said emperor.' Should any mischance happen to him (and Moscow was to be burnt by the Tatars in 1571) he would, of course, be as 'friendly received' as if a formal pact had been ratified.

Anxious to conciliate both the Muscovites and the Baltic powers, the English were already conducting a characteristic diplomacy: keeping in with all parties to promote their own trade; and already they show a characteristic detachment and insularity. Randolf's secretary, George Turberville, was a Wykehamist from New College; a Dorset country gentleman who would write rhymed treatises on sport and who now turned his pedestrian talent to disapproving descriptions of the Muscovites. During the tedium of the Russian winter, *Certain Letters in Verse* were written by 'Master G. T. out of Muscovia', and described the Russian way of life in laborious couplets. He observed their capacity for drink:

The soberest head doth once a day stand needful of a guide;

[2] Quoted in B. H. Sumner's *Survey of Russian History*, London, 1944, p. 260.
[3] Calendar of State Papers, Domestic, 1547–1580, p. 338.

and he thought their religion sordid :

> Devoutly down they duck with forehead to the ground
> Was never more deceit in rags and greasy garments found.

Their women, 'mewed up' by the stove, painted their 'smoakie' faces to counteract its effects, and rode astride in a manner unseemly to the English; while during the appalling winter the peasants slept hugger-mugger in the same hut as their animals, whose meat tasted 'watrish—the flesh not like English beefe'. And Muscovite gambling was reckless :

> At play, when silver lacks, goe saddle horse and all;

while the men were hideous—pot-bellied and 'flat headed'. In a word—and what worse term of abuse could he then employ?—

> Wilde Irish are as civil as the Russes in their kind,
> Harde choice which is the best of both, each bloody rude
> and blinde.

Among all this insular prejudice, Turberville also observed that, by English standards, the Muscovites had no certain laws and no security of property or inheritance before the autocracy of the Tsar: among them, he writes, 'Will in Commonwealth doth beare the only sway.'⁴ It was an observation which, in varying idioms, as they penetrated further east, the English would often make.

Such was the already characteristic reaction to an alien autocracy. But the trade would flourish. By 1618, when the Muscovy Company petitioned James I to grant credits to Mikhail, the first Romanov Tsar, they referred to an 'ancient amity of three score years', and to the profitable trade down the Volga where English cloth and tin could be exchanged for the silk and indigo of central Asia. Credit was arranged up to 100,000 marks. And after Peter the Great had won access to the Baltic, Anglo-Russian trade became greater for the Russians than their trade with any other state. This mutual interest would resist Napoleon's continental system, and even contribute to its break-up. The attempt to find a northeast passage had failed; but the later Tudor missions to Moscow would have a momentous long-term sequel.

II

On his expedition to Persia in 1562–3, Jenkinson was acting both for the Muscovy Company and for the Tsar, who was glad to use

---

⁴ For the full and entertaining text, see Hakluyt *Principal Navigations*, Vol. III, pp. 124 ff.

this knowledgeable expert. And here the English first encountered the most sophisticated Muslim civilization in central Asia. Its exponents were a formidable elite—'comely', as Jenkinson observed, 'and of good complexion, proude and of good courage, esteeming themselves to be the best of all nations, both for their religion and holiness, which is most erroneous ... They be martial, delighting in fast horses and good harnesses—soon angrie, craftie and hard people'.[5] Here a different style of diplomacy was demanded; and Jenkinson ingratiated himself with the Khan of Shirvan by comparing English and Persian methods of hawking.

But at Shah Tamasp's court at Casbeen he was ill-received. The Shi'ah Muslims of Persia hated and despised the Sunni Muslim Turks; but the conflict was then in abeyance, for Shah Tamasp had just done Suleiman the Magnificent a good turn. He had decapitated the Grand Turk's eldest and rebellious son, a refugee at his court: and the Turkish ambassador was about to return to Istambul with a present of the head to the grateful father. During this *détente*, the Turk's enemies were the Shah's; and the Turks, who depended on the Venetians for the spice trade, had warned him that the English were a particularly pernicious kind of Frank. So the Shah gave rein to his natural fanaticism. Did Jenkinson, he asked, believe that Jesus was the Son of God and the greatest of the Prophets? ' "Yea, that I do," said I. "Oh thou unbeliever," said he, "we have no need for friendship with unbelievers." '[6] And the envoy was escorted from the Presence, an attendant sifting sand behind him to the very gate. Extricated by the Khan of Shirvan, who wanted good relations with Moscow, Jenkinson returned by Astrakhan to the relatively dependable tyrant in the Kremlin, to whom he presented the robe of honour belatedly accorded to him by the Shah. The reception had been bleak, but here also trade prospects were good: the most rewarding product was raw silk, exchangeable for cloth; but there were other profitable commodities—cotton-wool, alum gum for dyeing, and a big potential traffic in spices from the East.

By the 'nineties Shah Abbas the Great was at war with the Turks, and the political omens were more favourable. The Shah wanted European experts and armaments; the English 'to get goods to and fro outside Turkey'. And, by 1616, English ships were in the Indian Ocean. An agent at Bahrein was urging the good prospect for cloth in Persia, and that an English fleet should 'curb the passage of the Portugals in the Persian gulf', though he advised of the great cost of

---

[5] Hakluyt, *op. cit.* p. 95.
[6] Hakluyt, *op. cit.* p. 89.

transport of goods inland.[7] Moreover Sir Anthony Sherley had been sent by James I to Persia, and his brother, Robert, who had remained as military instructor to the Shah's army, had proved highly adaptable. By 1599, married to a Christian Circassian, a relative of one of the Shah's wives, he was sent to Europe, 'brave in diet and expences' and wearing Persian dress, as the Shah's ambassador. After visiting Spain and Italy, he was well received in 1607 by James I, who assigned him the large allowance of £4 a day. Indeed, this adventurer's exotic appearance helped to further Persian prestige.[8]

Though the Levant merchants opposed the Gulf enterprise round Africa, diplomatic correspondence continued. Confronted with a letter from James I, Shah Abbas remarked that if the king would write in Persian he would reply in 'Franks'; and the English at Jask developed trade not only in cloth, which was limited by the poverty of the people, but in candy, steel, hides, walrus teeth and sugar, in return for carpets and raw silk. And when in 1627 another English embassy visited Persia from India, Thomas Herbert described the luxury of the court, then at Asharoff on the Caspian, though the big deal in raw silk for cloth which the Shah had sanctioned never came off.[9] Herbert vividly depicts the terrifying potentate, symbolic of many eastern despots whom the English would encounter; a small man with drooping mustachios, and the profile of a hawk, sitting cross-legged in plain red, quilted calico and a great white turban amid his silent and apprehensive entourage. Herbert was impressed by the silence and by the elegant simplicity of the palace—very different from his own baroque court—and by the crystalline pools, the walled gardens, the purling streams, the goblets, the flowers and the very curious erotic paintings in the royal apartments. For the Jacobean English, Persia at the height of its civilization was, indeed, an eye-opener. The Native Safavid dynasty which had ousted the Mongol and Turki rulers who had dominated the country since the time of Tamerlane, now presided over the most brilliant phase of Persian culture. It was based, indeed, upon the usual poverty and illiteracy of the masses, but it disposed of much

[7] Calendar of State Papers, Colonial East Indies, 1513–1616.

[8] In 1624 Sherley's second embassy to England was marred by a fight with a Persian impostor who claimed to be the Shah's true representative, and both were packed off to Persia. But Lady Sherley, who, like her husband, had been painted by Van Dyck, remained in Europe. When Sherley died, out of favour, in 1628 in Persia, Shah Abbas later remarked he had done more service than any of his other subjects.

[9] See Thomas Herbert, *Some Years Travel in Africa and Asia the Great*, especially describing the famous Empires of Persia and Industan, London 1638.

wealth and is commemorated by the Masjid-i-Shah at Isfahan and the Golden Mosque at Meshed. It produced the finest carpets in the world, splendid miniature paintings, bookbinding and calligraphy; Shah Abbas, the great warrior, was also a connoisseur of porcelain as well as of dancing-girls, 'ganimed' boys, polo and the chase. The English found Persian manners, wine and gaiety highly congenial, though they complained of the discomforts of the climate and were wary of the pitfalls of the despot's diplomacy. They were already learning to keep their heads, both literally and metaphorically, amid the splendours, finesse and treacheries of arbitrary power. And they would soon have their fill of such negotiations in their main field of Eastern exploitation and responsibility—the Indian sub-continent.

The constricted area of late-medieval commerce had thus long been superseded; the English were gaining footholds that would lead to empire in the east.

III

The first contact with India and the Far East had been made through the Mediterranean and the Levant. In 1583 the merchants John Newberry and Ralph Fitch had sailed to Tripoli in the *Tyger* and, crossing the Syrian desert to Baghdad, had been imprisoned by the Portuguese at Ormuz, whence they were shipped as prisoners to Goa. Here they escaped and made their way south to Golconda; then north to Akbar's court at Agra. Newberry perished attempting to return; but Fitch went on through Burma to Siam and the Far East, returning to England by Colombo and the Persian Gulf. His report encouraged the English ventures round the Cape to Surat, Masulipatam, and Bengal on the estuary of the Ganges, with all the immense consequences. Newberry and Fitch had revealed at once the immense opportunities of the Far East and how impracticable it was to go by land. By 1589 the English were aware of the riches of the Malabar and Coromandel coasts, and in 1591 Elizabeth I sanctioned the first expedition to the East Indies by the Cape. Malaya, Indo-China and, above all, Indonesia were the main objectives, though not yet India.

In 1580 the union of Portugal with Spain had made Portuguese shipping legitimate prey. Three 'tall ships' were now dispatched by the Cape of *Buona Esperanza* to Zanzibar 'on the backside of Africa', and so by Cape Cormorin to Malacca and Sumatra. The venture was costly in lives: one ship had to return, nearly all her crew having died, and another foundered near the Cape of Good Hope; but Captain James Lancaster of the *Edward Bonaventure* brought back a valuable report. The voyage also gave the English their first contact with South Africa, where they did some smart business, trading knives for oxen with the 'negroes', killed their first big game—'an antelope as big as a young colt, and another beasts unknown to us'—and observed 'great store of overgrown monkeis'—presumably baboons.[10]

Arrived at Sumatra, the *Edward Bonaventure* had wrought havoc among the Portuguese shipping in the Malacca straits, but by December 1592 the surviving members of her scurvy-stricken crew were so mutinous that Lancaster had to return to the Cape, and thence they sailed to St Helena, where the 'excellent green figs, oranges and lemons' restored their health. Then, caught in the doldrums, they had to run for the West Indies, where they suffered complicated disaster —the survivors being brought back by a French ship to Dieppe, whence in April 1594 they crossed to Rye.

But Lancaster's report confirmed the opportunities of the Far East, already stressed by Thomas Cavendish, who in 1586 had reached the East Indies by the Straits of Magellan. Thus, by the end of the century, English ignorance of the Far East had been dispelled, and the rottenness of the Portuguese monopoly revealed.

So, with royal backing, on 31st December 1600, a decision was taken which would lead to empire. The Company of 'the Merchants of London trading with the East Indies'—or 'East India Company'—was incorporated; for the Indies 'being so remote from hence, they could not be traded with but in a joint or united stock'. The original capital was £30,133-6s-8d in sums ranging from £3,000 to £100, and the Company was accorded a fifteen-year monopoly of trade between the Cape of Good Hope and the Straits of Magellan. The main investment was in the ships; then in specially minted coin—'rials of eight'; and the least in goods. Destined at first directly, then nominally, to control India until 1858, the Company was originally designed for a quick profit in the Spice Islands and the luxury trade with the Far East.

The highly speculative venture proved an immediate success. In 1607 the profits of the fourth voyage were estimated at £12,000; two years later, when cloves were making a profit of twenty-five per cent, the Company was given the monopoly of pepper sales at a fair price, and James I himself launched 'the great Indian ship'. In 1613 the courtier Chamberlain wrote to Sir Dudley Carleton of the great promise of the trade 'if we can agree with the Dutch';[11] and in 1616

---

[10] Hakluyt, *op. cit.* p. 401. The whole vivid account was dictated by Lancaster's Lieutenant, Edmund Barker of Ipswich.

[11] Calendar of State Papers, Colonial, p. 264.

the English Ambassador in Madrid reported 'the Portugals very disconcerted with the great success of the English in the East Indies'.[12]

The enormous archipelago which the Portuguese, the English and the Dutch were now exploiting, and which the Dutch were long to dominate, had already been controlled by two sea-borne commercial empires before the arrival of the Europeans: the first Indian, the other Arab, superimposed on a great variety of peoples in a rich tropical environment. Besides the coveted spices, ginger and cinnamon, cloves and nutmeg, it produced cotton, cassava, rice, sugar-cane, yams and bananas, as well as gold, diamonds and rubies. The civilized population was generally concentrated on the coasts, while a tangle of estuaries, mountains and jungle was inhabited by primitive aboriginal peoples, including the Dyaks of Borneo 'who lie in rivers on purpose to take the heads of all they can overcome'.

Since the fourth and fifth centuries A.D. in the time of the Gupta Empire, Indian colonists, known as 'Klings' since they came from the Kalinga coast on the Bay of Bengal, had moved into Indo-China and Indonesia. A Buddhist kingdom of Shri Vishaya had grown up at Palembang in Sumatra and had included western Java. In eastern Java the Indian Cholas are remembered by the superb sculptures of Borobudur—one of the greatest monuments of Asian art. And although by the mid-fourteenth century Muslim Arab traders and colonists from Aden and the Hadramaut had come to dominate much of the area, the Hindu kingdom of Madjapahit had held its own until the late fifteenth century, and has left its trace in Bali, if Islam had also captured the Moluccas and the Philippines. When in 1511 the Portuguese had arrived at Malacca, they were on the fringe of a rich, highly complex and original society.

Such were the prospects that now excited the ambitions of the northern Protestant nations, the English and the Dutch. But Chamberlain had been right that only in harmony with the Dutch could the full profits be reaped. And the Dutch, who had got in first, had no more intention of sharing this lucrative commerce with the English than with the Portuguese. As early as 1596, Cornelius van Houtman with four ships had arrived at Bantam in Java, then proceeded to Djakarta, which they named Batavia. In the next year no less than five Dutch expeditions had been launched, and by 1600, besides making contact with Siam, Canton, the Philippines and Japan, they had established a fortress at Macassar in Celebes and at Amboyna in the Moluccas. By 1602 the Dutch United East India Company was founded, with a much larger capital than the English merchants

[12] *op. cit.* p. 268.

could raise. Well-armed fleets systematically broke the Portuguese monopoly and Dutch sea-captains bullied or cajoled the native rajas, who already detested the Portuguese. A Dutch Governor-General was appointed: the most redoubtable and high-handed Jan Peterzoon Coen.

The Dutch had turned their desperate struggle against Spain in their own country to a triumphant offensive in the Far East, and the English could neither compete with nor appease this state-subsidized attack. By 1622 as the President of the East India Company reported, the English were finding the Dutch exactions intolerable; and, being less single-minded, would 'murmur at three meals of meat a week. The Dutch have been content with rice alone for a year together.' The English also detested the climate: 'he that escapes disease', they said, 'from that stinking stew of the China part of Bantam, must be of strong constitution of body'.[13] And the Dutch told the Indonesians that the English were a 'rude and ungoverned nation, given to drunkenness and abusing of women, quarrelling and fighting'.

The conflict came to its climax in 1623 with the notorious massacre at Amboyna. The English merchants were framed and deliberately degraded before the populace. After a Japanese in English employment had enquired the strength of the garrison, the English were arrested, tortured and hung spread-eagled on doors while a cloth over their mouths and noses was half filled with water, so that to breathe they had to swallow and 'soon after they had drunk a body full water came out of their eyes and ears'. Others had candles lit under the soles of their feet and armpits. After these 'torments of fyre and water', they confessed to anything. They were taken in procession round the town, and ten of the English, one Portuguese and nine 'Japoneses' were decapitated.

The 'Amboyna massacre' achieved its objective. The English withdrew from the Moluccas and, although in 1654 the Cromwellian government obtained some compensation after the first Dutch war, the English were compelled to turn their main effort to India. The affair was a turning point in what would become imperial history. For, in fact, by concentrating on the Spice Islands and spending great sums in maintaining a military and naval power, the Dutch diminished the profits of their commercial empire, and when, after the introduction of root crops in Europe, animals were no longer salted down for the winter, the spice trade fell off, though coffee and tea plantations long proved profitable. Dutch-planned political strategy thus proved less successful than the more opportunist and purely commercial policy of the English, who were indirectly and casually

[13] C.S.P., Colonial, p. *lix.*

to obtain a more massive and politically much more important empire in India.

The other commercial contacts followed up were often successful, but as yet much more limited. In 1614, for example, English merchants were at Patani, Bangkok and Ayuthia in Siam; but in Cochin China they were 'attacked and killed in the water with harping irons', the local ruler having been given counterfeit dollars by the Dutch who looked just like the English. Though the Chinese were contemptuous and suspicious of the foreigners, so that little business was done, a chance contact opened up what would be a brief phase of intercourse with Japan—'the most remote part of the world'. In 1598 William Adams, a 'pilot major' hired by the Dutch, had escaped disaster in the Straits of Magellan and fetched up destitute on the shores of Japan. Here the aristocratic and anarchic Ashikaga regime had been replaced by a military and social revolution, led by Oda Nobunaga and his follower, the peasant soldier Hideyoshi. In 1600 the formidable Tokugawa Ieyasu, the first of the Tokugawa Shoguns, had consolidated this military—literally 'tent' (bakafu)—government, and from the new capital at Yedo had imposed an unwonted peace. The English thought his regime 'the greatest and powerfullest tyranny that ever was heard of in the world', for those whom the Shogun distrusted were 'made to cut their bellies'.[14] Ieyasu had also expelled the Jesuits—active since the coming of the Portuguese in 1542 —and massacred more than a quarter of a million of their converts.[15] But he knew a useful foreigner when he saw one. The Protestant William Adams was commissioned to design a ship, and even to teach mathematics and geometry to the Shogun himself. He was rewarded with a large estate and remained in Japan for life.

When, therefore, in 1613 the English arrived in Japan, they found a friend at court. He advised them that tobacco would not be welcome—the Shogun executed anyone who smoked it—but that bars of iron, steel and lead for armaments were in brisk demand. For the Shogun in person, the factor reported to London, Russian glass and lambskins would be acceptable and three or four pairs of spectacle glasses—a convenience still particularly in demand among the Japanese.

[14] C.S.P., Colonial (Eastern), p. 351.

[15] The Chinese also, reported another anti-Catholic Englishman, 'could not abide to hear of any padres, who had come in swarms, begging without shame'. Op. cit. p. 352.

IV

The English reconnaissance to the east had thus extended from the original and vain attempt to find a passage to Cathay by the eastern Arctic, down into Muscovy and beyond as far as the Caspian, Bokara and Persia; round the Cape to Socratra and the Persian Gulf; and to India and the Far East as well as across the Pacific. The objectives had been purely commercial—to obtain 'vent of cloth', to secure fabulously profitable spices and any gold that could be had. There was no attempt, as by the Portuguese and Spaniards, at political empire in the Roman tradition: merely by private initiative sponsored by government to obtain the bases for permanent trade, and during the war with the Iberian powers to supplement the finance for these ventures by plunder—preferably of rich carracks laden with the produce of the East.

The reconnaissance had been remarkably far-flung—though its original objective, Cathay, had not been properly attained. It had comprised countries literally unknown to the provincial fifteenth-century English, and the sudden opening out of new horizons had combined with the Northern Renaissance to make the late Elizabethan and Jacobean ages the most creative in the literature of the English-speaking world. To nineteenth-century Protestant historians, the Elizabethan sea-dogs conducting their religious warfare westward in the Atlantic and Caribbean against Catholic Spain and the Inquisition, while plundering the Spanish Empire of Central and South America, seemed a more romantic subject than the eastward ventures here described. But these expeditions, all of them to countries with ancient and well-established civilizations in Muscovy and the Middle and Far East, were in fact as significant. For they opened the way for a main commitment which, with the decline of the Mughal Empire in India, would lead to the British *raj*, strategically the massive basis of British power in the East. This paramountcy in India would profoundly affect the English in their own island, after the main empire in North America had seceded, and link up with the colonies of settlement in Australia and New Zealand, if for world history the rise of a predominantly Anglo-Saxon civilization in North America would be even more important.

CHAPTER 3

The Foothold in India

The English footholds on the huge Indian sub-continent, at first only
incidental to the East India Company's ventures to Indonesia and
the Moluccas, were early consolidated. In 1608, three years after the
death of Akbar, the richest and most powerful ruler in Asia and the
main architect of the Mughal Empire, William Hawkins, a Levant
merchant who spoke Turkish, brought the 500-ton *Hector* into harbour off Surat, while the main expedition proceeded to Java on the
company's third voyage. Here he was within reach of Agra and the
court of Jahangir (1605–28), a bored, talented, inconsequent and
frequently inebriated aesthete, liable to moods of sadism.[1]

In spite of the apathy and corruption of local officials, and the
natural hostility of the Portuguese, Hawkins reached Agra with a
formidable escort of Pathans, and presented a letter of recommendation from James I. The Great Mughal, *Anglice, The Grand Magoare*,
was intrigued by this foreigner who spoke Turkish, still his own
family speech; and Hawkins soon found himself a Commander of
Four Hundred with a high notional salary and an Armenian Christian
wife. The Mughal allowed the English to build a warehouse or 'factory'—a place for 'factors' to live—at Surat. But the Portuguese were
experienced intriguers and, after cancelling and renewing his *firman*,
Jahangir finally rescinded it. Hawkins left Agra, with or without his
Armenian, his mission a failure.[2]

Such was the first reconnaissance. But it was soon followed up.

[1] For a vivid account of him, see Bamber Gascoigne *The Great Moghuls*,
London, 1971, pp. 131–79—a splendidly illustrated book.

[2] When, in England, a widowed Mrs Hawkins petitioned the Company for
arrears of salary, the Company 'would not allow her extraordinary charges'
and assigned her 200 *jacobus* in final settlement. It was alleged that she in fact
had a diamond worth £2,000 and smaller ones worth £4,000, but whether
she was the Armenian or an earlier Mrs Hawkins is obscure. C.S.P., Colonial,
East Indies, *op. cit.* p. 277.

The Company decided to buy cotton goods in India—then the main centre of textile manufacturers in Asia—and ship them to tropical Indonesia instead of cloth. In India, on the other hand, English cloth was in brisk if limited demand, particularly if dyed red, yellow or green and if the dye did not run in the heat. By 1616 one factor could report sales worth 50,000 rupees, most of them to the Mughal himself, and the profits could be reinvested in indigo. In contrast to the prospect in Japan, tobacco also found a promising market, as did iron, tin and lead. So, in 1613 the English were still at Surat, reporting 'a great trade in red coral', though 'wanting a sufficient place ... to anchor, free of danger from the Portugals'. Had they shipping here from England, they believed, they could sweep the board. But the Mughal, wrote Thomas Kerridge, was 'proud and covetous and took himself for the greatest monarch in the world'—which, after all, he was. And Jahangir was a connoisseur who had commissioned a superb tomb for his father, and superciliously 'viewed a standing cup of Mr Canninge's a little and delivered it to an attendant, not esteeming it'.[3] He had then demanded Kerridge's beaver hat. And the 'prattling' Portuguese Jesuits had just presented him with a real Neapolitan juggler. The English again petitioned for a 'place of safety for their ships to ride in', but could get no firm answer.

Obviously, a higher-powered mission was required. So in 1615 James I sent out the first English ambassador to the 'Grand Magoar or Emperor of the Oriental Indies'. And he had been chosen with care. In general the Company preferred not to employ gentlemen, who were apt to be feckless and unsystematic, but Sir Thomas Roe was a distinguished and experienced courtier and man of the world. He had been Esquire of the Body to Elizabeth I; he was accomplished, observant and imperturbable, and he was the first Englishman of quality to be officially sent out to India. Although he failed to obtain a trade treaty, for negotiation between equals was unthinkable to the Mughal, 'the King observing the custom of the Grand Turk not vouchsafing to article with any nation whatsoever',[4] by character and diplomacy Roe enhanced prestige. As his chaplain wrote, 'There can be no dealing with the King on very sure terms, he will say and unsay, promise and deny. But yet we Englishmen did not at all suffer ... but there found a free trade, a peaceable residence and very good esteem with that King and people.'[5] Like the English confronted with Ivan the Dread whose 'will in common-

[3] C.S.P., Colonial, East Indies, p. 255.
[4] op. cit. p. 486.
[5] Quoted by Philip Woodruff, *The Men who Ruled India: the Founders*, London, paperback, 1963, p. 34.

wealth' was 'the only sway', Roe declares that the King 'by his own word ruleth', and is 'everyman's heir'. In this precarious situation, he wrote, English aims should be strictly commercial, for 'the Portugal never profited from the Indies since he defended them. Let this be received as a rule that, if you will profit, seek it at sea and in quiet trade'. It was a rule that would long enhance commercial empire.

Such quiet trade was now also already developing on the other side of India in two other enclaves, one strategically well-placed at Masulipatam commanding the Coromandel coast southward, and one in 'Bengala' in the Ganges estuary commanding its rich hinterland. The *Solomon*, it was reported in 1616, had arrived at the former, though the *Thomasin* laden with nuts and mace had been lost; and in 'Bengala' it was already 'stock, not new residences' that was urgently required. But the decisive place was still Agra : and here the English reputation had been advanced by a minor naval victory over the Portuguese. From the first the Mughal had received the ambassador graciously, though very 'inquisitive about his presents' which included a looking-glass framed in ebony. And soon, wrote the ambassador, he was demanding more presents. He liked rich gloves, coloured beaver hats and silk stockings for the women of his harem, indeed any new invention, particularly striking clocks. 'Velvets and dogs were enquired after.' Roe recommended greyhounds and 'well-fed water spaniels'; though when one batch were landed, only a young mastiff had survived. He promptly fought with a tiger and killed it, then faced a bear which the Persian dogs would not touch. A coach and horses also arrived, complete with a former coachman of the Bishop of Lichfield, and the Mughal was pleased to ride in it. In 1617 a musician of the Lawes family played to him on the virginals : he thought little of them, but was delighted with Robert Tully's cornet. A picture of Diana also 'gave great comfort'.

Roe now suggested that since the Mughal bought jewels so lavishly, some 'old ones' from the Tower might be sent out. Large knives, swords, velvets, light Hague armour and arras would all be well received. But a picture of Venus and the Satyr must be really good or it would be despised. In return Roe had himself received presents worth £500—roughly the cost of a year's expenses; but already in 1616 he was complaining that the Mughal's court was 'not a place for a Christian ambassador, in regard of their disrespect and pride'. He disliked following the court about with goods; 'the King', he wrote succinctly, 'drinks and is indifferent'.[6]

To another Englishman the Mughal showed a better face. Tom

[6] C.S.P., Colonial, East Indies, 1617–21.

Coryat, an amiable rogue Wykehamist, son of the rector of Od-combe in Somerset, was a bohemian and a buffoon. He had already walked to Italy and back, written a lively description of Venice, and hung up his old shoes in Odcombe Church. As Roe is the first ambassador, so Coryat is the first recorded English eccentric to reach India. He had now visited the site of Troy, then walked through Turkey and Persia, travelling for safety, as he reassured his mother, in the large caravans that made their slow journeys through the passes down to India. And Coryat, unlike Sir Thomas Roe, could live on twopence a day; he had got from Aleppo to Agra on £3, counting the ten shillings stolen by an Armenian; and 'in case he should happen to be destitute—'a matter very incidental to a poor footman pilgrim' —he had picked up Turkish, Arabic and Persian, so as to earn his living if pressed.

Arriving at the Mughal's court at Ajmir, he made an oration in Persian beginning 'All Hail, Lord Protector of the World', and explained that he had come from England 'the Queen of all the Islands', mainly to see a monarch 'whose fame had resounded over Europe'. He had also, he said, 'wanted to see the Mughal's elephants' (he greatly enjoyed the elephant fights which occurred twice a week); to observe the famous River Ganges, and to 'intreat a gracious pass to Samarkand to see the Tomb of Tamberlain, the Lord of the Four Corners of the Earth'.

The Mughal, whose family had been hounded from Samarkand by the Uzbeks, replied that there, of all places, his recommendation would be fatal: they would kill Coryat at once. But he threw the supplicant a hundred pieces of silver—the equivalent of £10. He did not give more, he explained, since Coryat was evidently mad and no *dervish* needed money. And here the Mughal was kinder than James I, who, told news of Coryat, had remarked 'Is that fool still alive?', and more humane than Sir Thomas Roe could afford to be. The ambassador had already complained of 'volunteers' who came by sea and were a 'disgrace to our nation'; like many ambassadors after him, he had to disown such characters. But privately Roe gave Coryat a gold piece.[7] Coryat never saw Benares: he seldom, he said, drank anything but water, and not surprisingly ended his 'laborious pedestrial peregrinations' in 1617 when he died of the flux at Surat.

Already by 1618 three distinct English types had appeared in India: the merchant or office *wallah*, the lordly *Sahib*, and the eccentric, the last probably the most congenial to the Indians. And although 'nothing effective' had yet been secured 'with the Emperor for

[7] See *Coryat's Crudities*, to which are added his *Letters from India*, London, 1776, Vol. III *passim*.

a settled trade in these parts', the Company had maintained their unassuming foothold. The Portuguese, still bearers of the faith and the sword, had established the Inquisition at Goa, and their Jesuits, as in Japan, had briefly penetrated to the centre of power; but wisely no Anglican divine debated theology with Jahangir. Nor could the commercial English, though masterful at sea—an element uninteresting to the Mughals—yet attempt to assert a military command on land. Among the uncouth but technologically interesting Europeans tolerated by the Mughal, the English must have seemed the most unobtrusive.

II

The great civilization, on whose fringes the Company was now installed and into which they would infiltrate, contained an extraordinary variety of peoples and climate. Cut off from Central Asia, though not from Central Asian invaders, by the gigantic barrier of the Himalayas and the Hindu Kush, the northern plains extended southwest through predominantly arid country to the estuary of the Indus on the Arabian Sea. Eastward, a broad landscape of cereal crops and cattle gave place to sub-tropical cotton and rice fields, bamboo and mango clumps and elaborate irrigation extending to the mouths of the Ganges on the Bay of Bengal. Southward a contrasting country of broken hills and irregular plateaux, of forest and jungle and red earth, tapered down to Cape Cormorin, on the west along the shores of Malabar and on the east along the Coromandel coast. The north, an area of sparkling winters and arid heat, lay in the same latitude as Central Arabia, the Sahara and the northern deserts of Mexico; the tropical south in that of Uganda, the Gold Coast and Guatemala. And all but the lush extremity of the south depended on the summer monsoons which swept in with varying intensity from the equatorial ocean.

Though the townspeople had long developed a great variety of specialized crafts and textile manufactures, India was, and is, a peasant country. Its civilization had derived from the prehistoric cultures along the Indus and the Ganges, on which peoples from the north had long descended: most decisively in the mid-second millennium B.C. when Aryan-speaking pastoral tribesmen had mastered the strategically important Punjab—the Land of the Five Rivers. In spite of an inhibiting caste system designed to perpetuate their difference from the native Indians, these invaders, their traditions and epic literature now preserved in Sanskrit, had blended over the centuries with the native culture to create the classic Buddhist India which had flourished under Ashoka, the greatest of the Maurya emperors. Following the brief incursion and Hellenistic influence of Alexander, he had ruled over most of the sub-continent in the third century B.C. And during the fourth and fifth centuries of the Christian era, when the Guptas had ruled from the Punjab to the Bay of Bengal, their empire, the second to unite most of the north, had seen the climax of what had now become a great Hindu culture. This long-established and superficially wealthy civilization—based on a primitive agriculture and harassed by endemic famine—had created a superb variety of art, sculpture and architecture, an elaborate literature and drama, and a strange contradiction of ascetic and orgiastic cults, of pacific and martial traditions.

By A.D. 1001 the first Muslim invaders had fallen upon northern India. Their cultures had been Persian (their leader, Mahmud of Ghazni, had been a patron of the poet Firdausi), their religion monotheist, and they were fiercely intolerant of Hindu polytheism and image worship, phallic cults, suttee, infanticide and veneration for sacred cows. They had been conquerors, encamped, like the Turks, among subject peoples, and they had exacted all the tribute they could get.

Most of these Muslim paramountcies had proved short-lived, as successive invaders had fought over the spoils. Muhammad of Ghor in 1193 defeated the Rajputs at Tarain, and in 1206 his viceroy, Kutub-ud-din, became Sultan of Delhi, now the centre of an elaborate Muslim culture; but the wars of Afghans, Turkis and 'White' Huns, of Rajput *rajas* in the northwest and Hindu *rajas* in the Deccan, had not eradicated the peasants over whose heads these storms had passed. And when, in 1526, Babur, the sophisticated and ruthless founder of the Mughal Empire, whose autobiography remains a classic, had conquered Hindustan, the most lasting of these Muslim dominations had been established. It had proved the third successful attempt to unite most of India.

Babur's grandson, Akbar, had been one of the greatest rulers of world history. Building in part on the work of an intervening Afghan conqueror, Sher Khan, he had established the first comprehensive government since the Guptas. His court had been richer and more magnificent than any in Europe, and he had himself been a lavish and discriminating patron of the arts. Miniature painters in the Persian style had depicted him in battle, mastering wild elephants for fun, or massacring big game in spectacular *battues* with the aid of cheetahs; but they had also depicted him discussing theology with Muslim *imams*, Hindu ascetics and Jesuit confessors, and visiting holy men on foot. Thick-set, bandy-legged, immensely strong, this descendant of Timur Lenk and Genghis Khan was Indian through his mother; and he endeavoured to transcend the hatred of Muslims and Hindus in a divine monotheism known as *Din Slahi* and summed up in the ambiguous phrase *Allahu Akbar*, 'God is Great', which also means 'Akbar is God'.

A brilliantly successful soldier, a pioneer in the use of artillery and expert in the organization of supply, he had secured an immense and permanent revenue by taxation systematically assessed on land according to its crops. He had maintained a sound currency and administered and financed his Empire through a central secretariat and district 'collectors'—a term inherited by the English. These officials extracted a third of the crops grown by the villagers, to be sold for the imperial revenues and for their own ample salaries. Since land belonged not to individuals but to the village community, this tribute raised from the village commune remained in Akbar's time an onerous but tolerable imposition. But under his successors the peasants would often be taxed to ruin, and desert their villages in despair, leaving the land to itself.

Yet the Mughal system provided a rational and lasting framework: better than farming out taxes to the highest bidder, a frequent custom in areas outside Mughal government. Though clogged with bureaucratic delays, and with even the greatest officials on precarious tenures, the administration united the Empire, while the tributes of the princes to the paramount Mughal added to the wealth which made the court a centre of fantastic luxury and of formidable military power.

So vast was the Empire that the revenues were enormous, but the spruce Turki boys in Persian coats set off by jewelled turbans and curved swords, the fiercely bewhiskered Rajput princes glittering with gems, the wily grey-beard officials in their robes of office, were an elite amid a sea of poverty. The armoured war elephants, the sleek horses, the mules and camels which transported the acres of tents and the oxen that dragged the great guns, were paid for by the tribute of villages in the precariously irrigated plains and in clearings in an encroaching jungle. In 1632, traversing the country between Surat and Agra, one of the Company's factors described the dead heaped by the road, mothers selling their own children, open cannibalism. Confusion, squalor, disease, mendicancy were then taken for granted; but in India among the teeming population of the Mughal Empire, then estimated at about eighty million, these things were on a vaster and more hopeless scale. And at the heart of this civilization was an entirely arbitrary power. All that Aristotle had said about tyrants is confirmed in the political record of Mughal India. No ruler was safe from poison or assassination; Shah Jahan conspired against his father, Jahangir; Aurangzeb against his father, Shah Jahan. Brothers fought over their inheritance, and the dynastic conflicts of Merovingian Gaul were fought out, on a much greater scale, in seventeenth-century India. But the unobtrusive civilian English— to the Muslims rapacious and common, low caste and unclean to the Hindus—came from an early modern world, a world of tenacious purpose, of political system, of order and plain common sense. A new and insidious element had been added to the Indian scene.

III

In this ancient and various society, at once static and confused, highly organized but subject to incalculable despotic power, in a climate then dangerous to Europeans, the English had to shift for themselves, and proved well able to do so. Surat remained their principal coastal base, with access to Agra where the most ambitious of their 'factories' was established. But by 1639 they had also extended their hold on the Coromandel area near Armagon by a strip of coast six miles long by a mile wide, in full possession; it would become the sovereign enclave of Madras Patanam. Here they found textiles in good demand, in particular if coloured a 'pleasant green' or 'carnation colour'. And here, as at Surat and Agra, they lived in what they termed a 'College' behind substantial walls. By 1641 Masulipatam had been founded and from these bases the Company's factories in Bengal and Orissa could be developed. The more so since at his accession in 1628 Shah Jahan—another royal aesthete who commissioned the Taj Mahal and combined good taste with political murder—had evicted the Portuguese in Bengal for supporting Jahangir and so backing the wrong horse.

Naturally Charles I, never a businesslike monarch, gave the Company little backing, and during the Civil Wars it was mulcted by both sides. But in 1656, under the efficient Protectorate, the Company's charter was confirmed and in 1658, under a new charter, its monopoly was enhanced. The merchants now lived better and, of necessity, in some state. The death rate could be one in three, but the survivors lived well in a European–Indian style, their curries washed down by arrack punch and beer; by the mid-century they also had tea and coffee. They wore turbans and light cottons in Indian style and, when they did not ride, were carried in palanquins by bearers. Attended, like all people of any consequence in India, by a swarm of servants, they now observed some formality. Moreover, since their convoys had to be guarded, they regularly hired soldiers. It was necessary to maintain face, proceed with some pomp, and carry 'St George, his colours swallow-tailed in silk'.[8]

And when, in 1665, the English at last gained possession of the island of Bombay—part of the dowry of Catherine of Braganza, whose marriage to Charles II had consolidated a Portuguese–English colonial interest in common detestation of the Dutch—they could assert a naval power with which no Asian ruler would care to compete. The foundations of the three 'Presidencies'—Bombay, Madras and Bengal—had been laid. And although in 1650–1 the Navigation Acts of the English Republic struck at the far-flung Dutch commerce and foreshadowed three Anglo-Dutch wars for colonial objectives, since the affair at Amboyna the English had abandoned any major ambition in Indonesia and beyond. They had established themselves firmly in India, whence they could prosecute their trade with Persia up the Gulf, their ventures to Indo-China, and in time—though after 1640 excluded from Japan—to their original objective of China, the fabulous 'Empire of Cathay'.

[8] Woodruff, *op. cit.* Vol. I, p. 56.

CHAPTER 4

West Africa and the Caribbean

In 1531 'Olde Mr William Hawkins of Plimmouth, a man for his skill in sea causes much esteemed, and beloved of Henry the 8', who had brought the Brazilian *Cacique* to Whitehall, had already been to West Africa as well as to Brazil. West Africa meant gold-dust, ivory, pepper and slaves: since 1482 the Portuguese had been exploiting the area and shipping slaves to their Brazilian plantations, and English adventurers were keen to take a hand. They now penetrated new territory, founded trading-posts which would lead to greater commitment and even, in the nineteenth century, to colonization; they also contributed to the development of a traffic which would reach nearly a million 'blacks' by the end of the sixteenth century, about seven million during the eighteenth, and become integral to the economy of the first or Old Colonial British Empire.

The slave-trade was, of course, no European innovation: 'there had been slavery in Kongo, as in every other part of Africa long before Europeans began to export negroes overseas'.[1] To ship Negroes to the American plantations seemed the obvious thing to do, since the Amerindians were incapable of sustained labour, and if coerced, apt to lie down and die. Moreover since the slaves could become Christians, the trade combined duty with profit. It came to determine the economy and social order of vast areas in the Americas and of the Caribbean islands, leaving a social problem still unresolved.

But though old Hawkins' reconnaissance was followed up by his more famous slave-trading son, it was gold, ivory and pepper which first lured the English to West Africa as far as the Bight of Benin and the estuary of the Niger. The Portuguese had come to the coast to circumvent the Muslims in Morocco who had interrupted the trade

[1] Roland Oliver and J. D. Fage, *A Short History of Africa*, Harmondsworth, 1962, p. 126.

in gold across the Sahara from the medieval centres of Old Ghana, Mali, Songhai and Kano. And this gold had derived from what is now northern Guinea and the rain-forest lands of modern Ghana. Here in the tropical *Ahaln-Ignuinawem* (Berber for 'Negrolands' and the original of 'Guinea') was the most densely populated and wealthy region of West Africa. The people raised millet, sorghum, yams and gourds; poultry, hogs and goats; and the more affluent minority wore rich bark-cloth and gaily coloured cottons, with gold for ornament.

These Negro kingdoms of the sixteenth century, the heirs of an ancient civilization, were wealthy and formidable powers. Mali, Songhai and Bornu in the interior; Akan and Benin on the coast; above them, Oyo and Nupe. In 1602 a Dutch observer would compare Benin in size to Amsterdam, his highest compliment. The portrait heads of Yoruba Ife and the ivory masks of Benin are famous. So the Europeans did not, as is often supposed, only raid, swindle and plunder the savages of Senegal or Sierra Leone, but dealt with rulers of large kingdoms who monopolized commerce and gladly traded their produce, their subjects and any victim in the interior they could catch, for European novelties: preferably drink and fire-arms. So a few Europeans established themselves along the coast, where the mid-Atlantic broke in tremendous surf, and the tropical sun, dispersing the mists over the mangrove swamps, glittered on mosquito-ridden estuaries.

II

To those fever-stricken shores in 1553, the year that Chancellor's expedition had set out for Muscovy, came the *Primrose* and the *Lion* out of Portsmouth, with Captain Thomas Windham from Somerset in command. This hard-bitten sea-dog, whose portrait reveals his character, had successfully traded cloth and arms for sugar, dates and molasses in Morocco. He was now after pepper. So by way of Madeira and the Canaries and the Sestos River, he had pressed on to Benin, against the advice of his Portuguese pilot not to go so far at that season. 'This whoreson Jew,' he had said—for such was Pinteado's race—'hath promised to bring us to such places as are not, or as he cannot bring us unto: but if he do not I will cut off his ears and nail them to the mast.'[2]

In Benin, the formidable Oba proved to be 'a black moore (although not so black as the rest) who sate in a great hall long and wide ... the roofe of their boords open in sundrie places ... to let in the aire'. He had thirty or forty hundredweight of pepper in store,

[2] Hakluyt, *op. cit.* p. 33.

and soon collected much more, so that they obtained sixty tons. But Pinteado had been right: the crews died off, four and five a day, and Windham, 'all raging', wrecked the pilot's cabin and possessions, then died himself. The crews, deserting their colleagues at the Oba's palace, then sailed for England. Seven days out, Pinteado succumbed, out of sheer chagrin, it was said. On the first Tudor expedition to West Africa the 'white man's grave' had found its victims, and the 'mad' English sea-captain of nineteenth-century fiction his proto-type.

Undeterred, the English sent out other ventures after the pepper, the ivory and the gold. But John Hawkins had wider ambitions. Like the Portuguese, he saw West Africa as the catchment area for the most profitable of all commodities: slaves for the Spanish settlements in the Caribbean and on the Spanish Main of South America. The planters needed labour so much that Hawkins, who still claimed to serve the King of Spain as well as Elizabeth I, hoped for a quasi-legitimate commerce. And, indeed, assured that Negroes were 'very good merchandize in Hispaniola', and trusting the Spaniards no further than he was able to master them, he twice got away with it. But his voyages had been horrible: the 'middle passage' took two months, with the 'blacks' battened down in conditions so appalling that it was reckoned a quarter of them would die. Only brutal discipline prevented mutiny; but as they were herded blinking in the unwonted sunlight on the quays of dilapidated Caribbean settlements, the Spanish planters, with or without the connivance of the authorities, were eager to buy.

In 1563 Hawkins had returned to England with a cargo of sugar, pearls and hides, having sold three hundred Africans at a big profit. On this early venture the Negroes were savages who wore necklaces of their enemies' bones and teeth, but the other Africans from the big states further east, who came to form the bulk of the slave-trade, had more to lose. Their social order disrupted, some acquiesced in numbed servility, some irrepressibly revived; a few plotted revolt. These the English would use against their Spanish masters, then often kill them in the interests of white solidarity. Such was the first English contribution to the slave-trade, already, within limits, long-established by the Spaniards and Portuguese.

III

In 1568 Hawkins, on his third voyage, with ten ships had crossed from Africa to the Caribbean, where he had again sold his cargo at a profit. But the large and obsolete royal ship *Jesus* had needed repairs;

so he had put into San Juan de Ulloa, the port of Mexico. There, when the Spanish Viceroy's big fleet arrived, they had found the English in the harbour. Hawkins could have kept them out of their own port; but unwilling to risk unauthorized battle, he had admitted them. And, once inside, the Spaniards, in spite of a written pledge not to do so, had attacked the intruding heretics and overwhelmed them. Half the English crews had surrendered and in the ships that got away, most of the crews had perished on the voyage home across the North Atlantic. Only the young Francis Drake in the *Judith* managed, characteristically, to escape intact.

The affair ended the old understanding with Spain; set off a systematic English assault on Spanish America and the gradual occupation of many Caribbean islands from Trinidad and Barbados up to Jamaica—an area that proved one of the richest of the Old Colonial British Empire. And immediately the encounter provoked the Elizabethan government into the first global strategy in English annals, which led to Drake's circumnavigation of the world—a spectacular prelude to naval supremacy.

Drake was the first English seaman to win international fame and to establish the captain's absolute authority at sea.[3] He was very conscious of that authority in an unmedieval way. When he had to execute Thomas Doughty, his second-in-command and Burghley's spy, he acted with macabre correctness, improvised a trial by jury, took communion with the culprit, preached a sermon: the 'gentleman', he said, 'must haul and draw with the mariner and the mariner with the gentleman'. For Drake combined aggressive Puritan piety with brilliant tactical flair; indeed the English generally sacked towns, settlements and churches with godly conviction. He was also a Renaissance man: his panache and fine manners surprised his ad-

[3] Sir Francis Drake (1541–96) came of yeoman stock at Tavistock, Devon, where his godfather and patron, Francis Russell, son of the first Earl of Bedford, owned a manor. His father became chaplain at the Medway dockyard, and the boy first went to sea in barques plying between the east coast and the Low Countries. He sailed with Hawkins to West Africa; by 1572–3 he was raiding the mule-trains which carried silver from the Pacific to the Caribbean. After his circumnavigation of the world, he made spectacular raids in 1585–6 on San Domingo in Hispaniola and on Carthagena on the Spanish Main. In 1587 he made a successful foiling attack on Cadiz, and in the following year played a major part in the defeat of the Armada. He made a substantial fortune from his voyage round the world: if it was not much compared with the colossal sum of £320,000 which it made for Elizabeth I, Drake netted £10,000 and had doubtless laid by some more, so that he could buy Buckland Abbey in his native Devon. Here he retired after the failure of the attack on Lisbon in 1589 until his last and fatal expedition to the West Indies in 1595, when he died of fever.

versaries, unaccustomed to civilized behaviour from heretic corsairs —instead of keeping only the gentlemen for ransom and throwing the rest overboard, he would actually spare the entire crew.

Drake was also the first great English explorer. On the Californian coast, for example, when he landed, probably at Drake's Bay near Point Reges for he never found San Francisco harbour, he had the country and the Miwok Indians carefully described: they took the strangers for gods, performed ceremonial dances of goodwill and misguidedly enough, welcomed the Europeans. Drake then set up a brass plate 'nailed to a great firm post' and claimed the country, which he named New Albion, for Elizabeth I.[4] And if the Spaniards, needing to service their galleons from the Philippines and determined that no one else should dominate the Strait of Anian, should it exist, now hastened their explorations of northern California, the first English contact with far western America would have its sequel in the days of Cook and Vancouver.

When Drake crossed the Pacific, he was also the first English commander to arrive from the east. Here, by contrast, he found a rich and ancient civilization, ruled by the Sultan of Ternate, 'from his waiste down ... all cloth of gold ... and about his neck a chain of perfect gold, the links whereof were great and one fold double'. What was more, at Batareve, 'linnen cloth was of good merchandise for turbans and girdles', and the island rich in 'gold, silver, copper and sulphur and in nutmegs, ginger, long pepper, lemons, cucumbers, cocos, figs and sago'. Fortified with these luxuries, the English sailed to Java major and Drake returned by the Cape; to be knighted, at the Queen's command, by the compromised hand of the French Ambassador at Deptford.

The exploit, the second circumnavigation of the world, had 're-verberating effects in every direction. It was a sudden and brilliant demonstration that a new power had arrived on the oceans.'[5] And

---

[4] 'The Indians were extremely fond of dancing which they engaged in not only for amusement, but also in connection with the numerous ceremonials with which they celebrated any important event, public or private. The North West Indians ... had a salmon dance; special dances for the new-born child, for the black bear, for the new clover, for the white deer, and for the elk; the dance of welcome to visiting Indians; the dance of peace,' Andrew Rolle, *California: A History,* second edition, New York, 1969, p. 22. The country had already been named California from a 'second-rate romance of chivalry known to Cortez about a wonderful island of tall bronze coloured Amazons ruled by a pagan queen Calafia' (pp. 33–4). 'Drake's plaque' found in 1934 is probably the original.

[5] A. L. Rowse, *The Expansion of Elizabethan England,* London, 1955, p. 186.

this power would be confirmed in 1588 by the defeat of the Spanish Armada. For in spite of a dangerous sequel and subsequent gruelling campaigns in Ireland and the Netherlands, by 1604 the peace with Spain marked Spanish recognition of an accomplished fact. Thenceforward, first the Dutch, then the English, dominated the Channel and the trade routes radiating out from it about the world, confirming the shift of economic opportunity from the Mediterranean to the Atlantic, and opening new prospects of trade and even settlement.

IV

The English, though not yet as strong as the Dutch, now used this sea power in the Channel and Atlantic more systematically to break into the Spanish colonial empire in the Caribbean—a project which already obsessed Sir Walter Raleigh. The Spaniards dominated, and retained, the Greater Antilles, Cuba, Hispaniola and Puerto Rico, Central America and the 'Spanish Main'—the mainland of what is now Colombia and Venezuela; but the Lesser Antilles, strategically placed athwart the Spanish sea-routes, were soon colonized by the northern Europeans. And the English would clinch their hold on what would long be the most valued of their colonial possessions, when in 1655, in pursuit of Cromwell's ambitious and far-flung Western Design against the Spanish Empire, the government of the Republican Protectorate—the first deliberate imperialists of settlement—seized upon and colonized Jamaica, commanding the vital 'Windward' passage between Cuba and Hispaniola into the Florida Channel, the main route to Europe out of the Caribbean.

The area which the northern Europeans would wrest from the Spaniards during the first half of the seventeenth century, and which would become the scene of fluctuating but hectic prosperity and brutal conflict for the most-prized area of colonial empire, seemed much more attractive than North America. But it had its major disadvantages, climatic and social.

When Columbus had landed in the Bahamas, the Arawak Amerindians, a pacific and tractable people who had colonized the West Indies from South America, had lately been exterminated from all the Lesser Antilles, save Trinidad, by fierce man-eating Caribs— the original 'Cannibals'. In contrast to the easy-going Arawaks, the Caribs were a formidable people, fine seamen and swimmers. But they had certain inhibitions: they would not 'eat pigs lest their eyes should become small, nor turtles, to avoid becoming stupid'; so, although they were partial to plump iguanas, these 'fierce and bloodthirsty warriors ... ate the bodies of their enemies', and 'boucanned'

—that is, dried and smoked—the 'more distinguished' ones 'whom they had killed in battle, and handed them round to be gnawed at special festivals'. In 1564 they ate the crew of a Spanish ship, and in 1596 that of a French one—'the French they declared made most delicate eating, while the Spaniards were the hardest to digest'. It was also said 'that Arawak boys captured by the Caribs were emasculated and fattened for eating'.[6] While the Arawaks were enslaved by the Europeans—in the Bahamas they were told they were being taken to meet their ancestors—they soon died of broken hearts or committed suicide; but the Caribs, in their great *piragua* canoes, darted about the islands or lurked in tropical jungle, armed with poisoned arrows, and in some islands long remained unsubdued.

Such were the original human inhabitants of this neolithic and exotic world. They had no domestic animals save some little dumb dogs—also eaten on occasion—and poultry; but parrots, pigeons and flamingoes, turtles and a great variety of fish, oysters and conches were all abundant. Cotton and coconut, maize and tobacco, avocado pears, guava and the delicate papaya were indigenous. But toredo and banksia worms infested the hulls of European ships; poisonous ants, scorpions and tarantulas were a menace.[7] In Trinidad there were vampire bats. The climate, apparently ideal even to the dour Puritans who incongruously attempted settlements in the Bahamas and Old Providence Island, in fact included appalling seasonal hurricanes, while volcanoes and earthquakes were more intermittent but more terrible dangers.

Until the twentieth century the worst hazard was disease. Mosquito-borne malaria and yellow fever—the latter imported from West Africa—wrought havoc among new settlers and garrison troops, unaccustomed to the tropics. And since the exploitation of the islands seemed to demand negro slave labour, a new dimension was given to the problems already presented by the Amerindians and the climate. Though the successful planters attained great wealth, for most settlers the prospects of affluence amid palm-fringed islands, white sands and translucent waters proved less substantial than the rewards of colonizing the wilderness of Virginia and New England.

The English settled mainly on the islands. Though Raleigh's hopes of finding *El Dorado* had been disappointed, Guiana on the Main looked promising for sugar and timber; and a settlement was also made at Belize on the Moskito Coast of Honduras for log-wood and

[6] Sir Alan Burns, *History of the British West Indies*, London, 1954, pp. 44–5. To this admirable and standard work the following pages are indebted.
[7] Burns, *op. cit.* p. 20.

later for mahogany; but between 1620 and 1642, twenty thousand settlers had gone to Barbados alone (only about thirty thousand had gone to North America) and already by the 'twenties, Sir Thomas Warner, disillusioned with Guiana, had settled St Kitts and Nevis. By 1632 Montserrat and Antigua were taken over, and in 1630 Lord Warwick and other Puritan magnates, with John Pym as Treasurer, formed a company, in which Oliver Cromwell took shares, to settle Old Providence, an island strategically placed off modern Nicaragua between Cuba and Panama.[8] But the western Caribbean soon demoralized even the Puritan planters. The company soon had to order cards and dice to be burned, and to put down 'mixed dancing and other vanities'; virtuous clergymen were hard to come by, and one who could not even preach extempore was thought 'more fit for a buffcoat than a cassock'. Another clergyman favoured the negroes, and became very unpopular. Piously concerned at employing Christians, the colonists left the slaves unconverted. There was a slave revolt, and by 1641 the place had become a haunt of pirates; then the Spaniards captured the island, now a Dutch possession.

The West Indies, like the East Indies, were still dominated by the sea power of the Dutch, now engaged in the Thirty Years War; and in 1628 their admiral, Peyt Heyn, captured or sank the entire Spanish treasure fleet in the Florida channel—a more crippling blow than any struck by the Elizabethan corsairs. But they were more interested in trade than in plantations and the English took advantage of the Spanish defeats to establish themselves on the islands.

The most successful English colony was Barbados, where rum-drinking was early notorious. 'The Chief fudling they make in the Iland is Rumbullion, alias kill Divill, and this is made of suggar cones distilled, a hot hellish and terrible liquor.'[9] In 1625, a sea-captain, returning from Brazil in the service of a Bristol company headed by Sir William Courteen, had annexed the uninhabited island; then, backed by Lord Pembroke and Montgomery, the company began to exploit it. But in 1628, Charles I, with characteristic insouciance, granted Barbados to a bankrupt courtier, the Earl of Carlisle, and made him Governor Palatine of all the Lesser Antilles. He soon handed over a vast acreage to his London creditors. In the ensuing conflict, the Crown decided for Carlisle, and the Courteen interest, as might have been expected, lost heavily on the enterprise.

But Barbados prospered in spite of continuing friction between the

---

[8] A colony distinct from New Providence, with its capital Nassau, in the Bahamas.
[9] Burns, *op. cit.* p. 218.

Carlisle interests and the planters, and of 'such aboundance of small knatts by ye shore' ... and a 'multitude of little black aunts on the trees'.[10] Cotton, tobacco and indigo crops began to flourish on small plantations so that in 1639 there were more than thirty thousand settlers. Then, under the governorship of Captain Philip Bell in the 'forties, sugar was planted on a much bigger scale. Affluence for the major planters and ruin for the lesser ones were on the way. The Civil Wars now brought out some well-to-do royalists to take refuge in Barbados, and when, following the Navigation Acts against Dutch and other foreign shipping, the Republican government imposed sanctions on the island to prevent their trading with the Dutch, the Governor, Lord Willoughby, the Council and the Assembly made one of the earliest and most eloquent assertions of colonial rights against the first centralizing English government, the original architects of the mercantilist Old Colonial system.

They had, after all, they declared, developed the islands themselves; why, they asked, should they obey 'those that stay at home'? Like the Americans in 1776 and Rhodesian 'rebels' in our day, they repudiated a parliament in which, they said, 'we have no representative and persons chosen by us'. That would be 'a slavery far exceeding all that the English nation has yet suffered'. Their own regime, they insisted, was the 'nearest model ... to that under which our predecessors of the English nation have lived and flourished for a thousand years ... a right-well settled government'. Then, repudiating economic sanctions, they declared that they would never be 'unthankful to the Netherlanders', whose goods, anyway, were the cheapest. Nor would they ever, they concluded, 'alienate themselves from those old heroick virtues of true Englishmen, to prostitute our freedom and privileges to which we are borne to the will of anyone'.[11]

The royalists in Barbados were soon overwhelmed by a squadron of the Cromwellian navy, which had hunted Prince Rupert out of the Mediterranean and which now hunted him out of the Caribbean. Puritan laws were hopefully enacted to put down blasphemy, swearing and sin. But by 1659 the Barbadian Council had made a clean sweep of the Republic's authority, and declared all patents from Oliver and Richard, late Protectors, 'void and null'.

But Cromwell's neo-Elizabethan concern with the West Indies, part of his wars against the Dutch and Spain, had other more lasting results. His Western Design of 1654 was nothing less than to establish a colonial empire on the ruins of the Spanish possessions in the

[10] Burns, *op. cit.* p. 226.
[11] Burns, *op. cit.* pp. 745–7.

Greater Antilles and on the Main. It failed in its more ambitious objective, but it secured Jamaica, a major permanent asset. And if the mishandled expedition contrasted with Drake's brilliant but transitory exploits, it had lasting results and anticipated later successful muddlings through.

In 1655 the Cromwellian fleet, based on Boston, sailed down to Barbados, thence westward to attack San Domingo on Hispaniola. But the assault was a fiasco: Drake had taken the town with a thousand men in a day; but now, wrote an observer, 'God was not pleased to deliver it unto us though with 9,500 men ... so that never were men more disappointed.'[12] 'I hope,' wrote Colonel Sedgewick, 'God hath brought down our comfortable spirits for some more noble work.'[13] General Venables, Admiral Penn and Vice-Admiral Goodson now turned on Jamaica. The Spaniards fled to the hills, leaving only 'niggers' and Portuguese, and 'God seemed to smile' on the English; but the soldiers soon died of dysentery and fever, and refused to plant vegetables even for their own benefit. Sedgewick was soon writing 'Unless God in His mercy stay his hand, it will be sad for us in the island.'[14] At present God seemed displeased; and a brilliant guerrilla leader, Cristoval de Ysassi, took to the hills and organized the maroons and negroes against the incompetent English commanders of almost the only Cromwellian campaign to be mishandled.

General Venables now went sick and returned to England; Admiral Penn, anxious to vindicate himself, hastened to leave first; and Cromwell put them both briefly in the Tower for desertion. Then Venables' successor died; Vice-Admiral Goodson, now in command, reported 'great complaints of the squadron of the bread sent out in old liquor casks and great increase of vermin, as cockroaches, weevils, ants, earwigs, mites and such-like'. He asked for copper-sheathed ketches and carpenters, and twine for turtle nets. As for the soldiers, he wrote, they were dying fast, 'forced to work in the heat of the sun'. What they endured, he considered, proceeded from the army's own neglect.

Two thousand bibles were now dispatched for the troops,[15] but Ysassi, the maroons and the negroes soon killed another thousand of the invaders. And Sedgewick's personal reading of the intentions of the Almighty proved correct: by the following summer he was

[12] Burns, *op. cit.* p. 251, quoted from *The Narrative of General Venables*, ed. C. H. Firth, Royal Historical Society, 1900, p. 136.

[13] C.S.P., Colonial, Addenda, p. 96.

[14] C.S.P., Colonial, Addenda, p. 96.

[15] C.S.P., Colonial, 1574–1660, p. 426.

himself dead of fever, and his widow had been meagrely and briefly pensioned from Royalist 'delinquent's' estates.[16]

Somehow the island was held. The Spaniards had not the forces to regain it; and already in October the Council of State discussed sending out a thousand Irish boys and a thousand Irish girls over fourteen to help populate the place. To the annoyance of Boston, they also tried to induce New Englanders 'who knew and feared the Lord' to leave their 'wilderness' for 'this land of plenty', offering all males twenty acres a head. Only about three hundred arrived. But experienced planters were brought over from Nevis, and by 1660 the Restoration Government, continuing the imperialist designs of the Protectorate, thought the settlement well enough established to pay off the 2,200 soldiers who had survived and send out respectable 'poor maids' rather than women from Newgate. Charles II himself accepted a private plantation, and the government, now exploiting the slave-trade from both sides of the ocean, urged the Royal Africa Company to establish the staple for the 'sale of blacks' in the island. From being a garrison Jamaica had become a colony, and the potential base for a lucrative trade in slaves as well as in sugar, cotton, tobacco and dye woods. It remained, too, a strategic base; and what with the booming sugar industry and the lavish spending of the bucanneers who soon made it their headquarters, a phase of riotous prosperity set in. With the development of slavery and sugar and the formal Spanish recognition of English possessions in the Caribbean in 1670, the major West Indies were to become the richest, the most favoured and the most fought over of the British colonies in the Americas.

[16] C.S.P., Colonial, p. 452.

CHAPTER 5

The Virginia Settlement; Bermuda

The plantations of Virginia and New England, at first small and amateurish in comparison with the great crusading conquests of the Spaniards in South and Central America and their hard-won settlement of California; with the far-flung explorations of the French; or even with Drake's highly professional exploits in the Caribbean and the Pacific, marked the greatest event in the history of the English-speaking peoples since the Old English had come to sub-Roman Britain. These North American ventures were thought less promising than the plantations of Bermuda and the West Indies; Raleigh, the main pioneer behind the reconnaissance of Virginia, turned again to Ireland and then to Guiana; while the so-called 'Pilgrim Fathers' arrived at Cape Cod by mistake, having originally planned to settle further south within the jurisdiction of Virginia. The Spanish *Conquistadores* in the Roman tradition of empire—*Un Monarca, un Imperio y una Espada*—had cut straight to their staggering objectives, a steel-clad elite seizing the strategic key points of populous and wealthy, if technologically primitive, societies; and they had been followed up by dedicated and often highly educated Erasmian *padres*, who planted an adapted Christianity among the demoralized Amerindians and so mitigated and consolidated the Spanish exploitation.

The small English settlements, on the other hand, were often made with dangerous casualness. The settlers tried at first to conciliate or ignore the savage inhabitants, pushing them out rather than mastering them at one paralysing blow; and they made their plantations on the fringes of a vast and sparsely inhabited wilderness.

The first, Elizabethan, reconnaissance was made on the initiative of Raleigh and Grenville in 1584. It was a proprietary venture, interrupted by the Armada campaign. But after the peace with Spain, James I's government took a hand and set up a Council for Virginia. The Virginia Company was backed mainly by London merchants

already behind the Muscovy and East India trade. Sir Thomas
Smythe, with his massive interests in the Muscovy and East India
Companies, was its treasurer; and Sir Edwin Sandys, who attacked
his administration, an influential parliamentarian appointed to the
Council in 1607, became assistant to Smythe in 1617 and Treasurer
in 1619 and 1620.

Sir Thomas Smythe (1558–1625), the grandson of a clothier from
Corsham in North Wiltshire, was the son of Thomas Smythe of West-
hanger in Kent, haberdasher and 'customer' of the Port of London.
His maternal grandfather was Sir Andrew Judd, Lord Mayor of
London under Edward VI, one of the founders of the Muscovy Company and the founder of Tonbridge School. In 1604 he himself went
to Muscovy, and from 1603 to 1621 (save for 1607) he was Governor
of the East India Company. From 1609 he was also Treasurer of
the Virginia Company. Though he was ousted by Sir Edwin Sandys
on charges of corruption and incompetence, the accusations were
never accepted by James I. This City tycoon had a vast range of
enterprise, including a governorship of the Somers Islands Company
for Bermuda. Like his grandfather, he was a major benefactor to
Tonbridge, to both town and school. The origins of his family fortunes in the Wiltshire cloth-trade is characteristic, as is their expansion into the East and America.

Sir Edwin Sandys (1561–1629) was the second of the seven sons of
Edwin Sandys, Archbishop of York, who had remarked, 'These be
marvellous times. The patrimony of the Church is now laid open to
all the world,' and founded a flourishing family. Educated at Merchant Taylors' and Corpus Christi College, Oxford, Edwin had collaborated with Richard Hooker in his *Ecclesiastical Polity*. He had
entered Parliament in 1588–9 as M.P. for Andover, and in subsequent
Parliaments sat for Plympton, Stockbridge, Hindon and Penryn. He
served on the Committee of the East India Company and was a
member of the Company for the Somers Islands (Bermuda). He had
also travelled extensively on the Continent when young, and wrote
Europae Speculum, or a View of the State of Religion in Europe.
As a Puritan and a constitutionalist, he opposed the policy of James I;
but although dismissed by the King in 1621, and briefly imprisoned,
he remained influential in the Virginia Company, of which Henry
Wriothesley, third Earl of Southampton and Shakespeare's patron,
was now governor. And when Virginia became a Crown Colony the
representative institutions there encouraged by Sandys were not
eradicated.

Such were the interests behind Virginia: part of the worldwide
trade speculation now established in the City. The New England

Plantation of 1629, though also backed in London, was most consistently promoted by Sir Ferdinando Gorges, Governor of Plymouth, by investors in Bristol and Dorchester, and by East Anglian Puritan gentry.

With this kind of backing by merchants of the City and Puritan opposition magnates, English representative institutions were early and firmly established. The patent of 1606 for the first settlement of Virginia limited the Colony to a hundred miles along the coast and a hundred inland, and established a miniature Jacobean administration 'designed for the propagation of the Christian religion and the bringing of infidels and savages to a settled and quiet government'.[1] The settlers under their own Council had the same liberties as Englishmen born; at Jamestown by 1619 an assembly of twenty-two burgesses represented eleven 'incorporations', 'hundreds' and plantations, and 'sat in the choir of the Church, the most convenient place they could find'.[2] Thus a conciliar but representative government was established, with decisive effect for the future of Virginia and the United States.

The early settlement was extremely precarious: of the one hundred and four men and boys who went out in 1607, fifty-one were dead of disease or starvation by the next spring. The settlers were mainly artisans, some idle and unadaptable; or inexperienced apprentices, or country boys, as Henry Spelman who had emigrated from Norfolk, 'beinge in displeasure of my frendis and desirous to see other countryis'; or youths 'given to excess of drinking together with the quarrelsome condition of young fyery spirits'.[3]

But in spite of Amerindian attacks, a 'noisesome' original site, dissension among the settlers and crises of confidence and finance at home, the plantation pulled through. In 1612 Chamberlain wrote to Carleton that he feared the plantation would fail 'because of the extreme beastly idleness of our nation'; a lottery had to be started to raise more capital and the underwriters were being sued in Chancery for their subscriptions. The only administrators who could control the colony were career soldiers—Captain John Smith and Sir Thomas Dale. And by 1617 Smythe's administration of the Company was under attack.

Further, pro-Spanish interests at Court were hostile to Sandys, who was personally detested by James I; and by 1624 the Company's charter was annulled. In 1625 Virginia became a Crown Colony.

[1] It was a 'pious and heroic enterprise'. C.S.P., Colonial 1574–1660, London 1860, p. 11.
[2] op. cit. p. 13.
[3] 'or disorderly persons, profane and riotous'. op. cit. p. 12.

During the Civil Wars most Virginians were for the King, and though
the Republican Government, having 'reduced them to obedience',
granted favourable articles of surrender, most of the planters, as in
Barbados, remained Royalist.

So in Virginia a politically and economically sound, if sometimes
'ungodly', version of Jacobean society was established; mainly exploiting tobacco, maize, silk, vines and livestock in what proved in
the long run a rewarding country with relatively mild winters in the
latitude of southern Spain and Morocco. In New England, in a
harsher setting, but still in the latitude of Vigo and Bordeaux, and
with a brighter if more extreme climate than England, the godly
Puritan colonists struck root and created the most redoubtable
centre of the East Coast establishment in America.

These small colonies, which in 1632 included the proprietary
colony of Maryland under Lord Baltimore, at first competed with
French and Dutch settlements up and down the coast, but they
struck such firm roots that throughout the entire North American
continent Anglo-Saxon forms of government, language and civilization would be paramount—a fact of even greater weight in the world
than the Spanish-American Empire.

II

Before these Jacobean and Caroline settlements are surveyed, the
Elizabethan reconnaissance, backed by Raleigh, demands attention.
In the summer of 1584, at the reverberation of a shot, a great flock
of white cranes, their cries 'doubled by many echoes', rose over a
well-wooded island off the mainland of what would become North
Carolina and heralded the first English foothold in that part of
America. Soon an Alconquian Amerindian, greatly daring, came
on board one of the ships. He was wined and dined and given a
shirt and a hat; then, to return the stunning hospitality, he presented
the English with a large catch of fish.

The country appeared, on the face of it, entirely attractive. There
were 'melons, walnuts, cucumbers, gourdes, pease' and 'diverse
roots'; 'fruits very excellent good', and 'country corn' (maize) of
which there were three harvests; and fat bucks, conies and fish 'the
best in the world', so numerous that the explorers tried to catch
them with a frying-pan, but found it 'a bad instrument to catch fish
with'. Moreover, when the local *Cacique*'s brother arrived with a
company of divers boats, he proved as 'mannerly and civill as any in
Europe'[4] and brought his wife and children aboard the ship—'his

[4] Hakluyt, *op. cit.* pp. 286ff., q.v.

Elizabeth I, Queen of England, France, Ireland and Virginia: from a late
16th-century engraving

North American Indian tribal dance, at about the time of
Raleigh's settlement of Virginia

Map of New England, 1614, with inset portrait of Captain John Smith, Admiral
of New England

The taking of Quebec by the British, 13 September 1759

The Battle of Bunker Hill, 17 June 1775

British Army Camp in New England, 1780

reet in
hiladelphia
1775

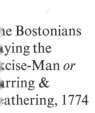

he Bostonians
aying the
xcise-Man *or*
arring &
eathering, 1774

The Red Lake Chief making a speech to the Governor of Red River at Fort Douglas, 1825

The Sargent family, New England, 1800

Sugar-cane plantation in Antigua, 1823

Making sugar in Antigua, 1823

wife being well favoured'. Even allowing for a probably interested exaggeration, these were just the noble savages that men of the Northern Renaissance hoped to find. Next year, after this glowing report, Raleigh's cousin, Sir Richard Grenville, came out to see for himself, and established a plantation on Roanoke Island in Pamilco Sound. The expedition included John White, the best watercolour artist of his day, and Thomas Hariot, a scientist who accurately described the country and its people and probably brought back the first potatoes. From Roanoke they reconnoitred Chesapeake Bay, where better anchorages offered. Then, planning to return the following year, Grenville returned to England. In spite of complaints of his tyrannical conduct, 'intolerable pride and insatiable ambitions',[5] the settlers had declared themselves 'resolute to stay rather than lose so noble a kingdom for the Queen'.

The first idyllic contacts with the Alconquians soon turned sour; and when in 1586 Drake appeared, fresh from raiding in the Caribbean, the famished colonists took the chance of going home. In 1587 Raleigh and Grenville sent out a new venture; but during 1588, the year of the Armada, they had other things to do than prospecting in America. And when in 1590 a final expedition was sent out under John White, he found only the macabre traces of an abandoned settlement.

Such had been the disappointing prelude to the Elizabethan settlement of Virginia. Now in 1606, the Elizabethan charters were revoked and a committee of the Privy Council set up: under Charles I it would become the standing Committee for Plantations.

It was against this background in 1607 that the first real settlers, under Sir Charles Newport, landed in Virginia on a swampy, reed-fringed peninsula. They made a log fort and called the place Jamestown, and the Alconquian inhabitants naturally soon attacked them. These Alconquians were part of a widespread confederacy of tribes dominated by a great *Cacique* or *Werowance*, called by the English the great Powhatan, though his proper name was Wahunsomacock. They probably amounted to about seven thousand tribesmen, and the entire Amerindian population of what is now Virginia to about eighteen thousand. They had a relatively advanced economy and practised rudimentary hoe-cultivation, hunting and fishing. In small plots round the huts the women grew maize and beans, pumpkins, squashes and tobacco. Sugar maples were tapped, mulberry trees cultivated; chestnuts, walnuts, hickory nuts and groundnuts were abundant, as were sturgeon, 'caveare', shellfish, crabs and turtle. The

[5] Hakluyt, *op. cit.* p. 3.

main meat was venison and squirrel, and James I, petulant when told that Lord Salisbury had received some Virginian flying squirrels, had hastily to be given one as well.[6] Deer were rounded up in elaborately organized hunts, or stalked in palaeolithic style by men disguised in skins. The more vulnerable kind of bears were chased up trees, where they were shot with arrows. Deer-hides and bear-pelts were staple clothing, and one of the few forms of work performed by the men was chewing and dressing skins. Fishing was skilfully organized by weirs and canoes and canoe-borne flares at night. There were wild turkeys, partridges, huge flocks of pigeons—so thick that they darkened the sky. With such materials the Amerindians lived well, their diet supplemented by a great variety of cultivated and wild fruits. But during the first winters the settlers, pent up in a small infertile area, were half-starved and survived by trading copper for food.

Like most primitive peoples, the Alconquians had elaborate rituals, centring on the seasons of the agricultural and hunting year. They worshipped a Sun God of order and light, but he demanded human sacrifice. 'For the most part,' wrote young Spelman, 'they worship ye diuell.' Once a year the whole community would troop out in the woods, when the medicine men made a circle of fire out of which a voice would choose two or three children to be bound and thrown into it. 'Be it the King's son, he must be given; after this, the men depart merrily, the women weeping.'[7] Their sports, the boy observes, "are much like ours in England', and their dancing 'like our darbyshire Hornepipe. They use beside football play, while women and young boys do much plaie at. They made their goals as ours, only they never fight nor pull one another down.'

The Amerindians were dangerous enemies. But they would never attack in the open, only among reeds or behind trees, whence they would stalk their enemies with arrows and tomahawks; or they would glide up estuaries in canoes, 'which is a kind of boat made in the form of an Hogg's trough, but somewhat more hollowed out', and softly steal towards their enemies. They had no drums or battle trumpets, but relied on 'howling and Howbabub';[8] and in the event, since by civilized standards they had no discipline, there was 'no great slaughter of neither side'. The rulers were supported by heavy tribute in kind, and by sheer terror. One method of execution was to dismember the victim limb by limb; another to flay him alive. One

[6] C.S.P., Colonial, p. 8.

[7] Henry Spelman, *A Relation of Virginia* (1609), reprinted London, 1872, p. 11.

[8] Spelman, *op. cit.* p. 19.

Werowance, interrupted in a spate of eloquence, tomahawked the interrupter with one blow and then went on with his oration.

Such was this neolithic society, one of the most advanced in North America east of the Rockies. In the consequent 'treacheries and encounters' Captain John Smith, a character justly famous in the history of the Empire, first became the immediate saviour of the colony, then went on to prospect New England—he invented the name—and his narrative is a classic of description and propaganda.[9] For Smith was a professional, seasoned in European wars: one panegyrist wrote of

> savages who shake
> At bruit of thee, as Spain at name of Drake.

Another, more specifically and simply,

> Fast by the hair thou ledst the savage grim
> Thy pistol at his breast to govern him.

Indeed, Smith, who had fought against the Turks, 'with sword and target made such a passage among these naked devils that they next him tumbled over one another'. But though Smith saved the colony, in 1609–10, after the flagship of the supporting expedition had been wrecked on Bermuda, the colonists were in the act of abandoning the settlement when Lord de la Warr's ship appeared in the estuary.

Then in 1611 Sir Thomas Dale, another professional soldier, took charge. Since under communal cultivation the settlers were apt 'to slip away' from their labour, he assigned each man 'three English acres of clear corn [maize] ground'. He also assigned much larger holdings—some up to 1,500 acres—to raise tobacco in commercial

---

[9] See *The Generall Historie of Virginia, New England and the Summer Isles* by Captain John Smith, 'sometymes governor of those countryes and Admirell of New England', London, 1624. This elaborate edition includes an anthology of earlier adventures, and is embellished by tributes to Smith in verse. As one eulogist wrote, he was no brutish mercenary Captain:

> I never knew a warrior yet, but thee
> From wine, tobacco, debts, dice, oaths so free.

Another wrote, in an obvious pun,

> Smith's forge mends all, makes chaines for savage nation,
> Frees, feeds the rest; then reade the Bookes narration.

The lower part of the title page includes an attractive picture of the country, with cedars, maize-fields and Amerindian huts and canoes. The upper half depicts the Indian Princess Pocohuntas in a coarser, thicker-faced version than the more elegant picture of her as a Jacobean lady which is generally familiar.

quantities. He also approved the politic marriage of John Rolfe to Powhatan's 'delight and darling, his daughter Pocohuntas' and so brought that 'subtle old revengeful' *Cacique* to apparent friendship.[10] He thus diminished the danger of 'emnity with the naturals' and the 'bruit of famine'.[11]

The Spaniards, infuriated at the intrusion of the English in Bermuda and Virginia into their American monopoly, now threatened to extirpate the colony, and the English ambassador in Madrid reported that they could do so 'unless we undertake the business much more thoroughly and roundly than we hitherto have done'; so the government decided to reinforce the plantation.

Virginia was strategically and economically worth defending: by 1616 Dale reported that it could 'put such a bit into our ancient enemies mouth as will cure his haughtiness of monarchy'. But, although, since the Tudor inflation, poverty in England was acute and the country 'pestered with multitude', colonists were hard to find. The English seemed 'wedded to their native soile like a snaile to his shell'.[12] Moreover, it cost £500 to transport even a hundred boys and girls who 'lay starving in the streets', though an enterprising Welshman offered to ferret out maidens who had fled from their parishes and of whose whereabouts their parents professed ignorance. Ill-disposed children, it was thought, might be brought to 'goodness' in Virginia, if the planters were strict. And the colony was now doing well. 'It did me good,' wrote one observer, 'to view our English wheat how far formed it was ... and English barley very hopeful.' By 1619 there were about 2,400 colonists; five hundred cattle; some horses and goats and 'infinite hogs in herds all over the woods'. 'Virginia wheat, called Maize', was even 'much commended for an excellent strong meat and hearty for men at sea—indeed, more wholesome on shipboard than beef'.

And the more affluent English were now thoroughly addicted to tobacco—probably introduced by Hawkins in the 'sixties—so the government forbade tobacco to be imported by foreigners or grown in England: 'If it must come,' people said, 'it had better come from beyond seas and not misemploy our soil.' The Virginians grew it on even bigger plantations.

Such was the environment of the first session of the first representa-

[10] Rolfe was in two minds about marrying an 'unbelieving creature', considering the fate of the sons of Levi who married strange wives: the fame of the episode shows how unusual it was.

[11] Ralphe Hamor, *A True Discourse on the Present State of Virginia*, London, 1615, p. 16.

[12] C. Bridenbaugh, *Vexed and Troubled Englishmen*, Oxford, 1968, p. 396.

tive Assembly in North America, convened by the new Governor, Sir Thomas Yeardley, in the church at Jamestown—in part still extant—on 30th July until 4th August 1619. Its proceedings are characteristic. First they secured a revenue by a tax of a pound of tobacco on everyone over sixteen to pay the expenses of the Speaker, the Clerk, the Sergeant and the Provost Marshal. They assigned seats to the twenty-two burgesses, and set up a committee to examine the laws of the settlement. They then discussed the assignment of land and, hopefully, the prospect of setting up a university or college, as well as 'changing the strange name of the Kiccowton plantation'. They fixed the price of tobacco at three shillings for the best and one and sixpence for the second quality, discussed the conversion of the Indians to Christianity and the planting of corn, of mulberry trees, of flax, hemp and vines. Finally, they sentenced Tom Garnett, servant to Captain Powell, to stand nailed by the ears for four days in the pillory for extreme neglect of his master's business and impudent abuse, and degraded Captain Spelman to act as interpreter for seven years for disparaging the government of the colony to the Indians. Then, since most of the assembly were overcome by the heat of a Virginian August, they closed the session.[13]

The proceedings are what one would expect: no declaration of rights, no covenant, no rhetoric, no drama. The concerns of this first representative assembly in the British Empire had been entirely practical.

The problem of attracting settlers remained. In 1620 a hundred children of the 'surplus multitude' at home were sent out as bound apprentices; and next year a considerable group of Walloons and Flemings was accepted—most of them skilled artisans. But the Amerindians had now realized the full implications of the settlement: they decided to wipe it out, and they nearly succeeded. Stealing up through the woods and reeds, they massacred 347 colonists. The disaster, commented Chamberlain, was the settlers' own fault —through 'supine negligence—no other nation could be so overtaken'. Here, too, was an aspect of empire which could be characteristic.

In spite of this tragedy, the Virginian plantation flourished. In 1622 the first negro slaves were brought in—harbingers of a vast social problem, but immediately useful; and when in 1625 the plantation became a Crown Colony, it was over the worst. To be sure, as in all pioneer societies, the law was not always enforced. Dr John Potts, for example, convicted of murder, got away with it as the only physician in the place. Women were still scarce—as late as 1635 a

[13] C.S.P., Colonial, p. 12.

batch of women was sent out from Newgate under threat of execution if they set foot in England again; and a highway robber was pardoned on condition that he emigrated. But in 1625 Charles I had worn Virginian silk at his coronation; and though the early investors had lost their money, there were now fine prospects for 'such a main continent as in Virginia and boundless for ought we have discovered'.

During the Civil Wars, the Virginians, always firmly Anglican, were royalist. The Governor, Sir William Berkeley, was a cavalier, and the big planters were socially reinforced by a few substantial royalist gentry, though most preferred the continent of Europe. The planters took advantage of the paralysis of the royal government to trade with the Dutch for negro slaves. When, therefore, the victorious Republican government attempted to reimpose trade restrictions, the Virginians, like the colonists in Maryland, Bermuda and Barbados, defied them. As already recorded, the Republic replied to this colonial revolt with the momentous Navigation Acts of 1650–1: stating the first clear doctrine of the sovereignty of Parliament over all the colonies and permanently forbidding any foreign ships to trade without licence with any of them.

But once they had recognized the new regime and its restrictions, the Virginian planters were left to themselves. Indeed, the Republican governments, though they encouraged emigration, were often indifferent to the society that would result. We have seen that their idea of populating Jamaica was to ship out Irish children and Newgate prisoners; so long as the political forms were observed, Virginian purchasing power, not Virginian loyalties, was what interested them. The Republican regimes imposed a mercantilist policy, enforced by sea power, the foundation of the Old Colonial Empire, and the Virginians adapted themselves to it.

By the Restoration the development of the colony was thus unimpaired; no internecine conflicts, as in Barbados or Maryland, had occurred, and a new generation of settlers was being acclimatized. Along the creeks and estuaries of the tidewaters of Virginia the big plantations spread; inland, as the primeval forest was tamed, a country of broad fields and woods, in parts reminiscent of the Yonne Valley in France, began to prosper, while the Blue Ridge and the Appalachian mountains sheltered the colony from the blizzards that howled over the great lakes out of Canada and the Arctic. Here, in due time, Washington would develop his estates along the Potomac, Jefferson build Monticello and the University of Virginia, and James Madison represent Orange County, his first introduction to political life.

III

The uninhabited Bermudas and their reefs and tides, discovered by the Spaniard Juan Bermudez early in the sixteenth century, had an evil reputation: the Spaniard, it was said, 'durst not venture there but calls them *Daemoniorum insulam*—the Isle of Devils'. In 1593, Henry May, the first Englishman to describe them, was cast ashore in a French ship, and the oldest English island colony in the western hemisphere was settled through shipwreck. In 1609 the supporting expedition of Sir Thomas Gates and Sir George Somers to Virginia had been badly timed, for they arrived off the Bermudas in late July, well within the hurricane season. The winds and seas became 'mad' in a 'hell of fury and darkness'; thunder and lightning stupefied the mariners, and though the rest of the ships struggled on to Jamestown, the Admiral's ship—the *Sea Venture*—went on the rocks at the northwest corner of the main island.

Far from being the evil place expected, the islands proved to be swarming with hogs and the seas with fish—'which they took enough with their hands in half an hour that did suffice the whole company for one day'.[14] Rockfish, mullets, pilchards, greyfishes and turtles all proved excellent. As for the equally unwary hogs, the first hunt secured thirty-two. There were pigeons and many white herons. The islands were then covered with cedars, and out of them and from the iron and tackling from the wreck the explorers built seaworthy if clumsy boats. Under Somers' command, and laden with much-needed supplies, they reached Virginia in May 1610. The reputation of the 'remote Bermudas' was now transformed, and their settlement 'was at first considered the business of the greatest hope ever begun in our territories'. It was thought to call them Virginiola; but they were spared this fate, to become the Somers Islands, in compliment to the man who had in person done most to plant the settlement.

Here was a good harbour, and through clear waters darted swarms of brilliant fish. By 1614 a London company was formed for the plantation of the Somers Islands, the backers including Henry, Earl of Southampton, Lucy, Countess of Bedford, Lords Pembroke and Paget, the Earl of Warwick, Sir Edwin Sandys and Sir Thomas Smythe—most of them still commemorated in the Bermudan parishes. Settlers now began to 'nestle and plant there very happily'— the air 'so temperate the country so fruitful'—thinking so remote a place was safe. Overlooking coral beaches, their sub-tropical smell

---

[14] See Silvester Jourdain, *A Discovery of the Bermudas*, ed. J. Q. Adams, New York, 1940, for a first-hand account on which this description is based.

of gulf-weed strange to Europeans, and in the sheltered interior of the main islands, they built cottages reminiscent of Dorset and Devon and raised tobacco, mulberries, maize and palmito trees. Ambergris was found on the beaches, and the whales were heard 'blowing in the night'.

But there was soon trouble. Escaping from the ships, rats infested the islands; some planters became claustrophobic in a place which, in all, covered only twenty-one square miles, and five of them built a wherry and sailed off home in it. But in 1620 an Assembly was in being—still uninterruptedly extant; and the main fabric of a church erected, with its well-wrought cedarwood altar, three-decker pulpit and heavy, late medieval, West-Country font. By 1628 there were already two thousand settlers.

During the Civil Wars the majority declared for the King; the more so as the Bermuda Company, including the share-holding Earl of Warwick, was mainly Puritan. In 1644 a Parliamentary fleet put a Puritan governor in power; but the King's execution—'that horrid act of slaying his Majesty'—so roused the people that they replaced him by a royalist. Then in 1651–2, when Ayscue's squadron had mastered the Caribbean, the Puritan regime returned, supported by 'unconformable ministers' who had 'preserved their schismatic humours'. It inaugurated extensive witchhunts in which a number of harmless old women were executed. More permanent than the strife of religious factions, the tension between the settlers and the London Company remained unresolved. In 1658, on Warwick's death, a city merchant named Trott bought his interests and came to live on the island, where he supported the settlers against the company. But it was not until 1684 that the islands became a Crown Colony—afterwards important mainly for their strategic position: the Gibraltar, it would be said, of the western Atlantic.

CHAPTER 6

The American Arctic, Newfoundland, New England

'We reade,' wrote Richard Hakluyt the younger in his *Divers Voyages* which appeared in 1582, the year before Sir Humphrey Gilbert annexed Newfoundland, the first North American colony of the Empire, 'that the Bees when they grow to be too many in their own hive at home are wont to be led by their captaine to swarm abroad.'[1] The English had long been determined both to find the Northwest Passage to Cathay, the main inspiration of the northern ventures, east and

[1] *The Original Writings and Correspondence of the two Richard Hakluyts*, ed. E. G. R. Taylor, Hakluyt Society, Second Series, 2 vols, Vol. I, p. 175. Richard Hakluyt the younger, one of the many eminent Englishmen educated at Westminster and Christ Church, had a pervasive influence on his age. He came of a family of Herefordshire gentry near Leominster, through a younger branch who went into business as skinners in London. His interest in navigations and discoveries was inspired by his cousin, a lawyer, Richard Hakluyt the elder, and together their writings were decisive. 'I do remember,' he writes, 'that being a youth, and one of her Majesties scholars at Westminster that fruitfull nurserie, it was my nappe to visit the Chamber of my cousin, a gentleman of the Middle Temple ... at a time when I found lying open upon his boord certeine bookes of Cosmographies with an universall mappe: he seeing me somewhat curious in the view thereof began to instruct my ignorance ...' So inspired, he resolved to 'prosecute that knowledge', and as a Student of Christ Church gave the first lecture in Oxford on geography. It was Hakluyt the younger who most fired the Elizabethan English with enthusiasm for the American 'plantations' as a counterbalance to Spanish preponderance in the New World, and whose indefatigable industry collected the vast material on which modern knowledge of the Elizabethan exploration is based. His *Divers Voyages* was dedicated to Sir Philip Sidney, who had leased a big tract of the land to be discovered from Sir Humphrey Gilbert. His *The Principall Navigations, Voiages, Traffiques and Discoveries of the English Nation* appeared in 1589, the year after the Armada. But already in 1583, the *Discourse on Western Planting* had put the case confidently to the Queen, not simply for finding the route to Cathay or plundering the Spanish American Empire, but for settlement.

west, and to 'share a part stakes (if we will ourselves) both with the Spaniard and the Purtugale in parts of America and regions yet undiscovered'. The Gospel, after all, promised that 'everlasting riches await those who are zealous for the advancement of the Kingdom of Christ'.

They had early asserted their claim. The Letters Patent granted to John Cabot and his sons—'the first finders out of all that great tract of land stretching from the Cape of Florida into those islands which we now call the New Found Land', were still regarded as valid; and he had reached Cape Breton and Nova Scotia in 1497, only five years after Columbus' voyage.[2] Then, in 1576, a West-Country seaman, Martin Frobisher, his ship so low built that he could drag an Eskimo and his kayak on board, had penetrated beyond Labrador to Baffin Land into what is now Frobisher Bay, past great icebergs or 'Islands of Ice' which 'split with a roar as if a great cliff had fallen into the sea'.[3] Here he found black-haired Eskimoes 'like Tartars ... tawnie in colour'; and here he lost five men, whom they probably devoured. He also brought back a sample of black iron pyrites, certified by an Italian expert to contain gold.

The Queen herself and the Court magnates invested heavily in the potential goldmine; and an expedition carrying forty-one miners set out for Friseland, as they called what is today Baffin Land. The Eskimoes now welcomed them with a noise 'like the mowing of bulls', to which Frobisher answered in kind, and a wary barter was conducted. An Eskimo whom Frobisher tried to kidnap shot him with an arrow in the buttock; so a Cornish seaman 'served another such a wrestling trick that they took him alive' and 'with this strange new prey we repaired to our boats'.[4] The Eskimo igloos—two fathoms underground, 'having holes like a Foxe and Coney berry'—seemed even to the Elizabethans to be 'noisome dennes' defiled by their inhabitants' 'beastly feeding'; and after further brushes with the inhabitants, who when wounded would throw themselves into the icy sea to escape capture, the expedition returned laden with a mass of ore. Unhappily it proved worthless: badly stung, the London investors lost interest in northern exploration for some time.

But the West-Country interest was undeterred. John Davis, a mariner born at Stoke Gabriel near Dartmouth, wrote a work to prove that a Northwest Passage must exist, as indeed it does, though iced up, through Lancaster Sound, Barrow Strait, Melville Sound and

[2] See Samuel Eliot Morison, *The European Discovery of America A.D. 500–1600*, O.U.P., 1971, for the best account of the background.
[3] Hakluyt, *op. cit.* p. 151.
[4] Hakluyt, *op. cit.* p. 166.

McClure Strait, north of the magnetic pole. He was backed by Adrian Gilbert, brother of Sir Humphrey Gilbert and half-brother to Sir Walter Raleigh, and though later killed by pirates in Sumatra, he handled the Eskimoes better than had Frobisher. On Davis's second voyage in 1586 the Eskimoes flocked round the *Mermaid* (120 tons) in their kayaks, eager to barter sealskins for knives, and amicably wrestled and played football with the sailors. 'They eat all their meat raw,' he recorded, 'they live most upon fish, they drink salt water and eat grass and ice with delight: they are never out of the water but live in the nature of fishes.'[5] The word for sealskin was *Lethicksaney* and *Canyglow* meant 'kiss me'. Davis reconnoitred Baffin Land and Greenland up the broad strait that bears his name, proved that Greenland was separate from North America, and returned with five hundred sealskins, the Northwest Passage undiscovered.

An even more extensive reconnaissance was made by Henry Hudson who, failing by the eastern Arctic, tried the western. On Dutch service, he explored the Hudson River right up to Albany, but perished in 1611, marooned on the southern shore of Hudson's Bay, at the hands of mutineers.

Such, in brief, is the picture of the first English exploration of the Canadian north. But it would be fur and fish, not the Northwest Passage or iron pyrites, which would lead to settlement, first in Newfoundland, then in New England.

II

In 1578, Sir Humphrey Gilbert, a courtier educated at Eton and Oxford and, in contrast to Frobisher and Davis, no sea-dog, who had written a discourse not merely on the Northwest Passage, but advocating permanent settlement in North America, had obtained a patent to 'discover and occupy barbarous lands ... not actually possessed by any Christian Prince or people'. After an initial failure, he set out again in 1583, with four ships—the largest the *Delight*. He undertook the 'Westerne discovery of America', to 'plant Christian inhabitants in places convenient upon those large and ample countryes extended northward from the Cape of Florida lying under very temperate climes', and to convert the natives to Christianity. According to the sanctimonious but observant narrator of his voyage, their conversion was particularly urgent; the end of the world was obviously imminent, and now would be their last chance.[6] Gilbert

[5] Hakluyt, *op. cit.* p. 308.

[6] *A Report on the Voyage and the successe thereof attempted in the year of our Lord 1583 by Sir Humphrey Gilbert Knt, written by Mr Edward Hale, gentleman*, Hakluyt, *Selection*, pp. 236–82.

followed the normal trade course to the already long-established Newfoundland fisheries, distinguishable far off by the yelping gulls that preyed on the offal of the catch. He planned then to 'follow the sun' and took along a German mineralogist and a learned Hungarian refugee to write up the venture in correct Renaissance style.

The voyage was at first propitious. Though the navigator ran the flagship on to a rock in a calm sea and broad daylight when making an impressive entry to the harbour of St John's, the cosmopolitan and hard-bitten crews of thirty-six fisherboats, who had long been managing by sea-custom, thought it prudent to acknowledge Gilbert's annexation of the country—symbolized by the 'Arms of England in lead affixed to a pillar of wood'.

The Labrador current makes North America in winter much colder than the same latitudes in Western Europe, whose climate is modified by the Gulf Stream. But the explorers, arriving in summer, argued that the Newfoundland climate must be like that of Anjou, and that the cold could not be as bad as in Muscovy. The narrator dilates on the wild roses and strawberries of a Newfoundland summer; on the vast wealth of fish—not merely cod but salmon, bonitos and trout, as well as lobsters. The timber could provide resin, pitch and masts; there were swarms of geese and duck and a great white fowl called a 'gaunt'—Flemish for a big cormorant. Bears, black foxes, otters and beavers would provide rich furs: a live sable was caught to be shipped to England—though it never arrived.

Well supplied, they now turned south to disaster. Off Cape Breton Island in the mouth of the St Lawrence, the *Delight*, again carelessly handled, went aground. A hundred men perished, including the German expert and the Hungarian refugee, along with Gilbert's books and charts and a lump of ore which the German had sworn contained silver. Gilbert brooded over the loss and 'beat his boy' who had failed to retrieve this treasure into the *Squirrel*—the pinnace in which the Admiral was now navigating to explore the coast.

Then the weather got worse and they turned to run for England as a sea beast like a 'lion' passed them 'roaring'. They got more than half-way home; but north of the Azores a great gale hit them; Gilbert was last seen in the pinnace overcharged with netting and small artillery, which he had refused to leave, 'sitting abaft with a book in his hand'. 'They were as near to heaven by sea as by land,' he shouted, as a last encouragement, but that night the pinnace was overwhelmed. The other ship struggled back to Falmouth and ended her voyage at Weymouth.

In spite of the disaster, Newfoundland had been annexed. And in the following year, as we have seen, Gilbert's half-brother Raleigh sent the first reconnaissance to what is now the North Carolina coast and, the year after, planted Roanoke.

The hold on Newfoundland was not consolidated until well after the peace with Spain. English fishermen had frequented the banks since the time of Henry VII, but their trade had been seasonal and ill-organized: now in face of the hostility of the fishermen, the merchants established more economic fisheries based on Newfoundland itself. In 1610 John Guy, a London merchant, 'the first Christian who planted and wintered in the island', obtained a patent to colonize the more temperate southern and eastern parts, so that in 1613 the French were protesting against the settlement of what they called *Nova Francia*. The English government replied that they had 'presumed an interest in an English enterprise ...' Then, in 1617, Sir William Vaughan, a highly articulate Welshman, planted a colony, which 'proved hopelessly incompetent'.[7] He had called the plantation Cambriol; and, although he soon abandoned the enterprise, he wrote *The Golden Fleece* by 'Orpheus Junior', attacking those who 'reaped the fruits of all painful trades without wetting [their] cat's feet, though the fish be never so dearly prized'.[8] Another colonist, Robert Hayman of Exeter College, Oxford, praised the New Foundland:

> Exempt from taxings, illness, lawing, fear,
> If clean and warm no matter what you wear.[9]

And where Vaughan had tried to relieve Welsh poverty, Sir William Alexander obtained a patent for needy Scotsmen to colonize Nova Scotia. He also, in 1611, induced James I to extend the new order of baronets, originally devised to encourage the settlement of Ulster, to Nova Scotia, and so made a curious contribution to English social history. Like Vaughan, Alexander was a writer and very pedantic: in 1624 he published *An Encouragement to Colonise*, beginning with the 'Exodus of the Jews'.[10]

The feud between the original and seasoned 'Channel' fishermen and the later settled 'boatmen' of Newfoundland itself rumbled on through the seventeenth century. The government favoured the Channel interest, as a source of employment and a school of sea-

---

[7] *Cambridge History of the British Empire*, Cambridge University Press, 1929, Vol. I, p. 91.

[8] Quoted by A. L. Rowse, *The Elizabethans in America*, London, 1959, p. 174, q.v., for an account of this 'interesting Welsh fanatic'.

[9] Quoted *op. cit.* p. 177.

[10] Rowse, *op. cit.* p. 179.

manship, and Charles I tried to put the Channel fishermen under the mayors of the major seaports from Southampton round to Barnstable. In 1634–7, before the Civil Wars disrupted them, the Channel fisheries exploiting Newfoundland employed about three hundred ships and eighteen thousand men.[11] These fisheries were contemporary with the momentous colonization of New England, in a brisker climate and harder surroundings than the Virginian tobacco estates, and of the slave-worked sugar plantations of the West Indies.

So, in quest of the Northwest Passage through the Arctic, the far north of the American continent was explored; then 'the New Foundland' was annexed and settled and the Atlantic fisheries developed. But outside informed circles the new knowledge did not penetrate far. In 1597 some innocent Brownists petitioned to be let go 'to a far country that lieth to the West of Canada, where they may not only worship God but annoy the bloody and persecuting Spaniard about the Bay of Mexico'.[12]

III

By 1614 there was a seasoned professional to hand, determined on further expansion, who had already won reputation in Virginia. After a turn at whaling off the American coast, Captain John Smith had now set himself to promote the settlement of the country, then still called North Virginia or *Norumbega*. A considerable expedition from Virginia had already reconnoitred the coast up to Maine; and now, when after the peace with Spain piracy had diminished, a few independent settlers had tried to exploit the fisheries. It was Smith, who devoted far more of his time to New England than to Virginia, who first properly surveyed and appreciated the scale of the country —not only 'as God made it when he created the world'; but 'such as could equalize the famous kingdoms in its latitudes'. His *Description of New England* (1614), written to distract his mind when he was captured by a French pirate, claims that the New England fisheries 'better than the richest mine known, could serve all Europe', and that the timber could bring vast profit. There was also a great potential fur-trade, particularly in otter and beaver. Smith humbly entreated Prince Charles, now heir to the throne, to change 'their barbarous names to such English as posterity might say Prince Charles was their Godfather'. So the Prince named Cape Cod, Cape James, though the

[11] J. A. Williamson, *The English Channel*, London, 1959, p. 229.
[12] C.S.P., America, p. 31.

name never took on; the Massachusetts River became the Charles; and Bahannah became Dartmouth.

Smith had an influential and dedicated backer behind him. Sir Ferdinando Gorges, perhaps because of his peculiar name, has had less recognition than such obviously sound characters as Governor Bradford and Governor Winthrop. But in fact he was 'the man to whom more than any other, New England owes it that the idea of colonization was kept before the mind of the public and attempts made with constancy to carry it out, as the result of which scattered settlements took root before ever "Pilgrim" or Puritans appeared: the man who held on tenaciously to his fixed idea, in spite of all setbacks, personal losses and discouragements'.[13]

Coming of an ancient family in Somerset and descended through his mother from John Howard, first Duke of Norfolk, and so distantly related to the Queen, Gorges had some influence at court, and, having distinguished himself in the wars in the Low Countries and in France, and ruthlessly extricated himself from the Essex Rebellion, he had been appointed in 1605 Military Governor of Plymouth.[14] Here he had charge of three Amerindians—'a Godsend to an energetic soldier with time on his hands, at Plymouth Fort'[15]—who learnt enough English to give him an attractive account of their country.

So Smith had a knowledgeable and reliable supporter, with contacts in Bristol and Plymouth and with the court, and in 1614 he had canvassed his projects among the West-Country gentry and in the major seaports. Thus, by 1620 the original West-Country enterprise had won decisive court backing. The Lord High Admiral, the Duke

---

[13] A. L. Rowse, *The Elizabethans in America*, London, 1959, p. 122. See the whole chapter, 'Sir Ferdinando Gorges and New England', pp. 89–123.

[14] Born in 1566, second son of Edward Gorges of Wraxall, he made his way as a soldier, and administrator. Besides his military duties at Plymouth he was in charge of the regulation of the pilchard fisheries, and of measures taken to put down piracy. He collaborated with Lord Chief Justice Popham, formerly recorder of Bristol, in launching successive western enterprises, and recouped his own fortunes by marrying well four times. Though tolerant of the Congregationalist Pilgrims and Massachusetts Calvinists, even if the latter in effect broke into his monopoly, Gorges took the King's side in the Civil Wars and in old age helped to defend Bristol, where he died in 1647. His son succeeded to his rights in Maine, which the Massachusetts Puritans annexed in 1652. His grandson was bought out after the Restoration for a poor compensation. In 1621 Gorges wrote *A Brief Relation of the Discoveries and Plantations of New England*, and in retirement *A Briefe Narration of the Originall Undertakings of the Advancement of Plantations into the parts of America, especially showing the Beginning, Progress, and Continuance of that of New England*.

[15] Rowse, *op. cit.* p. 96.

of Buckingham, the King's favourite, was now its chairman; it was called 'the Council established at Plymouth in the County of Devon for Planting, Ruling, Ordering and Governing of New England in America', and Captain Smith's and Gorges' ambitious propaganda was behind it. But, as often in the history of empire, the man of vision got little advantage. Though appointed Admiral of New England, the Captain died in comparative poverty in London in 1631: a wreck, as he put it, 'upon this shelfe'—by which he meant a reef.[16] The Plymouth or New England Council, however, had been granted vast territories—extending between latitudes 40° and 48° and across the entire and unknown territories to the west. And it was, formally, in this area that both the Pilgrim Fathers and the Puritan settlers of Massachusetts would establish themselves.

It was thus not, as often supposed, on an unknown coast that the 'Pilgrims' (who had in effect told Smith that they preferred his maps to his company) arrived in November 1620 off Cape Cod—'only ... sand overgrown with shrubbie pines, huckleberry, and such trash, but an excellent harbour for all weather'.[17] The expedition of the 'Pilgrims' had been licensed, mainly through Sandys, by the original Virginia Company, and financed and equipped as a joint stock enterprise by merchants in the fish- and fur-trade who wanted a permanent base in America, the assets to be distributed among both parties after seven years. But whatever the motives of their backers, the Plymouth colonists came not for gain but for religion. In spite of fears from 'casualties of the seas, change of air and diet', and savages who flayed people alive with fish shells, these redoubtable and inexperienced enthusiasts were convinced that 'all great and honourable actions' were only accomplished through difficulties that 'might and must be emprised and overcome'. Independent Congregationalists, who had emigrated to Holland from Nottinghamshire, Lincolnshire and Yorkshire, they found 'great labour and hard living' among the Dutch. And, what was worse, their children were being not only overworked but corrupted by 'the great licentiousness of youth in that country' and 'getting the reins off their necks'.[18]

---

[16] Smith's veracity has been as much impugned over his account of New England, as over his adventures in Virginia; but his most authoritative editor has largely vindicated him. After he left Virginia the remaining twenty-one years of his life were devoted to the colonization of New England. See S. E. Morison, *Massachusettensis de Conditoribus or the Builders of the Bay Colony*, Boston, 1930, pp. 8–9 and 20. This admirable work opens with an enticing pastiche of a seventeenth-century table of contents.

[17] William Bradford, *History of Plymouth Plantation 1620–1647*, Massachusetts Historical Society, 1912, 2 vols, Vol. I, p. 152n.

[18] Bradford, *op. cit.* p. 55.

The famous but then insignificant voyage of the *Mayflower* in 1620 took nearly two and a half months, but only one lusty and 'profane' young seaman, who had laughed at the 'Pilgrims' for being seasick, had died—showing the 'just hand of God upon him'. At Southampton a nucleus of Independents, reduced to thirty-five, had been joined by others of less pious condition; but when, on 11th November, they 'fell on their knees and blessed the God of heaven ... who had brought them over the vast and furious ocean [and] set their feet on the firm and stable earth, their proper element ...' it was 'no marvel', writes Bradford, who soon became Governor of the settlement, 'if they were then joyful, seeing wise Seneca was so affected with sailing a few miles on the coast of his own Italy'.[19]

In the late fall they found the country 'with a weather-beaten face'; and though the Amerindians thought that winter a mild one, to the English it was 'sharp and violent'. In December the sea spray on their coats 'froze like glass'; from behind their barricade they could hear wolves howling, and the 'savages' come 'skulking about them ... readier', they thought, 'to fill their sides full of arrows than otherwise'. That winter at least forty of the hundred-odd settlers died of scurvy and exposure. Smith, the expert, comments rather acidly that they 'endured a wonderful degree of misery with infinite patience'.

At last the swift American spring 'put new heart into them'. They tilled their fields and placed a fish weir; the Amerindians, doubtless by a special providence, had for three years been stricken by a 'wasting plague'—probably virulent typhus—and were unusually thin on the ground. One of them, Tisquantum—they called him Squanto— had been sold in Spain and then, having escaped to Newfoundland, come to England with Gorges; he became their interpreter and advised them where best to plant maize. That year, with Bradford as Governor, they obtained a formal land grant from the Plymouth and New England Company against competing fishermen who were objecting to the settlement. Soon they were raising good enough maize to trade it with great profit for furs. In 1627, 220 otter skins with mink and musquash brought in £78-12s-0d, and 494 lb of beaver £383-14s-3d. In all the shipments were already worth £659-16s-11d. They appointed a goldsmith as their London agent, and that year, according to their contract, they bought out the London shareholders.[20]

But moral contamination pursued them. A reprobate settler,

[19] Bradford, *op. cit.* p. 155.
[20] Bradford, *op. cit.* II, p. 33.

Thomas Morton, already established near New Plymouth, had set up a maypole at his home at Merriemount. This pioneer of another aspect of New England life invited all and sundry, including the natives, to 'frisk in beastlie and Bacchanalian' orgies, and composed 'sundry rhymes and verses tending to lasciviousness'.[21] He also sold arms to the redskins and taught them to hunt on his behalf, and they got 'mad'. He had to be besieged and taken by Miles Standish, the colony's man of action. Nor was Morton the only settler guilty of this nefarious trade.

In 1630 Charles I's government, alerted of this danger, forbade all trade in arms with the 'savages'. But it was impossible to prevent it. Fortunately for the settlers, the 'savages' were at odds—Pequots against Naragansetts and the rest, and remained so, even when some of them realized that the Europeans would take their whole land. But the settlers were not above encouraging them to beat up another reprobate, Sir Christoper Gardiner, who, accused of concubinage, had gone native.

A much more important venture was now in train, drawing on resources in the West Country, London and East Anglia. In 1623 John White, the conforming but Puritan rector of Holy Trinity and St Peter's Dorchester, a Wykehamist from New College, Oxford, who had the ear of the Puritan Earl of Lincoln, had formed a Joint Stock Company, the Dorchester Adventurers, partly 'in compassion towards the [unemployed] fishermen and partly in some expectations of gain', under patent obtained from the New England and Plymouth Company. They had sent an expedition to Cape Ann, northeast of Boston. But it had not been a success: 'rarely', as White observed, 'any Fisherman will work at the land, neither are Husbandmen fit for Fishermen but with long use and experience'.[22] The Dorset investors lost £3,000, though a remnant of the settlers built the first huts down at Naumkeg under the leadership of Roger Conant, a settlement which was to become Salem.

Undeterred, the West-Country interests persisted in the enterprise, this time with the backing of the Skinners and Merchant Taylors and other interests in London, as well as from Puritan landowners in East Anglia—where there was now a slump in the wool-trade—a divine hint, thought John Winthrop, the future governor of the Massachusetts colony, that they ought to emigrate, or, as their enemies put it, 'Shuffle themselves into New England.'[23] By now

[21] Bradford, *op. cit.* II, p. 48.
[22] Morison, *op. cit.* p. 29.
[23] Perry Miller, *The New English Mind: From Colony to Province*, Harvard, 1953, p. 4.

Charles I and the Anglican bishops were hardening against the Puritans, and economic and religious motives combined.

So in 1629 a new company was incorporated, again under patent from the New England and Plymouth Council. Unlike the patent of the New Plymouth Pilgrims it would 'create something that had not existed before: the right of these men as a corporate body to rule and administer the territory under their authority and to exercise complete sway over any colonies or plantation that might be set up on its soil'. How they had managed it, nobody knows. One thing is clear: they managed it when nobody was looking.[24] It was called the Governors and Company of Massachusetts Bay in New England. Already in 1628 White had sent out fifty colonists from Weymouth, under the formidable Captain John Endicott, who settled at Salem. These Dorset emigrants took 'a generous stock of supplies, including five tuns of beer, thirty hogsheads of malt and two of aquavity, twelve runlets of 'strong' waters and two pipes of Madeira'.[25] Then in 1630 the Dorset expedition was followed up in a much bigger way. The company transferred itself to North America. John Winthrop went out as Governor of the colony until 1649, and proved the ablest of these pioneers. The Massachusetts colony was thus something new: it was designed not merely for profit and the relief of unemployment, but to establish a new, if necessary independent, model commonwealth for the Calvinist elect.

In contrast to the haphazard ventures in Newfoundland and up and down the coast, and to the small-scale settlement at New Plymouth—not more than three or four hundred people—the Massachusetts plantation was an enterprise of high purpose led by substantial men. Most of the leaders had been educated at Cambridge and, set on their own exclusive form of worship, they established an exclusive theocracy.

Civil government and local administration were dominated by their Calvinist pastors, and 'Englishmen emigrating to Massachusetts became subject to a government which differed radically from anything known before. Between 1629 and 1640 its population rose from less than 300 to more than 14,000, but not more than one in every five adult males possessed full Church membership or political rights.'[26] But they prospered: by 1634 they were strong enough to defy the Committee for Plantations, headed by Laud and Gorges. And when in 1635 the Massachusetts Charter was superseded by the

---

[24] Rowse, *op. cit.* p. 115, quoting C. M. Andrews, *The Colonial Period of American History*, Vol. I, p. 368.

[25] Morison, *op. cit.* p. 35.

[26] *Cambridge History of the British Empire,* Cambridge, Vol. I, p. 161.

direct authority of the Crown and Gorges was appointed Governor-General of New England, he could never assert his authority, though it was reinforced by his being made Lord Proprietory of Maine. Then, with the Civil Wars, the autonomy of Massachusetts was *de facto* confirmed.

The doctrinal differences of the elect encouraged expansion. By 1635–6 some settlers, led by the radical Thomas Hooker, hived off from Cambridge, Massachusetts, through a then daunting wilderness of forest and lakes to the Connecticut valley at Hartford. Here they were better placed for the fur-trade and out of the range of Pastor John Cotton, who dominated the Bay Settlement. But there is no evidence that Hooker was a 'democrat'—nearly all these Calvinist divines were determined to impose an oligarchic discipline on their own version of a model and godly commonwealth.

Roger Williams, who also seceded and founded Providence, Rhode Island, and whose community survived against Massachusetts only by an appeal to the English government, was the exception—a radical Independent like the extremer sectaries of the Cromwellian army, who declared for liberty of conscience and denied that God had decreed uniformity of worship. Like them, he appealed to natural rights. Moreover he was determined, like John Eliot in the 'forties, to convert the Amerindians, whom most of the settlers regarded as vermin.

John Eliot is the more attractive personality. He was an evangelist, not a theologian, and his charm and courage made him a Protestant 'Apostle of the Indians'. At least they found no difficulty, they said, in keeping the Sabbath, having, even on weekdays 'not much to do'.[27] They were 'induced to sit down orderly in self-governing villages'.[28] Various Sachems and Sagamores proved amenable and, under the English Republic, large sums were sent to the colony—in 1654 as much as £7,625 for the Propagation of the Gospel to the 'praying Indians'. Eliot's Bible of 1661 became *Mamusse Wunneetupana-tamwe up-Biblum God Nameeswe Nukkome Testament Kah Wonk Wusku Testament*. Many 'praying' Indians, who often suffered the enmity of both sides, proved allies when the colonists were attacked by the better-organized tribes of the interior. But, after these wars and massacres, missionary fervour fell away. North America became a white man's country.

The Calvinist theocrats, the religious radicals and the evangelists of the Amerindians all showed the intellectual power of Puritan New England. Colonies had hitherto been settled mainly by brisk ad-

[27] *C.H.B.E.*, Vol. I, p. 290.
[28] *C.H.B.E.*, Vol. I, p. 295.

venturers, dilapidated courtiers or remittance men, and often populated by jail-birds and the sweepings of the London streets; the West
Indies, and, to a less extent, Virginia had become dependent on
negro slave-labour. Here, in New England, were substantial men of
principle—if of narrow principle—single-minded witnesses to the
spirit of the Lord, united in a determination to build a model
commonwealth from which England itself might be redeemed. They
were not, of course, democrats: by Cavalier standards, they were a
canting oligarchy with their Puritan nasal twang, and the penalties
they imposed on non-conformists were far heavier than those inflicted in England by the Anglican Court of High Commission. But
the leaders, bred in the Puritan colleges at Cambridge, were determined from the first to maintain and transmit their own intellectual
standards. Hence, within four years of the settlement, the foundation
of Harvard, consolidated from 1640 to 1655 by President Henry
Dunster, who firmly reproduced the curriculum and way of life of an
English college: 'Dinner in hall at eleven o'clock or noon; high
table for the Masters and Fellow Commoners ... ancient good wives
of unblemished reputation ... serving as bedmakers; butlers drawing beer at the buttery ... Fellows' Orchard where the master might
enjoy seclusion ... a prodigious commencement feast.'[29]

There was another side to this humanism. Witches were even more
fiercely persecuted in New England than in the old country, and the
standards and good intentions of the highly educated minority could
not be maintained as the frontiers were pushed to the west. The hard
lives of the frontiersmen made them think that the only good Indian
was a dead one. And the settlers' children were now young Americans, impatient of the reins which the Plymouth Congregationalists
had tried to keep on their necks.

The New England way of life thus soon diverged from that of
Anglican England. When, in 1634, Charles I attempted to re-examine
the original charter, and depose Winthrop, the Governor at once put
Boston into a posture of defence and erected the original beacon on
Beacon Hill to detect any English descent on the coast. And during
the Civil Wars and the rule of the English Republic, the colonists
were wary even of favours from a government sympathetic to them,
in case their independence were compromised.

The Plymouth Congregationalist settlers had been anxious merely
to escape and to practise, unmolested, their own kind of religion,
but the Calvinist elect of Massachusetts had been set from the beginning to 'practice the positive part of Church reformation and
propagate the Gospel in America'. They were proud, formidable,

[29] *C.H.B.E.*, Vol. I, p. 202.

shrewd and legal-minded; by the standards of the Caroline court, philistines:

> I am obnoxious to each carping tongue,

wrote their first poetess, Anne Bradstreet,

> Who says my hand a needle better fits.[30]

But they were representative of just the people in England who would bring down the last northern Renaissance monarchy in Europe. And, unlike the Virginian settlers, they did not carry with them aristocratic and manorial traditions, rather one of small townships directed by the godly. Their middle-class realism and respect for good management and thrift, along with their dour sense of election and mission and order, would enable them to strike root; then to push out west into the unknown interior and exploit its enormous potential wealth. These English Puritans could be hard as steel and cold as a North-wester out of the Arctic, and their descendants would predominate in the mastery of a continent. Though their independence made them secede from the British Empire, they in fact began its most important achievement in world history, the Anglo-Saxon domination of North America.

IV

The settlement of Virginia and New England, like the annexation of Newfoundland and the exploration of the American Arctic, was only the most decisive and western aspect of a worldwide English reconnaissance. The original and sustaining motive, rooted in medieval commerce, had been to find new markets for cloth, but during the northern Renaissance new horizons and objectives had opened out. By the mid-sixteenth century the great map of Pierre Descallier of Arques had depicted the whole world, an elegant and much more comprehensive advance on the best medieval cartography, if still vague on northwestern America and *Terra Australis Incognita*. The reports of explorers and merchants accumulated, to be collected and popularized by Hakluyt and Purchas, while, as big oceanic trading companies kept records—if often of loss—more reliable statistics became available. Under Elizabeth I this new efficiency blended with the widest prospect of loot, exploration and adventure and the Renaissance cult of heroic fame.

[30] Which indeed it did, when she compared herself when missing her husband to 'the loving Mullet, that true fish', who, 'her fellow lost, nor joy nor life doth wish'.

Then after the dismantling of the archaic Conciliar monarchy of Charles I, a new standard of administration came in—the main constructive legacy of the Civil Wars. The Republican governments were deliberately imperialist, set on creating a self-sufficient colonial empire, following the new mercantilist theories formulated in Thomas Mun's *England's Treasure by fforraign Trade*, already circulating, though not yet published, in the 'thirties. And as the English economy now developed, giving employment to a larger population, the 'Plantations' were no longer thought of merely as a place for 'bees to swarm abroad' or 'a means of disburdening this country of its inhabitants' and of setting up younger sons. They were to be part of a great self-sufficient protected area fostered by government in the interests of the home country and, in return, protected by a formidable navy.

The early Tudor English had first felt their way towards empire through 'vent of cloth', the lure of the spice-trade and of Asian, African and American gold. Now, after brilliant explorations and with substantial footholds and settlements in being, their descendants were developing their first or Old Colonial Empire. And it was significant in this time of the rivalry of great oceanic powers, that Thomas Hobbes' *Leviathan* appeared in 1651, the year of the second and most important Navigation Act, defining the relationships of sovereign states as a 'posture of warre'.

BOOK II

The Old Colonial Empire
1660–1784

CHAPTER 7

The Mercantilist Exploitation

The Old Colonial Empire, originating from the Elizabethan and early Stuart reconnaissance and settlement, and first developed under the English Republic with a new and formidable sea power deployed against the Dutch (1652–4) and then against Spain (1655–9), was extended under the later Stuarts. They fought the second and third Dutch Wars (1664–7 and 1672–4), and achieved a new dimension of power by King William's War (1689–97) and the War of the Spanish Succession (1701–3). It was a commercial much more than a political empire, casually administered over vast distances, with much freedom of local government; but it firmly subordinated the colonial economies to the home country.

It reached its climax in the major War of the Austrian Succession (1742–8) which followed on the 'War of Jenkins' Ear' with Spain (1739) that ended Walpole's peaceable regime, and in the Seven Years War (1756–63) with the conquest of Canada, paramountcy in Bengal and the Carnatic, and the domination of the western Mediterranean and the Caribbean. Under pressure of these great wars with France, Elizabethan projects in the 'South Sea'—the Pacific—were also revived, to control what was thought to be a vast southern continent, still unknown. In 1740–4 Anson circumnavigated the world, and Cook's brilliant exploration of 1768–9 opened up vast prospects, at first little regarded, in Australia and New Zealand.

The East India Company, though now mainly concerned with India, also exploited Indo-China and even contacted the Chinese, though the promising trade with Japan had petered out. The Tokugawa Shoguns had become implacably isolationist; particularly since Charles II had married a Portuguese, a nation the Japanese particularly detested. They wished the English merchants a pleasant voyage and long lives, but refused to treat with ships wearing any sort of cross.

English commerce, which had long included the slave-trade out of West Africa, had now become worldwide; and while the Old Colonial Empire was diminished by the American revolt, a new and, in due course, free-trading empire was building up. The British contested the Spanish claim to monopolize the entire Pacific—a claim only formally relinquished in 1790, when, after the Spaniards had impounded a British sealer in Nootka Sound, north of Vancouver, the Younger Pitt's government called their bluff.

This expansion of commercial empire was gradual and cumulative. In 1659 the Republican government had followed up its seizure of Jamaica in 1655 by annexing St Helena; in 1704 Gibraltar was captured, in 1708 Minorca (retained until 1783); while in 1766 the British briefly occupied the strategic Falkland Islands to which, despite Spanish-American claims, they would return.

The Navigation Acts of 1650 and 1651 had been passed by the much-maligned Rump Parliament, ostensibly to prevent foreign ships carrying royalists to Barbados and Virginia and to blockade the royalist colonies. But they in fact had a much wider purpose: to cripple the predominant Dutch commerce and enhance British sea power. The Act of 1651 specifically aimed at 'the Increase of the Shipping and Navigation of the Nation'. Then, following the Navigation Act of 1657, an Act of Trade of 1660 enumerated all the essential colonial goods—sugar, tobacco, cotton, indigo, ginger and dye-woods—which could be exported only to England or to another of the colonies in English or colonial ships; while in 1663 a Staple Act directed that all foreign goods destined for the colonies must be shipped from an English port. These Acts of Trade were designed to co-ordinate the sub-tropical colonial plantations with the flourishing English economy, and were reinforced by the Plantations Duty Act of 1673 which imposed duties even on enumerated goods traded between the colonies themselves. On balance, though it would become a main cause of the loss of the American colonies, this mercantilist policy succeeded: it enlarged the merchant navy and helped pay for the strategic protection it accorded to the colonies.

It was naturally beyond the limited naval resources of the Restoration government to enforce the Navigation Acts thoroughly or, indeed, to protect their West Indian colonies from the raids of the French, the Spaniards and the buccaneers—let alone to administer the colonies at such a distance with so primitive a bureaucracy. But the later Stuart governments had able administrators—Samuel Pepys, for example—and were as successful as their resources would permit. Such was the expansion of colonial trade, import and re-export, that where in 1640 the old medieval cloth-trade still accounted for over three-quarters of English exports, by the end of the seventeenth century the enumerated colonial products accounted for about half of them. In 1688 outward bound shipping amounted to 190,000 tons: by 1700 to 273,000; by 1763 to 561,000. Following this expansion, the Navy now outclassed the Dutch, and already by 1692 defeated the French off La Hogue in the 'Trafalgar of the seventeenth century'. In spite of much smuggling and evasion, economically and strategically the Navigation Acts had paid off.

With greater resources than the Dutch, whose *tour de force* in the seventeenth century had overstrained their limited resources, and better organized than the French, whose population and economic potential were both superior, the English with their relatively fluid hierarchy and adaptable establishment, freedom from internal customs barriers and growing moneyed interest, now went ahead. Following methods of banking and insurance pioneered by the Dutch, the establishment of the Bank of England in 1694 and the funding of a National Debt created a new financial stability and scope. A new class of investors grew up, who put their money not into land and plate but into joint stock companies and 'annuities' secured upon the public funds. Socially and politically again predominant since 1660, the great landowners also adapted themselves to the times, and the rich merchant families who had been assimilated into the landed aristocracy and gentry since the later middle ages now became even more closely connected with a plutocratic establishment. The sugar millionaires from the West Indies and the Nabob millionaires from India were accepted into the oligarchy and both became formidable pressure groups in Parliament. The insular and conservative 'Tory' interests hostile to Whig and 'Dutch' finance and tainted with Jacobitism, gave way to a predominantly Whig regime as the kaleidoscopic and hectic strife of factions behind the Marlborough wars subsided into a consensus of politics under the Hanoverians. It was symbolized by Walpole, that adroit and commercially minded politician, the first effective 'Prime' Minister and political boss able to carry on the King's government in a more permanent way. And from this broad and briefly pacific base was launched the next and most aggressive phase of the Old Colonial Empire, which came to its astonishing climax under the elder William Pitt, when the British obtained the greatest sea-borne empire in the world.

All had followed from the commercial imperialism of the Republic backed by a new dimension of sea power, from the reconciliation of the monarchy with the great magnates and City men, the defeat of the briefly influential radical democrats of the Interregnum, and the supersession of the 'rage of party' by the 'pursuit of place' against a background, contrasting with Tudor and early Stuart times, of stable prices until the inflation during the Napoleonic Wars.

II

In the reign of Charles I, while the court was much concerned with masques and music and the King making the greatest collection of pictures of the day, a young Cornishman was kidnapped by Moroccan pirates and enslaved. Compelled to pilot another raider to his own coast 'in search of English women', he had incited the Christians on board to seize the captain and brought the slaver into a West-Country harbour. But his exploit was not representative: most of those whom the pirates carried off never saw England again, and such was the incompetence of the government that little could be done.

With the advent of the Republic, the now expanded Navy became master of the Channel; Blake would even attack Tunis and release English captives from the galleys at Algiers. The ship money belatedly raised by Charles I had now got through to the fleet, whose defection to Parliament had been decisive, and by 1652 the Republic had begun the first of the wars for trade and empire which were backed by a better-organized state. They were fought over more than a century and a half, first with the Dutch, then with France, which became the main enemy; and intermittently, with Spain. And they would culminate in the global struggle against Napoleon, from which the British emerged with the world supremacy on the oceans which was behind the second, nineteenth-century, Empire.

These gruelling battles, fought out in all weathers between heavily gunned ships able to stand prolonged battering and hard to sink, demanded high professional skill. Losses were far heavier than in Elizabethan times. During the long fight between Monck and De Ruyter in 1666 the English alone had nearly two and a half thousand casualties, and in 1672, in the third Dutch War, when the English *Royal James* was rammed by the *Groot Hollandia* and set ablaze by fireships, only a hundred men out of a thousand survived unscathed. The Admiral Lord Sandwich and most of his officers perished. And the decisive naval actions of the eighteenth and early nineteenth century, culminating at the battles of the Nile and Trafalgar, brought similar carnage. The price of empire was here paid in blood.

In a hard world the cost was written off. The rich were accustomed to discomfort and illness unmitigated by scientific medicine, and for most of the population life was cruel and precarious. States went to war because that was what states did, and the prize was the exploitation of the world. The wars had relatively little impact on the civilian population within the island, but the mass of the people were now more politically conscious and militant. After the union with Scotland in 1707, the United Kingdom of Great Britain and Ireland was becoming the major commercial, naval and colonial power in Europe, destined to be the victor in the wars for the world domination which fell to Europeans from the sixteenth to the early twentieth century.

The seventeenth- and eighteenth-century British were as enterprising and ruthless and much more systematic than the Elizabethans, with far better resources of wealth and sea power behind them. Many were even more brutal to the 'blacks'—Indians and Amerindians came into this category as well as Negroes—than were the Spaniards, whose missionary friars regarded the 'natives' as souls capable of salvation, an idea that the Protestant Dutch and English generally disregarded. The architects of the first British Empire were out for substantial and lasting profit, and ready to take on formidable political responsibilities to ensure it. Clive of India, for example, an East India Company civilian turned soldier, fought his way to fame and wealth at Arcot and Plassey.

At the summit of affairs, William Pitt, first Earl of Chatham, was a manic-depressive genius whose melodramatic eloquence and strategic and political flair struck a new note of high-flown if commercial 'imperialism'. Carrying the politically articulate nation with him, he was a new portent in British history, in contrast to Walpole, whose humdrum consensus politics had made Chatham's enterprise possible.

Wolfe, who conquered Canada, was as highly-strung as Chatham: he was a dedicated soldier with an oddly neurotic touch; Cook, on the other hand, the greatest of English explorers and the son of a Yorkshire labourer, showed an imperturbable humanity and professional skill. Nor were the lesser men lacking in vigour, whether they kept to the right side of the law or went beyond it. The original Pitt, Governor Thomas, for example, was the second of nine children of the Rector of Blandford St Mary in Dorset, whose living was worth no more than £100 a year.[1] His rather shady transactions culminated in the purchase of the 'Pitt diamond', bought after fierce haggling for forty-eight thousand pagodas—about £17,000—and sold for two

[1] There is a pious memorial put up to him by the Governor, in elaborately impeccable Latin and adorned with palms, in his father's church.

million francs—about £125,000; and some of this nabob's 'uncontrollable explosions of wrath and disgust which occur only too persistently throughout his correspondence ... would have done no discredit to the most untutored peasant in his native country'—which is saying much.[2] Job Charnock, who founded Calcutta, is said to have hacked through a chain across the harbour with a sword, set fire to the Calcutta seafront with a burning glass, rescued a Hindu widow from her funeral pyre and married her; William Dampier, part buccaneer, part explorer, though without power of command, shows an indefatigable courage and vivid powers of observation and narrative. And even among the ruffians who infested the Caribbean, Sir Henry Morgan, who unofficially sacked Panama, and then became Vice-Governor of Jamaica, had preternatural luck. He was expert at blatantly whitewashing his nefarious transactions, though, as he put it, 'I left the schools too young to be a great Proficient [in law], and have been more used to the Pike than the Book.' The most notorious of them all, Edward Teach, 'Blackbeard', the prototype of all legendary pirates, who from Nassau in the Bahamas terrorized the West Indies, the Spanish Main and the Carolina coasts in a French prize rechristened *Queen Anne's Revenge*, and ended, his decapitated head slung over a bowsprit of an avenging English frigate on the James River in Virginia in 1718, enjoyed his brief prosperity with genial riot.

After the original godly and formidable impetus of the Protectorate, the Restoration and eighteenth-century English thus created the first or Old Colonial Empire with a robust self-confidence and without the inhibitions or introspection and aloof evangelical sense of duty of many soldiers and administrators of the second.

In India, of course, like the other Europeans of the time with their immense technological advantages, the British took their superiority for granted. Often, like Clive and Warren Hastings, set on rehabilitating their families at home, they were not too nice in their dealings abroad. They also took great risks: for the few who made history there are dozens who perished in battle or shipwreck, from drink or disease, and have no memorial. No wonder that, like all the conquerors of India before them, the survivors were hard men. But their descendants would bring peace to all India.

[2] Sir C. M. Dalton, *The Life of Thomas Pitt*, Cambridge University Press, 1915, p. 6.

III

The theory behind the Old Colonial Empire as established by the English Republic and the much-maligned later Stuarts, who here had their major success, was 'mercantilist'. Already defined by Thomas Mun, it was elaborated by the pioneer economist and East India administrator, Sir Josiah Child, whose *New Discourse on Trade* appeared in 1665, 'wherein are recommended several weighty points, companies of Merchants, the Act of Navigation, ... the Balance of Trade and the Nature of Plantations'.

In 1660 the old monarchy, though battered, still held the initiative; and Charles II—who remarked 'Odd's fish, they have put a set of men about me but they shall know nothing'—saw the Crown Colonies as an area in which the royal prerogative was still untrammelled. 'Distance of place', he insisted, could remove no one from 'our justice and power'. This outlook was shared by James II: indeed, 'though the Stuart monarchy is not reckoned a successful institution ... it won at least a sizeable victory in America'.[3] And if 'the old English monarchy fell for ever in 1689, the old colonial system that was the product of its partnership with Parliament survived its fall for a century and a half'.[4] The system was based mainly on the Americas and the West Indies, and on the slave-trade out of West Africa: in India and the Far East exploitation was more indirect, but the East India Company, whose profits were booming during the later seventeenth century, was encouraged by government. Charles II combined business with pleasure by demanding Indian spotted deer, 'small green parrots', and oriental screens from the Company; and although under William III it came under attack, it was virtually refounded and its monopoly confirmed in the reign of Anne.

Through the enterprise of Prince Rupert, who had been much about the world during the Interregnum, the Hudson's Bay Company now exploited the fur-trade in the Canadian sub-Arctic, getting in behind the fur-traders based on the eastern seaboard, and penetrating deeper into the North American interior. Rupert, who had been off the West Africa coast in the 'fifties, also inspired an expedition to Gambia, where Fort James was founded in the oldest English colony on that continent: by the 'seventies English factors were on the Guinea coast and at Accra. In 1672 the Royal Africa Company was founded to exploit gold-dust and slaves, and its elephant crest ap-

[3] A. P. Thornton, *West Indies Policy under the Restoration*, Oxford, 1956, p. 19.
[4] Thornton, *op. cit.* p. 3.

peared on the first golden 'Guineas' fixed at twenty-one shillings when Newton made his recoinage in 1717. The slave-trade, greatly increased during the seventeenth century, continued to bring profits both to the Company and to the interlopers who infringed its monopoly. It reached its climax for the English slavers after the turn of the eighteenth century, when Bristol and Liverpool became the greatest ports in Europe, for this then well-regarded traffic, contributing to the prosperity of the planters of the West Indies and the American colonies, conferring the benefit of Christianity on its victims—better off, it could then be argued, than they would have been in their own land. 'I can assure you,' wrote John Pinney, to his Dorset family in 1764, when he first visited his sugar plantation on Nevis, 'I was shocked at the first appearance of human flesh exposed for sale. But surely God ordained them for the use and benefit of us, otherwise the Divine will would have been made manifest by some particular sign or token.'[5]

IV

It was of course the men of property, great and small, and their younger sons who benefited from the Old Colonial Empire. But it would be misreading history to imagine that this exploitation was resented by the mass of the people. On the contrary, in Great Britain itself, particularly after the Hanoverian settlement which had mercifully assuaged religious passions—still, however, to continue in Ireland into the twentieth century—the monarch and the political and social establishment commanded the loyalty of a robust, insular and self-confident nation. Most of the people were still semi-literate and led lives which would be regarded as typical of 'underdeveloped' countries today, and sanitation, medicine and public order were rudimentary and punishments were savage, but the English enjoyed liberties unknown over most of the continent. There was no centralized bureaucratic monarchy as in France; there was freedom from arbitrary arrest and from incarceration without trial; there was trial by jury, and freedom, within the bounds of poverty and communication, to move about. There were no internal customs dues, such as those imposed in Germany which still handicapped trade along the Rhine; there were no serfs, as in Eastern Europe, bound to the land and sold with it. The misguided but well-intentioned Tudor attempt to regulate and retard a naturally dynamic and changing social order had been abandoned, while the riots, bribery and general excitement of elections still held under an extraordinary medieval franchise gave

[5] Quoted by Richard Pares, *A West India Fortune*, London, 1950, p. 121.

the people a brisk illusion of participating in politics. Hence a robust insular patriotism which went right down through this hierarchical society—from the ostentatiously arrogant and often cosmopolitan nobility and the brilliant minority culture which they patronized, the independent and wealthy squirearchy and upper clergy of the Established Church, through the rich merchants, the professional classes, the Army and Navy, the farmers, local tradesmen and artisans, down to the urban and agricultural masses, who for all the poverty and insecurity of their lives, generally felt themselves part of a great and prosperous state. 'Rule Britannia', composed by Arne in 1740, and 'God Save the King', popularized during the last Stuart attempt to upset the Hanoverian settlement in '45, expressed not the feelings of an exploiting landowning and capitalist minority, but of a nation; and though Dr Johnson remarked that in politics patriotism was the last refuge of a scoundrel, he was a monolithic patriot himself.

Unsophisticated and old-fashioned as this picture may seem to some historians dedicated to the analysis of social conflict, such, in spite of poverty and illiteracy, are the facts: they are apparent from the political literature, the newspapers, the pamphlets and records of the time. By the later eighteenth century there was indeed a popular reaction, repressed at home during the French Revolutionary wars and tamed by prosperity during the mid-nineteenth century; more comprehensive and successful in the American colonies, where it led to secession. But it never upset an apparently representative hierarchy.

As wealth increased and resounding victories acclaimed by the populace extended and consolidated a huge commercial empire, this political and social establishment became more complacent, arrogant and obtuse. The sovereignty of King-in-Parliament became more concentrated, claiming powers unknown in the seventeenth century; and George III, no tyrant but a conscientious monarch who identified the Crown with Parliament in the terms established by 1688–9, roused the opposition of aristocratic Foxite Whigs and of radicals led by Wilkes and Tom Paine, reasserting old seventeenth-century liberties, and provoked the Americans to revolt against an innovating and overriding power. Yet the magnates who distributed patronage with a bland disregard of the recipient's abilities if he had a 'claim', who muddled distant campaigns and looked down on the colonists as provincials and rebels, were still more representative of articulate political opinion than the Whig reformers and popular radicals; and during the French wars most of the populace rallied to the establishment, in spite of the distress, mainly among old-fashioned artisans, caused by that other and greater innovation, the Industrial Revolution, and by rising prices and the destruction of the traditional sense of community.

The American colonies might secede, since their leaders, asserting a seventeenth-century and conservative doctrine of the separation of powers before an innovating assertion of impracticable sovereignty overseas, commanded wide popular support, reflecting the contrast between the rich hierarchy of the greatest mercantile power in the world and the colonies, with debt-ridden planters, doubtful currencies and pioneers determined to exploit their western frontiers. Because, too, at the critical moment, the French and their allies seeking to reverse the consequences of the Seven Years War, briefly won command of the Atlantic. But the British establishment, who detested the Americans the more for their influence on their own radicals, retained their authority in their own island: and during the final and most dangerous struggle with the French, in spite of Irish discontent and the social dislocations of the Industrial Revolution, they still had the articulate majority of the country behind them. For the raffish adventurers of later Stuart times, who had brought a brisker virulence and a more deadly prose to political warfare in the island, the coarse and cynical plutocrats of the Walpolean consensus and the high-strung predators of the Seven Years War had all been representative of their people and at one with most of them.

So the first or Old Colonial Empire came to its climax in the mid-eighteenth century. It formed the basis of the commercial capital that financed the Industrial Revolution, which enabled the British to defeat Napoleon by wealth as well as by sea power. It suffered eclipse in North America, but there was no political revolution in the island base, where a brash patriotism swamped radical discontent. And the first Empire carried on into the second, which would include areas of the Far East, Africa, Australasia and the Pacific unknown to the age of Chatham.

CHAPTER 8

India: Poachers turn Gamekeepers

'Hindustan', wrote Babur, the founder of the Mughal dynasty in 1526–7, after 'gaining the vast empire of Hind', is 'a country of few charms ... there are no good horses, no good dogs, no grapes, musk melons or first rate fruits; no ice or cold water ...'[1] He had been as alien to India as the English, now consolidating their 'factories' in Bombay, Madras and Bengal. And Muslim intolerance, in abeyance under Akbar, was now intensified by Aurangzeb who ousted his father, Shah Jahan, in 1659, and died in 1707 aged eighty-eight.

The Mughal Empire, long over-extended, now began to break up. A meticulous Sunni Muslim, Aurangzeb, had imprisoned his father, killed two of his brothers and exiled a third; and like Charles v, who had attempted to revive the Holy Roman Empire, he was constantly moving over the even vaster distances of an impracticable realm. In his declining years a bent and slender figure, his olive skin contrasting with a white beard, Aurangzeb is depicted in plain white muslin, with one enormous emerald in his turban. Under an exquisite politeness he was extremely cruel: he paraded the son of the rebel Maratha King Shivaji in cap and bells on a camel, to the sound of trumpets and drums, had him blinded and his limbs hacked off one by one and thrown to dogs. He would render his captives imbecile by drugs and go 'through and over' a crowd with elephants, thus making peaceful protest ineffectual. And he tried to suppress both Hindu festivals and Muslim gambling; discountenanced poets and even historians, and refused to appear at his palace window lest he should encourage idolatry. He also imposed an inconvenient lunar calendar which did not correspond with the Indian seasons. With an appalling grasp of detail, he over-centralized the administration, and carried out his devious policies behind the backs of his ministers, all of whom

[1] Cited by Sir Percival Griffiths, *The British Impact on India*, London, 1952.

were utterly dependent, as was the entire Empire, on his will and caprice.

Such was the last effectively great Mughal of the vast Empire which the Europeans were beginning to exploit. Though it had not been ill administered, it remained an encampment of Central Asian conquerors on an alien civilization, and the fanaticism of Aurangzeb provoked the martial races of India to war. The Princes of Rajputana had always been warriors; now Guru Govind Singh transformed the unworldly precepts of the original Sikh religion into a fierce cult of comradeship and prowess, and the Maratha guerrilla leader Sivaji founded the last great Hindu state and launched a confederacy which by the late eighteenth century nearly mastered India.

In Aurangzeb's own lifetime the Empire was under attack; under his successors the great officials began to carve out their own principalities, as in Hyderabad and Mysore. Then new invaders descended from the north. In 1739 Nadir Shah of Iran, sacked Delhi and looted the Peacock Throne itself; in 1761 the Afghan Ahmad Shah Durani overran much of northern India 'and Afghans on superb Khorasan horses traversed the country offering five rupees for every Hindu head'.[2] The Mughal, Shah Alam, still reigned in distinguished but dilapidated state in Delhi, from 1759 to 1806, during the crucial phase of the English takeover, but first as the puppet of the Maratha Rao Scindia of Gwalior, then of the British themselves.

Such was the setting in which the East India Company was transformed from a successful seventeenth-century trading enterprise into the paramount power in India, and of the successive wars between the British and the French and their Indian allies, part of a world conflict in which English sea power proved decisive in India as elsewhere. But the takeover was reluctant: as late as 1767 it would be laid down in London that it was 'not for the Company to take the part of Umpires in Hindustan'; and the civilian directors resented the political commitments forced upon them by Clive and Warren Hastings as the price of the Company's survival. 'You seem so thoroughly possessed of military ideas,' they wrote to the former, 'that you forget your employers are merchants.'[3] Nor did Hastings himself, though ready to extend the Company's influence by subsidies, want further conquests. 'An extension of territory beyond certain bounds,' he wrote in 1777, 'must in the course of time prove fatal to the authority of the Company.'

This reluctant takeover may be considered in three phases: the

[2] Keith Feiling, *Warren Hastings*, London, 1966, p. 29.
[3] Feiling, *op. cit.* p. 30.

first, from 1660 until Clive's victory at Arcot in 1751, assured British power in the Carnatic; then secondly, when, following growing anarchy in Bengal, Clive's victory at Plassey in 1757, consolidated at the more important battle of Buxar in 1764, made the Company *Zemindars* under the Mughal and a great political power; finally, and coincident with the crisis in North America and Cook's exploration of the Pacific, when Warren Hastings would defeat the French and their Indian allies and establish the paramountcy conceded by the Treaty of Versailles in 1784, accepted by Pitt's India Act of the same year, and extended and secured during the Revolutionary and Napoleonic Wars. Forced into a political role, the East India Company, now increasingly under the control of Parliament, took over the *raj* that nominally remained with Shah Alam, blinded in 1788 and politically powerless, but still the august and highly sophisticated descendant of Babur and Akbar.

II

The decadence of the Mughal Empire was nothing new. For centuries Afghans, Persians, Turks and Mongols had established their often ephemeral dominations; and nobody expected—any more than they had in the medieval West, in Muscovy or China—'that by means of political action life could be made better ... in Indian literature there are no Utopias'.[4] It was a familiar pattern. 'Since the time of Sir Thomas Roe the only thing that had really changed was the Emperor's power. The dull round of bribery and intrigue, into favour and out again, procrastination, evasion and deceit—all that was unchanged; only the Emperor was weaker, his viceroys stronger, their whims no longer liable to reversal if his ear could be reached. And in Bengal the tale of the viceroys and their governors is the familiar sequence of idle debauchee alternating with merciless tyrant—though one can detect a hint of individuality in the tyrant who, to make recalcitrants pay their arrears of land revenue, compelled them to put on loose trousers into which were introduced live cats.'[5]

Political collapse, moreover, had not meant economic or cultural decline. The civilization was vast and populous—if its wealth was in the hands of a few—and India was still the most important centre of small-scale industry in Asia, with a substantial export trade not yet swamped by the products of the Industrial Revolution in Britain. The ferocious rulers who competed for the spoils of empire were vigorous and astute: often self-made adventurers, if some were the products of

[4] Guy Wint, *The British in Asia*, London, 1947, p. 44.
[5] Philip Woodruff, *The Men who Ruled India: The Founders*, p. 79.

a 'satiated cult of beauty and sensation',[6] bored with government, who despised the European *banias* and the upstarts, Muslim or Hindu, who fought for it. Some, like the more sensationally criminal Roman emperors, went mad: as the Maratha Raja of Indore who 'put scorpions in the clothes and slippers given to Brahmins and venomous snakes in pots of rupees'.[7] Others, like some Yuan Mongols in China or some Ottoman Grand Turks, became sodden with drink and drugs, or enervated by the varied sensualities of that cradle of eroticism, the Muslim Middle East, long-elaborated in Hindu India. But in general—and English historians have often ignored the fact—'it is a mistake to suppose that the public stage was filled by weak-kneed or effeminate triflers. These are the by-products of prosperity and power. With few exceptions, the actors were vigorous and hardy, brave and warlike. There were brilliant feats of arms, there was stolid endurance and desperate courage ... It was not a case of anaemic courtiers falling before the onset of northern vigour, but rather of sword clashing upon sword, of fierce men giving and receiving stroke for stroke'.[8] Well might a servant of the East India Company complain in 1680 that 'the native rulers have ... got the knack of trampling upon us and extorting what they please'; while an Indian recorded with satisfaction that 'the Bengal Viceroy was oppressing the infidels without fear and he did so without mercy'. India was no place for compromise: the English had to fight and win, go under or get out.

III

For all its civilian bias the Company proved well able to fight. The Charter granted in 1661 and afterwards extended had given them many attributes of government: they could strike coins, appoint governors, enlist soldiers and arm ships; impose martial law and do justice on their countrymen in their territories. And decisions in London were now made by the more substantial holders of the stock, which rose from £250 a share in 1657 to £750 in 1682. During the 'eighties Sir Josiah Child, originally a naval contractor at Plymouth and a pioneer economist, became Governor, and he was not a scrupulous man. The laws of England, he declared, were 'a heap of nonsense' in Indian conditions, and under this nabob and nepotist the Company prospered. In 1681 Charles II had merely accepted a

[6] Wint, *op. cit.* p. 45.
[7] Wint, *op. cit.* p. 45.
[8] Sir Percival Spear, *Twilight of the Mughals. Studies in late Mughal Delhi*, Cambridge, 1951, p. 10.

present of £10,750 from the Company in return for his royal favour; but the Duke of York held £3,000 of stock, increased in 1685 when he became James II—a holding transferred in 1698 to his supplanters.[9] By 1684 Sir Josiah, whose early caution had provoked defiance from the speculators in Bombay, was writing, 'It is our ambition ...' to make 'the English nation as formidable as the Dutch, or any other European nation are or ever were in India; but that cannot be done only in the form and method of merchants ...'. And in the following year he was even aiming to secure 'Such a Polity of Civil and military power and create and secure such a large revenue to maintain both as may be the foundation of a large well-grounded secure English dominion in (not over) India for all time to come'.[10]

The Company was now so prosperous and so much identified with the Stuart court and the Tories that, after the Revolution in 1688, Whig politicians and interlopers combined to form a rival concern. In 1690 'Reasons' were being 'humbly offered-... for dissolving the Present East India Company, founded and planted in direct opposition to the native liberty of the subject and cultivated ... by the hand of Tyranny and arbitrary power'. And monetary theorists also reprobated the Company's massive export of silver. But by 1708, following a loan of £1,000,000 to the government and some judicious bribery to the tune of £80,000,[11] the original Company absorbed its rival and became the United East India Company—in fact, 'the same good old Company again'—a compromise which rested on a self-interest, 'so enlightened that it resembled public spirit'.[12] Successive extensions of its monopoly followed after 1711. In 1744 the Company lent another £1,000,000 to government while homeward imports 'rose from nearly £500,000 in 1708 to about £1,100,000 in 1748. and its exports to India from £576,000 to £1,121,000 between 1710 and 1750; while its dividends rose from 5 per cent in 1708–9, to 10 per

[9] Sir William Foster, *John Company*, London, 1926, p. 133. The fashion for Eastern drinks, tea and coffee, and for Eastern ornaments and fabrics was enhanced when exotic animals arrived from India. 'I went, with Sir William Godolphin,' wrote the diarist John Evelyn in 1684, 'to see the Rhinoceros or Unicorn being the first that I suppose was ever brought to England. She belonged to some East India merchant and was sold (as I remember) for about £2,000.' *Op. cit.* p. 85.

[10] Cited, Woodruff, *op. cit.* p. 62.

[11] The Duke of Leeds got £8,000, but during the subsequent investigations 'the flight to the continent of the Duke's Swiss factotums who had received the money ... destroyed the link in the chain of legal evidence'. Beckles Willson, *Ledger & Sword*, London, 1903, Vol. I, p. 428. This work is dedicated to the 'Venerable Governor of the Still surviving Merchant Adventurers of the West, Lord Strathcona and Mount Royal'.

[12] Sir George Clark, *The Later Stuarts. 1660–1714*, Oxford, 1934, p. 340.

cent from 1711 to 1721, and thereafter fluctuated between 7 and 8 per cent till 1755, when the war in India had increased its expenses'.[13] Of course, British exports to India were less important than to America and the West Indies: in 1761–5, for example, they averaged £976,000 a year as against £3,710,000 across the Atlantic; but there was already a prosperous background to the vast extension of the Company's responsibilities in Bengal. By contrast, in 1769, the French Compagnie des Indes, a state enterprise that had never commanded the public confidence or public influence of its rival, and which had lost 169,000,000 francs of capital since 1725, would be wound up.

In India the servants of *Jehan Company* or *Koompani Bahadur*, as it would be called, since the Hindus thought it a person—indeed, the more literal-minded, an old woman, her children being the Governors-General[14]—worked hard for their employers and harder for themselves. Separated from England by a voyage of at least six months and often more, they made their own decisions and feathered their own nests. As Governor Pitt, that redoubtable opportunist, observed, they became too astute. 'When the Europeans settled in India, they were mightily admired by the natives, believing that they were as innocent as themselves; but since the example they are grown very crafty and cautious; the more obliging your management the more jealous they are of you.'[15] Undeterred by any colour bar, the English threw themselves with zest into Indian business, went into partnership with Indian merchants, and piled up what fortunes they could. Not that the great nabobs were representative: they were survivors of ferocious competition and of a mortality reckoned as one in five. Indeed, if most of the Company's servants lived well in India, they came home, if they did, with only moderate fortunes.

By the end of the seventeenth century the original enclaves had been consolidated. There were three Presidencies: Bombay, held in full sovereignty as the dowry of Catherine of Braganza handed over to the Company by Charles II in 1669 and strategically better placed, was now superseding Surat; in Bengal, where Job Charnock founded Calcutta in the 'nineties, by 1700 Fort William had become a Presidency; while Fort St George in the Madras Presidency commanded the Carnatic and the trade to the Far East. All were cities of refuge as well as bases for commerce: and all now drew substantial customs revenues.

[13] Basil Williams, *The Whig Supremacy, 1714–1760*, ed. and revised C. H. Stuart, Oxford, 1962, p. 325.

[14] Beckles Willson, *op. cit.* Vol. II, p. 249 n.

[15] Willson, *op. cit.* p. 431.

Within these enclaves the Europeans lived in some state. 'A Gaudy shew and great noise,' wrote a Madras factor, 'adds much to a public person's rank in this country. As for soldyers they are an absolute necessity and especially whilst we are thus infested with interlopers.' So the President would be accompanied by three hundred 'blacks', with drums and trumpets and a flag of 'two balls on a red field'. In Surat his palanquin was preceded by a 'horse of State, and sheltered by a mighty fan of ostrich feathers'. But within the Madras 'factory' in 1685 the young men were supposed to live a quasi-collegiate life: no one to drink 'more than half a pint of arrack and brandy and one quart of wine at one time'—an amount considered a 'modest allowance'.[16] And the Company kept a pious face and sent out chaplains, though even after 1784, when the *raj* had become more respectable, missionaries were long discountenanced. In 1669 the clergyman sent out to Bombay learnt Portuguese, and was rewarded by £50 for his first sermon in that language. 'Young ingenious seamen' were recruited as pilots for the Bay of Bengal, and in 1669 eight youths from Christ's Hospital were bound apprentices for eight years on the Coromandel Coast and at Bantam. They each had £5 assigned for clothes.[17] By the 'seventies trade was already booming. Where in 1660–1 ten ships had been sent out, by 1667–8 fourteen were dispatched: six for Madras, three for Surat, four for Bantam and one for Sumatra. In 1670 eighteen went out and in the late eighteenth century the average would be twenty-five. They were fine ships—by the 'seventies well-armed three-deckers—built mainly in the Thames dockyards, at Chichester Harbour and at Bucklers Hard. St Helena, taken over from the Dutch, was permanently occupied in 1673 as a place of refreshment for the Company's ships.

The Company's main exports to India were cloth, metals for armaments and silver bullion. Broadcloths, 'casimirs' and tabinets found a variable market; but in a warlike country it was easy to sell copper, lead, bar-iron and steel, cutlery and sword-blades. Cloths, hats, wine, beer and cider, brandy, pickles and rum helped to make the private fortunes of the Company's officers. And for the Far East in 1670 the Company shipped 'looking glasses, amber, agate and ivory hafted knives, scissors, barber's cases, magnifying, burning, perspective and drinking glasses, spectacles and sword blades'. From India the Company imported muslins, cottons, calicoes, raw silk; ivory and pepper; vermilion, saltpetre (a constituent of gunpowder) and indigo. But until the takeover of Bengal which the English promptly drained of

[16] Willson, *op. cit.* Vol. I, p. 385.
[17] *Calendar of Court Minutes of the East India Company, 1668–1670,* Oxford, 1929.

Indian silver, there was an adverse balance on bullion—a cause of constant criticism. It was partly for this reason that the Company's servants were grossly underpaid and recouped themselves by private trading; as their powers extended, they used their monopoly to blackmail interlopers, or to take a rake-off from their own countrymen, excused the internal taxes still paid by Indian merchants. Interlopers and sometimes the Company's officers would buy up salt, opium and betelnut free of duty and undersell their Indian competitors. Added to this, and increasing as the powers of the Company advanced, were the 'presents' which, as in medieval Europe, normally accompanied business transactions in the East, and the Eastern cult of personal power, now being transferred to the English Governors.

Indeed, this was the heroic age of the early Presidents and Nabobs. Job Charnock—'honest Mr Charnock who has served us for twenty years and never been a prowler for himself', turned Lt-Colonel and defied the whole might of the Mughal Empire. He blockaded the food supply of Bengal and, after desperate vicissitudes, consolidated his foundation of Calcutta, to be the main basis of British power in India. Elihu Yale, Governor of Madras, hailed originally from Boston, Massachusetts: he was said to have hanged his groom, and was himself suspended from his Governorship: but in 1699 he returned to England to auction his spoils. And when, in 1718, Cotton Mather asked him to help his struggling college in Connecticut, the ex-Governor sent him a cargo of books and pictures. They were sold for £560, and the college called Yale. Thomas Pitt, 'the rough colt of an impecunious household', had gone out to India, probably as mate on the East Indiaman *Lancaster* in 1673, and first made his way as a 'prowler' in 'ways by no means delicately scrupulous'; then, poacher turned gamekeeper, as Governor of Madras. By 1688 he could buy estates near Blandford and at Stratford-sub-Castle, with its rotten borough of Old Sarum, politically so useful to his grandson, William Pitt the elder. But all these adventurers worked in terms of an armed commercial monopoly, not of a *raj*.

The collapse of the Mughal order and administration now threatened anarchy. The Deccan had been overrun by the Marathas, based on Poona in the Western Ghats, within striking distance of Surat. The great leader Shivaji (1627-80) had welded the ninety-six clans of these predatory horsemen into a formidable confederacy. He had built strategically placed forts in the hills, as at Parandar and Sinagad above Poona, and four naval bases 'which even the great Mughal emperors had never thought of'. Shivaji is still a national hero. From a brilliant guerrilla leader, expert in disguises, who would 'dexterously imitate the voices of birds and beasts', and who was 'a consummate wrestler and an accurate shot with a catapult or match lock',[18] he became a just and humane ruler, the Maharajah Chatrapati, and established an independent power.

In western India, failing the protection of the Mughals, the Company thus had to fend for itself. Having made Bombay a rudimentary naval base, they had come to their own terms with Shivaji. It was the first step to independent power. And when, in the 'seventies, the Marathas threatened Madras, that too had been put in a rudimentary posture of defence. In Bengal, Charnock's foundation of Calcutta, fortified in the 'nineties, had been the sequel to war first with the Mughal Viceroy, then with Aurangzeb himself. In all three areas the Company was being pushed out of being an armed monopoly into becoming a military and political power. Then during King William's and the Marlborough wars, the French, hitherto apt to collaborate with the English against the long-established Dutch, began a mounting attack. In 1664 Colbert had founded the *Compagnie des Indes Orientales*; by 1673 the French had established themselves at Pondicherry, south of Madras; and by 1690 at Chandranagore in Bengal. And in that year they had also occupied Mauritius which had been developed in conjunction with Madagascar into a naval base.

IV

So when, in the mid-eighteenth century, the French launched the first European attempt at political domination in India, the Company was forced to fight not only to protect its territories against Indian incursion and administrative collapse, but against European enemies: Indian affairs took on a new dimension and became part of a European world conflict. French ambitions were logical, comprehensive and far-flung. Here, as in North America, their vision eclipsed the more pedestrian English concern with immediate commercial interests. And they had a brilliant leader. Joseph François Dupleix had arrived in India in 1721: the son of a substantial tax farmer, he had some capital; within a decade he had made a fortune and his sanguine and vivid imagination envisaged not merely commercial success but political domination. By 1742 he was Governor-General under the *Compagnie des Indes*, while at Mauritius lay a French squadron under the command of Admiral Mahé de la Bourdonnais. And although, like the concurrent chairman of the English Company, who wrote, 'It would be in our interests at all events to get

---

[18] G. S. Sardesi, *A New History of the Marathas*, Bombay, 1946, Vol. I, p. 263. During his fiercest campaigns, it is alleged, he was careful not to molest women, children, brahmins, husbandmen or cows.

men-of-war there . . . as the French are now laden richly,' the Admiral was out more for prizes than conquest, when in 1744 the news of the outbreak of the War of the Austrian Succession reached India, Dupleix at Pondicherry took his chance. A clever diplomatist, and an extrovert who revelled in the splendours of Indian princely life, he established an able and high-born pro-French candidate, Chandra Sahib, as Viceroy of the Carnatic. Soon the English puppet, Muhammad Ali, was put down, and Madras, where the bastions of the fort were placed 'contrary to all rules', was overrun by the French and their Indian allies. But Dupleix had started a dangerous game, he had shown the superiority of European and European-trained troops in the still medieval battles of eighteenth-century India, and set off a competition which could be decided only by commercial and naval power based on Europe.

A more practical English adventurer now took up the challenge. Robert Clive came of a family of small squires of Old Styche Manor, a timbered house near Market Drayton in Shropshire. After a brief attendance at Merchant Taylors' and other schools, he had been shipped out to Madras at seventeen. And there, in 1743, in immense, meticulous letters, he had recorded his expenses and described an exotic world of aloes and pineapples, limes, mangoes, guavas, and tulip trees 'planted as in St James's Park'. But he had soon been dis-illusioned with most of his colleagues: 'The World seems vastly de-based of late,' he wrote, 'and Interest carries it entirely before Merit.'[19] Clive had been bored.

He set about trading on his own account, but now with the war he sensed real opportunity. In 1748 Major Stringer Lawrence, 'a stout hale man of fifty', who had served at Gibraltar and probably at Cul-loden, arrived at Madras, now restored to the English, to command the forces of the Company. Following the French example, Stringer Lawrence at once formed the English into the First Battalion of the Madras Fusiliers, and trained a considerable force of Indian *Sipahis*, 'Sepoys', the Hindi and originally Persian term for soldier. They were drilled and taught the latest techniques of close fighting with the new ring-bayonet. As a politician the Major was too hasty: when, with misplaced chivalry, he returned the body of a fallen *raja* in his own palanquin, far from returning it, the enemy paraded it as evi-dence of his own demise; but Stringer Lawrence—afterwards Major-General—would become the 'father of the Indian Army' and attain a monument in Westminster Abbey. He would also help to secure southern India in the second French bid of domination during the Seven Years War.

[19] Sir George Forrest, *The Life of Lord Clive*, London, 1918, Vol. I, p. 16.

And he now gave Clive his chance:[20] though peace had been made in Europe, the fight went on in India. In 1748 Dupleix and the French Admiral de la Bourdonnais had quarrelled, and Vice-Admiral Edward Boscawen had removed the strategic threat from Mauritius. But the now restored Muhammad Ali was besieged in Trichinopoly; and Clive, with correct strategic insight, planned to attack Arcot, Chandra Sahib's capital, to draw him off. Thomas Saunders, the civilian President of Fort St David, backed the idea: Clive, at twenty-five, was given local rank as Captain and dispatched with two hundred English troops, three hundred sepoys and three field-guns to his objective.

In the sweltering heat of August 1751 they quickly captured the town. 'Arcot stands in a stony plain; the sterile red rock does nothing to temper the harshness of the sun. The fort is not raised up on a height that might catch a breeze; the houses cluster thickly round the walls. It was September, close, hot and moist; in red coats and tight stocks, heavy felt hats, belts and pouches, the men must have poured with sweat. Water was bad and short; food was short.... Clive went the rounds with a sergeant by his side; on three separate occasions the sergeant was killed and Clive saved.'[21] Arcot was held; Chandra Sahib and his French allies were drawn as by a magnet to the politically important town. They soon vastly outnumbered the English, but the stubborn defence held. In November the final assault led by iron-plated elephants collapsed; the animals, wounded by musket fire, trampled on their masters. After fifty days Arcot was relieved by a column under Captain Kilpatrick from Madras, and by the threat of the Maratha allies of the Company, who now thought that the English were likely to win. In the next year the French and their allies surrendered at Trichinopoly.

The French would remain a major power in the country; but the miniature victory resounded over southern India and beyond: the strongest European power was no longer French or Dutch, it was British. The news penetrated to Bengal, to Bombay, to Surat and to Delhi. The Company was now a great political force, with commitments far beyond the defence of a commercial monopoly. And behind these victories was English sea power. The outcome of the siege of Arcot, among its barren rocks and granite hills, had confirmed the superiority of the English and given them a new prestige.

In 1752 Clive's father was writing that at dinner with Sir Philip

[20] Clive afterwards returned the compliment by augmenting the General's pension by £500 a year.

[21] Woodruff, *op. cit.* Vol. I, p. 86.

Chetwode, 'our neighbour in the country at Oakley', Clive's exploits had been discussed: 'Your five sisters are now most of them grown women and your two brothers, the one eleven and the other seven, all rejoyce at your welfare and are not a little proud of their relation.' Clive's mother wrote: 'I can't express the joy your letters to your father gave me. Your brave conduct and success that providence has blessed you with is the talk and wonder of the Publick.'[22] In the following year Captain Clive married the attractive niece of a high official of the Company, and he could also write, 'I have left in the hands of Mr Levi Moses the sum of 50,000 Arcot rupees to be invested in diamonds.' The sum was only a small part of his fortune: in addition to the profits of his trading ventures since 1743, he had obtained the contract for supplying the Company's troops in the campaign. He returned to England; he bought Walcot Park; he lived high and lavishly in London. In 1754 he was presented by the Company with a sword set with diamonds, worth £500. He was elected Member of Parliament for the rotten borough of Mitchell in Cornwall, though, owing to some irregularity, the election was set aside. Clive had put his family on its feet. But his way of life proved very expensive: in 1756 he went out to India again and founded the British Empire in Bengal.

V

When Clive returned to the East to enlarge his fortunes and promote the profits of the Company, he was still wary of political commitments. The south was now relatively secure, but soon events in Bengal forced the Company to accept political control. Calcutta was now a great city which presented a tempting prize: in 1739, when Nadir Shah of Persia, had invaded the Punjab, Ali Vardi Khan, a Tatar adventurer—called *Mahabat Jang*, 'the terror of war'—and Subadar or Viceroy of Bengal, Behar and Orissa, had revolted from Delhi, fought off the Marathas and set up an independent power. But he had been wary of attacking the European merchants, whom he considered an asset. In 1756, the year of the outbreak of the Seven Years War in Europe, his grand-nephew, the Nawab Suraj-ud-Daula, aged nineteen, inexperienced, inconsequent and unaware of the sea power and military resources of the foreigners, decided to be rid of the infidels and plunder their wealth. He seized the city, and the civilian British Governor and his entourage took to the ships in the estuary, and abandoned a hundred and forty-six compatriots, including women and children, to the invaders. Elated with his success, the

[22] Forrest, *op. cit.* p. 218.

young Nawab laid on a debauch, having casually ordered the captives to the nearest prison: they might well, in the conventions of Indian warfare, have been impaled. But if the Nawab's intentions had been relatively humane, they were frustrated. Herded into the 'Black Hole of Calcutta'—eighteen feet by fourteen—'one agitated wave impelling another', only twenty-three out of the hundred and forty-six prisoners survived the stifling night. The result of incompetence more than of cruelty, at which few Indians would have batted an eyelid, the affair rankled among Europeans.

The Seven Years War being now imminent, a force including the 39th Foot—later the First Battalion, Dorset Regiment, *Primus in Indis*—and a naval squadron under Admiral Watson, were poised at Madras to attack the French in southern India. So the expedition was switched to Bengal, with Clive, now Colonel and Vice-Governor of Madras, in command. The combined operation swiftly recaptured Calcutta, and Clive, anxious to eradicate the French from Bengal, cajoled Suraj-ud-Daula into an alliance. With his nominal connivance, the French settlement at Chandanagore was mopped up; but when the Nawab proved shifty, the Admiral threatened to 'kindle such a flame in your country as all the waters of the Ganges shall not be able to extinguish'. But Suraj-ud-Daula still tried to play the foreigners off against each other, so the English decided to get rid of him: in shady manoeuvres, which included forgery, they conspired with Mir Jaffar, Ali Vardi's brother-in-law, and with the real powers behind the throne—the Hindu and Armenian bankers of Murshidabad and Calcutta—to depose a ruler whose violence had become unpredictable. So when at Plassey in June 1757, Suraj-ud-Daula with an enormous host gave battle, Mir Jaffar, like the Stanleys at Bosworth, simply stood aloof. As the monsoon mist lifted over the green plains of Bengal, the 39th Foot and the Sepoys broke up the Nawab's Persian and Pathan guard. Under the English fire the elephants panicked, the crack mounted swordsmen overran the bullock-drawn guns: the French troops were engulfed. 'The blow,' wrote Clive to his father, 'obliged the Nawab to decamp'. Mounting a fast riding camel, Suraj-ud-Daula made off—recaptured, he was soon done to death. 'The last attack,' wrote Clive, 'was the warmest I was ever yet engaged in'; the booty was immense: 'two hundred boats with flags flying and music blaring carried the treasure to Calcutta'.[23]

Mir Jaffar now became Nawab and the French were evicted; 'the success', Clive informed his father, 'has probably saved the Company. Press my interest now ... I am desirous of being appointed Governor-General of India if such an appointment should be neces-

[23] Feiling, *op. cit.* p. 25.

sary.'[24] Vast sums, too, now compensated for the outrages at Calcutta : huge 'presents' were distributed. Clive himself obtained about £240,000; then, after the Mughal had made him a magnate of the Empire, a *jagir* or land revenue of £30,000 a year as well. It came in fact from the Company's *Diwani* of the twenty-four Pergunnas south of Calcutta and, though it would revert to them at Clive's death, some people even then thought the arrangement peculiar.

In the south, meanwhile, Sir Eyre Coote, who would again save the British power in the Carnatic under Warren Hastings, had scotched a renewed French attack.[25] In 1758 the French Governor-General Lally de Tollendal, with strong naval backing from Mauritius, had besieged Madras from Pondicherry. But in 1760 Coote defeated him at Wandewash, and captured the French commander, the Comte de Bussy—a disaster blamed on Lally de Tollendal who was afterwards executed in France. In the same year Colonel Clive had left India in a haze of fame: in 1761 he became Member of Parliament for Shrewsbury and an Irish peer.

But Bengal was still in chaos. Clive himself had seen only one solution : in 1759 he had written to Pitt, then at the height of his power in the 'year of victories', that the Company ought to be 'sovereign' in Bengal; but since the directors would never consent, government itself would have to take over. Pressing domestic and diplomatic reasons made the project impossible, so the Company's power still had to be masked : while they exploited the country and collected the revenues, a crippled and bankrupt Indian administration was supposed to govern Bengal. And Mir Jaffar soon proved disappointing. He had two royal Begums drowned, and the expenses of his *seraglio* were inordinate : he had to be dethroned and his son-in-law, Mir Kasim, installed. But the occasion brought the Company the untaxed revenues of Midnapore, Burdwan and Chittagong, worth half a million pounds a year. Then Mir Kasim, an abler ruler, soon found this dual system impossible : in final exasperation, he massacred the English at Patna. So he, too, had to go, and the dilapidated Mir Jaffar was restored. On his demise in the next year, his heir lavished further sums on his protectors.

[24] Forrest, *op. cit.* Vol. I, p. 363.

[25] Sir Eyre Coote—'Coote *Bahadur*' (1726–83)—was descended from the Coote Earls of Bellamont and Mountrath in County Limerick. He had campaigned in the 'Forty-five and played a major part at Plassey. He accumulated a large fortune at which his superiors connived, and purchased extensive estates in Ireland. He is not to be confused with his nephew of the same name, who inherited his property and after an education at Eton and a distinguished career in the Napoleonic Wars, became Commander-in-Chief in Jamaica, but displayed eccentricity at Walcheren and in conduct which afterwards perhaps occasioned the expression 'queer as a coot'.

It was decided that Clive should go out again. In 1765 Lord Clive, began his eighteen months' term as Governor of Bengal, to cleanse, as he himself put it, 'the Augean stable'. The Company now 'stood forth as Diwan' or revenue collector, under the Great Mughal at Delhi, for the whole of Behar Orissa and Bengal. It was a great political turning point. The English *Banias* were now a formidable and recognized political power in the declining Empire—the more formidable as the Mughal's own authority was a shadow. The Company became in effect paramount in the most vital area of India— with a revenue exceeding its income from its commercial investment. All Hindustan was open to exploitation up the waterways that converge on Calcutta.

But the Augean stable was too much even for Clive; in part, perhaps, because he netted another £200,000 for himself. The Company's servants, still grossly underpaid and trading on their own accounts, were inextricably involved with Indian agents. Nor had anyone the power to unravel the welter of their transactions or the activities of the independent merchants in the bazaars on whose profits they took a commission. A ramified and long-established interest was determined to thwart reform. So now, back in England, Clive had to set about strengthening his own political interest—his family, he wrote, 'would come very strong in Parliament' in 1768, 'seven without opposition, probably one more'. He had need of Parliamentary interest, for enemies at home and in India were on his track, but he continued to live in quasi-ducal magnificence in London and at Walcot, rebuilt Old Styche and bought up wider estates.

The Company shares and dividends had now reached unprecedented heights; but though long-term prospects were sound, the depredations of the rulers, Indian and British, aggravated by famine and war, had been too much even for the resources of Bengal. Though in 1771 the Company paid a higher dividend, by the following year the crash came. The shares fell by sixty points and the Company had to ask for a loan of £1,000,000 from government.

Lord North, George III's Chief Minister, had to appoint a secret Committee of Enquiry, and Clive was ferociously attacked. The English in India, wrote Horace Walpole, had surpassed the atrocities of the Spaniards in Peru. Clive repelled the onslaught, but the strain of his career and its sequel had told upon him. He had never been healthy; he travelled, in vain, to Avignon and the south of France. In 1774, tormented by gallstones—a disease, he wrote, that made life insufferable—he shot himself. He was only fifty-three. His commanding statue still overlooks St James's Park.

VI

The success of the East India Company had made it many enemies. The social dislike for *nouveaux riches* nabobs; the vendettas in Bengal, transferred to London; the administrative muddles and corruptions of a typically eighteenth-century administration which flourished in tropical luxuriance in India, combined to provide the enemies not only of Clive but of government with ammunition for attack. Yet the Company was far too important to the English economy to be allowed to default.

In 1773, following the Committee of Enquiry, North's government intervened. The loan asked for was accorded, but a Regulating Act in effect subjected the Company to Parliament. Dividends were limited to 6 per cent until the loan was paid off; private trading by the Company's servants was discountenanced, and a Governor-General appointed with authority over Madras and Bombay as well as Bengal. And if, by a typical eighteenth-century balance of power, he had only a casting vote in a council of four colleagues, Parliament had now acknowledged an ultimate responsibility for British India.

In 1774 Warren Hastings, already Governor of Bengal, became the first Governor-General, with headquarters at Calcutta. This remarkable man, who saved and consolidated the British position and thwarted another attempted takeover by the French and their shifting collaborators during the American War, proved the greatest eighteenth-century ruler of British India and the most sympathetic to Indian civilization, Muslim and Hindu. Unlike Clive, he was an intellectual, who spoke Bengali, Urdu and Persian, and was already touched with the insight of the romantic age. He came of an impoverished collateral branch of a great medieval family, and his ambition, in which he succeeded, was limited: to buy back his ancestral estate at Daylesford Manor in the Cotswolds.[26] Hastings would write

[26] Warren Hastings (1732–1818) was brought up by his grandfather, the Rector of Daylesford, and by a paternal uncle in the London Customs service. Of his father, who emigrated to Barbados, he wrote that there was 'not much' in his history worth repeating; his mother, Hester Warren, died at his birth. His uncle sent him to Westminster School, where as a King's Scholar he showed great academic promise, but his uncle died and the boy on his own initiative went into the East India Company's service, and arrived in India aged seventeen. He found Bengal 'a swampy land where giant bats flew at night and the jungle behind was full of tigers and where each hot weather, with the assistance of heavy drinking and incompetent doctors, bore off a large crop to the burial ground' (Feiling, *op. cit.* p. 10) but where the survivors made fortunes. In 1758 Hastings was made President at the great city of

to his second wife, on parting, in terms that Nelson would use to
Lady Hamilton—('Oh God, what a change in my existence within
the compass of a few minutes!' etc.). He was physically frail, Spartan
in habits, indifferent to field sports—even tiger shooting—more at
home riding and driving, gardening and farming. Though he kept up
formal state and his waistcoats were sumptuous even by the standards of the time, he saved no more than £75,000 out of his salary
of £25,000 a year and the previous opportunities of commerce, and
his tastes were relatively simple. He acclimatized English flowers
and vegetables at Calcutta, kept a stable of superb Arab horses and,
in retirement, a fine herd of Jerseys at Daylesford. But he was a
lavish patron of Indian arts, encouraged the easy social intercourse
still taken for granted between the English and Indian aristocracy,
and admired not only Persian poetry and civilization but the literature of the Hindus. It 'proceeded', he wrote, 'from an Antiquity preceding our own' and would 'survive when the English dominion in
India shall have long ceased to exist'.[27] Recommending Colebrook's
translation of the *Bhagavad Gita* to the current chairman of the Company, he asserts its 'wonderful fertility of genius and pomp of language',[28] and states that he has always thought it his duty to encourage
'liberal knowledge' among the servants of the Company. He was a
world away from the leathery, hard living, military atmosphere of

---

Murshidabad in Bengal; in 1769 he was posted as Deputy-Governor to Madras,
then in 1772 back to Bengal as Governor. After 1774 he ruled British India
until 1785, when he resigned and returned to face attacks which he found
incomprehensible. His notorious trial on impeachment lasted from 1787 to
1795 spread out over 145 days and, though he was acquitted, the legal costs
ruined him. But the Company awarded him a pension of £4,000 a year, and
he lived at Daylesford in amiable retirement for the rest of his life. In 1814 he
became a Privy Councillor and the Prince Regent wanted to make him a
peer. In 1757 Hastings married the widow of a Captain Buchanan, but both
she and their children died. In 1777 he married a German, Marian Imhoff,
whom he had met on the outward voyage eight years before and who had
obtained a divorce in Germany from her husband, Baron Imhoff, a painter.
They had no children, but Hastings looked after her two sons by the Baron.
There is a large plaque to his own and his wife's memory in Daylesford
Church, which Hastings, by 1816, had 'rebuilt with much the same materials as
constituted its primitive structure ... and the uniformity of its Saxon architecture ... restored'. In vain: the Victorians destroyed the building, though they
preserved the plaque in a church now appropriate to the Rhineland. In the
churchyard there is a plain urn on a pedestal simply inscribed 'Warren
Hastings'.
[27] P. J. Marshall, *The British Discovery of Hindiism in the Eighteenth
Century*, Cambridge University Press, 1970, p. 189.
[28] Marshall, *op. cit.* p. 185.

Clive, though as much a realist in policy, well knowing the Company's only claim to dominion to be 'founded on the right of conquest'. A man of his time, Hastings never tried to westernize the Mughal administration; only to revive and adapt it: 'To subject Indians to our legal code,' he told Lord Mansfield, 'would be wanton tyranny'; they should rather 'found the authority of the British Government in Bengal on its ancient laws'.[29] Yet he was the first British ruler 'to suggest that the Company's territories in India were not just a place of investment for shareholders but a responsibility, an obligation requiring sympathy, understanding and good government'.[30]

The Company, having obtained a conditional loan of £1,500,000, half a million more than its original request, Parliament now had the last word—and Hastings a new kind of authority. But it was circumscribed by an ill-chosen Council. Yet in the Indian setting, his rule was bound to be personal and, given Hastings' own temperament, autocratic. Though never the tyrant depicted by the Whig propaganda of Burke and Sheridan and afterwards by Macaulay, Hastings naturally ruled more in the personal style of Akbar than of an aloof Victorian pro-consul. His worst handicap was his own Council, and he fought a duel with one of its members, Philip Francis, a man ignorant of India, and his most virulent enemy.[31]

He took on an immense task. In Bengal the need for peace and good government was urgent, and Hastings accepted the responsibility. British sovereignty was now openly asserted, and Hastings centralized the administration of both revenue and justice on Calcutta. But neither the Company's servants, deep in private trade and dependent on their Indian agents, nor the Indian *Zemindars* who rendered an arbitrarily assessed revenue and salted away anything more that they could extract, were reliable agents. Mistakenly, Hastings plumped for the *Zemindars*, seeing in them the equivalent of the English squirearchy; though, owing to their influence in London, the British collectors survived, later to become the key men of later British administration. But the taking of 'presents' and private trading

[29] Keith Feiling, *Warren Hastings*, London, 1966, p. 86.

[30] Michael Edwardes, *British India 1772–1947: a survey of the nature and effects of alien rule*, 1967, p. 24.

[31] It was an amateurish duel. 'Francis said he had never fired a pistol in his life, while Hastings could only remember doing so once or twice.' They fought at fourteen paces and 'once Francis' pistol missed fire, twice he went to the present and came down again. A third time and they fired, almost together. Francis narrowly missed, while Hastings' bullet struck his right side, was turned by a rib, and lodged under the left shoulder. He fell crying "I am dead"; Hastings ran across, saying "Good God, I hope not". . .'. Feiling, *op. cit.* pp. 208–9.

were diminished, the diversion of revenues checked, land surveys made, currency reformed. The threatened collapse of government itself in Bengal was averted.

Concurrently Hastings had to face a mounting threat to the very existence of British India. With the American War, the French and their Indian allies, in combined strength superior to the Company, save for British sea power, mounted a formidable attack. In western India war broke out with the Marathas over Salsette, a strategic island off Bombay, and in the south with Haidar Ali, Sultan of Mysore, backed by the French from Mauritius. Hastings dispatched an army across the whole breadth of India to Poona, the Maratha capital: by 1781, after the capture of Gwalior, the Maratha Scindia, 'King of Hindustan', had been brought to terms by the Treaty of Salbai. In the Carnatic Sir Eyre Coote, the veteran of Clive's wars, paid by Hastings £16,000 a year and £18,000 expenses, defeated Haidar Ali at Porto Novo, and the French forces withdrew. His successor, Tipu Sultan, was brought to a truce. Eastern and southern India had been saved.

Hastings at a time of the worst British defeats in North America had thus succeeded on both fronts, internal and external. To do so he had raised revenues by ruthless means and put down conspiracy with a high hand. He had Nuncomar, his most inveterate Indian opponent, hanged, ostensibly for forgery—hardly a capital offence in India at that time.[32] And he had extorted money from Chait Singh, Rajah of Benares, and from the eunuch treasurers of the Begums of Oude. But 'whatever their interest to the political moralist, historically the significance [of these episodes] is small; and they are perhaps valuable today simply as illustrations of the ways in which power tends to operate in India. They must not be thought of just as episodes of a vanished age ...'[33]

Be that as it may, Hastings' enemies after his return seized upon this aspect of his rule. With melodramatic rancour, the Whig opposition launched their attack, and briefly whipped up the political nation into one of those fits of moral indignation to which the English are susceptible. But the trial was a nine days' wonder. The public got bored with it; Hastings was acquitted and in the perspective of history his greatness in the history of the Empire is entirely apparent. He saved British India from internal collapse and external attack during the crisis of the American War, when most European powers were united in hostility to the British: and if the limits he accepted

[32] See Woodruff, op. cit. Vol. I, pp. 125–6.
[33] Sir Penderel Moon, *Warren Hastings and British India*, London, 1947, pp. 5–6.

of direct British rule could not last, for his policy of subsidizing Indian rulers failed to pacify the country and led to further intervention to maintain the interests of the Company, he did, evidently, set a new tone of responsibility towards India and its peoples. In the raffish society described by William Hickey—often comparable to that in the West Indies—where most of the Company's servants and army officers consoled themselves for exile by a lavish and precarious ostentation, maintained hordes of servants and were concerned mainly with gambling, adultery and drink, Hastings was a scholar and an orientalist, who doubtless found intelligent Indians better company. In retirement he would write to another Governor-General, 'Among the natives of India, there are men of as strong intellect, as sound integrity and as honourable feelings as any of this kingdom ... by your example make it the fashion among our countrymen to treat them with courtesy and as participants in the same rights of society with themselves.'[34]

This eighteenth-century enlightenment would not survive into Victorian times, but Hastings in his day commanded the respect and affection of many Indians, and during his trial those he was said to have exploited and oppressed were loud in vindication of his rule. It is common form for the British to treat their greatest empire-builders with ingratitude, and Parliament never, as he wished, reversed his impeachment; but in 1813 when he was called to give evidence on Indian affairs, the House of Commons paid him a spontaneous and moving tribute of respect. 'I was heard,' he wrote, 'with the most respectful attention; all rose and uncovered, an honour which none in the power ... of the state to bestow can equal, either in the intrinsic worth or in its impression on my mind.'

[34] Cited Woodruff, *op. cit.* p. 124.

CHAPTER 9

Slavery, Slaughter and Sugar in the West Indies

While the British were consolidating and extending their enclaves in India, the Guinea coast of West Africa, from Senegal to Gambia and along the Ivory and Gold Coasts to the estuary of the Niger and the Bight of Benin, had become increasingly important. The small and casual trade in ivory, gold-dust and pepper, which had lured Windham and his kind to their deaths in a climate lethal for Europeans, had long given place to the much more lucrative slave-trade, pioneered, for the English, by the Hawkinses during the sixteenth century. 'Elephants' teeth' were being superseded by 'Black Ivory'.

The traffic was no innovation. Aristotle had taken it for granted; Christ had not denounced it; the Egyptian, Roman, Byzantine, Arab and Turkish Empires had imported slaves; and the early Anglo-Saxons exported their own kindred and the Welsh. But apart from Russia and the Caucasus, the main sources had always been African. Now the trade became Atlantic, part of a maritime domination, and even its abolition would lead to the predominance of the British in West Africa: for only the Royal Navy could put the traffic down, and for strategic as well as commercial reasons the British would gradually, if often reluctantly, take over the other European forts which in Renaissance or Baroque style had long protected the sweltering barracoons. Since the Portuguese had shipped slaves from Angola to Brazil and the Hawkinses had made their voyages from West Africa to the Caribbean, the demand had steadily increased. Planters in the West Indies and Virginia, then in the Carolinas and Georgia, in Spanish America and Brazil, like the dealers in the Hadramaut, Baghdad and Basra, provided profitable markets, and a forced migration of millions of Negroes descended on the Caribbean and the Americas. In West Africa itself the drain on the population was probably more than offset by the import of American food plants; and at first a hectic prosperity accrued to the rulers of already wealthy states. But the long-term consequences were disruptive.

At first the trade mainly affected the maritime states: European traders and their forts and depots were still peripheral, and the British made no contacts with the well-established sub-Saharan states of the interior. It was in the contrasting 'negrolands' of the tropical rain-forest that extended from modern Portuguese West Africa to the Volta in present day Ghana and, again, across southern Nigeria, that the slaves were rounded up and the Europeans got the footholds they would develop in colonial times.

By the late seventeenth century the most vigorous kingdoms in the southern area were Akan, Akwama, Ashanti and Yoruba Oyo with its capitals at Lagos and Ibadan. Here the slave-trade spread first along the Gold Coast, then through the rain-forest, the mangrove swamps and intricate waterways of the Niger.

To Europeans these West African cultures appeared a blend of sophistication and superstition: highly organized and wealthy, yet by European standards, barbaric. In Oyo, for example, when the Alafin died, all his closer relatives had to commit ritual suicide, and their strictly secluded existence had not given them much to live for. Even in the late eighteenth century, every year a living girl was impaled to propitiate the rain goddess, and human sacrifice would be taken for granted in Benin well into the nineteenth. The population was the densest in Africa. Ibos and amphibious Ijaws multiplied in flourishing settlements among the forests and lagoons east of the Niger; while, north of Benue, sparse and naked Pongos, head-hunters and bowmen, would eat 'anything from rats, mice and bats to their own deceased relatives'[1]—a people, as already observed in 1588, 'of beastly living'.

By the late seventeenth century the hunt for slaves had spread deeper into the interior: pleasantly demoralizing to rulers who were paid in alcohol and firearms, and hideously demoralizing to the victims shipped overseas. If, in fact, as the slavers set course over the mid-Atlantic, the prospects of the Negroes were not necessarily worse, their accepted and reassuring social order was certainly disrupted.

In this mounting tragedy the British played an increasing part. By 1661 Charles II and his advisers, as eager to promote the economies of the American and Caribbean colonies as the trade of Surat, Madras and Bengal, set up a Council for Foreign Plantations, which, among other objectives, encouraged the British trade in 'blacks' out of West Africa. Spanish slavers now had to pay a duty of ten pieces

[1] A. C. Burns, *A History of Nigeria*, London, 1929, p. 64.

of eight for each Negro, while the British could import them duty free;[2] and the Royal Africa Company had its monopoly in the British West Indies confirmed. But such monopolies were hard for any government to enforce. West Africa was the haunt of interlopers and pirates, and in theory the British were still excluded from Spanish America.

Hence, the signature in 1713, after the War of the Spanish Succession, of the Asiento contract by which the Royal Africa and South Sea Companies obtained the right, hitherto supposedly enjoyed by the French, to supply '4,800 prime slaves at agreed prices' to the Spanish colonies. And soon, such was the demand—for the Spaniards had no sufficient catchment area of their own—this agreement, too, proved inadequate; and in 1750, following the Wars of Jenkins' Ear and of the Austrian Succession, the Spaniards bought out the Company for £100,000. A diminished Royal Africa Company was subsidized to maintain the forts in West Africa, but the trade was thrown open to all competitors, among whom the English proved the most successful.

Meanwhile within the Old Colonial Empire the slave-trade had come to rival sugar, and from 1750 until its abolition in 1807—when the British had half the entire trade—the fortunes of Bristol and Liverpool were largely made by it. Already in 1749 a journalist was writing, smugly and representatively, that 'the trade of Africa is the branch which renders our American colonies and Plantations so advantageous to Great Britain, that traffic affording our planters a constant supply of negro servants for the culture of their lands ... The negro trade, therefore, and the natural consequences resulting from it, may be justly esteemed an inexhaustible fund of wealth and naval power to this nation'.[3]

After the Seven Years War, when in 1758 the French possessions of Senegal and Goree had been captured, the British grip on the West African slave-trade was confirmed. 'The accepted Foreign Office figure for the annual average of slaves transferred in the later eighteenth century was 100,000 a year ... of the 192 vessels sailing for the Slave Coast from British ports in 1771, 107 sailed from Liverpool, 58 from London, 23 Bristol and four from Lancaster. The profits of the round trip, as it came to be called, made it the most paying of all regular trade routes.'[4] Cloth, strong drink and obsolescent muskets were traded for slaves, and after the notorious Middle Passage, the slavers

[2] C.S.P., Colonial, 1661–1668, p. 169.

[3] Quoted by C. E. Carrington, *The British Overseas: Exploits of a Nation of Shopkeepers*, Part I, Cambridge, 1968, p. 331.

[4] Christopher Lloyd, *The Navy and the Slave Trade*, London, 1949, p. 5.

returned laden with sugar, tobacco and rum. For the crews probably only the 'Middle Passage' was really unpleasant.

In 1783, for example, the 'good ship *Bloom* (Robert Bostock, Master) ... took on board 307 slaves who were sold by auction at Antigua for £35–£45 a head. Having loaded a cargo of molasses and tobacco, the *Bloom* returned home, making a profit for her owners of £9,635-9s-7d of which the Captain's commission amounted to £360-14s-3d.'[5] The conditions in the ships had now slightly improved —obviously it paid to preserve the cargo—but two years before, when the water supply on board proved inadequate to keep his full cargo alive, the captain of the slaver *Zang* had pitched 132 of them overboard so as to claim the insurance of £30 a head, a claim upheld by the law to protect the rights of property. And in spite of Lord Mansfield's judgment in 1772 that any slave in England automatically became free since no such status was recognized there, the agitation which opened in Parliament in 1776, when the crisis over the American colonies coincided with the ventilation of radical ideas, did not become effective till 1787, when the Society for the Abolition of Slavery was founded, and the campaign was properly launched which would lead to the abolition of the trade within the Empire in 1807, and of slavery itself there in 1833.

II

In the West Indian colonies, now being developed by slave-labour, piracy and depredation were giving place to a booming trade in sugar. The 'vast and slip-shod' Spanish American Empire, which had 'pre-empted a continent',[6] was breaking down; and in 1670, by the Treaty of Madrid, Spain had tacitly recognized the facts of British sovereignty in the Caribbean. Unofficial neo-Elizabethan depredations went on, but the main source of really massive wealth was now sugar, and under the later Stuarts the West Indian planters attained a fabulous prosperity, coincident with the growing wealth of the East India Company on the other side of the world.

The demand for sugar both in England and for re-export to the continent was insatiable and a great West Indian Parliamentary 'interest' grew up. Following the Portuguese development of sugar-cane in Madeira and on a great scale in Brazil, sugar had become not merely a luxury but a necessity for the masses.[7] There was room for

[5] Lloyd, *op. cit.*

[6] Richard Pares, *War and Peace in the West Indies, 1739–1763*, Oxford, 1936, p. 1.

[7] See J. H. Parry, *Trade and Dominion: The European Overseas Empires in*

British enterprise as well. Jamaica experienced roaring prosperity as sugar exports surpassed tobacco; cocoa, indigo, hides and logwood were booming, and pirates and privateers returned to base to spend their gains. Barbados became even richer, Nevis prosperous. And if, as Portuguese production increased and other sugar colonies were developed by the French and the Dutch, recession set in, so that in 1733 the British tried harder to force the American colonists to buy their rum and molasses only within the Empire, profits often remained substantial on the better-run plantations. Then, with the Revolutionary and Napoleonic Wars, when foreign competition was dislocated and the armed forces badly needed much more rum, the seventeenth-century boom was restored, in a comparable if final prosperity.

The interests of the West Indian planters, as of the slave-traders, thus contributed to the great wars of commercial imperialism which culminated in the Seven Years War and the widest extensions of the Old Colonial Empire. As the Portuguese, Spaniards and Dutch became second-rate powers, the British and French fought one another over the declining but tenacious Spanish Empire. The Caribbean became a cockpit of great naval campaigns with global strategic objectives, part of a conflict which extended from Canada and the North American interior to India and the Far East. The West Indies became strategically vital for bases in a battle for the Western Atlantic, and as bargaining counters in negotiations which changed the balance of world power.

Through more than a century of this fluctuating and amphibious warfare the English possessions in the Caribbean emerged intact. During King William's War, fought in alliance with Spain, Irish Jacobites rose in Antigua and Montserrat, the French captured Anguila, for what it was worth; the Caribs raided where they could. Nature also took a hand : in 1692 the worst earthquake ever recorded there destroyed Port Royal in Jamaica, when 'with a hollow rolling noise like thunder, the earth heaved and swelled like rolling billows' and 'cracked open and shut', so that inhabitants were 'swallowed up ... or caught by the middle and pressed to death, and in others the heads only appeared, in which condition dogs came and ate them'. 'Scarce a plantation or sugar work was left standing in all Jamaica.'[8] About two thousand people were killed, and nature put the human conflicts in their place.

---

the Eighteenth Century, London, 1971, pp. 33–6, for the scale and importance of the Portuguese sugar-trade and its effect on Portugal.
    [8] Burns, *op. cit.* p. 381.

In the War of the Spanish Succession, that crusty tarpaulin, Admiral Benbow, tanner's son and former cabinboy, provoked such offence by his brusque manner of command that his own captains disobeyed orders and came to disgraceful defeat off Santa Marta on the Spanish Main. Two were court-martialled and shot; Benbow, his legs riddled with grapeshot, died in Jamaica. The French took Nevis and nearly wiped out the English settlement at Nassau, Bahamas, while the British seized St Kitts and nearly captured Guadaloupe.

Then, in the Wars of Jenkins' Ear[9] and of the Austrian Succession, Vice-Admiral Vernon captured Puerto Bello—an event still commemorated by the Portobello Road and taverns called 'The Vernon Head'—and in 1741 he destroyed a Spanish fleet off Cartagena. In 1740–4, Commodore Anson was dispatched to foment rebellion on the Pacific Coast of South America, and, more profitably, circumnavigated the world. In the Caribbean thousands of unacclimatized soldiers died of yellow fever, and the planters refused to conscript their slaves for transport and supply. But at the Peace of Aix-la-Chapelle, none of the major islands changed hands; and the French who had agreed to evacuate Dominica, St Lucia, St Vincent and Tobago, which were to be abandoned to the expectant Caribs, failed to do so.

[9] The War of Jenkins' Ear was a retrospective put-up job. In 1731 Robert Jenkins, Master Mariner of the brig *Rebecca* and his crew, bound from Jamaica to London, had been intercepted off Havana. The Spaniards had plundered the brig and, Jenkins declared, had tied him to the mast and sliced off part of his ear. But Jenkins and his crew brought the crippled vessel into the Port of London and the story got about. Seven years later, after Jenkins had been appeased in 1732 by being promoted to the command of an East Indiaman, the affair was cooked up into a political *cause célèbre*. It was, perhaps 'the habit of dining out, so to speak, on his ear', which prompted the revival of the story as anti-Spanish propaganda in 1738 (J. H. Parry, *op. cit.* p. 154). Before a committee of the House of Commons, the Master Mariner produced what he swore was the severed portion of his ear which had been pickled in brandy. Political enemies declared that he lost it in the pillory, and Pares—no mean authority—remarks that 'if perhaps they had looked under his wig they would have found both the celebrated ears in place' (*op. cit.* p. 612). On the other hand, the Commander-in-Chief West Indies had reported the mutilation. Whatever the truth, in 1738 Jenkins, perhaps suitably coached, rose to the occasion. Questioned on his feelings in his predicament, he replied in the best high eighteenth-century manner, 'I committed my soul to God and my cause to my country.' He had given the politicians their cue: the 'story of Jenkins', it was observed, 'will raise volunteers'. The trade war was on. Jenkins proved a very successful sea-captain in the East India Company's service and was briefly Governor of St Helena before he died of fever at Bombay in 1742.

The Seven Years War, the climax of British eighteenth-century belligerence, was more decisive. Hawke's victory off Quiberon Bay, and Boscowen's off Lagos, secured control of the Atlantic, and in 1759 Guadaloupe was captured: in 1762 Rodney occupied Martinique, St Lucia and Grenada. When the main Spanish battle fleet was crippled at Havana, the loot was worth three-quarters of a million pounds in doubloons and pieces of eight. Even Manila in the Philippines was captured. Such warfare was on a new scale. 'Between 1756 and 1762, 5,451 boys were drafted from the streets into the Navy, and 4,787 enlisted as Naval volunteers. Youth flocked to both branches of the service ... in 1762 upwards of 337,000 men were employed on land and sea in British service, of whom 57,000 were German mercenaries and 20,000 colonials.'[10] By the end of the conflict the British were masters of the Caribbean, as they were of Canada and India.

But the sugar planters of Jamaica, Barbados and Nevis wanted no extra competition within the mercantilist Empire; so Martinique and Guadaloupe were restored to France—the latter, incredible though it may seem, in exchange for Canada—an arrangement then thought greatly to the French advantage. But the English retained Dominica, Grenada, St Vincent and Tobago, and swapped Havana for Florida in the Olympian way in which eighteenth-century European statesmen decided the fate of the outer world. And when, in 1778, following the outbreak of the American War, the British briefly lost control of the Atlantic, the Spaniards regained Minorca, if not Gibraltar, and the French admirals, more concerned with the West Indies than with liberating Americans, captured all the lesser British islands, the main bases in Jamaica and Barbados held. In 1782 Rodney and Hood intercepted de Grasse who, after his appearance in Chesapeake Bay, was preparing to attack Jamaica. They defeated him and captured the French flagship in the battle of the Saints—so-called from the names of some islets between Dominica and Guadaloupe off which the action was fought, and though the British failed to annihilate the enemy, they saved the West Indies. In 1783, by the Treaty of Versailles, they restored St Lucia and ceded Tobago; but retained St Kitts, Nevis, Grenada, St Vincent and Dominica, though Florida was handed over to Spain. The sparse British settlements on the mainland of Yucatan, where the reefs, mango-swamps and matted forests had repelled the Spanish pioneers, had struggled on around Belize and developed their trade in mahogany and logwood. The West Indies, save for Cuba and Hispaniola and Puerto Rico, remained, and

[10] G. B. Hertz, *The Old Colonial System*, Manchester, 1905, pp. 12, 13, 21.

would remain, predominantly British, and prove their economic and strategic importance in the campaigns of Nelson and Villeneuve.

III

The successive tides of battle which swirled in and out of the Caribbean, like the summer hurricanes and earthquakes which periodically struck the islands, spread their occasional devastation. But the prosperity which had culminated in the late seventeenth century was not permanently undermined. Though tropical diseases could account for 4,700 out of the 5,260 casualties at the siege of Havana, the planters themselves were better acclimatized: indeed, they were pickled. 'They eat like cormorants,' it was observed, 'and drink like porpoises.' They enjoyed a rich blend of cookery—European, Creole, Negro and Amerindian—and in the 1660s it was already calculated that in Port Royal in Jamaica there was one tavern to every ten inhabitants. Rum was, of course, the ubiquitous drink: in its diluted form called grog—after Admiral Vernon, who imposed this precaution and habitually wore a boat cloak of grogrham.[11] As in India, madeira, though hardly the most salubrious drink in the tropics, was the favourite wine, and brandy, next to rum, the main standby. The rich planters and their European and Creole dependents competed with reformed pirates in raffish ostentation. The formal contemporary dress of Europe was adapted to the climate—'thread stockings, linen drawers and vest and handkerchief tied round the head and a hat above. Wigs are never used but on Sundays or in Court time, and the gentlemen appear very gay in silk coats and vests trimmed with silver. The ladies are as gay as anywhere in Europe.'[12] But this easy-going society, at once merry and contentious with its constant litigation over ill-defined boundaries and misinterpreted laws, appeared dull and provincial to sophisticated eyes. The wealthier proprietors looked down on the Creoles, and spent all the time they could in England or on the Continent.

As the sugar-trade developed, the big planters ousted the lesser ones. Sugar-mills, boiler-houses and a labour force of hundreds of slaves demanded big capital; while 'poor whites', some of whom turned pirate, added to the racial variety of the Caribbean. And as the slavers arrived from Guinea, 'loaded with negroes, elephants' teeth and gold dust', the influx of slaves created an overwhelming preponderance of negroes over whites. On the more prosperous and

---

[11] From *gros grain*—coarse grained. It was made of mohair and wool and stiffened with gum; a forerunner of the macintosh.

[12] Burns, *op. cit.* p. 451.

well-run estates in the tropical climate they toiled and multiplied with a cheerful resilience; but on the estates of absentee or impoverished planters they were often hideously exploited, inefficient and resentful. There were revolts, ruthlessly suppressed, as the white minority became more uneasy. 'The minutes of the Council of Barbados for 1693 record an order for payment of 10 guineas to Alice Mills for castrating 42 negroes according to the sentence of the Commissioners for the Trial of Rebellious Negroes.'[13] In Montserrat in 1698 a runaway slave was hung, drawn and quartered; and in 1740, in Jamaica, a negro who had struck a white man could be burnt alive or starved to death—a loaf hanging before his mouth; pepper and salt would be rubbed into the weals inflicted by flogging. These punishments were considered 'exemplary'.

Naturally most of the richest planters became absentees and cut a figure in their own country, where the origin of their wealth could be forgotten, and the Old Colonial Empire in the Caribbean produced a rich variety of character: ruffians who, like Sir Henry Morgan, ended their days in the taverns of Jamaica; the worthy and tenacious Pinneys of Nevis, who slowly built up the wealth that would establish them as squires in their native Dorset; the highly sophisticated and brilliant Governor Codrington of Barbados, who endowed the finest college library in Oxford and, at the summit of wealth, the Beckford millionaires and eccentrics who contributed to English politics, and to romantic and sporting literature.

IV

Some representative personalities are worth attention. They illustrate the brutality that wrested the islands from competitors, the way in which the mercantilist Empire worked and the humane or eccentric personalities nourished on West Indian wealth. The first is a colourful pirate, still notorious; the second is typical of the abler and shrewder planters; the last three had their impact on the home country. They form a varied consequence of the massive forced migration out of West Africa and the appalling hardships which made their wealth possible.

Born in 1635, the son of a Welsh farmer in Glamorgan, Sir Henry Morgan was kidnapped or enticed out of Bristol when still a boy. He was sold as a servant in Barbados, then fetched up in Jamaica, and his nefarious exploits were described by an eyewitness, 'In a Piece of Natural and Humane History (that) Informeth as (with huge novelty) of as great and bold attempts, in point of military conduct and valour

[13] Burns, *op. cit.* Appendix D, pp. 737–8.

as ever was performed by Mankind'.[14] He was knighted, but, even as Lieutenant-Governor of Jamaica, Morgan was never really on the side of the establishment.

He had got his start through an uncle in 1668 when, with the connivance of the authorities, he sacked Puerto Bello in Costa Rica. Here he compelled nuns and friars to fix the scaling-ladders and, though the Spaniards shot them down, 'with great loss to the said religious people'[15] with 'Fire Balls and earthen pots full of gunpowder', the assault succeeded. The loot amounted to a quarter of a million pieces of eight and three hundred slaves. The money was soon spent in Jamaica as Morgan's followers 'wasted their gains on strumpets and wine', of which they bought 'pipes', and forced all and sundry at pistol point to drink it. And when the Spanish Governor of Panama, surprised at Morgan's brisk Welsh tactics, asked him for 'some small pattern' of the arms wherewith he had taken so great a city', Morgan sent back a pistol and some small bullets, desiring him 'to accept this slender pattern of arms and keep them for twelve months, after which time he proposed to come to Panama and fetch them away'.[16]

In 1669, in a captured French frigate off Maracaibo in Venezuela, Morgan had a near shave. He had 'drunk many healths, and discharged many guns, as the common sign of mirth among seamen used to be', and 'by what accident is not now known, the ship was suddenly blown up in the air'. Morgan, naturally, was in the Great Cabin: he survived along with thirty others, though the rest of the crew of three hundred and fifty and an unrecorded number of French prisoners in the hold perished. Moreover, he fished up the bodies of the victims to secure their rings.

So he survived for greater exploits. In 1670, guided by local bandits, he made a terrible march across the Isthmus of Panama with 1,200 men. They chewed broiled leather helped down by gulps of water, and when the Spaniards attacked them with two thousand wild bulls driven by Negroes and Amerindians most of the animals bolted in all directions at the noise. Even those that got through went

---

[14] See *Bucaniers of America*, or 'a true account of the most remarkable assaults committed of late years upon the coasts of the West Indies, by the Bucaniers of Jamaica and Tortuga, both English and French, wherein are contained more especially the Unparalleled Exploits of Sir Henry Morgan, our English Jamaica Hero, who sacked Puerto Bello. Written originally in Dutch by John Esquemeling [more usually spelt Exquemeling] one of the Bucaniers, who was present at these tragedies; and thence translated into Spanish . . . now faithfully rendered into English,' London, 1684.

[15] Esquemeling, *op. cit.* p. 97.

[16] Esquemeling, *op. cit.* p. 102.

for the English colours, not the men, and were shot dead or turned back on their masters. So the Spaniards were routed, horse and foot; the great city of Panama, with its cedarwood houses, stately churches and eight monasteries, sacked and burnt. Morgan kept his men off the wine by pretending the Spaniards had poisoned it; but they failed to catch a rich treasure galleon through 'the lascivious exercises wherein they were totally ... involved with women'[17]—and indeed, their leader himself 'gave them no good example on this point'. But Morgan knew how to find out where treasure had been stowed away: he would hang men up by their private parts, 'thus lacerating the most tender parts of their bodies', bind their heads with rope so that the eyes protruded like eggs, 'disjoint' them on racks, and singe their faces with burning straw, until they revealed their savings. So the ransom and loot were colossal; and Morgan himself, to the fury of the other pirates, decamped with most of it.

It was his final major escapade. In 1670, following the Treaty of Madrid, this sort of thing had to be officially disowned: and in 1672 he was sent back to England in apparent disgrace. But Charles II soon knighted the resourceful ruffian, and 'reposing peculiar confidence in his loyalty, prudence and courage', sent him back as Lieutenant-Governor. Here he proved an astute adversary to his former colleagues, though not above occasional connivance, as when in 1677, he was accused of corresponding with the pirates. And, seaman that he was, Morgan would 'ridicule the guards' and 'traduce the officers'; nor could he abide the Nonconformists, left over presumably from Cromwell's time. Indeed, he curried favour with James II by denouncing the authorities for encouraging them.[18] He set up The Loyal Club at 'The Point', where, especially in drink, he and his cronies 'cursed and damned the Dissenters'—behaving so 'extravagently' that the Point was 'worse than Algiers'. If at fifty-two Morgan was done for, he ended his life in a congenial atmosphere.

In contrast to this flamboyant but now old-fashioned predator, representative of the phase of conquest and slaughter, the canny and unobtrusive Azariah Pinney of Nevis was more in tune with the mercantilist exploitation. Born in 1661, the youngest son of the eight surviving children of the Rector of Broadwindsor near Bridport in Dorset, Azariah, like his father and unlike Morgan, had leanings to Dissent and in 1685 he took part in the Monmouth Rebellion. So, transferred from Dorchester gaol via Bristol to Barbados, with a pardon for his life obtained for £65, the black sheep of the family

[17] *op. cit.* Vol. III, p. 59.
[18] C.S.P., Colonial, America and the West Indies 1681–88, p. 103.

'sailed for the West Indies equipped with a Bible, six gallons of sack and four of brandy for the voyage and £15 in his pocket ... the escapade under Monmouth's standard had diverted the whole course of his life; it had turned him from a Dorset yeomen and lace-maker into the founder of a great colonial fortune'.[19]

Azariah now proved cunning and persistent. Anyone with luck, judgement and a smattering of the law, who was not Jacobite Irish, and who did not drink to excess or blatantly embezzle the funds, could find an opening; and by 1696 he became an overseer of a small plantation in Nevis. He was paid five thousand pounds of sugar a year for doing 'all things fit for an overseer to do'—that is to look after the sugar mills and boiling houses and the planting and cutting of the cane and supervise the work of the slaves, who otherwise 'would slack; or run away, or hurt themselves in the machinery or steal the rum'.[20] By 1701 he was also attorney to an absentee proprietor, and a general 'factor' handling English and American imports on commission : four years later, he acquired a plantation of his own. He also became Collector of Liquor Duties and Treasurer of Nevis. In a 'small and close-grained society, surrounded by men of another colour, liable to sudden ruin from hurricanes, fires or French invasions', he had 'concentrated on getting rich quick in a trying climate and a. strange landscape'. His property survived the brief French occupation of the island; he returned to England in 1710–12 and in 1719, and he died the next year in London.

His son John, as befitted this prosperity, was very differently brought up. He became a Gentleman Commoner of Pembroke College, Oxford, married the heiress of extensive plantations in Nevis and Antigua, and learnt enough law in the Middle Temple to become Chief Justice of Nevis. His heir, John Frederick, owned one of the biggest plantations on Nevis, with a fine house whose inventory of 1722 includes 'elbow chairs' stuffed and covered with striped Holland and silk, a damask and 'China' bedstead, and 'Bermuda chairs ... covered with calaminco', and a great quantity of linen and silver— the whole worth over £500.[21] Typically, John Frederick, a third generation proprietor, disliked the West Indies. He only visited this property twice, in 1739–42 and 1749. His roots were in England; as Member of Parliament for Bridport, he lived 'the life of a West Country squire, visiting London in the Parliamentary season, but leaving his

[19] Richard Pares, *A West India Fortune*, London, 1950, p. 10. He had also turned 'witness', presumably against the other rebels, whose average age was twenty-three—ploughboys, weavers, clothiers, tanners.

[20] Pares, *op. cit.* p. 18.   [21] Pares, *op. cit.* pp. 336–9.
[22] Pares, *op. cit.* p. 54.

heart behind him in Dorset'.[22] He built the house at Racedown afterwards occupied by Wordsworth, and inherited another at Bettiscombe from a senior branch of his family. But he died childless in 1762 leaving, as might be expected, an encumbered West Indian estate.

But the Pinney fortunes were now retrieved and greatly enhanced by a distant and humble relation. John Pretor, the son of a 'gauger' or small revenue officer at Dulverton, assumed the name and arms of Pinney under John Frederick's will, went out at once and managed the West Indian properties himself. He proved able and meticulous and returned to England only in 1783; when he died in 1818 he was worth on paper as much as £267,000, of which £136,000 was in the West Indies and the rest in land, houses and mortgages in England and in the public funds. In addition he had money on current account in West Indian mortgages and in shipping, which brought his whole estate to £340,000.

Thus the Pinney fortune, created under the protection of the mercantilist Old Colonial Empire, and starting with Azariah's £15, and worth about £23,000 at his death, fluctuated according to the attention devoted to it and in concurrence with the recession in sugar during the mid-eighteenth century; then, reflecting the revival during the French Revolutionary and Napoleonic Wars, reached its climax in the early nineteenth century. The Pinneys and their kind enriched the landed and moneyed establishment of late Georgian England and their characters, ranging from the mean and calculating to the expansive, are representative of their kind.

The millionaires are more interesting: variously exotic products of a tropical background. Christopher Codrington was far the most distinguished—a scholar, soldier, administrator and wit, the finest flower of slave-begotten wealth. Thomas Beckford, twice Lord Mayor of London, was the richest; his son, William Beckford of Fonthill in Wiltshire the most talented; and his nephew, Peter Beckford of Steepleton Iwerne, Dorset, and M.P. for Salisbury, who wrote the first standard work on fox-hunting, the most popular in his neighbourhood.

Only Codrington, whose neo-classical statue by Cheere adorns the superb Codrington Library he founded at All Souls College, Oxford, did anything for the West Indies. He came of a junior branch of Gloucestershire gentry, whose main estates were at Doddington between Chipping Camden and Bristol, and his first ancestor to settle in the West Indies had married the sister of a Colonel Drax, who, arriving with £300, had already 'raised his fortune to such a height that he would not look towards England till he was able to purchase an estate of £10,000 yearly, which he hoped in a few years to accomplish ... and all by planting sugar'.[23]

So the son of this marriage, General Christopher Codrington, inherited what was then the greatest personal fortune in the West Indies. He had become Deputy-Governor of Barbados under Willoughby, bought sugar plantations in Antigua, and in 1690, as Governor-General of the Leeward Islands, he had captured St Kitts from the French. Like Governor Pitt of Madras, he had combined official status with illegal private enterprise, and in defiance of the Royal Africa Company and of the Navigation Laws, regularly traded in slaves and sold sugar to foreigners. When this rugged and masterful planter died in 1698 he had left an immense fortune to his son.

Born in Barbados in 1668, Christopher the Second came up to Christ Church, Oxford, in 1685, and his career was 'swift, short, kaleidoscopic and brilliant'.[24] 'No spark', it was said of this 'dapper' Creole squire, 'walk'd up High Street bolder'; and 'besides his skill with the Great Horse he was expert in dancing also to a high degree'. He was also a first-rate scholar, and in 1790 he was elected to a Fellowship at All Souls, at that time, following the suppression of the old custom of the retiring Fellows selling out to the highest bidder, in one of its most creative incarnations. Like others after him, he 'ever accounted this election one of the greatest blessings of his life'—the 'Happy Opportunity which Providence indulg'd him of being bred up in that fruitful seminary of good literature'.[25] A friend of Addison and Boyle, the chemist, he now collected a library of 12,000 books, 'as curious as any private one in Europe'. But academic brilliance was not enough: in 1692 he took part in the expedition to the West Indies which led to Benbow's failure and death, and in 1694, aged twenty-six, he left Oxford for good to join William III's campaign in Flanders, where he 'did signal service in the taking of the town of Namur'. Here he soon 'caught the monarch's eye' and became captain, then colonel in the First Foot Guards. Then in 1699, after a hectic social and literary life in London and Paris, Codrington was appointed to his father's old office as Governor-General of the Leeward Islands, and in 1700 he left England, never to return.

As Governor-General he showed high qualities, though his metropolitan self-assurance made him enemies. From his headquarters in Antigua, Codrington at once tried to reform the chaotic and corrupt administration of the islands, and he ruined his health leading a campaign against Guadaloupe. 'I have been not only General,' he wrote,

---

[23] V. T. Harlow, *Christopher Codrington, 1668–1710*, Oxford, 1928, p. 7.

[24] Harlow, *op. cit.* p. 47.

[25] Harlow, *op. cit.* p. 55.

'but engineer, serjt and corporell.'[26] He had 'dispatcht', he declared at the outset, 'more business and done more justice in three weeks than had been done in thirty years before ... I think I have acted with the sincerity of a Magistrate in a Platonick Commonwealth'.[27]

The sincerity was little appreciated by the local politicians and 'little animales' who called themselves lawyers, for there was 'grave disorder in the judiciary'. Moreover, racial tension was acute—in 1701, fifteen belligerent Corromantee slaves in Antigua cut off their owner's head, 'washed it in rum and triumphed over it'. As for the local clergy, they could not even 'do any service to the white heathens, let alone the blacks'. And the state of the militia was farcical. In Barbados 'not a single pound of gunpowder remained in the island, the little there had been having been fired by Colonel Norton when he and his council and asembly, after falling out, got drunk together and grew friends again'. Moreover, wrote Codrington, 'Ye Barbadoes has noe inclination to serve or save these Ilands, Nor have any of these Ilands to help Another, because if a suger Iland be lost, so much ye less of the commodity is made, and consequently ye price raised.'

High-handed and impetuous, Codrington cut through the tangle of intrigue and corruption. When a Commissioner of Customs was himself caught smuggling, he told him, following Aristotle, that government ought to be 'Ye Empire of Laws not men', and swore that 'Justice shall be too powerful for ye wealth, ye art, ye avarice and ye insolence of any man whatsoever'.[28] The case went to a committee of the House of Commons: Codrington was entirely vindicated; but Boyle, speaking in his defence, well summed up the position: 'This gentleman has too much merit to be endured by those that have none.'

And Codrington was a Whig, and the Whigs were in eclipse. When, following his gallant attack on Guadaloupe, he was stricken with fever and asked for leave, he was superseded, to be replaced by a Tory nominee who died within weeks of his arrival. Then a Colonel Peake, who had brought the news of Blenheim to Queen Anne, was appointed,[29] only to be murdered in 1710 in Antigua after provoking an armed rebellion. Codrington wrote in retirement in Barbados; 'I

[26] Harlow, *op. cit.* p. 128.

[27] Harlow, *op. cit.* p. 118.

[28] Harlow, *op. cit.* p. 134.

[29] Peake, much disillusioned with this reward, was soon writing, 'If I have my brains knocked out the Queen must send some other unfortunate Divel to roast in the sun.' He was in fact roasted himself, for, wounded in the rebellion which followed his attempts on the planters' wives, he was stripped and left to die in the open in the heat.

will pass my time in my library and be buried in my garden.' Too ill to risk the voyage to England, he died in 1710, aged forty-two.

He divided his benefaction between Oxford and Barbados, showing a rare sense of his West Indian obligations. If he was not to enjoy his English library, he had seen to it that others should. He left £10,000 charged on his estate at Doddington to All Souls: £6,000 to build a library; £4,000 and his own books to stock it. Begun in 1716 and completed in 1756, the stately Codrington, built on West Indian wealth and slave labour, has served generations of scholars from the whole university, and by his own wish, its founder lies interred in the College chapel.

But Codrington's other benefaction was to promote better education in the West Indies. He left the rich endowment of Codrington College in Barbados in trust to the Society for the Propagation of the Gospel in Foreign Parts: celibate medical missionaries were to be trained to serve the Negroes and Amerindians—'the idea of a large-hearted Oxford schoolman brought face to face with the colour problem'.[30] For the slaves, he insisted, must be not only converted but educated. And his purpose was in part achieved. The project to train celibate missionaries was abandoned, but the alumni of Codrington College, which had no colour bar, have played a decisive part in the development of the Caribbean. Christopher Codrington, the most brilliant, high-minded and versatile of the great West Indian planters, is one of the more attractive figures in the history of the Old Colonial Empire.

The Beckfords belong more to metropolitan than colonial history. Their first authenticated ancestor was a tailor in Maidenhead, one of whose sons became a minor City magnate and the other the founder of a fortune even greater than Codrington's. Peter Beckford had been one of the earliest settlers in Jamaica, and his son, Colonel Beckford, who died in 1710 'in a fit of passion at being contradicted by a member of the Council' had owned twenty-four plantations and 1,200 slaves. He had been the father of Thomas, Lord Mayor in 1762 and the redoubtable champion of the liberties of London, whose son, William Beckford, one of the most colourful of the early romantics, wrote the oriental tale *Vathek* (1786) and rebuilt Fonthill as a famous 'Gothick' fantasy.[31] This ebullient millionaire was a

---

[30] *op. cit.* p. 213.

[31] This talented and versatile eccentric lived to be eighty-four, having never, he declared, known a moment's *ennui*. He also wrote travel books of proto-Sitwellian brilliance. See Guy Chapman, *Beckford*, London, 1951, for a fascinating biography; and Lewis Melville, *The Life and Letters of William Beckford Of Fonthill*, London, 1910.

writer, traveller and aesthete. By contrast, Thomas's nephew, Peter Beckford of Steepleton Iwerne, Dorset, wrote the first standard work on foxhunting—*Thoughts on Hunting in a Series of Familiar letters to a Friend.*[32] All these characters, though, unlike Codrington, they contributed nothing to the West Indies from which their wealth derived, represent, like the Pitts, if on a less important scale, the impact of the riches of the Old Colonial Empire on the home country.

V

So out of ruffianly and precarious beginnings and the exploitation of slavery and sugar, the West Indian colonies became extremely important for the Old Colonial Empire: even more so at first than the expansion of the East India Company in Bengal and the Carnatic. The islands were at once economically and strategically of the first concern, and without them the British might well have lost control of the Atlantic in the critical wars with France and Spain. The basis of West Indies wealth was rum, slavery and the lash; but the British themselves paid a price. Some elegant buildings, well placed forts and strategic harbours, still recall the Old Colonial domination; more poignantly, in deserted churchyards dilapidated headstones recall those who died young of yellow fever and 'ague', or were killed in battle or lost in shipwreck during the long wars of the eighteenth century. More lasting were the immense economic and social problems created by the implanted and greatly predominant negro population, among whom the British were a tiny minority, and who, whether slave or free, would be the most permanent legacy of an exploitation paralleled in the colonial empires of the other European powers.

[32] The original title is *Thoughts upon Hare and Foxhunting with an account of the most Celebrated Dog Kennels of the Kingdom,* 1781. 'Hunting recommended' they begin, 'not as an entertaining exercise only but also as a wholesome one'. 'The kennel described', they continue; then 'the perfect hound described'; and they proceed to a discourse on feeding hounds, on breeding and naming them, and on the treatment of whelps; of 'rounding' them and spaying bitches and 'coupling your hounds and breaking them from sheep'. He thinks it better to 'enter' them at a marten cat rather than at the hare. Beckford also prescribes a cure for mange 'either in man or beast', before 'a description of the fox chase attempted', and a 'discourse of style in killing a fox'. He then makes observations on the 'Casting of hounds (riding too close upon them Censured)' and some 'remarks on Haloos, and on when a fox ought not to be given up to hounds and when it is best for them to eat him'. The whole work then proceeds with a digression in favour of the sport to 'a Frenchman's opinion of the Fox Chase', and concludes, after badgers had been objected to, with a hunting song.

CHAPTER 10

Colonial America and the Conquest of Canada

During little more than a century between 1660 and 1763, when the Old Colonial Empire in America reached its climax with the acquisition of Canada, the British colonies spread over the entire eastern seaboard from Florida, through Georgia, which became a Crown Colony in 1752, up to New Hampshire and Maine. And with the capture of French Acadia they linked up with Nova Scotia, where by 1749 the strategic base at Halifax had been established. Northeast lay Newfoundland, the oldest colony, and northwest the Hudson's Bay territories and the American Arctic: their full development long restricted by French competition, but after 1763 freer to expand.

Whatever their record in the frenetic politics of Great Britain, Charles II and James II were both architects of empire—the one improvising, the other dogmatic—and they left an ineradicable imprint on North America. Under the Old Colonial system the economic interests of Great Britain and the colonists were bound to diverge as the Americans moved west into the interior; while the gradual trend towards the untrammelled sovereignty of King-in-Parliament in the home country was incompatible with the seventeenth-century concepts of 'liberties' and fundamental laws enshrined in charters, still rooted in the colonies. As the social and economic gap widened, and as, after 1763, the casual and ramshackle administration was tightened up, a traditional friction mounted between colonial governors and assemblies. But so long as the French and their Amerindian allies remained a menace on the frontiers, ties of common strategic interest kept the colonists in line. Paradoxically, as the shrewder French politicians foresaw, the spectacular success of the British in evicting French power from Canada, the Middle West and the South, and the Spaniards from Florida, removed this common tie; and by opening up, yet thwarting, the prospect of expansion to the vast western hinterland, increased the economic and social divergence between the colonists and the home country.

In 1664 James, Duke of York, won for his medieval title an enduring and world-historic fame. Following the Stuart grand design of a centralized North American Empire under direct control of the Crown, he launched five hundred regulars, with Connecticut auxiliaries, against the Dutch city on Manhattan at the mouth of the Hudson, long known as New Amsterdam. Without a shot being fired, Battery Point, Wall Street—along the landward defences—and the 'Dutch garden' or Bowery, were taken. In due course New Amsterdam would be renamed New York. With it went the entire area hitherto known as New Netherland; and in exchange for the restoration of Dutch Surinam in South America, the colony was retained.

New York was always cosmopolitan, and the well-established Dutch families, the Germans and Scandinavians and Jews soon accepted an English Governor and a Council. By 1683 they had their own Assembly. The Dutch sphere of influence was thus taken over on both sides of the Hudson; north up to Albany, the Mohawk Gap and the Adirondaks beyond, now known as New York State; while their territories west and south of the harbour became New Jersey.

In Massachusetts the original Calvinist oligarchy, that would-be model community of 'saints', had during the Civil Wars 'purposely withdrawn from the King's Government', as if 'they intended to suspend their absolute obedience to the King's authority'.[1] They were now disciplined themselves, for they could hardly 'subsist without our protection'. Governor Endicott hunted down the regicide Goffe; and the Calvinists, who had given Quakers thirty stripes apiece with a three-cord knotted whip, hanged the Quakeress Mary Dyer in 1660 and executed witches with so much conviction, were forced to an unwonted tolerance. But 'their way of government', reported the Commissioner of 1665, 'is Commonwealthlike; their way of worship rude and called congregational. They are zealous of it and persecute all other forms.' They also smuggled extensively, in defiance of the Navigation Acts. So in 1684 James II declared the Massachusetts charter invalid, set up a Dominion of New England, appointed Sir Edmund Andros Governor and sanctioned Anglican services in Boston itself. And although in 1688–9 the Bostonians took the chance to imprison their Governor and James II's Dominion collapsed, the new charter granted in 1691 by William III extended the franchise from the Congregationalist elect to all owners of substantial property. The political power, not of the 'Commonwealth-like' spirit, but of the sectarian oligarchy, had been tamed.

[1] C.S.P., Colonial, 1661–1668, p. 25.

Meanwhile, to the south, a peculiar colony had come into being. In 1681 Charles II, not above employing Sir Henry Morgan in Jamaica, gave a contrasting personality an opening, and granted 'a province in America which his Majesty was pleased to call Pennsylvania',[2] to a Quaker, William Penn. He was the son of an admiral who had commanded both Commonwealth and Restoration fleets against the Dutch, and to whom the Crown owed £20,000—a debt which the grant redeemed. Penn had already written *The Great Cause of Liberty and Conscience*, and he was determined on a haven of toleration in the vast area assigned. It had rich pastures, fertile arable and trackless woods, and its vague southern boundary was defined in 1702 by the Mason–Dixon line (from the surveyors who made it), which afterwards divided the slave states from the north.

English, Dutch, Germans, Swiss, Huguenots and Scandinavians soon settled in, while Scots and Ulster Irish pioneered the high wilderness west of the Susquehanna. Philadelphia, the capital, laid out on Wren's rejected designs for London after the Great Fire, soon became a considerable metropolis. For the new colony prospered: 'by the middle of the eighteenth century, there were more Quakers in the Western hemisphere than in Great Britain ... From a wilderness,' Richard Townsend observed in 1727, 'the Lord, by his good hand of providence, hath made it a fruitful field.'[3] But the pacifist Friends found government difficult. During the wars of the mideighteenth century when the supposedly tame Delaware Indians massacred the settlers, the Quakers, 'though apparently indifferent to the fact that the Indian leaders with whom they dealt were sometimes half-demented with drink', had to decide whether to 'stand or run'.[4] When in 1756 the Delawares and Shawnees plainly had to be stopped, the vintage Quakers in the Assembly could only abdicate in favour of the more realistic Benjamin Franklin. If Penn's original vision founded the colony, the orthodox Quakers now had to give way to the world.

[2] *Aubrey's Brief Lives*, ed. O. Lawson Dick, London, 1949, p. 235: William Penn (1644–1718), educated at Christ Church, Oxford, had his first sense of God 'when he was 11 years old at Chigwell ... so suddenly surprised with an inward comfort and (as he thought) an externall glory in the roome, that he has many times sayd that from thence he had the seale of divinity and immortality ... He speaks well the Latin and the French tongues and his own with great mastership. He was chosen, *nemine contradicente*, Fellow of the Royal Society with much respect' (*ibidem*).

[3] Daniel J. Boorstin, *The Americans. The Colonial Experience*, New York, 1958, pp. 41 and 43.

[4] Boorstin, *op. cit.* p. 56.

South of Maryland, Delaware and Virginia, a more representative Restoration enterprise had also succeeded. In the hinterland of the coast and islands south of Virginia which the Elizabethans had explored, settlers had now penetrated from Virginia and the West Indies, and in 1668 Clarendon, Albermarle (formerly General Monck) and Ashley Cooper, Earl of Shaftesbury (whose attempt to exclude York from the succession would lead to his own ruin) had combined with Virginian speculators to exploit the Carolinas: an area promising not only for hemp and flax, but for the wine, fruit and silk normally purchased from Mediterranean countries. They commissioned John Locke to devise a very unpractical constitution; and the colonists had hard times until they turned to big cotton and tobacco plantations worked by slave labour. Then South Carolina began to prosper; and Charleston, the main port for the slave-trade, in its rich sub-tropical setting, became the most elegant centre of the old South where the 'gentleman planters', as Dr Garden, who gave his name to the 'Gardenia', observed, were 'absolutely above every occupation except eating, drinking, lolling and smoking ...'.[5]

But these halcyon days of entire independence did not last: after the proprietors had failed even to defend the country from the Amerindians, the Carolinas were declared a royal province. By 1729 they obtained a charter as a Crown Colony.

Then, in 1733, the last British colony was founded. That able prison reformer, General Oglethorpe, and Lord Percival, afterwards first Earl of Egmont, decided to give a fresh start to those in prison for minor debt and to some of the urban unemployed, and they raised subscriptions to buy out the debtors and settle the 'deserving' poor in land between South Carolina and Florida. Walpole countenanced the venture as a base against Spanish attack: it was named Georgia. The settlers were planted on fifty-acre holdings to grow mainly hemp and flax, and these holdings were bought, not just appropriated, from the Amerindians. It was hoped that, in the New World, the settlers would now lead peaceful and virtuous lives. Methodist missionaries, including the Wesleys and Whitefield, were imported to evangelize both the colonists and the aboriginals. The venture, of course, was to combine profit with benevolence; and it was calculated that in Georgia a family which lived poorly in London on an annual income of twenty pounds, of which ten came from charity, could here be self-supporting and earn sixty pounds a year. The immigrants were carefully vetted and equipped, and the importation of both rum and negroes was prohibited. But when timber for the West Indies proved the best export, it could only be paid for in rum; and when slaves

[5] Boorstin, *op. cit.* p. 212.

became essential for the big plantations which alone were viable, both prohibitions were rescinded. The colonists had hoped to market silk, but it turned out that only white mulberries nourished the silk-worms, and white mulberries did not thrive. Silk winding, too, was a specialized art. There was nothing for it but to turn to slavery, cotton and tobacco.

Most of the original settlers had now abandoned what had become the least attractive of the colonies. In 1739 Oglethorpe defeated a Spanish incursion from Florida; but he, too, left, disillusioned, in 1743. Then in 1752 the trustees threw in their hands, and Georgia, like the Carolinas, became a Crown Colony. In the 'sixties Goldsmith was still citing the hardships it had offered to the inhabitants of his *Deserted Village*, evicted to a country of

> matted woods where birds forget to sing
> But silent bats in drowsy clusters cling . . .
> While oft in whirles the mad tornado flies
> Mingling the ravaged landscapes with the skies.

But in the swamps and pine-barrens of Georgia the Methodists had learnt to preach in the open air; and if the Wesleys had their main influence at home, Whitefield tried to evangelize other colonies and founded a formidable religious movement in America.

In 1763 at the end of the Seven Years War, when Florida would be briefly added to them, the thirteen colonies thus extended in a broad sweep between the Alleghenies and the ocean from Georgia and the Carolinas to Virginia, Maryland and Delaware; then, above what would be the Mason–Dixon line, to Pennsylvania, New Jersey and New York; and beyond them through Connecticut and Rhode Island, to Massachusetts with Maine, itself, like New Hampshire, on the Canadian border. The colonies were still administered by the Commissioners for Trade and Plantations, by 1696 given wider powers; and the Crown ruled directly over all. But the proprietary colonies, Maryland, Delaware and Pennsylvania, and Rhode Island and Connecticut under their own charters, came nearest to auto-nomy.

Here was a great range of climate and environment, reflected in social structure and in mind; but all the colonies possessed what no other colonies on the American continent had been allowed—repre-sentative institutions and a tradition of inefficient but genuine self-government. And if the interests of the French colonists were West-ern and continental and the main interests of their British counter-parts were oceanic and European, they were both subject to an un-European influence. It was a great swathe of frontier, of 'backwoods' that stretched along the Appalachians and the Blue Ridge up to the Catskills and the Adirondacks, through which they were already moving westward over the mountains into Kentucky, West Virginia and Ohio, and which brought a pervasive stimulus to American life. What sort of people had these colonial Americans now become?

II

By the mid-eighteenth century the population of the colonies was about one and a half million, as against about 100,000 in the much larger French territories of Canada and the Middle West. The Amerindians, even including the more numerous and advanced tribes of the Pacific northwest, are thought to have numbered well under half a million in the whole of North America. When, therefore, in April 1759, the Reverend Andrew Burnaby sailed from Spithead for Virginia in the *Dispatch* to travel from Virginia up to New Hampshire, he traversed what was already the potential base of a continental civilization, well enough established to make it likely that the Anglo-Saxon influence would predominate and last. Burnaby had a sharp eye and a pleasant style: his *Travels through the Middle Settlements of North America 1759–60*, published in 1775, would become a classic description of the established colonies; as William Byrd of Westover's *A Journey to the Land of Eden*, an account of the surveying of the bounds of Virginia and North Carolina in 1728, would become a classic of the frontier.[6]

From the moment when his ship entered Chesapeake Bay, Burnaby sensed the 'fragrance of the pines'; and he was soon riding through fine tobacco plantations up to Williamsburg. He describes the rich variety of woods—myrtle, cedar, cypress and magnolia, redwood and acacia; the quantities of snipe and duck along the tidewater, and of pheasant, turkey and woodcock inland. Here the planters, if 'much given to convivial pleasures', supervised their estates themselves; and they already exported not only tobacco, but cider, pork, grain and 'peach-fed Virginia ham', while their horses were 'fleet and beautiful'. Yet not a tenth of the country appeared cultivated; though land was cheap and navigation 'commodious'. The wild fauna included beaver, deer, opossum, racoon and even moose, and a 'species of pole cat ...

---

[6] Burnaby (1734–1812) was a well-to-do clergyman, educated at Westminster and Queen's College, Oxford. He served as Consul at Livorno and visited Corsica, and succeeded to broad estates in Leicester. He was thus 'a person of address and affable behaviour', everywhere well-received.

commonly called a skunk'. 'This animal,' Burnaby recorded, 'when assailed emits such a fetid and insufferable stench as almost to suffocate whatever is in reach of it.[7]

He approved the 'royal' colonial style of government, with a Council of twelve and an Assembly of 108–110 burgesses, two for each county, the virtual absence of Dissenters and the predominance of an Anglican Clergy; but he found the people uncultured, and the College of William and Mary disappointing. He also observed that the planters' women seldom improved their minds, but were immoderately fond of dancing, particularly of 'negro jiggs'. Moreover, the planters obviously lived beyond their incomes and were most of them in debt, while their 'authority over their slaves renders them vain and imperious'.[8] Indeed, they seemed 'scarcely to consider the negroes or the Indians human'. And many already 'considered the colonies as independent states, unconnected with Great Britain, otherwise than having the same common King and being bound to her by natural affection'.[9] The cost of the current Seven Years War had already put the colony £400,000 in debt.

Very different were the good 'industrious Pennsylvanians', who 'seized any opportunity to struggle with innumerable difficulties', while the Virginians lived 'from hand to mouth'. Indeed, Pennsylvania was different from anything hitherto observed in America: 'much better cultivated and beautifully laid out with fields of clover, grain and flax'. Philadelphia already had 20,000 inhabitants; the streets were well paved and well lighted; there were public libraries and even accommodation for visiting Indian *sachems* in the state house. It was a 'wonderful province', in which Quakers, Calvinists, Lutherans and Catholics lived in mutual toleration; it exported lumber, flax, iron, leather, furs and the 'best beaver hats'. The people appeared frugal and industrious—'by far the most enterprising people on the continent'. But, Burnaby had to note, 'they are great Republicans'.[10]

In New York, a city of sixteen to seventeen thousand people, where he observed 'innumerable porpoises in the harbour', over half the citizens appeared to be frugal and industrious Dutch. But, save for Broadway, the streets were cramped and narrow. There was a college, a military headquarters and a synagogue, and the villas of the rich on Long Island were already imposing. The New Yorkers had turtle feasts, elegant entertainment, sleighing parties. There was

[7] *op. cit.* p. 23 n.
[8] *op. cit.* p. 39.
[9] *op. cit.* p. 43.
[10] *op. cit.* p. 108.

a big export trade in grain, pork, furs, glass and lumber, as well as in West Indian molasses, re-exported as rum.

Rhode Island, on the other hand, with its 'democratical government', Burnaby found repellent. 'The character of the Rhode Islander,' he wrote, 'is by no means engaging, or aimiable,' indeed, 'the public men frequently act without the strict regard for probity and honour which ever ought ... to direct mankind'. And although people took immense catches of fish, lobster and sea bass, raised good horses and exported much timber, the 'arts and sciences were almost unknown'. Moreover, the 'wretched state' had already lost a hundred and fifty ships to the French, and its paper money was particularly bad.[11]

Burnaby was more at home in Boston. Here was a flourishing metropolis of twenty thousand people with a spacious and noble harbour and a splendid prospect from the Beacon. Of all the states, Massachusetts was pre-eminent in the arts and sciences and in shipping. The people were hospitable, if 'precise and formal', with their Congregationalist puritan tradition; though they had 'very indifferent teeth', and the 'lower classes' were 'impertinently curious and inquisitive'.

Such are the vivid impressions, revealing both of the country and himself, which this urbane English clergyman recorded during the crisis of the Seven Years War. The potential causes of conflict are already as apparent as the vast prospects of the future, and Burnaby was aware of both. All the colonies, he observed, were deep in public debt for paying the provincial militia for 'Pitt's War'; their currencies were unstable, and the British maintained exasperating restrictions—as in New Hampshire, where the forty-foot masts of white pine were cut for the Navy and the British kept a monopoly of the woods.

Moreover, such were the differences between the states that 'union seemed almost impossible'. Consider, he wrote, the contrast between the lazy life in the south, where half the population was Negro, and the energy and puritanism of the north. Fire and water could not be more incompatible. Burnaby even foresaw civil war from one end of the continent to the other, with the Negroes and Indians waiting to exterminate their masters.[12] And with their long and vulnerable coast, the colonies would be at the mercy of any hostile power which controlled the Atlantic—'half a dozen frigates could ravage them'; disrupt communications, fisheries and West Indian commerce. The very existence of the American Empire must depend on the British mastery of the ocean. Yet, he wrote, separated as they are by three

[11] *op. cit.* p. 159.
[12] *op. cit.* p. 203.

thousand miles and 'removed from the reach of power', the Americans will not be subordinate; and in spite of their strategic weakness they have the idea, 'as strange as it is visionary', that Empire is travelling westward; 'everyone is looking forward ... to that desired moment when America is to give Law to the rest of the world'. Burnaby's classic, if relatively lightweight description merits some comparison with that of Tocqueville.

While the settled colonies had thus consolidated their ways of life, the frontier formed their common background. Thirty years earlier, another, more hard-bitten and cynical observer had described the borders of Virginia and North Carolina. Colonel William Byrd III (1674–1744) who owned the huge estate of Westover on the northern reaches of the James River, founded Richmond, Virginia, had a library of four thousand books and died with a property of 179,440 acres, had the sense of public duty which would inspire the natural political leaders of the American Revolution. He filled many public offices, and served on the commission to fix the boundaries of North Carolina. He had travelled much in Europe, and his judgement was realistic and worldly. He considered, for example, that 'a sprightly lover is the most prevailing missionary', and deplored that, unlike the French, who had 'not been so squeamish in Canada', the English colonists had not interbred with the Amerindians. Nor did he object to trading guns with them; they would then depend on the colonists for ammunition; and arrows, anyway, were more silent, rapid and lethal in the forest than a musket shot.

He had no illusions about North Carolina. There even the frontiersmen were 'cloyed with the felicity of having nothing to do', the Indians tended to 'stupid idleness' and, as elsewhere, nothing was 'so fatal to them as their passion for rum'.[13] Even those educated at the College of William and Mary—at once hostages, and, hopefully, being civilized—generally lapsed into barbarism on return to their families. Their women were dirty and stank of rancid bear-oil, and their cruelty was appalling. The braves had a grim dignity, but they rode worse than a Dutch sailor; they barbecued captives, and their children tortured them. Their inter-tribal hatreds were implacable.

Byrd found the animals and the scenery more congenial. He traversed the Great Dismal Swamp, when the long moss dangled from the trees ('not even a turkey buzzard will venture to fly over it'); the quagmires, the mosquitoes, the agueish mists, counteracted by big fires; the cedar bogs, where the sparse inhabitants would cook fat

---

[13] *A Journey to the Land of Eden,* and other papers by William Byrd, ed. M. Van Doren, New York, 1928, p. 99. It had first been published in 1841.

bacon in a pint of rum—that 'cordial of life ... in this dirty place'.[14] Surprisingly, the wildcat—twice as big as the household animal and much the fiercest beast of the woods—tasted good to eat, like veal. But bear was the meat most prized by the hunters: it promoted sexual prowess and could be eaten in bulk 'without rising in the stomach'. 'Certainly,' he observed, 'no Tartar ever loved horsemeat or Hottentot guts and garbage than woodmen do bear.' It has a particularly high relish in the fall. Racoon, also, makes good eating; and the opossum is 'a harmless little beast: if you take hold of it, it will only grin and never bite'; while the small wolf of North Carolina will run away from a man, 'as from an animal more mischievous than himself'. The bison is immensely strong: but 'the portly figure of the animal' is 'disgraced' by a little tail, and it grunts 'with no better grace than a hog'.[15] It is the beaver, of course, which is the most intelligent and industrious creature, especially in the matter of self preservation.[16]

Byrd is extremely observant of the forest—the vast wilderness of poplar, hickory and oak entangled with bushes and grapevines, on whose black grapes the bears loved to gorge. And he records the flight of cranes going south and the flocks of pigeon that darkened the sky and wrought havoc when they alighted.

Indeed, Byrd's narrative vividly conveys the fascination of the frontier. His expedition lived off the game; in spite of hardships they were never ill; their feeling of adventure and far horizons pervades the book.

For all their political and economic and social diversity the settled colonists still took their close relationship with England for granted. They spoke the same language, if, as usual in colonial societies, class and local accents had been ironed out. By 1724 'the planters and even the negroes', wrote one observer, 'generally talk good English without idiom or tone, and can discourse handsomely' (one can well believe it) 'upon most common subjects'. In 1764 a Scots traveller, himself accustomed to dialect, remarked upon 'the propriety of language ... the English tongue being spoken by all ranks, in a degree of purity and perfection surpassing any but the polite part of London.'[17] Save in pockets of backwoods poverty, as in North Carolina, the society was too mobile for local dialects to form; the colonists clung to their old speech and the children of foreign immigrants had to learn it. Hence the deliberate enunciation of every

[14] *op. cit.* p. 58.
[15] *op. cit.* p. 216.
[16] *op. cit.* p. 220.
[17] Boorstin, *op. cit.* p. 272.

syllable which still makes American English easier for foreigners to understand than the more clipped and casual native accents of the old country.

Free from the weight of the English hierarchy, a basic, if more superficial, education was now more widely diffused. In England, Oxford and Cambridge alone had the legal right of granting degrees; in America the local colleges simply assumed it. And they all had regional roots: they were not Anglican, exclusive and clerical; they even had laymen on their governing bodies. Harvard already had a high prestige; the College of William and Mary had been founded by 1691; Yale by 1701, though not formally incorporated until 1745. King's College, New York, would become the nucleus of Columbia; the College of New Jersey, that of Princeton; the College of Philadelphia that of the University of Pennsylvania. All these and others were well established before the American Revolution.

Since the founders of Jamestown had hopefully planned a college, Americans had been concerned to train lawyers, doctors, accountants and surveyors as well as clergy. Men had to be versatile and self-reliant: life might be crude, but there was no need to cringe in the ante-rooms of the great or traverse labyrinths of patronage and of academic and family interests. In a more open and self-assertive world, there was more room: men were valued, and felt valued, for themselves. Hence the confidence, the brashness and the pragmatism: the assumption that almost any problem can be understood and fixed. Later enhanced by the vast expansion of the frontier, this pragmatic outlook, so admirably and typically American, stems from colonial times.

Naturally, few books of distinction were yet written—the standard works were European—moreover, print was bad and hard to come by, and paper inferior. But handbooks, almanacks and newspapers were in great demand. Boston, the most bookish colonial capital, was still mainly concerned with theology; Charleston, the least bookish, with racing, gambling and sport.

The most earnest and best-informed public was in Quaker Philadelphia, where Benjamin Franklin early founded subscription libraries and centres for self-improving debates. But all over the colonies the favourite reading, next to the Bible, was almanacks, giving the schedules of the public year and the details of rudimentary public transport. There was a wide market for dictionaries and handbooks on spelling, on agriculture and medicine, on the care of horses and livestock. So, when more recondite subjects came into view, they, too, had to be explained. Popularized information was wanted, not arcane and scholarly erudition; on this level learning ceased to be an awesome mystery : perseverance and common sense, it was assumed, could grasp any subject.

As almanacks and handbooks provided the facts, newspapers and advertising early catered for a mobile and scattered population. *The Boston Newsletter*, published in 1704, soon had its equivalents in other colonies; by the time of the Revolution there were thirty-four. Though no longer subject to clerical censorship, these newspapers were liable to suppression and so relatively restrained. But by the 'sixties they had made their readers more politically minded and they would play a decisive part in the American Revolution.

On the eve of the Revolution, colonial America was already a restless and forceful society. Representative government, if on a restricted franchise, had been rooted in America since the first elected assemblies. No other European settlements had these liberties. There was no Anglican equivalent of the Catholic hierarchy of French Canada, or of the far-flung archbishoprics and bishoprics of Spanish America or Brazil; no imperial capital or centralized bureaucracy taking the right of taxing colonies for granted. A casual and lethargic administration across three thousand miles of ocean had long allowed the colonies substantial political, if not economic, independence. And this at a time when Bourbon absolute monarchs were ruling France; when from 1740 to 1788 a military martinet ruled Prussia; when even the 'enlightenment' of a Charles III of Spain or a Joseph II of Austria were being frustrated by their own bureaucracies and the conservatism of their peoples. In Russia the peasants were then being thrust deeper into serfdom under a regime ruled, first, by the almost illiterate Tsarina Elizabeth II, then by the autocratic, if 'enlightened' Catherine the Great, who in 1762 had attained power by conniving at the murder of her own husband Peter III. And outside Europe the Grand Turk in Constantinople maintained a dilapidated tyranny tempered by assassination. In Persia the Safavid dynasty had gone down in a welter of dynastic crime. India was being fought over by military adventurers, native and European, in the collapse of the Mughal Empire, while in the Far East the Manchu emperors were at the climax of their arbitrary power and in Japan the Tokugawa Shoguns had imposed order and isolation only by the sword. Apart from the small cantons of Switzerland, there was no country as democratic as North America : if compared with the various tyrannies by which most of the world was governed during the eighteenth century, the sovereignty of King-in-Parliament which the governments of George III tried to impose on the colonists was mild.

Yet they resisted it and broke the bonds of empire—just because the colonial experience had been British—and they thus asserted seventeenth-century liberties threatened in Great Britain and long swamped on most of the continent of Europe. And that tradition proved well enough set in the new environment and would draw so much strength from it that, by 1787, in spite of apparently overwhelming difficulties, Americans were able to combine a federal union with state liberties; and within that framework contain the massive immigrations and continental expansion of the nineteenth century. When fumbling British politicians and inept commanders managed to lose their American colonies, they would, in fact, make one of the greatest contributions of the British Empire to world history. For the emancipated Americans who would develop the United States into a far more cosmopolitan and forceful society than they could have made it within the Empire, gave the Anglo-Saxon forms of government and ways of life a more dynamic, broader and ultimately much more powerful base; so that, within a different balance of world power, they would again defend fundamental liberties against new and more monstrous kinds of tyranny, now potentially global.

III

This future could not have come about unless the British had mastered the North American continent by the conquest of New France, French Canada. The name, an Indian term, *Kannat*, originally applied only to the area between the Ottawa and Saguency rivers on the north bank of the St Lawrence, came to apply to half the continent of North America. Although English navigators had early explored the eastern coasts, the French in the interior had long surpassed these tentative explorations. The enormous territory containing the greatest series of inland lakes in the world, and a vast potential wealth in minerals and agriculture, fur and fish, extended across the western prairies to the 'abrupt glistening rampart' of the Rockies,[18] and to the warm and rainy Pacific coast. Northwest it extended to the sub-arctic tundra beyond Hudson's Bay and northeast to Labrador and the Ungavar peninsula overlooking Hudson's Strait, with Baffin Land beyond. The St Lawrence, the natural entrance to the interior, had early been explored by the French. Cartier had reconnoitred it; in 1608 Champlain had founded Quebec, reached the site of Montreal, explored the lake called after him and penetrated down to Ticonderoga, with its strategic access to the Hudson Valley. Frozen for five months of the year, the St

---

[18] See J. Bartlet Brebner, *Canada. A Modern History*, Michigan, 1960, for a fine evocation of the country.

Lawrence gave a seasonal passage only, and the primeval conifer forests which hemmed it in were inhabited by fierce neolithic Amerindians, whose way of life, though socially elaborate and interesting, was hard, cruel and precarious. Well adapted to the climate, they were skilled trackers and hunters with their snowshoes, toboggans and canoes; adept also with the tomahawk, and though a people of impressive dignity, obsessed with a strange cult of formalized war: 'a game for status and prestige in which the greatest bravery was displayed after capture in a grim, almost stately, progress through the most ingenious tortures to death'.[19] In Canada, as in Virginia, in spite of Byrd's realistic impressions, an undeserved halo of romance has been accorded these savages, though their way of life was well adapted to their surroundings. Before the inexorable advance of the colonists, their fate would be tragic; they had high qualities of skill, endurance and honour; but they practised ritual cannibalism and were so filthy as to disgust seventeenth-century Europeans, who used them as allies against each other.

After 1628, when Richelieu had founded the Company of New France, the fur-traders and missionaries had come to terms with the Amerindians better than those negotiated by the Puritan Anglo-Saxons. 'An unseasonable nicety,' as Byrd remarked, had deterred the latter from mixed marriages and 'a good natured alliance'; but the French, with their greater social aplomb and adaptability, had no such inhibitions, and half-breed *coureurs des bois* contributed to vast continental explorations. Moreover, they had the political state behind them. Where the English colonization had been commercial and individualistic, by 1661 New France had become a Royal Province, and Colbert 'had already done to the French Empire what James II failed to do to the English'.[20] Military governors and financial intendants carried out 'a mercantilism more rigid and consistent than that of the English Restoration Government'; while New France was colonized by picked settlers, subsidized and strategically located. And the French had vision. La Salle, for example, in the 1680s explored the entire Mississippi down to the Gulf of Mexico, and projected strategically placed forts and trading-posts from Canada to New Orleans. During King William's War the redoubtable Comte de Frontenac cowed and cajoled the pro-English Iroquois, and defeated an English attack on Quebec; while d'Iberville, best known for his exploits in the West Indies, struck north against what had become a more threatening English enterprise.

But he failed to destroy it. And here the English fur-traders had

[19] Brebner, *op. cit.*
[20] J. H. Parry, *The Age of Reconnaissance*, p. 270.

already outflanked the French. In 1666 a French adventurer, who called himself ironically *Sieur des Groseilliers*—Lord Gooseberry Bushes, from a patch of land he had acquired fit only to grow them —had cut across this wilderness by land to Hudson's Bay. He had got no response from his own authorities, but had managed to obtain an interview with Charles II. That shrewd monarch, always open to suggestions, had been interested; moreover some English merchants were still hankering after the Northwest Passage, and others had their eyes on the fur-trade. A reconnaissance had been made. The Hudson's Bay Company had been founded, with Prince Rupert its first Governor, and its second the Duke of York. By 1670 the Crown had assigned it a vast area, covering what is now Northern Ontario, Manitoba and the entire Northwest as well as Labrador. Stockaded trading posts were placed at the mouths of the sluggish rivers, frozen for half the year—'Forts' Albany, Severn, York, Nelson and Churchill, the last founded in 1685 when John Churchill, afterwards Duke of Marlborough, was Governor of the Company. The French soon overran most of them, but all were restored by the Treaty of Utrecht which confirmed the Company in its original possessions. The English had found and kept the entrance to one of the greatest fur-bearing regions in the world. Shelving the question of the Northwest Passage, the Company now swiftly developed an immensely profitable trade, paid huge dividends and increased its capital. So long as British sea power dominated the North Atlantic, the Company was secure.

Such was the background to the final conflict between the French and the British for North America. The British controlled the entire eastern seaboard from the border of Florida to Nova Scotia and French Acadia, and around Hudson's Bay a base for expansion north and west. But thrusting between these two areas, the French held a great curve of strategic forts from Louisburg, on Cape Breton island at the mouth of the St Lawrence, through Quebec, Montreal and Niagara, and beyond to Detroit and Chicago; then southwest to Fort Duquesne, the modern Pittsburgh at the junction of the Allegheny and the Ohio, and St Louis, at that of the Mississippi and Missouri and linked by the huge river with New Orleans; while the Spaniards held Florida.

In America the Wars of the Austrian Succession and the Seven Years War thus merged into one another. In the conflict, conducted by small armies for strong points in an enormous wilderness, the Europeans used Indian allies, and the parade formations and rigid command structure of Europe generally proved irrelevant, often disastrous. The Irish-American, Colonel Sir William Johnson, proved more effective, leading his Indians in guerrilla warfare from his estates on the Mohawk Valley,[21] than the British General Braddock, who, in 1755, after a dogged but strategically inept crossing of the Alleghenies in column of route to attack Fort Duquesne, marched straight into a French–Indian ambush, lost his own life and more than half his men and three-quarters of his officers. 'Who would have thought it?' were the dying words of his aide-de-camp; but another of his officers, George Washington, here got his first experience of extricating an army from disaster.

It required the strategic insight of Pitt the Elder to bring these confused frontier wars to a decision; and like Pitt himself, the general chosen to command the first brilliantly successful combined operation in the history of the Old Empire was extremely peculiar. The master plan was a three-pronged attack: at Fort Duquesne from Pennsylvania, since it commanded the Ohio and the communications to the West; against Ticonderoga, where in 1758 the British had suffered defeat and whose capture would threaten Montreal up the Champlain Valley; and, most critically, against Quebec.

James Wolfe was chosen for the most difficult enterprise.[22] He was

[21] Sir William Johnson (1715–74) came of Irish gentry in County Down, and emigrated to America in 1733, where his maternal uncle, Admiral Sir Peter Warren, who had married a de Lancy of New York, put him in charge of his estate in the Mohawk Valley. Here his charm, vigour and adaptability so ingratiated him with the Indians that they made him their *Sachem*, and in 1746 he became Commissary of New York for Indian affairs. He built 'Castle' Johnson, a fort on the Mohawk, and in 1755 his victory over the French at Lake George limited the consequences of Braddock's defeat at Fort Duquesne. He was voted £5,000, made a baronet, and Superintendent of Indian affairs in the entire area. In 1759 he took the surrender of Fort Niagara, and in 1768 concluded a treaty with the Indians at Fort Stanwix. He spent the rest of his life developing vast estates in the Mohawk Valley; surrounded by a large family, legitimate and illegitimate, and living with an Indian wife, who was the sister of a Mohawk chief and by whom he had eight children. He wrote a *Treatise on the Languages Customs and Manners of the Six Nations of the Iroquois*, i.e. the Mohawks, Oneidas, Onodagas, Eayugas, Senecas and Tuscaroras, still well worth perusal.

[22] He was born in 1727 at Westerham, Kent, eldest son of Lieutenant-General Edward Wolfe and Henrietta Thompson. Ten years later they moved to Greenwich, where the boy was briefly educated. At fourteen he was commissioned in the 44th Foot (Marines), then as an ensign in the 12th. In 1743, during the Wars of the Austrian Succession, he fought at Dettingen, at Culloden and at Laufeldt in the Netherlands. At twenty-three he was Lieutenant-Colonel and stationed in Scotland, where, bored with peacetime routine, he studied hard and read Thucydides and Montesquieu. From 1752 to 1753 he was in Paris, where he became more sophisticated and learnt the language. He was then posted to Kent where he devised new methods of manoeuvre. Wolfe now had a great reputation as an infantry officer, and at the outbreak

a brilliant soldier, highly critical of military muddle. 'We are the most egregious blunderers in war,' he wrote in 1756, 'that ever took the hatchet in hand.' They told George II that Wolfe was so eccentric as to be mad. 'Mad is he?' replied the King, making one of the better Hanoverian remarks, 'then I hope he will bite some of my other generals.' This general, who came of Anglo-Irish and Yorkshire gentry, was red-headed, tall, gangling, thin and goggle-eyed. 'His nose was thin and pointed, his jaw undershot to the verge of deformity, his pale blue eyes were strangely prominent his pallor alarming ... he was touchy, imperious, moody, vain and heroically brave.'[23] Though still in his early thirties, he suffered from gravel, rheumatism, scurvy and nervous exhaustion. But this neurotic and dedicated professional was a tiger for detail; and often contemptuous, even sadistic, to his subordinates. He was also impervious to women, gambling and drink—a characteristic that further alienated his officers—and his celebrated assertion that he would rather have written Gray's *Elegy* than take Quebec was not a statement of principle but a retort to his staff, who had grown restive when the general had recited the entire poem. Even Wolfe's charm sounds rather forced, and his wit was certainly unkind: as when, after an officer's head had been blown off at Laufeldt, he remarked that he had never known before that the fellow had so many brains.[24]

He had been set an almost impossible task. While Amherst, in overall command, advanced up the Hudson Valley,[25] Wolfe's ex-

---

of the Seven Years War served as quartermaster-general in a muddled amphibious expedition against Rochefort, where his ability sharply distinguished him from his colleagues. Hence his appointment as Brigadier to Amherst's expedition against Louisburg, based on Nova Scotia. In 1759 he was promoted Major-General to command the attack on Quebec. He is buried in the Church of St Alphage at Greenwich.

[23] Christopher Hibbert, *Wolfe at Quebec*, London, 1959, pp. 1–2.

[24] Hibbert, *op. cit.* p. 34.

[25] Jeffrey, Baron Amherst (1717–97), who came of a Kentish family, and owed his first advancement to the Duke of Dorset, his father's neighbour at Knole, was a Guards officer who had made his reputation under Cumberland in Germany. In 1758 Pitt selected him as the Major-General in charge of the entire expedition: though he was younger than Wolfe, he was thought more reliable. After his capture of Louisburg in that year, he was promoted Commander-in-Chief in Canada. In July 1759 he captured Ticonderoga, and was thus enabled to clinch Wolfe's success at Quebec by completing the converging movement on Montreal the following year. He was less successful in suppressing the Indian resistance, led by the French-inspired chieftain Pontiac, which demanded unconventional warfare. In 1772 he became officially Commander-in-Chief, but saw no more service in the field. He was created Baron Amherst in 1776 and Field Marshal in 1796, there being no age limit to that office.

pedition had to wind its way up the St Lawrence to assault a menacing fortress, impregnable to direct assault. The slow campaign in the wilderness proved gruelling and horrible, as the French-Canadians and their Indian allies skulked and scalped amid the trees, with knives like 'kitchen carving knives ...' They would first rip their victims open, then 'cut round the top of the crown to the skull bone and raising up one side of the skin with the knife, with a jerk ... tear it off ... and the work is done; upon which they set up the Indian whoop'.[26]

In this harsh environment, the crucial victory was the result more of the efficiency of the Navy, under Admiral Saunders, who had served under Anson in his famous voyage, than of the Army; and it was brought off in desperation, when all else had failed and before the ice would block the mouth of the river. But Wolfe had insisted that, since the fortress had defied direct assault, a battle had to be forced in the open. For months the British had been charting the river—James Cook here first got his opening—and now the assault barges, moving up with the tide, came down again on it in silence in the dark, so that, in spite of the fierce current, they actually landed the troops near the right beach. The soldiers then scrambled 170 feet to the top, up a path sheltered by trees then in full leaf, deployed upon the Plains of Abraham and routed the defenders, now forced to give formal battle. And the attack had been co-ordinated, with a timing rare in the eighteenth century, with a diversionary direct assault by the fleet. The whole affair was an astonishing feat of organization due to the skill of the Navy and to Wolfe's command of detailed planning and his imperious will. And the final touch of eighteenth-century melodrama was given by his own death. 'But tell me, o tell me how goes the battle there? Just then came some officers who told him that the French had given ground and our troops was pursuing them ... he was then lyin in my arms just expiring. That Great Man ... Raised himself up on the News and smiled in my face.'[27] He died murmuring of victory: his ambition, perhaps his death-wish, fulfilled.

The sequel was grim, but the precarious success was consolidated. To avoid being frozen in, the fleet had been withdrawn, but through the appalling winter the garrison held out against formidable counter-attack, sickness and privation. Relieved by a British squadron in the spring, they then combined with Amherst, who had taken Ticonderoga, to force the capitulation of Montreal. Johnson and his In-

[26] Cited, Hibbert, *op. cit.* p. 156.
[27] Quoted from a description by one of Wolfe's soldiers in Hibbert, *op. cit.* p. 156.

dians from the Mohawk Valley had captured Fort Niagara and, beyond the mountains, Fort Duquesne had at last fallen, to become Pittsburg. All French Canada and the French territories down to Louisiana and the Gulf had been won, and a predominantly Anglo-Saxon, not a French, civilization would dominate North America. For the northern flank of the mountains that had cut off the British colonies from the interior had been turned, and the Middle West was now more open to settlement. The maritime colonies still looked to the ocean, Europe and the West Indies, and were only tentatively exploring to the west, but the natural prospect of the St Lawrence Valley was towards the Great Lakes, the Middle West and beyond, across a continent.

CHAPTER 11

The American Revolution

The American Revolution, a politically cosmic event, decided that a United States of America would become an independent power, deriving, within an originally British political structure and civilization, as much from Continental Europe as from Great Britain. It contributed to the Revolution in France; and it set up the first liberal-democratic federation on a continental scale, 'unentangled' as Washington put it, 'in the crooked policies of Europe'. Why it happened, how it happened and why it succeeded are themes of perennial import.

For the British the apparent catastrophe disrupted the old mercantilist colonial Empire; but it also provoked a characteristic adaptation. The sequel would be the rise of a second and even more extensive free-trading empire, backed by a world industrial and naval supremacy—the basis of the nineteenth-century *Pax Britannica*, a peace maintained, in a somewhat negative sense, not in Europe but outside it. 'It was not that British warships were everywhere, but that there were no other warships in significant concentrations anywhere.'[1] For the real threat to the Empire was not the secession of the American colonies; it was another bout of world conflict with France, and when first the French and then the Spaniards entered the war, the American crisis fell into second place. As in the Revolutionary and Napoleonic Wars, the threat of invasion was frustrated, the mastery of the oceans reaffirmed. India was held, and with it a huge sphere of influence in the Far East; and, under the stimulus of French rivalry, Cook was already opening up the prospect of a new expansion in the Pacific and Australasia. In the event, Anglo-Saxon world influence was not diminished. And when in the twentieth century, after two world wars, the British Empire was eclipsed and dismantled, and air power and ballistic missiles rendered the always

[1] J. H. Parry, *The Age of the Reconnaissance*, p. 334.

limited *Pax Britannica* obsolete, the might of America was to restore a power balance in Europe and the Pacific.

The famous events of the Revolution have been exhaustively examined, and only the main conclusions of modern research can here be reviewed. They are very different from the partisan *idées reçues* long popularly accepted. Both sides were caught in the grip of forces they could not control, and if any event appears historically inevitable it is the American Revolution. On the British side the loss of the colonies marks an abysmal failure of statesmanship and singular incompetence in war; but, in the sequel, a perennial and characteristic commercial imperialism re-emerged. In spite of the affront to the pride of an insular and arrogant society, the British ruling classes managed to pursue their traditional aims with a rather fumbling realism. For in the long run the British and the Americans had that essential basis of accord—a common interest. Both were consciously or unconsciously determined that the English-speaking peoples should dominate North America and the Atlantic. Through a fog of mutual resentment and even after renewed conflict, this fact determined policies.

After the British defeat and the fall of Lord North's government in 1782, the Rockingham–Shelburne administrations accepted the accomplished military facts; but the Americans, though now independent, faced a precarious future. Soon after the surrender of Cornwallis at Yorktown, Rodney had regained the mastery of the North Atlantic at the battle of the Saints. British troops still held New York; Canada, still extending far to the southwest, remained British, reinforced by a large migration of loyalists. The French, though their brief command of the ocean had been decisive, had always been more concerned with the Mediterranean, the West Indies, the Newfoundland fisheries and the war in the Atlantic—part of a global strategy —than with the liberties of republican Americans. And the Spaniards detested the heretics only less than they did the British, still inexpugnable in Gibraltar. The colonies themselves, in spite of accepted Articles of Confederation, still lacked an effective common government in the essential fields of law, finance and foreign policy. They were not even united in a common policy towards the Indians; they were erecting tariffs against one another and there was mounting conflict between the radicals and the rich. How the Founding Fathers of the American Constitution responded to the crisis and created a viable Federal Union is a chapter in American, not in British imperial history; but the hated British indirectly contributed, in their own interest, to its hard-won and momentous success. If King and Court were bitterly resentful, the governing classes as represented in Parliament saw their interest clear. They cut their political loss. Lord Shelburne, who succeeded Rockingham in July 1782, has been termed by Disraeli 'one of the suppressed characters of English history'. But his strategy of conciliation, though modified after his political fall, in the long run and in essentials survived. An individualist contemptuous of party and loyal only to the policies and memory of Chatham, he held power only for a year. But in that time the government negotiated a realistic settlement. As was befitting a descendant of Sir William Petty, the pioneer economist, Shelburne had an unusual grasp of economics; and as a pioneer free-trader he was determined to turn the Americans from rebels into customers, if not allies.[2]

Anxious almost to the last to keep the Americans within the Empire, he thought coercion and limitation 'infatuate', and was ready at the sacrifice of mercantilist principles to broaden the basis of the American economy to the west. He was also determined, like his colleague Charles James Fox, if by different tactics, to detach the Americans from the French alliance. And since the Americans no more wanted to be satellites of the French *ancien régime* than to return to the British Empire, he succeeded. Shelburne thus won his immediate diplomatic object, at the price of recognizing the accomplished fact of American Independence.

There was, indeed, no alternative. A separate regime under a King in America was then obviously impracticable: since 1688 the Crown in Great Britain had been increasingly identified with Parliament, and the idea of a concurrent relationship with colonial legislatures

[2] Sir William Petty, K.G., Lord Shelburne, 1737–1805, first Marquis of Lansdowne (1784), was the elder son of the Hon. John Fitzmaurice, whose father, Thomas Fitzmaurice, Earl of Kerry, had married Anne, only daughter of the original Sir William Petty. Shelburne himself declared that she had brought into the Fitzmaurice family 'whatever degree of sense may have appeared in it and whatever wealth is likely to remain in it'. Brought up by his grandparents in Ireland, he was briefly educated at Christ Church, Oxford, then entered the army and fought at Minden. In 1760 he was M.P. for High Wycombe, and in 1766 Secretary of State (Southern department) in Chatham's administration. He resigned in protest at Townshend's coercive policy to the Americans, but in 1782 accepted the same office under Rockingham. Shelburne was widely detested as a politician, being termed the 'Jesuit of Berkeley Square', and accused of 'constant and notorious falsehood'. It is said that Gainsborough refused to paint him with the remark, 'Damn it, I never could see through varnish and there's an end.' But Shelburne was a great patron of art and literature, a friend of Bentham, Morellet, the French economist, and of Adam Smith. He accumulated an enormous library and set 'Capability' Brown to lay out his estate at Bowood near Calne, which had come to him with his second wife, an heiress of the Carterets.

recalled Stuart ambitions for independence, a royal colonial power.
And since George III had consistently done what he believed to be
his constitutional duty and identified the Crown with Parliaments
which, despite an eloquent minority, had been, as he was himself,
overwhelmingly anti-colonial, he had become detested in America.
But Shelburne, if not the King or most of the British establishment,
had accepted the secession of the colonies with a good grace, and
though Burke's resounding opinion that 'magnanimity in politics
is often the truest wisdom' and 'a great empire and little minds
go ill together' had been disregarded, it influenced the final settlement.

Following the defection of Fox, in February 1783 Shelburne's
government collapsed, but the subsequent Fox–North coalition had
ratified the Treaty with the Americans. Negotiated in Paris in 1782
between the British diplomats and Franklin, John Adams and Jay,
it gave the Americans favourable terms. It recognized their authority over a vast area between the Alleghenies and the Mississippi;
and the Canadian border, though fought over in the war of 1812-14,
and the cause of much subsequent friction, would be peacefully
adjusted. American pre-war debts to English creditors were not
cancelled, but the British undertook to compensate the dispossessed
American loyalists in Canada. And if the subsequent British treaty
with Spain assigned the Spaniards Florida and Louisiana—a vague
potential threat—the settlement, along with an economic recovery
after 1786, made the United States viable. Though Shelburne had
been displaced, and the British still hankered for the old colonial
restrictions, the treaty brought in returns for both sides. When the
French Revolution and the Napoleonic Wars convulsed Europe,
the new republic had time to consolidate, and following Napoleon's
takeover of Louisiana from Spain, Jefferson saw his chance. Napoleon knew he could never hold it: in 1803, badly in need of cash
and calculating that a stronger United States would become more
hostile to the British, he sold the entire territory to the Americans
for fifteen million dollars. Jefferson, on his own initiative, thus
rounded off the great area of the middle and southwest already within the Union. So far, in less than one generation, had the United
States advanced: from a vigorous but disunited and indebted
colonial society, it had become a great independent power expanding
westward over a continent. How this transformation came about will
now be considered.

II

The causes that led up to the American Revolution have been elaborately analysed. The most obvious cause is social. The Great Britain of George III was an old and wealthy society, long set in its ways, with a rich elite culture. The ruling oligarchy, highly sophisticated and complacent, had emerged out of the savage political and religious warfare of late Stuart times: 'George and pudding time' had come in, and though the House of Commons was elected on a medieval franchise, it was representative of the political nation.

In 1763 that nation had just won the first of the world wars, it possessed the strongest navy in the world and it was backed by the piled up wealth of its own centuries-old commerce and by new fortunes accumulated in the West Indies and in India. The court had lost the glamour of Stuart times, and George III, though a musician and a connoisseur, would make it duller; but the nobility, who dominated political life and who had recovered from the attempted middle-class and radical revolution in the mid-seventeenth century, were, in their fashion, part of a cosmopolitan European civilization which looked to France and which was immensely creative in its own right. For heartless brilliance Horace Walpole's *Memoirs* have not been surpassed in English; inspired commonsense has never been better propounded than by Dr Johnson, polymath and lexicographer; and Gibbon's prose still has a sweep and vigour that only the blandest self-confidence can produce. Moreover, though the majority of the people were hardly literate, the condition of the villages and towns by modern standards appalling and the law only sketchily if brutally enforced, the ordinary English were a vigorous, still overwhelmingly rural people, accustomed to hard conditions and to accept the social order and its values, materialistic and intelligible. They identified themselves with victories won by a small professional army, reinforced by German mercenaries, and by battle fleets whose crews were augmented by the press gang. The rhetoric and grab of Pitt's commercial imperialism had caught the imagination of the people, shown the British what they could do and promoted a self-confidence that would survive the loss of the American colonies and the ordeal of the Napoleonic Wars.

This close-knit British hierarchy, with its crown, nobility and bishops, its ancient universities, its civic pomp and popular acclaim, had the momentum of tradition and success behind it. In comparison the American colonial society was open, provincial and diffuse. The patroons of Virginia, on their vast plantations, lived off slave-labour and, though they retained an English sense of political obligation, they had not the rural and civic English social structure to support them. They were in business and conducted it themselves, and most of them were deep in debt to British creditors. In the north the exclusive Congregationalist oligarchy in Boston had now to take account of Yankee merchants and shipowners who had prospered under the Navigation Acts. New York had always been cosmopolitan, open to wealth whatever its origin; Connecticut and Rhode Island had always been radical; and in Pennsylvania the original Quakers, in spite of their attempts to keep the country respectable, were being swamped by Irish, Scots, German, Dutch and Scandinavian immigrants. Along the frontier, if there was less rough democracy than is often supposed—for pioneering needs organization and the skill to survey—the old European social outlook was, of course, irrelevant. Moreover, in spite of great American discrepancies in wealth, capital was not yet substantial or concentrated. Society was more egalitarian and opportunist : anyone had a chance to make good without the social probation still exacted even by the relatively fluid English establishment. This 'democratic' aspect of the colonies —the word was then one of abuse—provoked hostility in Great Britain, since the example might encourage radicals to subvert the hierarchy at home—as indeed it did. The deepest, if most impalpable cause of alienation between the British and the Americans was thus social, aggravated by distance and a contrasting environment.

Economic grievances were also decisive, though less so than often believed. The Old Colonial system, for which there was economically much to be said, in that the raw materials of the colonies naturally supplemented British needs and British manufacturers the needs of Americans, made all the colonies dependent on British capital. Most of the American currencies commanded little confidence and the colonists were at a disadvantage. Two-thirds of the tobacco exported from Virginia and Maryland, for example, was re-exported at a profit from Great Britain; while the colonists had to pay 25 per cent more for wine, oil and fruit from the Iberian peninsula since all had to come through this 'roundabout' route; while the 'enumerated' products which could only be indirectly exported to the continent included sugar, tobacco, cotton, rice and furs. Further, nascent American industries were penalized—wool, textiles, iron and steel foundries and even, in the interest of the British West Indian trade, the distillation of rum from molasses imported from the French or Dutch plantations.

On the other hand, the Navigation Laws greatly benefited American shipping, and bounties encouraged the production of many goods, such as tobacco, flax, hemp, raw silk, fish oils, logwood, pitch, turpentine and tar—the latter important for the British Navy. The British demand for timber benefited northern Virginia and Pennsylvania, while the pine forests of New England supplied masts which could compete with Baltic timber, though colonial methods of shipment and classification were inferior to European.

The two economies were, indeed, naturally complementary: by 1790, even after the war—and a justification for the moderate settlement—three-quarters of American trade was still with Great Britain, whence the Americans took all but 10 per cent of their imports. And it was worth more.

In a world of economic nationalism, when all the colonial powers aimed at self-sufficiency, the Old Colonial system had long been taken for granted; and if, on balance, the colonists suffered, it was more from the way it was enforced and from their dependence on British creditors than from the system itself. Indeed, as late as 1774 the Continental Congress was ready to continue their obedience to the Navigation Laws, if the proposed new taxation was remitted, and most Americans sought rather to adjust the system than abolish it. The restrictions on colonizing to the west were a new grievance, both among rich prospectors, of whom Washington—whose estates amounted to 50,000 acres with three hundred slaves at his death—is the most famous, and also among the radical frontier pioneers.

Yet the leadership of the revolt came from Virginian aristocrats and well-established Bostonians, more than from the western radicals; and the American Revolution does not reflect economic class warfare between the frontier and the maritime east. While, therefore, economic grievances contributed to the revolt, they were less unanimous and decisive than is frequently supposed. Indeed, the Old Colonial system of a self-sufficient empire, which came in for so much criticism in the nineteenth century when free-trade was thought an economic panacea, appears more intelligible today, when a favourable 'balance of payments' is thought crucially important, and currency restrictions and variations in exchange rates reflect an economic nationalism now less realistic than the old system in its day.

The political causes of the Revolution are also far from the simple confrontation, between tyranny and freedom, of popular belief. The old image of George III, determined to be absolute abroad as well as at home, depicted by Whig historians, is as false as the image of enlightened colonial radicals determined to create a democratic state. The monarch forfeited his original popularity in America just because he conscientiously played the role assigned to him by the Hanoverian settlement and identified himself with Parliament. He still believed that the colonies could be subdued after Lord North's government and the generals had muddled them away; and only reluctantly acquiesced in Shelburne's settlement. But he was never the would-be despot of political mythology. Nor was the cry for 'no taxation without representation' then realistic. Neither in Great Britain nor the colonies was there any democratic franchise, and taxation by colonial assemblies would not have been imposed by representatives of the 'people' elected on a franchise of one man one vote. The leadership of the revolt came predominantly from the established classes, and the Constitution, as devised by the Federalists and represented by Washington as the first President of the United States, was socially and economically conservative. It could, indeed, be adapted to democracy; but if the Declaration of Independence was resoundingly liberal, it was so only in the sense that John Locke was a liberal. The proclamation of human equality does not mention the slaves.

Like the seventeenth-century English Revolution, the Revolution in America owed much to propaganda. The precociously developed colonial newspapers were anti-British and anti-loyalist, and the eighteenth-century passion for oratory found full scope. The writings of the English radical, Tom Paine, an international revolutionary later acclaimed in France, had extraordinary influence. Propaganda cannot create revolution, but it can make latent feelings articulate and widespread, and where in the seventeenth century religious enthusiasm had inflamed men's minds, the pamphleteers and orators of the American Revolution created its own secular ideology.

But when all these causes and symptoms are reviewed, social, economic, political and ideological, the fact remains that the original revolution was made reluctantly, and carried through only by a minority—at most, perhaps, by a third of the population. There was civil war among Americans, particularly in the south, where Captain Lynch, who persecuted loyalists, gave his name to 'Lynch law'; in the event, the majority, as usual in political revolution, accommodated themselves to the shift of power.

If the long-term causes of the Revolution, here of necessity simplified, remain complex, the immediate cause of its success is plain—the sheer ineptness of British governments and British generals. Had a Marlborough or a Wellington been on hand, Washington's army, whose one hope was to outlast the enemy, would have been sought out and destroyed. And this incompetence decided the French to intervene—first with arms and supplies, then directly at Yorktown, Virginia, where the capitulation of Cornwallis's army saw the end of a war not so much won by the Americans as lost by the British.

III

The American Revolution thus reflected divergent ways of life, and the exaggerated grievances that led up to it were symptomatic. To the British, the colonists appeared raw provincials; to the colonists, the British seemed arbitrary and arrogant. For the days of casual neglect were over. After the conquest of Canada and much of the Middle West, the British commercial empire was becoming immense and territorial; with a new sense of concern, successive governments were trying to cope with the change. 'After 1763, the Spaniards attempted to rationalize and pull together their South American Empire, and the French to consolidate what remained of theirs. But the British Empire was the most unmanageable and its sheer diversity and geographical extent ... invited improvisation, hasty decisions and muddle.'[3] Burdened with a massive national debt and mounting occupation costs, with eighty thousand French-Canadians on their hands and threatened, following Pontiac's revolt of 1763, with Amerindian wars in the interior, perhaps overestimated, the British tried to consolidate their gains and limit their commitments. The American problem was only one aspect of immense responsibilities: in India, in the Mediterranean, in the West Indies and West Africa. With the potential economic mastery of the world in their hands, and French power checked, if not eradicated, the political cliques in London, through whom the king was trying to govern, faced a challenge that would have tried better men. Moreover, during the phase of mounting friction that preceded the crisis in America, there were four successive ministries. In 1763 Grenville succeeded Bute; in 1765 the Marquess of Rockingham followed Grenville; then the Duke of Grafton, for the first two years in coalition with Chatham, governed from 1766 to 1770. And if Lord North's government managed to last for twelve years, it was twelve years too long. In 1782, after North had been forced to resign, the second Rockingham administration only lasted four months; Shelburne's but eleven; and the Fox–North coalition, which fell through the rejection of Fox's India Bill, only eight months. Not until 1783 would William Pitt the Younger form a government that would last until 1801.

To the British the most urgent problem in America was the control of immigration to the west. The colonists, from the big prospectors to the small farmers, hungered for land; but the British were more concerned with the fur-trade and so with tolerable relations with the Indians. They hoped, in vain, that settlers could be diverted to

[3] Parry, *op. cit.* p. 136.

Quebec or Florida. As the colonists moved in, they provoked fierce resistance from tribes in a wilderness that was almost impossible to control, and government tried to slow down the migration and create a vast Indian reserve. It was in part to finance this expedient, which involved ten thousand troops and cost £350,000 a year, that in 1764 Grenville, in the course of a general attempt to balance the budget, imposed a Plantation or Sugar Act, which revived Walpole's duty on molasses imported from the French and Dutch colonies. He halved its amount, but enforced its collection. Since the importers of molasses—the syrup of raw sugar from which rum was distilled—had largely evaded this duty, even its collection at a lower rate was resented. Then a Revenue Act also imposed stiff duties on wines, coffee and linens, and when, in the same year, a Currency Act disallowed the bills of credit issued by the colonial administrations, the colonists had to pay their taxes in hard currency.

But it was the notorious Stamp Act of 1765 that provoked the most violent indignation. Here was a direct internal tax, something apart from the normal duties imposed under the Old Colonial system; and though there had been stamp duties in England since 1695, they were new in America. They applied to important transactions— the clearance of ships' cargoes, the registration of legal business and the issue of newspapers; merchants, lawyers and journalists combined in protest, and the Americans declared they had not the currency to buy stamps. In view of these protests, which were backed by powerful interests in London, the Stamp Act was repealed. But not before radicals in America had organized resistance under the famous slogan, 'no taxation without representation'. And Rockingham's government, covering its climb down to conciliate opinion at home, spoilt the effects of the concession in the colonies by a pedantic Declaration Act, which asserted, in principle, the British Parliament's right to 'bind the colonies' in any circumstances. Yet, in spite of this face-saving gesture, colonial opinion was in fact considerably appeased. Most Americans still wanted a return to the traditional pre-1763 inertia.

Then in 1767, the Duke of Grafton's administration returned to the attack. The Townshend Acts imposed import duties on tea (then a popular drink in America), on paper, always in short supply, and on glass and paint. These measures were, again, not routine mercantilist Acts of Trade, but directly designed to raise revenue to pay the customs officials, the colonial governors and the judiciary. They provoked another and more formidable storm: the colonial governors, it was declared, would become independent of the colonial assemblies.

The colonies thus became united as never before. As Washington —no radical—wrote in 1768, 'at a time when our lordly masters in Great Britain will be satisfied with nothing less than the deprecation of American freedom, it seems highly necessary that something should be done to avert the stroke and maintain the liberty which we had derived from our ancestors'.[4] He still considered armed resistance a 'last resource', but he mentioned it; and in 1770, in face of indignation common to Yankee merchants and Virginian planters, the British again climbed down. Lord North repealed all the Townshend duties, save that on tea; but, once more, the British government threw away the colonial goodwill won through appeasement by a saving of face at home. North had insisted that the tea duty be retained 'as a mark of the supremacy of Parliament and an efficient declaration of the right to govern the colonies'.

Twice the imperial government had attempted the impracticable, twice retreated and twice, for domestic reasons, infuriated the colonists, now in the grip of a trade recession. But save for the fracas termed the Boston 'Massacre' in 1770, when British troops guarding the Customs' Commission were provoked into unauthorized retaliation, and for the burning of the revenue cutter *Gaspée* by some tough smugglers from Rhode Island in 1772, the conflict simmered down. Then, in 1773, Lord North and his advisers had an unfortunate inspiration. The East India Company, as already recorded, was now verging on bankruptcy; North brought in his Regulating Act in that year, and two years later he would appoint Warren Hastings as Governor-General with enhanced, though fettered, powers. The American market for tea had been falling off, the tea duty had further diminished sales and most of what was left of the trade had been taken over by smugglers. So the British government, while maintaining the duty for Americans, decided to allow the Company to sell their tea in America direct at a cut retail price. The Boston merchants, some of whom had done well out of smuggling Dutch tea, were outraged; those politicians already set on Independence saw their chance; in December 1773 the famous Boston tea-riot was staged, the chests flung into the harbour.

It was not, on the face of it, a sinister occasion. But it provoked a change of policy in Great Britain that led to war. At first it was a rather phoney war, with the colonists still 'rebels' within the Empire; then, after the Declaration of Independence in 1776, it became all-out conflict in which the French and Spanish Empires were to be involved, for the British government now reacted with anger. The

[4] Quoted by Esmond Wright, *Washington and the American Revolution*, London, 1957, p. 48.

Massachusetts colony had always been disliked as republican in sentiment and dissenting in religion: Coercive Acts were imposed, the Massachusetts charter called in and revised, a military Governor, General Thomas Gage, appointed,[5] the port of Boston closed to shipping.

These drastic measures alarmed the Virginians, hitherto not greatly concerned with the grievances of Massachusetts; and when the Governor, the Earl of Dunmore, newly installed in the elegant palace at Williamsburg, had dissolved a recalcitrant assembly, the burgesses met in the Raleigh tavern and, amid scenes of celebrated enthusiasm, transformed themselves into a Convention. The representatives of the oldest and most conservative colony now boycotted the export of their own tobacco and, that September, sent delegates to the first Continental Congress in Philadelphia. Among these was Washington, the conservative landowner, and Patrick Henry, the radical orator: the British had managed to unite contrasting Americans in a common cause. On the other side of the ocean, opinion also hardened. 'The die is cast,' the King would declare with heavy Hanoverian finality, 'the colonies must either triumph or submit.'

IV

Even so the first phase of the war was half-hearted. Informed contemporary opinion, so often in history proved wrong, believed that the colonists had little chance. The French and Spanish governments reluctantly concluded that the might of the Royal Navy, the weight of professional troops and the vast financial reserves of England would bring the colonial rebels to heel; and the American leaders were themselves apprehensive. In fact, the logistic difficulties of fighting a war across three thousand miles of ocean, the dispersal of effort by hide-bound commanders in guerrilla-type conflicts that dragged on for six years over fifteen hundred miles of difficult country, the tenacity of the American command and the marksmanship and initiative of men accustomed to Indian wars in the wilderness, soon changed the prospect. By 1777 Burgoyne's capitulation at Saratoga on the Hudson decided the French that the Americans were worth an alliance. But before the momentous treaty could be concluded, the Americans had to set up a sovereign power; and this, by 1776, after the resounding Declaration of Independence, they had done.

The war opened with a British tactical reverse and an American

[5] Thomas, first Viscount Gage (1721–87), had fought in Braddock's disastrous expedition to Fort Duquesne, and during the conquest of Canada he had been made Governor of Montreal.

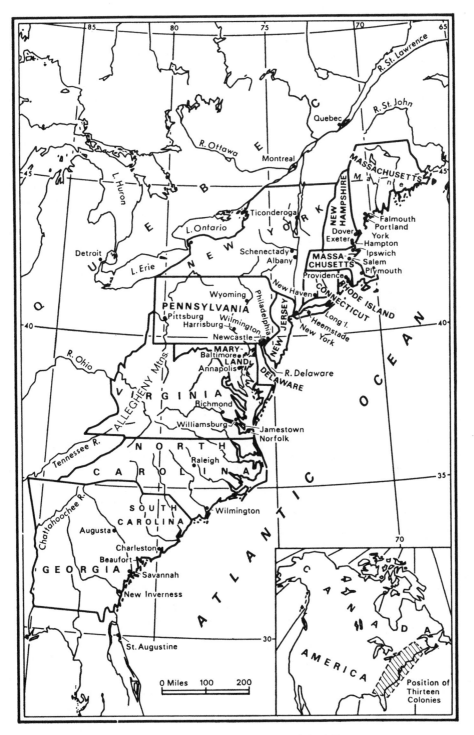

Eastern North America: The 13 Original States.

strategic failure. Both sides reacted predictably: the British redcoats —'lobsters' the Americans called them—showed their usual disciplined courage, but their commanders were generally incapable of adapting themselves to colonial conditions. The Americans, on the other hand, armed if undisciplined civilians, were often seasoned in warfare against the savages.[6] Among them were trackers and marksmen, and their Pennsylvania rifles were handier, more accurate and easier to re-load, than the heavy muskets of the British and Hessian infantry. While the latter were conspicuously and uncomfortably clothed, many Americans wore dark hunting-shirts and long breeches, and most of them had been accustomed to shoot game since boyhood. The colonial militia could seem a rabble, but they were better paid and better supplied than the British, and exempt from the ferocious British punishments. Because of their provincial loyalties Washington had great difficulty in creating a nucleus of a continental army, but he 'took wise advantage of his opportunity to fight a war *seriatim*—first in New England, then in the Middle Colonies, then in the South'.[7]

The war in New England and Canada was decided during the winter of 1775–6. In the opening skirmish at Lexington and in the attack on the supply depot at Concord the British rushed 'shouting and huzzaing' to meet the embattled farmers;[8] but in their harassed retreat from Concord they lost 273 casualties to the American 95. And when the British, who might have cut the neck of the Charlestown peninsula commanding Boston, captured Breed Hill—in a battle afterwards known from the neighbouring Bunker Hill—by frontal attack at a third assault, this time in column, they lost 1,054 men out of 2,200.

Such tactics were too much, even for the authorities in London: Gage was superseded and, after a winter shut up in Boston, the British withdrew to their base in Halifax, Nova Scotia, there to mount, correctly, a strategic attack on New York which could cut the colonies in two.

Meanwhile, Washington himself had arrived at Cambridge, Massachusetts, and organized an attack on Canada. The Americans under

[6] Danger was part of their lives. Even the 'Indian summer', now thought of as a pleasant time, was in fact dreaded by the frontier families. They had welcomed the hard weather that prevented Indian attacks, and when, after its apparent onset, 'the weather became warm ... this ... "Indian summer" gave the Indians another chance to attack and the apprehension of another visit from the Indians was painful to the highest degree'. Cited Boorstin, *op. cit.* p. 349.

[7] Boorstin, *The Americans. The Colonial Experience*, p. 366.

[8] Hertz, *The Old Colonial System*, p. 175, q.v., for some shrewd comment.

Richard Montgomery advanced from Hartford, Connecticut, on Ticonderoga, captured its guns and, by way of Lake Champlain, took Montreal. Benedict Arnold, the brilliant American commander who later deserted to the enemy, also advanced from Maine by Lake Megantic and the Chaudière River on Quebec. But Sir Guy Carleton, afterwards Lord Dorchester, the ablest British soldier and diplomatist in America who as Commander-in-Chief in Canada in 1782–3 would do much to assuage the bitterness following the war, saved Quebec. Escaping from Montreal with a handful of followers, he defended the fortress from a night assault in a mid-winter snowstorm. Montgomery was killed; Arnold severely wounded.[9] In May 1776 a British fleet relieved Quebec and the Americans had to evacuate Montreal. As a spoiling attack the American initiative had succeeded; but Canada remained under British control—the base for the advance down the Hudson Valley on New York.

The second phase of the war now centred on the middle colonies, and here the Americans came nearest to defeat. The British had ridiculously small forces to hold their entire Empire: they thought any standing army a menace and twenty thousand regulars too many. So the government, as usual, hired troops from Germany. The Swiss were not allowed to serve across the Atlantic, and though 'Gibbon welcomed the idea of purchasing troops even from barbarian Russia',[10] Catherine the Great refused to export her subjects. Germans, anyway, were of course regarded as far the best soldiers, and their rulers made a business of hiring them out. By the following year, nearly fifteen thousand Hessians were in America, better trained and better at taking cover than the British and Scots troops. Both sides used Indian auxiliaries.

The British now meant business. At first the war had been unpopular; but, following the disgrace at Boston and the gallant defence of Canada, most opinion was now solid behind the government. The Whig politicians, and even Chatham, whose eloquence would later have momentous consequences, were thought to be exploiting the revolt for party advantage; and they were themselves no more ready to grant away the right of Parliament to legislate for the colonies than was the King. The Tory squires and clergy were solid against the colonials. 'Though of American original,' wrote one of them in Wilt-

---

[9] Carleton was thought too valuable in Canada to succeed Gage, and 'Howe, Carleton's inferior in rank and efficiency, was given supreme command of thirteen colonies. Had Carleton occupied the post, the American rebellion might not have blossomed into a Revolution'. J. R. Alden, *The American Revolution*, London, 1954, p. 58.

[10] Hertz, *op. cit.* p. 166.

shire of his dog, Pero Grande, 'he was no rebel.' And the war relieved the current depression in trade: the Birmingham armaments industry was now doing well; Liverpool, Bristol and Glasgow provided transport and supplies; the clan chieftains of the Gordons and Macdonalds, since Culloden no longer allowed to raid in their own country, each raised one thousand Highlanders for the fray, now perforce loyal to the House of Hanover.

So, on 4th July 1776, the very day the Americans proclaimed themselves a sovereign state, a formidable expedition from Halifax under General Sir William Howe descended on Staten Island, off New York. Eight days later, his brother Admiral Richard, Earl Howe, arrived from England with a great fleet and an army which would amount to thirty-four thousand men—the largest expedition ever sent to America. Yet the campaign of 1776 failed: Washington's army was not trapped in New York, or destroyed when pursued into New Jersey. Indeed, crossing the icy Delaware on the 25th December and turning upon the King's troops at Trenton when the Hessians were recovering from Christmas, Washington inflicted a spectacular if minor defeat, for Sir William Howe, though a first-class fighting soldier, was strategically obtuse. He had already sent in his resignation in October 1777; he now muffed his chances and Washington showed his mettle. The British captured and held New York, but Washington's legend began to grow. After Trenton, wrote an English eye-witness, 'the Americans', previously in despair, 'are all liberty mad again'.[11]

The obvious British strategic move was now to attack again from Canada down the Hudson Valley, link up in New York and isolate the northern colonies. But here, as in 1776, they failed and, still pursuing this objective, next year they came to disaster. Carleton, indeed, won control of Lake Champlain; but he failed to take Ticonderoga, and since he was disliked by Lord Germain, Secretary of State for the American colonies, he was now in effect superseded by a political soldier of high social connections and apparent dash. In July 1777 this general, John Burgoyne, with 9,500 troops, captured Ticonderoga; but advancing recklessly with insufficient reconnaissance or supplies, he was surrounded in September by superior American forces under General Gates, in tactical collaboration with Arnold. The British in New York then divided their forces and sent an expedition to relieve him—but it proved too little and too late. In October Burgoyne surrendered under a convention—not observed —that his troops should be repatriated on condition of taking no further part in the war. In fact, they were shipped to Virginia.

[11] Cited Alden, *op. cit.* p. 111.

This American victory proved the turning point of the war. In 1778 the French, who had already heavily subsidized the Americans, signed a treaty of alliance, in 1779 Spain entered the war, and in 1780 the British declared war on the Dutch. The Baltic powers formed a League of Neutrality, hostile to Great Britain. In India, the French and their allies launched a formidable attack.

Howe, meanwhile, having already resigned, spent a comfortable, even merry, winter in Philadelphia; a course perhaps justified by difficulties of military supply. But Washington, now undergoing great hardship at Valley Forge, still held the initiative. In the spring of 1778 Howe was superseded by Sir Henry Clinton, another gallant but limited Guardsman who had fought in Germany and who, as cousin of the Duke of Newcastle and M.P. for Newark, had political pull. He proved no more successful in hunting down Washington, and, following instructions from London, switched his objective to the south, inaugurating the third and final phase of the war, undertaken only after the Americans had rejected North's offer of a favourable peace.

This southern campaign, an effort to retrieve the disasters in the northern and middle colonies, was attended, as Clinton himself observed, 'with great risks unless we are assured of permanent superiority at sea'. And during this crucial phase the British Navy lost command of the western Atlantic.

At first the bold stroke paid off: the King's troops could move faster by sea than could the Americans by land. In December 1778 they captured Savannah in Georgia; then, in May 1780 Clinton himself took Charlestown, the principal city of the south, along with over six thousand men, among them some of the best Virginian troops, and more than three hundred guns. And that August, Cornwallis[12] routed the Americans under Gates at Camden—their worst defeat in the war.

Clinton had now returned to New York, leaving Cornwallis with instructions to proceed with caution. But Cornwallis was determined to follow up success. He advanced into Virginia, while the renegade American, Benedict Arnold, combined with him to devastate the

[12] Charles, 1st Marquess and 2nd Earl Cornwallis, 1738–1805, came of a Suffolk family, allied to the Townshends of Raynham. During a game of hockey at Eton he suffered injury to one eye at the hands of Shute Barrington, afterwards Bishop Durham, but this did not deter his military ambitions. In spite of his loss of reputation in America his career proved much more than military. In 1786 he was appointed Governor-General of India; in 1797 Viceroy of Ireland. He then went out to India for a second term and died there, having taken, in his two terms of office, immensely important decisions for the future of British India.

country, and Pennsylvania loyalists rose in revolt. There now seemed little to oppose the British advance. Richmond was taken and sacked; Jefferson, the American Governor of Virginia, was chased out of Montecello, making off down one side of the hill while Carleton's cavalry sweated up the other, and escaping to the next eminence through his woods.[13] Cornwallis now begged Clinton to collaborate in mastering Virginia, even at the risk of losing New York. But Clinton's reinforcements proved wholly inadequate, and Cornwallis had to dig himself in at Yorktown on the southern bank of the York River.

The campaign had involved risks of which Washington and the French, as well as Clinton, had been well aware. The British Navy had now to cope with the French and Spanish fleets as well as the Americans: the naval war would involve 171,000 men, and if only 1,240 were killed in action, 42,000 deserted and 18,500 died of disease.[14] By August, Admiral de Grasse had brought twenty ships up from Haiti with substantial reinforcements to Chesapeake Bay, while Washington and Lafayette, with 16,000 troops, had moved down from Philadelphia to Williamsburg. This well-timed operation brilliantly succeeded. Cornwallis was trapped. The British no longer controlled the sea and a weak British expedition from New York to relieve Cornwallis was driven off by de Grasse: the entire British army at Yorktown, outnumbered and surrounded, was forced to surrender. As is well known, some wit instructed the band to play a piece called 'The World Turned Upside Down'. Another relieving expedition under Clinton arrived too late and sheered off to New York. 'All depended upon a fleet,' Cornwallis wrote, 'Sir H. Clinton promised one, Washington had one.'[15]

The British troops in the south, harassed by American levies, now lost their tenuous hold on the country. They could only hold Savannah and Charlestown, surrendered to the Americans at the peace. The third and final effort to subdue the colonies had failed.

V

Such, in a broad view, were the three stages of disaster suffered by the British in America. The military and political experts had been confounded, for Washington's continental army had never been destroyed. Hunted about, it had always made a comeback; diminished

---

[13] See Dumas Malone, *Jefferson and his Time* and *Jefferson the Virginian*, Boston, 1948, pp. 355–8, for a vivid account.

[14] J. H. Parry, *op. cit.* p. 217.

[15] Alden, *op. cit.* p. 247.

by desertions, it had attracted fresh recruits. It had included Indian auxiliaries not above eating their prisoners, 'squads of negroes, and ... outposts of black men with white shirts';[16] it had suffered terrible hardships and defeats—but it had been better led. And the Americans had been less encumbered; they could attack in mid-winter—as through the snow at Quebec or across an icy river at Trenton; they had taken advantage of their own vast country from the northern wilderness to the swamps of the south. They had out-lasted their opponents; then, with the French command of the sea, they had closed in for the kill. Washington, unlike most of his op-ponents, had a quick eye.

Apart from the decisive long-term causes for separation described, the British lost their colonies through the incompetence of their politicians and their commanders: their failure to discern the essen-tial, the vacillation of their strategic aims. And the contrast between American adaptability and improvisation and the ponderous and slow manoeuvres of the British reflects the difference between the two societies. In the plethoric Great Britain of George III those in power often no longer had the hard realism of the Elizabethan rulers, whose own lives, from the Queen downwards, were at risk. Sheltered, padded about by eighteenth-century convention, shielded by grandeur and wealth, George III and most of his advisers had little sense of the facts of the American scene. The bureaucracy was not well enough developed to administer distant colonies, nor rudimentary enough to leave them alone. The generals, who would already fight their battles over again in contradictory memoirs, had won promo-tion in gallant but conventional warfare on Continental battlefields or by political and family influence. The Navy, as usual, after great victories, had been run down, and though it soon recovered control of the Atlantic, it had temporarily lost it. The foreign sympathizers with the Americans, Lafayette, Kosciusko, for example, were skilled and enterprising: the French and Spanish governments gave large subsidies. As Jefferson put it, 'the English cannot hold out long be-cause the world is against them'. And, indeed, for them, the Ameri-can conflict, in retrospect so immensely important, had taken second place to a threat to the whole Empire: to Gibraltar, to India and the West Indies, even, when France and Spain entered the war, to the island itself. Nor were there prizes in America to attract men of the neo-Elizabethan quality of Clive or the political subtlety of Warren Hastings, both fortunately separated from London by at least a six months' voyage, while America could be reached, with luck, in a month. The British still had their greatest phase of empire before

16 Hertz, *op. cit.* p. 169.

them, and during the Industrial Revolution and the Victorian climax would show their old enterprise; but in the earlier reign of George III they were saddled with governments whose incompetence was quite outstanding. It was the leaders of the American Revolution who displayed the *élan* of their Tudor and Stuart past, and who now stood for the kind of political liberties defined in England in the seventeenth century, to which the Declaration of Independence now gave a worldwide and eloquent appeal.

CHAPTER 12

The South Sea: the Reconnaissance of Australasia

While in Europe and Asia great civilizations had been long established, and elaborate, if still neolithic cultures had arisen in Mexico and Peru, the peoples of the Pacific had led primitive, original and easy-going lives in a vast, isolated and favourable environment. Deriving mainly from Southeast Asia and Indonesia, they had spread out over Melanesia, New Guinea, the Solomon Islands, the New Hebrides and, peripherally, Fiji; over Micronesia, which included the Marianas, the Marshall and Gilbert Islands, between Melanesia and Japan; and over the much larger area of Polynesia which ranged from Hawaii in the northeast down to the Marquesas and Pitcairn, to Tahiti, Samoa and New Zealand.

This huge colonization probably began, by European reckoning, about 300 B.C., soon after the death of Alexander, and it had reached New Zealand by about the mid-tenth century A.D., during the climax of the West Saxon monarchy and the Ottonian Holy Roman Empire. The Polynesian culture was the most elaborate, amiable and enterprising; even if their immense voyages have been too much romanticized. Their deliberate expeditions seldom exceeded two hundred miles—less than the length of the English Channel or the passage from New York to Cape Cod, and Hawaii, Pitcairn and New Zealand were probably colonized when the great canoes were blown off course by survivors of local expeditions, most of whom perished. There is no firm evidence for the legends of deliberate colonization, though conceivably some navigators may have managed to return. The Polynesians certainly shared dialects of the same language, and claimed a common origin. For the British, New Zealand proved the greatest Polynesian discovery, if the great continent of Australia, sparsely inhabited by much more primitive peoples, became the basis of more massive settlement.

The great islands, termed by their Maori inhabitants *Te Ika a Mani* and *Te Wai Ponnamu* in the great ocean of Kiwa, had first been observed by Abel Janzoon Tasman, a sea-captain from Groningen, commissioned by the Dutch East India Company to investigate the 'southland' from Batavia, in 1642, twenty years after the Amboyna 'massacre', and at the height of Dutch colonial power. The Dutch had called the country, which they at first thought part of a continent, *Statenlandt*, then *Nieuw Zeelandt* or *Nieuw Hollandt*, but they had found a martial and defiant people. The earliest inhabitants, who had lived off and exterminated the moa, a flightless bird as big as a man, had been followed, probably in about A.D. 1350, by more advanced immigrants, who had created a socially elaborate but politically anarchic neolithic culture geared to ferocious tribal war: they built stockaded hall forts and efficient war canoes, and they ate their enemies. They were the only Polynesians who had to adapt to a temperate climate and they gave the Dutch such a reception that they sheered off. It was not until 1769 that another European, Captain James Cook, the greatest of British explorers, made his landfall, charted the coasts and, after initial conflict, came to terms with the inhabitants.

Australia, too, had first been discovered by the Dutch. After tentative and discouraging contacts along the Gulf of Carpentaria and the northwestern coasts by earlier navigators, Tasman had found what he called *Athooney van Deimanslandt*, now Tasmania, in the far south. The north and the northwest appeared a waste of sandy desert with sparse, unfamiliar, vegetation; and the inhabitants, in fact dark brown, seemed to be 'blacks', owing to the layers of dirt and pigment with which they were encrusted. Their earliest ancestors probably were roaming the continent about 14,000 B.C. when there was still a landbridge; they were related to the Negritos of Southeast Asia, the Ainu of Japan and the Veddas of Ceylon, and they were palaeolithic savages. Well-adapted to their peculiar environment, with their initiation rites, orgiastic corroborees and numinous cave paintings, these hunters and scavengers had remained technologically very primitive, and their way of life was doomed by contact with European civilization. Here, again, the Dutch had sheered off, disappointed of hopes of gold, spices and commerce in *terra Australis incognita*, though, optimistically, they had named the land *Nieuw Hollandt*.

Such was the hazy European knowledge of the fringes of New Zealand and Australia in the mid-seventeenth century. And knowledge of the lesser Pacific islands was even vaguer: their strategic potential was not yet realized, and the Polynesians, happier had the Europeans never intruded upon them, were left for nearly two centuries on their own. The West would then inevitably 'open up' the Pacific, too often with disastrous results. The Maoris, warred down first in casual and then in official battle, recovered and adapted themselves to civilization; but the aboriginal Australians were largely wiped out and the remnant demoralized. The Tahitians, the Samoans, the Fijians and the rest were swiftly overrun and exploited —the indigenous population of Tahiti at the heart of Polynesia diminished from about forty thousand to six thousand within less than a century. Cannibalism, infanticide and tribal warfare were, indeed, put down, but the original social order was often wrecked. By the time of the annexations made mainly by the British, the French and the Americans, in the mid-nineteenth century, a well-adapted culture had been largely destroyed by the European adventurers and puritanical missionaries, though much would be done to save it.

For the British Empire the sequel to these discoveries would be momentous: the foundation of two major nations of European descent in New Zealand and Australia, and some successful experiments in indirect rule, particularly in Fiji and Tonga in the late nineteenth century.

II

The first Englishman to describe part of the northwestern fringe of Australia was a determined and original character. William Dampier, one of the prowlers and adventurers who haunted the oceans after the Caribbean had been made too hot to hold them, was a cartographer and observer of genius; an intelligent buccaneer with an astonishing capacity for survival.[1] His casual privateering and

[1] Born in 1652, the son of a tenant farmer at East Coker near Yeovil, Somerset, Dampier early sailed to Newfoundland and Bantam; then he fought in the Second Dutch War. He went out to Jamaica to manage a plantation, but soon took to trading rum in Yucatan and buccaneering in Panama. In 1683–91 he made his first and famous voyage round the world on a privateering expedition which crossed from Virginia to Sierra Leone, then rounded the Horn to plunder the Spanish-American colonies in the Pacific. Having traversed the ocean to Guam in the Marianas, the crew marooned the captain, then cruised off New Guinea and New Holland, where Dampier made his first observations. They then marooned Dampier as well, on the Nicobar islands in the Indian ocean, whence he escaped in a native craft to Sumatra, returning by an East Indiaman to London. The fruit of this extraordinary experience was Dampier's *Voyage Round the World* (1697), which won him immediate celebrity and which was followed in 1699 by *Voyages and Descriptions*. In 1698–9 he made his second great voyage, this time in the *Roebuck*, when he

amateurish methods of command contrast with the steady professional competence and magnanimity of Cook, who had much more substantial backing; but Dampier's vivid and commonsensical descriptions are often worthy of Defoe.

He already had a hunch that Australia was enormous: 'It is not yet determined,' he wrote, after his first brief contact with the northwestern coast in 1688, the year of the 'Glorious' Revolution in England, 'whether it is an Island or a Main Continent, but I am certain that it joynes neither to Asia, Africa nor America.' But the country was unprepossessing—'low even land with sandy banks against the sea'—and the inhabitants appeared 'the miserablest people in the world'. 'The *Hodmadods* of *Monomatapa*, though a nasty People, yet for wealth are gentlemen to these; who have no houses and skin garments, sheep, poultry and fruits of the earth.' The cadence is reminiscent of Hobbes on primitive man and almost as familiar. Suffice it that Dampier, who observed some of the most primitive of aboriginals in Australia, created a highly unfavourable impression of them: a tall bottle-nosed people, with slender limbs, fuzzy hair, with 'great heads, round foreheads, and great brows',[2] their eyes screwed up against the ubiquitous flies. 'There is neither herbs, roots, pulse or any sort of grain' for them to eat, he wrote, 'that we saw, nor any kind of bird, or beast they can catch'. They subsisted mainly on small fish trapped by the receding tide in primitive stone weirs. 'The colour of their skins both of the faces and of the rest of their body is coal black, like that of the negroes of Guinea.' Naturally, they were 'much disordered at our landing, snatched up the infants and ran away howling, and the little children ran after squealing and bawling'. But the men attempted some resistance, standing their

---

again explored Western Australia; but the ship was wrecked on Ascension Island on the return voyage, whence Dampier returned, again on an East Indiaman, to face a court-martial which declared him unfit for command. But in 1703 he was again sent out on another and disastrous expedition to the Pacific, on which Alexander Selkirk, the original of Robinson Crusoe, was set ashore on Juan Fernandez, and the Manila galleon, the main object of the exercise, escaped. Finally discredited as a commander, Dampier was now employed as a pilot (1708–11) on the *Duke* privateer under Captain Woodes Rodgers, who left an interesting account of the expedition—*A Cruising Voyage Round the World*. They rescued Selkirk and captured a Manila galleon worth £200,000 though the officials so delayed the distribution that Dampier died in 1715 before he got his substantial share of it. But he left some property to his cousin and to his brother who lived near Bridport, so died solvent. For a modern edition of his writings, see *Dampier's Voyages*, ed. John Masefield, 2 vols, London, 1906.

[2] Dampier's *Voyage Round the World*, 7th edition, in *A Collection of Voyages*, London, 1793, Vol. I, pp. 464–7.

ground, while 'some of the women lay by the fire making a doleful noise, as if we had come to devour them'. Some, captured when swimming, were brought aboard, but, like animals, they only noticed the food—boiled rice, turtle and manatee, which they greedily devoured, indifferent to the ship, unable to take in a spectacle so far outside their experience. They spoke, unintelligibly, 'somewhat through the throat'.

On his second voyage ten years later in the *Roebuck*, Dampier landed at Sharks' Bay in western Australia and found aborigines of more spirit. They had a 'chief, a young and brisk man ... more active and courageous' and 'painted with a circle of white paste or pigment—a sort of line ... about the eyes and a white streak down his nose from the forehead to the tip of it'—not 'for beauty', but to 'look terrible'. But Dampier concluded that the aborigines of these parts were 'just the same blinking creatures as the others. There being also an abundance of the same kind of flesh flies, teasing 'em, and with the same black skins and hair frizzled'.[3] The English had found the country no more attractive than had the Dutch; but Dampier's writings had literally and metaphorically put a fringe of it on the map. He had sensed the immensity of the land; and his books, so well written, were widely read.

He had also spotted many huge green edible turtles and the whales that swarmed and spouted in the surrounding ocean, whose quest, spreading originally from the Quaker seamen of Nantucket to the southern hemisphere, would give rise to the first and horrible phase of European–American exploitation. 'The sea is plentifully stocked,' he wrote, 'with the largest whales I ever saw; but not to compare with the vast ones of the northern seas.' For the rest, there were parakeets and duck, but hardly any animals: 'two or three beasts like hungry wolves'—probably dingoes—a 'racoon', which was probably a bandicoot, and at Sharks' Bay another 'racoon' with short forelegs—probably a kangaroo rat.

III

The British, like the other north Europeans, had little chance to find the many small and attractive islands of the Pacific, intent as they were on the exploitation of the Far East, on the capture of one of the Manila galleons bound from Acapulco to the Philippines, or still hankering to find a Northwest Passage from Lake Superior to the north Pacific. The prevalent east to west winds made a relatively northerly route the best, and groups of islands, even if observed,

[3] Dampier, *op. cit.* Vol. III (*Voyage to New Holland*, etc., 1699), p. 102.

were difficult to find and recognize again. The Spaniards kept any discoveries they made to themselves and claimed suzerainty over the whole area. It was not until the second half of the eighteenth century that exploration was backed by governments. Plunder, commerce and political subversion rather than exploration were still the British objectives; and though their next famous circumnavigation of the world was made by Commodore Anson (1740–4), not like Dampier as a privateer, but under orders from the Admiralty, his objectives were still in principle Elizabethan.[4] So were the hardships suffered by his crews from scurvy and fever, the difficulties of manning the ships, and the resource and enterprise displayed against apparently overwhelming odds.

In spite of crippling losses, Anson's voyages, designed to rouse the Spanish-American colonies against their Iberian rulers and 'for the extension of our commerce and power', was both a navigational and a predatory success—'no voyage I have yet seen furnished such a number of views of land, soundings, draughts of roads, ports and charts and other matters for the improvement of navigation'.[5] Anson was, indeed, a precursor of Bougainville, Wallis and Cook; but the contrast in professional competence is emphatic. Anson only succeeded because he somehow overcame the inefficiency of his equipment and the losses among his crew; Cook succeeded because his requirements were better catered for and his methods understood, and because, by the second voyage in 1772–5, he had mastered the scurvy and fever, which had still plagued Anson's crews.

The squadron as it eventually got into the south Atlantic was made up of the *Centurion* and the *Gloucester*, fifty-gun men-of-war, with crews, in theory, of 400 and 300 men; in fact, with only 170 seamen

[4] George Anson was born in 1697, of Staffordshire gentry, related through his mother to the Earl of Macclesfield, in 1718 Lord Chancellor. This political pull ensured rapid promotion, and he saw service in the Baltic and the eastern Atlantic. By 1723 he was a Captain, commissioned to put down piracy off the Carolinas and the Bahamas. In command of the *Centurion* in 1737, he served in the West Indies before being ordered to the Pacific on the voyage here described. Anson's reputation was then made, and he entered Parliament as Member for Hedon, Yorkshire. In 1746 he defeated the French off Cape Finisterre, captured £300,000 worth of coin and was created Baron Anson. As First Lord of the Admiralty, Anson radically reformed the administration of the dockyards and supply, and his administration was behind the successes won during the Seven Years War, in particular Hawkes' victory at Quiberon Bay. He died in 1762, an Admiral of the Fleet.

[5] *A Voyage Round the World, in the Years MXCCXL–IV*, by George Anson, Esq., Commander-in-Chief of a Squadron of His Majesty's ships sent to the South Seas. Compiled ... by Richard Walter, of His Majesty's Ship the *Centurion* on that expedition; 2 vols, London, 1748.

aboard, with auxiliary victualling ships. Having called at Madeira to take on 'the wines ... designed by Providence for the refreshment of the inhabitants of the Torrid zone', and touched at Brazil and Buenos Aires, they rounded the Horn at the worst time of the year. When they reached Juan Fernandez, half the crews were dead: but the survivors found Robinson Crusoe's verdant island delectable—'judge the emotion with which we eyed a large cascade of transparent water'. Here were quantities of seals and fish, and the Commodore set up his tent in a meadow surrounded by well-timbered hills.[6]

Disappointed of their political objectives in rousing the Spanish colonies to revolt, and then of plunder in Mexico, the expedition now stood off southwest to cross the Pacific for Canton, 'hoping to enjoy the advantages of an amicable and well-frequented port, inhabited by a polished people, and abounding with the conveniences and indulgencies of civilized life'.[7] In May 1742 they did not abound on *Centurion* or *Gloucester*: both by this time were 'extremely crazy'; the latter even had to be set on fire and 'blew up in black pillar of smoke'. *Centurion* then proceeded, with the remnants of the combined crews, across the enormous wastes of the Pacific; the scurvy got worse, due, they thought, to the sea-mists which contaminated the air. 'Perhaps,' writes the representative narrator, 'a distinct and adequate knowledge of the disease may never be discovered.' The blend of smugness and blank ignorance is characteristic. Yet the evidence stared them in the face, for at Tinian in the Marianas, their sick at once so much benefited from the fruit, particularly of the 'acid kind', that they recovered within a week. Limes, coconuts, guavas, bread-fruit abounded amid wonderful scenery and 'fortunate animals —sole lords of the happy soil'. But even here the 'Indians' had not escaped the violence of the Spaniards—'that haughty Nation, so fatal to a large proportion of the human race'; and there were mosquitoes too, and ticks. Then, arrived at Portuguese Macao, the British found the Chinese at Canton bored and incurious; but Anson took on some Lascars and Dutch seamen and made southeast for what was now his main objective—the Manila galleon, as it came into the Philippines from Mexico.

Sure enough, it appeared on schedule—the big *Nostra Signora de Cabadonga*, 550 men, 36 guns—and Anson had well prepared for the 'happy crisis' which might 'balance the account of all the past

[6] Anson, *op. cit.* The picture (in Vol. II, of plates) taken from the life, shows the officers walking elegantly in tricorn hats and formal coats in the tropics. Crusoe's island was in fact very attractive, so his physical hardship was not severe.

[7] Anson, *op. cit.* Vol. I, p. 278.

calamities'. He still had far too few men, and they mostly youths, but he had drilled them hard in 'the use of great guns', trained thirty marksmen to go aloft and, since there were not enough crew members to man the guns, assigned 'roving gun firers' who would fire any pieces that were ready, thus maintaining a more continuous fire. The Spaniards elected to make a fight of it, but the galleon was soon taken with a loss of sixty-seven killed and eighty-four wounded. Anson lost only three killed, and one lieutenant and fifteen men wounded. 'So little consequence,' runs the narrative, with justified complacency, 'are the most destructive arms in untutored and unpracticed hands.'

Having taken twice as many prisoners as his own crew, Anson soon brought *Nostra Signora de Cabadonga* into Canton, where the Chinese now treated him with much greater respect. They might well do, for the galleon contained 1,313,843 pieces of eight and 35,682 ounces of virgin silver—worth together nearly £400,000. It also contained valuable charts of the Pacific. So the Cantonese now thought Anson a more 'official person, the acquisition of wealth being a matter greatly adapted to the estimation and reverence of the Chinese nation'.[8] But they crammed the ducks and chickens sold to the English with stones, to increase their weight, and, for the same purpose, injected water into dead hogs. Tension mounted, and the mandarins prevaricated until, with 'trustyness and resolution', Anson's sailors extinguished a great fire in the city and stopped the consequent pillage. The Chinese authorities, then in better mind, gave them licence to depart; but the British left disillusioned with this 'polished' people with their 'affected evenness of demeanor'. In contrast to the '*philosophes*' in France, who made a cult of the Chinese from a distance, they thought the magistrates corrupt and the people thievish.

Anson's luck now held. Proceeding round the Cape—'the best provisioned port of call in the whole world'—they escaped a French fleet cruising in the Channel in a fog, and returned with their loot to immense civic rejoicings in London.

IV

After the conclusion of the Seven Years War in 1763, the British, already had more than they could manage, but they were alert for further enterprise. 'It was then possible,' after all, 'to make a peace that was an act of release, for untapped energies and expanding thought, in which action was not necessarily tied to fear, nor the future grimly dubious ...'. And now, though the fashionable conventions were urban, the 'romantic age' was beginning to stir, and

[8] *op. cit.* Vol. I, p. 389.

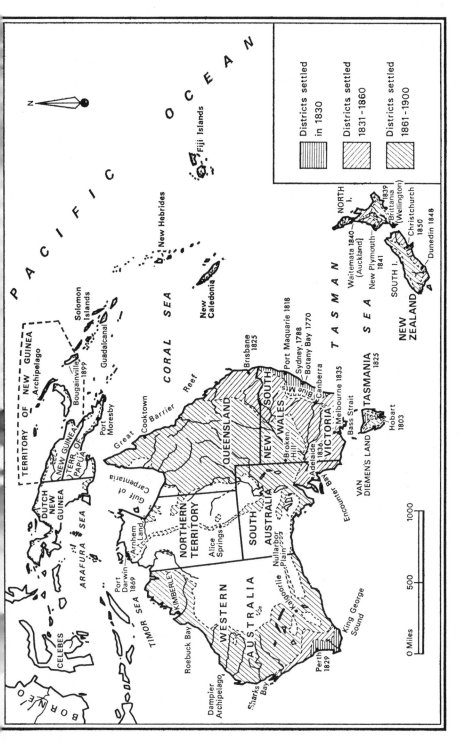

Settlement of Australasia 1770–1900

'down the well-disposed façades, stirring the curtains of tall and elegant windows, blew a stranger air, a wind that carried a wilder scent than that of the neat English hedgerows, that sounded too the echo of tempest that was now warm, now icy as from a pole. Salt-laden and astringent, or relaxing into a magical softness, it was the breath of islands magical and enchanting, of the greatest and most inscrutable of oceans'.[9]

The Elizabethan and Jacobean ambition for far-flung exploration now revived, though the rewards would prove, in the short term, less valuable. British governments were again determined to exploit, to be the first in discovery in the South Sea, and to forestall any French or Spanish colonizations of a great southern continent that might upset the then favourable balance of world power. They therefore resolved to give official backing to expeditions 'to search for unknown tracts that might exist within the immense expanse of ocean that occupies the whole of the southern hemisphere'.[10]

Magellan, Mendana, Drake and Quiros in the sixteenth century, Le Maire, Shouten and Tasman in the seventeenth, had all failed to find the answer; and Anson had been intent on other objectives. In 1764 Commodore John Byron, the grandfather of the poet, unaware that the French explorer Bougainville had been there already, had surveyed a potential strategic base for southern exploration in the Falkland Islands, where the first short British occupation followed while Cook was making his first voyage.

Byron's main objective had been to reconnoitre the Pacific entrance to the Northwest Passage; but the Commodore, who well deserved the appellation 'foul-weather Jack', had been nearly wrecked in the Straits of Magellan, and, with scurvy-stricken crews, had ignored his instructions and made direct across the Pacific for Batavia.

Then in 1766 Captain Wallis and Philip Carteret, in the *Dolphin* and the *Swallow*, baffled by contrary winds from the Antarctic off

[9] *The Journals of Captain James Cook: The Voyage of the Endeavour 1768–1771*, ed. J. C. Beaglehole, Hakluyt Society and Cambridge University Press, 1955. General introduction Vol. I, pp. *xxix–clxx*. This superb edition, in 4 volumes, covering all Cook's voyages, with its magnificent illustrations, is definitive. It includes a full account of Cook's colleagues, a substantial introduction on Polynesian history, a thorough account of the manuscript sources and many illustrations and maps. The great quarto volumes of the eighteenth-century editions are still worth consulting for their fine form and plates, but Dr Beaglehole's edition alone is based on the original manuscripts of Cook's own narrative.

[10] *A Voyage to the Pacific Ocean undertaken by Command of His Majesty*, Vols I and II by Captain James Cook, F.R.S., Vol. III by Captain James King, Ll.D., F.R.S.

southern Chile, proceeded to more genial latitudes, and Wallis fetched up on Tahiti, which he named, with singular banality, George III Island. Here the British first came upon a South Sea island with highly sophisticated inhabitants, where, 'under the bright day the air was soft, ... and after the day came the quick dark, flooding over the heights, the sombre tree filled valleys, the cascades'.[11]

The public now became more interested in the Pacific. Carteret, moreover, having found nothing more attractive than Pitcairn, turned northwest, rediscovered the Solomon Islands, first found by Mendana, discovered 'New Ireland' between New Guinea and New Britain and proceeded to Batavia, having at least proved the emptiness of a large area of ocean southwest of Chile. Meanwhile, Bougainville who, as A.D.C., had shared the hardships of Montcalm at Quebec, had also discovered Tahiti, which he named, more romantically, *Nouvelle Cythère*; he had also observed Samoa, failed to make the passage through Torres Strait, and returned to Europe by way of the Solomons, Batavia and the Cape.

Such was the limited knowledge available when the British government commissioned Cook to find out once and for all 'whether the unexplored part of the Southern Hemisphere be only an immense mass of water, or contain another continent as speculative geography seems to suggest'. Tahiti was already familiar and New Zealand known to exist. Cook's first expedition made for both.

James Cook was neither a shady privateer, like Dampier, nor a high-ranking sea officer with powerful political connections, like Anson: he was a self-made professional of transcendant ability who had come up the hard way. The son of a Yorkshire labourer of Scots descent and of a Yorkshire mother, at eighteen he had gone to sea in Newcastle colliers, and transferring in 1755, when the Seven Years War was imminent, to the Royal Navy as an ordinary seaman, had soon made his reputation by his masterly conduct of the charting of the St Lawrence and the Newfoundland coast.[12] In the Army he

---

[11] Beaglehole, *op. cit.* Vol. I, p. *xciv*.

[12] Born in 1782 at Marton, Cleveland, Yorkshire, Cook worked as a boy on the farm, then in a grocer's store near Whitby. Tiring of this incongruous employment, he signed on as apprentice, then mate, in Whitby colliers trading to London, Scandinavia and the Baltic, thus becoming inured to the North Sea. He joined the Royal Navy in H.M.S. *Eagle*, captained by Sir Hugh Pallisor, another Yorkshireman, who discovered his qualities. By 1759 he was Master of the *Mercury* on Wolfe's expedition to Quebec, then of the flagship *Northumberland*. When Pallisor became Governor of Newfoundland, in 1762, he appointed Cook to the command of the *Grenville* schooner, as Marine Surveyor of Newfoundland and Labrador, an appointment which led to Cook's publishing his *Marine Directions*, a standard work. Promoted Lieutenant on

would hardly have stood a chance of promotion; but in the Navy merit could count. From the beginning Cook knew what he was about and summed up the facts. 'All the ships,' he wrote, 'which attempted it before the *Endeavour* were unfit for it; although the officers employed in them had done the utmost in their power.'[13] The barque *Endeavour* was therefore chosen as peculiarly adapted to his purpose—a ship of 'shallow draught but sufficient burden, not to be found in ships of war of forty guns, nor in frigates, nor in East India Company ships, nor in large three-decked West India ships, nor indeed in any but North Country built ships, of such as are built for the coal trade'.[14] Unobtrusive and sturdy, the *Endeavour* and *Resolution* ploughed slowly through the long Pacific swell; but Cook had plenty of time and achieved explorations which dwarfed anything ever attempted before.

On his first voyage of 1768–71 in the *Endeavour*, 368 tons, cat-built at Whitby on an originally Scandinavian design, he rounded the Horn, unlike Anson, at the best time of year, the height of the southern summer; then, after a stay in Tahiti to observe the transit of Venus, which owing to the then defective techniques his expedition in fact failed to do, though they thought they had accomplished it, he proceeded to New Zealand which he charted in the next southern summer. He then turned northwest to discover an entirely unknown country in southeastern Australia which he called New South Wales. Cook next explored north into the tropics along the Great Barrier Reef, on which *Endeavour* was nearly wrecked, and, rounding Cape York, passed by the southern shore of Torres Strait, proving for the first time that Australia was a huge island separate from New Guinea, for Torres had not set eyes on the shore of the sub-continent. Cook then returned to England by Batavia and the Cape in July 1771.

The second voyage, 1772–5, 'Towards the South Pole and Round the World', in the *Resolution* (452 tons) and *Adventure*—which in 1773 lost contact with Cook—proved that the supposed great southern continent did not for any useful purpose exist. Sailing due south from the Cape, then east along the fringe of the Antarctic which he

his appointment to the *Endeavour*, Cook was made Commodore in 1771 and Captain in 1775, with a sinecure at Greenwich Hospital to increase his income. In 1776 he was awarded the Copley Medal of the Royal Society. In 1762 Cook married Mary Batty of Barking by whom he had six children, of whom three sons survived. The eldest, who reached the rank of Commander, was drowned at sea, the second died young at Cambridge and the third was lost in a storm in the West Indies; Mrs Cook lived to be ninety-three.

[13] *A Voyage towards the South Pole and Round the World*, written by James Cook, Commander of the *Resolution*, London, 1778, p. *xxvi*.

[14] Cook, *op. cit.* p. *xxv*.

penetrated more deeply than had any navigator before him and where he sensed the existence though not the size of the land mass, Cook returned to New Zealand and Tahiti. He discovered the Society Islands, came back to New Zealand, discovered Easter Island and turned south again far into the Antarctic and there found Georgia. He returned by New Zealand and the Cape, and on this voyage for the first time, he fully mastered scurvy.

His final voyage (1776–9) was made in the *Resolution* and *Discovery* (336 tons) 'to the Pacific Ocean for making Discoveries in the Northern Hemisphere to determine the position and extent of the west side of North America, its distance from Asia and the Practicability of a North passage to Europe'. For now, following the shift of emphasis in the Empire from the disaffected American colonies to India and the Far East, the old idea of a Northwest Passage had again been taken up. So, sailing again for the Cape, Tasmania, New Zealand and then Tahiti, Cook discovered the Sandwich Islands, of which the most important was Hawaii, proceeded to Nootka Sound north of Vancouver, coasted northeastern America and went on into the Behring Sea until blocked by the pack ice. Returning to Hawaii, Cook was taken for a God; but in 1779 he was murdered by the inhabitants when, after an apparently final farewell, the British returned to repair the foremast of the *Resolution* in Kealakekua Bay. Next year the expedition returned to the Behring Sea, but, again baffled by the pack ice, gave up the attempt to find an eastern exit from the Northwest Passage and returned by China and the Cape.

Such, in bare essentials, was Cook's enormous exploration: New Zealand charted, eastern Australia and the Great Barrier Reef and Cape York discovered, and Australia proved separate from New Guinea; Antarctica circumnavigated and the myth of a temperate great southern continent dispersed; a Pacific exit from the Northwest Passage proved impracticable. And besides all this, he had discovered whole new archipelagos in the Pacific. 'Cook's competence [had] changed the face of the world.'[15] The achievement, though it brought little profit at the time for no civilization was discovered, was decisive for the second British Empire—leading to the settlement of New Zealand and Australia, and linking up with the now more effective domination of India and the expanding commerce with the Far East; though only in late Victorian times would the British establish themselves in strategic islands in the Pacific.

[15] Beaglehole, *op. cit.* Vol. I, p. *xxiii.*

V

The enquiring minds of Cook and of his forceful colleagues Joseph Banks, a young man of great fortune who accompanied and recorded the first expedition,[16] and the botanist, Dr Solander, show the eighteenth century at its best; and Parkinson's admirable drawings vividly recall the explorations. Cook, who was probably a sceptic in religion, had no desire to convert the savages he encountered, but he recorded their behaviour with singular fairness, without moral indignation or contempt.

His account of Tahiti is famous, but irrelevant to the Empire.[17] His observations on New Zealand and Australia are here more pertinent, and though 'from an apprentice boy in the coal-trade to a Post Captain in the Royal Navy', he had 'no opportunity of cultivating letters', his style is all the more direct.

Cook's rule for dealing with savages was realistic but humane: first show them the use of firearms to convince them of European 'superiority of force', then, though always on guard, deal with them 'gently and honestly'. And these principles he carried out, both in New Zealand and Australia.

The Maori of New Zealand had to be convinced at once: on 7th October 1769, soon after dawn, a ship's boy, Nicolas Young, descried the high country behind the east coast of the North Island. Unlike Columbus, who diverted a promised reward to himself, Cook awarded the boy a gallon of rum, and named the nearest promontory Young Nick's Head—though, justly or not, a midshipman thought him a 'son of a bitch', whose 'evil communications corrupt[ed] good manners'. Cook and Tupia, the Tahitian interpreter whose language proved easily intelligible to the Maori, now went ashore in the pinnace and some ship's boys in the yawl; whereat the Maori tried to cut off and spear them. Cook and the marines had to shoot to kill. The next day the Maori staged a war-dance, 'distorted their mouths, lolling out their tongues, and turn'd up the whites of their eyes with a strong hoarse song'; their canoes had again to be fired upon and men killed—though three Maori youths, captured, clothed and fed, at once became 'cheerful and merry'. Cook's men concluded that the New Zealanders were a 'sett of very obstainate and stubborn kind of

[16] See *The Endeavour Journal of Joseph Banks, 1768–1771*, 2 vols, ed. J. C. Beaglehole, 1962.

[17] See Alan Moorehead, *The Fatal Impact*, London, 1966, for a vivid popular account, both of the contact with Tahiti and of the other explorations.

People', and he termed the place Poverty Bay 'because it afforded nothing that we wanted'.

Even in the Bay of Plenty, where the Maori brought them lobsters, mussels and eels, there was soon a quarrel and the Maori shook their paddles and *Pattoos* (war clubs) in defiance. Indeed, wrote Cook, 'They handled all their arms with great Agility, particularly their long pikes and lances, against which we had no weapon that is an equal match except a loaded musket'.[18] They were a 'strong raw-boned well made active People, rather above than under the common size, all a very dark brown colour with black hair, thin black beards and white teeth'. And they appeared healthy and long-lived. One war canoe, designed like a New England whaler, measured over sixty-eight feet, by five-foot beam and three-and-a-half-foot draught. The Maori sang songs 'harmonious enough, but very doleful to a European ear, and in most of their dances they appear[ed] like madmen, jumping and stamping with the feet, making strange contortions with every part of the body and a hideous noise at the same time'.[19] They wore 'thrummed matts and cloth like sail cloth', and the warriors round caps with black feathers, and they lived well, off fern roots, fish and wildfowl, and baked tame dog: there appeared to be no other mammals but a few rats. They viewed sheep and goats with 'a kind of stupid insensibility'. As to religion, apart from a belief in a supreme God, 'these people trouble themselves little about it'. They had lived for generations in the mountainous, well-wooded islands—robust, cheerful, head-hunting cannibals. Yet, in spite of their initial belligerence, Cook's methods worked. 'After they found that our Arms were so much superior to theirs and that we took no advantage of that superiority, and a little time given to reflect upon it, they ever after were our good friends.'[20] Significantly, he concluded that it 'did not appear to him at all difficult for strangers to form a settlement in this country. They seem to be too much divided among themselves to unite in opposing, by which means and a kind and gentle usage the colonist would be able to form strong parties among them.' One could divide and rule.

VI

The British experience in Australia was very different. On 19th April 1770, at 6 a.m., with topsails close reefed, *Endeavour* first came

---

[18] Beaglehole, *op. cit.* Vol. I, p. 189.

[19] Beaglehole, *op. cit.* p. 285.

[20] Beaglehole, *op. cit.* p. 282.

in to the southeast coast of what would be New South Wales, so-
called from the apparent resemblance to part of the northern shore
of the Bristol Channel. Cook named the first promontory Point
Hicks 'because Lt Hicks first discovered this land'.[21] They observed
a 'round hillick, very much like the Ramhead going into Plymouth
Sound ... and the country appeared green and woody, the seashore
... all white sand'. As the yawl came inshore, the Pacific surf prevented their landing and the few aborigines around decamped.
Only one man, greatly daring, stood his ground. As the sailors rested
on their oars, Tupia shouted in Tahitian across the surf, but neither
he nor the Australian understood each other. The few aborigines,
who now half-heartedly resisted, only had 'darts' and were soon dispersed with a couple of musket shots: in Botany Bay 'all they seemed
to want was for us to be gone'. They had long, four-pronged spears
pointed with fish-bones, more for spearing fish than humans, but
their throwing sticks could send 'darts' accurately up to fifty yards:
'I do not,' wrote Cook, 'look upon them as a warlike People, on the
contrary I think them a timorous and inoffensive race, little inclined
to cruelty.'[22] Both men and women were entirely naked, and appeared
to live on small fish, mussels and oysters which they roasted or
stewed. There are, of course, worse diets. They also greedily devoured turtle, but rejected bread. Indeed, as in Dampier's experience,
they were totally uninterested in everything the Europeans showed
or gave them.

Further up the coast, behind the Great Barrier Reef in tropical
Australia, Cook found that the people had their noses pierced with a
transverse bone, and painted their bodies 'the colour of wood, soot,
or dark chocolate', with streaks of red ochre and white pipe-clay. Unlike Dampier in the northwest, Cook considered that these northeastern Australians 'had far from disagreeable features'; and their
voices, far from being guttural, were 'soft toned'.[23]

As for the country, the trees and bush were flimsy and sparse so that
settlers need not, as in North America, fell thick forest; Cook
admired the brilliant 'Cocatoos, Lorryquets and Parrots'. And Europeans now first observed a proper kangaroo: 'I saw this morning,'
he wrote, 'one of the animals before spoke of. It was of a light
mouse colour and the full size of a greyhound and shaped in every
respect like one, with a long tail which it carried like a greyhound, in
short I would have taken it for a wild dog, but for its walking or
running in which it jumped like a hare or a deer.'[24]

Where the Maoris had been belligerent, then briefly tamed, the

[21] Beaglehole, *op. cit.* p. 299.
[22] Beaglehole, *op. cit.* p. 396.
[23] Beaglehole, *op. cit.* p. 395.
[24] Beaglehole, *op. cit.* p. 352.

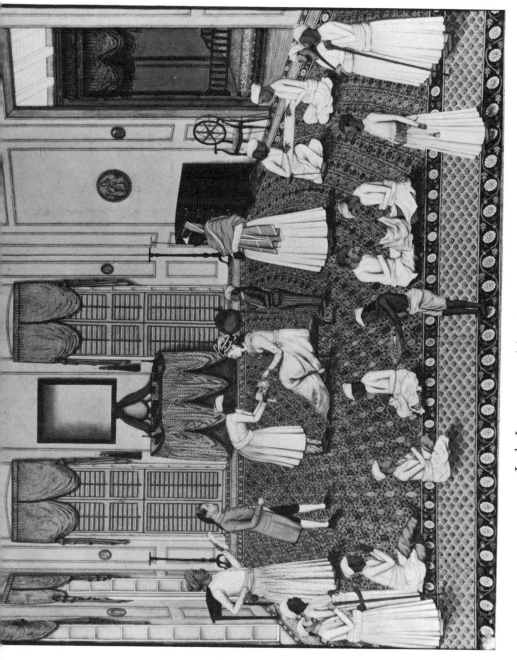

Lady Impey supervising her Indian household

Tea-planter overseeing his Indian workers (from a late 18th-century Indian painting)

An Englishman smoking a hookah, *c*. 1750 (from a miniature by Dip Chand)

Warren Hastings, first Governor-General of India

Lord Clive of Plassey, by Gainsborough

1st Afghan War: troops in the Kojak Pass

Soldiers in the Bengal Infantry, *c*. 1790

Mutineers' attack on the redan battery at Lucknow

Mutineer cavalry attacking infantry square at the Battle of Cawnpore, 1857

Blowing up the Kasmir Gate, Delhi

Captain Hodson arresting the King of Delhi

19th-century Indian 'Bazaar' painting

Prison ship in Portsmouth Harbour (drawn and etched, 1828)

Port Jackson, the first chief British settlement in New South Wales

Australian aborigines had been entirely evasive—they had baffled even Cook. But he thought better of them than had Dampier. Apparently 'the most wretched people on earth', he thought them, in this fine climate 'far more happier than we Europeans, being wholly unacquainted not only with the superfluous but the necessary inconveniences so much sought after in Europe, they are happy in not knowing the use of them. They live in a tranquillity which is not disturbed by inequality of condition.' No intellectual, and untouched by the romantic cult of the noble savage, Cook, who had known the eighteenth-century social order from below, may well have reached this sad conclusion through his own experience.

By 1779, when he was hacked to death on Kealakekua beach in Hawaii, Cook had become the most important of all British explorers. But it was not for his navigations that he had been made a Fellow of the Royal Society and awarded the Copley Gold Medal. It was for his conquest of scurvy.

As early as 1754 the Scots physician James Lind (1716–94), horrified at Anson's losses by the disease, had published the first *Treatise on the Scurvy* written from observation at sea, and had recommended fresh vegetables, orange and lemon juice, as a remedy. And although the Admiralty did not order lemon juice for the navy till 1795, Cook was ready to try out his advice. During his first expedition he had lost thirty men out of eighty-five, but mainly from fever at Batavia; in the second he lost only one through illness, and that consumption. The recorder of Anson's voyages had attributed the apparently irremediable illness to sea-mist; and Cook himself met two Dutch East Indiamen, one with a hundred and fifty and the other with forty-one men down with it. But by observation, common sense and the discipline of an unpopular hygiene, Cook had found the answer. And if 'marmalade of yellow carrots inspissated till it is the thickness of fluid honey'—recommended by the knowledgeable Baron Storche of Berlin—had been disappointing, in Cook's own quasi-Germanic phrase, it was 'the never enough to be recommended' sauerkraut, the galoup of lemons and oranges, the infusion of sweet wort and water at sea, along with the scurvy grass, celery and fruit obtained in Tahiti, New Zealand and the other islands, that had proved the sovereign remedy.[25] Most of the Elizabethan, Stuart and early Hanoverian admirals had seen dozens of their men regularly die in undermanned ships; one could now make huge voyages with a new confidence.

Further, though the basic design of ships was little altered during the eighteenth century, great improvement had been made in steering when the tiller had been superseded by yoked rudders controlled by a

[25] Cook, *Voyage Towards the South Pole and Round the World*, p. xxxii.

wheel; fore and aft sails had been better developed to sail nearer the wind, and copper sheathing introduced.[26] And although the problem of finding longitude remained baffling until accurate chronometers were invented by 'Longitude' John Harrison in 1775, Cook had one on his second voyage—'our trusty guide the watch'.[27]

While the politicians and the generals were losing the American empire, Cook thus presented his country with the prospect of a new if undeveloped one in the south Pacific, and the promise of a more far-flung and regular sea power to maintain it. His magnanimity and fairness would also promote a more humane concept of empire, while he had precisely fulfilled his stated purpose: 'to continue for Britain the reputation of taking the head of all nations in exploring the globe'.

[26] See J. H. Parry, *Trade and Dominion*, pp. 203–57.

[27] Parry, *op. cit.* p. 227. Harrison (1693–1776), from childhood 'attracted to machinery on wheels', had received a scanty education and was never able to express his ideas clearly in writing'. But this obstinate Yorkshireman, who was abominably treated by the authorities over the promised award of £20,000 for an accurate determination of longitude, got the full sum three years before his death through the personal intervention of George III. His chronometers are on view in the Meridian House at Greenwich.

BOOK III

Industrial Revolution and the Second British Empire

1784–1867

CHAPTER 13

Powerhouse of the World

The American decision to leave the Empire proved a turning point in world history; for the British at the time it was only one aspect of the mortal conflict with France, the climax of a second Hundred Years War. Since the Wars of William III and of the Spanish Succession, this intermittent struggle had determined the fate of western Europe and its dependencies in America and the East. And if the American colonies were lost, the wars with France and Spain were won.

As a result the British retained and augmented their paramountcy in India and extended it to Burma, consolidating the massive strategic base for their power in the East and Australasia. They regained control of the Atlantic, the Caribbean and the western Mediterranean, and, after the Napoleonic Wars, extended it by the annexation of Malta and the control of the Ionian isles to the Levant. They took over the Cape Colony and Ceylon from the Dutch, and Mauritius from the French; under the Regency they established themselves at Singapore, and in 1842 at Hong Kong. The second war with the United States of 1812–14 fended off the American attempts on Canada, and a strategic base on Vancouver Island could be developed on the north Pacific; while the convict settlement made in Australia in 1782 began to take on strategic importance both for the south Pacific and New Zealand. The British emerged from a struggle for existence, when the island base itself was threatened with invasion, to become the greatest world power of the nineteenth century with an overwhelming naval and industrial supremacy.

In the wars with revolutionary and Napoleonic France they had disposed of an unprecedented and extra-European power. Their navy now dominated the oceans and the sea routes to the markets in the Americas and the East, soon to be exploited by the Industrial Revolution of which the British had been the pioneers. The commercial wealth accumulated by a maritime trading people had financed a new dimension of production, following the mechanization of textile industries by water and steam power; new techniques in heavy industry based on coal and iron; and, in the early nineteenth century, the application of steam power to transport on railroads. This Industrial Revolution and the cumulative technological developments that followed, in which the British had so long a start, provided the staying power and paid for the alliances which proved decisive against Napoleon. It then developed by leaps and bounds into the immense British prosperity of the 'fifties and 'sixties, with its individualist enterprise and unprecedented wealth, culminating in the mid-Victorian *Pax Britannica* based on naval supremacy and extended, in the absence of competition, by bluff.

The changes of political power in the island which coincided with these events and determined the future of the Empire, from the Younger Pitt taking office in 1783 to the death of Palmerston in 1865, divide roughly into three phases.

The first, from 1783 to 1832, was overwhelmingly Tory in the old style, its governments elected on the old and very limited franchise— a continuation of the eighteenth-century order under which the British fought off the French and attacked and contained social discontent at home. The second began with the Reform Bill, with its momentous extension of the franchise, and, ending in 1846, saw a new kind of government bent on 'improvement', a novel idea, and reflecting a consensus in politics between the reforming Whigs and the Tory followers of Sir Robert Peel. The third phase of renewed Whig ascendancy followed Peel's attempt, which temporarily wrecked the Tory Party, to bring in free-trade: it lasted for nineteen years, culminating in Lord Palmerston's last administration (1859 to 1865), which witnessed the climax of mid-Victorian power, prosperity and enterprise.

If internally the political theme was adaptation and 'improvement', externally it was the assertion of sea power backed by industrial supremacy and immense wealth. If one recalls only the most decisive naval actions, it will be observed that, despite reverses in the West Indies and on the Continent, Pitt's essential purpose was achieved. In 1794, on the 'glorious first of June', the French Atlantic fleet was destroyed off Brest; by 1797 the Spaniards had been defeated off Cape St Vincent and the Dutch fleet crippled off Camperdown. In 1798 Nelson won the Battle of the Nile, more decisive than Trafalgar, wrecking Napoleon's strategy for the conquest of the East and bringing the whole Mediterranean under British control. Finally, in 1805 the Battle of Trafalgar confirmed that the French attempt on the island base had failed, and British sea power as predominant throughout the world. With this command of the oceans, in 1808 the British could regain a foothold on the Continent—this time on the Iberian peninsula—and help directly, as well as financially and by blockade, to wear down Napoleon's over-extended empire. And it was sea power that confirmed the British position in India and Canada on opposite sides of the world.

Emerging victorious from the last of these French wars for empire, the British were thus able to restore the balance of power in Europe in their own interest. They rehabilitated France, created a buffer state in the Low Countries and prevented the partition of Germany between the autocrats of Prussia, Austria and Russia. Further, as the interests of the Continental autocracies and the West again began to diverge, British sea power and diplomacy supported liberal and nationalist movements in Greece and later in Italy, and greatly contributed to the independence of Latin America and to maintaining the sovereignty of Portugal. And when in the 'fifties the Russians tried to dominate the Balkans and the Levant, an ambition already apparent under Catherine the Great, a Franco-British alliance checked them in the Crimean War and gave the decadent, but politically necessary, Turkish Empire a new lease of life. It was not until the Franco-Prussian War that this power balance would be upset and the initiative pass to Imperial Germany, a great but still entirely European power, which would be twice contained by the mobilization of extra-European resources, continental and oceanic, in which the British Empire would play a decisive part.

II

In spite of the immense political and strategic commitments of this still essentially trading empire, made during the French wars and their aftermath and in early and mid-Victorian times, the Whig and Peelite governments after the Reform Bill had little imperialist vision. Palmerston, attempting to influence the power game in Europe, took a more aggressive stance, but it was not until the later nineteenth century, when Disraeli came to power with a new sort of party organization and a mass electorate to manage, and when British wealth and power had provoked increasing envy and British influence in Continental Europe and competitive power in industry were beginning to wane, that a much more deliberate imperialism set in. This policy reflected the growing popular nationalism infecting all Europe, that would be the curse of the nineteenth century and, by 1886, had found its academic voice in J. R. Seeley's *The Expansion of England*.

Meanwhile, the Whig–Peelite governments were mainly concerned not with the Empire but with 'improvement' at home and increasingly with free-trade with the entire world. If the concern with India and the Far East, constant since the seventeenth century, was now enhanced after the loss of the American colonies, governments still thought the colonies of settlement relatively unimportant and likely to hive off. They were far more preoccupied with the power balance in Europe, where the decisions were made, and with their own mature and immensely prosperous and creative civilization at home.

Sir James Stephen, for example, Permanent Under-Secretary of State for the Colonies from 1837 to 1847, was typically cautious and unforthcoming to projects of settlement and expansion. Born in 1789, son of an anti-slavery reformer of the same name, he married into the evangelical 'Clapham Sect'. A successful barrister, in 1825 he was appointed permanent counsel to the Colonial Office. He only once violated the sabbath, and that was in 1833 to draft the Bill abolishing slavery throughout the Empire. He overcentralized and overworked, and resigned through ill health. Then, in the casual fashion of the time, in 1849 he became Regius Professor of Modern History at Cambridge, where he was accused of heresy for denying the reality of hell-fire. He died at Koblenz in 1859. A high-minded evangelical lawyer, he was guyed unmercifully by the enthusiasts as Mr Oversecretary Stephen and Mr Mother Country, the embodiment of procrastination and indecision. It was not government policy that extended the early Victorian Empire, but mainly a spontaneous initiative of commerce and emigration.

At the beginning of the century the population had been about eleven million; when in 1867 Disraeli lowered the franchise it was nearly twenty-six. During the first half of the century roughly seven and a half million emigrants left the United Kingdom and, if half of them went to the United States, one and a half million went to Canada and about a million to Australasia. Such was the United Kingdom's contribution, voluntary or forced, to the vast emigration out of Europe at that time. The second British Empire would reach its greatest extent and most imposing appearance in the late nineteeth and early twentieth centuries; but it was this mainly voluntary early- and mid-Victorian migration that laid the foundation of the White Dominions, as it was the timely concession of self-government that kept them within the Empire.

India, on the other hand, had long been of great concern to governments and it was there, between Pitt's India Act of 1784 and the Mutiny of 1857, that the British did their greatest administrative work. They now gradually brought the entire sub-continent under one rule, direct or indirect, and under a peace which was more far-flung even than that of the Mughals. It is not the later, sometimes blatant and imperialist phase of empire, celebrated by Kipling and Elgar, which was the most important in world history. In spite of the heady imperialism of Joseph Chamberlain, the late-Victorian and Edwardian Empire was a satiated power, vast but vulnerable and on the defensive: reluctantly undertaking great new commitments out of strategic necessity. It was the mid-nineteenth century Empire which was the more creative and lasting.

Indeed, both in the Dominions of settlement and in India, at a time of great versatility, vigour and creativeness at home, the mid-Victorian British, like their kinsmen in the colonies, produced personalities of a neo-Elizabethan force and eccentricity; and in spite of much indecisive and dilatory manoeuvre, the statesmen and civil servants in the home country managed to combine the recognition of colonial self-government with the maintenance of empire. The mid-Victorian Empire, however casual, was bound together by the need for British protection and the need for British capital, while the new railroads and steamships overcame problems of communication which in the eighteenth century had appeared insuperable. And the mid-Victorians, both in the island and overseas, also fully maintained Cook's achievement of 'taking the head of all nations in exploring the globe'; in the Canadian Arctic and Far West, in Australasia, in Africa and in the Antarctic. The Victorian missionaries, also, though they often now appear provincial, even misguided, made an effort comparable to the Anglo-Saxon conversion of the Germans and Scandinavians, and more far-flung. If they were now, in Catholic eyes, schismatics, their influence nevertheless became world-wide.

The inventors, economists and entrepreneurs of the Industrial Revolution, the railway engineers and shipbuilders, the British scientists of the age of Darwin, the pioneers of the study of institutions, of the origins and comparative study of law, of anthropology and medicine, the surveyors and cartographers, all developed a new kind of thought and action. The nineteenth century saw the greatest British impact on world history: politically in the creation of new nations in Canada and Australasia, in the unification and pacification of India, in bringing modern administration and the prospect of self-government to vast populations in Asia and Africa; economically in the Industrial and Technological Revolutions; and intellectually in promoting a scientific outlook which gradually altered the prevalent view of the human condition throughout the world. Victorian literature, if not architecture or art, vastly enriched English speaking civilization. Mid-Victorian empire was only one aspect of this original vitality: at its centre was a dynamo of economic, administrative and intellectual enterprise. Though the mid-nineteenth century governments were far from imperialist, at the heart of the second British Empire were men of much greater range and influence than the hard realists who had sought commercial objectives within the first. It is significant that both Darwin and Huxley drew their original inspiration from expeditions of worldwide scope undertaken for the Royal Navy.

III

This tremendous impact, political, economic and intellectual, which would briefly make the British Empire the greatest of all the European dominations, could be made because the island base had not only survived the threat to its existence posed by the Revolutionary and Napoleonic Wars, but contained the threat of social disruption which accompanied and followed them. But the English Revolution never came off. Politically, the old establishment was adapted. Economically, in spite of much hardship, real wages rose by 40 per cent between 1824 and the mid-century. By the 'fifties and 'sixties great industry had broken the pre-industrial Malthusian cycle into a new dimension of growth. Nor, in spite of much recent opinion, was the Industrial Revolution built on a ruined countryside. The agricultural population doubled between the mid-eighteenth century and 1830: it provided the work-force for the expanding industrial towns, and the migration to the colonies of settlement. The Chartist protest in the 'forties, like the class war predicted by Engels, did not develop; with greater prosperity, the radical front broke up, as skilled workmen themselves formed craft unions to maintain their own rising standards of living against the mass of the unskilled. Modern research has exploded the myth that the 'trauma' of the Industrial Revolution so divided the nation that it never fully recovered. On the contrary, in spite of the sufferings of the farm-labourers and submerged urban poor in the 'twenties and 'thirties, most of the early- and mid-Victorians of all classes supported or took for granted the existing social order; and since revolution and reaction, menacing in the early nineteenth century, had been avoided, the country went forward with unimpaired momentum and confidence behind an adapted but traditional leadership. Mid-Victorian England was vigorous, up-to-date and versatile, with the skilled work-people, as well as the expanding professional and *rentier* classes, behind a still predominantly aristocratic ruling class which had come to terms with a new business plutocracy. From a commercial nation

Great Britain had become the greatest industrial power in the world, if at the price of a top-heavy economy and a population out of scale with its agricultural resources; while, as usual, the colonial Empire —not as yet, save in India, much valued—remained a commercial proposition rather than one of territorial domination and ambition. But it too now felt the impact of a dynamic, improving society, as did India and the underdeveloped countries outside the Empire: for the aims of free-trading mid-Victorians were expansive and cosmopolitan not, as in the Old Colonial system, restrictive; and the colonies of settlement, coming of the same stock, now began to show their own initiative, often backed by colonial reformers at home.

The modifications of the Old Colonial system forced on the British during the French wars had palpably benefited oceanic trade. In 1825 Huskisson at the Board of Trade made the first important move to allow foreign countries to trade direct with the British colonies, so long as the goods were the product of the country which shipped them—a measure which safeguarded British shipping, but which otherwise allowed free competition. In 1819 the return to the gold standard had restored stability, and after the repeal of the Corn Laws in 1846, of the Navigation Acts in 1849 and after Cobden's Treaty with France in 1860, British and French capitalists settled down to exploit the enormous extra-European sources of raw materials and the expanding markets of a free-trade economy.

As the old restrictive policy was discarded, and a worldwide commerce and industry were unshackled, the mid-Victorian Empire began to look more promising. In the early nineteenth century British capital had been invested mainly in Continental Europe, and in North and South America, but in the mid-century it financed vast railway projects in India and Canada and made big loans to colonial governments. And although trade with the British colonies of settlement at first appeared relatively unimportant in this global exploitation, as their population increased and developed their resources, they began to appear no longer liabilities but assets. And both in Australia and Canada, the discovery of gold stimulated the world economy.

The development of communication was also decisive. Until the mid-century, shipping remained predominantly under sail, but governments could not ignore the promise of faster mail services. In 1837 the Peninsula Steam Navigation Company was accorded a contract to carry mails to Lisbon, Cadiz and Gibraltar. In the following year the service included Malta and Alexandria, where Thomas Waghorn independently organized an overland service from Alexandria to Suez, where mails and passengers transferred to a mail ship from

Bombay.[1] The journey to India, which in Warren Hastings' time had generally taken six months, was now cut to not much more than two. In 1840 the Company contracted to carry mail and passengers right to India and became the Peninsula and Oriental—the Imperial P & O.

In *topees* and *puggarees*, or veiled and swathed, the passengers were laboriously conveyed across the desert in *tongas*, stopping at the equivalent of motels; and, if the 2000-ton P & O's were stiflingly hot and reeking of coal, the ticket did, at least, include unlimited whisky, brandy and wine. It was not until 1858 that a railroad linked Alexandria and Suez, and not until 1869 that the Suez canal was opened and the passage to India cut to six weeks; but the mid-Victorians no longer faced the hazards and tedium of the voyage round the Cape. By 1856 the P & O's even went on to Australia.

The Atlantic passage was faster but more exacting. In 1842 Dickens described the discomforts of an Atlantic voyage in January in the *Britannia*, the crack ship of the Cunard line. He called his 'state-room' a 'preposterous box',[2] and compared the salon to a 'gigantic hearse'; once on deck, the 'bright cold sun, the bracing air, the crisply curling water, the thin white crust of morning ice which cracked ... beneath the lightest tread was irresistible'.[3] But two days out, the Atlantic had crushed the lifeboat like a 'walnut shell' and torn the planking from the paddle boxes; the ship's cook had been found drunk and the stewards fell down the companion-way. But when they all fetched up, unexpectedly, near Halifax, Nova Scotia, with 'the sun shining as on a brilliant April day in England, and the land streaked with light patches of snow', and thence proceeded to Boston, the *Britannia* had crossed the ocean in eighteen days.[4]

The British and American Royal Steam Packet Company had been founded in 1839 by Samuel Cunard, an American owner of

---

[1] Waghorn (1800–50) born at Rochester, the son of a shopkeeper, had worked in the Bengal pilot service, and observed the efficiency of a primitive steamer during the first Burmese war. Coal consumption was such that long voyages were still impracticable, so he organized camel caravans from Cairo to Suez, and in 1829 himself proved it possible to get to Bombay and return within three months, as against the normal six one-way by the Cape. He induced the local Arabs, with whom he got on good terms, to collaborate with rather than rob the caravans, and became a pioneer of tourism to Egypt, where Shepheard's Hotel was already established by 1844.

[2] *American Notes* for general circulation, London (1850 edition), p. 1. The frontispiece depicts a wooden paddle steamer with an enormous funnel, also rigged for sail to be on the safer side. On her maiden voyage, in July 1840, she had crossed the ocean in a fortnight.

[3] *ibidem* p. 4.

[4] *ibidem* p. 14.

whalers out of Halifax, and had contracted, like the P & O, to carry mails for the British governments.[5] By 1855 the steamers were iron, and by 1862 powered by screws. In the eighteenth century, the crossing had generally taken over two months. Now even the fast American clippers were superseded. Cunard had to come to Great Britain to get his ships built, where Isambard Kingdom Brunel was already the most famous shipbuilder in the world.[6] He had designed the *Great Western*, which in 1838 had crossed the Atlantic in fifteen days, and by 1845 the iron *Great Britain* was screw-propelled. By 1851 Brunel was advising the Australian Steam Navigation Company, and in 1853–8 he had constructed the *Great Eastern*, far the largest ship afloat. She had an original double-skin construction, and though commercially a failure and relegated to laying cables, anticipated the great liners of the early twentieth century. In the 'fifties other lines had also developed: the Royal Mail Steam Packet to the West Indies and South America, the Union Castle to South Africa.

So in the first half of the nineteenth century a revolutionary network of swift communications by sea was linking up the Empire; and by the 'seventies the British had as enormous a lead over all competition in the merchant marine as in the Royal Navy, now equipped with 'ironclad' coal-burning capital ships, to the disgust of those trained to the clean, silent and traditional skills of sail. Railroads, too, had now startlingly diminished distance, and here, also, the British were far ahead. During the 'thirties, Brunel had designed and carried through vast projects for the Great Western Railway. By 1859 his bridge spanned the Tamar at Saltash, and he had advised on railroads in Bengal and Australia. By 1853 a railroad ran from Montreal to Maine, in the United States, and by the 'sixties the strategic Grand Trunk Railway from Halifax to Montreal had been financed by the British government. The construction of railroads in India, begun under Dalhousie and financed by Indian taxation, proceeded during the 'sixties and 'seventies, on a massive scale. These enterprises by sea and land, unheard of in the slow-moving eighteenth century, were spreading a network of rapid transport over the vast Empire, now drawn closer by the electric telegraph, and in the

[5] Cunard, who was on board the *Britannia* on her first voyage, settled in England, and was made a baronet; he died in 1865, worth about £350,000.

[6] I. K. Brunel (1806–59), son of Sir Marc I. Brunel, a French *émigré* of genius from Normandy, who had first made his name in America, came to England in 1799, where he had greatly cheapened the construction of ships, improved the Chatham dockyard and pioneered steam navigation on the Thames. Isambard was as great a railway engineer as designer of ships, but over-reached himself in the construction of the 20,000-ton *Great Eastern*, had a stroke at her trials and died ten days afterwards.

'seventies by reliable cables, first laid across the Atlantic in the 'fifties and now operating under the oceans to Bombay, Canada, and to Melbourne and Wellington in the Antipodes.

IV

Thus the mid-Victorian Empire backed by the great industry, increasing wealth and unchallenged naval power that had emerged from the Industrial Revolution and the Napoleonic Wars, developed with a spontaneous drive of commerce, settlement and exploration. On the darker side, even the appalling conditions of the rural and urban poor in the early nineteenth century, and the famine in Ireland, had contributed to the dispersion.

By the mid-century great problems had thus become urgent. How to combine imperial administration with local self-government; assuage the friction between modern and primitive societies; deal with the status of Europeans in Asian civilizations and with traders and missionaries who had outrun the flag? Most urgent, a new relationship had to be worked out between the home country and the colonies of settlement. But, contrary to most early nineteenth-century expectation, as the decades passed, the question became clearly not whether they would stay within the Empire, but on what terms.

Pervading all was a profound change of intellectual climate. Humanitarian improvement, Christian evangelical zeal, professional scientific method and technology, and romantic insight had all derived from the eighteenth century; but they had developed in contrast to the eighteenth-century orthodoxy, and they now gave the nineteenth century a new, more high-minded tone, more constructive and professional, and even more self-confident. How the problems of the Empire were tackled and the power structure which made them manageable was maintained will now be considered. They were tackled, as might be expected, in a piecemeal, empirical and often casual way, but on balance with success: in India, Canada and the West Indies; in Africa, now including the Cape; in Australia, New Zealand and the Far East.

CHAPTER 14

Koompani Bahadur; Burma; the Mutiny

In 1793, the first year of the war with Revolutionary France, an able report appeared on the affairs of the East India Company,[1] and it dwelt at length on 'the difficulties of extending our commercial pursuits under the native governments'. The Raja of Benares, for example, 'like most of the Chiefs of this country', was 'too jealous of his own personal importance to assent with sincerity to Rules which included the very necessary regulation of his own conduct';[2] while the 'capricious imposts of the rulers of Oudh combined with the disordered state of Upper Bengal' and 'interruption from the lawless subjects of a weak government' to disrupt the Company's trade.

In 1783–4 the loss on wool exported to Bengal had been nearly £5,000; and the net loss over 1783–9 more than £26,000. Even 'the accoutrements of Maratha Cavalry [were] not now made of woollen cloth but of chintz'.[3] Only the trade in metals for armaments had held up, with a profit of £4,917. But cotton and silk goods were still much better and more cheaply made in India, and 'their calicoes better than our linen'. Bombay showed a loss on woollens at £42,000, profit on metals £10,855, while the illicit and immense private trade still eroding the Company's monopoly was so fluctuating as to 'baffle computation'. Although, on average, twenty-four of the big East Indiamen went yearly out to Asia and earned profits by their passenger and carrying trade, the quantity and value of private goods on board and on the foreign ships—particularly American—which defied the monopoly, exceeded the legitimate commerce.

---

[1] *The First, Second and Third Reports of the Select Committees appointed by the Court of Directors of the East India Company to take into consideration the export trade from Great Britain to the East Indies*, London, 1793.

[2] *ibidem* p. 11.

[3] *ibidem* p. 13.

The Company, of course, had great revenues from the territories it controlled, but these were eaten up by war, and since 1773 the deficit had been financed by loans from government. The main asset was now the trade to Canton, where opium was exchanged for tea, and where other Europeans were still excluded. Indeed the profits of the China trade alone maintained the dividend, fixed at 10 per cent in 1793, roughly $3\frac{1}{2}$ per cent on the price of the stock. Although the perquisites and patronage of the Directors remained substantial, the East India Company was becoming more insolvent; yet it was bound to extend its control of Bengal and Bihar, the Circars and Madras and the protected areas of the Carnatic, of Malabar and Bombay, as the Mughal Empire lapsed into final anarchy. India was no decadent civilization; but outside the Company's territories it was being fought over by Mughal viceroys and military usurpers— by the Nizam of Hyderabad, the Sultan of Mysore, the Maratha potentates of central India, while in the northwest the Afghans continued their traditional incursions. French influence, scotched but not eradicated, had revived, and Bonaparte's invasion of Egypt was aimed at the East. The civilian East India Company could only protect its dividends by a military expenditure it could not afford; while the mastery of India had become essential to British power in the whole of the East.

By 1805 the first phase of this undesired but inevitable expansion had been achieved. Lord Cornwallis, the first Governor-General (1786–93 and 1805) under Pitt's India Act, and a forceful successor to Warren Hastings, checked the ambitious Tipu Sultan of Mysore; then Lord Mornington, from 1801 Marquess Wellesley, and his formidable brother Arthur, later Duke of Wellington, had crippled the Maratha power. The Company now controlled Delhi, still the imperial capital, the Circars and the Carnatic on the eastern coast, and the southwestern coast up to Kanara, as well as the original base at Surat above Bombay. Oudh, Hyderabad, the remnant of Mysore and the Maratha territories along the east coast and in central India were now 'protected' states. After Trafalgar, French sea power had been destroyed: and in 1810, after their base in Mauritius had been mopped up, French influence was finally eradicated.

The aged Mughal, Shah Alam, blinded in 1788 by the Afghans, was now a pensioner of the British, who accorded him and his successors, Akbar II and Bahadur Shah, a formal respect and sanctioned their own rule by Mughal political and cultural prestige. 'Shah Alam, was a brave and cultured man, though a shifty diplomatist and an unsuccessful ruler'; Akbar II was 'exceedingly good looking . . . a venerable white beard added dignity to his countenance, while his dark intelligent eye impressed all in his favour'. Bahadur Shah, the last of the Mughals, deported to Rangoon after the Mutiny at eighty-two, was 'a poet and a literary patron ... with his own niche in the Urdu pantheon ... still affectionately remembered by the people', whose court was a cultural influence of great value. With the royal patronage it became the centre of the second Delhi period of Urdu literature, whose brightest star was the great Ghalib'.[4]

Horrified at the expense of these conquests, the Directors recalled Wellesley in 1805 and sent out Cornwallis again, who died within the year; but when in 1813 their charter was renewed, it was their political responsibility that interested the government. The monopoly was curtailed, and ten years later, save for that over the China trade, abolished. Finally in 1833, the Whig government bought the Company out for an annuity of £630,000 charged on the revenues of British India and the India market was opened to free-trade. This decision amply paid off: the volume of trade greatly increased and the trade balance became favourable; the old problem of finding bullion to pay for Indian goods was solved as Lancashire cotton manufacturers entered the Indian market. 'Between 1834 and 1856 the export trade of India increased by 188 per cent from £7,990,000 to £23,000,000 and the import trade increased by 227 per cent from £4,260,000 to £13,400,000. This economic transformation was the background to the extension of territory and improvement of administration under successive Governors-General between 1815 and 1857,'[5] though its price was the ruin of the old-style Indian productivity.

The political expansion went on. After the third Maratha War all central India was pacified; and the Gurkhas of Nepal were diverted from their normal depredations to become the most formidable fighters in the Company's armies. Then the British secured their frontiers in the northwest. In 1834 Sind was conquered, and in 1849, after ferocious wars with the Sikhs, Dalhousie annexed the Punjab. In 1856 Oudh was taken over. The entire sweep of northern India from Baluchistan and the Afghan border to the mouth of the Ganges was now under British control. Burma, too, in part conquered in 1824–6, was annexed in 1852. Save for Gujerat, Kashmir and Rajputana and the numerous protected states, the sub-continent was now ruled directly by the Company, whose regime reached its climax under Dalhousie. For it was not until 1858, after the Mutiny, that the government of India was transferred to the Crown.

This enormous area was still ruled by the Company under Pitt's

[4] Sir Percival Spear, *Twilight of the Mughuls*, Cambridge, 1951, pp. 66–83.
[5] E. L. Woodward, *The Age of Reform, 1815–1870*, Oxford, 1938, p. 389.

India Act of 1784. Cornwallis, though he had accepted the appointment 'against his will and with grief of heart',[6] was more successful in India than in America, he had tackled the casual, corrupt aspects of the eighteenth-century regime, and administration became more disinterested, if more aloof. As the Company's responsibility increased, men of formidable creative power found scope. Soldiers turned administrators; administrators soldiers: they ruled provinces the size of European states. Residents and Agents dominated the courts of dependent princes, and threaded the mazes of Baluchi, Afghan and Central Asian intrigue. For, while southern and central India remained at peace, the British became involved on and beyond the Northwest Frontier in fierce campaigns and cloak and dagger risks against supposed Russian designs on India, part of complicated manoeuvres to control the Middle East.

II

Pitt's India Act had been designed 'to give the Crown the Power of Guiding the Politics of India with as little means of corrupt influence as possible', and its purpose was in time largely achieved. The Act had created a political Board of Control to superintend the Court of twenty-four Directors, whose powers had been strengthened over the stockholders. The Secret Committee—an executive originating in the days of Child—now comprised a Chairman, a Vice-Chairman and only two other members to deal with urgent political decisions, and it was distinct from the Committee of Secrecy that dealt only with shipping. Between 1784 and 1832 the powers of government over the Company increased and the parliamentary interest of the Directors and stockholders diminished: from 103 seats in 1806 to 45 in 1834.[7] Meanwhile, the standard of administration improved both at the centre and in the field. In the London office Charles Lamb, James Mill, Edward Strachey and Thomas Love Peacock were all able men; and John Stuart Mill, who entered the Office in 1823, served the Company until he resigned as head of it in 1858, in protest against the transfer of power to the Crown.

So while the French *Compagnie des Indes Orientales* had collapsed and the Dutch East India Company went bankrupt, the Eng-

---

[6] 'I have a great deal more business,' he wrote to his son, 'than you have in a whole schoolday, and I never get a holiday. I have rode upon an elephant, but it is so like going in a cart, that you would not think it very agreeable.' (*D.N.B.*)

[7] C. H. Philips, *The East India Company 1784–1834*, Manchester, 1940, p. 299.

lish improvised and adapted. An apparently unworkable dual control worked, and a faltering eighteenth-century Company notorious for nepotism at home and corruption abroad was proved able to rule a vast Asian empire.

The adaptation was made easier during the French wars, when the politicians concerned with India and officials of the Company were both much left to themselves as the curious compromise was worked out. For the first sixteen years Pitt's convivial Scots crony and political manager, Henry Dundas,[8] dominated the Board of Control and maintained his influence in Scotland by exploiting his patronage in India. 'After 1784 Dundas used all the skill that he had acquired plus the authority of the Board of Control, to induce the East India Company to distribute jobs in the East as he desired. The thirsty plains of India absorbed the stream of Scotland's young men of energy.'[9] Cornwallis, too, with typical understatement, wrote: 'It must be universally admitted that without a regulated body of Europeans our hold over these valuable dominions will be very insecure,' and tried to replace the old Indian hands with their 'splendid sloth and languid debauchery', with better men, better paid. As Warren Hastings had long ago recommended, miserable stipends, immense perquisites and openings for private trade now gave place to regular and substantial salaries. And by 1809, following an experiment with a college in Calcutta, an East India College was established at Haileybury. Samuel Henley, a Virginian loyalist who had taught at Harrow and translated Beckford's *Vathek*, originally written in French, was the first Principal, and Malthus one of the professors. Haileybury would train the Company's cadets for half a century.[10]

In the 'thirties and 'forties the administrative improvement made in Great Britain under the consensus of Whig and Peelite governments would be applied to India by an enlightened Asian despotism. But the first generation administrators and soldiers under Pitt's India Act—Sir John Malcolm, Sir Mountstuart Elphinstone, Sir Charles Metcalfe, who came to the front under Wellesley—had an eighteenth-century realism and caution, though this was touched with a new romantic insight. 'Their criterion was the test of reality ... To them, the most dangerous thing that could happen would be for a young man with no experience, no vision, no sense of the past or

[8] Raised to the peerage under Addington as Viscount Melville in 1801, before his impeachment and narrow acquittal for corruption in 1806.
[9] Edward Thompson and G. T. Garrett, *Rise and Fulfilment of British Rule in India*, London, 1935, p. 175.
[10] See Philip Woodruff, *The Men who Ruled India. Vol. I. The Founders*, pp. 279–86, for a good short account.

of the heroic nature of politics to be let loose on their conquests. "Were I to remain in India," wrote Malcolm in 1821, "I do not think that there is a human being (certainly no Nabob or Maharaja) whom I should dread half as much as an able Calcutta civilian ..." A simple administration, protection for the peasant—especially from such dangerous sophistications as English law—were all that was needed. It is the political philosophy ... of the romantic movement in Europe.'[11]

Indeed, the generation who created the main structure of empire were conservative, steeped in experience of India and convinced that change must be slow—'Great and beneficent alteration in society,' wrote Malcolm, 'to be complete, must be produced within the society itself; it cannot be the mere fabrication of its superiors, or of a few who deemed themselves enlightened.'[12]

In contrast to these sophisticated late-Georgian and Regency administrators and diplomats, the new insular Benthamite improvers, Evangelicals and the missionaries were brisk reformers who believed in progress. By 1843 the Governor-General, Lord Ellenborough, wrote that he could 'see no limit to the future prosperity of India, if it be governed with due respect to the interests of the people, with the resolution to make *their* well-being the chief object of government, and not the pecuniary advantage of a nation of strangers to which providence has committed the rule of this distant empire'. But in fact the reformers alienated the Indians, Muslim and Hindu. In 1835, for example, Macaulay, out to reform Indian education, dismissed in a notorious minute the best Muslim and Hindu literature with contempt, though at the dilapidated court of Delhi he would have found a culture more subtle than his own. Then, as communications improved, and the *memsahibs* came out, the British began to create a caste within a caste-ridden society. Where Malcolm, Elphinstone and Metcalfe really understood their subjects, and many early Victorian civilians shared their human approach, there would grow up a new type of administrator, intent on imposing Western standards on a medieval and alien civilization and raising a new class of Western-educated Indians uprooted from their own culture. This alienation, enhanced under Dalhousie by the impact of Western technology, as great roads, railways and canals were built, contributed to the Mutiny of 1857 that brought the Company's regime to an end—no nationalist war of liberation, but a conservative revolt. The contrast between the late eighteenth century and Regency rulers of India and their successors is symbolized by the change from the elegant neo-

[11] Michael Edwardes, *Glorious Sahibs*, London, 1968, p. 235.
[12] Edwardes, *op. cit.* p. 236.

classical British official buildings of the early nineteenth century to the incongruous Gothic of Victorian times and the heavy semi-oriental palaces that housed the bureaucracy in the final phase of empire.

III

The soldiers and civilians who mastered and ruled the vast territories of the Company, which now extended from the Northwest Frontier to Burma, and from the Himalayas to Ceylon, are quite as interesting as the Elizabethans. They had no illusions about the basis of their power. 'Our dominion in India,' wrote Sir Charles Metcalfe, acting Governor-General in 1835, before he went on to administer Canada, and echoing Warren Hastings, 'is by conquest; it is naturally disgusting to the inhabitants and can only be maintained by force.'[13] And on this basis the Governors-General and their officials tackled their problems in different ways. The first of them, Cornwallis, a soldier and a Whig aristocrat who followed Hastings' policies, tried to create in Bengal the kind of landed establishment he knew in England, and convert the hereditary Zemindars into landed gentry. He thus secured a limited but reliable revenue, at the expense of the peasants. Munro in Madras, on the other hand, based his revenue on security of tenure for the peasantry, a system that proved socially more advantageous.

Richard Colley Wellesley, 1st Marquess Wellesley, Governor-General from 1798 to 1805, was a very different character from Cornwallis—a talented emotional aristocrat from the Anglo-Irish ascendancy: arrogant, brilliant and aloof. 'I stalk about,' he wrote, 'like a royal tiger without even a friendly jackal.' The eldest son of the Earl of Mornington of County Neath, he had been removed from Harrow for 'barring out' a new headmaster; but he had found Eton more congenial, and at Christ Church, Oxford, won the Chancellor's medal for Latin verses on Captain Cook. Elected to a Studentship, he had left Oxford on succeeding to his father's estate. He wrote Latin verse all his life and made a study of Dante: his eloquence was Ciceronian.

In India he found most of the Europeans boring and vulgar and said so, quarrelled with the Directors of the Company over patronage and was furious at being made merely an Irish Marquess, a title he called a 'gilded potato'; but he created a secretariat of promising young men and his restless initiative proved as important as Clive's. His high-strung character and relatively liberal opinions

[13] Cited Woodruff, *op. cit.* Vol. I, p. 274.

contrast with the personality and opinions of his laconic and conservative brother, the first Duke of Wellington.

Wellesley was by temperament a conqueror and the French wars were his opportunity. He finished off the French-supported Tipu Sultan, the ruler of Mysore, checked but not destroyed by Cornwallis. Seringpatam was stormed, Tipu Sultan slain: it was the Plassey and Buxar of southern India. His brother, Sir Arthur Wellesley, who now gained the logistic experience to be brought to bear in the Peninsular War, then crippled the Marathas, organized under French officers. At Assaye in 1803 he won his first major battle, clinched by the defeat of the Bhonsla Raja at Argaon. In 1805 the British occupied Delhi. Wellesley then placed his political Residents and Agents in the courts of the 'protected' princes, and only Scind, Rajputana and the Punjab remained outside the Company's control. When in 1805, the Directors 'found this dazzling activity too much for their ledger'[14] and recalled the Governor-General, the last French influence had been eradicated and the British were paramount in India.

Pitt had always envisaged that the Governors-General under the India Act should not, like Warren Hastings, be career servants of the Company, but aristocrats, like Cornwallis and Wellesley, above the battle for promotion in India. These men were most of them able and disinterested, and they wielded great power.

No longer preoccupied with a fight for survival, the Company was now paramount. They greatly extended the bounds of British India. Among their proconsuls were Lord Moira (1813–23), in 1817 created Marquess of Hastings, and a veteran of the first American war; William Amherst (1823–8), in 1826 Earl Amherst of Arrakan, and Edward Law (1842–4), Earl of Ellenborough. All moved respectively against the Gurkhas of Nepal, the Burmese, and the Afghans, Baluchis, Sikhs and Marathas. Probably the ablest was the Marquess of Dalhousie (1848–56) through whom the Company extended its sway 'from the seven mouths of the Ganges to the five tails of the Indus'. James Andrew Brown Ramsay, first Marquess of Dalhousie (1812–1860), was the third son of the ninth Earl, one of Wellington's generals in the Peninsula and afterwards Commander-in-Chief in Canada and the West Indies. He came of ancient Scots nobility, with a touch of French ancestry.[15]

[14] Michael Edwardes, *British India*, London, 1967, p. 27.

[15] Like Wellesley, he had done badly at Harrow. 'I did little,' he wrote, 'but smoke, drink and dawdle.' ('While Winchester,' writes his biographer, 'was sending out many distinguished men, the years at Harrow were particularly lean.') And though Dr Butler commuted expulsion for breaking windows for the horrid but lighter penalty of translating six pages of Paley's *Evidences of*

In 1843 Peel appointed him Vice-President of the Board of Trade, and here he overworked on the problems created by the railway boom. In 1847 Lord John Russell appointed him to India, where, in spite of ill health, he stayed three years beyond the normal period of office. Dalhousie was extremely good-looking, with a fine voice and presence. He died at forty-nine, mainly from overwork in India.

The British now controlled all northern India, up to the natural frontiers in the northwest, and ended the centuries-old incursions out of central Asia that had been regular in Indian history. And, thinking in terms of eastern Europe and Middle Eastern politics, they became concerned with a potential threat from Russia, though the Russian frontier was two thousand miles away. The peoples of Nepal and the northwest were therefore recruited for the British armies in India.

This expansion was the sequel to initial disaster. In 1840–2 Lord Auckland (1836–42), one of the few incapable Governors-General, had sanctioned an ill-planned invasion of Afghanistan, a disgraceful disaster followed by an ephemeral revenge. In 1843 the spectacular reverse had led to a Baluchi rising in Sind and to the annexation of the country and the entire valley of the Indus. Under Dalhousie, following the first Sikh war of 1845, the second Sikh war of 1849 led to the annexation of the Punjab. Kashmir, also annexed, was sold to the Hindu Raja of Jummu, with lasting political consequences. This huge extension of territory involved the British in the power politics of the Northwest Frontier: British agents, playing the 'great game' against Imperial Russia, infiltrated Baluchistan, Afghanistan, Iran and the Khanates of central Asia. These wars, annexations and political intrigues necessary for the pacification of northwestern India and the perennially warlike Northwest Frontier, if incongruous with the still civilian intentions of the Company, gave scope to many outstanding men. As, for example, Sir Charles Napier and Lord Lawrence of the Punjab, who in 1863–9 was Viceroy of India under the Crown, and Sir James Outram and John Nicolson. Napier, best known as the conquerer of Sind (and by the pun—made not by him, but by *Punch*—'*Peccavi*, I have sinned') was a descendant of Charles II through the Lennox Dukes of Richmond, and on his father's side of Napier of Murchiston who had invented logarithms. He was a veteran of the Peninsular War, and also of the deplorable American War of 1812–14, and he had been Military Resident on Corfu. Like many early Victorian generals, he was fiercer than the

---

Christianity into Latin, the boy had to be removed. At Christ Church he took an honorary fourth class in Greats. See Sir William Lee Warner, *The Life of the Marquis of Dalhousie*, 2 vols, London, 1904.

steady and cynical professionals of Wellesley's time, and his appearance was alarming—'under bushy eyebrows gleamed a pair of piercing and brilliant eyes. High nose, highly aquiline by nature, was made still more so by a bullet at Busaco.' 'If you draw it again,' he remarked, returning a sword to a beaten enemy in India, 'I will tear it from you and kill you like a dog.'[16] Like most of these conquerors, Napier was austere and religious, in contrast to his eighteenth-century counterparts, and as keen an administrator as soldier. Sind, annexed, he observed, 'by a very advantageous, useful, humane piece of rascality', had been ruined by nearly a century of tyrannical government. It was in fact 'capable of immense production, the soil rich beyond description. My efforts are directed to controlling the waters of the Indus.'[17] He was vividly aware of the drama of his conquests. 'It is not easy to describe,' he wrote when Commander-in-Chief in India, 'how picturesque my march is through the roots of the Great Himalaya, with an escort clothed in such various uniforms, all of bright colours and striking forms. They and their wild horses winding through passes, crossing rivers and ascending hills, mixed with swinging camels and the sober, strong elephants.'[18] At sixty-eight, he records, 'I got up at four o'clock but rode my elephant till daylight; then mounted my beautiful white Arab Mosaic, and galloped him for ten miles ... A hearty breakfast at seven and from that time till five o'clock write, write, write, and my horse is now waiting for me to go and review two regiments.'[19] In physical decline he lamented: 'Just as a man feels he is able to command as a general, so far as mind goes, his carcass gets the staggers and down he goes.'[20]

Napier's exploits were extraordinary. In 1842, without declaring war, he seized the Baluchi stronghold at Imamghar by a dash with camelry across the eastern desert of Sind; at Miani in the next year, with twelve guns and 2,200 men, only 500 British, he held 22,000 Baluchis by gunfire and swamped them by a cavalry charge in the rear by 'Jacob's horse': 'the Seidlitz', as Napier put it, 'of the Sind army'.[21] At Dubba, near Hyderabad, Napier personally led the charge

[16] Thompson and Garrett, op. cit. p. 360.

[17] Lt-Gen. Sir William Napier, The Life and Opinions of Sir Charles Napier, London, 1857, 4 vols, IV, p. 8.

[18] Napier, op. cit. p. 224.

[19] Napier, op. cit. pp. 242–3.

[20] Napier, op. cit. p. 284.

[21] Brigadier John Jacob (1812–58), the son of a Somerset clergyman, attained a legendary reputation on the frontier. He served with the Bombay artillery, and was commissioned to raise the Sind Irregular Horse, which after its exploits at Miani, became the crack cavalry regiment of its kind in northern India. Jacob had only four British officers to command it, and trained his men

that routed the Baluchi Amir Sher Muhammad, killing 5,000 of the enemy for his own loss of 270 men in temperatures of over a hundred in the shade, and after the battle of Shahdulpur, evicting him from the country.

As an administrator Napier was just as dynamic. He organized the entire government of Sind, and himself inspected the main mouths of the Indus, intent on making Karachi a great port. In 1844 he held a Durbar at Hyderabad, attended by about three thousand Baluchi chieftains, come to do honour to the Queen. He deeply admired Wellington, whom he compared as a hundred-gun ship to his own cockboat, and appropriately ended his career through catching pneumonia when a pallbearer at the great Duke's funeral. His statue glowers across Trafalgar Square.

Sir John Lawrence, Bart, G.C.B., first Baron Lawrence of the Punjab and Viceroy of India 1863–9, is another dynamic Victorian. He was a rough character: 'so brusque in speech that he used to say very sharp things to the Punjab chiefs, under which they winced, though he was half in fun'.[22] The eighth of twelve children of a minor and nomadic military family, and of Irish descent through his mother, he obtained a cadetship to Haileybury though he wanted to enter the Army. He soon mastered Urdu, Persian and Bengali, and, though invalided home for three years, returned against medical advice to India, saying, 'If I can't live in India I must die there.' The Sikh wars gave him his chance. By 1846 he was Resident in Lahore, and as President of the Board of Administrators created the British Government of the Punjab. He codified the laws, built roads, extended irrigation, commuted feudal dues and payments in kind for fixed taxes in money, and so dominated the Punjab that he saved northeast India for the British during the Mutiny.

When Palmerston, following the takeover by the Crown from the Company, made him Viceroy after Lord Elgin, Lawrence carried on Dalhousie's work in building railroads and canals, consolidated the defence of the Northwest Frontier and created a department of forestry. Often ill, but indefatigable, he was careless of appearances, as witness his statue in Waterloo Place; he combined ferocious effici-

---

to scour the country and attack at sight. Having pacified Upper Sind, he so transformed the village of Kanghur that Dalhousie had renamed it Jacobabad. Jacob negotiated a treaty with the Khan of Kelat, became acting commissioner in Sind and commanded the cavalry in Outram's expedition to Persia. After the Mutiny he raised two infantry regiments—'Jacob's Rifles'—and invented a new kind of rifle firing explosive bullets. He died of fever at Jacobabad, having never again set foot in England after he had left it in 1828.

[22] Thompson and Garrett, *op. cit.* p. 377.

ency with evangelical fervour, and by force of personality won a resounding prestige.

Many other such characters created the military and administrative structure of British India. Sir James Outram, for example, the 'Bayard of India', was the son of a Derbyshire engineer and a Scots mother. Left in poverty on his father's death, he went out to India in 1819, and between 1825 and 1834, always 'ready for dangerous sport', killed one hundred and twenty tigers, twenty-five bears, twenty-five buffaloes and fifteen leopards.[23] He then traversed the mountains of Afghanistan in disguise, recruited a regiment from the defeated Bhils and won a sensational reputation during the Mutiny. John Nicolson, 'Nickkul Seyn of the Punjab' who was slain during the Mutiny could write, 'Sir, I have the honour to inform you that I have just shot a man dead who came to kill me.' It was said of Nicolson that 'the sound of his horse's hooves was heard from Attock to the Kaibar'.

Such were some of the early and mid-Victorian pro-consuls: no longer adventurers intent on becoming Nabobs and pushing their political fortunes in England, but militant Christians dedicated to India, as convinced of their own superiority as Babur or Akbar, and more humane. In general 'their work was superb and in the days of the Mutiny enforced with terrific vigour, it stood. They were almost without exception intensely religious in a manner compounded of Cromwell, the Thirty-Nine Articles and the public schools of England.'[24] With their alarming sense of mission, and often Irish or Scots descent, they had less in common with the prosperous civilian majority in their own country than with the central Asian conquerors whose descendants they mastered mainly with Indian troops with a stiffening of Europeans; and whose own austere fanaticism had created and provoked the fierce military traditions of northern India, Muslim, Rajput and Sikh. As such they now appear in world history —a strange extrapolation of mid-Victorian zeal.

IV

The British in India, still nominally under the East India Company, but with their country's wealth and naval power behind them, thus revived, adapted and improved the Mughal administration, transformed traditional regimes of plunder into more constructive government, guarded the frontiers of the Punjab and Sind, and within this political framework secured an unwonted peace over the

[23] *D.N.B.*
[24] Thompson and Garrett, *op. cit.* p. 376.

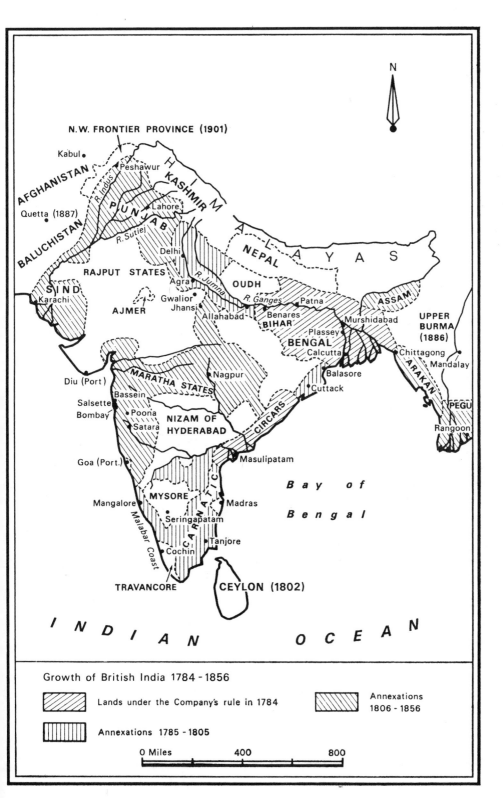

N.W. FRONTIER PROVINCE (1901)

Kabul

AFGHANISTAN

Peshawur

HIMALAYAS

KASHMIR

Quetta (1887)

R. Indus

PUNJAB

Lahore

BALUCHISTAN

R. Sutlej

NEPAL

Delhi

SIND

RAJPUT STATES

Karachi

Agra

R. Jumna

OUDH

ASSAM

AJMER

Gwalior

R. Ganges

Patna

Jhansi

Allahabad

Benares

Murshidabad

UPPER
BURMA
(1886)

BIHAR

Plassey

Diu (Port)

MARATHA STATES

Nagpur

BENGAL

Calcutta

Chittagong

Mandalay

Balasore

Bassein

Salsette
Bombay

Poona

NIZAM OF
HYDERABAD

Cuttack

ARAKAN

Satara

CIRCARS

PEGU

Goa (Port.)

Masulipatam

Rangoon

Bay of

Mangalore

MYSORE

Madras

Bengal

Seringapatam

CARNATIC

Malabar Coast

Cochin

Tanjore

TRAVANCORE

CEYLON (1802)

I N D I A N   *O C E A N*

Growth of British India 1784 - 1856

| | Lands under the Company's rule in 1784 | | | Annexations 1806 - 1856 |

Annexations 1785 - 1805

0 Miles   400   800

Growth of British India 1784–1856

entire sub-continent. Within it the life of India went on, in all its conservative variety, impervious to campaigns in which casualties were seldom more than a few thousand even among the vanquished. Over vast areas of British India, ordered administration had been established and the independent states, most of them under British 'protection', were no longer able to conduct the wars rampant during the decadence of the Mughals. The spectacular atrocities and reprisals of the Mutiny, which in parts of northern India embittered rulers and ruled, were still to come. 'Benthamite' improvement, which would in part provoke the crisis, was now well under way; but throughout the rule of the Company, the prospect of Indian self-government, though early envisaged, always appeared remote.

To secure the economic and strategic advantages of their paramountcy the British had first to secure an adequate and regular revenue, enforce existing law, British, Muslim and Hindu, to train a minority of their subjects in Western administration, stabilize the currency, build the canals, roads and railways and, by the 'fifties, the telegraphs through which they could govern and develop the sub-continent. These aims, natural to nineteenth-century western Europeans, were alien to India : that vast agglomeration of religions and languages, with its contrast between the way of life of Muslim conquerors and the ancient civilization of the Hindus, the whole based on a primitive and conservative peasant economy.

The eighteenth-century British had accepted, even admired, this colourful Asian society, and, if necessary, left ill alone while they exploited it; but now, as the political anarchy described by the Company in 1793 had worsened, the 'old interest and respect for Indian civilization was changing to criticism and distaste. New intellectual and moral gods had arisen in Europe, who frowned upon the gorgeous East.'[25] In Great Britain after 1832 eighteenth-century conditions were reformed, but India was naturally much more recalcitrant. Indeed, 'the British reformers were unduly optimistic. They thought that by converting the top layer of Indian society, they would convert the masses. In this they were sadly mistaken.'[26] In fact, they created a new sort of friction by promoting a Western-style education and disseminating liberal ideas, yet not conceding social equality : indeed by diminishing it from the easier ways of the eighteenth century, they provoked mounting discontent. The Hindu higher castes had always looked down on the foreigners, reeking of cigar smoke, alcohol and beef: the Muslims, more impervious in their proud conservatism and just as intolerant of other creeds, had tended to

[25] Spear, op. cit. p. 51.
[26] Edwardes, op. cit. p. 118.

confine their interest in the *Feringhi* to serving in their armies or collaborating in sport.

The immediate task of the reforming British was to put down the Hindu customs which they found most outrageous. Human sacrifice was still practised among certain tribes, generally of pre-Aryan origin; but it was hard to detect and took long to extirpate. Female infanticide, a common practice, as in ancient Sparta, in the island paradise of Tahiti and in West Africa, had survived among the highly cultivated upper-caste Rajputs, so many of whom died in battle. Male infants were prized; but females were poisoned with opium or their own excrement, and ceremonially buried beneath the floor which was then smoothed over with cow-dung. Very gradually this selective method of birth control was eradicated.

The custom of *Suttee*, when widows 'died in company' with their lords, was again paralleled in other cultures—as in early Mesopotamia and among the pre-Christian Celts and Scandinavians. It was still fairly common among high caste Rajputs, and maintained in the interests of male heirs. In India, life in itself often seemed less attractive than in the West; widows who survived were socially ostracized, and in view of the danger of losing caste and being reincarnated in a lower form of existence, the custom was widely followed. Aurangzeb had failed to put it down: women, after all, are more conservative than men. By 1829 the venerable custom, though it long persisted, was made illegal in British India.

Another grand old Hindu custom was more drastically stamped out. Dedicated Thugs had long strangled travellers in sacrifice to the Goddess Kali: it is estimated that in their finest hour these fanatics accounted for twenty or thirty thousand travellers a year. Between 1831 and 1837 over three thousand were convicted, four hundred hanged. When apprehended they were unrepentant: on the eve of execution one remarked that 'his only regret was to have been caught before he had reached his target of a thousand murders'.[27] So, at a cost of a slight increase in an already excessive population, the British put down four of the more macabre customs of ancient India. They won little popularity by doing so.

They also enforced the law with new vigour. It was administered through district courts, courts of civil and criminal appeal, and supreme courts in Calcutta. Indians, adept in Muslim and Hindu codes, took with relish to the novel intricacies of English law, though the codification and rationalization of their own codes, begun in 1834 by the Macaulay Commission, was only achieved after India came directly under the Crown.

[27] Edwardes, *op. cit.* p. 104.

In education, on the other hand, radical and swift innovations were made. Neither the classical Sanskrit of the Brahmins nor the Persian of the Mughal court would have been acceptable both to Muslims and Hindus; and the Indian intellectuals who were interested, like the merchants and bankers, preferred English. It was the only world language available. Moreover its use would consolidate British power, and Macaulay hoped that through this medium 'idolatry' might be quickly eradicated. The mid-Victorian Christian missionaries, who loathed the erotic cults of the Hindus, and regarded Muslims and Sikhs as 'heathen', shared his hopes. The eighteenth-century British rulers had been tolerant men of the world. In Warren Hastings' time, Sir William Jones had been a great orientalist as well as a judge; Zoffany had found it worthwhile to paint Indian landscapes. In the early nineteenth century James Prinsep, besides reforming the coinage, had deciphered the Pali edicts of Asoka and founded Indian archaeology; early Baptist missionaries had edited Indian texts and compiled dictionaries. The British had revealed India to its own people.

Yet, as we have seen, Macaulay could 'challenge any orientalist to deny that a single shelf of good European literature is worth the whole native literature of India and Arabia'. The great Sanskrit epics —the *Mahabharata*[28] and the *Ramayana*—the pantheist idealism of the *Upanishads*, the highly sophisticated dramas of Kalidasa, the Shakespeare of Hindu India, and the wealth of Persian and Arabic literature, were alike written off. It was a staggering provincialism and led to a shallow westernized kind of culture.

The decision to make English the language of instruction was inevitable, but the content was often inappropriate and debilitating and the 'intelligentsia', who assimilated Western liberal and nationalist ideas, would become the militant leaders of the emancipation of India from British rule.

The massive material progress, then in full swing in the West, was only gradually introduced into India, but by the mid-century it was making a decisive impact: canals had preceded railways in Great Britain, and some of the broken-down Mughal canals were now adapted. By the 'twenties the big east and west Jumna canals had been constructed; by 1850, the Ganges canal, four hundred and fifty miles long. Massive irrigation projects, as advocated by Napier, had already begun in the Indus Valley. But agriculture, so entirely bound up with the structure of peasant society, remained archaic, in terms of creaking water-wheels worked by oxen, of hand-operated water-hoists and of primitive ploughs, while relays of horses, the

[28] *Bharata* is the ancient Sanskrit word for India.

palanquin and the sedan chair, remained the usual manner of transport until the 'fifties, when the first railways were built.

After that, as in Europe, transformation was swift. Better posts and the electric telegraph contributed to the economic expansion which reached its climax in the 'sixties, early encouraged after 1830 by the establishment of the rupee as a stable and general currency, and the introduction of Western-style printing.

In spite of these innovations, most Indian life continued at the slow pace habitual in the East and, in default of air-conditioning and modern devices, the British, like other Indian elites, employed hordes of specialized and generally inefficient servants to sustain an often singularly ill-adapted way of life: for their ample meals and heavy drinking were hardly suitable to the climate. In shuttered bungalows they sweltered during the hot weather under the swaying *punkahs*, and took their exercise in the dawn or in the cool of the day. Disease was bad enough: the causes of cholera, typhoid and malaria were still unknown, and many of the most dynamic proconsuls were constantly down with 'fever' or, at intervals, invalided home. The convention that, only when protected from the sun by spine-pads and topees, could Europeans venture out was now accepted—hence a great variety of headgear, from the wideawake to the jockey, military, mushroom and toadstool topees and to the casual 'farmer's hat'. But the British most easily adapted themselves to the life of the camp elaborated by the Mughals, and became adept at riding, polo, pigsticking, shooting snipe, duck and quail, and hunting big game—here finding common ground with the Indian aristocracy, Muslim and Hindu. But, as more English women came out, they created replicas of their own middle-class society, which the patrician Governors-General and their entourage found so vulgar —provincial Western enclaves in an old and alien civilization. They saw the 'natives' only as servants and dependents, thus adding another deterrent to the already tricky and intractable apartheids of religion and caste.

V

In their Regency and early Victorian expansion the British had undertaken a new and exotic commitment, originally to protect their northeastern frontier, then to exploit the country. The colourful and volatile civilization of Burma, centred on the rich tropical valley of the Irrawaddy from Mandalay and Ava down to Rangoon, a city founded hopefully in the late eighteenth century as the 'place of peace' and part of an Indo-Chinese culture which included Thailand

and Cambodia, had more affinities with Tibet and China than with India, from which it was divided by the mountains and forests of the Arakan. Here Hinayana Buddhism had long flourished; and from the reign of King Anawrahta in the eleventh century to the successful resistance of King Bayinnaung to the Portuguese in the sixteenth, the Burmese, relatively wealthy and self-sufficient with their abundant rice-fields and timber, had been singularly impervious to Western influence.

Though their environment and way of life were genial and even gay, and their Buddhist religion pacific, the rulers were second to none in Asia for hysteria, tyranny and caprice; and it now chanced that in the late eighteenth century King Bodawpaya, 'the great grand-father King' (1782–1819), after ousting his elder brother, 'an in-efficient young man who was bored with palace routine and spent his time making pilgrimages to pagodas',[29] developed megalomaniac ambitions. Having massacred most of his relations ('His predecessor's queens and lesser ladies were burnt alive holding their babies in their arms')[30] and in one area of conspiracy destroyed every living thing, man and beast, he had conquered the Arakan in 1784 and so brought his frontiers up to those of British India. He then turned east, proclaimed himself the 'Coming (and belligerent) Buddha' and invaded Siam: indeed 'the Chronicles of his reign are full of the white elephant myth'.[31] Though soundly defeated, he consoled him-self with building 'dozens of pagodas' by forced labour, and provoked a revolt in Arakan, savagely repressed. Refugees escaped through the jungle into British territory, with consequent tension over their re-turn. Then the monarch intrigued with the French, still active in Mauritius and southern India, and invaded Assam where he ac-counted for or deported half the population. Finally, with the acces-sion of the ineffective King Bagyidaw (1819–37), a talented Burmese general, Bandula, advanced into Bengal, equipped with golden fetters for the Governor-General, Lord Amherst.

In 1824 the British declared war. An amphibious expedition based on the Andaman Islands seized Rangoon—the correct strategic move; and although the Burmese, tattooed with fierce animals to make them invulnerable, put up a gallant resistance, and the British, bogged down during the rains, so grossly mismanaged their supply and medical services that fifteen thousand out of forty thousand men perished mainly from dysentery and malaria, the campaign ended in 1826, after a nightmare of riparian and jungle fighting, in the Treaty

[29] D. G. E. Hall, *A History of South Asia*, London, 1961, p. 354.
[30] F. S. V. Donnison, *Burma*, London, 1970, p. 56.
[31] Donnison, *op. cit.* p. 503.

of Yandabu. The Burmese surrendered Assam, and any claims on Manipur on the Bay of Bengal, Arakan and the entire Tenasserim coast; and they paid an indemnity of a million pounds.[32] Shorn of their conquests, but still in possession of the heartland of Burma itself around Ava and Mandalay, the Mon capital of Pegu, and the delta of the Irrawaddy, the Burmese remained intransigent. King Bagyidaw, having lost so much face, now became insane; and his successor, King Tharrawaddy, repudiated the treaty. By 1845 King Tharrawaddy, too, went out of his mind, and was succeeded by King Pagan Min, 'the fourth in succession to be both mad and bad',[33] who made the usual massacres in the royal family as well as ordering about six thousand other executions. In this political setting the British were now beginning to exploit the teak forests and mineral wealth of the country, and, after the Burmese court had resisted by various exactions and insults, the merchants clamoured for annexation.

So, by 1852 Dalhousie had launched the second Burmese war. Eight thousand British and twenty-two thousand Indian troops captured Rangoon and Bassein, and advanced to Ava itself. The British now annexed Pegu, thus joining Tenasserim and Arakan. King Mindon, Min, who was sane and a Buddhist of outstanding piety and calm, and in 1871 would crown the Shwe Dagon Pagoda at Rangoon with a new gold-plated and jewelled *hti*, was installed in upper Burma instead of Pagan Min, and normal diplomatic relations were established. In 1855 Sir Arthur Phayre, who wrote the fascinating *Narratives of the Mission ... to the Court of Ava* and the first elaborate history of Burma in English, was well received. Burma—now upper Burma—itself remained independent, but in 1862 the Province of British Burma was established, including all the annexed territories except Assam, which came under the Bengal administration.

Thus the British extended their rule over a rich but, on its borders, geographically difficult country. It was very different from India, containing a great variety of peoples, from the sophisticated inhabitants of Rangoon and Bassein, who now greatly prospered through the export of rice which boomed after the opening of the Suez Canal, to the Shans, akin to the Thais, on the eastern plateau, the Karens, Chins and Kachins of the country that borders Yunnan, and the hillmen and head-hunters of the rain-forest mountains of the north and east.

[32] Captain Marryat, R.N., the Victorian novelist who afterwards wrote *Peter Simple, Mr Midshipman Easy* and *Children of the New Forest*, gained a C.B. for his services in Rangoon.
[33] Woodruff, *The Men Who Ruled India*, Vol. II, *The Guardians*, p. 120.

VI

In India, during this time, the tension which broke in the Mutiny of 1857–8 had long been building up. The mounting tempo of 'improvement' now produced a crisis out of proportion to the numbers and areas concerned, ended the Company's rule in India and at last officially brought the sub-continent under the British Crown. In this clash of civilizations the conflict appears tragically inevitable, stemming from the characters of those concerned. The impact of the Mutiny on Victorian England, then at a height of confidence and prosperity, was sensational, and the rising was later misinterpreted by Indian Nationalists as a war of Independence. In fact it was mainly confined to the privileged—even pampered—Sepoys of the Bengal Army, and 'from every aspect it was localized, restricted and unorganized. Only one of the three provincial armies rebelled and it is doubtful if a quarter of the sepoys were ever in arms against the government.'[34] It centred on Hindustan proper, the area between Patna and Delhi, and spread into Oudh, annexed only the year before. But southern India below a line from Surat to Bombay was not affected; and the Sepoy mutinies of the Punjab were swiftly put down with the help of formidable Sikh and Muslim levies. For the Sikhs and Punjabi Muslims detested the Hindu Sepoys, who would never, they felt, have defeated them without British leadership and arms. Nor was the Mutiny a peasant revolt or an organized attempt to restore the Mughal Empire: it was a spontaneous, confused expression of alienation and panic, of the incompatibility between the well-paid high-caste Brahmin mercenaries and the Europeans they served.

The British, who ruled India by prestige and 'face', were a tiny minority: in all, fewer than a hundred thousand in a population of about two hundred million, and their own forces amounted at most to forty-five thousand men to nearly a quarter of a million Indian troops. Their reaction was therefore fierce; and the atrocities—and atrocities they were—committed by both sides lived up to the worst standards of Asia, though on a miniature scale compared to those of Mongol, Afghan and Pathan invaders. British women and children were hideously massacred; Sepoy mutineers ceremonially blown from guns, shot by the hundred and hanged.

There had already been Sepoy mutinies, all savagely repressed. In 1766 mutineers had been blown from guns, and at Barrackpur in 1823, most of a regiment had been shot down with grapeshot

[34] Thompson and Garrett, *op. cit.* p. 436.

for refusing to cross the sea to Burma, since it ·would thereby have lost caste. The realities of power in India had always been stark.

And now the very success of the British administration had scared conservatives. As Woodruff well writes: 'No Indian, surely, of warm intelligence and lively ambition could fail to be aware of something a little chill and clammy near his heart when he regarded the conquerors who were bringing his countrymen so marked a progress in things they would hardly have chosen for themselves. The colour and danger of the old fierce, merciless India, the intoxicating possibility of servants and slave girls beyond counting one day and the next of death, bashed to bloody rags at the feet of an elephant—all this was being filmed over by a viscous monotony of precedents, regulations and law suits, against which it was as useless for him to struggle as for a fly to swim in treacle.'[35]

Although, therefore, the Mutiny was local and limited, there was plenty of tinder lying about. The fire spread, so that at first it was touch and go. The dominant Brahmins were afraid of the breaking down of the rules of caste and purdah; even of the imposition of Christianity. The former Muslim rulers resented the destruction of their old supremacy; while the Muslim peasants thought that the British favoured the Hindu money-lenders to whom they were in debt, though, in general, they regarded the Hindus with too much contempt to take sides with them.

The immediate causes are familiar. By the mid-century the Sepoy army was becoming an anachronism: the fighting races of the Punjab and the Gurkhas of Nepal were now better suited for campaigns of the Northwest Frontier and in Burma. Lord Canning's decree of 1856, enforcing an oath on recruitment to serve anywhere, had alarmed the Sepoys; and the immediate and imbecile blunder, perpetrated by the War Office in London, of issuing cartridges greased with cow-fat and cockades of leather, had outraged their religion. And as the usefulness of the Sepoys had declined, so had the quality of European regimental officers.

The Mutiny broke first in May 1857 at Meerut in the hot weather; the mutineers, with the advantage of surprise, seized Delhi and were joined by others who had murdered their officers. The aged Mughal, Bahadur Shah, was proclaimed Emperor of Hind. The British Commander-in-Chief was at Simla; the British forces available were minute, and the revolt spread to Cawnpore and Lucknow; to Jhansi and Bareilly. But the Sepoys who mutinied in the Punjab were themselves attacked by the peasants, and at Lahore, Multan and Pesha-

[35] Woodruff, *op. cit.* Vol. I, p. 322.

war, they found no popular support. In due course, Madras troops put down rebels in Benares.

The rebels now failed to exploit their initial success, or to set up a coherent alternative government. At Cawnpore, that June, the Maratha Nana Sahib, one of the few rulers to take advantage of the revolt, had proclaimed himself Peshwa; and after the British defence had been overwhelmed, massacred the British troops when they embarked under a safe conduct for Allahabad. He also ordered his palace servants to finish off their women and children with knives, a crime for which the Sepoys were not responsible.

The British now struck back. In July, Cawnpore was recaptured; the atrocities of Nana Sahib ferociously avenged. In September, Delhi was relieved; the Mughal captured and three of his sons shot. The city was sacked and non-combatants massacred. Havelock and Outram then relieved Lucknow: by the end of September the crisis was over. Those waiting to see which side would win hastened to support the British.

Then a ruthless sequel began. Through the cold weather the rebels were attacked, besieged and, after fierce fighting, put down. Lucknow and Cawnpore were again fought over; but the outcome was not now in doubt. Pathans, Afghans and Baluchis, watching from the frontier, decided not to move. The Marathas put up the most formidable resistance; but by July 1858 Canning could declare the conflict officially over. The disciplined fury of the British troops and of their Punjabi and Gurkha allies had routed forces which had greatly outnumbered them, and all was over in less than fourteen months. The 'Mutiny' had demonstrated what might have been expected: that the Muslims loathed the Hindus more than they did the British; that the Sikhs, Punjabi Muslims and Gurkhas were now the decisive force in the British Indian armies, and that the Hindus, rulers or mercenaries, were in no condition to create an alternative *raj* for a sub-continent.

CHAPTER 15

The Dominion of Canada; Caribbean Decline

In contrast to the ancient sub-tropical and tropical civilizations of India and Burma, where fewer than a hundred thousand Europeans dominated more than three hundred million Asians, the huge sparsely inhabited area of British North America, most of it frozen up for half the year and much of it hardly explored, lay open to European settlement. But so long as communications were rudimentary, its potential was obscure. New England traded with Europe and the West Indies; but much of the British North American interior was forbidding and inaccessible. 'Old and sombre and ravaged', its mineral wealth untapped, the forested Lawrentian shield extended from Labrador down to the Great Lakes, then northwest to the Mackenzie River. It was a 'solemn country, with that ungainly splendour evoked by great crude sweeping lines and immense and clumsy masses'.[1] But the St Lawrence waterway, its settlements dominated by Quebec and Montreal, skirted this desolation, and by way of Lakes Ontario and Erie gave access to the Ohio and the Middle West; for British North America then also extended deep into this immense area, down to the former French forts and trading posts on the Missouri and Mississippi. There were 'two societies in two different American landscapes':[2] one faced east to the Atlantic; the other west into a continental wilderness inhabited only by a few Amerindians and European pioneers. The conquest of Canada, formally recognized in 1763, had thus presented the British with a country very different from the maritime American colonies, and one already settled on the St Lawrence by Catholic French Canadians, long set in their own way of life.

The new commitment was at first reluctantly undertaken. But the

[1] Donald Creighton, *The Empire of the St Lawrence*, Toronto, 1956, p. 4.
[2] Creighton, *op. cit.* p. 3.

revolt of the Americans made the country more important. It became
the base for the British campaign in the north and a refuge for
thousands of American loyalists, better aware than the conservative
French *habitants* of the prospects of expansion to the interior. And
there was one constant interest common to the English, the Scots,
the French voyageurs, the *coureurs des bois* and the Amerindians—
the lucrative fur-trade, mainly exploited by the Hudson's Bay Company since the seventeenth century.

In 1791 Pitt's government, determined to reconcile the British and
French-Canadians, divided the country into two provinces: Lower
or French Canada including Quebec and Montreal; and Upper or
British Canada west of the Ottawa with its capital at York, now
Toronto. And by the Canada Act of that year they tried to graft a
balanced eighteenth-century-style constitution on the British model
on to these obstinately different societies. It was an attempt at assimilation, following the lessons of the American War, instead of the
traditional eighteenth-century neglect. And it was so far successful
that in 1812–14, during the war with the United States, the French-
Canadians showed no desire to be liberated. By the Treaty of Ghent
of 1814 the British kept Canada, though relinquishing great untenable areas below the 40th parallel. And that artificial and at first
unfinished boundary, though contradicting the natural economic
pattern of the interior which runs geographically from north to south
—for the mountains and prairies are an extension of the United States
—would serve its turn. It would be extended to the Pacific by the
Oregon Treaty of 1846, and in spite of mounting political and
economic pressures at their climax after the American civil war, be
confirmed by the Washington Treaty of 1871, four years after British
North America had become the Dominion of Canada.

Internally Pitt's Canada Act was less successful. The two provincial assemblies had little control over the legislative council appointed by the Governors-General, from which, even in the French
province, the French-Canadians were excluded. Hence in Upper
Canada a raucous republican opposition; in Lower Canada a sullen
and increasing resentment. Such a government was particularly unsuitable in a colonial society: in Upper Canada without a squirearchy or established clergy; in Lower Canada, feudal, peasant and
Catholic. Hence, riot and rebellion so severe that in 1838 even Lord
Melbourne had to tell his colleague Lord Durham to 'go out and put
it right'—a move that led to the historic Durham Report.

Such was the political background to vast exploration in the west
and north. The Hudson Bay Company now controlled territories
from Labrador to the Yukon, from Lake Superior to the Columbia

River on the Pacific, though the North West Fur Company long infringed its monopoly. In 1784 Alexander Mackenzie, a 'North-Wester', knighted in 1802 by George III, explored the Great Slave Lake, and the Mackenzie River to its mouth in the Arctic or Beaufort Sea. Then, in 1792–3, he became the first European to cross the Rockies north of Mexico.[3] In 1790 Captain George Vancouver, a veteran of Cook's voyages, dispatched to the north Pacific coast after the crisis with Spain over Nootka Sound, surveyed it from San Francisco to Southern Alaska, and planted an outpost on Vancouver Island.[4] Thus, although in 1805 the Americans Lewis and Clarke made their famous exploration of the Columbia River, and John Jacob Astor, originally from Montreal, began his fur-trade round the Horn to New York, Vancouver and the Scots who had pioneered what they called 'New Caledonia' had established a prior claim. But it was not until 1849 that Vancouver Island with its trading port and afterwards naval base at Esquimault was made a Crown Colony. Then, following the gold-rush to Cariboo on the Frazer River in the 'fifties, the administration of British Columbia had to be improvised. Finally in 1866 the two were merged into an enlarged British Columbia.

Back in the Middle West in what is now Manitoba, where the Red River runs into the southern extremity of Lake Winnipeg, the fifth Earl of Selkirk had founded a settlement at Fort Garry. A major shareholder in the Hudson's Bay Company, he brought over Highland crofters from his own tenantry, and his documents of possession were attested by the marks of the Amerindians—wolf, bear and fish.[5] The settlement all but succumbed before the hostility of the local half-breeds and Amerindians, but when bought back by the Company, Fort Garry would be the nucleus of Winnipeg and a base for a vast expansion west into the Prairies.

All these settlements, in the Far West and around Hudson's Bay itself, were of log cabins round tiny stockaded forts in the wilderness. Only railways could link them with the St Lawrence and the Atlantic, and for any substantial commerce the Pacific settlements would still be reached only round the Horn or from the Far East. Hence, after 1867, it would be the railways that would consolidate the politi-

[3] He wrote *Voyages on the River St Lawrence and through the continent of North America to the Frozen and Pacific Oceans in the years 1789 and 1793*, with a preliminary account of the 'Rise, Progress and Present State of the Fur Trade in that country', London, 1801. Mackenzie did well enough to buy an estate in Rosshire, Scotland.

[4] See his *A Voyage of Discovery to the North West Pacific Ocean and Round the World in the years 1790–1795*.

[5] See John Morgan Grey, *Lord Selkirk of Red River*, London, 1963.

cal union of Canada, and politics would be much determined by
their competition.

In the Canadian sub-Arctic the neo-Elizabethan lure of the Northwest Passage now again inspired much dangerous enterprise. In 1818
Commander John Ross had entered Davis' Strait 'for the purpose of
exploring Baffin's Bay and inquiring into the possibility of a North
West Passage'; an expedition followed up in 1829–33, when King
William's Land was discovered. In 1819–20 Commander William
Parry, who had sailed with Ross, actually reached Melville Island;
but his expeditions in the 'twenties were blocked by the ice—in fact,
the only barrier. In 1818, too, Lieutenant John Franklin, a Lincolnshire man intended for the Church, whose passion for the sea had
survived all deterrents, who had fought at Copenhagen and Trafalgar
and sailed to Australia, tried to reach the Behring Straits by way of
the passage between Greenland and Spitzbergen and the Pole—
naturally in vain. His two other expeditions to the Canadian Arctic
also failed; but they increased knowledge and enhanced Franklin's
fame. Then in 1845–7 his last expedition, heading for the Behring
Straits in H.M.S. *Erebus* and *Terror*, perished to a man, twelve miles
north of King William's Land, where both ships were trapped and
crushed in the ice. Ironically Franklin and his crews, the last victims
of the Northwest Passage, had in fact struck the strait between King
William's and Victoria Lands through which, with modern ice-
breakers, the passage can be made. But the courage of these explorers
was not enough; all explored new territories, all were knighted, but
in the old objective all failed.

Such were the vast but daunting opportunities presented by British
North America: the overriding need was to unite it.

The Maritime provinces, Nova Scotia, New Brunswick (French
Acadia) and Prince Edward Island, made the first move. Here in
1864, when it was becoming clear that the North was going to win
the war between the States in America, a convention was held at
Charlottetown, attended also by representatives of the now combined
Upper and Lower Canada. Its aim was to create a Federal Union
under the Crown—perhaps an 'auxiliary' Kingdom of Canada. As the
British Canadian John Alexander Macdonald, its principal architect,
observed, 'the weakness of Canada is an embarrassment to England.
For the sake of securing peace for ourselves we must make ourselves
powerful. The great security for peace is to convince the world of our
being united ... we want to make a transcript of the British Constitution.'[6]

[6] *Memoirs of the Rt Hon. Sir John Alexander Macdonald*, ed. Joseph Pope,
London, 2 vols, 1894, Vol. I, p. 269.

It never became a kingdom. During the Westminster Conference of 1866, when Lord Carnarvon, as Secretary of State for the Colonies, took the Chair, the Foreign Secretary, Lord Derby, vetoed the term. He feared, he indicated, 'that the name would wound the susceptibility of the Yankees'.[7] But it chanced that Leonard Tilley, a descendant of one of the American 'Pilgrim Fathers' and delegate for New Brunswick, exhausted by the discussion, had sought solace in Westminster Abbey, where they were singing the seventy-second psalm—'His dominion shall also be from one sea to another'. The word sank in: he seized upon it and Canada became the first 'Dominion', its motto *a mari usque ad marem*—from sea to sea.

Meanwhile, the West Indies, long considered far more important than British North America, had witnessed the final bout of Anglo-French colonial conflict. It had coincided with negro revolts against the owners of both French and British plantations and also with the last boom in sugar and cotton provoked by the Napoleonic Wars; then, following the abolition of slavery and the coming of free-trade, a steady decline set in.

Historians have denounced the naval strategy of Pitt's government which sent thousands of men to their deaths in the West Indies, mainly from tropical disease; but the West Indies had long been the source of great wealth, and in fact there was method in it. Sugar and cotton were always essential to the Old Colonial economy, and the West Indian naval bases essential for the control of the Atlantic. In the event, the British maintained their hold on the Caribbean and took and kept Tobago and St Lucia with its strategic harbour. In 1833 when slavery was abolished, the West Indian planters managed to absorb most of the £20,000,000 assigned as compensation throughout the entire Empire; but only the more adaptable economies, as Barbados, Trinidad and British Guiana, were able to face the competition brought in by mid-Victorian free-trade.

The emancipation of the Spanish-American colonies had been an aim of British policy since the late seventeenth century. Desired by Walpole, attempted by Anson, backed by Canning, it was now achieved with the help of Great Britain and the United States, as France had helped to emancipate the British colonies: for the Monroe Doctrine of 1823, elicited by Russian claims on Alaska and by the threatening gestures of the Holy Alliance towards South America, had coincided with British commercial interests.

[7] 'Had United Canada,' wrote Macdonald, 'been declared to be an auxiliary Kingdom, as in the Canadian draft of the Bill, I feel sure (almost) that the Australian Colonies would even be placed in the same rank as the Kingdom of Canada.' *Op. cit.* Vol. I, p. 313.

In the south Atlantic, in 1832 the British re-established a naval station in the Falkland Islands, and by 1844 had planted a settlement at Port Stanley, when the islands were developed, as a sheep-run, a whaling station, and a base for the exploration of South Georgia and Victoria Land in the Antarctic.

Thus, despite the loss of the American colonies, vast tracts of British North America and the sub-Arctic were retained, augmented, organized into the Dominion of Canada; the British increased their hold on the West Indies—now less valuable but still, with British Guiana, strategically important—and extended their influence in South America, while in the Arctic and Antarctic huge and desolate areas were explored.

II

Compared with these achievements, the brief war with the United States in 1812–14 was insignificant. As Charles Napier, afterwards famous in India, observed, it was 'a most unnatural war; a sort of bastard rebellion' in which the small farmers suffered most. 'It is hateful,' he wrote, 'to see the poor Yankees robbed.'[8]

But the war was due to causes outside British or American control. During the Napoleonic Wars, Jefferson, who had taken his chance to purchase Louisiana, tried hard to stay neutral. But, inevitably, both belligerents interfered with American commerce, as British Orders in Council were answered by the Berlin Decrees. Desperate for crews, the British combined a brisk search for contraband with impressing American sailors, as well as their own deserters found in American ships. 'It is my duty,' said one British officer, 'to keep my ship manned, and I will do so wherever I find men who speak the same language with me.'[9] So under mounting popular pressure enhanced by Mid-Western politicians with their eyes on British North America, President Madison declared war. He could not have chosen a worse time for the declaration—to coincide with Napoleon's disaster in Russia and defeat in Spain.

So the outcome was never in doubt. This time the British controlled the Atlantic and could convoy all the necessary troops. The blockade soon crippled American commerce and though American captains won brilliant successes and the British were heavily committed in the Baltic, the North Sea, the eastern Atlantic and the Mediterranean, the British Atlantic fleet alone greatly outnumbered

[8] Napier, *op. cit.* Vol. I, p. 225.
[9] Graham S. Graham, *The Empire of the North Atlantic*, Toronto, 1950, p. 239.

anything the Americans could muster. Based on Halifax at one end of the St Lawrence and on Kingston, Ontario, at the other, the British attacked the Middle West by way of Lakes Ontario and Erie, and the Hudson Valley by Lake Champlain. The Americans regained Detroit, burnt York and in improvised amphibious campaigns won minor victories; but they failed to invade Canada. And in the south, from Chesapeake Bay, the British attacked Baltimore, an event that inspired the composition of the 'Star Spangled Banner', later the American national anthem—'a beautiful and animating effusion', wrote a contemporary, 'which was long to outlast the occasion'.[10] By 1814, in reprisal for the burning of York, the Peninsular veterans had burnt the government buildings in Washington, and President Madison's official residence as well. After repairs and a repaint it became known as the White House. Finally, in January 1815, not knowing that the war was over, Sir Edward Pakenham—who at Wellington's order, 'Now's your time, Ned,' had charged to win the battle of Salamanca—was killed in an assault against New Orleans, which cost over three thousand casualties, an action in which Andrew Jackson first won fame.

The reverse did not affect the terms of the Treaty of Ghent. The Americans emerged with their Canadian ambitions frustrated but their frontiers intact, while the British and French-Canadians returned to their rancorous domestic politics.

III

The frictions in British North America now forced governments to face the problems which variously would confront them throughout the immense territories of the second British Empire. When, in 1838, Melbourne appointed the able but temperamental Lord Durham, whom he was anxious to exclude from his cabinet, as High Commissioner for Canada, the Report that he and his collaborators produced proved one of the great classic state papers of imperial history.

John George Lambton, first Earl of Durham, only visited Canada from late May to early November of 1838; but the Durham Report of 1839 made him the greatest constitutional theorist of the British Empire. Lambton came of an ancient Durham county family, enriched by collieries; his mother from a branch of the brilliant Villiers

---

[10] Francis Scott Key of Baltimore, on a mission to release a friend and detained by the British during the attack, had to watch the American flag on Fort Henry under bombardment all night, and wrote his poem when he saw Old Glory still flying in the dawn. The tune was one already familiar to the Anacreontic Society in London and its branches in the United States.

stock. Educated at Eton, he went into the 10th Dragoons, but in 1813 resigned to become M.P. for County Durham. He married a daughter of Earl Grey and, as Lord Privy Seal, collaborated with Lord John Russell in preparing the Reform Bill of 1832. Known in political circles as 'Radical Jack', Lambton, who was made a baron in 1828 and Earl of Durham in 1833, had been Ambassador to St Petersburg in 1832 and 1835–7. He was *grand seigneur* and remarked that 'a man could jog along on £40,000 a year'. He was extremely handsome, impetuous and forceful; but his health was precarious and he died at Cowes, Isle of Wight, in 1840, aged forty-seven.

Immediately, his mission was hardly a success; for this arrogant and fiery aristocrat treated the French-Canadian rebels with a high hand and transported the ringleaders to Bermuda. Indeed he soon exceeded his powers and Melbourne disowned him; he resigned, sacrificed, like many other able men, for actions necessary in the country he had to govern. Though it is widely believed that Durham wrote little of the Report, the best authorities now give him the main credit. 'No-one,' wrote Lucas, 'would suppose that he drafted every line of the document himself. On the other hand, to maintain that Lord Durham, of all men in the world, allowed someone else to dictate what he would recommend is ridiculous. Whether Lord Durham's own pen actually wrote much or little of the Report, in form and substance it is his and his alone, able as were the members of his staff.'[11] And Coupland wrote, 'Durham's enemies were quick to belittle his report. They even denied him the credit of its admirable style. It was written, they said, by Buller and Wakefield. On both points they were mistaken. Careful research has put it beyond question that, though certain sections of the Report may have been drafted by other hands, the main parts of it, and especially the section on Lower Canada, were written by Durham himself.'[12]

If Durham's was the master mind, he had able collaborators, official and unofficial. Charles Buller and Edward Gibbon Wakefield[13]

[11] Sir C. Lucas, *The Durham Report*, 3 vols, London, 1912, Vol. I, p. 3.

[12] Sir R. Coupland, *The Durham Report*, an abridged version with introduction and notes, Oxford, 1945, p. *i*.

[13] Born in 1806, Charles Buller, who came of a Cornish family, had been removed from Harrow (otherwise 'his future', it was alleged, 'would have been jeopardized') in 1821, to be tutored by the young Thomas Carlyle. He had then read law at Trinity, Cambridge, and became M.P. for Looe in 1830, and for Liskeard in 1832–48. Like Durham, he was a radical Whig reformer, and well versed in the law: two years before his death in 1848 he became Judge Advocate-General. Wakefield (1796–1862) was the son of a farmer, land agent and philanthropist in Essex, and distantly related to the historian Gibbon. He had been educated at Westminster which he had disliked, and in Edinburgh.

were both formidable men, the latter destined profoundly to influence the destinies of New Zealand.

Unlike most of the eighteenth- and early nineteenth-century statesmen, Durham at once saw the potential of Canada. Its agriculture, timber and minerals, he observed, were all scarcely touched. The country had the greatest and richest fisheries in the world, ample water-power, safe and spacious harbours, great rivers and vast inland seas.[14] And all this area was the rightful patrimony of the English people: 'the ample appanage which God and nature have set aside in the New World for those whose lot has assigned them but an insufficient portion of the old'. Yet this great future was being jeopardized by political mismanagement. One part of Canada was set against the other; settlement had fallen off, and until better government was established no emigrants would settle. Yet the forms of government, not the Canadians, were to blame, and 'we need not despair of governing a people who really have hitherto very imperfectly known what it is to have a government'.[15] 'The experience,' Durham continues, with a touch of irony, 'of keeping colonies and governing them well ought at least to have a trial, ere we abandon forever a vast dominion which might supply the wants of our surplus population, and raise up fresh consumers of our manufacturers and producers of a supply for our wants.'[16] For, unless the Canadians were given greater liberty, he concluded, they would secede from the Empire like the Americans and be absorbed in the United States. 'No large community of free and intelligent men will long feel contented with a political system which places them, because it places their country, in a position of inferiority to their neighbours.' The colonists were 'linked, it is true, to a mighty Empire, . . . but they were 'in

---

After a brief service under the British envoy at Turin, he had then, in 1816, aged twenty, eloped with his first heiress, Eliza Pattle, a ward in chancery. He had returned to diplomacy, this time in Paris; four years later his first wife had died. So in 1826, being evidently good at such enterprises, he had eloped with a second heiress, a schoolgirl named Ellen Turner. Pursued to Calais, the couple were retrieved and Wakefield got three years in prison. His younger brother, William, who had collaborated in the adventure, also got three years; but he made good, commanding British auxiliaries in Spain, and became a Portuguese knight. In 1839, under Edward's auspices, he sailed for New Zealand. It was thus in Canada, as a rather shady éminence, that Wakefield spread his pervasive influence on the history of the British Empire. Here he had his first experience in the field, and already, and in vain, recommended his main policy—the controlled distribution of public land to substantial settlers who could pay for it.

[14] See Coupland, op. cit. pp. 11 ff.
[15] Coupland, op. cit. p. 179.
[16] Coupland, op. cit. p. 180.

remote dependence on it; confined in a 'narrow subordinate community', parochial and relatively undeveloped, with unworkable political institutions, bad communication, bad municipal government, bad education.

The Report, with an easy casual style, as later used by Bagehot, was a prospectus and an indictment. When, save for the West Indies, colonies were thought a liability and certain to hive off, 'to keep colonies and govern them well' was to some people impracticable. The Report gave it official backing and just when an American take-over appeared likely. Moreover, wrote Coupland, 'the Report as a whole belongs to a small company of state papers that may be classed as literature',[17] and 'the present (1945) status of the Dominions has been its almost automatic outcome'.[18]

The Report, to be decisive for the whole Empire, had a mixed reception in Canada. Following its recommendations Upper and Lower Canada were reunited, and, along with the Maritime colonies accorded 'responsible' self-government through an elected assembly, though foreign affairs, defence and the regulation of external trade were 'reserved'. It was hoped that the British republicans would be appeased and the French-Canadians assimilated.

But the Tories called it 'Chartism for the colonies', the Radicals resented the reserved powers and the French-Canadians, who feared they would be swamped, complained that they were not properly represented. From 1843 to 1845, the Governor-General, Sir Charles Metcalfe, though mortally ill, contended with rancorous colonial politicians in a tragic epilogue to his career in India. And when, in 1848, under the Governor-General Lord Elgin, a responsible government was formed, including French-Canadians, British loyalists burnt down the Parliament House in Toronto, then the political capital. It was only the mounting fear of an American takeover that made the Canadians gradually sink their differences. Much as the British and French-Canadians disliked one another, they detested the Americans more, and the British, who maintained a large garrison to guard the frontier, wanted to hand over all the responsibility they could to a single Canadian government. If they lacked vision, the British at least felt that it would be more convenient to deal with one colony than with half a dozen. But it was not until the victory of the North in the American War between the States made the American threat seem more urgent that the Canadians took a decisive line.

Canada owes more to Sir John Macdonald than to anyone in Whitehall. This remarkable man, not at all the rough colonial poli-

---

[17] Coupland, *op. cit. XLVII.*
[18] Coupland, *op. cit.* p. 1.

tician but a rather Disraelian character, dominated Canadian politics for the best part of quarter of a century and became one of the foremost statesmen of the Empire. Born in 1815 in Glasgow, he was the son of Hugh Macdonald of Dornoch and his wife Helen Shaw of Highland descent. His father, an unsuccessful haberdasher, had emigrated to Canada and the boy, briefly educated at the Grammar School of Kingston, Ontario, had fought his way out of poverty by the law. In 1844 he had represented Kingston as a Conservative in the new Parliament of the united Canadas, and had been a leading advocate of the transfer of the political capital to Ottawa effected in 1859. In 1870 he became Prime Minister of the first government of the Dominion, and, though his ministry was defeated three years later for accepting contributions by an American railroad company to party funds, he regained office in 1878 and remained Prime Minister until his death in 1891. With his 'casual air of jaunty distinction' and 'of assured friendly expertise', he 'evoked a ghost of the old eighteenth-century idea that government was a craft which could be practised best by gentlemen amateurs.... Politics was simply the art of the possible in the management of living men.'[19]

The natural economic development of North America being from south to north, the Americans had long hankered to rule the whole continent; now in 1865 'the conclusion of the Civil War released all the pent up power of the United States'.[20] Indeed, as Macdonald put it, 'but for the absorbing interest of the late internecine war' the Canadian northwest 'would have already been overrun'. Irish Fenians, demobilized from the Union army, now raided across the Canadian frontier, and the victorious Americans cancelled the Reciprocity Treaty of 1854 and again raised tariffs against Canada. They even demanded half the Canadian continent in settlement of their claims for the depredations of the Confederate frigate *Alabama*, which had been harboured in British ports. In face of this hostility the British and the Canadians found their minds wonderfully concentrated on uniting British North America.

Following the convention at Charlottetown, a Canadian delegation went to London, intent on founding a 'vigorous general government ... of British Americans under the British sovereign'. The Derby–Disraeli government was then in power, and Henry Herbert, fourth Earl of Carnarvon, Colonial Secretary, brought in the British North America Act: though he resigned over the franchise bill— Disraeli's 'leap in the dark'—before the Act was passed, this came into operation on 1st July 1867. In spite of Carnarvon's enthusiasm

[19] Donald Creighton, *The Dominion of the North*, London, 1958, p. 323.
[20] Creighton, *op. cit*. p. 313.

—he showed similar zeal with less success over the Union of South Africa—the casual British officials, though thankful to simplify colonial administration and shift responsibility, in Macdonald's view, 'treated the union as a private bill uniting two or three parishes'.[21]

The Federation created by the Act was much closer than the American model, with less emphasis on state rights, the 'Guy Fawkes' of the United States which had brought Civil War, and, though it was written and elaborate, it was in spirit nearer to the British constitution. Ontario, Quebec, Nova Scotia and New Brunswick were brought into the Dominion of Canada. There was a Governor-General, a parliament of a Senate and House of Commons, with lieutenant-governors and legislatures for the provinces. Newfoundland would not join until 1949, but in 1870 Manitoba was added, in 1872 British Columbia and Prince Edward Island in 1873.

So Canadian and British pragmatism combined. Cobden, the free-trading little Englander, might ask, why 'guarantee three or four million of North Americans living in Canada against another lot of Americans', but the first of the Dominions was made, to be consolidated during the rest of the nineteenth century and to set a precedent for the rest of the Empire.

IV

For centuries the Caribbean had been a cockpit of European conflicts, which came to their climax in the war with Revolutionary and Napoleonic France. Investments of £70,000,000 were at stake, as were the rich French sugar islands and the Dutch colonies. In London and Paris business interests urged on the war, and 'yellow Jack', rum and vile eighteenth-century administration cost both sides immense casualties. Whole armies perished, particularly when the authorities had planned campaigns in the hurricane season. Only Sir John Moore, later killed at Corunna, insisted on precautions against tropical disease; and the British suffered eighty thousand casualties, about half of them fatal, mainly from dysentery and yellow fever—twice the number killed in the Peninsular War. But strategically these campaigns were not a failure. At a terrible price, the lucrative French sugar-trade was diverted, extensive cotton plantations captured and the best of the French islands secured and kept. On the balance sheet

[21] But the Canadians had their lighter moments. They all went to the Derby with 'Russell of the *Times*' and Macdonald bought the ebullient George Brown, leader of the Tory 'Old Grits', a peashooter with which he took aim at people on the tops of buses. Macdonald also won twenty guineas.

of cold economic advantage, if not of human lives, the expeditions paid off. Revolutionary movements among the negro majorities were put down—often by both sides. In British Honduras, on the other hand, in 1798 settlers and slaves had combined to beat off a major Spanish attack; and the whole territory would be made a British Colony in 1862, under the Governor of Jamaica.

But although the wars had created a hectic prosperity among the sugar planters, since French competitors were put out of action, their economy had long been precarious; now the abolition of the slave-trade, 'amelioration', and finally abolition of slavery itself, demanded an adaptation of which most of them were incapable.

Nelson, who had spent much of his youth in the West Indies—'bred', as he remarked, 'in the good old school'—had always defended the 'just rights of the planters' on the questions;[22] and the West Indian interest still commanded over fifty seats in Parliament. They fought abolition to the last ditch; but save for the defence of property on principle—a strong card—they had a poor case. The planters themselves were not generally prepossessing: 'no civilized society on earth', wrote Sir James Stephen in the Colonial Office, is 'so entirely destitute of learned leisure, of literary and scientific intercourse and even liberal recreations'.[23]

They had not much chance against the tide of humanitarian and evangelical zeal now setting in, and which would affect the whole Empire. Pitt had thought the slave-trade both iniquitous and bad business; while the reformers and evangelicals inspired by Sharp and Clarkson, were represented in Parliament by Wilberforce and Sir Thomas Fowell Buxton. Both greatly influenced imperial and world history, and both combined eighteenth-century enlightenment with evangelical and Quaker religion. William Wilberforce (1759–1833) came of a Yorkshire family, with a rich Baltic business behind them. At St John's and at Pembroke Colleges, Cambridge, he had become a friend of Pitt; and he was M.P. for Hull at twenty-one.[24] A sociable young man of great charm, he was widely popular. Then in 1784

[22] See John Ehrman, *The Younger Pitt. The Years of Acclaim*, London, 1969, p. 390.

[23] Woodward, *The Age of Reform*, Oxford, 1938, p. 356.

[24] He remained in Parliament until 1825, and increased his following by writing a bestseller, *A Practical View of the Prevailing Religious Systems of Professed Christians in the Higher and Middle Classes of the Country contrasted with Real Christianity*. This perennially topical work had enormous sales both at home and in the United States. Wilberforce in his declining years lost most of his fortune: his third son, Samuel, became successively Bishop of Oxford and Winchester and was worsted in public controversy by T. H. Huxley.

he became serious: he was converted to evangelical religion, founded a 'Society for the Reformation of Manners' and joined with the evangelicals and Quakers in the campaign against slavery. Abolition, already carried in the Commons by 1796, had been blocked by the Lords, and it was not until February 1807 that it became law—by a majority in the Commons of 283 to 16. There still remained to abolish it throughout the Empire, and in 1823 Wilberforce, who had identified himself with the evangelical Clapham Sect, wrote his celebrated *Appeal to the Religious Justice and Humanity of the Inhabitants of the British Empire on behalf of the Negro slaves in the West Indies.* He just lived to know that the Abolition Bill of July 1833 had passed its second reading in the Commons. It became law that August.

Sir Thomas Fowell Buxton (1786–1845), who had brought in the Bill, was a wealthy brewer of Quaker stock in Essex, and married into the Gurney family of Earlham Hall, Norfolk. He was M.P. for Weymouth from 1818 to 1837, and by 1824 successor to Wilberforce in the leadership of the anti-slavery group in Parliament. He was a zealous penal reformer and, after slavery had become illegal, tried to have it stamped out in West Africa in areas outside the Empire.[25] Both these reformers had ample private means and devoted their lives to their objective: their careers coincided with the rise of Benthamite 'improvement' and humanitarian evangelical reform, and the impact which they made became worldwide.

Against this kind of attack the West Indian interest could put up only a rearguard action, while the long-term solution—more efficient cultivation, diversification of crops and technical education for the free Negroes—demanded broader resources and horizons than they possessed. But, in the British way, compensation tempered the wind: by 1837 and during the 'forties, indentured coolies from India provided some more skilled labour, while the sugar planters were still protected by tariffs. But as the British had to pay nearly twice as much as the price on the Continent, this protection gradually diminished, to be abolished in 1854. The West Indies were not yet ruined; but they had lost their eighteenth-century political and economic priority.

Already in the late 'fifties when free-trade exposed the planters to

[25] Buxton, who had a successful academic career at Trinity College, Dublin, early joined the firm of Truman, Hanbury and Buxton at Spitalfields, where he tried to improve the conditions of the poor—raising over £93,000 for them by a speech at the Mansion House. He also founded the Society for the Reformation of Prison Discipline. In 1820 he settled at Cromer Hall, Norfolk, and developed a model farm at Runton. He was keenly interested in forestry and in animal life.

full competition, there were bankruptcies, riots and political friction. In Jamaica, in 1795 during the French Revolutionary wars, the British had taken two years to put down a maroon revolt, part of a widespread upheaval in the European colonies following the French Revolution. These risings which had emanated in 1791 from the revolution in Saint Domingue (afterwards Haiti) led by the Negro, Toussaint Louverture, whom Napoleon wrote off as a 'gilded African' and who ended as a prisoner in France, had given the Blacks of the Caribbean their next and promising opportunity for revolt. A groundswell of revolution had continued into the mid-century; and in 1865 a Scots-Negro, Paul Bogle, inspired by revivalist religion and with the connivance of certain Baptist missionaries, again raised rebellion in Jamaica. It was promptly and ruthlessly suppressed by the Australian explorer and administrator, Governor Eyre, who lost in Jamaica the humane reputation he had gained in Australia. Indeed, his conduct and recall gave rise to a long and violent set-to among some redoubtable Victorians—Huxley, Herbert Spencer and J. S. Mill, against Carlyle, Ruskin and Tennyson, who defended the Governor; Carlyle, typically, calling Eyre's accusers 'a knot of nigger philanthropists', and insisting that Eyre was just, valiant and humane.[26] As the emancipated Negroes outnumbered the white population by about twenty-seven to one, Eyre had taken no chances, and when at Morani Bay twenty Europeans had been murdered, Eyre proclaimed martial law in the district and cordoned the rebellion off. But he also authorized the execution of the missionary agitator, George William Gordon, outside the area of martial law, and by the end of the affair over six hundred rebels had been killed and hundreds flogged and their huts destroyed. Following a Commission of Enquiry, Eyre was commended for acting swiftly, but blamed for excessive and sometimes illegal severity, recalled and retired. The ancient Jamaican Assembly was dissolved and, after two centuries of relative independence, the island became a Crown Colony with a nominated legislative council.

The brisker economies of Barbados, of Trinidad and of British Guiana, on the other hand, adapted themselves to free-trade; and although Mauritius, now a British colony, produced even more sugar than Guiana, by 1870 Trinidad's production had doubled and Guiana's increased by more than half. But the smaller, less adaptable, islands began to drift into a casual if picturesque poverty.

[26] Though not employed again, Eyre was accorded the normal pension of a colonial governor, and his acts thus implicitly condoned. See Hamilton Hume, *The Life of Edward John Eyre*, London, 1867.

V

Such in outline were the fortunes of the British Empire and British influence in the Americas from the recognition of American independence in 1783 to the Federation of Canada in 1867. In spite of the brief Anglo-American war of 1812–14 and of American ambitions to take over Canada, always secondary to expansion to the southwest, the two Anglo-Saxon powers had together come directly and indirectly to dominate the whole area. The West Indies had lost the economic priority they had long been accorded, and the development of Canada, like that of the United States, had become continental, the country now extending from Nova Scotia to the Pacific. In this, the first British colony of settlement now within the Empire, responsible self-government had been developed, and railroads were beginning to unite the enormous country. While Canada could not compete with the massive industrial expansion of the United States, its potential was now being understood, and although the French-Canadian problem remained unresolved, another secession from the Empire had been avoided. It was, indeed, over Canada, that predominant opinion in Great Britain became convinced that properly governed colonies of settlement could be an asset. All these events, like those already recorded in India, the strategic base of British power in the East, and Australasia, were the result of the defeat of Napoleon and the final decision of the century-old struggle with France for colonial Empire on both sides of the globe. This victory had been achieved by a combination of continental manpower, drawing on central and eastern European and Eurasian resources, with the industrial and naval power of Great Britain; it had left the British supreme on the oceans, a world supremacy unchallenged until the late nineteenth century. The *Pax Britannica* was thus created not so much by colossal naval armaments, as because no one, until Germany entered the armaments race, now seriously challenged the British at sea. Based on established prestige, it enabled them to extend a mainly commercial Empire in Africa, the Far East, Australia, New Zealand and the Pacific—as usual a spontaneous rather than a state-run expansion.

CHAPTER 16

West African Commitment; Boer and Bantu; East Africa

When the slave-trade, 'that inexhaustible fund of wealth and naval power,'[1] became illegal for British subjects, and even when slavery itself was abolished within the Empire, most of the interior of Africa and the ancient, well adapted and intensely conservative societies it contained, was still unknown to Europeans, while the Muslim traders and slavers of East Africa kept their knowledge a secret. Now European explorers, British, German, French and Italian, began to infiltrate the vast continent. In this enterprise the British would predominate. And, gradually, following the lead of traders and missionaries, they were forced into political domination.

The process took over half a century. In 1770 a Scots laird, James Bruce, had arrived in Ethiopia, found the source of the Blue Nile and vividly described an ancient, peculiar and original Coptic Christian civilization, already known to the Portuguese. In 1795 on the other side of the continent, Mungo Park, another Scotsman, under the auspices of the African Association, whose president was Cook's shipmate, Sir Joseph Banks, discovered 'the long sought after, majestic Niger glittering in the morning sun, as broad as the Thames at Westminster and flowing slowly eastward'[2] at Sego. But it was not until another Scot, Captain Hugh Clapperton, R.N., and the Cornishman Richard Lander had reached Kano, first in 1823–5 across the Sahara, then in 1825–7 from Badagri on the West African coast, that Lander, after Clapperton's death, proved that the river flowed into the Bight of Benin.

It was not until the mid-century that the most important explorations were made. In West Africa, William Baikie, who used quinine against fever, thoroughly explored the Niger and the Benue, while

---

[1] *vide supra.*

[2] Margery Perham and J. Simmons, *African Discovery*, London, 1942, p. 80, citing Park's travels pp. 191–200.

in 1849 Dr David Livingstone, a Scots missionary set out across the Kalahari from Bechuanaland in South Africa to Lake Ngami, and, two years later, struck the great Zambesi at Sesheke on its middle course. In 1853 Livingstone followed the river northwest and emerged at Luanda in Angola; then, retracing his route, turned east and found the Victoria Falls, where the river, 'a thousand yards broad leaped down a hundred feet, and then became suddenly compressed into a space of fifteen or twenty yards ... giving off a dense white cloud ... with two bright rainbows on it',[3] with a smoke of steam two or three hundred feet high, and a sound like thunder. Accompanied by John Kirk, afterwards British consul at Zanzibar, he then went down the Zambesi to Quilimane on the Indian Ocean. For the first time the whole breadth of southern tropical Africa had been traversed by a European. Then, in 1858–64, Livingstone, whose main obsessions were to put down the slave-trade and discover the source of the White Nile, moved north from the Zambesi into the highlands of East Africa and discovered Lake Nyasa; and in 1867–73 struck out beyond it to Lake Tanganyika and the Lualaba in the southeastern headwaters of the Congo. Here Stanley could have rescued him;[4] but determined to explore the source of the Nile, Livingstone went on, to perish near Chitambo, southeast of Lake Bangweolu near the frontier of modern Zambia and the Congo Republic.

Meanwhile, by 1858, after service in India and perilous journeys to Mecca and Harrar, Richard Burton, a much more worldly and cosmopolitan character who described both West and East Africa and was far the best writer among the explorers, with his colleague, the Somerset country gentleman John Hanning Speke, had already found Lake Tanganyika—'in the lap of the mountains, basking in gorgeous tropical sunshine. Below and beyond a short foreground ... shelves towards a ribbon of glistening yellow sand, here bordered by sedgy rushes, there cleanly and clearly cut by breaking wavelets. Further in front stretch the waters, an expanse of the lightest and softest blue, in breadth varying from thirty to thirty-five miles, and sprinkled by the crisp east wind with tiny crescents of snowy foam.'

In 1862–4 Speke and Grant came upon Lake Victoria and the elaborately organized Kingdom of Buganda, where Speke's entire self-confidence outfaced the able but capricious Kabaka, Mtesa. They went on to Lakes Kioga and Albert; they, and not Burton, found the sources of the White Nile.

[3] Perham and Simmons, citing *Missionary Travels* pp. 518–25, *op. cit.* pp. 135 ff.

[4] *op. cit.* pp. 175–6, citing Sir Richard Burton, *The Lake Regions of Central Africa*, Vol. II, pp. 40–4, in Perham and Simmons.

These, and other European expeditions, coincident with the greatest period of Victorian enterprise and prosperity, had traversed tropical Africa from sea to sea. They had been made in order to suppress the slave-trade, to propagate Protestant Christianity, for commerce and for curiosity. And they cost many adventurers their lives.

European governments took little interest in these explorations: they had enough to do already to protect the enclaves of trade and influence already established. In 1808 the British had founded Freetown at Sierra Leone as a base against the slavers; by 1821 the British forts on the Gold Coast were taken over; but the country was only made a Crown Colony, after a long hesitation, by 1874; though Lagos, captured in 1851, became one by 1861.

On the other side of Africa, the flourishing Arab island of Zanzibar was gradually made a British base against the slave-trade in the Indian Ocean. In 1861 the Sultanate of Muscat was separated from Zanzibar; and by 1873 the British had abolished the greatest slave-market of East Africa.

Away to the northeast, in Egypt and the Sudan, over which Muhammad Ali and his descendants had established their rule as Viceroys to the Sultans, British official interest was still confined to the railway built in the 'fifties from Alexandria to Suez. As Palmerston put it, 'We want to trade with Egypt, and to travel through Egypt, we do not want the burden of governing Egypt.' It was not until the Suez Canal was completed in 1869 that the British became deeply committed to protect the route to India, though in 1839 they had already established themselves at Aden and by 1830 had British political agents on the Trucial coast and at Bahrein.

In spite of their footholds on the fringes of West and East Africa and extensive exploration of the tropical interior, the British thus still controlled only one area of real settlement, and that in the extreme south. At the Cape of Good Hope in 1652 the Dutch had established a port of call for their East Indiamen and other shipping, and soon many pastoralists had trekked off into the huge hinterland. During the Napoleonic Wars the British took over this strategic colony; first in 1795–1803; then in effect permanently, in 1808, when the colonists numbered about 77,000. Friction between British administrators and missionaries and the more obdurate Dutch *Afrikaaners*, coincident with the worst crisis in Canada with the French Canadians, led, in 1836–7, to the Great Trek to the East; and here the Boer *Voortrekkers*, who were only a minority of the Cape Dutch, collided with a new and dangerous power, the Bantu Nguni clans, organized under Shaka Zulu from 1818 to 1828, and under his half-brother Dingaan between 1828 and 1840. After a long and horrible war culminating in the Boer victory on 'Dingaan's Day', 16th December 1838, the Boers mastered the Zulus and finally got what they wanted, two pastoral republics outside British control, the *Oranjie Vreistaat* (1854) and the *Transvaal* (1852) bounded by the Limpopo. Thus both the depredations of the Zulus and the land-grabbing of the Boers had wrecked the basis of Bantu society and created famine and disorder. The essential conflict was now for the land.

The British government, still mainly concerned with the Cape as a naval base, had now to think of their own frontiers, and were forced by the British traders exploiting the lush areas of Natal to annexe the country in 1845. This move, along with malaria and tsetse fly, would cut off the Trek-Boers on the hinterland from the sea : but they remained pastoral and self-sufficient on their great ranches in their archaic way of life, while the British developed the richer resources of the Cape Colony and Natal. In their own seventeenth-century African world, the Boers remained dourly 'apart'; and continued to regard the Bantu as *skepsal*—creatures—not *Mense*—people. By contrast to the Boers, now as African as any other pastoral people, the immense if casual British Empire represented a wider and a modern world.

And now more British settlers had arrived—as the five thousand colonists at Port Elizabeth in 1820. During the period of reform in Great Britain in the 'thirties, the normal patterns of British Parliamentary government were introduced : legislative and executive councils for Cape Colony; even, by 1854, a parliament in Cape Town, both houses elected on a franchise limited not by colour, but by a low property qualification. Moreover, as early as 1826 British law allowed slaves to bear witness against their masters and buy their freedom. And the evangelical missionaries, now active in South Africa as in other parts of the Empire, and without Boer memories of 'Dingaan's Day' on the Blood River, refused to treat the Bantu as animals.

Further, the imperial government, responsible for order and defence, was reluctant to allow the *Afrikaaners* the expansion that their pastoral needs and large families required. The fundamental conflict which runs through the history of South Africa is thus early apparent. Since both European minorities depended on Bantu and coloured labour they had essential interests in common, and political union was in their obvious mutual interest. But the project, already handicapped by daunting barriers of communication and distance, was long made impracticable by a fundamental contrast in outlook and ways of life. And even when it had been achieved, after two wars, the Dutch majority's policy of *apartheid* would cause the Union to leave the Commonwealth.

II

To suppress the long-established slave-trade out of West Africa was a daunting enterprise, but the British soon became deeply committed. It had, of course, to be put down, both on humanitarian principles and because it had made other major commerce impossible. The trade had indeed been so profitable that it had swamped anything else; and once the British had outlawed it within their own Empire, interest as well as sentiment drove them to suppress it elsewhere. Moreover, though the traffic was prohibited by most countries during and after the Napoleonic Wars, only the British Navy then had the power to suppress it. After 1808 a British squadron patrolled the Atlantic coast of West Africa and in 1817 the Spaniards and Portuguese were assigned £400,000 and £300,000 to allow ships sailing under their flags to be searched north of the equator. But the trade went on: the slaves were, in fact, worse treated, since only the more disreputable kind of slavers now operated. They would resort to any atrocity.

The British also had long to deter African rulers who still exported their subjects and captives, for in North America and Brazil the brisk demand ended only with defeat of the Southern States in 1865, and the abolition, in the 'eighties, of Brazilian slavery. So the British Navy kept a considerable squadron on patrol in the sweltering climate off West Africa: 'Quinine and mosquito nets were unknown, and the common treatment of fever was by bleeding. Even as late as 1859 H.M.S. *Trident* lost eight officers and thirty-six men from yellow fever in two months, and such a death-roll was not uncommon.'[5] The officials sent to regulate legitimate trade died off even faster and in 1862 Burton would describe the residence of the consul at Lagos 'as a corrugated iron coffin or plank-lined morgue, containing a dead consul once a year'.[6] When even in 1912, 'Saki' sent his anti-hero Comus Bassington to West Africa, 'that heat blistered, fever scourged wilderness where men lived like groundbait and died like flies',[7] the reader took it for granted he would die there, which he did.

But both missionaries and traders urged government to maintain their humanitarian and commercial interests. The Baptists, the Congregationalists, the Society for the Propagation of the Gospel, had

[5] A. C. Burns, *History of Nigeria*, London, 1929, p. 113.
[6] *Wanderings in West Africa*, p. 213, cited by Burns, *op. cit.* pp. 138–9.
[7] *The Unbearable Bassington*, London, 1912, p. 228.

all been founded in the late eighteenth century; in 1799 the evangelical Anglicans founded the Church Missionary Society; by 1803 the British and Foreign Bible Society was in being; nor were the Scots Presbyterians remiss. And they all had scope: in 1841 King Pepple of Bonny 'celebrated the anniversary of his father's death with a cannibal feast' ... saying 'it was the custom of his country; that his father did it and his forefathers also'.[8] The missionaries were not yet so numerous and enterprising as in the later nineteenth century; but they reinforced the political campaigns of Wilberforce and Buxton. The traders, meanwhile, scented great profit from palm-oil and groundnuts—now, with the Industrial Revolution and population explosion, in greater demand for soap, candles and machine lubricants. On the Gold Coast alone the value of exports through the British ports increased from £70,000 in 1831 to £325,000 in 1840, and of imports during the same period from £131,000 to £423,000'.[9] The prospects at Lagos and on the oil rivers were even more promising; British merchants established themselves in armed 'hulks' on the estuaries, and 'the palm oil exported to Liverpool rose from 150 tons in 1806 to 13,600 tons in 1839.[10]

All this activity, of course, was still peripheral. Many West African states, as already observed, were highly organized; and though Benin was now in decline, two major powers had emerged during the eighteenth century—Ashanti in the rain-forest behind the Gold Coast, and the Fulani *emirs* north of the Niger and the Benue. The former, now under their fierce Ashantihene, Psei Kojo, a well-organized military power, had attacked the Fantis of the coast; by 1806 they were menacing the British forts, and in 1824 they killed Sir Charles McCarthy, British Governor of Sierra Leone. So began the long Ashanti wars which flared up most savagely in 1863–5 and 1873–4, when Sir Garnet Wolseley burnt Kumasi, and drove King Kofi Kari Kari from his capital. They concluded only in 1896–1901, when Ashanti was annexed, and the Golden Stool, which harboured the spirit of the people, disappeared, to be recovered only twenty years later by some roadmakers and, in 1935, restored.

The Fulani *emirs* who, by 1804–9, had overrun Hausaland in a *Jihad* had been led by Usman Dan Fodio (1775–1817) of Sokoto, and his son, Muhammad Bello, both highly intelligent rulers influenced by a Muslim renaissance of the ancient cultures of Mali and Songhai described by Ibn Battuta in the mid-fourteenth century. And the Bornu to the east only resisted the Fulani attack under another

[8] Burns, *op. cit.* p. 118.
[9] J. D. Fage, *A History of West Africa*, Cambridge, 1969, p. 136.
[10] Burns, *op. cit.* p. 115.

Muslim, Muhammad al Kameni, who took on Dan Fodio in theological controversy as well as in battle. The big trading cities south of the Sahara had prospered under this new Muslim order, and the animist Yorubas were driven back on Abeokuta and on their military headquarters at Ibadan; but the European coastal trade in palm-oil, palm-kernels, groundnuts, forest rubber and cotton was now in fact superseding the Sahara caravans.

Such were the dominant economic and political facts behind the still tentative fringe commitments of the British in West Africa—in Sierra Leone, the Gold Coast and Lagos. All three areas would now be gradually consolidated, if only in late-Victorian and Edwardian times would the British be pushed into outright colonization during the scramble for Africa.

The Regency and mid-Victorian consolidation was thus limited, tentative and uneven. Freetown had proved a successful base for the Navy, and here, between 1825 and 1865, 130,000 slaves would be liberated. In 1821 Bathhurst on the Gambia, south of it, became a Crown Colony. But a forward policy on the Gold Coast, based on Sierra Leone, was checked by the death of McCarthy at the hands of the Ashanti; and government, which had taken over the Gold Coast from the British Company of Merchants in 1828, soon shifted responsibility to a committee of the merchants still concerned. And their representative, George McClean, more tolerant than the missionaries—much too tolerant, said his enemies—of the African way of life, established more informal and effective relations with the coastal chiefs, extending the range of British influence and exploitation.

Then, in 1841, government had to impose a kind of protectorate with a Legislative Assembly of local rulers. The Ashanti, prevented from exporting slaves, were planning their major counter-attack from the interior, which would erupt in the 'sixties and 'seventies, when the British had taken over more forts from the Dutch.

Further down the coast, the island of Lagos remained the principal centre of the slave-trade. Here the slavers, as in Dahomey, continued to flourish and the British now intervened, in the event to lay the foundations of Nigeria, their biggest West African colony. In 1845 King Akitoye of Lagos, evicted by his nephew, Kosoko, who supported by the slavers had exterminated his uncle's family, appealed to the British from his refuge at Badagri. 'I need not tell you, Sir,' he wrote to the British Consul, 'what a calamity it is for a King to be reduced to my distressed circumstances.'[11] He was given refuge on the Spanish island of Fernando Po, then under British control; and

[11] Burns, *op. cit.* p. 126.

the British seized their chance. In December 1851, with humane objectives but, using literally the 'gunboat diplomacy' now maligned, H.M.S. *Bloodhound* led a small squadron into the lagoon. She went aground and the British withdrew. But on Christmas Day, reinforced by H.M.S. *Sampson*, H.M.S. *Teazer*, by the Consul's barge fitted for rockets and by boats from H.M.S. *Penelope*, they again attacked, blew up Kosoko's magazine and fired the flimsy town. Akitoye was restored; the slave-trade in Lagos abolished.

Within weeks the monarch died, probably poisoned. His son, Dosumu, proved unable to put down the slavers or even maintain order. So by August 1861 Lagos had to be annexed; the Union Jack was unfurled and the ceremony concluded with a salute of twenty-one guns and the singing of the National Anthem by the children of the mission schools.[12] That June, the British Foreign Secretary had written, 'It is not without some reluctance that Her Majesty's Government have determined, by the occupation of Lagos to extend the number of British dependencies on the West African coast; but they have been induced to come to that determination because they are convinced that the permanent occupation of this important point on the Bight of Benin is indispensable to the complete suppression of the slave-trade in the Bight, whilst it will give great aid and support to the development of lawful commerce, and will check the aggressive spirit of the King of Dahomey',[13] who had a regiment of Amazons at his disposal. Further east, on the Oil Rivers, King Pepple of Bonny had also to be deposed; though, in spite of his anthropophagous past, he was fêted by the missionaries in London; and in 1875 King Jaja of Opobo, a slave who had fought his way to the top and knew the winning side when he saw it, was accorded a sword of honour by Queen Victoria for token assistance in the Ashanti War. Unfortunately, he took to massacring the Kwa Ibos, and the sequel in the 'eighties was less happy. He had to be deported to St Vincent.

III

In 1691 William Dampier, returning from the Far East, had described the Dutch Colony at the Cape. It was 'a high and very remarkable land,' he wrote, 'and off at sea it offers a very pleasant and agreeable prospect.' It was backed 'by a high mountain with a flat even top, which is called the Tableland'; the grass was short, 'like that which grows on the Wiltshire or Dorsetshire downs', and crops were excellent: wheat, barley, stone fruit and grapes; indeed, the Cape

[12] Burns, *op. cit.* p. 137.
[13] Burns, *op. cit.* p. 136.

British Possessions in South, East, and West Africa 1806–1914

Dutch made 'abundance of wine like a French high country white wine, but of a pale yellowish colour ... sweet, very pleasant and strong'.[14] And though this dry country was not 'proper for great cattle', sheep were large and fat; and there was 'a very beautiful sort of wild ass, whose body is curiously striped with equal lines of white and black'. There were fowls and ostriches, fish and seals, and the town had fifty to sixty houses, 'low and well-built', as well as a 'stately garden', well irrigated and 'hedged apart'. Dampier only regretted the exorbitant taxes on liquor and tobacco, and that he could find only three taverns in the place.

Founded by Jan van Reibeeck in 1652 for the Dutch East India Company, the Cape had been only a refreshment station, not a colony; and its white population by 1778 was still only 9,721. The Company accepted it as a liability, essential to shipping and, like the English East India Company, expected its officials to recoup their small salaries by perquisites and private trade. But in spite of occasional drought and the small fertile area cultivated, there was already a small export of wheat to Batavia and even Holland, and sometimes a glut of wine.

The only way to exploit the interior was by sheep- and cattle-ranching, an enterprise that appealed to those colonists 'unanchored' (*eenlopende*) in Cape agriculture. Up in the Karroo—the dry country at between 1,000 and 6,000 feet—was and is 'a region of flat topped hills with slopes untidy with rubble and tussocks of wiry dry grass ... underfoot the earth is brown, hard and compact. In the distance it is purple save where the dry west wind whirls the sun-baked ground into dust and fills the air with the haze which causes the breath-taking sunsets of winter.'[15] The *Trekboers*, as these pastoralists were termed, were not officially encouraged; but they were allowed to pay only nominal rents for their vast ranches—6,000–10,000 acres for a family. They pushed off, with their households, their oxwagons and livestock, already Africans who knew no other country, and well-adapted to their environment. By 1780 they had reached the Great Fish River, five hundred miles east of the Cape. They were patriarchal, old-fashioned Calvinists, pastoralists and hunters, who spoke their own dialect or *taal*, and who had already adopted a life 'much closer to that of the *Khoikhoi* (Hottentot) pastoralists than to that of seventeenth-century Europe whence their forebears came'.[16] Like the

---

[14] *Voyages to New Holland*, Vol. III, 1699, p. 531.

[15] C. W. de Kiewiet, *A History of South Africa, Social and Economic*, Oxford, 1941, p. 15, q.v., for the best short account.

[16] *The Oxford History of South Africa*, ed. Monica Wilson and Leonard Thompson, Vol. I, *South Africa 1870–1970*, p. 67.

rest of the Cape settlers, Dutch, Huguenot and German, they had always taken slavery for granted and there had always been rather more slaves than whites in the colony, for both the agriculturalists at the Cape and the Boers on the *Veldt* were a tiny minority among the large indigenous population—palaeolithic Bushmen or *San*, neolithic Hottentots or *Khoikhoi*, and, to the east, the much more numerous Iron Age Bantu.

When, following the occupation of 1808, the British in 1815 officially took over the colony, the principle of social, if not sexual, apartheid was already firmly established. 'By the late eighteenth century the distinctions between Christian and non-Christian, free and non-free were giving way before the growing gulf in social status between white and non-white.'[17] Yet, as experienced administrators, the British had to come to terms with the pre-colonial African majority, ancestral to most of the present population.

It was composed of a variety of peoples. The *San* were an extraordinary survival: hunters and scavengers, with no domestic animal save the dog, living off the game they brought down with poisoned arrows, stalked disguised as animals and drove on regular beats into pits and fences. Their artists, like their equivalents in the Sahara and in Europe, could depict the animals to the life. The *San* 'worshipped the praying mantis, mimed animals in dances, and danced to the sun and moon'. They were little yellow people with crinkled hair; expert thieves as well as huntsmen.

The *Khoikhoi*, on the other hand, were neolithic pastoralists and *strandlopers*, who spoke with a strange inimitable 'click' and herded many fat-tailed sheep and some long-horned cattle. Their chiefs rode slowly upon oxen, under sunshades of ostrich feathers on sticks and they had copper ornaments, ivory and beads. The people wore garments of sheepskin and oxhide; they dried meat and made mead, and built circles of huts round their cattle kraals. They sacrificed to the sky-god for rain, built cairns and propitiated their ancestors, and their weapons were spears and throwing sticks. To most Europeans their prominent lips and buttocks were unattractive. Sometimes the *San* would become their clients; or if opportunity served, kill them with poisoned arrows.

Though unwilling to part with their sheep and cattle, the *Khoikhoi* could not resist the beads, brandy and tobacco of the Europeans, whose offspring by their women proudly termed themselves Bastards. The *San*, on the other hand, were hunted down, and 'many white farmers thought and spoke of them as if they were animals'. But the children of both *San* and *Khoikhoi* could be tamed to be servants

[17] *O.H.S.A., op. cit.* p. 232.

and farmhands, and they soon mingled with descendants of West African and Indonesian slaves imported in the early years of the colony.

The Bantu were far more numerous and formidable. They had been moving south for generations, for 'the Dutch were not the first Trekkers in South Africa ... like the herds of wild game the native peoples had a slow rhythm of movement and change ... they moved freely, especially as their primitive and wasteful agriculture exhausted the soil. Thus they developed the half-nomadic habits which were best suited to a land of low fertility and irregular rainfall.'[18] They were part of that widespread Iron Age culture that extended from the Kenya highlands down through modern Zambia into Rhodesia, where their rulers had traded iron and ivory with India, China and Indonesia, built the Great Zimbabwe in the Middle Ages, extended and rebuilt in the seventeenth and eighteenth centuries. And the Monomatapas of the Lower Zambesi had early traded at Sofala with the Portuguese.

The Bantu ranged from the primitive herdsmen and villagers of the north to the more 'elaborately organized societies of the fertile coastlands and of Natal: they had in fact occupied the only parts of the sub-continent with a climate and rainfall suitable to primitive agriculture'.[19] Though they had never invented the wheel or plough, they were skilled herdsmen and reckoned wealth in cattle, valued more for number than condition. They raised millet, sorghum and beans, yams and melons, and they brewed beer; they were also miners and metal workers. By Western standards they were conservative, lazy and improvident; but their society was elaborately organized in terms of age groups who had shared an alarming initiation. Their chiefs had immense prestige and embodied the traditions and the luck of their peoples; but save when some great warrior, a Shaka among the Zulu, or a Moselekatze among the Matabele, broke out into arbitrary power, they were enmeshed in a complex web of custom and precedent and bound by law. In their tribal councils the chiefs would arbitrate disputes; but they ruled by consent more than force. Indeed, an intolerable ruler could be deserted or put to death. Bantu society was pervaded by witchcraft and sorcery; but the rulers, unlike the potentates of West Africa, very seldom sold their people into slavery. The land belonged not to individuals but to the tribe.

It was thus no empty land that the Cape settlers were cultivating and the Afrikaaner *Trekboers* beginning to occupy, and, as already

[18] Kiewiet, *op. cit.* p. 23.
[19] R. Oliver and J. D. Fage, *A Short History of Africa*, Harmondsworth, 1962, p. 130.

From a sketch by
Mungo Park: a
view of a bridge
over the Ba-Fing
or Black River

The Benin
Expedition: a
trader returning
to the coast

The Siege of
Rorke's Drift
Zulu War

Zulu warriors

Johannesburg
Market Square in
the 1890s

British troops
crossing the Sand
River during the
Boer War

Cecil Rhodes, by Mortimer Manpes

Christmas Day entertainment for the troops at Port Said

'Chinese' Gordon

Lord Kitchener of Khartoum

The Opium War, China 1841

Sale of English goods in Canton

Sir Stamford Raffles, Lieutenant-Governor of Benkulen in Sumatra and founder of Singapore

Sir James Brooke, Raja of Sarawak

Court of the Sultan of Borneo

recorded, by 1818 the Zulus had become extremely formidable. Most of the Bantu were 'an agricultural and pastoral people, with little sense of time and less of purpose'.[20] But in the late eighteenth century Dingiswayo, King of a small Nguni Zulu clan—the *ama-Zulu*, People of the Heavens—had made himself paramount over about fifty clans of the Nguni. He had then been ousted by Shaka—a royal bastard, who, like Genghis Khan, had survived appalling handicaps and vicissitudes. For Shaka had invented a short, heavy stabbing assegai— 'the *iklwa*, so-called from the sucking sound it made as it was withdrawn'[21]—and had also disciplined his head-ringed warriors into regiments—the *Chest, Horns* and *Loins*, with a *Haze* of youths for reconnaissance, known as *Shaka's Own*. They were ferocious warriors of limber and magnificent physique. Decked in complicated finery of leopard skins and ostrich feathers, and carrying great oval shields, Shaka's impis out to 'wash their spears' were the most martial of surviving Iron Age peoples. The Zulus devastated vast areas and sent ripples of migration and terror through the hitherto fairly static and well-adapted tribes. Shaka was murdered in 1828, at forty-one, by Dingaan, his half-brother, and ten years later Dingaan massacred an expedition of *Voortrekkers* under Piet Retief, whom he impaled: an atrocity amply revenged by Pretorius' commandos on the Red River on Dingaan's Day. Other hard-bitten Boers now drove another formidable people—the Matabele—north across the Limpopo, and thus both outflanked the Bantu along the Drakensburg above the richer country facing the Indian Ocean, and took over large areas of the High Veldt to the northeast.

Though defeated, the Bantu remained the predominant demographic fact. Unlike the sparse Amerindians, they were numerous and they never faded out. As their lands were overrun, their labour became all the more necessary. If with defeat and encroachment, the authority of their chiefs was undermined and their cohesion disrupted by land hunger, war and devastation, they always outnumbered both whites and coloureds in the racial structure of South Africa.

IV

The first British government at the Cape was military and autocratic. Lord Charles Somerset, the Governor, was a veteran of the Napoleonic Wars: a high Tory, out, it was said, to recoup his racing

[20] Donald R. Morris, *The Washing of the Spears: A History of the Rise of the Zulu Nation and its Fall in the Zulu War, 1879*, London, 1966, p. 39.

[21] D. R. Morris, *op. cit.* p. 97.

debts. He briskly organized frontier defences, and encouraged the first and not very successful major British settlement at Port Elizabeth. English replaced Dutch as the official language of the law courts and an advisory court and British judges were appointed. Already in 1812, on the 'Black Circuit' so notorious to the Dutch colonists, the grievances of Hottentots against their masters had been heard; now in 1828 'Ordinance 50' abolished the 'passes' restricting the movement of slaves. To the fury of the conservative settlers, already short of labour, non-whites could now even buy land and leave masters whom they disliked. The law was indeed officially extended to protect all British subjects whatever their colour. In 1829 a South Africa College was founded, ancestral to Capetown University; by 1847 there was an Anglican bishop. And now, with the tide of reform and humanitarianism running high at home, the missionaries were weighing in. John Philip is a representative figure. The son of a Scots schoolmaster in Fife, he had become a Congregationalist minister at Aberdeen, and he arrived in Capetown in 1819. He at once campaigned on behalf of the London Missionary Society to secure equality of status for the non-whites. Sued for libel by the principal official he had denounced, he was convicted and fined, to the delight of most of the colonists. But returning to England in 1836, three years after the emancipation of the slaves, he staged lecture tours accompanied by a converted Hottentot and a Kaffir—though the former afterwards lapsed and joined in raids on the colony. And such was Philip's influence with the Whig government and the Colonial Office, that he got Sir Benjamin D'Urban, a relatively liberal governor, recalled. Philip wanted to organize independent native states on the frontier: unpopular among the British, he was detested by the Dutch.

Far to the east, the *Voortrekkers* on the High Veldt were now outflanking the populous Bantu territories in Natal, where British traders and 'white hunters', coming by sea, had already established themselves in the time of Shaka. After the defeat of Dingaan in 1838, a Boer Commando had fought against British troops sent to protect the traders; and finally the exasperated Boers again took themselves off into the interior, leaving a situation so disordered that in 1843 the British had to annexe the country. They were now facing a problem then familiar in British India, as in the Roman Empire: whether or not an extension of the frontier would be an asset or a liability. And behind them was the Treasury in London, determined in those days of low taxation, on strict economy. Hence, often, a policy of two steps forward, one step back.

The territory between the Orange River and the Vaal, for example, first taken over by Sir Harry Smith in 1848,[22] was relinquished to the Boers by the Bloemfontein convention of 1854. In 1852 the Transvaal between the Vaal and the Limpopo had already been recognized as independent. But when, in 1865, the Boers of the Orange Free State went to war with the Basuto, the British intervened, and two years later annexed the mountainous area of Basutoland, between the Free State and the coastal plain. The two Boer republics remained cut off from the sea. In these circumstances projects of federation, advocated at the Cape by Sir George Grey, afterwards Governor and then Prime Minister of New Zealand, naturally petered out.

Such, in broad outline, had been the development of South Africa up to the 'sixties: the Cape and Natal had prospered, but they were still miniature agricultural economies; and the pastoral Boer Republics, though self-sufficient, were extremely poor. There was no staple product comparable to Canadian timber, fur and fish, or West Indian sugar and cotton. The wines of Constantia had become popular in England and, after the Napoleonic Wars, were still given preference over those of France; but in 1861, in the interests of European free-trade, Gladstone abolished duties on French wines, thus crippling the South African trade. Wool was the nearest thing to a staple product, and by the mid-century the main source of profit; but its export could not compare with the great wool-trade out of Australia. South Africa in the 'sixties was a poor country, and save for its strategic importance often considered, with its uniquely complicated racial problems, a liability. Nor was it a place for immigrants: the great tide of migrations went to America, Canada, Australasia.

Then, following finds on the Orange River in 1867, the prospect was transformed. At Kimberley in Griqualand, annexed by the British in 1871, prospectors discovered the greatest diamond reefs in the world. Not, as in other countries, alluvial diamonds, but deep 'pipes' of diamond-bearing soil which could only be exploited by expensive machinery. The early rush of prospectors soon gave place to great capitalist concerns; and the economy and infrastructure of the country began to be swiftly developed. And in 1886 this wealth of diamonds was surpassed in the Transvaal by the discovery on the Witwatersrand of the greatest gold-fields in the world. 'South Africa

[22] Sir Harry Smith had the most remarkable war record of all Wellington's Peninsular veterans sent to govern South Africa. He had fought in the Americas, both at Washington and at New Orleans, and won a resounding victory against the Sikhs at Aliwal. Lady Smith, who gave her name to a town famous in the Boer War, was a Spaniard, rescued by him from outrage at the battle of Badajoz.

[had] advanced politically by disaster and economically by wind-falls.'[23] Modern great industry had come to the country, with all that it implied.

V

The interior of Eastern tropical Africa, long a huge catchment area for the Arab traders in slaves, ivory and rhinoceros horns from Zanzibar and for the Egyptian conquerors of the southern Sudan, was now reconnoitred by Livingstone, and the sources of the White Nile discovered by Speke and Grant coming from Zanzibar, and by Baker from the equatorial Sudan. This magnificent and diverse country which includes Kenya, Uganda and Tanzania and extends from the Sudanese and Ethiopian borders down past the great lakes Albert, Victoria-Nyanza and Tanganyika to Lake Nyasa and the Zambesi, had in medieval times formed the hinterland to a more extensive trade in slaves, ivory, gold and iron with southern Arabia, southwestern India and even the Far East. A cosmopolitan Muslim culture had dominated the coast from Kilwa and Zanzibar through Mombasa and Malindi up to Mogadishu, part of an Indian-oceanic world that had contacts with China. 'Under the Ming dynasty (1368–1644) Mogadishu, Brava and Juba were reckoned as Imperial tributaries ... Ming porcelain has been found at every late medieval site on the East African coast', though 'the great part of such wares were probably acquired by Muslim Indian merchants in Western India and exchanged by them for African goods for the Indian market'.[24]

The irruption of the Portuguese into the Indian Ocean round the Cape had dislocated this old and far-flung economy; and by the early nineteenth century, when the British dominated the Indian Ocean, the main economic focus of the area was the island of Zanzibar, the greatest centre of clove plantations in the world and the main market for the slave- and ivory-trade into the interior. As in West Africa, the British now set about putting down the slave-trade; and the Imam Seyyid Said of Muscat and Oman, who by 1840 had moved to Zanzibar to conduct a flourishing traffic with the interior in collaboration with the Nyamwezi of Tanganyika at Tabora and Ujiji, had now to reckon with them. In 1840 a British Consulate was established at Zanzibar, and a British squadron was operating in the western Indian Ocean. As already recorded, although the economy of the place de-

[23] Kiewiet, op. cit. p. 89.
[24] See Roland Oliver and Gervase Mathew, History of East Africa, Chapter IV, 'The East African Coast until the coming of the Portuguese' by Gervase Mathew.

pended on it, by 1873 the slave-market in Zanzibar would be suppressed.

It was from this base that the British explorers Livingstone, Burton, Speke and Grant, penetrated the highland zone of East Africa, while Baker proceeded up the White Nile from the Sudan. The explorers themselves are all interesting in their determination and eccentricity. And, even beside the explorers already cited, Sir Samuel Baker was outstanding. He was the son of a wealthy shipowner with West Indian interests, had shot big game in Ceylon, and directed railway works on the Danube. Now with his intrepid German wife, he explored far up the Blue Nile, then in 1862 set out from Khartoum up the White Nile, reached Gondoroko and after two years even Lake Albert. A forerunner of Gordon, he was then appointed by the Khedive Ismail governor of Equatoria, supposedly to put down the slave-trade, and also to limit the indiscriminate slaughter of elephants for ivory.

All the explorers wrote vivid accounts of their adventures in many volumes, eagerly bought by the Victorian public, for whom their exploits had the sort of interest now evoked by the exploration of outer space. Few of them coveted money. Livingstone was sustained by an ineradicable sense of mission; Burton by anthropological curiosity, dislike of Victorian conventions and the desire for fame; Speke by love of adventure and sport; Baker by a rich man's love of adventure and by social and political ambition. Only Sir Henry Stanley, originally a workhouse boy from Wales, a naturalized American and the most efficient explorer, was out for gain: a pioneer journalist who had reported Napier's extraordinary Abyssinian campaign of 1868 before he went in search of Livingstone.

The country which these explorers penetrated contained a great variety of predominantly Bantu peoples, ranging from the non-Bantu Masai, aloof and proud pastoralists who lived off their vast herds of small cattle in which they reckoned their wealth, to the elaborate settled civilization of the Buganda, with its Bahima aristocracy. It also contained an immense and teeming variety of wild animals—buffalo, wildebeest, zebra, kudu, impala, waterbuck. Elephant and rhinoceros were hunted for their ivory and their horns, the latter passionately coveted as an aphrodisiac by the Chinese;[25] while lion, leopard and cheetah lived off the game; as the Masai off their cattle. And on the slopes of Kilimanjaro lurked that majestic ape—the huge jet-black gorilla, whose vegetarian, monogamous and pacific way of life was travestied by Victorian gorilla-hunters into one of appalling

[25] No scientific evidence supports their belief, but it was psychologically stimulating, particularly as the commodity was very expensive.

ferocity, since the animal defended itself when attacked, screaming and drumming on its barrel chest and twisting the heads off the enemies it could catch.

The exploration of these territories, like the exploitation of West Africa, was no deliberate prelude to colonialism, and the British government long evaded responsibility for them. Yet, here, too, the explorers were forerunners of a massive if reluctant takeover, following the 'scramble for Africa' set off in Europe during the 'eighties.

Many of the peoples discovered, though illiterate, were highly organized. When, for example, in 1862 Speke in Uganda approached the 'palace' of King Mtesa at Bandawarogo, he thought it magnificent: 'A whole hill was covered with gigantic huts, such as I had never seen in Africa before.' The etiquette observed was complicated, and though Speke wore his best clothes, he felt that he 'cut a poor figure in comparison with ... the dressy Waganda. They wore neat bark cloaks, resembling the best yellow cordoroy cloth, crimp and well set, as if stiffened with starch, and over that ... a patchwork of small antelope skins ... while their headdresses generally were abrus turbans, set off with highly polished boar tusks.'[26] The musicians danced 'like bears at a fair', and from the monarch downwards, the consumption of *pombe* beer was gargantuan. The Kabaka himself was splendidly attired: 'Everything was light, neat and elegant in its way, not a fault could be found with the taste of his getting up.'[27] Here in Buganda the Kabakas, whose power was absolute, for their brothers were generally all put to death on the royal accession, made much of their wealth by exporting slaves and ivory to the Arabs of Zanzibar; while northern areas suffered the sinister exploitation of the Turko-Egyptians at Khartoum and Gondoroko whence they raided for slaves and ivory. If the slave-trade were to be put down and European trade to be established instead, British governments would have to become involved in East as in West Africa. For the present, the field was left to the explorers, the missionaries and the Arabs who, but for European penetration, would have probably established a wider Muslim civilization in Equatorial Africa.

VI

Although the British were still politically uncommitted in East Africa, save for their informal control of Zanzibar, there was one

---

[26] Perham and Simmons, *op. cit.* p. 190, quoting Speke's *Journal of the discovery of the Source of the Nile.*

[27] Perham and Simmons, *op. cit.* p. 192.

area in which they had already become entangled. The ancient Coptic Christian kingdom of Ethiopia, described in the eighteenth century by Bruce, had since, on its broad and fissured plateau, with mountains rising to over 15,000 feet in the latitudes of Madras and Guiana, gone its often sanguinary way. But when British traders had established themselves at Massawa on the Red Sea to tap the trade with Southern Arabia, they became involved with the politics of the country.

In 1855 an obscure adventurer who had become the great feudatory, Ras Kassa, had proclaimed himself Negus Tewodorus (Theodore III) at Axum, with his main stronghold at Magdala, east of Lake Tana near the source of the Blue Nile. He had subdued the Muslim Galla of the south and dominated Tigre, Amhara and Shoa, and his regime had to be taken seriously by the British concerned with their interests along the Red Sea, particularly as the Suez Canal was already under construction.

Theodore was a ferocious despot, who had tried, in vain, to 'abolish slavery, to reform taxation, to pay his soldiers instead of allowing them to plunder, and ... even introduced into the country those extraordinary white jodhpurs in which Ethiopians still go about'.[28] Crazed at once with frustration and power, he developed megalomaniac ambitions and an inordinate craving for *tej*—the mead of the country—and for arack. And when he wrote an elaborate letter to Queen Victoria offering friendship the missive got lost in the Foreign Office. Furious at receiving no reply, the Negus imprisoned and even tortured the British Consul and incarcerated other Europeans, played a cat and mouse game over their release and even accorded similar treatment to the British envoy, Hormuzd Rassam, a naturalized Iraqi, belatedly dispatched with an acknowledgment which combined appeasement with menace.

Theodore still refused to release his captives, and the British, in the interests of their prestige in Africa and the Near East, decided to act. In 1867 a well-equipped expedition based on India was mounted, with Sir Robert Napier, afterwards Lord Napier of Magdala, in command.[29] He was an engineer who had constructed great irrigation works in the Punjab, fought on the Northwest Frontier, defended Lucknow during the Indian Mutiny and commanded the British

---

[28] Alan Moorehead, *The Blue Nile*, New York, 1962, p. 206, q.v., for a vivid account.

[29] Napier, no relation to Sir Charles Napier of the Punjab and Sind, came on his mother's side from the Codringtons of Barbados. He was a geologist and an artist: one of the more versatile and popular of mid-Victorian soldiers.

contingent on the Anglo-French expedition to Peking. The Ethiopian expedition was thus an unwonted logistic success. As has been well written, 'There has never been in modern times a colonial campaign quite like the British expedition to Ethiopia in 1868. It proceeds from first to last with the decorum and heavy inevitability of a Victorian State banquet, complete with ponderous speeches at the end.'[30] Huge piers were erected at Zoulah on the Red Sea and connected by rail to the main base, forty-four elephants transported the heaviest equipment and reservoirs were installed. Theodore's Ethiopian enemies helped the British march of four hundred miles to Magdala, which was taken by assault. The Ethiopians fought with their accustomed ferocity, but modern fire-power and organization was too much for them. The Negus Theodore committed suicide; the European captives were released. But the shrewd Rasses learnt their lesson—to import more European fire-arms at once. Napier, loaded with honours, became a hero of mid-Victorian England: Commander-in-Chief in India, Governor of Gibraltar. And the martial Ethiopians became much better equipped: so much so that when, in 1896, during the scramble for Africa, the Italians invaded their country, they would inflict on the invaders a singularly painful defeat.

[30] Moorehead, *The Blue Nile*, p. 230.

CHAPTER 17

The Settlement of Australia and New Zealand

Asked by Pitt's government his opinion of New South Wales, in the continent still known as New Holland, as a place to settle convicts whom the former American colonies would no longer absorb, the celebrated Sir Joseph Banks testified to its excellent climate: 'similar', he affirmed, 'to that of Toulouse in the South of France'. Moreover, there were no beasts of prey or major wild animals, except '*Kangourous*' which were 'almost the size of a middling sheep and harmless if hard to catch'.[1]

The matter was urgent. There were still a hundred and sixty crimes punishable with death: not only stealing a sheep but stealing linen, breaking down fishponds, making off with plated shoe-buckles when in drink, and purloining a master's goods worth over £2. But 'so dreadful a list' now defeated its own purpose: the justices would not enforce the law, the major criminals often escaped. Transportation was the answer; 'to restrict the number of capital inflictions ... and make guilty persons serviceable to the public and correct their moral depravity'. Between 1717 and 1776 thirty thousand British convicts had been shipped to North America; now, with the revolt of the colonies, the practice had 'become attended', to put it mildly, 'with considerable inconvenience'.

As a temporary expedient, the convicts had been set to clean the Thames by raising sand, soil and gravel, and accommodated in overcrowded and stinking 'hulks'. Such vessels—the *Dunkirk* at Plymouth, for example—contained two hundred and fifty prisoners in conditions of squalor and, it was feared, of 'nameless' vice. Indeed, during the Regency, conditions improved; but respectable people now complained of the goings on with lights and music on board, and declared that a sentence to the 'hulks' was no longer a deterrent. The

[1] C. M. H. Clark and I. J. Prior, *Select Documents of Australian History, 1788–1850*, Sidney, 1950, p. 26.

Gambia or the Gold Coast in West Africa had early been considered as dumping grounds for the most dangerous criminals; but field labour there was impossible and the climate threatened to kill every-one, warders and convicts, with fever and flux. Hence the consulta-tion with Banks, and hence a momentous decision.

For in 1787, under the command of Captain Arthur Phillip R.N., a half-pay officer lately farming in Sussex, seven hundred and fifty convicts, most of them with sentences of seven years, some of four-teen, and only thirty-four for life, and of whom a third were female 'unfortunates', set out in six transports for the Antipodes. They were accompanied by a guardship, H.M.S. *Sirius*, and by store ships, and 'attended for the first hundred leagues by the frigate *Hyena* (24 guns)'. There was 'no part of the planet', it was argued, 'except New Holland to which we can have recourse, though we found a new centre for buccaneers'.[2]

Captain Phillip could hardly afford to reject the appointment as Captain-General and Commander-in-Chief. Born in 1738 he was the son of Jacob Phillip of Frankfurt, who had come to England and taught German, and of Elizabeth Breach. He had fought at Havana and in the Seven Years War; then taken service with the Portuguese. He had afterwards become Post-Captain of the H.M.S. *Ariadne* in 1781, aged forty-three, but he was not in the class of those with influence who rose rapidly in the service. He proved an able Governor, and his papers are the foundation of a splendidly pro-duced account of the early days of the settlement and of the plants and animals of the country.[3]

By the standards of the time the voyage of the First Fleet was pro-pitious. Many convicts had petitioned to go to Botany Bay rather than to Newgate or the hulks; some were countrymen of good stock with the short names of their kind, if the London malefactors were often past caring and 'showed no sign of distress on the occasion of their exile from their native land'.[4] Sailing by the Canaries, Rio de Janeiro and the Cape, the fleet was well provisioned *en route*: the marines each got 1 lb of bread, 1 lb of beef and a pint of wine a day

[2] Ehrman, *op. cit.* p. 409.

[3] *The Voyage of Governor Phillip to Botany Bay, with an account of the Establishment of the Colonies at Port Jackson and Norfolk Island*, ed. Stockdale, London, 1789. It includes superb coloured plates of a 'Kanguroo' (p. 106, the orthography of the word, derived from its oral sound, is arbitrary), of vulpine and spotted opossums; of a bronze-winged pigeon, a kingfisher and a cassowary 'with wings, so short as to be totally useless for flight'. The title page has an elegant vignette of *Hope* encouraging *Art* and *Labour* under the influence of *Peace*.

[4] Manning Clark, *A Short History of Australia*, London, 1964.

(the convicts got less and, of course, no wine). So the transports *Scarborough, Lady Penrhyn, Friendship, Charlotte, Prince of Wales* and *Alexander* arrived on 20th January 1788, at the height of the Australian summer in Botany Bay, with relatively slight loss; the convicts 'looking forward doubtless with very varying emotions to that unknown region which, for a time at least, they were destined to inhabit'.[5]

Secured by 'native good sense from the seduction of romantic reveries', Governor Phillip and his subordinates had no illusions. By 26th January, a day still celebrated, they had transferred themselves to Port Jackson on Sydney Cove with its magnificent harbour.[6]

The Governor, particularly instructed to 'cultivate the affections of the natives', gave them beads and red baize, and they brought in plenty of fresh fish. But after the first excitement on 6th February, when the women landed and the entire community got drunk on rum, the convicts began to go down with dysentery and scurvy. Already, too, their 'habitual indolence' made it 'hard to clear the bush', alien and sombre to Europeans. So Phillip gave them a lecture. He thanked the marines for 'their steady good conduct', pointed out to the convicts that they were lucky to be alive, that there was not much to steal, and that thefts would easily be discovered. He stressed that 'illegal intercourse between the sexes encouraged a general profligacy of manners', and recommended marriage. Fourteen couples complied: but by the end of the month a convict had to be hung for robbing stores. So 'inveterate were their habits of dishonesty,'[7] it was thought, that some men would steal for the fun of it. Such was the beginning of the settlement of Australia: it contrasts with those of Virginia and New England; it was less casual than the first and much less high-minded than the second.[8]

The expedition, made by government policy, had been at first strictly organized and sensibly planned, and, unlike the Pilgrim Fathers, the settlers arrived at the right time of year. Banks' view of

[5] Stockdale, *op. cit.* p. 15.

[6]   Where Sydney Cove her Lucid bosom swells
          Courts her young navies and the storm repels.

The poet even foresaw a time when

          Embellished villas crown the landscape scene
          Farms wave with gold, and orchards blush between.

[7] Stockdale, *op. cit.* p. 76.

[8] Though the Society for the Propagation of the Gospel had selected an edifying library: 200 copies of *Exercises against Lying*; 50 *Cautions for Swearers*; 100 *Exhortations to Chastity*; 100 *Disuasions from Stealing*, and 50 *Religion Made Easier*. (W. K. Hancock, *Australia*, London, 1930, p. 37.)

the climate was fully vindicated; Phillip thought it 'on the whole equal to the finest in Europe', if the huts of soft wood and cabbage palm were 'very perishable'. Vegetables at first did well, and the Governor even hoped that the 'wines of New South Wales may perhaps hereafter be sought with avidity, and become an indispensable part of the luxury of European Tables'.[9] But the sheep promptly died from eating rank grass and Phillip did not foresee that wool would make the fortune of Australia. About the Aborigines he concurred with Dampier: 'the bodies of these people smell strongly of oil and the darkness of their colour is much increased by dirt'.

II

Port Jackson was a tiny enclave in a vast continent, one half of its arid interior in the equivalent latitude to the Sahara. The settlement, indeed, long remained deliberately restricted. The place was essentially a gaol, and the convict population was long out of balance: 'up to the year 1817 [only] twenty per cent of the total appear to have been women, and more than three-quarters of them were serving sentences of only seven years transportation'.[10] Most of them remained in the colony, having no better prospects. Until 1819 most of the 'new chums' had to shift for themselves for shelter and pay for it by overtime labour. Food was appalling and scarce; clothing and bedding dilapidated. Conditions in the few barracks put up by 1819 were atrocious, and 'the feelings of the men were petrified by the hardness of everything about them'.[11] Many were boys, taken up for petty theft, pickpockets from the slums, accorded the mercy of flogging not across the back but on the buttocks. In 1800 there were three times as many men as women; even by 1820 a proportion of 100 women to 270 men. Morals were loose and 'unnatural crime' was rife.[12]

With further settlement the system of 'assignment', begun in 1789, was developed, so that by 1817 in New South Wales only a third of the convicts depended on government provision. The employers had to house, feed and clothe their 'assigned' convicts, who worked ten hours a day for five days a week, six hours on Saturdays. Some found fair, even generous, masters; others were savagely exploited. The more hardened convicts worked in chain-gangs, guarded by soldiers.

[9] Stockdale, op. cit. p. 129.
[10] Gordon Greenwood, Australia: A Social and Political History, London, 1955.
[11] Greenwood, op. cit. p. 20.
[12] ibidem.

Discipline was enforced by flogging, freely administered in the barracks, and magistrates could order it for those 'assigned'. It was generally agreed that 'the great persuader to work and good order was the lash'. Hanging, generally in public, was the final sanction.

In these conditions the economy long remained restricted, even if the infrastructure of roads and bridges and houses was made. It was not until 1835, when free-trade and enterprise were the fashion and the wool-trade began to boom, that the economy fully broke out of its original coastal limitations, and not until the Gold Rush of 1851 that the population decisively increased. During the first half of the nineteenth century the population rose only to 405,000. Convicts—known as 'canaries' from their yellow garments—long predominated, and even the most liberal governors were autocrats with military authority. Transportation was not abolished in New South Wales until 1840, in Van Diemen's Land not until 1850, and in Western Australia not until 1868. Contrary to widespread belief, there were very few political offenders, like the Tolpuddle martyrs of 1834—not more than a thousand out of the eighty thousand transported between 1820 and 1840—and 'an examination of the records of transportation of any period between 1790 and 1840 would show that spirited poachers and political prisoners and even picturesque intelligent villains were but a small leaven in the lump, which was wretched and listless and forlorn'.[13] They had, after all, 'left their country for the country's good'.[14] About 130,000 were transported over the first thirty years; but now 'what proportion of Australians are descended from convicts can hardly be guessed'.[15] Already it was reported that the first generation of native-born Australians were finer than their parents—'generally tall in person, and slender in their limbs, of fair complexion, and small features ... active in their habits, but remarkably awkward in their movements ... quick and irascible but not vindictive'. They appeared 'not to inherit the vices of their parents'.[16] By 1827 the native-born Australians seemed 'little tainted by the vices so prominent in their parents', and modern Australia mainly derives from the enterprise of the great 'squatter' sheep-masters and from the 'digger' democracy of the 'fifties. The 'old lags' looked down socially on the subsidized free immigrants. 'Thank God,' said one of them, 'I was not a bloody immigrant ... It was not

[13] Hancock, *Australia*, p. 38.
[14] See C. E. Carrington, *The English Overseas*, pp. 212 ff.
[15] Carrington, *op. cit.* pp. 353 ff.
[16] *Report of Commissioner Bigge on the Colony of New South Wales*, 1822, cited R. M. Crawford, *Australia*, London, 1970, p. 42.

for nothing I came out.' But the enduring effects of Australia's convict stage are probably small and that intangible.[17]

The political and economic crises of the first settlements are now of little concern. After Phillip, a series of military or naval governors was sent out, of whom the most colourful was Bligh of the *Bounty*, or 'Breadfruit' Bligh (1805–9).[18] He quarrelled as vigorously with his subordinates and colleagues as he had with his crews, and tried with his usual impetuosity to break the various rackets established by the officers of the garrison, and to stop the unlimited importation of rum from Bengal and its use as wages and currency. What was worse, he fell out with the most enterprising adventurer in the colony, Captain John Macarthur, the pioneer of the sheep-ranching that would make the fortune of the country. He was therefore deposed and spent over two years in detention.

'Wool would make Australia a solvent nation, and in the end a free one',[19] but it took long to reach solvency and freedom, let alone wealth. Whaling and sealing were early developed—the female aborigines being employed to swim out to the seal colonies, lie down among them, and when the animals' suspicions had been lulled, club them to death at a concerted signal. But during the first decades mere self-sufficiency was the aim; and here Australia owed much to two remarkable Scotsmen, the main founders of the early fortunes of the colony. Macarthur, who came of Jacobite Highland stock, had arrived in New South Wales in 1790. He had obtained land, fought a duel and been recalled under arrest to London, where he resigned his commission. But he came out again, better equipped; and in 1797 imported merino sheep from the Cape, originally presented by a king of Spain to the Dutch. And in 1805 George III presented him with a royal ram. The fine long wool of the merinos was superior to the short coarser wools of most English sheep and by 1821 it could compete with continental wools to supply the huge demand occasioned by the Industrial Revolution. On his vast estate at Camden near Parramatta, 'the residence of John Macarthur, Esq.', south of Port Jackson,

[17] Crawford, *ibidem*.

[18] William Bligh, F.R.S. (1754–1817) came of an originally Cornish family of Plymouth, and had sailed with Cook on his second voyage, fought at Gibraltar under Howe and in 1787 arrived at Tahiti in the *Bounty*, to collect breadfruit for plantations in the West Indies. In 1789 he was set adrift by mutineers, and with a crew of eighteen in a boat twenty-three feet long, navigated the Pacific to Timor, while the mutineers colonized Pitcairn Island. Bligh also helped to quell the Mutiny at the Nore and in 1801 distinguished himself at Copenhagen. He ended his career as Vice-Admiral of the Blue, despite his failure in New South Wales.

[19] Hancock, *op. cit.* p. 12.

he planted olives and fruit-trees, as well as breeding sheep. In 1817 he planted the first vines; he also, in spite of Bligh, made substantial profits from rum. As the founder of both the Australian wool- and wine-trades, he is memorable.

In 1809 another Scot, Governor Lachlan Macquarie (1809–21), descended from the lairds of Ulva near Mull, came out to take over from Bligh.[20] He, too, was an autocrat and used his power to develop the colony, to sponsor exploration by sea and land, to replan Sydney and develop Hobart in Tasmania. He was detested for emancipating convicts and even making them magistrates; but his administration of the convict settlement was a turning point in the history of Australia.

It was during his time that the long exploration of the great continent began. Flinders had already explored the Bass Strait and the entire coast of southern Australia; in 1813 Blaxland, Lawson and Wentworth crossed the Blue Mountains which cut off the colony from the interior, to begin an epic of enterprise and endurance that would go on until the 'seventies.

These journeys and these explorers are less famous but quite as interesting as the celebrated contemporary adventurers in Africa, though they lack the evangelical fervour which made Livingstone so attractive to the Victorians. They all deserve more attention than the lesser and strident broils of colonial politics.

The explorers faced vast distances and constant drought; and while their African counterparts could buy or attract human aid, the sparse Australian aborigines, deeply attached to their tribal territories, soon realized the menace of the Europeans.

The explorers generally had wide horizons. They were British officers, bored with the Victorian peace; professional surveyors and botanists; or bushmen born in Australia and backed by local sheep-ranchers; there was a Pole, who naturally named the highest mountain on the continent Kosciusko, and a very accurate Prussian scientist. One of the earliest, William Charles Wentworth, who accompanied Blaxland across the Blue Mountains in 1813, became a leading politician in the squatter interest. Most of them wrote admirable accounts: as, for instance, Blaxland's expedition, which included four servants, four horses and five dogs who killed the kangaroos, drove off aborigines intent on a night attack and made the native dingoes frantic. The party hacked and climbed their way

[20] He had served in America (1777–83) and in India, then in 1800 in Egypt and again in India, 1805–6. He ruled the Australian settlement without a Council, and overruled all opposition. He bought back Ulva, which had been sold by his father's creditors, and died in 1824.

across fifty miles of mountain and bush and descried beyond them 'forest and grassland sufficient ... to support the stock of the colony for more than thirty years'.[21] George Evans, who followed them up and discovered the Lachlan and Macquarie rivers (for the Governor liked to be commemorated), could not 'speak too much of this country; the increase of Stock for some 100 years cannot overrun it; the grass is so good and intermixed with a variety of herbs'.[22] The Macquarie abounded in geese, duck and fish: Evans compared the country to an 'Ocean ... small hillocks are seen at great distances of pale blue ... on a calm evening near Sunsetting'.[23]

Very different were the terrible journeys into the arid outback undertaken by Edward Eyre and by McDouall Stuart; or by Burke and Wills who, in 1860–1, made the first crossing of the continent from south to north and perished; or by the more successful Forest and Giles.

In 1830 Stuart, an Harrovian who had fought at Waterloo, was appointed by Governor Sir Ralph Darling to trace the course of the Murrumbigee, if possible, to the sea. He proved that it joined the Murray, which emerged at Lake Alexandrina in south Australia, where he refused to shoot the seagulls which he thought 'messengers of glad tidings' that 'ill deserved such a fate';[24] and where he described the roar of the ocean and the 'silvery and melancholy note of the black swans',[25] elegant creatures in stippled shades of charcoal with carmine beaks.

Sir George Grey, later to serve in New Zealand and South Africa, was the first to describe the big aboriginal cave painting in Kimberley in the northwest: the most conspicuous 'an uncouth and savage figure ... Its head encircled by bright red rays ... inside a broad stripe of very brilliant red ... The face was painted vividly white and the eyes black ... the body being curiously painted with red stripes and bars.'[26]

In 1841 Edward John Eyre, whom we have already met in Jamaica, made the first crossing of the continent from east to west from Adelaide to King George's Sound through the wilderness that borders the great Australian Bight. The sand got into water, hair and eyes; most of the horses died; his native servants stole the fire-

[21] Kathleen Fitzpatrick, *Australian Explorers*: a selection from their writings with an introduction, Oxford, 1958, p. 38.

[22] *op. cit.* p. 44.

[23] *op. cit.* p. 49.

[24] *op. cit.* p. 119.

[25] *op. cit.* p. 112.

[26] *op. cit.* p. 165.

arms, decamped and shot one of his companions.[27] But he survived, along with the one reliable aborigine. Succoured by a French whaler on the coast and with renewed supplies, they struggled through to Albany.

In 1844 Leichhardt, the Prussian botanist and geologist, made the first expedition north into tropical Australia from Brisbane: he is the most scientific of the explorers. He describes the wealth of bird life, 'the noisy call of the laughing jackass (*Dacelo gigantea*); the scream of the white cockatoo; the hollow sound of the thirsty emu'.[28] He observed the brilliant tropic stars, the crocodiles, the flying foxes whose 'membranous wings' sounded 'like a hail storm'.[29] His expedition traversed Queensland to Arnhemland in the Northern Territories; but his final venture perished near Cooper's Creek in Central Australia.

The explorers, some led on by the hope of a central sea, found a terrible country. Stuart, who reached the Simpson Desert and wisely turned back, describes the 'tractless solitudes', and how, actually threatening them, a huge flock of kites swooped on the expedition. Here the horses displayed little sense: indeed, writes Stuart, disillusioned, 'I am satisfied that a horse is not capable of strong attachments to man, but that he is a selfish brute.' A dog would stay with a man to the end and, 'though carnivorous, guard the hand that fed him'; but 'turn a horse loose at night, and when will you find him in the morning?'[30]

Camels were the answer. But, in 1874, John Forrest, who later became the first Premier of Western Australia and the first Australian peer as Baron Bunbury, got through with horses from Perth to Adelaide. Then, in 1875, Ernest Giles, a Bristol man educated at Christ's Hospital, who won the gold medal of the Royal Geographical Society but died poor, made his famous east–west crossing through the interior, with fifteen pack and seven riding camels, and an Afghan to manage them. These animals were better adapted to the howling wilderness of red sandhills and blistering heat, some of it totally uninhabited by 'either man or animal ... a region utterly unknown to man and utterly forsaken by God'.[31] But they got through: 'When I say,' wrote Giles, 'that the personnel of the expedition behaved as well as the camels, I cannot formulate greater praise.' He even broke into verse.

> Though the scrubs may range around me
> My camel shall bear me on.

---

[27] *op. cit.* p. 17.   [28] *op. cit.* p. 228.   [29] *op. cit.* p. 250.
[30] *op. cit.* p. 266.   [31] *op. cit.* p. 483.

Such, in brief, was the immense and contrasting range of these explorations. By the mid-seventies the continent was roughly known, though only when rail and air transport became normal would the outback be fully opened up.

III

Already, by 1834, South Australia, with Gibbon Wakefield and the South Australian Land Company behind it, had been founded and financed by a more realistic price of land grants. Meanwhile, still mainly round the fringes of the continent, settlement had been going on. Western Australia, founded in 1829 and economically a private venture on the Swan River, had precarious beginnings, and in 1849 asked for labour forces of convicts to enable it to become properly viable. Even in the older colonies there was no Anglican established Church—there were too many Catholic Irish and Scots Presbyterians—and no squirearchy in the English sense; but agricultural conditions were unfavourable to a small-holding farmer. Here a rich oligarchy of great sheep-masters now blended with the bankers and merchants of the towns. The first small sheep-masters had pushed off beyond the state borders into the outback and 'squatted'—the word derives from the French—without formal title on crown lands. But this officially reprehensible habit became different if done in a big enough way; by 1836 the word was 'coming to include persons of respectability as well as bush looters'.[32] The original humble adventurers had been outclassed, for the booming factories of industrial Europe now demanded vast quantities of fine wool, and anyone with capital 'put everything in four feet'. By 1836 government had to recognize the accomplished facts of widespread occupation.

The first forebears of the squatter aristocracy and their dependents made good the hard way: 'there is no romance in monotony and mutton fat',[33] in isolation, unleavened *damper* bread and strong tea. Whiskered and bearded, in great 'cabbage tree' hats, essential adjuncts skilfully woven of the leaves of the cabbage palm, they would periodically invade the cities to forget their boredom in riot. But if one of the richest, James Tyson, started as a hired overseer, most of the big sheep-masters and cattle-men of the 'forties had capital behind them. They were a mixed lot: adventurous old Etonians, retired officers, sons of local officials, Scots with small capital swiftly increased—Wallaces, Macmillans, Robertsons and an Urquhart who

[32] S. H. Roberts, *The Squatter Age in Australia 1835–47*, Melbourne, 1965, p. 65.
[33] Roberts, *op. cit.* p. 284.

obtained 400,000 acres. They combined with the established land-owners of the Macarthur vintage—termed ironically 'pure merinos' —and with the businessmen who financed their huge sheep-runs. And during the mid-century, save for fluctuations in the market as in 1839 and 1843-4, which big capitalists could outlast, they had it all their own way. The shepherds and labourers, who had long com-peted with the convict labour, a virtual slavery which had made the fortunes of their employers, remained as poor as in Great Britain, but the climate was better and rum was cheap: 'Everybody drank the execrable Bengal rum ... all smoked Brazil twist.'[34] But the slums of Sydney were among the worst anywhere. And though the squatters and bushrangers loom large in Australian tradition, the majority of the population was urban and would remain so.

Wool had first launched the Australian economy out of mere sub-sistence and created a tradition of hardy enterprise and self-reliance; now gold would give it brisker stimulus—the first instalment in the exploitation of the mineral wealth of the country. In 1851 one E. H. Hargreaves, who had prospected in California, noticed that the geo-logical formation at Summer Hill Creek on the Macquarie near Bathurst looked similar to that of the Californian gold-fields. Told he was crazy, he persevered. And he struck gold. Soon bigger deposits were found at Bendigo and Ballarat in Victoria near Melbourne and there was a rush of 'Diggers', some from Australia and many more from beyond. In Victoria the population rose from 77,000 in 1851 to 540,000 ten years later. It was not quite a gold rush American style, for the government of Victoria handled it better; but it pro-duced raging inflation and changed the social order and outlook; for the resulting massive immigration would undermine the pastoral ascendancy, though this community put up a stubborn resistance. With the Diggers, most of whom were unsuccessful, mass democracy began to come to Australia, and their defiance of the authorities became legendary.

The most notorious episode became a political myth. In Decem-ber 1853, at the Eureka Hotel, Ballarat, one of them was murdered; but the landlord, though strongly suspected, was acquitted. A mob of Diggers, who resented the licence fees exacted and had already clashed with the police sent to collect them, burnt not only their licences but the hotel. Then a hundred and fifty of them fought the Victoria state troops from a stockade: twenty-five were killed, thirty-five wounded. Three soldiers lost their lives.[35] It was a brutal episode; most of the Diggers were not penniless proletarians but small

[34] Roberts, op. cit. p. 273.
[35] See Manning Clark, A Short History of Australia, London, 1964, p. 122.

speculators, out to abolish the fees. And since they had no alternative, the state government compromised: the monthly licence fee of £1 became annual, the revenue being recouped indirectly by a duty on the gold export.

> They gave us what we asked for,

wrote an insurgent,

> When we asked for it in blood.[36]

But the protest, if mainly of small capitalist speculators, had its radical overtones; there were demands, in Chartist style, for manhood suffrage, annual parliaments, payment of representatives. In retrospect, the affair would be regarded as a triumph of radical democracy, of the popular vote over the old representation of capitalist interests. And when, in 1857, over twenty-three thousand Chinese were brought in to develop the gold-fields, a new nationalism was provoked in the demand for a white Australia.[37]

After the 'fifties the number of Diggers fell from 155,000 in 1858 to 75,000 in 1866, and the oligarchy would long in effect predominate; but an egalitarian and nationalist outlook would increase. Not that there was yet much positive nationalist feeling. Attempts at Federation were ill-received: but by 1850 Lord Grey, Secretary of State for the Colonies in the government of Lord John Russell, had given the states an instalment of 'responsible' government as recommended in the Durham Report, and the Parliament Act of 1855 fully secured it. There were, indeed, nominated Upper Houses in the state parliaments, and the constitutions were weighted in favour of the rural districts, but the franchise for the Lower Houses were rapidly extended. By 1858 manhood suffrage had been established in all the colonies save Tasmania. And trial by jury and freedom of the press were now taken for granted. To the disgust of the Burkeian conservative, Wentworth, colonial democracy had arrived. So, by 1859, with the founding of Queensland, there were five self-governing colonies: New South Wales, South Australia, Victoria, Tasmania (for such by 1850 was the former Van Diemen's Land, where Hobart had become the biggest whaling station in the Empire). Only Western Australia, with its capital at Perth, still harboured a convict settlement.

Sydney, as T. H. Huxley described it in 1847 in his voyage on the

---

[36] Clark, *op. cit.* p. 123.

[37] As in South Africa in 1904, the Chinese arrived with practically no women, and the Diggers accused them of 'immorality caused by this absence'. The Chinese replied, very politely, 'As soon as we get a little money we will try to get home to our aged parents', Clark, *op. cit.* p. 124.

Rattlesnake, and where he met his future wife, already had a thriving social life. In Georgetown, Van Diemen's Land, 'everything from the rosy-faced girls and children to the fruit trees bent down under their weight of apples or pears put us in mind of England'. The clearings along the River Tamar were 'yellow with stubble ... and in the far distance lay the blue summits of the distant hills of the interior'.[38] The country, originally occupied to fend off French settlement and a separate colony by 1824, had outlived its past of exterminating the aborigines and fighting bush-rangers. And at Melbourne, the flourishing capital of Victoria, Huxley was 'much surprised, knowing that the place had not been more than ten years in existence, to observe its size and the many tall chimneys which rose near the river'.[39] There were already about twelve thousand inhabitants. He also liked the sub-tropical country behind Brisbane, where in the country that would become Queensland, the road lay through thick bush, with its 'beautiful, dense, dark foliage and whimsical festooned creepers'.[40] But he considered that Port Essington on the Gulf of Carpentaria was 'fit for neither man nor beast'.[41]

The original tiny convict settlement in New South Wales with its penal and military discipline had thus come a long way. The free immigrants now outnumbered the convicts; for in 1831 the British government, influenced by the colonial reformers and by Edward Gibbon Wakefield, whose *Letters from Sydney* (1829) had painted Australia in unwontedly attractive colours, had launched a campaign for assisted emigration financed by the sale of unsettled crown lands.[42] Australian employers, short of labour, could now obtain 'bounty' tickets issued to shipowners who now packed the emigrant ships. By 1841 over twenty thousand settlers had arrived, and since men still far outnumbered women, the redoubtable Mrs Caroline Chisholm now took a hand. Whole families, she insisted, should go out, and unmarried women should be looked after. Since life on the emigrant ships was 'lax', the *Family Colonization Loan Society,* which in 1850 financed a hundred and fifty emigrants bound for Melbourne and Adelaide in South Australia in the *Slains Castle* (503 tons), appointed 'six females of appropriate age selected by Mrs Chisholm to see that all the young females [were] in their sleeping

---

[38] *T. H. Huxley's Diary of the Voyage of H.M.S. Rattlesnake,* ed. Julian Huxley, London; 1935, p. 105. There is a drawing made by Huxley of himself in an immense 'cabbage tree' hat; plate 6.

[39] Huxley, *op. cit.* p. 102.

[40] Huxley, *op. cit.* p. 91.

[41] Huxley, *op. cit.* p. 148.

[42] Published under a pseudonym.

appartment at the proper time'.[43] They were allowed no strong drink, and the surgeons who looked after them had to be over twenty-six.

Both the colonial reformers and Mrs Chisholm—who ended life in poverty on a Civil List pension—fought for the small settlers against the big squatter and bourgeois oligarchy in the interests of a much broader national colonization to supersede the old convict-based social order. And even the colonial establishment, in its own interest, now encouraged local education. In the 'thirties, both King's School, Parramatta, and Sydney Grammar School had been founded; in 1836 a Church Act had given state aid to schools of whatever religious denomination; and by 1849–52 the University of Sydney was founded. There was much good colonial architecture, comparable to that in America and the West Indies, and the Australian cult of all kinds of outdoor sport was already established. The country was now self-supporting in agriculture and enriched through wool and gold— a place now safe for investment. By 1861 the population numbered nearly one and a half million, and most of the immense interior had been traversed. But only in the late 'seventies and 'eighties, with the big gold strike in Queensland, the discovery of zinc at Broken Hill, of copper at Mount Morgan and of coal in New South Wales, with the development of Queensland sugar and cotton, and of huge meat exports following the invention of refrigerated ships, would the biggest expansion come about, to bring the population to four million by the end of the century and create the assumption of 'Australia Unlimited.'

IV

In contrast to the vast Australian continent, New Zealand was relatively manageable. It presented an intricate and attractive variety of scenery and climate. And while Australia was sparsely inhabited by palaeolithic savages, the North and South Islands, *Te Ika a Maui* and *Te Wai Poumamu*, contained at least two hundred thousand neolithic Maori or 'normal ones'—a name they coined to distinguish themselves from the *Pakeha*, the whites. They were the most

---

[43] Margaret Kiddle, *Caroline Chisholm*, Melbourne, 1950, p. 149. Mrs Chisholm, whose tight little mouth and questing profile recall Miss Nightingale's in a more plebeian way, was the wife of an East India Company captain who shared her enthusiasm. If Dickens caricatured her as Mrs Jellyby in *Bleak House* 'a touch of her in Mrs Jellyby being a characteristic quirk of his exuberant humour—it did not detract from his good opinion of Caroline Chisholm', p. 168.

advanced and warlike of Polynesian peoples; and it would be more than fifty years after the first settlement in Australia that New Zealand would be annexed, and that reluctantly, following a free-for-all between missionaries, settlers and Maoris, and an apparent threat of a takeover by the French.

The superb landscape of New Zealand varies from the 'mangroves and mudflats' around Auckland, with its 'reefs, volcanic cones and dark islands reminiscent rather of Fiji than of a temperate land', to the rich pastures and willows behind Christchurch, and the gorse, fiords and snows of the Southern Alps. And the light 'not veiled as in England, stares with a Mediterranean boldness.'[44] Cook had, indeed, annexed the land; but the British government had imposed only the vague authority of New South Wales over its own subjects in New Zealand. The whalers and missionaries were more interested in this fine country, and a riff-raff of European adventurers and beach-combers from the Pacific had early fetched up on the North Island. But by 1797 British missionaries had also arrived in Tahiti; and by 1814, Samuel Marsden, a Yorkshireman educated at Magdalene College, Cambridge, and chaplain to the convicts at Parramatta, arrived in New Zealand on the first of his seven visits. The Maoris, like the Anglo-Saxon rulers in the seventh century, remained wary but ready to exploit the missionaries, some of whom were themselves glad to do some land-grabbing, and liable, indeed, to worse lapses. Deeply impressed by European firearms, the Chief Hohgi of Ngahitau so well adapted himself that he was exhibited as a convert at Cambridge and presented to George IV—an interesting confrontation. But he was in fact intent only on obtaining muskets. Armed with these, Hohgi soon massacred his hereditary enemies. Then a younger chief, Te Rauparàha, long terrorized both settlers and Maoris; underneath the impassiveness of one 'habituated to wield authority he concealed the savage ferocity of a tiger ... plainly discernible on a nearer view'.[45] Not a Maori was baptized until 1825, and he was on his deathbed. When conversion came, as in Frankish Gaul and Anglo-Saxon England, it was wholesale.

On the European side some of the whalers 'went native': as George Bruce, who married a chief's daughter and became a tattooed chieftain himself. These whalers and sealers, with their Maori wives, were formidable characters 'in whom the frankness and courage of the

---

[44] Kèith Sinclair, *A History of New Zealand*, Harmondsworth, 1959, pp. 222–3.

[45] Edward Verningham Wakefield, *Adventurers to New Zealand from 1839–1844*, London, 1845, p. 113. The author, the son of Edward Gibbon Wakefield, went out to New Zealand aged nineteen: he was a born writer.

sailor mingle[d] with the reckless daring of the convict or lag'.[46] They were called Long Bob, Butcher Nott, Horse Lewis, Flash Bill and Black Peter; and, being seamen, they kept their houses as ship-shape as 'a Dutch coaster'.[47] Some skippers even lent themselves to traditional Maori atrocities; as when in 1830 the crew of a brig hired by Te Rauparàha connived at the kidnapping of one of his rivals and his family and to their being cooked and eaten on board.

In 1835 Governor Darling of New South Wales dispatched a Resident to the Bay of Islands; and, in the following year, the indefatigable Edward Gibbon Wakefield turned his full attention to New Zealand, where he would have his greatest influence and end his days. The evangelical missionaries were against colonization, they wanted to create a Christian Maori culture; Wakefield was determined that New Zealand should be settled by white men. He promoted the New Zealand Association, under the patronage of Lord Durham and other influential reforming Whigs. And when government had to reconcile the interests of missionaries and colonizers, its hand was forced.

In May 1839, before the authorities could prevent her sailing, the Tory (400 tons) chartered by the Association and with Wakefield's brother William, the colonel, and one of Wakefield's own sons on board, set out from Plymouth. Commanded by a former master of The Beagle, on which Darwin had made his world voyage, the ship was well-found, with a small library; and the tedious voyage was relieved by 'an occasional battle of albatrosses' when boiled pork 'caught the gigantic birds by the beak' and they were made into 'sea pie'.[48] That August, the colonists arrived in Queen Charlotte's Sound. Here friendly Maoris came on deck, shaking hands and 'chattering', to barter pigs and potatoes for red blankets; and less friendly Maoris appeared in a war canoe, which 'silently paddled round the stern', the crew armed with tomahawks and green stone clubs.[49] Colonel Wakefield lost no time: by September he had bought an immense tract of country from the chiefs.

Back in England, government had reluctantly decided that New Zealand must be annexed, and Captain Hobson, R.N., had been dispatched to take over the country. He arrived in the Bay of Islands in January 1840, and by February he had negotiated the Treaty of Waitangi. Forty-six head-chiefs and some five hundred lesser ones assembled under large beflagged tents. The missionaries in high clerical collars and shovel hats, the French Catholic equivalent, who had suborned his converts to oppose annexation, fully robed, and the British officers in full dress, confronted the head-chiefs, who squatted

---

[46] Wakefield, op. cit. p. 311.   [48] op. cit. p. 20.
[47] Wakefield, op. cit. p. 331.   [49] op. cit. p. 34.

in a half circle opposite. The Maoris, who made a cult of oratory, spoke at length: some against, more in favour.[50] Finally, the British 'being desirous to establish a settled form of civil government', obtained 'full and clear recognition of the sovereign rights of Her Majesty over the northern parts of this island', with a government monopoly of the right of land purchase. In May, sovereignty was also proclaimed over the South Island 'by right of discovery'. In return, the Maoris obtained 'royal protection' and all the rights and privileges of English subjects. 'You must be our fathers,' said one Chief, 'you must not allow us to become slaves, you must preserve our customs and never permit our lands to be wrested from us.' Another, more pessimistic, remarked, 'We shall lose our power as Chiefs, and the end of this will be that the Chiefs of the Country will have to break stones to make roads for these white people.'[51]

Neither event occurred; the government proved unable, sometimes unwilling, to prevent exploitation and 'native' wars; on the other hand, the Maoris who long remained the great majority adapted themselves and revived. There was war but not apartheid. Wakefield himself wanted to maintain a native aristocracy with equal status, if on diminished territory.

There had been no alternative to annexation. Under the threat of European land-grabbing, even the missionaries thought it the lesser of the two evils. And the Maoris, in the short term, were all too anxious to sell, though their way of life needed broad territories. For it was not that of peasants. They lived well; as Sir George Grey, the greatest mid-Victorian administrator in New Zealand, would write, they 'live on fern-roots, fish, eels, duck and wild pig'; they should not, he insisted, be deprived of their 'wild lands', and left only with patches of cultivation.[52] They should sell their lands to government and then have the use of them; otherwise they would become 'lawless borderers'.

If annexation was unavoidable, and the long-term result a success, the immediate sequel to the Treaty of Waitangi and the founding of Auckland by Governor Hobson, was disastrous. Before annexation, the Colonial Secretary, Lord John Russell, had authorized the New Zealand Company to take over four acres for every pound spent in their venture, and in 1841 more colonists came out to take over a big area. They founded New Plymouth at Taranaki and,

---

[50] *Selected Documents on British Colonial Policy 1830–1860*, ed. Kenneth N. Bell and W. P. Morell, Oxford, 1928, p. 56, *q.v.* for a brilliant vignette of Edward Gibbon Wakefield, pp. xxviii–xxxiii.

[51] *op. cit.* p. 565.

[52] *op. cit.* p. 577.

under the leadership of another Wakefield, Nelson on the South Island. But Hobson died, and under his incapable deputy, the Maoris believed that the government was ratting on the terms of Waitangi. So the redoubtable Te Rauparàha now massacred and devoured Arthur Wakefield and his settlers at Wairau; a crime condoned, to the fury of the colonists, by the authorities, anxious to show their good faith. Then in 1843 a new governor, Captain Robert FitzRoy, Darwin's old shipmate in *The Beagle*, grandson of the third Duke of Grafton and inventor of the FitzRoy barometer, stood up for the Maoris with naval forthrightness and, by 1845, had to be superseded. In the confusion, it seemed that the relatively few settlers might be overwhelmed.

But in 1845–53 (Sir) George Grey, aged thirty-three, and already Governor of South Australia, saved the colony from collapse.[53] This able liberal imperialist defeated the Maoris, restored *Pakeha* prestige, confined the aged Te Rauparàha on a warship; removed the worst local officials; secured and limited the claims of the settlers. He collaborated with George Augustus Selwyn, the equally formidable first Anglican bishop of New Zealand, appointed in 1842. Together they restored the colony and in 1855 its six provinces would be federated, with an emphasis on state rights.

Wakefield, meanwhile, had not been idle. He was now promoting sectarian settlements—in 1848, Scots Free Churchmen at Dunedin in the South; in 1850, High Anglicans at Christchurch. Here, after early vicissitudes, the best-planned and most grandly sponsored settlement was made with singular success. By 1858 seven thousand settlers were developing sheep-runs, cattle pastures, farms and orchards. Though hardly typical of the main stream of spontaneous immigration, the Christchurch colony proved the most successful of the settlements Wakefield had inspired. In 1853 he himself came out to live in New Zealand, and became a member of the first parliament. He still obtained no official recognition; but this indefatigable and

[53] Sir George Grey (1812–98) the son of an army officer killed at Badajoz, had resigned his commission in 1839 to explore Western Australia, where, as already recorded, he had survived great hardships. As Governor of South Australia from 1841 to 1843 he had marked success. He governed New Zealand until the colonists obtained self-government, with much local autonomy for their six provinces. Grey then became Governor of Cape Colony, but failed, as we have already observed, to achieve the federation he desired, and in 1861–8 was again appointed to New Zealand. In 1871, after he had retired, he settled in the country and by 1877 he was Prime Minister. Grey was a scholar and bibliophile, who wrote books on the language of the Australian aborigines and a pioneer work on *Polynesian Mythology and Ancient Traditional History of the Polynesian Race*, London, 1855. He is one of the most talented and interesting of mid-Victorian pro-consuls.

often maddening eccentric had a touch of genius. He remains one of the most important founders of the British colonies of settlement.

But self-government within a loose federation did not solve the racial problem. As the settlers encroached and government wavered, there arose a new kind of united Maori nationalism. In 1859 Wiremu Kingi of Waitara in Taranaki had defied the Governor—'none of this land,' he said, 'will be given you, never, never, till I die.'[54] In 1860 they proclaimed a Waikato Chief, Wherowhero, as 'King' Potatau I. 'Let the mad drunkards get off to Europe,' runs a "Kingite" song, 'To the diggings—the sugar, flour, biscuit, tea consumers,'[55] so crystallizing their hatred for the British colonial way of life. In that year there was open war. The home government were horrified: 'England,' wrote an official, 'cannot undertake against a nation of warlike savages the defence of a number of scattered farms or villages, selected not with any view to such defence.'[56] Any help available must depend on other, greater, commitments. The current Secretary of State for the Colonies thought the Maoris had a right to a King, 'whether his name be Potato or Brian Boru'.[57]

But the metropolitan British were forced to intervene. The wars, fought mainly in the southwest of the North Island, were never on a great scale—about a thousand whites were killed; perhaps two thousand Maoris. By 1864 European weapons had broken the main Maori resistance, though a sporadic guerrilla warfare by fanatics of a new religion, who thought themselves invulnerable if they chanted *Hau Hau*, dragged on until 1872. The Maoris, whose gallantry won the admiration of the British troops, who often sympathized with them against the land-hungry colonists, were beaten; their lands confiscated, their social order disrupted. In the North Island they would lose over half their territory.

So, before the economic realities of colonial settlement, as harsh here as in North America, South Africa or Australia, ended the evangelical attempt to found a model colony on Christian principles. But in New Zealand the sequel was less divisive. Already in 1865 white land-grabbing had been checked by a Land Court; and already in 1867 the Maoris were represented in the Lower House of a Federal Parliament, and five years later two of the chiefs were included in the Upper House. In the 'seventies the Maori population even began to increase, to become an integral part of modern New Zealand.

Peace having been imposed, the settlers, if long handicapped by lack of capital investment, now had a lot to go for; and from the 'seventies until the advent of the radical Liberal government of

---

[54] Sinclair, *op. cit.* p. 124.
[55] Quoted in Sinclair, *op. cit.* p. 112.
[56] Bell and Morrell, *op. cit.*
[57] Sinclair, *op. cit.* p. 132.

Premier Seddon in 1893, the better-off immigrants remained politic-ally predominant. 'The country,' wrote Samuel Butler, artist and topographer as well as writer, who came to New Zealand in 1860 and placed his *Erewhon* Utopia in it, thought the country the 'grand-est that can be imagined'. 'How often,' he wrote, 'have I sat on the mountainside and watched the waving downs, with the two white specks of huts in the distance, and the little square of garden behind them, the paddock with the patch of bright green oats above the huts, and the yards and wool sheds down on the flat below; all seen as through the wrong end of a telescope, so clear and brilliant was the air.'[58]

Butler doubled his investment of £4,000 in four years by buying a sheep-run at Rangitata near Canterbury; he was typical of the lesser capitalists who made good through pastoral farming. As in early Australia, the first wealth of the colony would come in this pastoral way. And the average immigrant, without such resources, but in a more favourable environment for small farming than Australia, often obtained his own smallholding and became self-sufficient, if not yet farming for a substantial market, let alone for export. The areas around Wellington, Nelson, Canterbury were mainly pastoral; those round Auckland and Taranaki agricultural. The Maori wars had hardly affected the South Island, and in 1861 gold was discovered at Otago, so that Dunedin became a boom town. Then in 1864 there was another gold strike in the west coast; later one near Auckland. A substantial establishment would predominate till the 'seventies when, following financial crises, a much more democratic political order would come in.

Thus in New Zealand, as in Australia, a vigorous and potentially egalitarian colonial society grew up, though in the former the native population survived and would even prosper, for, on balance, and thanks a good deal to the work of Grey, the Treaty of Waitangi was 'the best bargain, from the Maori point of view, ever made by any native race'.[59] Moreover, there had here been no convict settlement. And if mid-Victorian New Zealand was still debt-ridden and the settlement sparse, and Wakefield's vision of a transplanted British social hierarchy had not materialized, many settlers of good British stock had escaped the industrial life of their own overcrowded islands, and founded a new nation, akin to Australia but distinct from it, on the other side of the world in the south Pacific.

[58] *Erewhon: or Over the Range*, London (fifteenth impression) 1922, p. 6. See also Butler's *A first year in Canterbury Settlement*, London, 1863.
[59] E. L. Woodward, *The Age of Reform*, 1815–70, Oxford, 1938, p. 376.

CHAPTER 18

The China Trade, Singapore and Sarawak

While British colonies of settlement were being founded in Australasia, British traders, independent or backed by government, were developing their interest in the Far East, while missionaries as well as adventurers from Great Britain and Australasia were settling on the major islands of the Pacific. The fortunes of the East India Company, otherwise in decline, had long depended on its trade monopoly in the Far East. Anson's unpromising contact with Canton in southern China had now been developed, and by 1773 the Company was established outside Chinese jurisdiction; if subject to the extortions of the imperial officials, *en rapport* with the local merchants or *Hong* who, at a safe if inconvenient distance from Peking, were alone allowed to trade with foreigners. The British sold opium (carried not in the Company's ships but in English vessels registered in Indian ports), as well as cotton, spices, tin and lead, in exchange for silk and, above all, for tea. The British imported four million pounds of tea in 1783 and twenty million only eight years later. The national addiction to tea had now spread to the rapidly increasing and industrialized work people, who already consoled themselves for their cooking by its grateful warmth, and the Company was netting a profit of about £500,000 a year. Moreover the directors again had their eyes on the potential riches of Indonesia, still dominated by the Dutch. Indeed, the convict settlement in Australia had been regarded by its more sanguine projectors as a foothold for trade with the Far East. And after the Napoleonic Wars a valuable base for expansion had been secured. In 1814 Ceylon, with its strategic harbour at Trincomalee, had been finally taken over from the Dutch. It had already been seized by the British in 1796 and, two years later, made a Crown Colony; but the high and forested interior was still ruled by the King of Kandy, an incalculable despot who naturally resented the

European intrusion. Though guerrilla resistance long continued, he was deposed in 1815.

Apart from being the main surviving centre of Buddhism in southern Asia, Ceylon had long been linked culturally and commercially with Indonesia, in particular with the medieval Buddhist kingdom of Sri-Vishaya in western Java, still famous for the superb sculptures at Borobadur. Westward, too, Ceylon, 'the island Palaesimundu called by the ancients Taprobane',[1] had since Graeco-Roman times been connected with the Persian Gulf, southern Arabia and East Africa, and the Emperor Claudius had received envoys from the island.[2] In a very different context, it was now to be developed for world markets: first for coffee, then for tea plantations, and its possession enhanced British commerce and sea power in the East.

Eastward British influence was now further extended by two men of genius. In 1819 Sir Stamford Raffles, a brilliant linguist and diplomat, founded Singapore: 'what Malta is in the West,' he wrote, 'that may Singapore become in the East.'[3] After the abolition of the East India Company's monopoly in 1833 it would become much more than Malta: the strategic and economic hub of a booming cosmopolitan trade with the Far East. Then, in 1841, James Brooke, who had begun a spectacular career by absconding from Norwich grammar school, became Rajah of Sarawak on the northwest coast of Borneo. He was an independent oriental ruler: it was easier, he told Queen Victoria, to govern thirty thousand Malays than to manage a dozen of Her Majesty's subjects, and in 1864 his regime was recognized by the British as an independent state.

Further acquisitions could have been made. Raffles, backed by Lord Minto, Viceroy of India, had first tasted power in 1811 as Lieutenant-Governor of Java, taken from the Dutch; the Moluccas —the famous 'spice islands'—could also have been held. But, in spite of the arguments of those experienced in the East, diplomatic decisions in Europe prevented these annexations. To restore the European power-balance, a buffer state, including Belgium, was set up in the Netherlands, and the Dutch colonies in Indonesia, in jeopardy while the Batavian Republic had perforce sided with Napoleon, were restored.

So, while great colonies of settlement were developing in Canada and Australasia, and Europeans were spreading out in South Africa,

---

[1] Sir Mortimer Wheeler, *Rome Beyond the Imperial Frontiers*, London, 1954, p. 123, citing the Greek author of the *Periplus of the Erythaean Sea*.

[2] Wheeler, *op. cit.* p. 134.

[3] D. G. E. Hall, *A History of South East Asia*, London, 1961, p. 433.

the British coped with 'government at a distance, furious assemblies, foolish governors, missionaries and slaves',[4] and with the general friction between advanced and primitive societies, as the tides of European industry and population swept into new continents. Concurrently, British entrepreneurs, with the strategic naval and military power broad-based on India behind them were exploiting the commerce of the Far East. How they did so, and the responsibilities that government accepted, evaded or muddled through, make an interesting study. By the mid-nineteenth century, though administrators in Whitehall were loath to admit it, the British Empire, like British sea power, was worldwide.

II

In 1795 when the conflict with Revolutionary France was raging in Europe, the Manchu Emperor of China, Ch'ien-lung, abdicated after sixty years of great power. His reign had seen a climax of imperial expansion, luxury and cultural achievement, and the beginnings of decline. He had ruled over a vast civilization, the equivalent not of any European state but of Europe itself, and which, of all the great cultures, had the most massive population and ancient continuity. The Manchu Sons of Heaven, like the thirteenth-century Mongol conquerors, had quickly been assimilated—by the mid-eighteenth century they could not even speak their own language; and they had encouraged the intensely conservative Confucian learning and literature of the scholar gentry, with whom for the needs of government they had come to terms. Massive encyclopaedias had been commissioned, writers encouraged—by the mid-eighteenth century the *Dream of the Red Chamber*, the greatest Chinese novel, had been written—traditional drama had flourished, the ancient porcelain industry had revived, and, in the unwonted peace, the swarming populace had increased from about 184·5 million in 1754 to 374·5 million in 1814. At the expense of the Kalmuks of the Ili region and of western Turkestan they had infiltrated to the southwest as well as moving north into Manchuria.

The Chinese Empire, like the Roman and the British at their greatest extent, had been forced to expand to defend what it already held. The Manchus were perforce as much imperialists as the Europeans. The mid-eighteenth-century campaigns which had overwhelmed the Kalmuks and taken Kashgar, which in 1789 had

[4] Bell and Morrell, *op. cit.* Oxford, 1928, p. xiii, citing Henry Taylor summing up the raw material of his duties at the Colonial Office.

reasserted Chinese overlordship in Burma and Assam, and which, even in 1790–1, had overwhelmed even the Gurkhas of Nepal, had been made for security, not profit, and they had strained even the immense resources of the Empire. Already by the late seventeenth century, the Chinese had collided with Russians on the Amur, and their Office for the Regulation of Barbarians had condescended to make the first 'capitulation' with foreigners, when in 1727 a Russian embassy had been admitted to Peking. Such 'capitulations'—and the term is misleading, for it means the agreed headings on an unequal treaty between the Son of Heaven and ostensibly abject foreigners, never regarded as properly reciprocal by the Chinese—would in fact gradually allow the virtual economic and political subjection of China to the Western powers, including the United States.

The British, from their vantage point near Canton, were determined to exploit the interior; but they were long kept out. The Emperor, who mediated between Heaven and Earth, exacted the full ritual of the Kow Tow; and when in 1793 Lord Macartney's mission arrived, it was preceded by a banner announcing the 'Embassy from the Red Barbarians bearing Tribute'. 'The Celestial Empire,' the ambassador was informed, 'possesses all things in prolific abundance and lacks no product within its borders. There is therefore no need to import the manufactures of outside barbarians in exchange for our own products.'[5] Moreover, Macartney, 'being inhibited by Ulster obstinacy, refused to perform the Kow Tow. He was prepared to go down on one knee and bow as often as they liked; to descend on all fours and touch the earth with his forehead was more than he could endure. His mission was a failure, and he departed without a Treaty of Commerce being concluded. Lord Amherst, who came on a second mission in 1816, announced in advance that he would not perform the Kow Tow and was, with all courtesy, conducted back to his frigate.'[6]

To the rulers of Manchu China such complacency seemed natural. They were blankly unaware of the contemporary Western world; and their 'extreme conservative outlook was shared by the whole official hierarchy, Chinese and Manchu alike ... the type of mind that entered the Civil Service was a mind closed to all ideas of progress; almost incapable of grasping the possibility, still less the need, for change ... The real cause of the rapid decline of the Manchu Empire in the nineteenth century was the intellectual stagnation brought about by a small alien ruling class, itself dominated by a petrified cultural

[5] Cited by C. P. Fitzgerald in *China, a Cultural History*, London, 1954, pp. 557–8.

[6] Harold Nicolson, *Monarchy*, London, 1962, p. 46.

tradition."[7] This stagnation, which had lasted for centuries, was reflected in the economy. Though medieval Chinese technology had been more advanced than that of Europe, here no industrial revolution confuted the Malthusian law, and peasant agriculture could not keep pace with a population explosion. Peasant risings thus broke out under popular leaders—as in Shantung and Honan, suppressed at heavy cost of heads and money, and culminating in the great T'ai-Ping rebellion of the mid-nineteenth century which, but for European intervention, would probably have brought down the Manchu regime itself. Already, on the accession of the Emperor Hsuang Sung (1821–50), the Chinese government was in no condition to resist the penetration of the 'outer barbarians dwelling at the ends of the sea'.

The first British commercial objective was to break out from the inconvenient confines of Canton and open up other ports to the interior all up the coast. In 1838 their opportunity arrived. Chinese officials had long connived at illegal imports of opium: between 1823 and 1832 they had risen from 6,000 to 20,000 chests on the Canton estuary alone. But contrary to much modern opinion, the British were not forcing opium on the reluctant Chinese government and deliberately debauching their customers. The Chinese in fact thought it a harmless drug, if taken in moderation; and 'opium sots in China are as rare as dypsomaniacs among ourselves ... [Chinese] public opinion refused to condemn a habit that appeared to the ordinary observer to be socially harmless'.[8] Indeed, when the authorities tried to suppress the trade, they did so not as a European attempt to corrupt their subjects but because it paid no duty, drained silver out of the country and reversed a favourable trade balance.

Twenty million pounds of opium were confiscated, a British warship was attacked and the British were excluded from trade with Canton. They answered by blockade. In 1840–2 troops from India, supported by gunboats, moved up the coast to the Yang-Tse estuary and upriver to Nanking in the heart of China. Under the imposed Treaty of Nanking, a large indemnity was paid, Hong Kong island ceded, new treaty ports opened—Amoy, Fuchou, Ningpo—most profitably, Shanghai. Next year, the British, like medieval merchants in backward areas of Europe, obtained 'extra-territorial' rights to trial in their own courts, thus avoiding the old Chinese custom of torture to extract evidence; and a 'most favoured nation' clause, later extended to other powers, entitled them to any further privileges granted to anyone else.

This breakthrough, confirmed by similar treaties of the Chinese

[7] Fitzgerald, op. cit. p. 563.
[8] Fitzgerald, op. cit. p. 565.

with France and the United States, led to a vast extension of commerce in tea and silk, porcelain, wall-papers and lacquer, while swift-sailing *lorchas* conveyed even more contraband opium to an expanding market, besides doing some slave-running and piracy on the side. The southern Chinese merchants prospered, if at the expense of the north and of an increased loss of silver, with resulting inflation. Hong Kong flourished; Shanghai became even richer than Canton; and European and Chinese merchants combined to create a board of Customs Control. In 1864, following the disturbances during the T'ai-Ping rebellion, an independent Chinese Maritime Customs Service was set up under an able Irishman, Sir Robert Hart: it would survive all the vicissitudes of Chinese politics until the Japanese invasion of 1937, and protect and regulate an enormous trade.

Thus Western business 'opened up' China. And with commerce came Western religion, science and political ideas. Missionaries, banned in the early eighteenth century, were now protected; and the T'ai-Ping rebellion itself was inspired by an odd mixture of Protestant Christianity and Chinese pre-Manchu conservatism. Its leader, Hung Hsiu-Chu'an, was a Cantonese, who had been ploughed in the Civil Service examination. He therefore became very radical and, inspired by a vision, demanded equal distribution of land, communal centres to collect any surplus, the emancipation of women (they would no longer bind their feet), prohibition of opium, alcohol and tobacco and, though the Manchu treaties were rejected, a more friendly attitude to foreigners. Hung soon won a big following among the peasantry, who plundered the Buddhist monasteries; and by 1853, master of the Yang-tse valley, he established himself in great splendour, with thirty wives and a hundred concubines, as *T'ien Wang* (Heavenly King), in the great city of Nanking. He thus looked well set to establish a new dynasty and in anticipation appointed subordinate *Wangs* to rule his empire.

During this crisis the British and French, feeling the time ripe for new concessions, also attacked the harassed Manchu government. In 1858, following the seizure of a probably piratical *lorcha*, the *Arrow*, and the imprisonment of her crew, Palmerston sent troops from India to occupy Canton—a move that coincided with a Russian advance in the north which led to the development of Vladivostock, as well as with a severe Muslim rising in Turkestan. In 1860 the French and English occupied Peking: a campaign in which the future Lord Napier or Magdala participated; and since the Emperor had maltreated British diplomats and even murdered the correspondent of the *Times*, James Bruce, 8th Earl of Elgin, formerly Governor-General of Canada and afterwards, briefly, of India, ordered the Imperial Summer Palace to be destroyed. It was an eighteenth-century building in the rococo style, and Elgin showed the ruthlessness, if not the artistic flair, of his father, the 7th Earl, who had removed the Elgin marbles from the Parthenon.

The consequences of this Second China War were decisive. Tientsin, the harbour for Peking, became another Treaty port; a fortified legation area was planted in Peking; and the British acquired Kowloon opposite Hong Kong. Only the T'ai-Ping could upset these satisfactory arrangements; so the Europeans decided to help the now subservient Manchu Emperor to suppress them.

Strangely enough, that militant Christian, Captain Charles Gordon, R.E., was seconded to the Chinese for the good work. For the T'ai-Ping, though their name meant Eternal Peace, had not lived up to their professions of Christianity, and were committing major atrocities and devastation. So the commercial opening up of Imperial China by Western business interests was clinched; and 'Chinese' Gordon, at thirty, won the kind of reputation long after enjoyed by T. E. Lawrence, another very peculiar man of action. Gordon already had extraordinary magnetism and strategic insight. Appointed to command about three thousand motley troops, under Chinese authority but subsidized by the European merchants of Shanghai, he galvanized them into deserving the title they already claimed—The Ever Victorious Army. He used the Yang-Tse waterways to infiltrate behind the T'ai-Ping outposts and to mop them up, and led his troops into battle carrying a small walking-stick. In 1863 he captured Soochow, and although, following the execution of some T'ai-Ping *Wangs* contrary to the terms of surrender, Gordon resigned, he returned that autumn and finished off the campaign. The Manchu Emperor offered him vast sums, which he declined; but he could not refuse the immense gold medal, or the yellow sash and peacocks' feathers of a mandarin of the First Rank; still less the C.B. and promotion to Lieutenant-Colonel with which the British government rewarded his services. Nor could he avoid the reputation which would lead to his great appointments and celebrated fate in the Sudan.

Thus the vast and splendid façade of Manchu China crumbled before the advance of a technologically superior civilization; Russia encroached in the north; the British, French and Americans up to Tientsin from the south.

The eclipse of the massive Chinese civilization would not last. But during the nineteenth century, outclassed in technology and administration, politically incoherent and economically run down, handicapped by the very success of a system which had long served its turn, the Chinese suffered another foreign exploitation. It was nothing unusual in their history; but now it was imposed by Europeans; not Mongols or Manchus.

Among these Westerners the British were the most enterprising. Their 'China Trade'—which Galsworthy would make the Victorian foundation of his *Forsyte Saga*—became a source of immense profit; Shanghai and Hong Kong became centres of a far-flung network, the latter still a British possession. Only after the Japanese invasion and the Second World War, the rise of another indigenous peasant leader in the mid-twentieth century and the assimilation of Western technology and Marxist–Trotskyite ideas, would China again become a world power of the first consequence.

III

Since the coming of the Portuguese, the Dutch and the British, the huge tropical islands of Indonesia, like the Moluccas, had long been exploited by Europeans. Now the Revolutionary and Napoleonic Wars gave the British a strategic and economic opportunity to overreach the Dutch. The Batavian republic being now dominated by the French, the Dutch East Indies were swept into Napoleon's strategic campaign to dominate the Indian Ocean, planned from the Dutch bases on the Cape, Ceylon, Java and from the French naval base on Mauritius. Hence the swift British takeover of the Cape and Ceylon, and afterwards of Mauritius; and Java and the Straits of Malacca had also become strategic objectives. Already at Penang, the British now occupied Malacca, a base for a brief conquest of Java. Then, as we have seen, in 1819, Sir Stamford Raffles, one of the most interesting Regency architects of Empire, founded Singapore. Raffles, who had risen in the service of the East India Company by sheer ability and tact, and who had at once mastered Malay, combined diplomatic skill with strategic insight. He was born in Jamaica, son of the unsuccessful master of the cargo ship *Ann*, and brought up in penury—they could hardly afford candles. He early entered the East India office as a clerk. By 1805 he was promoted to a post at Penang at £1,500 a year, married Olivia Fancourt and began his lifelong study of Malay and Indonesian civilization and environment. Appointed in 1811 Lieutenant-Governor of Java, he introduced radical but not controversial reforms, and the Dutch, resuming possession of the island in 1816, accepted most of them. Made President at the dilapidated island of Bencoolen off Sumatra, where, he wrote, Government House was infested with dogs and polecats, Raffles was invalided home; and, like Warren Hastings, he had to defend his forward policy against the directors of the Company. But he was knighted by the Prince Regent and backed by Lord Hastings, the Governor-General in India, before he occupied Singapore. Raffles was a pioneer naturalist and anthropologist, and one of the earliest Europeans to appreciate and understand Malay and Indonesian culture. He made a large collection of animals and plants at Bencoolen and explored the Sumatran jungles; but in 1824 most of his collections and documents perished when the ship on which he had embarked for England caught fire. In London the Company then presented him with a bill for £22,000 for going beyond his instructions. Though he was personally exonerated. Raffles was burdened by this debt, settled by his widow by £10,000 paid to the Company. In retirement he became the principal founder of the London Zoo.[9] The Dutch had overlooked the economic potential of Singapore; and, in February 1819, a month after getting permission to find a base inside the Dutch area of monopoly, Raffles could write, 'Here I am at Singapore true to my word, and in the enjoyment of all the pleasure which a footing on such classic ground must inspire. The lines of the old City and its defences are still to be traced, and within the ramparts the British Union [Jack] flies unmolested.'[10]

A disputed succession, after the death of Sultan Muhmud of Johore had given Raffles his opening. He had backed Hussein (the 'Singapore Sultan'), the legitimate claimant, and soon 5,000 Spanish dollars a year to the Sultan and 3,000 to the local Temenggong had confirmed the deal. They both thought the British a lesser evil than the Dutch.

Singapore was singularly well placed; the focus of trade routes radiating to the Indian Ocean and the Bay of Bengal, to China and Japan, to Indonesia, the Moluccas, Australasia and the Pacific. In 1826 a British administration of the 'Straits Settlements'—Penang, Malacca and Singapore—was set up. Planned and reorganized by Raffles in 1824, the government of the island was well suited to harmonize the interests of Malays, Chinese and Europeans. Between 1833, when the Company's monopoly was dissolved, and 1862 the population rose from 22,000 to 90,000.

Already in control of the Cape and Mauritius and by 1823 with a foothold in Burma, the Regency British had gained another important strategic and economic base. They were long reluctant to take over Malaya itself, but following the mining of tin in the late nineteenth century, then the boom in rubber, they would come to administer much of what had become one of the richest areas of the world. And though never taken over, the vast tropical areas of Indonesia,

[9] See R. Coupland, *Raffles, 1781–1826*, Oxford, 1926.
[10] Cited by Coupland, *op. cit.* p. 90.

long exploited by the Portuguese and Dutch, also came within a British economic sphere of influence. It was a world of contrasting sophistication and savagery; as in the great islands of Sumatra and Java, the picturesque enclave of Hindu–Malay civilization in Bali, in Borneo and beyond to Celebes, the Moluccas and Timor. Cosmopolitan Singapore would become the economic focus of the whole area. Here was a wealth of metals, sugar and rice; of timber and fruit and spices; of animals and birds exotic to Europeans; and here were peoples, uninhibited by the caste system of India or disciplined by the intense commercial drive of the Chinese, who appeared singularly attractive to those who, like Raffles, understood their way of life.

IV

Under the Kingdom of Sri-Vishaya in the eighth century and the Hindu maritime Empire of Madjapahit in the thirteenth, which had beaten off a Mongol invasion launched by Kublai Khan, life in Indonesia and on the eastern seas had been relatively pacific. But with the collapse of Muslim Mataram in Java, following the advent of the Portuguese and the Dutch, piracy, slave-raiding, the age-old depredations of the Dyak tribes in the estuaries, forests and mountains of Sumatra, Java and Borneo had all increased. Before the Europeans could exploit and develop these vast territories, piracy and headhunting had to be put down. Sir James Brooke was mainly responsible for doing so. Like Raffles, he was fascinated by the peoples and environment of the Far East. The son of one of the East India Company's administrators in Bengal, and commissioned in an Indian regiment, he had fought in the first Burma campaign. And when in 1835 he inherited £30,000, then a considerable fortune, he bought his own yacht, *Royalist*. Then, in 1838, he set out for Borneo, with a doctor, a naturalist, two mates, twelve sailors and a couple of boys, originally to trade at Singapore. By August 1839 he arrived at Kuching in Sarawak, where Muda Hassim, then Governor, under his nephew the Sultan of Brunei, welcomed him as an ally against a current revolt. By 1840 Brooke, who had also visited Celebes, had so much assisted him that he was offered and accepted the rajaship of Sarawak, a position confirmed by the Sultan and formally ratified in 1842.

Brooke delighted in the place. 'For this country,' he wrote, 'you could not want a richer; its soil is fine and admirably calculated for the culture of rice, coffee, nutmegs, cotton . . .' It had 'a noble river, a healthy climate and woods' which 'could supply the dockyards of

Europe'.[11] Inspired more by the kind of goodwill, often apparent in the well-to-do Victorian gentry, and by desire more for reputation than for profit, Brooke transformed the usual exploitation into a juster government, which he conducted mainly himself. 'It is essential,' he observed, 'to the good government of the natives to treat them on a footing of equality. On this point Europeans are most grievously wanting. They always adhere to their own customs, feeling and manners, and in a way force the natives to conform to them.'[12] Raffles was here a 'brilliant exception'.[13]

Outside his own territory, where he lived with little contact with Europeans, Brooke collaborated with Captain Henry Keppel, R.N., who was based on Singapore, to put down the Dyak pirates who infested the seas and estuaries of Borneo, and the Muslim slave-raiders who carried off anyone they could with the connivance of the Sultans. But Brooke liked and understood the Dyaks, who often reciprocated his interest. When a young man needed to take a head, they explained —for without having done so he could not take his proper place in society—he was always careful to go outside his own territory to collect one. Brooke believed that once the area had been pacified and developed, Dyak initiative and resilience would invigorate the country.

His success in developing Sarawak and putting down piracy now obtained official recognition; and in 1848 he was knighted and appointed consul for North Borneo. But he had his political enemies. Cobden and some radicals accused him of being cruel to the pirates and Dyaks; an accusation that led Lord Aberdeen, to appoint a Commission of Enquiry at Singapore, by which Brooke was entirely exonerated. But, characteristically, the radical politicians had done much harm on the spot. The rumour of the accusation and the Commission got round to the Chinese, who had swarmed into a now more lucrative Sarawak. In 1857, confident that Brooke had lost the support of his own government, they attacked and destroyed his residence and his library. Brooke escaped by diving under their boat but they accounted for several of his English colleagues before the Malays and Dyaks came to the rescue and massacred most of the Chinese.

This typical sequel to liberal sentiment was soon eclipsed by the long-term advantages of Brooke's paternalist regime, which proved

[11] *Narrative of Events in Borneo and Celebes ... From the Journals of James Brooke, Esq.* by Captain R. Mundy, 2 vols, London, 1848, Vol. I, p. 325.

[12] Mundy, *op. cit.* Vol. I, p. 356.

[13] Mundy, *op. cit.* p. 351.

well suited to the country to which it brought a novel order and prosperity—one of the better aspects of colonialism. Brooke died in 1868,
but his family retained his position until the Japanese invasion of
1941.

V

Out beyond Borneo and Celebes the vast Pacific Ocean had not
yet been divided into spheres of influence by the great powers. It
was not until 1874 that the British government accepted the
sovereignty of Fiji from Thakombau, who had presented his favourite war-club, named the Blood Bather, to Queen Victoria so that she
might rule 'justly and affectionately' and they all 'might live in peace
and prosperity'.

In fact it long looked as though Tahiti would be the first major
island to be brought into the Empire. Here Wallis and Cook had
come ashore, and here the English missionaries had won their earliest
influence. As in New Zealand, the first Europeans had been whalers,
beachcombers and adventurers, whose often nefarious activities came
to include 'blackbirding' or kidnapping *Kanakas* as labourers and
ranchhands, or, in the 'sixties, as coolies to grow cotton and sugar
in the major islands and in Queensland. But the missionaries were
also early in the field: Cook's account of Tahiti had made it famous;
and in 1795 the London Missionary Society had been founded, originally to convert its pagan inhabitants.[14]

Two men of versatile if incongruous vigour and ability soon made
their mark: John Williams, a former apprentice ironmonger in London, was sent out in 1816; and in 1824 George Pritchard, originally
a brassfounder in Birmingham, who later became British consul for
the area. Both put their training to good use: Williams could build
a boat sixty feet long out of improvised materials himself and sail
it eight hundred miles; he reduced the language to writing and set up
a printing press. And he wrote *A Narrative of Missionary Enterprise
in the South Seas* (1834), before being killed and eaten by the inhabitants of Erromanga in the New Hebrides, who mistook the good man
for a 'blackbirder'. Pritchard had better luck, though the French de-

---

[14] One vocabulary, compiled in Cook's time in the Society Islands, well
indicates the interests of the Polynesians. It includes *Poheea*, it is very hot;
teepy, being lazy; *Ahooa*, my legs ache; *my'neena*, to tickle; *e'hoee*, to kiss;
mo'hoe, scented oil. Gastronomic words include *Boa*, hog; *erooy*, belch; and
O'opya I am full up. Activities include *Ehopoo*, to dive; *Horo'wai* means surf;
and *Mao*, a shark. *Ewona* signifies pulling the hair; *Toa*, a warrior; and *Toe*,
an axe.

ported him from Tahiti after their takeover in 1843; he wrote *The Missionary's Reward* (1844) and died in retirement at Hove in 1883.

Subjected to these influences, the Tahitian way of life, which had shocked Cook and intrigued Bougainville, had apparently been transformed. The merry pagan islanders had acquired a Wesleyan sense of sin and decorum: there was a Temperance Society, and they regularly said grace before meals. When in 1835 Darwin described them, they still had 'the dexterity of amphibious animals in the water' and appeared honest, neat and clean; and though the missionaries had prohibited 'the flute and dancing' they were still cheerful.[15] Darwin was struck by their grace and intelligence: the missionaries, he pointed out, though criticized as kill-joys, had abolished infanticide, tribal warfare and human sacrifice. He thought that some European visitors had attacked them because they were disappointed that the Tahitians had reformed. Queen Pomare, though 'a large and awkward woman ...' had 'one royal attribute: a perfect immobility of expression under all circumstances';[16] and with ironic humour remarked that one boisterous sailors' chorus could hardly be a hymn. She thought highly of Pritchard, and she was furious when, in 1843, after two Catholic French missionaries had been thrown out with ignominy by their Protestant colleagues, the French annexed the island as a supply base, and the 'missionary kingdom' was wound up under culturally more congenial masters.

Fiji, on the other hand, the British would retain. Here was a base and coaling station on the route from Panama to Sydney, and by the 'fifties strategists were thinking that it might be 'inconvenient to be excluded'. A zealous consul, Thomas Pritchard, son of Pritchard of Tahiti, tried to force the Colonial Officer's hand; and in 1858 King Thakombau, the precariously paramount chief, in debt to Americans for $45,000 for destruction of some property, offered the island to the Queen. But the British government, with a Maori war on its hands, rather sanctimoniously replied 'that it must continue to entrust the propagation of the Gospel in distant parts of the world ... to the piety and zeal of individuals. The hope of the conversion of a people to Christianity, however specious, must not be made a reason for increasing the British dominions.'

The situation in Fiji now became impossible. By 1874 Commodore Goodenough reported: 'We can see no prospect for these islands should government decline the offer of cession but ruin to the English planters and confusion to the native government.' And

[15] Charles Darwin, *The Voyage of the 'Beagle'*, ed. Leonard Engel, New York, 1966, p. 413.
[16] Darwin, *op. cit.* p. 410.

Thakombau now had another able adviser. In 1864 John Thurston, after farming in Australia and botanizing in the south Pacific, had been wrecked on Samoa. An excellent swimmer, he had survived and lived happily among the people; then, four years later, armed with this knowledge, he had arrived in Fiji. He had soon become the unofficial secretary to the king, then acting consul. But such was now the disorder that Manchester cotton interests and Australian farmers in New South Wales had long been urging annexation—a rich sheep-master even offered to pay the debt to the Americans himself. For the hunt for *Kanakas* was now in full swing; and the notorious 'Bully' Hayes, son of a Mississippi bargeman, was only one of many ruffians who battened on it. Indeed, he prospered until knocked on the head by his own ship's cook and thrown overboard, bound to an anchor, with the words 'Fore sure massa Hayes dead this time'. Cheated over their indentures, signing contracts they could not read, or simply hi-jacked, the *Kanakas* were being rounded up. Further, in Fiji alone, there were already more than two and a half thousand whites; some substantial planters, others insolvent absconders, drop-outs and drunks. The former had already petitioned the Americans to make the country a protectorate—a request refused.

Hence, in 1874, Commodore Goodenough's Report; and hence— since there was no alternative—the decision to accept the sovereignty offered by Thakombau as paramount king and chief. In that year Sir Arthur Gordon, one of the best Victorian pre-consuls, was appointed Governor of Fiji, and by 1877 he would also be High Commissioner for the Western Pacific. Reluctantly, another and enormous sphere of influence had been acquired.

BOOK IV

The Defensive Climax

1867–1931

CHAPTER 19

Zenith of Imperialism

When in 1883 Professor J. R. Seeley, the Cambridge historian, published his lectures on *The Expansion of England*, he reflected and encouraged a changed outlook on the Empire. With singular prescience, he pointed out that the accepted supremacy of Europe was already on the wane: 'If,' he declared, 'the United States and Russia hold together for another half-century, they will, at the end of that time, completely dwarf such old European states as France and Germany, and depress them into the second class.' 'They will do the same,' he added, 'to England if at that time England still thinks of herself as a European state, as the Old United Kingdom of Great Britain and Ireland, such as Pitt left it.'[1]

The British Empire, 'the last survivor of the European sea-borne empires', was now faced either with expansion and consolidation or with decline. 'At once commercial and warlike,' it was now potentially a vast British nation, and when Napoleon had shut the British out of the continent of Europe, they had proved that they could do without it. In fact, 'a fine covetousness mixed with heroism' had enabled the British 'to leave Europe altogether behind and become a world state'.[2] And this position Great Britain must now consolidate. Already 'our terrible hive of population at home' gave rise 'to most anxious politics'; and if the Empire were not developed, the country would subside into mediocrity, 'as the lustre of Athens grew pale as soon as Macedon rose, and Charles v speedily brought to an end the great days of Florence'. Yet instead of drifting into the resignation of played-out empires, the British, who had shown the world how liberty could be adapted to the conditions of a nation-state, had now in fact been even more original as the founders of a Greater Britain. Turgot had compared colonies to 'fruits that cling to the tree only

[1] *The Expansion of England,* two courses of lectures, London, 1883, p. 75.
[2] *ibidem* p. 293.

until they ripen'; but the logic of British political history had led to empire on a world scale.

These sentiments would have shocked most civilian mid-Victorians devoted to *laissez faire* and free-trade, and, until 1895, when Joseph Chamberlain came to the Colonial Office, few of those in control in the inmost circles of power were ever much attuned to them; but they now took on an aspect of the mounting nationalism then gripping all the great European states, and they were in tune with fashionable views of Darwin's doctrine of the 'survival of the fittest', then misinterpreted as the survival of the most belligerent rather than of the most adaptable.

And there were many other reasons for this change of political climate. While the world financial supremacy of London remained unchallenged and the British merchant marine, like the Navy, was still twice that of any power in the world, Great Britain was no longer its workshop. As pioneers of the Industrial Revolution the British had obtained a tremendous start: they were now often beginning to pay the price in obsolescent technology, restrictive practices, unemployment and the amateur and complacent management of their wealth. Even in the heavy industries, they no longer set the pace; Germany and the United States were now producing the best, cheapest and most abundant iron and steel; while inventions and discoveries in electrical, chemical and oil industries were being better exploited outside Great Britain. Long accustomed to economic supremacy, the British were becoming less adaptable, less professional; their management less open to talent from below. Where free-trading Victorians asked only to go their own way uninterrupted by the state, the Edwardians and their heirs clamoured for 'Tariff Reform'—that is protection—while with the great financial crisis of 1929–31 and the abandonment of the gold standard, the medium of exchange would be disrupted whereby a free-trading country had prospered and more harm be done to an economy dependent on world trade than even by the First World War. Already by the 'seventies British farming was in decline, as vast prairies and ranches were exploited outside Europe, and their products transported by rail and refrigerated ships to feed a top-heavy urban population determined on cheap food.

This loss of industrial competitiveness, an excessive population and agricultural malaise were still masked by enormous wealth drawn from land and real estate, by massive overseas investments and by the worldwide financial power and services of the City of London. And the enterprise of British finance capitalists, constant since Tudor times, was well deployed: most massively in North and South

America, then in India, Australasia and the Far East. Africa was comparatively unimportant and never became a major interest until the discovery of diamonds at Kimberley and gold in the Transvaal. But by the 'eighties the still mainly aristocratic political and social establishment was, as usual, assimilating new men. Joseph Chamberlain, the self-made Birmingham manufacturer, and his kind, thought that the colonial Empire should be better developed on business lines. He declared that the British must 'think imperially' and his ideas are in close harmony with Seeley's. Cecil Rhodes, who could have thrived in the seventeenth century Caribbean or in Clive's India, who was worth over a million pounds a year and left a vast fortune, most of it to promote his large ideas, unofficially added vast territories to the Empire in pursuit of a project as visionary as anything Elizabethan—the world supremacy of the Anglo-Saxon peoples as a prelude to world peace. As new chances cropped up, the millionaires and their associates pounced: diamonds in Kimberley, gold on the Rand, tin and rubber in Malaya, oil in the Middle East.

Yet it was still, as throughout the history of the British Empire, a civilian expansion; part of the surge of capitalist development of which the British had been the pioneers. It was not, as in the Tsarist or Wilhelmian Empires, the work of the state, an expression of state absolutism for which 'any war would do', or of an atavistic military class who waged war as they 'would ride to hounds'; nor, in spite of the hysteria over Omdurman and Mafeking, of a deep-rooted *Volksimperialismus*, always alien to the majority of the British of whatever class.[3]

Nor can this basically commercial and financial expansion, which was cosmopolitan in a world of still predominant free-trade, be attributed to the supposedly 'inevitable' compulsions of a glutted capitalism in its final 'New Imperialist' decadence. This explanation, first formulated by the British economist J. A. Hobson[4] in the rueful aftermath of the Boer War, would be widely accepted and it would be developed by Lenin in *Imperialism, the Highest Stage of Capitalism* (1916), the foundation of the Marxist–Leninist, Stalinist and

[3] Joseph A. Schumpeter, *Imperialism and Social Class*, trans. H. Norden, ed. with introduction by P. M. Sweezy; Oxford, 1951, p. 81. The original of the work of this famous German economist appeared in 1919. Its range and profundity, sometimes reminiscent of von Ranke, show German scholarship at its best; and though the author was primarily an economist, it is one of the essential works on the theory of Imperialism. Schumpeter, who retained his objectivity during the First World War, won great reputation at Harvard in the 'thirties.

[4] *Imperialism. A Study*, London, 1902.

Maoist theory of colonialism, now of world influence in political warfare. When, argued Hobson, markets were glutted in the developed world, finance capital was inevitably driven to exploiting the underdeveloped. Hence a 'spurious' colonialism; no longer an expression of healthy patriotic enterprise, but 'in the interests of the leisured classes imposing their policy on the nation for their own advantage, diverting the people from troubles at home by wars abroad, and augment[ing] their own wealth from the toil of reluctant and unassimilated peoples'. Hence also an increasing conflict between the capitalist power for raw materials and markets leading to war.

This doctrine chimed well with Marx's theory of the inevitable collapse of capitalism through its in-built contradictions; but in fact Great Britain, the pioneer and then greatest capitalist power, was the least belligerent; Chamberlain's imperialism collapsed after the unpopular Boer War, and the final expansion was defensive, trying to protect existing interests rather than promote new ones. Indeed, British governments right up to those of Baldwin and Chamberlain were desperately concerned to maintain the kind of world in which the free-trading Victorians had prospered, and were only driven into protectionist policies. Indeed, 'a purely capitalist world', as Schumpeter demonstrates, 'can offer no fertile soil for imperialist impulses', and in England 'the imperialist wave never did more than beat against the mainland of social evolution'. Since there was 'an absence of warlike structure' in the state, Disraeli's imperialism, 'a fascinating vision ... unfolded before the provincial mind', had in fact never gone deep—it had been a 'political arabesque'. War for colonies, perhaps good business in the eighteenth century, was now unpopular with the majority of the electorate, and most of the colonial Empire in Africa was reluctantly created as part of a defensive strategy. Since trade with the tropical colonial territories amounted to only 1·2 per cent of British exports when Hobson wrote, and with the entire Empire to only a quarter of the free-trade with the rest of the world, the economic motive for the acquisition of Empire in the late nineteenth century has been much overstressed. 'The British were investing heavily and trading freely in regions which formed no part of the Empire: South America, the United States, western Europe. The large bulk of the newly acquired territories in Africa were of minimal economic value and were certainly not acquired solely for economic reasons. Strategy and prestige often played a large role. Had Disraeli or Gladstone so wished, the British could have had for the asking much larger areas of Africa than they took.'[5]

[5] David Dilkes, *Curzon in India*, London, 1969–70. Vol. I, p. 68.

Yet Hobson's theory both in his own country, and more importantly outside it, found a receptive audience. Beneath the thrusting plutocratic world of cosmopolitan finance and privilege and the more anxious world of realistic statesmen in office and of their advisers, who knew the strategic necessities and the precarious balance of power politics, the old Liberal 'little England' tradition went on, kept alive even by Gladstone, and now reinforced by Fabian Socialism and a Labour party hostile to the establishment. By 1867 Disraeli had nearly doubled the electorate by household suffrage, and the Ballot Act of 1872 and the extension of the rural franchise in 1884 had gone much further, coinciding with the formation of centrally organized mass parties, Liberal and Conservative. In 1889 *Fabian Essays* had given reformist socialism its programme, and by 1893 the Independent Labour Party was in being. By 1906–14 the Liberal governments of Campbell-Bannerman and Asquith would lay the foundation of a Welfare State, and by the 'twenties Lloyd George, originally a radical demagogue, would bring in manhood suffrage to all over twenty-one, a suffrage fully extended to women by the end of the decade on the same terms.

The last and apparently most imposing period of Empire would thus coincide with the advent of total mass democracy in the island. And while, as has been well written, 'what was left of the rough, happy, ignorant mass of Merry England'[6] was still 'Jingo' over the Anglo-Russian crisis of 1877, and the majority of all classes, not knowing what they were in for, went into the First World War with a brash solidarity, by the end of the 'twenties a gaunt popular disillusionment had set in, both with power politics and the Empire, thought of as an upper-class preserve; while a vague but genuine internationalism and pacifism emerged among many intellectuals and even among the leaders of the powerful Trade Unions. In 1924 the Labour party would form its first administration and supersede the Liberals, disrupted by the mercurial Lloyd George, as the alternative party to the Conservatives.

These profound changes had their bearing on the Empire. Already at the Imperial Conference of 1926, the door had been discreetly closed on the projects of Imperial Federation fashionable in the 'nineties and in Edwardian times, when Balfour declared with ambiguous virtuosity and Athanasian opaqueness that the Dominions of Great Britain were 'autonomous communities within the British Empire, equal in status, in no way subordinate to one another in any aspects of domestic or internal affairs, though united through common allegiance to the crown, and freely associated as members of

[6] Sir Philip Magnus, *Kitchener*, London, 1961, p. 31.

the British Commonwealth of Nations'. This formula was accepted by the Imperial Conference of that year, and in 1931 the Statute of Westminster, one of the earliest Acts of the new Coalition government in which the Trade Union leader, J. H. Thomas, was Secretary of State for the Dominions and Colonies, would recognize the right of the Dominions to legislate for themselves. The Colonial Laws Validity Act of 1865, whereby the Crown could disallow such legislation, and the right of a Governor-General to 'reserve' consent until the monarch's pleasure had been ascertained, were now abolished. And India had now been formally accorded the prospect of dominion status. Though the fact was seldom realized abroad, even in the United States, only the colonial empire now remained under full British sovereignty; and nearly all of that, within less than half a century, would be hastily accorded self-government and complete independence.

Moreover, beneath the surface of an apparently aggressive imperialism, and while the Empire of 372 million inhabitants of 1897 became the Empire of 493 million in 1933, most of those responsible for protecting the enormous imperial concern were in fact playing for safety, as befitted the rules of the richest and most vulnerable commercial and maritime Empire in the world. Liberals and then Socialists came to power, so that Curzon, the most glitteringly imperial pro-consul in British Indian history, and one of the greatest, and Kitchener, who had the bones of the Mahdi thrown into the Nile,[7] and ground down the Boers by concentration camps, sat in the same cabinet as the Radical Lloyd George and was an only slightly older contemporary of Ramsay MacDonald, the first Socialist Prime Minister.

The fact is hardly surprising. The British establishment had been adapting itself since the twelfth century, and had been assimilating the industrial bourgeoisie and the skilled workers since the English Revolution was avoided in the mid-nineteenth. The Liberal reformers of the school of T. H. Green in the 'eighties, like the contemporary Fabian Socialists, wanted to uplift the masses, but they were no revolutionaries. Protected by the greatest wealth and the biggest navy in the world, these reformers believed that their civilization could be extended to the people, who would in due time be able 'to make the best of themselves' within the adapted social order. Their gradual attack had not been revolutionary, but it was all the more formidable

[7] Magnus, *op. cit.* p. 137. He was only prevented by Queen Victoria from dispatching the skull to the College of Surgeons in London (the Mahdi, she objected, though very bad and cruel, was after all 'a man of certain importance').

for that: income tax, death duties, if still the thin end of a large wedge, and the curbing of the powers of the House of Lords, all had come in before the First World War. And when the war itself vastly extended the powers of the state, never shaken off, the landowners and plutocracy came under an increasingly comprehensive, if not conclusive, attack.

Within the Empire, the change would at first be gradual. It was tempered by inescapable facts; by British empiricism and by the advice of administrators on the spot; but in principle it was the same. Full democracy and socialism were incompatible with even Liberal imperialism, and in Great Britain itself the shift of power towards social democracy was well under way before the Second World War. Further, as most Englishmen of affairs understood, politics is the art of the possible, and what cannot be held is best relinquished with a good grace. Nor is there anything surprising to an historian that democracy and empire proved incompatible: Thucydides at the end of the fifth century B.C. made it the main theme of his history of the Peloponnesian War—a work written 'not to win the applause of the moment, but as a possession for all time'.[8]

II

The international setting of these domestic and imperial events was one of mounting menace. After the defeat of France in 1870–1, Germany had become the strongest power in Europe; by the turn of the new century challenging British supremacy at sea. France, long regarded as the main colonial rival in Africa and the Levant, had by 1904 become the partner in a *détente* which became an *entente cordiale* with Great Britain, who thus became involved with a Franco-Russian alliance against the Triple Alliance of Germany, Austria-Hungary and, supposedly, Italy. The British had not, of course, ever aimed at 'splendid isolation', a phrase used originally by Lord Salisbury to express fastidious detachment from the internal politics of the Turks; and in 1902, even before the outcome of the Russo-Japanese War, the British had realistically allied themselves with Japan—an unprecedented commitment for a European power. The British Navy would thus look after the North Sea, the Channel and the Atlantic; the French after the Mediterranean; the Japanese after the Far East. And the old commitment of 1839 to guarantee the integrity of Belgium still stood, for here, too, an historic 'vital interest' was at stake, the control of Flanders and the mouth of the Scheldt.

[8] *The complete writings of Thucydides. The Peloponnesian War*, translated by Crawley with introduction by John H. Finley, New York, 1951, p. 15.

As the huge rival power blocs manoeuvred heavily for advantage in a world in which prospective wars fought by vast conscript armies were taken for granted, the oceanic *Pax Britannica* of the nineteenth century, always in part a bluff, was breaking down. The rivalries of European powers now affected vast territories in Africa, hitherto immune; and the British collected the biggest share in the sudden 'scramble' for the enormous and hitherto relatively neglected continent. Here, during the 'eighties and 'nineties, they acquired enormous new colonial responsibilities, not for compulsive capitalistic lust for new territory but to keep strategic rivals out: as in 1882 by the occupation of Egypt and in 1899 by the Anglo-Egyptian Condominium over the Sudan and in most of East Africa. Then, after the First World War, they took over Iraq under a mandate from the League of Nations, mainly to protect the oil-wells of the area, and planted their residents in the oil-rich sheikdoms of the Persian Gulf and southeastern Arabia. And when in 1916 Balfour, Lloyd George and Samuel put the case for a 'national home'—with a small 'h'—for the Jews in Palestine, it was only accepted by the Asquith cabinet after they had been persuaded that a Jewish presence in Palestine would help to protect the Suez Canal.[9]

Indeed, the Liberal experiment, so civilian and humane, carried out within the island between 1906 and 1914, had been made in contrast with the barbarity of the power politics and armaments of the time; in contrast with the rampant militarism of the Prussian officer caste, the nationalist passions that seethed within the Austro-Hungarian Empire, the colossal social upheaval brewing in Russia. It was incongruous with the armaments race, with the great coal-burning battleships with fifteen-inch guns, the howitzers, cannon and machine-guns which would pulverize the battle of manoeuvre into trench warfare, and with the clumsy but, when properly deployed, effective 'tanks' which would break the four-year-old palaeotechnic deadlock. For the first time the British would accept the conscription normal on the Continent and suffer over two million casualties; their industries, geared to mechanized slaughter, turning out colossal armaments, the women, too, now herded into factories for the good work.

Already in 1877–8 the power conflict with Russia which had previously occasioned the Crimean War had almost come to another one over the moribund Turkish Empire, sustained by the British as a buffer state in the Levant to protect their communications with India. Following the purchase by Disraeli in 1875 of the predominant interest in the Suez Canal, the Levant and Egypt had become an area

[9] See my *Viscount Samuel, a biography*, London, 1957, pp. 166–80.

of tension between Tsarist Russia, France and Great Britain, as it has since between the Soviet Union and the West. In 1878 the British, further concerned by evidence of Russian expansion in central Asia and with the 'great game' on the Northwest Frontiers of India, occupied Cyprus, still nominally under Turkish suzerainty; by 1882 they had occupied Egypt, and a year later, following the Mahdi's revolt against the Egyptians, became reluctantly involved in the Sudan. And in 1899–1902 at the other extremity of Africa the British would fight the greatest of their modern colonial wars to retain paramountcy in South Africa, which now contained the greatest diamond- and gold-mines in the world, and to keep the strategic mastery of the south Atlantic and Indian Oceans.

III

The sequence of this imperial climax, satiety and defence is generally familiar; but the main political events within the island base and outside it may here conveniently be recalled. Following Gladstone's first Liberal administration of 1868–74, Disraeli's third Conservative government of 1874–80 inaugurated a more adventurous policy for the Empire. In 1875 he bought the controlling interest in the Suez Canal; tensions with Russia over the control of the Levant, the route to India and the Northwest Frontier became severe : in 1877, in part as a deterrent signal to the Russians, the Queen was proclaimed Empress of India. In South Africa the British, intent on a Federation, annexed the Transvaal, and in 1879 became involved in a formidable Zulu rebellion in Natal. Here they suffered severe reverses before their superiority in armaments was brought to bear. In 1880–5 Gladstone returned to power, to be forced, within two years, against his Liberal conscience, to occupy Egypt; and the fate of Gordon in the Sudan as well as Liberal dissensions over Home Rule for Ireland contributed to the Liberal defeat. For both parties imperial affairs were becoming much more important than in mid-Victorian times; and the Conservative preponderance which lasted, save for a brief interval under Gladstone in 1886, from 1885 to 1892, saw a vast, generally reluctant and defensive expansion in tropical Africa, which Gladstone's last government in 1892–4 and Rosebery's Liberal administration of 1894–5 did not reverse. There followed the long Conservative preponderance under Salisbury until 1902, then under his nephew A. J. Balfour which lasted until 1905. During this last phase of old-style patrician government which incongruously gave scope for the Liberal–Unionist Joseph Chamberlain's commercial imperialism and projects of Imperial Federation, the climax of the

Diamond Jubilee of 1897 was organized; in 1898 Curzon became Viceroy of India; the Sudan was conquered by Kitchener; the grip on tropical Africa was confirmed, and the conflict with the Boer proved the most exacting colonial war since the American Revolution.

Following the landslide election of 1905, the Liberals came to power, first under Campbell-Bannerman then under Asquith, until the formation of the Asquith Coalition of 1915 and the Lloyd George Coalition of 1916–22. These years saw a more Liberal imperialism: the Morley–Minto Reforms in India before the war were followed by the Montagu-Chelmsford guarantee of progress towards Dominion Status, and the First World War and its aftermath led to the international recognition of the independence of the Dominions.

During the 'twenties, following the disruption of the Coalition and the collapse of the Liberal party, the Conservatives again came to power: first in 1922 under Bonar Law, in the next year under Baldwin. Then the brief and embarrassed first Labour government of Ramsay MacDonald of 1924 was ousted that November by Baldwin, who remained in office until 1929. This period of Conservative rule saw the greatest territorial expansion of the Empire by Mandates under the League of Nations over Palestine, Trans-Jordan and Iraq and over German East Africa.

It would be interrupted in 1929 by the second Labour government, which collapsed in the financial crisis of 1931, the year in which MacDonald's National government formally recognized the independence of the Dominions by the Statute of Westminster.

So during less than a century the Empire passed through its late Victorian and Edwardian climax, survived the First World War and attained its greatest population and size, then began to transform itself into 'that extraordinary British paradox, a Commonwealth, whatever the term really meant'.[10] The climax of this defensive expansion, comprising more than a quarter of the globe, will be the theme of the ensuing chapters.

IV

The history of Ireland, part of the British Isles, has hitherto, in a survey concerned with the Empire outside them, formed no part of this narrative. But Irish affairs now so much affected British politics at home and abroad that a brief account must be taken of them. The Irish, never mastered by the Romans, had continued a tribal way of life into the sixteenth century, and preserved and propagated Chris-

[10] *New Cambridge Modern History*, Vol. XII, p. 532.

tianity during the Dark Ages. They had high qualities of courage, charm, imagination and wit; but their strategic position had wrecked them. The rulers of England had to control it. The ancient tale of wrong and recrimination which had begun in the twelfth century under Henry II, when Richard Earl of Pembroke (Strongbow) had invaded Ireland, continued through the Tudor reconquest and plantation, the rebellion in 1641 against the Protestant settlers of the north, the incursions and massacres of Oliver Cromwell and the conflict between James II and William of Orange at the Battle of the Boyne, had simmered on through the eighteenth century, beneath the landowning Protestant ascendancy.

Ireland had been a potential strategic base first for the Spaniards then for the French; and following the rebellion in 1800, the British had decided to abolish the fractious Irish parliament and accord the Protestant Irish representation at Westminster in an 'Imperial Parliament' of Great Britain and Ireland. Following Catholic emancipation, reluctantly conceded in 1829, Irish Catholic Members came to Westminster, and the appalling famines and massive emigrations in the 'forties had contributed to the Repeal of the Corn Laws and the temporary eclipse of the Tories.

The perennial feuds and grievances of the Irish at Westminster had now increasingly come to disrupt British politics, and in 1886 and again in 1893 Gladstone tried to get rid of them by creating an Irish Parliament with Home Rule within the Empire. In vain, for the archaic religious and social divisions within the poverty-stricken and depopulated island made a united Ireland impracticable. The Catholic and Nationalist Irish detested the Protestant landlords and gentry who owned most of the land and socially dominated the country; while the militant Protestants of Ulster equally detested the priests and peasants of the south. Hence, although the Irish Protestant gentry provided many outstanding soldiers and administrators for the Empire, and Irish volunteers some of the best regiments in the Army, Balkan-style vendettas between Catholics and Protestants and growing nationalist hatred of the British made Ireland an incessant problem for all concerned, and spread bitter enmity of the British among the immigrant Irish in the United States and the Commonwealth.

And when, at last, in 1914 Asquith looked like getting the principle of Home Rule accepted, the Great War intervened. In 1916, at a critical time in the war, the Irish nationalists rose in rebellion, with its sequel of reprisals and counter-reprisals. Following the atrocities committed both by Irish Republicans and British police auxiliaries, known from their uniforms as 'Black and Tans', in 1921–2 Lloyd

George's government in desperation shelved the problem by partition. An Irish Free State was set up, with Ulster remaining part of the United Kingdom of Great Britain and Ireland. This solution so enraged the extreme nationalists that they rebelled against their own leaders. In 1937 the Irish Free State went its own way as the Republic of Eire, a separate state, hostile to the British, officially remaining neutral during the Second World War and denying the Grand Alliance the use of bases in the crucial battle of the Atlantic. In 1949 Eire would leave the Commonwealth.

So, while the English, Welsh and Scots managed to reconcile their different temperaments within the main island, the relationship with the Irish had proved a tale of failure, of civil war and rebellion, recrimination and distress. Yet through all this political hatred and prejudice and misguided religious fanaticism, the charm and wit of the Irish and the Anglo-Irish had proved irrepressible: Wilde, Bernard Shaw, Yeats and Joyce would be among the most brilliant and original of writers in English, and the Empire which the nationalists and their kinsmen in the United States so detested would in fact be in part the creation of Irishmen.

Such, in broad outline, was the metropolitan imperial background of the final, mainly defensive and greatest expansion of the British Empire. Since the 1870s, the huge concern had been linked by cables and telegraphs sprawled across the world in a network covering a fantastic variety of peoples and languages. With the Indian and colonial Empires, it would contain more coloured peoples than Europeans and their descendants. They were ruled politically under the Crown, by the British Parliament, through the Indian and Colonial offices; and legally in spite of a fantastic variety of local codes and customs, by the Judicial Committee of the Privy Council, to which all British subjects had the right of appeal. The Empire thus ranged from the self-governing, still sparsely populated, but economically and socially advanced Dominions of settlement, through the great sub-continent of India—a civilization in itself, still ruled in fact, if not in form, as a liberal Asian despotism—to the huge and variegated African colonies, occupied Egypt, the Anglo-Egyptian Sudan, the tiny naval bases and coaling and cable stations strung across the oceans, and the mandated territories assumed after the First World War. What kind of people had the British now become, who ruled it with such confidence, defended it with such success and then, within half a century, would politically dismantle the entire concern?

V

The vagaries of fashion can give successive generations a misleading air of contrast, but the changes from the whiskered and bearded Victorians to Kitchener-moustaches, close-cut, centrally parted hair, and the starched wing or turn-over collars of the 'nineties, or to the more casual but equally expensive elegance after the Great War, are both representative. The ruling classes in Europe and America were immensely rich; and their *trains de luxe*, brassy automobiles and sleek liners, like their svelte clothes, were glossy with comfort and panache. The Edwardian women, like galleons under full sail, were elaborately elegant, and the whiff of recherché scent blended with the aroma of Havana cigars, no longer, as in Victorian days, confined to the smoking-room. This social world, so appropriate to the world of the millionaires and symbolized by the rotund and regal figure of Edward VII, was full of confidence and not too particular. It welcomed American heiresses and Jewish financiers from central Europe to a cosmopolitan exploitation and conviviality, in which some of the old aristocracy, still drawing immense revenues from land and urban property and investment, were glad to participate. In this plutocratic world, dominated more by financiers than Victorian society had been, the intellectuals were less central to the etsablishment than were the writers of the mid-nineteenth century: but they remained, most of them, still part of it even until the 'thirties. The inner circle of wealth and political power has never been intellectually more brilliant than when Balfour was Prime Minister or Margot Asquith hostess at 10 Downing Street, and most of the Front Bench Liberals, in spite of depending on the Nonconformist conscience, were part of the establishment. Strategically now imperialists in defence, they sanctioned the building of Fisher's battle fleets that maintained strategic supremacy under Jellicoe and Beatty. Anyone looking through the periodicals at the time of the Diamond Jubilee of 1897 will be struck by how military the pattern was: by the quasi-Prussian tropical helmets of the age of Kitchener and Curzon, the professional touch of the new *khaki* suited to the Northwest Frontier and the *Veldt*, the bemedalled chests of military magnates, the roar of applause with which the new popular press greeted exploits that made news. If Lord Roberts was the dapper and amiable embodiment of a peculiarly British tradition, Kitchener could hold his own with the most monolithic titan of the German army. And the fleet, spick and span with an impeccable tradition and officered by professionals who were almost a caste, was respected and romanticized even by the solid civilian majority to whom the army and the Empire in India appeared more of a class preserve.

And behind the Monarchy, the City and the Services, were a new generation of administrators, at home and in the Empire, recruited by competitive examination, mainly from Oxford and Cambridge and from the major public schools. They provided, beneath the often patrician and politically appointed pro-consuls, the cadre from which the real masters of administration were selected and the able men who ran the secretariats and the districts of India and the colonial Empire. The elite of this meritocracy—Cromer, Milner, Curzon, for example—were men of wide cultural interests and ability, in contrast to the cultural barbarism of many of the old, class-ridden army and hide-bound businessmen. But this high intellectual tradition of College at Eton and Winchester, of Balliol and New College, and Trinity Cambridge, became diluted in the raw post-Arnold public schools, with their oddly puritanical narrow and games-ridden outlook, hypertrophied by a narrow curriculum and Anglican provincial prejudice. They often turned the image of the British administrator into one quite uncharacteristic of the uninhibited and often magnetic characters who had made, and were still making, the Empire that the new late-Victorian and Edwardian public schools would help to lose. Middle-class snobbery and intolerance exported by these people and their wives, were apt to provoke a natural and justified exasperation, both among Asian representatives of ancient and sophisticated cultures, and among more primitive peoples in Africa, anxious not only for knowledge but for understanding and recognition.

Meanwhile, and in the long run far more important, the doctors, scientists, engineers and inventors, the anthropologists and historians, the investigators of comparative law, the cartographers and surveyors, carried on the brilliant creativeness of mid-Victorian times and made Great Britain a metropolitan intellectual powerhouse. The queer chameleon genius of Kipling reflected the push and the pride and, occasionally, the misgivings of Empire with an uncanny insight, if the poet laureate, Alfred Austin, wrote verse so inept that Masefield seemed a good poet by comparison. The greatest novelist, Thomas Hardy, who detested power politics, had little concern with the Empire; but H. G. Wells, who became a world influence, began life as a Liberal imperialist, and always hankered for a cosmopolitan revolt of the competent, which retained affinities with the vision of Empire that inspired the founders of the *Round Table*, whose ideals, if not European, were Oceanic and worldwide.

To this confident and final phase of the old order came the colossal disaster of the First World War; then its economically more crippling sequel in 1939–45. Given time, the British would have gradually liberalized and emancipated their Empire: the First World War overextended it and the Second brought it down with a run, with immediate consequences which were often, as in India and Nigeria, a terrible price for independence. But it was the twice attempted collective suicide of Europe that shattered the Empire, not so much the domestic politics or intolerance of the British before 1914. The fate of the British Empire must be mainly attributed, like the eclipse and partition of Germany, to the two World Wars and the spread of European-style nationalism beyond Europe.

The British Empire emerged apparently victorious from the first catastrophe, but the world which it represented and attempted to carry on had in fact collapsed. Revolutionary dictatorships had emerged in Russia, dedicated to the overthrow of capitalist society; a Fascist gutter elite had emerged with the breakdown of the bourgeois social order in Germany, dedicated, like their Italian prototype —a reversion to the traditional gangster politics of the Renaissance without their cultural veneer—to mob-nationalist aggression. Over large areas of the Continent parliamentary institutions collapsed or became demoralized, and the Americans, whose intervention had finally tipped the scales in 1917–18, withdrew from political responsibilities in Europe. The more conservative British and their Empire were left in a world economically disorganized and politically transformed—not knowing which was worst, the Marxist–Leninist attack on capitalism or insatiable Fascist aggression. The insular Baldwin–Chamberlain governments of the 'thirties, their nerve shaken, representative both of the rich and of the insular and masses indifferent to Empire, made the worst of both worlds, not understanding either.

Given their background, it was natural they did so. The horrors of the First World War, affecting millions as no conflict had done before, had roused the disgust of the more sensitive and articulate elites and the resentment of the politically conscious masses, now disillusioned by poverty and unemployment and never much aware of the realities of world power. Reeking from the carnage brought about by an international political system of which it had been part, the British establishment came under attack, and with it the Empire. Left-wing intellectuals and Trade Unionists identified the peoples of India and the colonies with their own kind, extrapolating insular social conflicts into alien settings, and clamoured for disarmament and the abdication of Empire when an even more dangerous storm was brewing up. By 1931, when the Statute of Westminster tried to define the transformation of Empire into Commonwealth, the hope of preserving even that was already precarious. The always limited *Pax Britannica* and the financial supremacy that had preserved it were breaking down, and revolutionary governments, hostile even to social democracy, let alone to capitalism, were in control of great states. A cosmopolitan class warfare now radiated from the U.S.S.R. and often joined with the forces of nationalism in the dependencies and colonies. But on the surface, after the stunning victory which ended the Great War, the old order and the old imperial grandeur went on. The British still dominated the largest Empire in history and the aura of great power still surrounded even that 'second eleven' of politicians, elected in a National government to restore a vanished normality, and it even concealed their purblind insignificance.

CHAPTER 20

The Indian *Raj*; Burma; Ceylon

Late in 1876, on the eve of the proclamation of the Queen as Empress of India, the Viceroy, Lord Lytton, held an immense Durbar at Delhi, vividly depicted by Sir Frederick Roberts, afterwards Lord Roberts (or 'Bobs') of Kandahar. 'The magnificence of the native princes' retinues,' he wrote, 'can barely be described; their elephant hangings were of cloth of gold or scarlet and blue cloths embroidered with gold and silver. The howdahs were veritable thrones of precious metals, shaded by the most brilliant canopies.' The war elephants, their tusks, 'tipped with steel, wore shields on their foreheads and breastplates of flashing steel; chain-mail armour hung down over their trunks and covered their backs and sides and they were mounted by warriors clothed in chain-mail and armed to the teeth'.[1] This medieval spectacle, obsolete yet symbolic of the rich variety of India, had been the prelude to a colossal parade and reception of the magnates of the sub-continent, mixed up as much as possible to avoid questions of precedence. Then, from under a satin canopy embroidered with gold, with a flourish of trumpets and a salute of a hundred and one guns, Lord Lytton, the *Shah in Shah Padisha*, proclaimed Victoria R & I. The guns, indeed, upset the elephants, who became 'more and more alarmed' and 'scampered off', dispersing the crowds; but since the ceremony was held on a wide plain, there was nothing for them to run into and no harm done. The Indian Empire, thus inaugurated on 1st January 1877, would last for seventy years until Earl Mountbatten, the last Viceroy, handed over power to the Republic of India and the Dominion of Pakistan into which the country had been hastily divided, a division accompanied by enormous mutual massacres by Muslims and Hindus.

[1] Field-Marshal Lord Roberts of Kandahar, *Forty one Years in India, From Subaltern to Commander-in-Chief*, London, 1897, 2 vols, Vol. II, p. 93.

This swift transformation came about mainly through events in Europe, and because the British rulers had willed it. In 1917 during the worst crisis of the Great War a liberalizing policy had been defined—'the increasing association of Indians in every branch of the administration, and the gradual development of self-governing institutions with a view to the progressive realization of responsible government in India as an integral part of the British Empire'. But independence came about far more rapidly than intended. Two World Wars, emanating from Europe and the second spreading to the Far East, along with their consequent social revolutions, violent or mild, undermined European power and even the will to rule. The Japanese conquests, though ephemeral, were erased mainly by the United States, and though India was never overrun, the Japanese inflicted such damage on European prestige in the East that the British, French and Dutch never recovered their political hold. The great world powers were no longer European: they were the United States, the Eurasian Soviet Union and, potentially, China. Within less than half a century the India of Curzon and Kitchener, even of Irwin and Wavell, would vanish.

The vast civilization thus to be hustled into partition and self-government on Western and incongruously nationalistic lines, was about the least homogeneous in the world; divided not only by physical type and geographical contrast between the peoples of Northwestern India, Bengal, Maharashtra, Mysore and Madras, but also by fundamental conflict between Muslim and Hindu, and in Hindu India by the elaborate strata of caste. And the vast majority of Indians were still illiterate peasants. The Asian sub-continent could hardly be a more inappropriate setting for Western parliamentary institutions, party government and the ballot box, or the doctrines of nationalism and economically determined class conflict then emanating from Europe. These facts the men who ruled India well understood. But governments in London were their masters, and as Liberal and Labour governments came to power, they reflected the changing outlook already described. Imperial problems were considered with the liberal idealism of the *Round Table*, or in terms of obsessional and extrapolated insular class resentments. When one man one vote was the accepted principle in the metropolitan country, this franchise ought, it was often believed, to be extended to the illiterate masses of Asia; and the rule of British officials and soldiers in India was equated with the resented preponderance of the establishment at home. As these changes of public opinion mounted in Great Britain and beyond, what had been designed as a slow and tentative process was hotted up; and when, after the Second World

War, the British position became untenable, the Attlee government cut their loss.

Such were the main and world-political causes of this swift abdication. But internal causes had also long been at work. The very success of the British *raj* produced its own nemesis. The unwonted unity and pacification of India and the style of education imposed had produced a militant and articulate Westernized minority—potential administrators and politicians. Then Hindu India itself produced a characteristic and, to Western eyes, extraordinary movement of non-violent resistance under the magnetic leadership of Gandhi—a blend of Tolstoian and Hindu mysticism—unique in the world, appealing beyond the intellectuals to the peasant masses and against relatively humane rulers, a success. From 1909, with the Morley–Minto reforms, the *raj* was thus gradually, if reluctantly, putting an end to itself; although in this 'land of formulated intentions' by 'a sort of desperate fatality the imperial formulation always came too late';[2] and when it came, 'the gift of conditional freedom called forth no thanks'.[3] Lord Cromer's apt citation from Gregorovius would apply to India as well as Egypt. 'The unhappy King (Theodosius) now learnt by experience that not even the wisest and most humane of princes, if he be an alien in race, in custom and religion, can ever win the hearts of the people'.[4] Inevitably, the European domination came to an end.

II

The Indian Empire, an *imperium* and a dependency, not a Dominion, was long ruled despotically by the Crown in Parliament, under a Viceroy who was at once 'the Great Ornamental' and a kind of Prime Minister. He had a Council of high civil servants, and heads of departments, which included a military representative and to which Indian nominees could be co-opted. The Viceroy continued to live in Eastern state and profusion, ruling first from Calcutta, from a replica of Curzon's own Kedleston of which Dr Johnson had said that it 'would do excellently well for a town hall'; then in 1912 from New Delhi (by Lord Irwin's time, from Lutyens's vast semi-oriental palace there), and during the hot weather from Simla, among the deodars and the pines, but where, it was said, one could not sleep at night for the grinding of axes.

[2] *New Cambridge Modern History*, Vol. XII, p. 551.
[3] *New Cambridge Modern History*, Vol. XII, p. 533.
[4] The Earl of Cromer, *Modern Egypt*, 2 vols, London, 1908, Vol. II, p. 571 n, quoting the *History of Rome in the Middle Ages*, Vol. I, p. 323.

The Viceroys moved about this enormous realm with an immense entourage. They were then paid £16,700 a year with £73,000 expenses; they had state elephants and a Viceregal train. They brought out their own upper servants, such as Curzon's French *chef*, detected, as his master observed, 'in some peculations of a character and extent that excited admiration even in the east'. Beneath this autocrat and his Viceregal Council and secretariat, were seven provincial governors ruling areas that could have been countries in Europe. These pro-consuls also lived in elaborate formality and state—as, in 1932, that model civil servant, Sir John Anderson, could still rather wrily inform his father in Scotland from Bengal.[5] These governors, too, had coun-cils and secretariats, which controlled a far-flung and complex administration. And beneath these great provinces were the districts, controlled by commissioners and deputy-commissioners, who were at once tax assessors, magistrates and heads of police. These districts and sub-districts were the foundation, and they were manned, like the whole elaborate structure, by the Indian Civil Service as devel-oped from its origins in the days of Haileybury and the Company. They were an elite, recruited by an exacting examination and they numbered no more than thirteen hundred. They were adequately, if not lavishly, paid; their tenure and pensions secure, their rewards in prized decorations, in wide authority and scope. They were all drawn from roughly the same British background and their own relation-ships were close and informal. All Indian civilians had district ex-perience, and all had the chance of sport, from pigsticking and polo to going out after snipe, duck and quail, while tiger and leopard could provide the thrill of danger. Moving about their districts in camp, doing justice in a stuffy courtroom or confabulating with village elders under a pipal tree in a fresh sub-tropical morning, or as wood-smoke ascended into a warm dusk, these expatriates came to under-stand and love a fascinating country; and the more adventurous could be seconded, like some army officers, to the Indian Political Service and posted on or beyond the Northwest Frontier, to southern Arabia or to the Persian Gulf. Though the secretariats might get notoriously bogged down, these vast responsibilities were discharged with rela-tively little bureaucratic fuss; one can imagine the much more meticu-lous pomposity, the mountains of *paperasserie*, that could have settled on India under most other European regimes.

Outside British India were about a hundred major native states and many more lesser ones, the more important 'advised' by British

[5] See Sir John Wheeler Bennett, *John Anderson, Viscount Waverly*, Lon-don, 1962, *passim*, for the grand but dangerous position of a governor at that time.

Residents. They covered about a quarter of the country and their rulers were often colourful: some Westernized and cosmopolitan figures of vast wealth, others enjoying the caprices and extravagance of older times. They ranged from the separate but 'protected' kingdoms of Nepal and Bhutan, to Hyderabad and Mysore and the states of Rajputana, Bikanir, Jaipur, to the Maratha Gwalior and the principalities of the Bombay presidency and the territories of minor rajahs in the Deccan or the foothills of the Himalayas.

Such was the vast legacy from precariously placed Jacobean and Caroline 'factors', the depredations, bluff and chicanery of Job Charnock and 'Diamond' Pitt, the brisk exploitations of Clive and the statesmanship of Warren Hastings; from Wellesley and the proconsuls of the Romantic Age, from the gaunt and casual mid-Victorians of the stamp of Lawrence of the Punjab, to the dapper leathery soldiers in the style of Roberts of Kandahar. But since the Sepoy Mutiny and the assumption of a direct and more elaborate *imperium*, the character of the *raj* had changed. It had developed the defects of all well-established bureaucracies, while the relatively fast P & O's now brought out a new sort of *memsahib* without the confident poise of the mid-Victorian upper class.

Good relations continued in unofficial enclaves, as in the Kulu Valley, where British families settled and planted orchards, and where some retired colonels married Kulu girls, always famous for their beauty and formerly in great demand for Mughal harems. But many officials and military families, in positions they would not have held in England, often created enclaves of quasi-suburban life, indifferent to and subconsciously afraid of their exotic surroundings, and practising an *apartheid* as rigid and more wounding than that of the Afrikaaners. They could create a provincialism, very different from the freedom of the district and political officer in camp or residency. Hence the tedium, the snobbery and the gossip; the pseudo-British food, the tomato ketchup and the doilies, the yapping little dogs, not much appreciated by Muslims; the resentment towards anyone of their own order who took up with 'natives', however friendly and interesting. It was a far cry from the days of Warren Hastings, when the British had adapted themselves better. These people and their even more philistine business colleagues, like their equivalents in the colonies, provoked a natural and deserved detestation, with mounting political effects.

At the summit where patrician viceroys and their visitors looked down on these middle-class enclaves, late-Victorian and Edwardian wealth and arrogance reinforced the studied grandeur natural to any Indian ruler, and the regime, with a certain hardening of arteries, proceeded to its external climax, well symbolized by the surly, enormous and apparently apoplectic figure of Kitchener, and the cold arrogance of Curzon's public face. This far-flung administration was supported by a small British garrison and by a much larger Indian army, recruited mainly from the fighting races of the north, which under British officers formed an imperial strategic reserve that raised more than a million and a half men for the First World War. It was also backed by immense British overseas investments, which dominated the economy, and by roads, railways and canals which were far the best in Asia.

Here, indeed, was the greatest British material achievement; an emanation of a regime more akin to state socialism than to *laissez faire*. Already Dalhousie had rehabilitated the Mughal Grand Trunk road, which now extended from Calcutta to Peshawar: the scene of that kaleidoscopic India celebrated by Kipling; of marriage processions with their 'marigold and jasmin stronger even than the reek of the dust', with the people, 'little clumps of red and white and pink and white and saffron, turning aside to go to their own villages, dispersing and growing small by twos and threes across the level plains', and the swift sunset 'driving broad gold spokes through the lower branches of the mango trees; the parakeets and doves ... coming home in their hundreds'.[6]

By the end of the century an immense network of strategic and commercial railways had been built, the most important ones state-owned. Vast irrigation works were constructed, as on the Chenab in the district of Lyallpore and on the Sutlej, tributaries of the Indus, and culminating in the 'twenties in the immense Sukkur barrage on the Indus itself: 'already by 1909 the 13,000 miles of primary and secondary canals with 42,000 miles of distribution irrigated 23 million acres of land. That is half the total acreage of Great Britain.' In the Punjab there was 'desert waiting to be peopled and a Utopia waiting for an architect. ... And there is something staggering about its success ... if the English were to choose one monument by which their years in India were to be remembered, it might well be the canals, the cotton, and the prosperous villages of Lyallpore.'[7]

In late medieval times India had been the greatest manufacturing area in Asia; but now, following the Industrial Revolution in Great Britain and free-trade, Indian traditional crafts and manufacturers were being swamped. On the other hand, British capital now developed big jute mills, and Indian capitalists a great cotton industry.

[6] *Kim*, London, 1908, pp. 86–90.
[7] Philip Woodruff, *The Men who Ruled India*, Vol. II, *The Guardians*, London, paperback edition 1963, pp. 111–14.

Like Egypt and Fiji, India benefited from the American Civil War, and if resentment of Western-style factory life led to the success of Gandhi's cult of the spinning-wheel, the new factories provided a livelihood, if a poor one, for some of the vastly increased population. For, by the end of the nineteenth century, the increasing conquest of famine and disease, hitherto the Malthusian controls normal in the East, had trebled the population to nearly 300 million; and by the mid-twentieth century it would be more than 400 million.

It was in this vast, peaceful and by previous standards relatively prosperous and still mainly peasant country, with its pockets of atrocious poverty, submerged untouchables and a literacy rate at the turn of the century of at most 10 per cent, and with its traditional religious contrasts and prejudices and fanaticisms basically un-assuaged, that in the early twentieth century the British slowly set about their declared purpose of handing over the political power of 'responsible' government within the Empire. In part they would do so on the now predominant principles of liberalism and self-determination, in part to retain the otherwise untenable within the Empire, preserve their strategic base in Asia and maintain the great investment and trading connections built up over centuries and still their most important interests in the East.

III

Until the Morley–Minto Reforms of 1909 the imperial *raj* proceeded with unimpaired momentum. The threat of invasion from the northwest, constant for millennia, had now been contained. But in the 'seventies, when the British and Russians had again come near to war over Constantinople, 'the Russian danger was no bogey of fad-dists',[8] and, following the steady and apparently insatiable Russian expansion, the 'great game' celebrated by Kipling flickered on. Only the defeat of Russia by the Japanese and the change of alliance in Europe led, by 1907, to agreed spheres of influence in central Asia.

So in 1876 'a great power', wrote Roberts in retrospect, 'was step by step creeping nearer our possession'. In the 'sixties the Russians had occupied Bukhara and the territories of the modern Turkmen and Usbek republics of the U.S.S.R. and were building strategic railways directed south. In 1877, the year of the proclamation of the Queen as Empress, the Russo-Turkish War which broke out in Europe threatened to involve the British, and Lord Lytton, following Disraeli's Eurasian strategy, was directed to make Afghanistan a British-controlled buffer state. And when a diplomatic mission had

[8] Woodruff, *op. cit.* Vol. II, pp. 149–50.

been rejected the British opened the Second Afghan War of 1878–80. The Amir fled, and his supplanter, Yakub Khan, appeared ready to negotiate; but, with or without the Khan's connivance, the British agents and their escort installed in Kabul were burnt alive in their quarters. So Roberts marched on Kabul, blew up the citadel, hanged some of those responsible and tried to make the country a protected state. And although in 1880 Gladstone's government, here as in the Transvaal, beat a retreat and the British were badly defeated by the Afghans at Maiwand, Roberts' avenging march down from Kabul to Kandahar reasserted British power. In the event, the Amir Abdurahman, though originally a *protégé* of the Russians, proved astute enough to get subsidized by the British, retain power and to pay a state visit to India. His successor, the Amir Habibulla, also proved amenable until assassinated in 1919, while his supplanter, Amanullah, after a traditional descent on India through the Khyber had been scotched, was also brought to terms. The buffer state had been achieved.

South of Afghanistan were the Baluchis, eastward the Pathans, in a no-man's-land between the Afghan and the former Sikh frontier, where 'the life of a border cattle thief was not one that encouraged a vague good will for one's neighbours. Nor was there likely to be tolerance in a country where there was no shade but the shade of a rock'.[9] Such was the poverty of the tribes that raiding the plains was necessary—not just exciting—and the British changed their originally defensive policy for intervention by diplomacy, subsidies and force. In 1894, 'to knit the tribes into one Imperial system',[10] Sir Mortimer Durand negotiated the 'Durand line' with the Afghans, asserting British 'protection' over the tribes east of it, and thereby diminished the tribesmen's chances of playing the Afghan Amir against the British and the British against the Amir.

Further to control the Northwest Frontier between Afghanistan and Jammu and Kashmir, in 1889 the British established an Agency at Gilgit, and west of it six years later advanced through the Malakand Pass through the inaccessible territory of the Ahkoond of Swat, to occupy the magnificent and fertile valleys of Chitral, whose horsemen were famous for their skill at polo. Cut off by a rising of the tribesmen behind them, the British had to be relieved in 1897 by the Malakand Field Force from Peshawar, an expedition vividly described in the dispatches of the young Winston Churchill. Apart from counteracting any strategic threat from Russia, these frontier wars and their cloak and dagger accompaniments gave the British public much

[9] Woodruff, *op. cit.* p. 138.
[10] Woodruff, *op. cit.* p. 147.

vicarious excitement. They were all necessary to arrest the normal and centuries old rhythm of invasion from Afghanistan and central Asia. The resulting and unwonted peace was not the least of the benefits of British rule in India.

With its frontiers secure, the pattern of the *raj* was set, and the important events would be internal. Lord Dufferin, who succeeded Ripon as Viceroy in 1884–8, proved an outstanding ruler. He was a grandson of the playwright Sheridan: a diplomat and grand seigneur of cosmopolitan experience and tact, a former Governor-General of Canada and Ambassador in St Petersburg and Constantinople. Like Curzon, he appreciated the civilization of India, and could write of a temple in Madras as 'quite superb, and as full of mystery as of beauty, with enormous gloomy halls and long corridors with golden and brazen animals . . . standing sentinel between the pillars'.[11] And unlike Curzon, he had a 'rare gift for carrying out great works with the minimum of friction'.[12] But he was always extremely cautious of importing British parliamentary institutions into India; though willing to adopt British rule to the 'expanding intelligence and capacity of the educated classes', he declared quite explicitly that the British would never abdicate 'their superior control of public affairs'.[13] And it was under Dufferin's regime that in 1885 Upper Burma was annexed.

IV

Under Lord Curzon (1899–1905) the *raj* reached its greatest grandeur and scope. Then, following the experiment in 'dyarchy' launched after the First World War, Lord Reading (1921–6) and Lord Irwin inaugurated more radical change.

Lord Curzon, a brilliant and able man, now widely regarded as a rather preposterous anachronism, was in fact a great Viceroy, the founder of the Indian archaeological survey and the restorer of Delhi and Agra, with a wider knowledge and understanding of Indian civilization than any ruler since Warren Hastings, and with a wider range. George Nathaniel Curzon was born in 1859 of an ancient but not hitherto important family of Norman origin. He was the eldest of eleven children of the fourth Lord Scarsdale, a clergyman of Calvinistic views; his mother died when he was sixteen and his family background and upbringing were bleak. After a brilliant career at Eton and Balliol College, Oxford, culminating in a Fellowship at All

[11] Sir Alfred Lyall, *The Life of the Marquis of Dufferin and Ava*, London, 1905, 2 vols, Vol. I, p. 137.
[12] Lyall, *op. cit.* Vol. II, p. 312.
[13] *ibidem*.

Souls, he entered Parliament and twice travelled round the world. He spent five months in arduous travel in Persia. He also visited Afghanistan, and, crossing the Pamirs, reached the sources of the Oxus.

Appointed in 1891 Parliamentary Under-Secretary of State for India, he had a high vision of his responsibility: 'As long as we rule India,' he would write, 'we are the greatest power in the world. If we lose it, we shall drop away to be a third rate power.' In 1895–8 he won greater authority and experience as Parliamentary Under-Secretary for Foreign Affairs, so that when, aged thirty-nine, he was appointed Viceroy, he was no patrician 'ornamental', but one who had made his own way, and was already an authority on Persia and Central Asia. He had also lived at the summit of London Society, when with Salisbury and Balfour as Prime Ministers, high-spirited intellect was in fashion.

In India he refused to be 'paper-logged' by the bureaucracy. 'I am prodding the animal,' he wrote, 'with most vigorous and unexpected digs, and it gambols plaintively under the novel spur. Nothing done hitherto under six months: when I suggest six weeks, the attitude is one of pained surprise; if six days, one of pathetic protest; if six hours, one of stupified resignation.' Until 1903 he proved successful; but his methods alienated colleagues and subordinates, and he was at odds with St John Brodrick, later Earl of Midleton, Balfour's Secretary of State for India.

Yet his major political decisions were sensible, if disliked. He had successfully created the Northwest Frontier province, independent of the Punjab, if for political reasons his partition of the unmanageable province of Bengal had to be abandoned. He had also clinched British control of the Persian Gulf. And if he had lectured the Princes like a priggish headmaster, he had, generally, associated them more closely and importantly with the regime, while, true to his determination to 'hold the balance even', he had insisted, despite the high feelings of the Army and their wives, on disciplining the fashionable 9th Lancers for outrageous conduct to 'natives'. He had attempted to galvanize Indian education, from the universities to the village schools, and taken care of Indian antiquities as no one had done before. If he had ignored the then unrepresentative Indian Congress, first convened in 1885, he had tackled immediate problems of agriculture, marketing and finance. 'We have to answer our helm,' he wrote, 'and it is an Imperial helm, down all the tides of time.' After his resignation Curzon was created an Earl in 1911 and a Marquess in 1921. He was Foreign Secretary from 1919 to 1924 but to his intense mortification it was not he but Baldwin who became Prime Minister in the latter year.[14] Curzon was Chancellor of Oxford University and President of the Royal Geographical Society, and author of many fascinating books, mainly on central Asia. He was a brilliant conversationalist, with a great sense of fun and on occasion a rollicking eighteenth-century humour. But since his youth he had fought against a crippling curvature of the spine and encased in a steel corset, appeared rigid, cold and pompous. He was apt to overwhelm rather than persuade. Given the assumption of temperament, age and background, it was natural that he 'failed to overcome his own anachronism'.[15]

The Morley–Minto reforms, devised between that spinsterish intellectual, John Morley, and a Viceroy selected mainly for his contrasting mediocrity to Curzon's old style egotism and independence, were very limited. Indians were nominated both to the Secretary of State's Council at the India Office, to the Viceregal Council and to the Councils in the provinces. The franchise was restricted, not unreasonably, to those who could read; and separate elections devised for Muslims and Hindus—not, as Indian nationalists believed, to enable the British to divide and rule, but because in any other arrangement the Muslims would be overwhelmed. These concessions only infuriated the Hindu nationalists in Bengal, and in 1912 a fanatic tossed a bomb with unwonted accuracy into the howdah in which Lord Hardinge was riding, severely wounding the Viceroy.[16] Then, after the First World War, an ingenious form of 'dyarchy' was attempted. As originally devised by Lionel Curtis, it meant, broadly, handing over internal responsibility for the provinces to elected representatives, while the provincial governments retained reserved powers. By 1920 Curtis could write 'the war compelled England, as nothing else could have done, to recognize that the principles for which she was fighting could not be restricted to the people of Europe, America or Australasia, but *must* [italics mine] be extended to Asia and Africa'.[17] And if immediate self-government was impracticable, Great Britain had now to 'put India in the way of taking responsible government for herself. That she has done and the rest remains for India to do.' But, as implemented, 'dyarchy' has been justly described as 'the technical term for handing over the steering

[14] See Lord Ronaldshay, *Life of Lord Curzon*, 3 vols, London, 1928. David Dilkes' *Curzon in India*, 2 vols, London, 1969; also Harold Nicolson's superb miniature in 'Arketall' in *Some People*, London, 1927.

[15] Harold Nicolson in *D.N.B.*, 1922–30.

[16] The story that he exclaimed 'save the elephant' is apocryphal.

[17] See his *Papers relating to the application of the principle of Dyarchy to the Government of India*, Oxford, 1920, pp. *lix–lx*.

wheel and retaining control of the accelerator, the gear lever and the brake'; and the Montagu–Chelmsford measures of 1919 still reserved finance, police and general administration to a governor whose 'right hand was despotic, his left nearly responsible to the electorate, but not quite, because he need not take the advice of his ministers in the last resort'.[18]

Further, this compromise now seemed inadequate. India's major contribution to the war, the current fashion for liberal democracy and self-determination, the political rise of the Indian National Congress from which the Muslims had in 1906 hived off into a Muslim League, made 'dyarchy' an anti-climax. Then the Mahatma Gandhi launched his campaign of non-co-operation and became a major political force, appealing to the peasant masses in a new way. Mohandas Karamachand Gandhi (1869–1948) was the son of the Chief Minister of Porbandar in Kathiawar, Gujerat. He came of the *bania* (merchant) caste, and his name means, literally, 'grocer'. He studied law in England at the Inner Temple, and in 1893 set up as a barrister in Natal where he defended the rights of Indians in South Africa. In 1907 he invented a technique of 'non-resistance' by *Satyagraha* (soul force) among Indians whose status was being threatened in the Transvaal, and incongruously set up a Tolstoian co-operative farm near Johannesburg. In the First World War he raised an ambulance unit, but after it, in collaboration with Congress, he led a resistance movement by the methods he had developed in South Africa, to which he now added the cult of hand-spinning. Imprisoned by the British in 1922–4, he emerged to conduct a campaign over vast areas of India and to win a huge following. In 1930 Gandhi led a march to the sea to break the law which imposed a tax on salt. He was again imprisoned.

Gandhi's hypnotic personality combined a mystic's single-mindedness with a shrewd lawyer's flair. He was in revolt not simply against the British but against the Western way of life: he rejected political violence and attacked caste discrimination against 'untouchables'. Doctrines of withdrawal and voluntary poverty, common in the East as in medieval Europe, were now combined with modern methods of publicity and mass communication. Gandhi's campaign would have stood little chance against Hitler or Stalin, but the British were ambivalent, already in principle committed to Dominion status for India.

In April 1919 there had been riots, savagely suppressed at Amritsar. Brigadier-General Reginald Dyer, C.B., in face, it seems, of a spreading anarchy, had ordered his troops to fire: they killed three hundred and seventy-nine rioters and wounded more than a thousand.

[18] Woodruff, *op. cit.* Vol. II, p. 211, q.v.

He had then ordered all Indians who passed along a street where a British female missionary had been beaten up, to crawl the length of it—a gesture which exacerbated feelings on both sides, for and against.[19] Moreover, in a civilian scene of action, the Simon Commission to report on the working of the Montagu–Chelmsford reforms had contained not a single Indian, an exclusion bitterly resented.

In 1926 a new Viceroy had arrived in India. Edward Wood, Lord Irwin, afterwards Earl of Halifax, was as religious as Gandhi, though he loved foxhunting. A high-church Anglican, he was ready to admit Gandhi—whom Churchill had called 'a half-naked fakir'—to long and soul-searching conversations. He got on much better with Gandhi than the imperialist Lord Curzon, or the lawyer Rufus Isaacs, Marquess of Reading, would have done, and he made a better success of his negotiations in India than those he conducted afterwards in Germany. Together the two mystics made a pact which for a time ended the civil disobedience campaign, and in 1931 Gandhi was invited to London, when he appeared in the English winter in his usual garb and created a considerable sensation, making a formidable impression at the ensuing Round Table Conference. No agreement, however, was reached, and Gandhi for the rest of his life continued his anti-British activities.[20] For the first time since the proclamation of the Queen Empress, a British Viceroy had been seen to negotiate on equal terms, and Curtis' vision of the 'candle of British representative institutions, lit in England centuries before, being lit in India' and 'extended to all Asia', was ousting a despotism in fact more akin to Asian history, but which was now incompatible with the liberal democratic ideas prevalent in the Dominions in western Europe and the United States.

V

In 1885, when Lord Dufferin was Viceroy, the affairs of Burma had reverted to their pristine violence. In 1837 the pacific King Mindon, who, it will be recalled, still reigned in Upper Burma, had transferred

[19] The Governor of the Punjab, Sir Michael O'Dwyer, supported Dyer, and the Guardian of the Har Mandar, the principal Sikh shrine, made the Brigadier an honorary Sikh; but Dyer was forced to resign his commission. He was compensated by £28,000 raised by subscription through the *Morning Post*.

Dyer had done well in the campaign in southern Persia during the Great War; and his father, the Managing Director of the Muree Brewery, had been the first to brew good beer in India.

[20] He was assassinated in 1948 by a Hindu nationalist as a result of his attempts to reconcile Hindu and Muslim aspirations.

his capital from Ava to Mandalay, where he had created an elaborate city whose gold-roofed pagodas behind machicolated walls and moats reminded one of its observers of a flimsy version of the Kremlin.

Though many of his subjects remained, understandably enough, intractable, resentful and pertinaciously unfriendly to the British, the monarch had remained on tolerable terms with the foreigners who now ruled the Arakan, Pegu and Tenasserim as a province of British India, and with the British merchants who were exploiting rice and teak and anxious to reopen the old road to China. But, like all Burmese rulers, Mindon was surrounded by palace intrigue. In 1866 he was nearly murdered in a conspiracy by two of his own sons and, since the British refused to sell him armaments, he took up with the French, then expanding their territory in Indo-China. Relations were worsened when, in 1875, the British envoy, Sir Douglas Forsyth, refused to remove his shoes and squat on the floor when negotiating at the court, a gesture he thought humiliating, but which in Burmese eyes was the very least he could do.

In 1875 King Mindon died, and the usual free-for-all set in among the royal family. Out of it there emerged King Thibaw, a puppet under the control of his ferocious consort, Supaya Lat. Under her inspiration—and when she lifted her little finger, it was said, the whole city trembled—he massacred nearly eighty of the royal relations, and Upper Burma fell into sanguinary confusion. Moreover, the new regime entered into a commercial treaty with the French, and the British merchants were loud in protest when King Thibaw heavily fined the British-owned Bombay–Burma Corporation on a trumped-up charge. The British government felt compelled to act.

Lord Dufferin was reluctant to intervene. The campaign in Afghanistan had been costly in men and money; but Burma, as much as Afghanistan, was considered one of the 'glacis' of India. If, he wrote, the French should try to 'forestall us in Upper Burmah I should not hesitate the annex of the country'; the more so as the principal Burmese minister was a 'savage brute, originally a member of Theebaw's bodyguard'.[21] It looked indeed as if 'in their folly and ignorance the Burmese were determined to rush upon our bayonets'.[22]

Lord Roberts was now Commander-in-Chief, and the campaign on the road to Mandalay was well organized. The Burmese were swiftly overwhelmed, and both Thibaw and Queen Supaya Lat, known to the British soldiers as 'Soup-plate', evicted. In 1886 the Viceroy and

[21] Sir Alfred Lyall, *The Life of the Marquis of Dufferin and Ava*, Vol. II, p. 118.
[22] Lyall, *op. cit.* Vol. II, p. 120.

Roberts visited the country, determined, in the absence of suitable puppet rulers, on outright annexation. 'Burmah,' wrote Dufferin, 'is a most delightful country and the Burmese people are extremely engaging, full of fun and jollity and light-heartedness and unlike our sombre Hindus.' He admired the freedom and beauty of the women in their flowered silks; the splendour of the pagodas—'wonderful nightmare kind of structures, all gold and high relief and topped in every direction like pavillions'[23]—and the 'great monasteries filled with enormous statues of silent Buddhas'. He found the Buddhist *poongyis* picturesque—their robes falling in classic folds and the 'dusky orange of their garments in perfect harmony with their dark skins'.[24]

But easy conquests are often the most difficult to follow up. It took three years before the country, a 'theatre of domestic anarchy and the playground of hereditary bandits', larger than France and with about four million inhabitants, could be pacified; not so much because of political resistance as because of sheer anarchy and 'an ingrained repugnance' to any discipline.

And in this context the British made their major mistake. For the whole area, like the previous conquest, was now administered from India, and the kind of bureaucracy there developed imposed on a very different country. In a society not ridden by caste, where women had much greater freedom, the British hardly established the kind of aloofness that they did in India; on the other hand, the Burmese were far too proud and set in their ways to be Westernized. During the Japanese war, 'the hill tribes showed ... a loyalty as moving as any in history. But of the rest of Burma one must conclude that this mature and self assured people were much less influenced by the English than the people of India ... The connection was in the first place much shorter—only fifty seven years.' And if 'in India nationalism was a product of British rule, in Burma it was there ready made'.[25]

But, the economic domination of the British was in proportion much greater than in India. In 1846 the rice-growing area had been well under half a million acres; by 1870, following the American Civil War and the opening of the Suez Canal, it was nearly one and three

[23] Lyall, *op. cit.* Vol. II, pp. 123–4.

[24] When Dufferin retired from the Viceroyalty, the Queen created him a Marquess. But he was reluctant to take a title from India. People would 'resent it', he wrote, 'if I called myself Marquis of Agra, or Delhi, or Benares or Lahore'. And when Salisbury suggested a place in Burma, he objected that all the names there were 'horribly uncouth and would sound like names out of Offenbach or the Mikado. The only possible one is Ava' (*op. cit.* Vol. II, p. 192). So Dufferin and Ava it was: at once euphonious and romantic.

[25] Woodruff, *op. cit.* Vol. II, p. 136.

quarters: by 1930 it would be more than twelve and a half million—
'the most spectacular development in [Burmese] economic history'.[26]
But the expansion, due to European capital, brought inflation of
land values, land speculation, the eviction of the peasantry, absentee
landlords; debt to India, moneylenders and European banks. Immigrants swarming from India provoked violent Burmese protest: the
dependence on exporting rice made the economy vulnerable.

The other major product was timber. Teak, iron wood for railway
sleepers, bamboo, lac, charcoal—all found a ready market in India.
The British-organized Burma Forest Department prevented indiscriminate exploitation, but the timber export was entirely in foreign
hands. And in 1886 the Burmah Oil Company—the original of the
Anglo-Iranian—began to exploit the oil-fields and controlled three-
quarters of the industry.[27] Tin and tungsten were mined by the British,
and the government of India built the railways—over two thousand
miles of them—but 'Burma was developed by foreign capital, Indians,
Chinese and Europeans owned all the large factories and industrial
concerns, the greater part of Burma's debt was foreign-held, and
Indian *Chettis* (money lenders) in 1930 had an investment of 750
million rupees in the rice lands'.[28]

Such was the economic situation with which governments had to
contend. It was further complicated by the Morley–Minto Reforms,
then, following the Montague–Chelmsford Report, by the experiment
of 'dyarchy'. The removal of the king and the disestablishment of the
Buddhist religion had further undermined the traditional order; now
the attempt at political 'education' on British lines produced first a
Legislative Council with a majority of Burmese voters but no final
authority; then in 1921 another council, elected on a very wide franchise, but with defence, finance and public order still reserved. Hence
the rise of a nationalist party determined on emancipation from
British control and on joining the proposed Indian Federation with
the option of secession, for the Burmese had no wish to exchange
British domination for one by an Indian government at Delhi.

The dominant theme of the brief phase of British rule over the
whole of Burma is thus the rapid economic development of the
country by foreign capital; the arrival of Indian immigrants, resented
by the people; and the persistence of the traditional Burmese way of
life—so different from that of India and now politically more
dynamic among Westernized exponents of the kind of nationalism
emanating from Europe. Though the British administration was not

[26] Hall, *A History of South East Asia*, p. 650.
[27] Hall, *op. cit.* p. 653.
[28] Hall, *op. cit.* p. 654.

unsuccessful, the resulting and accumulating resentments made it predictable that Burma would leave the Empire, even when it was called a Commonwealth.

VI

The ancient civilization of Ceylon, symbolized by the exploits of King Dutugemunu in the second century B.C., described in the spirited *Mahavamsa Chronicle*, and commemorated by the gigantic *Stupas* of Anuradhapura and the Ajanta style paintings at the rock fortress on the Sigiriya, built by the megalomaniac Kasyapa I when the Anglo-Saxons were invading Britain, was based on elaborate irrigation of the lowlands that border the Mahaveliganga. Here, in the northeast of the island, were canals and reservoirs unparalleled in ancient India; and in spite of sanguinary internal power struggles and Chola conquests from southern India, the Sinhalese—from *Sinha*, Sanskrit for lion—had established an aristocratic and theocratic society, still flourishing in the twelfth century under Parakrama Bahu I, and symbolized by the sacred tooth of the Buddha still carried in the annual Perahera procession. The natural focus of the seaways from East Africa, southern Arabia, the Persian Gulf and the China Sea, the island had early developed a considerable commerce; the more so as it was the only source of good cinnamon, which here grew wild.[29] The Sinhalese monarchs had also exported pearls, gems and elephants, trapped and tamed. Alien to the predominant Sinhalese, were the Dravidian Hindu Tamils of the northeast and Muslim Arab traders of the seaports; while Veddah tribesmen lurked in the rain-drenched high country in the south of the island around Adam's Peak.

Upon this medieval and by the sixteenth century politically deca-dent society the Portuguese had imposed their domination, mainly on the northwestern coast and on the stem of the mango-shaped island at Jaffna. By 1658 the Dutch had ousted them, seized Colombo and Trincomalee and established a solvent administration in the coastal areas they controlled. But, like the Portuguese, they had never con-quered the interior, the Kingdom of Kandy itself. When in 1795 the British had taken over the country, it had been administered from Madras and considered an economic liability annexed for a strategic purpose. But in 1803 it had become a Crown Colony, and in spite of the massacre of an ill-found expedition against Kandy in the hilly jungle in the following year, Sir Robert Brownrigg, consoled for his

[29] Hence the 'spicy breezes' of Bishops Heber's well-known hymn: not probably designed to reflect on the Sinhalese in particular but on humanity in general.

failure as a Quartermaster-General of the disastrous expedition to Walcheren, by the command in Ceylon, had managed by 1815 to crush the Kandyan resistance. The British had become the first Europeans to control the whole island.

During the early and mid-nineteenth century they had opened up the interior, constructed strategic roads and bridges and enabled European settlers to develop the large coffee plantations which first geared the island to a world economy and exploited the potential of the hill country. This coffee boom, in which local officials and wealthy Sinhalese participated and which came to its climax in the 'sixties, was based in part on coolie labour, imported, as in the West Indies, from India, and the self-sufficient but limited peasant economy was eroded. Hence the Kandyan rebellion of 1848, provoked immediately by taxes on the dogs and guns essential to small farmers on the outskirts of the jungle—a rising put down so fiercely that the Governor, Lord Torrington, though a relative of Lord John Russell to whom he owed his appointment, was hastily recalled.

The planters, the local aristocracy who had adapted themselves, and the Western-educated lower bourgeoisie were now powerful interests, and even when the market for coffee collapsed, tea took its place. It proved even more profitable. The masses in England preferred the 'stronger' brew of Ceylon to the more subtle brews of China, and from the 'eighties until the mid-twentieth-century tea plantations flourished. And in 1876, that enterprising civil servant, Sir Clements Markham of the India Office, had promoted another new and lucrative enterprise. Rubber, brought by devious·ways from Brazil to Kew and thence to Ceylon, was now acclimatized.[30] The predominant 'planter's *raj*' was thus reinforced; but, beneath it and its dependants, seethed peasant discontent, the hatred of Buddhist Sinhalese and Hindu Tamils, and the ambition of Eurasian 'Burghers', and Westernized intellectuals excluded from higher posts in government. Upper-class Sinhalese were now associated with government but, as in India, 'dyarchy' proved disappointing. There were major riots in 1915, mainly against Muslim merchants and harshly repressed. Then in the 1920s following the Montagu–Chelmsford reforms in India, ingenious but ineffective procedures were devised.

---

[30] Henry (afterwards Sir Henry) Wickham, a young English resident in Brazil, chartered a freighter liner, secretly loaded it with rubber seeds, bluffed the Brazilian authorities with the help of the British consul, and rushed the seeds to the orchid houses at Kew, cleared for the occasion. They reached the Botanical Gardens in Ceylon in good condition and their descendants were later transported to Malaya. See E. F. C. Ludowyk, *The Story of Ceylon*, revised edition, London, 1962, pp. 203–5.

Apart from Europeans, the population now comprised about three and a half million Sinhalese, half a million indigenous Tamils, three-quarters of a million immigrant Indians and three hundred thousand Muslims. These communities, though increasingly represented on the legislature, had no control of the executive and were constantly at odds. So in 1928 representation by communities was superseded, universal suffrage over twenty-one brought in regardless of religion and race, and a constitution devised, incongruously enough, on the lines not of the British Parliament but on those of the London County Council, doing most internal business by committees. But here, as in India, the essential powers over defence, justice and finance were still reserved, and the country administered through the British Ceylon Civil Service. The voters, of course, most of whom were illiterate, still elected their local magnates, and in spite of efforts to create it, they remained blind to the blessings of party government.

Although by the 'twenties the slogans of modern nationalism, Marxist–Leninism and even Trotskyite doctrines, were seeping in, the old system carried on, and with communal political strife diminished. There was appalling poverty and disease in many jungle villages, but between 1834 and 1915 the population had risen from roughly one and a half million to over four million, and exports, which greatly exceeded imports, had increased in worth from about a million and a half to nearly two and three-quarter million pounds. The First World War had increased the demand for rubber, and a wealthy establishment, British and Asian, was still apparently secure. It was rather the usual British social discrimination, not against illiterate 'natives' who accepted their rulers, but against just the people they had educated in the English language and way of life, that provoked exasperation. As Leonard Woolf wrote in his subtle evocation of Ceylon, 'the flavour and climate of one's life was enormously affected ... both by this circumambient air of a tropical suburbia and by the complete social exclusion from our social suburbia of all Sinhalese and Tamils'.[31] This ambience, prevalent over most of the middle reaches of the colonial Empire, was doubly incongruous in a colony containing the splendid art of the temples of Anuradhapura, where 'everything shines and glitters in the fierce sunshine, the great sheet of water, the butterflies, the birds, the bodies of the people bathing in the water ... the brightly coloured clothes. Along the bund grow immense trees through which you can see from time to time the flitting of a brightly coloured bird,[32] and in a climate where 'out of the

[31] Leonard Woolf, *Growing, an Autobiography of the Years 1904–1911*, London, 1961, p. 18.

[32] Woolf, *op. cit.* p. 28.

enormous sky all day long the white incandescence of the sun beats down upon the earth, and where 'towards evening it changes slowly to a flaming red or a strange delicate mixture of pink and blue'.[33] Naturally, there should be a passionate desire for an Asian and autonomous government; but unlike the Burmese, the leaders of Ceylon, a country dependent on oceanic trade, and historically with wider horizons, would elect to remain within the Commonwealth.

[33] Woolf, *op. cit.* p. 34.

CHAPTER 21

Continental Canada; the Caribbean; the Antarctic

By 1867, the year of the Confederation of Canada, the 'dreary waste of colonial politics', as its principal architect, Sir J. A. Macdonald, had remarked, had become less parochial. Politics began to turn on the rival intrigues of the railway magnates who would create the infrastructure of a continental economy extending from the Atlantic to the Pacific. The hostility of British- and French-Canadians, aggravated by the transplanted vendettas of Protestant and Catholic Irish immigrants, would spread to the new territories, already the scene of intense Amerindian resentment;[1] but the two main creators of a viable Dominion were the Scotsman, Macdonald (Prime Minister 1870–3 and 1878–91), and the French-Canadian, Sir Wilfrid Laurier (Prime Minister 1896–1911).

The political structure of the Dominion was swiftly made. In 1870 the Federal Government assumed sovereignty over the vast thinly inhabited and partly unexplored territories of the Hudson's Bay Company, extending from Labrador across the hinterland of the Bay itself to the mouth of the Mackenzie River and to the Yukon. In the next year, British Columbia joined the Confederation, on the promise of a transcontinental railway to be built within ten years—a pledge fulfilled in fourteen, when in 1885 the Canadian Pacific Railway, through colossal obstacles, completed an overland Northwest Passage from the Atlantic to the Pacific and made Canada more than a geographical expression. In 1873 Prince Edward Island joined the Dominion, and Winnipeg, the capital of Manitoba, in the geographical centre of Canada, was becoming the natural gateway to the

---

[1] The white settlers killed off the game, polluted the rivers and burnt the forest, while the Blackfeet Amerindians did not understand the settlers' idea of private property and declared that 'they had made no bargain with the white folks for their native country': G. F. G. Stanley, *The Birth of Canada*, Toronto, 1936, p. 276.

prairies and the far west. Then in 1880 the British transferred the huge Arctic Archipelago to the Dominion. In 1905 the prairie provinces of Saskatchewan and Alberta would be created: the former with its capital at Regina in the greatest wheat-growing area of Canada, the latter with its capital at Edmonton, originally the headquarters of the Hudson Bay Company's northwestern fur-trade, and destined to develop after the discovery of oil-fields and minerals into an industrial city. Calgary, too, would become the centre of the cattle-trade of the enormous ranches and of great oil refineries.

But it was not until 1896 that the real expansion began, coincident with Sir Wilfrid Laurier's Liberal and freer-trading government. In the far western Yukon territories gold had been found at Bonanza Creek on the Klondike, and the boom town of Dawson City had sprung up. From Skagway at the northern end of the panhandle of American Alaska—the entire country purchased from Russia in 1867 —the diggers had struggled over the White and Chilkoot passes into Canada, under the eyes of the Canadian mounted police—for in Canada there was no wild west. Then, as the world depression lifted, the agricultural and pastoral potential of the prairies had been realized, as combine harvesters, silos, elevators and railroads brought the grain east to be shipped to Europe, while the cattle ranches fed an insatiable American demand. Though the main population remained heavily in the east, the more so as the mineral wealth of the Laurentian shield was developed, the foundation of a continental economy and power had been laid.

Between the Klondike gold rush and the First World War over three million immigrants settled in Canada: Ukrainians, Central Europeans, Scandinavians, Jews and Italians, as well as about a million Americans and a million British. And although at the Imperial Conference of 1902 the Canadians had led the resistance to Chamberlain's policy for an imperial system of defence, and a Canadian navy was not built, in 1914 the Dominion at once voluntarily came into the war; and by 1916 Canada had put four divisions into the field in France. At Arras and Vimy Ridge they took all and more of their share of the carnage; indeed, during the whole war, Canada would raise over 600,000 men, though the French-Canadians proved recalcitrant to conscription. At the Peace Conference the Canadians were thus accorded separate representation; and if the slump in the 'thirties set back their economy and diminished immigration, the country was now a power in its own right. It was also now more cosmopolitan in origins, more Americanized—a process confirmed in the Second World War. Only the French-Canadians, contradicting Durham's expectation, refused to be politically and culturally swamped in the Anglo-Saxon tide: 'such', as Laurier had written, 'was the pride of the French people that they wished to remain what they were'.[2]

II

In 1871 the Treaty of Washington marked a politically tactical reverse for Canada, as Canadian claims had been sacrificed for an overall settlement. But it marked also strategic recognition, for it stabilized Anglo-American relations over the Empire. From the Federal capital at Ottawa, 'a sub-arctic lumber village converted into a political cockpit',[3] the government of the Dominion could now deal with its vast problems, social and economic, without the hitherto considerable menace of an American takeover.

The Canada Act had been realistic. The Federal government, first convened in 1867, was responsible to a Senate, its life members nominated by the Governor-General in accordance to the population of the original provinces—Ontario, Quebec, Nova Scotia and New Brunswick. A House of Commons of 181 members was to be elected in the same proportions every five years. And the provinces seemed under control. They had their own Lieutenant-Governors, appointed or removed by the Governor-General, and their legislatures dealt with local taxation, education and public works. The upper ranks of the judiciary were appointed from Ottawa; proceedings both in Parliament and the law courts were bi-lingual and the French in Quebec kept their old laws. In 1871 Ontario had the biggest population—over one and a half million; Quebec then had nearly a million and a quarter; Nova Scotia nearly 400,000; New Brunswick only about 285,000. Of the other provinces, Prince Edward Island had rather less than 100,000; Manitoba not much more than 25,000; and even British Columbia still only around 36,000. But they would vastly develop. The population of the entire gigantic Northwest Territory was returned at 4,800. Most Canadians, in all little over three and a half million, were thus still concentrated around the great lakes and along the St Lawrence. The problem and the challenge was how to develop the enormous interior in a country which, west of the lakes, was little more than a ribbon of frontier, until the slightly broader settlement of British Columbia beyond the Rockies.

The answer was to build railways, the basis for a real continental

[2] O. D. Skelton, *The Life and Letters of Sir Wilfrid Laurier*, Oxford, 2 vols, 1922, Vol. I, p. 73.

[3] *Cambridge History of the British Empire*, Cambridge, 1929, Vol. VI, p. 65.

confederation; in contrast to the Australians, the Canadians soon built them on the transcontinental scale. But the vision of those aware of the promise of the west and the Pacific coast was not shared by the peoples of the Maritime Provinces. Nova Scotia, far too dependent on its fisheries, with relatively barren soil, if a slightly better climate, and with its resources of hydro-electric power and timber still under-developed, looked mainly to its Atlantic trade, exporting salt cod to impoverished Catholics in southern Europe and lobster to affluent Americans in New York. Newfoundland had stayed out of the confederation and would not enter it until 1949. In face of the competition of steam, New Brunswick no longer built sailing ships; there was a sparse population of fishermen and small farmers.

To the Federal government the Maritimes were of political concern, but irrelevant to the development of the west. They early realized that it was essential to buy out the Hudson's Bay Company which controlled vast areas from Labrador to the Pacific, from Lake Superior to the Yukon and the 'backdoor to the North Pole'. Here, through snowbound primeval forests, the fur-traders brought their pelts by dog-sleigh and canoe in temperatures of 50° below, and over enormous prairies half-breeds and Amerindians hunted buffalo for their hides and tongues. And these venturesome and self-sufficient hunters had no wish to see their territories mined for minerals, ploughed up for mechanized agriculture and tamed by railroads.[4]

So when in 1869 the Canadian government bought out the Company's claims to sovereign power and trade monopoly for £300,000 and extensive freehold land grants, the half-breeds or *métis*, alarmed when the surveyors arrived and fearing for their tenuous land rights raised rebellion. They were led by a French-Canadian, Louis Riel, who proclaimed a Republic of the northwest. Irish Fenians took a hand, and Riel, the *méti* leader, had the most articulate British-Canadian shot for treason to the Republic. The resistance threatened to set off the old French against British feud across the country.

In this crisis two major characters in imperial history won fame. Colonel Garnet Wolseley, who had already gained reputation in the Crimea, during the Indian Mutiny and at Peking, arrived at Fort Garry from Lake Superior with 1,200 men, many transported by canoes. The rebellion was scotched and Wolseley, knighted, went on to campaigns in Ashanti and Egypt and, as Commander-in-Chief, to

[4] R. M. Ballantyne, the contemporary bestseller of books for boys, had taken service with the Company in Rupert's Land in 1841, and spent six years there. Hence the inspiration for the *Young Fur Traders* (1856) and the *Dog Crusoe* (1860), both better works than the even more popular *Coral Island* and *The Gorilla Hunters*—the equivalent of a popular thriller today.

try to modernize the British Army. But the settlement was due mainly to Donald A. Smith, afterwards Lord Strathcona and Mount Royal, one of the makers of modern Canada. Donald Alexander Smith, born in 1820 near Forres in Morayshire, Scotland, and on his mother's side of Highland descent, joined the Hudson's Bay Company at eighteen through the initiative of his maternal uncle, John Stuart; an occasion on which his mother remarked, 'They'll all be proud of my Donald yet.' He had spent thirteen years in the hardships of the fur-trade in Labrador—a country the size of Great Britain, France and Prussia combined—and by 1862 he had become chief factor for the Company and had also built up some capital by investing the savings of his colleagues on commission. As chief factor and one of the 'wintering partners' (local traders who had fixed shares in profits in the Company), he represented their interests. But when in 1868 Smith became chief executive of the Company at Montreal and the architect of the settlement with the government, he foresaw that the ordinary shareholders would swamp out the local traders. So, along with his Montreal associates, he bought up a controlling interest in the Company. When in 1871 the 'wintering partners', who demanded their share of the £300,000 paid by the government, had their minority claims settled on poor terms, Smith and the shareholders came off best. Now more popular with the shareholders than with his former colleagues, Smith became Chief Commissioner—in effect, the head of the fur-trade—then a Director, and by 1889 Governor of the Company.

He had meanwhile turned his attention to railways. And it was now that this formidable fur-trader became interested in politics as a means to developing them. Unlike Cecil Rhodes, who was interested in money as a means to political power, Smith was interested in politics as a road to wealth. Fort Garry, or Winnipeg, as it now became, was the natural centre for railroad development into the prairies and the far west; and there the St Paul and Pacific, an American–Dutch enterprise, and afterwards the Great North Railroad from the Red River to the Pacific, had been paralysed by the American Civil War. It was now bankrupt; but its owners could claim valuable land grants if it were completed. So in 1876 Smith and his able cousin, George Stephen, later Lord Mount Stephen, already President of the Bank of Montreal, along with other Montreal associates, bought out the Dutch bondholders in Amsterdam for a sum equal only to the interest on the arrears of interest due to them. They were thankful to get it.

The new proprietors then threw all they had into developing what became the St Paul–Minneapolis–Manitoba railways and extended them north and south; issued new bonds in New York and netted for themselves holdings in the now prosperous company which would become worth three hundred million dollars. So armed, in 1880 they founded the transcontinental Canadian Pacific Railway Company and pushed through the tremendous project in five years. In 1885 at Craigellachie, British Columbia, beyond Kicking Horse Pass, 'Mr Donald A. Smith, with a few words of congratulations, lifted a hammer, and the well-directed blows of a man not unaccustomed to manual exercise drove in the last spike'.[5] In 1896 Smith was knighted and appointed High Commissioner for Canada in London, and in the following year he was created Lord Strathcona and Mount Royal. He now settled in Great Britain, bought an estate in Scotland and died aged ninety-three in 1914. During the war of 1899–1902 in South Africa he had raised Strathcona's Horse at his own expense, and he left large endowments for schools and hospitals in Canada, Scotland and the United States.[6]

The development of the Canadian Pacific Railroad had been achieved with the collaboration of the Conservative government of James A. Macdonald, which had returned to power in 1878, and which had supplemented the original investment with massive public loans, and the grant of a vast acreage of land on either side of the track. For it was urgent to bring the rule of law to the prairies. Riel, who had fled to the United States, had returned to head another rising of French-Canadian *métis*, this time in Saskatchewan. Though he was taken and hanged for the murder of his British-Canadian rival in the previous resistance—and so became a political martyr in French-Canadian eyes—there had been a real danger that *métis* or Amerindians would overwhelm the sparse white population. The need to pacify the area had been underlined: it could only be done by railways.

Other entrepreneurs seized their chance. Aided and abetted by the politicians, they would build three other railway systems; the Grand Trunk, the Canadian Northern and the Canadian National. Canada thus had a superfluity of railways, tying up large public funds, and it would not be until 1917 that they would be reduced to the Canadian Pacific and the Canadian National. Macdonald's protectionist policy had also fostered new industries. The great Massey-Harris enterprise developed agricultural machinery so novel and efficient that it could

[5] Beckles Wilson, *Lord Strathcona and Mount Royal: His Life and Times*, London, 1902, p. 209.

[6] The coat of arms of this formidable tycoon was gules on a fess argent between a demi-lion rampant, a canoe and hammer; and his crest: on a mount vert a beaver eating into a maple tree, proper. Motto *Perseverance*. His peerage, by special dispensation, descended to his daughter.

be exported to Europe; and under Laurier's Liberal administration of 1896–1911, the massive immigration and mining and industrial developments already described would transform the scale of the economy. Moreover, successive governments managed to keep the original British- and French-Canadian incompatibilities within bounds, and assimilate the million Scandinavian and central European immigrants who flocked to the prairies. As in Australia, these newcomers diversified the British (though not here the French) way of life. Free land grants in the prairie states were made to selected immigrants, and from small beginnings in the 'seventies a colossal production of cereal crops was achieved and exported.

To European immigrants the life was hard; the climate exacting. In 1910 a young Wiltshire farmer, A. G. Street, arrived in Winnipeg. 'The men,' he wrote afterwards, 'were of all nationalities, but they nearly all had one thing in common. They were clean-shaven. There were townsmen in high shouldered suits and boots with funny bumps on the toe-caps, leathery faced miners, lumber jacks and teamsters; excited French Canadians come up from the East for the harvest, North West Mounted policemen, in high heeled boots and stetson hats, and one Indian in a blanket and mocassins, who surveyed the bustling crowd with haughty indifference. There were various types of peasants from central Europe with their families. Women were few, and these were chiefly Galician peasants' wives, who sat amongst their brood waiting patiently, oh so patiently, for someone to tell them when to continue this interminable journey from Austria.'[7] 'The whole scheme of things,' he reflected, after his first Canadian winter, 'was so different from my old life in that one told somebody else to do a job, whereas, in this there wasn't anybody to tell.'[8]

In 1911 Laurier's government, which had tried to lower the tariffs against the United States, failed any longer to contain the French-Canadian nationalist politicians and was replaced by a conservative administration under Sir Robert Borden (1911–20). The son of a farmer and station-master in Nova Scotia and of Scots descent through his mother, Borden had made his way as a barrister. He was a liberal Conservative, determined to use state power to clean up a rather casual administration and cut down on uneconomic public expenditure, and he was an early advocate of an independent Canadian navy. He brought Canada at once into the First World War, and, in 1917, brought Laurier into a wartime unionist coalition. Like the Australian and New Zealand Prime Ministers, he represented his

[7] *Farmer's Glory (1932)*, Harmondsworth, 1951, p. 74, q.v., for an illuminating account and comparison.
[8] Street, *op. cit.* p. 91.

country at the Peace Conference with plenary powers.[9] This new status confirmed the failure of any attempt to federate the Empire, whereby the Dominions thought they would be dominated by Great Britain. And it was on the Canadian model that the Irish Free State was accorded Dominion status in 1922—without much success.

When in 1921 Borden resigned through ill-health he was succeeded by the Liberal, William Mackenzie King, who held office with a brief interval until 1929, and who was even more set on Canadian autonomy. In 1925 he defied the Governor-General, Lord Byng, over his right to dissolve parliament; a gesture which had wide repercussions. For after the Imperial Conference of 1926 all Governors-General were confined to representing the monarch, not the current government in Great Britain, which was now to be represented by a High Commissioner.

It was thus on Canadian initiative, not shared by Australia or New Zealand, that the Statute of Westminster came to define the constitutional position of the Dominions: a fact that reflects the greater economic power of Canada, which under Mackenzie King's second administration, 1935–48, was able to send massive financial and military aid to the United Kingdom, and greatly promote the success of British–American collaboration in the Second World War.

III

If until the mass immigration of the early twentieth century, there had been too few people in Canada, in the British West Indies there were far too many: at the end of the nineteenth century about one and three-quarters of a million, and by the mid-twentieth century around two and a half million. All the Caribbean islands depended on sugar; and though sugar remained 'king' until the 1950s, the British planters were now outclassed by the big American factories in Cuba with vast capital behind them. Moreover, sugar-beet, inferior in sucrose but subsidized and protected, was now a major crop in continental Europe, where production rose from 451,584 tons in 1859–60 to 4,725,800 in 1894–5. Cane sugar prices fell by half; and in 1897 Joseph Chamberlain, who in 1890 had condemned his son Neville to grow sisal on 20,000 acres on Andros, Bahamas, for seven years on soil too thin for it, appointed a Royal Commission on the West Indian economy. They recommended more diversified crops—bananas and citrus groves, coffee, cocoa and cotton—the

[9] He wrote *Canada in the Commonwealth* (1929). *Robert Lord Borden, his Memoirs*, were edited by H. Borden, 2 vols, 1938.

last already profitable in the early nineteenth century. But the planters, who wanted any fresh land for sugar, opposed the recommendation, though their methods were often such that 'James Watt might never have lived for all the effect his invention had on West Indian production'.[10] Central factories were more economical; but production was still dispersed, and the windmills of Barbados, a picturesque anachronism, could not compete with the American factories in Cuba which in 1894 produced 1,054,214 tons of cane sugar to British Guiana's 102,502 and Barbados' 50,958. Further, though world demand still expanded, and British Guiana and Barbados staggered on, cane sugar was now grown in India, Fiji, Mauritius, Queensland and New South Wales and, outside the Empire, in Louisiana, Brazil, Java and the Philippines. The British West Indies were heading for bankruptcy.

During the First World War, when the beetfields of northern France and Belgium were put to other use, and the Germans needed all their own crop, the British Caribbean industry revived; but in 1921 the British themselves began to grow their own sugarbeet and restricted cane sugar imports, while during the trade depression of the 'thirties a glut of all tropical products set in. Emigration to Canada and the United States was stopped; and poverty and malnutrition worsened a long-standing social and political discontent. Save in parts of Jamaica, there was little adequate peasant agriculture; the descendants of slaves were naturally feckless; apt, it was said, to drink too much rum on Sundays to work with much conviction the next day. The East Indian immigrants who made up more than a third of the population of Barbados and of British Guiana, could be more enterprising; but wages were low and methods obsolete: the vast eighteenth-century profits that had built the Codrington Library at Oxford and Beckford's Fonthill had not been ploughed back into an industry then highly profitable without further investment, and tourism was still limited and seasonal. Though climate and temperament made poverty more endurable than in the north, the once most-prized British possessions in the Americas were now, as Lloyd George put it, becoming the 'slums of the Empire'.

Political institutions, too, were ramshackle and unrepresentative. In 1865 following the crisis under Governor Eyre, even the ancient Jamaican assembly had been abolished; in the West Indies proper, only Barbados, assertive since Cromwellian times, had self-government; and if the Bahamas and Bermuda also retained their assemblies, all were still elected on a restricted franchise. The economic and

[10] Eric Williams, *From Columbia to Castro. The History of the Caribbean, 1492–1969*, London, 1970, p. 369.

political grievance was mounting up, to erupt in the 1930s in strikes and riot.

In spite of the exploitation of aluminium and bauxite in Jamaica, oil in Trinidad, and of the variety of timber, of which mahogany and cedar were the most profitable, and the cultivation of yams, sweet potatoes, breadfruit and papaya against a background of warm seas and luxuriant vegetation, the islands remained too much dependent on sugar, with its by-products of molasses and rum and, after the invention of refrigerated ships, on the export of bananas, most fully developed in Jamaica.

Communication between the islands remained rudimentary until the coming of modern aircraft and, when, after the Second World War, the British and Caribbean governments devised a Federation mainly directed to increase the economic bargaining power of the islands, it would take ten years to bring this about and it would break up after four years, in 1962.

These adversities would hardly offset the natural climatic advantages of the area, which, in spite of relative poverty, was now no longer the scene of the piracy and major warfare of the seventeenth and eighteenth centuries, and which would remain within the Commonwealth as independence was attained.

IV

In the far south Atlantic, the Falkland Islands, finally annexed in 1832, had been a base for exploration. From Stanleyville, founded in 1843, the Antarctic had been investigated. Rear-Admiral Sir James Clark Ross, who had already located the magnetic pole in the Arctic, had also made an extensive reconnaissance in H.M.S. *Erebus* and H.M.S. *Terror*, both destined to destruction in Franklin's Arctic expedition. He had discovered Mount Erebus, a twelve-thousand-foot-high volcano in what he named Victoria Land, part of a range of mountains which fringed the Antarctic continent.

A Crown Colony by 1892, the Falkland Islands now proved their strategic worth in the First World War, commanding the Magellan Straits and the passage round the Horn. In December 1914 the German China Squadron under Admiral von Spee, with *Scharnhorst* and *Gneisenau*, crack ships of the new German navy, had crossed the Pacific and sunk the obsolescent British cruisers *Good Hope* and *Monmouth*, with all hands, off Coronel, south of Santiago in Chile. But, making for the Falklands, their commander observed with horror the tripod masts of the latest British battle-cruisers, *Invincible* and *Inflexible* in Stanley Harbour, dispatched in haste by Fisher under Sir Doveton Sturdee, his own Chief-of-Staff. Now themselves outclassed, *Scharnhorst* and *Gneisenau* were doomed; the first annihilated with her entire crew, the second sunk with only one hundred and sixty-six survivors out of a crew of eight hundred. Twentieth-century standards of slaughter had come to the south Atlantic; and although the predominantly coal-burning battle-cruisers were blinded by their own smoke, so that the execution, gallantly resisted, took a long time, the British based on the Falklands had cleared the outer oceans of dangerous enemies.

In politically more tranquil but climatically more lethal latitudes, the high and enormous Antarctic continent was still awaiting exploration and political partition. The British had already made South Georgia and the South Orkneys dependencies of the Falkland Islands, and claimed the South Shetlands, Graham Land and huge areas beyond the Weddell Sea as 'British Antarctic Territories'.

In 1901–4 on the other side of the continent, opposite New Zealand, Captain (then Commander) Scott, R.N., in the *Discovery* led an expedition promoted by the Royal Geographical and Royal Societies to explore South Victoria Land in the Ross dependency. Proceeding eastward along the ice barrier he discovered Edward VII Land, and returned to winter on Ross Island. Then he penetrated south with the great mountains topped by Mount Markham on his right: the coast of South Victoria Land was surveyed; the Ross Sea charted. The expedition got nearer the South Pole than anyone had before it.

Then, in 1907–9, Ernest Shackleton, who had accompanied Scott and been Secretary to the Royal Geographical Society, returned to the Ross barrier in the *Nimrod*; and after discovering the Beardmore glacier leading up on to the great plateau of the Antarctic, got even further south. One of his party discovered the magnetic pole. Shackleton was knighted and his expenses paid by Parliament.

After routine service at sea and at the Admiralty, Scott now determined to reach the Pole itself. In 1910 another expedition with official backing left England in the *Terra Nova* for a base on the Ross Sea, where it coincided with Amundsen's venture from Norway established on Whale Island. This expedition was equipped with dogs, ponies and motor sledges; but these primitive machines broke down, the ponies had to be eaten and the dogs sent back, so that the final attempt on the Pole had to be made by manpower alone. In November 1911 Scott's party advanced up the Beardmore glacier into the icebound interior. Though it was high summer, the climate was appalling; but by January 1912 Scott had reached the Pole, only to find that Amundsen had forestalled him. The return proved even more dangerous and finally fatal. In temperatures around 40° below zero, they got to the top of the glacier; but Petty Officer Evans died of exhaustion. Then they got down to the ice barrier; but frostbite crippled Captain Oates, who, to promote the others' chances, walked out into the blizzard. The survivors struggled on to within eleven miles of a major supply depot, but a blizzard stopped them. 'We shall stick it out to the end,' wrote Scott, 'but we are getting weaker and the end cannot be far. It seems a pity, but I do not think I can write any more.'

Eight months later, their frozen bodies were found; gear and records and specimens intact. Posthumously knighted, Scott became world-famous. He was commemorated by the Polar Research Institute at Cambridge, paid for by public subscription.

Undeterred, Shackleton planned a more ambitious attack: the Pole would now be reached by traversing the continent. By 1914 the *Endurance* sailed for the Weddell Sea; the *Aurora* for the Ross Dependency. But the *Endurance* was trapped in the ice; and drifting east, far from the objective, she was crushed. Shackleton and his expedition escaped by sledge and boat and reached Elephant Island, where Shackleton and the crew of a ship's boat traversed eight hundred miles of ocean to South Georgia, crossed its high and unknown interior and arrived at a Norwegian whaling depot. He then retrieved the expedition back to South America, and from New Zealand collected the other one from the Ross Sea. Scott had attained his objective; but the Antarctic had got him: Shackleton, who failed, had defeated the Antarctic Sea. He died in South Georgia in 1922, planning an expedition to Enderby Land. Shackleton and Scott were contrasting characters. The former was warm-hearted and enthusiastic; whereas Scott, who entered the Navy at fourteen, remained the impeccable naval officer. It was left for the American Admiral Byrd in 1928, using aircraft, to survey the enormous desolation.

Meanwhile, in 1923, the New Zealanders had annexed the Ross Dependency extending from Edward VII Land, round the ice barrier, to the fringes of Victoria Land; and in 1933, save for a small French enclave behind *Terre Adélie*, a huge territory including the interior of Victoria Land, Wilkes Land and Enderby Land, up to the boundary of the area annexed by Norway between Enderby Land and the Weddell Sea, was taken over by Australia.

The British, the New Zealanders and the Australians thus claimed about two-thirds of the Antarctic continent. As in Regency and Victorian times, they remained predominant over both the icebound extremities of the world.

CHAPTER 22

The Gold Coast and Nigeria; the Union of South Africa

The part of the world still most isolated from the rest of mankind, though the most ancient habitat of the human race and the home of socially complex, if illiterate and technologically primitive cultures, was still the interior of tropical Africa. Here the first major exploitation was begun in the Congo by Leopold II of the Belgians, 'a monarch whose ambitions and capacities far outran the introverted preoccupations of the country he had been born to rule'.[1] Then, after the British occupation of Egypt in 1882 and the swift German annexation of Togoland, the Cameroons, and Southwest and East Africa, the notorious 'scramble' for the continent set in. Of all the great powers, the British were the most concerned. They wished to maintain their trade with West Africa, protect their vital strategic base at the Cape, command the eastern seaboard of the Indian Ocean and the entrance to the Red Sea. With the opening of the Suez Canal, they found they had to control first Egypt, then the Sudan to maintain the Empire in India and the Far East.

In Africa the strategically important areas were often the least rewarding; but Europeans now took over almost the entire continent; and chartered companies, railways, lake and river steamers, began to transform conservative subsistence economies. Already the best-placed power, the British now created a vast new colonial Empire, not so much to extend their own territories, still less under the compulsions of the final stages of a surfeited and 'decadent' capitalism, as to keep others out. For more than half of British overseas investments were in the Americas and the next biggest in India, the Far East and Australasia; and though the discovery of diamond- and gold-mines now made South Africa important, tropical Africa had

[1] Roland Oliver and J. D. Fage, *A Short History of Africa*, Harmondsworth, 1962, pp. 183–4.

always been, and long remained, negligible. Yet 'against all precept and prejudice, against the experience and trends of previous expansion, the British occupied Egypt and staked out a huge tropical African Empire. And what was more, they were ready at the end of the century to fight major wars for Sudanese deserts and South African kopjes. Why after centuries of neglect, the British and other European governments should have scrambled to appropriate nine-tenths of the African continent within sixteen years, is an old problem still awaiting an answer. At the centre of late-Victorian imperialism in Africa lies an apparent paradox. The main stream of British trade, investment and migration continued to leave tropical Africa untouched, and yet it was tropical Africa that was now bundled into the Empire.'[2]

The swift partition of Africa radiated from Europe. It was part of the global strategic manoeuvres between the greatest European powers and of the armaments race between them: but it was relatively peripheral, a would-be insurance accomplished without major conflict. Though Indian troops were used against Africans, Europeans seldom mobilized Africans against other Europeans; and if the continent was artificially and arbitrarily partitioned by statesmen whose advisers were sometimes without proper maps, Africa was never balkanized. On the contrary, the brief phase of colonialism, so much reprobated since, generally set modern standards of administration, literacy and medicine, and went far to adapt archaic and intensely conservative tribal societies to the inevitable challenge of the outer world and in time to bring Africans into it.

The British colonies in West Africa were now greatly enlarged. The Gold Coast Colony now took in Ashanti, and Oil Rivers Protectorate and Lagos expanded into the big Nigerian Federation which included the sub-Saharan Muslim emirates of the middle and upper Niger. Thus the foundation of modern Ghana and Nigeria were laid, the latter combining incongruous cultures. In South Africa during the 'seventies and 'eighties, the economy was transformed and the political balance of power altered by the discovery of the greatest diamond- and gold-mines in the world. The Afrikaaner republics of the Transvaal and Orange Free State resisted the British attempts to create a federation on the Canadian model in the first Anglo-Boer war of 1880–1; they then attempted to defend Afrikaaner paramountcy in the second, 1899–1902. They were crushed by the tardily mobilized might of the British Empire; then in 1910 brought into the

---

[2] Ronald Robinson and John Gallagher with Alice Denny, *Africa and the Victorians. The Official Mind of Imperialism*, London, 1961, p. 17, q.v., for a penetrating analysis.

political and economic Union of South Africa, on terms that would lead, after a phase of Anglo-Dutch collaboration, to Afrikaaner political domination, *apartheid* and eventually to secession from the Commonwealth. Meanwhile the Chartered British South Africa Company, incorporated in 1889 with Cecil Rhodes' millions behind it, took over Matabeleland and Mashonaland between the Limpopo and the Zambesi; penetrated beyond into what became Northern Rhodesia; and absorbed the Africa Lakes Corporation which had developed Nyasaland, by 1889 a protectorate.

In East Africa the British had long controlled the strategically placed island of Zanzibar. They now moved into the interior. Uganda, infiltrated by Catholic and Protestant missionaries in the 'seventies and long nominally the sphere of influence of the Imperial British East Africa Company, now became part of an East African Protectorate, which by 1895 included Kenya and which was linked by 1901 by the strategic railway with Mombasa through Nairobi. So, when German East Africa or Tanganyika was taken over under a mandate of the League of Nations after the First World War, Rhodes' ambition of a Cape to Cairo British domination was in part realized. For at the beginning of the scramble for the continent in the strategically most important area of all, in Egypt, the most decisive move had been made. In 1882 Egypt had been occupied; and since the country depended on the Nile, the British became preoccupied with the Sudan. After a British attempt to pull out, which in 1885 cost Gordon his life, the huge area was ruled briefly by the Mahdi, then by his Khalifa. Then a threat of a French takeover in the southwest, in 1896–8, led to the British conquest of the entire area and an Anglo-Egyptian condominium that would last until 1953.

These vast responsibilities, extending round the whole African continent, from West Africa to Egypt, had been reluctantly assumed; part of a strategy to protect India, Australasia and the Far East. In spite of the popular imperialist excitements of the Diamond Jubilee of 1897, and Chamberlain's encouragement of Lugard in Nigeria and Rhodes in the Rhodesias, the annexations of East Africa had been much more a strategic insurance than an economic exploitation. Indeed in Edwardian times not much was heard of any of the tropical African colonies, then merely being laboriously organized to pay their way. Save for South Africa, the Rhodesias and the Kenya Highlands, Africa was still not attractive to immigrants or investors. Nor had African societies, fascinating to modern historians and sociologists, yet been much appreciated, or modern medicine brought most tropical diseases under control. The medieval dignity of Fulani Emirs, the Kinta'ed brilliance of Ashanti or Yoruba kings, the disciplined and superb courage of the Zulus, the contemptuous dignity of the Masai, the russet bark-robed elegance of the Baganda or the peculiar self-sufficiencies of the Shilluk and the Nuer, had not the glamour of the rich civilizations of India and the Far East. For most of the public, even in Jubilee year, Africa was still a continent of blazing deserts, dervishes and 'fuzzy-wuzzies'; of fever-stricken swamps and of hippopotami that crunched up canoes and their occupants; of hyenas who stole up in the night and ate off half one's face; of lions and charging elephants; of crocodiles and of cannibals who, provoked, would devour a missionary on sight.

In spite of these opinions, in part justified by the sheer malice of the African environment, and the current and reasonable reluctance of governments to spend taxpayers' money on risky enterprises, the tropical colonies would slowly become viable—mainly after the First World War and during the Second. These growing commitments, originally often undertaken with ridiculously inadequate resources to forestall rival powers, were only gradually enlarged. Indeed, they had often been forced on reluctant cabinets; 'the Marxist stereotype, of brutal imperialists riding to power over the machine-gunned corpses of defenceless Africans, is far further from the truth than its opposite, which would maintain that colonial occupation was a bloodless process'.[3] With a handful of Europeans to administer millions of Africans, 'indirect rule', already initiated in Fiji in the 'seventies, and adopted by Lugard and applied beyond Nigeria, was an obvious and realistic move. It can justly be regarded as 'the most comprehensive, coherent and renowned system of administration in our colonial history ... in which native chiefs had clearly defined duties and an acknowledged status and equality with the British officials'.[4] It cushioned the impact of modernity on archaic societies. Indeed, it would be criticized by Western-educated African intellectuals and potential rulers as maintaining a conservative social order too long. For with it went Western education, which produced, as in India, its crop of évolués, impatient of their own traditions and social order as well as better aware of their own past, and present potential in the world.

II

British influence on West Africa, hitherto peripheral, now became decisive, and a brief colonial rule and its devolution made modern

[3] Oliver and Fage, *op. cit.* pp. 197–8.
[4] Margery Perham, *Lugard. The Years of Authority, 1898–1945*, Vol. II, Oxford, 1960, pp. 138 and 144.

Ghana and Nigeria. In the 'seventies the prospect was still unpromising. These ancient societies had their own intensely conservative pattern. In the Gold Coast and Ashanti were gerontocracies organized around many 'enstooled' priest kings, who embodied the tradition and the luck of their tribes, and far from being the arbitrary monsters then generally depicted by Europeans, could be 'destooled' if refractory or too savage. These barbaric but elaborate and often wealthy cultures, have since been better appreciated. But to most Victorians they were intolerable—with their cult of human sacrifice and 'hideous performances on tom-toms, gong-gongs and native horns'.[5] Even the waning of slavery and tribal warfare and the well-meant efforts of the missionaries often undermined traditional authority and compounded confusion.

On the coast the relatively pacific Fanti so far adapted themselves that by 1885 a Fanti could be co-opted to the legislature, but despite, or because of, Wolseley's 'punitive' campaign, the warlike Ashanti of the interior remained irreconcilable. In 1898 King Prempeh, who had been enstooled with the normal ritual of human sacrifice, refused a British Protectorate. He was removed, and what was much worse, his people told to surrender the Golden Stool of Ashanti itself, the embodiment of their collective spirit. They rose against the impious foreigners but, subdued in a final Ashanti war, were incorporated in 1901 into an enlarged Gold Coast colony.

Meanwhile, Europeans had been mining the gold, bauxite and manganese, and during the 'twenties, with the boom in cocoa, the Gold Coast colony became more prosperous. Sir Gordon Guggisberg, an athletic Canadian brigadier of Swiss-American parentage, Governor from 1919 to 1928, had already surveyed the country in 1905. As an engineer he had collaborated with Africans, whose potential he understood, and he now created the deep-water port of Takoradi which, linked to the interior by railway, superseded the normal and risky service of surf-boats. In further collaboration with Africans he also founded Achimota College. If the peasants of the interior remained poor and the boundaries of the colony were artificial, cocoa and palm oil had made the Gold Coast solvent.

In the country which was to become Nigeria, a larger area with even more strongly contrasting people and environment, one of the most headstrong of late Victorians had made his mark. In 1854 William Baikie, a Scots naval surgeon, naturalist and philologist, had extensively explored the Niger and, three years later, made a settlement at Lukoja, where he had opened negotiations with Mupe. But he

[5] David Kimble, *A Political History of Ghana. The Rise of Gold Coast Nationalism*, Oxford, 1963, pp. 128 ff.

had died aged only thirty-nine in 1864. Sir George Taubman Goldie, like Guggisberg, had been a Sapper but after two years in the Army, into which he alleged he had passed his examination when 'blind drunk', resigned on inheriting some capital.[6] Indeed, he 'bolted' at once without sending in his papers, and decamped to Egypt. He greatly admired Rajah Brooke of Sarawak, and, arriving on the Niger, now set about amalgamating the rival trading concerns then trying to exploit the delta. By 1881 this Scots-Manxman had founded the National East African Company, and by 1883 it had absorbed its principal rival on the Middle Niger. He had done this just in time: and in 1884–5 at the West African conference in Berlin the British could present Bismarck with a *fait accompli*. Goldie's concern, now the Royal Niger Chartered Company, was empowered to protect and administer large areas, now the object of French and German ambitions.

Another individualist then took charge. Frederick Lugard had been born in 1858 in Madras, the offspring of a sadly incompetent but prolific clergyman and a strong-minded female missionary. After much misery at Rossall School, when his closest friend died of cold and 'exposure', Lugard had failed for the Indian Civil Service; but encouraged by General Sir Edward Lugard, his uncle, he had entered the Army, passing high into Sandhurst. A wiry, little, dark-eyed man, he had then fought in Afghanistan and Burma and developed a passion for tiger-shooting, pigsticking and polo. But after a disastrous love affair in India, Lugard went on half pay and set out to Africa as a deck passenger, ready to shoot elephants for ivory. There he began his main life's work. As will be apparent, he made his reputation in the service of the Africa Lakes Company at Blantyre in Nyasaland, where he had rescued some missionaries from the attacks of Arab slavers; and working for the Imperial British East Africa Company in Uganda, where he had pacified the conflicts between the *Wa-Franza* and the *Wa-Ingleza* and contended with Mwanga, that temperamental Kabaka.

In Nigeria under Goldie's Company, Lugard had full scope; and in 1894 with thirty Hausa and ten Yoruba, in tropical rain, he was the first European to penetrate to Borgu on the west side of the Niger.

[6] Born in 1846 the son of Lieutenant-Colonel Goldie Taubman, Scots Guards, and Speaker of the Manx House of Keys, Goldie detested Victorian England, even the sound of church bells. His eagle profile and fierce blue eyes furthered his design, and his influence in the City and at Westminster became formidable. Though widely distrusted, he was at length accepted as an authority on Africa and received the accolade of the establishment when appointed to the official inquest on the inadequate preparations for the Second Boer War. He also became President of the Royal Geographical Society.

In spite of fever, cured by 'ten grains of antipyrene and thirty miles marching under a blistering sun', and a poisoned arrow in his skull, hard to extract, Lugard won what the French, with an inaccurate metaphor, called the *Course au clocher* (steeplechase) to Nikki, where the blind and ancient ruler assigned the Company a 'Protectorate'. On his return to Yorubaland, Lugard was welcomed by the Alafin of Oyo, but narrowly escaped the fate of forty-three of the Company's African employees at Akassa, when a local chief and his tribesmen killed and ate them all.

In 1897, after prospecting for the British West Charterland Company round Lake Ngami in Bechuanaland, Lugard at last secured an official appointment. Alarmed at French and German competition, Chamberlain appointed him a Commissioner in Nigeria; then after the government had taken over the Niger Company, High Commissioner for the newly created Protectorate of Northern Nigeria. With a budget of little more than £100,000 a year, five European administrators and a West Africa Frontier force of about three thousand under less than a hundred and twenty European officers and N.C.O.s, Lugard managed to control a country with more than ten million inhabitants.

For north Nigeria contained an elaborate and still medieval civilization. From crenellated palaces in Kano and Sokoto, in the 'huge turbans, with the characteristic swathe round the chin ... flowing robes and brilliantly coloured equestrian trappings', the Fulani emirs 'would ride out among their earth stained Hausa peasantry who would fall prostrate in the fields'.[7] But before modern weapons their power crumbled: by 1903 Lugard had captured the big city of Kano and defeated the paramount Emir of Sokoto. Then perforce working through the existing hierarchy—for the Fulani, anxious for Western weapons and amenities, accepted the accomplished facts—he began his first phase of 'indirect rule', to be followed, after his return in 1912 and his appointment as Governor-General of a Federated Nigeria in 1914–18, by its consolidation.[8] As in the independent states of

[7] Perham, *op. cit.* Vol. II, p. 146.

[8] Lugard was Governor of Hong Kong, 1907–11, between his Nigerian appointments, and served on the Mandates Commission of the League of Nations and as Chairman of the International Institute of African Languages. He married Flora Shaw, one of the earliest women journalists of major political influence and colonial correspondent of *The Times*. In 1900 he was knighted and in 1928 created Baron Lugard. He died in 1945. Lugard wrote *The Rise of our East African Empire*, 2 vols, London, 1893; and the *Dual Mandate for Tropical Africa*, London, 1922, became a classic. The definitive and admirable biography is by Dame Margery Perham, *Lugard, the Years of Adventure 1858–98*, London, 1956, and *The Years of Authority, op. cit.*

India, British Residents were installed, and the Muslim rulers of the north and the pagan Yoruba and Ibo of the rain-forest and the coast worked on a light rein, appreciative, it was hoped, of British standards of justice and administration.

So within the tenuous but firm framework of order and taxation sanctioned by a few expatriate Europeans, both the Gold Coast and Nigeria became solvent and governments began to promote better agricultural and technological education. The welfare of colonial peoples in terms of their own cultures had now become an official objective. By the 'twenties, indeed, as in coastal West Africa, in a setting of ancient, wealthy and populous if hitherto absolutist states, Western-educated Africans became eager for authority. But they did not get much of it. It would be only after the Second World War, when European power had been crippled and African nationalism had become formidable, that a colonialist order that had seemed likely to last for generations with only a gradual transfer of power would come to an end, and Africans, though so often with Western standards of administration, revert to forms of government more congenial to them.

III

In South Africa the British had long tried to promote a customs union and a Canadian-style federation. But the Boer Transvaal and Orange Free State republics were only brought into a South African Union, not a federation, after a major conflict—to the British, the Great Boer War; to the Afrikaaners, *het tweede vryheid soorlog*, the Second War for Freedom.

Following the peace of Vereeniging in 1902 the British and their more open-minded opponents led by Botha and Smuts then tried to create the 'self-governing white community', defined by Chamberlain, 'supported by a *well treated* and *justly governed* black labour force from Cape Town to the Zambesi'.[9] Both Balfour's Conservative and Campbell-Bannerman's Liberal governments thus tried to swamp an unappeasable Boer resentment in a common prosperity within a favourable political settlement. But the settlement did nothing to emancipate the Bantu, the Coloureds or the Asians. Indeed, it was made at their expense: Anglo-Dutch white domination was taken for granted, and Smuts, the cosmopolitan philosopher, remarked that 'he did not believe in politics for the natives'.[10] South Africa had room for only one civilization and that was White.

[9] Cited in *The Oxford History of South Africa*, eds Monica Wilson and Leonard Thompson, 'South Africa 1870–1966', Oxford, 1971, Vol. II, p. 350.
[10] *O.H.S.A.*, Vol. II, p. 343.

In the long run this 'creative withdrawal' failed. The Boer *bitter-einders* proved more representative than Botha and Smuts, and any British concession to the Bantu at once raised the spectre of a 'black menace'. Calvinism and now fear enhanced Afrikaaner nationalism, and although Smuts brought the Union into the Great War when mainly South African troops conquered German East and West Africa, by 1924 the Nationalist Boer General, J. B. M. Hertzog, could form a coalition, and by 1929 would have an absolute majority in the Union Parliament. Formal *apartheid* and secession were still distant: but the tide apparently running after Vereeniging had turned. The vision of South Africa as a White Dominion of a liberal Commonwealth faded before the bitter logic of local history.

Indeed, from 1877 to 1902 there had been mounting conflict, exacerbated, not assuaged, by sudden prosperity. It first derived from the competition of Boer and Bantu for land. The Boer farmers thought 6,000 acres the smallest viable property, and by 1877 had pushed out into tribal territory and come near bankruptcy in conflict with Sekukuni, Chief of the Bapedi. The British, coming to the rescue, seized their chance in the interests of South African union to annexe the Transvaal. But hoping to appease the infuriated Transvaalers and the Dutch at the Cape, they neglected Machiavelli's maxim that political injuries, if committed, should be total. Their half-hearted domination was no less loathed. Then the British, too, became involved with the Bantu. The Zulus, now encircled by the Transvaal and Natal, numbered nearly half a million, probably more than all the Europeans in South Africa. A new generation of warriors were again eager to wash their spears and Cetshwayo, a nephew of Shaka, had to show his *Indunas* and *Impis* their traditional sport. Their *raison d'être* was war and they were the 'greatest menace to European civilization in South Africa.'[11] The British determined to strike first.

In 1878 the High Commissioner, Sir Bartle Frere, formerly a successful Governor of Bombay, told Cetshwayo to disband his *Impis* within thirty days, well knowing that no Zulu king could do so. He naturally refused. Then seven thousand British and seven thousand troops from Natal, advancing against thirty thousand Zulus but without reconnaissance or even entrenching their camps, came to disaster at Isandhlwana—the worst British defeat since the Crimean War. And the Prince Imperial of France, ill-protected by his escort, was ambushed and assegaied. It was a sensational setback and the report of it rang round the world. Lord Chelmsford, already superseded in command, then routed the Zulus at Ulundi. Cetshwayo,

[11] *O.H.S.A.,* Vol. II, p. 263.

deported, lionized in London and sent back to rule in 1883, was soon murdered. Zululand was divided among minor chiefs. By 1887 the whole territory had been annexed to the Transvaal or Natal. The *Impis* and the *Indunas* would sink into a proletariat.

The Boers in the annexed Transvaal had observed the British reverses, and chafed under the government taxes the British imposed. Piet Bezuidenhout, the Hampden of the Transvaal, refused to pay them, and Paul Kruger, the most intransigent leader, won wider influence. In 1880 the Boers rebelled. Incredibly, the British, repeating the blunders of Isandhlwana, occupied Majuba Kopje without entrenching their position, and the Boers stormed it in daylight. Gladstone was now in power, and under the Convention of Pretoria the British withdrew from the Transvaal. Save for a general assertion of British suzerainty, the Transvaal again became a republic. Isandhlwana and Majuba had finished Disraeli's and Carnarvon's attempt to unite South Africa, and the Boers, smarting with resentment, now held the initiative.

And this they could now better take. When, in 1867, near the Orange River, a farmer's children were found playing with *blink-clippies*, a momentous 'diamond revolution' had begun; to be followed in 1886 by an even greater 'gold revolution' on the Witwatersrand in the Transvaal. In 1870 diamonds were found at Colesburg Kopje or 'New Rush'—soon dignified as Kimberley, in Griqualand West—which was taken over by the British in the following year and in due course incorporated into Cape Colony. By 1880 Jagersfontein in the Orange Free State, bought by a farmer from the Griquas for £30, had produced the finest diamond yet seen in the country, so the New Jagersfontein Mining and Estate Company bought the mine from his widow for £89,000. They had a capital of over three-quarters of a million, second only to that of De Beer's Mining Company from which, in 1889, Cecil Rhodes would form De Beers Consolidated Mines, the leviathan of them all. For the original raffish competition of the diamond diggings, in which young Rhodes had begun to make his fortune, had given place, after massive financial strife, to this colossal amalgamation, when Rhodes and Otto Beit had called in the Rothschilds and bought out Barney (Isaacs) Barnato's Kimberley Central: 'with what purpose high finance had invaded the land of oxwagons and fat tailed sheep was seen when the house of Rothschild was involved in Kimberley and when the price of a single company's capitulation to the will of Rhodes was £5,338,650'.[12] Mud huts and corrugated iron had given place to the

[12] C. W. de Kiewet, *A History of South Africa*, p. 94. Born in 1853, the fifth of the seven surviving sons of the Rev. F. W. Rhodes, Vicar of Bishops

Kimberley club: 'a graceful low white building, arcades below, verandah above ... it reeked of success, lived by diamonds and was frequented by all the flashiest millionaires of the day'.[13] In London a diamond syndicate controlled the market. These plutocrats were known to their critics as Hoggenheimer & Co.

The discovery of gold was even more important, and made the near bankrupt Transvaal the richest state in South Africa. On the Witwatersrand—the greatest gold-field anywhere, 170 by 100 miles —the reefs went deep and coal seams were adjacent. If the gold content was low, the ore was abundant. Here was no swift plunder of surface gold, but a massive and lasting industry. Johannesburg—*Egoli* to the Bantu—was soon much bigger than Kimberley. Bantu labourers were brought to the mines, the incongruous apparatus of modern machinery settled on the pastoral land, and the world changed its monetary standard from silver to gold. Already experienced in amalgamation, by 1887 Rhodes and his associates had formed the Gold Fields of South Africa Company and in 1890 Rhodes had become Prime Minister of Cape Colony. There were vast resources for

---

Stortford, Hertfordshire, and Louisa Peacock of Kyme, Lincolnshire, Rhodes was descended from Cheshire graziers who had obtained property near Islington and in Essex. The vicar, like Curzon's and Lugard's fathers, no imperialist, wanted, wrote Rhodes, 'all his sons to enter the church as a preliminary to becoming angels; they preferred becoming angels through the army and I don't blame them'. The eldest a Wykehamist who had taken six wickets in the Eton match, and with whom Rhodes farmed in Natal, perished in his tent when some rum he was broaching caught fire. The second, an Etonian, who won the D.S.O. in Egypt, and narrowly escaped execution after Jameson's Raid, collaborated in many of Rhodes' ventures. Known as 'long headed Cecil', Rhodes retained more classical learning from Bishops Stortford School than he might have from Eton, and always admired Aristotle, Marcus Aurelius and Gibbon. At Oxford he lived in lodgings, because he disliked the food in Oriel College, joined Vincent's and Bullingdon Clubs and took a pass degree; but the inspiration of the place was lasting. After the political catastrophe of the Jameson Raid, Rhodes concentrated on the north and in his finest hour went unarmed among the Matabele to settle the rising of 1896. In 1902 he died of heart disease in his cottage at Muizenburg on the sea, his alleged last words, 'so little time, so much to do'. He was buried among the great rocks of the Matopo hills at a place he had called 'the View of the World'.

[13] James Morris, *Pax Britannica*, pp. 290–1. Barney Barnato, originally Barnet Isaacs, had adopted his name from his brother, a pugilist, barman and general entertainer who had taken a foreign-sounding *nom de guerre*. Barney had started with £30 and forty boxes of doubtful cigars and was soon making £1,800 a week as a diamond merchant or *kopje walloper*.

his major ambition—European settlement beyond the Limpopo to the Zambesi and beyond.

The proliferating railways and markets spreading over South Africa now urgently demanded the fiscal union that the Boer republic blocked. But the Transvaal's resources, multiplied twenty-five times, only made Kruger's regime more intransigent and ambitious. The price of prosperity had been a swarm of brash *Uitlanders*, who threatened to outnumber the Afrikaaners. Kruger's corrupt regime mulcted them by taxation and denied them political rights. A *Voorlooper* on the Great Trek at the age of nine, and now President of the Republic, Paul Kruger in old age, in his top-hat and ill-cut frock-coat, looked like a dilapidated undertaker; but in youth he had been a mighty hunter and athlete, who had shot a lion when only thirteen, fought against the Matabele and farmed a vast area under tobacco and citrus orchards at Rastenburg. Now, with sixteen children and more grandchildren, the patriarch *Oom* (Uncle) Paul and his spouse, *Tante* Sina, both authentic relics of the Great Trek, stood for the most archaic Afrikaanerdom. It was the life of the high-wheeled yellow oxwagons creaking across vast spaces of red earth and grey bush, the women in faded blue or pink sunbonnets, the men large and bearded in wide hats on their fast ponies, herding their thousands of sheep and cattle on the *veldt*. And Kruger was doctrinally a *Dopper*, an extinguisher of heresy; a lay preacher of the *Gereformeede Kerk* which followed the doctrine of the seventeenth-century synod of Dordrecht, and forbade even singing, save for the metrical psalms.[14] He was also a cunning captain-general of commandos and an obstinate, astute politician with a turn of homely phrase in the *Taal*. But in world politics he was out of his depth—as in table manners, for in 1883 entertained by the Kaiser, he drank out of his finger bowl, and his host, of course, did the same. But he counted too much on German support, when the German navy was not yet ready for *Der Tag*.

The contrast with Cecil Rhodes, with his world outlook, was total, even to physique. Kruger, in stuffy garments, slumped on his *stoep* dispensing homely burgher wisdom; Rhodes, as in the portrait in Rhodes House, Oxford, in light loose clothes, large, sunburnt and intense, the *veldt* tawny around him under a hot blue sky.[15] They had

---

[14] See M. Juta, *The Pace of the Ox: The Life of Paul Kruger*, London, 1937. The Krugers were originally German, though no one could look more of a Fleming than *Oom* Paul.

[15] Rhodes built Groote Schuur at Cape Town, which he bequeathed to the South African government, and left £3,383,691 net mainly to endow the Rhodes Trust and the Rhodes scholarships to bring able men to Oxford

nothing in common save the moral fervour endemic in the politics of South Africa.

For Rhodes money meant power. He wanted nothing less than Anglo-Saxon world domination to impose world peace, an objective now much denigrated as typical of the racialist social Darwinism of the day. But it compares well with the ideas of other racialists like Gobineau and Treitschke; and in fact Anglo-American world power would decide two World Wars. Better co-ordinated it might have prevented the First, and in fact it stabilized the situation after the Second.

Rhodes' immediate ambition was to promote European settlement between the Limpopo and the Zambesi, and beyond up to Lake Tanganyika. Long thought a shady megalomaniac by the Colonial Office, now, with the Transvaal restive and the Germans in southwest Africa, he was welcomed as likely to encircle the Transvaal on the cheap. In 1889 his company became the Chartered Company of South Africa, with wide administrative power. He went on and founded the Rhodesias, so-called by 1895.

But Rhodes was impatient. Chamberlain was Colonial Secretary, and that year Dr Leander Starr Jameson, Rhodes' hitherto brilliantly successful man in Bechuanaland, jumped the gun. The notorious Jameson Raid, by twentieth-century standards so amateurish, was a ghastly blunder.[16] The civilian *Uitlanders* in Johannesburg were not ready. They had much money to lose and little wish to come under a British government in London. Kruger remarked that one must 'give the tortoise time to put its head out before you cut it off'; Rhodes wired to stop the mad enterprise, but it is said that the telegraph wires were cut. Jameson's commando was rounded up. 'Yes, yes,' said Rhodes, 'it is true, old Jameson has upset the apple cart.'[17]

Politically Rhodes was ruined; he resigned as Prime Minister of the Cape, even, briefly, as Chairman of the Chartered Company. Chamberlain, too, had connived at the rebellion in Johannesburg, though not at the Raid. He was whitewashed by a Parliamentary Committee of Enquiry, and Rhodes kept his Charter. Nor was Chamberlain now averse from a well-prepared showdown. But the Boer

---

from the Empire, the United States and Germany. He also left £100,000 to Oriel, with the proviso that the College must consult trustees, as 'College authorities live secluded from the world so are children in commercial matters'. In the immense literature on Rhodes, the best biography is by J. G. Lockhart and the Hon. C. M. Woodhouse, *Rhodes*, London, 1963.

[16] See Elizabeth Pakenham, *Jameson's Raid*, London, 1960, for an excellent account.

[17] Lockhart and Woodhouse, *op. cit.* p. 323.

provincials got a wrong impression when the Kaiser wired to congratulate Kruger *en clair*. The Boers even thought they could defeat the British Empire in battle; and in 1899, with accumulated armaments and Mauser rifles superior to the Lee Enfield, they tried to overrun South Africa before the British troops could arrive.

The Boer War was fought in three phases. Save for intervention by the great powers of Europe, it could have only one end. Thirty-five thousand burgher commandos, superb horsemen, knowledgeable on the *veldt*, struck out to cut off the British garrisons and cut the railways. They struck west to Mafeking, defended by Baden-Powell; southwest to Kimberley; southeast to Ladysmith in Natal, aiming at Durban. And when Sir Redvers Buller, V.C., arrived, seasoned in colonial wars, he proved deficient in cavalry, supply and strategic insight. Attacking piecemeal to relieve all the garrisons at once, instead of to win strategic central objectives in the Orange Free State and the Transvaal themselves, he was defeated on all fronts: on the Modder River outside Kimberley; at Stormberg in Cape territory; most decisively at Colenso in Natal. The British had a 'Black Week' and their enemies rejoiced. Then, early in 1900 Lord Roberts of Kandahar, with Kitchener as Chief-of-Staff, took charge.[18] He raised

[18] Horatio Herbert Kitchener, 1st Earl Kitchener of Khartoum, K.G., was born in 1850 of a military family settled in County Kerry, Ireland. He learnt fluent French in Switzerland as a boy, and in 1868 passed into Woolwich, obtaining a commission two years later in the Royal Engineers. He first made his way as a surveyor in Palestine and Cyprus, but in 1882 took part in the British conquest of Egypt, where he made many reconnaissances in disguise. Appointed second-in-command of the cavalry in the Egyptian Army, he took part in the campaign to rescue Gordon; then after taking part in a survey of the boundaries of the Sultanate of Zanzibar, became Governor-General of the Eastern Sudan. Here he repelled the incursions of the Khalifa's forces, and by 1892 became Sirdar of the Egyptian Army. Having organized the conquest of the Sudan that culminated at Omdurman in 1898, he was created Lord Kitchener of Khartoum and Governor-General of the Sudan. After his service in South Africa, he became Commander-in-Chief in India (1902–7); then Consul-General in Egypt (1911–14). As Secretary of State for War he then planned the expansion of the army from six regular and fourteen territorial divisions to seventy. Unlike his colleagues in 1914, he expected a long war of attrition. Having made his career in the East, Kitchener was expert in the intrigues of the *souks*: as indeed, on the highest levels, in the Army, as when he worsted Curzon in India. But he could not cope with the civilian politicians, and his peculiar and over-centralized methods were unsuited to the conduct of a great European war. He never lost his great prestige with the public; but by 1916 he had little influence in Cabinet. He was drowned on a mission to Russia in June of that year. This enigmatic man, at once a military martinet and a passionate collector of works of art, has been admirably portrayed by Sir Philip Magnus, *Kitchener: Portrait of an Imperialist*, London, 1958.

cavalry commandos, supplemented by 'Strathcona's Horse', personally financed by the Canadian magnate to the tune of £1,000,000. He took Bloemfontein, the Free State capital, and a base for the relief of Ladysmith. Kimberley, which contained Rhodes, was relieved by Sir John French; Cronje defeated at Magersfontein. Buller relieved Ladysmith and saved Natal; in May 1901 Johannesburg and Pretoria were captured, Mafeking relieved, to hysterical rejoicing in London. Kruger fled to Laurenco Marques, later to be fêted in France, Germany and Holland, and to die at Clarens near Montreux. The Boer Republic was annexed.

But fifty thousand Boers continued to resist. They were broken only by what Kitchener termed 'a new system of kraaling the Boers into areas by lines of our patent blockhouses'. Contrary to widespread belief, he loathed this expedient; but thousands of combatants were deported and non-combatants herded in 'concentration' camps, where twenty-five thousand died through administrative muddle and their own ideas of sanitation, appropriate only to wide-open spaces. It was a suitable overture to the twentieth century.

So ended what Lord Salisbury called 'Joe's War', leaving a poisonous bitterness behind it. A force of 256,000 British regulars, 109,000 volunteers, 31,000 Canadians, Australians and New Zealanders and 53,000 British South Africans, had defeated 88,000 Boers in a white man's war. When Queen Victoria had declared, 'We are not interested in the possibilities of defeat—they do not exist,' she had been right, but the victory had been hard-won. The sequel was magnanimous, but though it kept South Africa within the Empire and Commonwealth in two World Wars, in the long run it was a failure. Sir Alfred Milner, High Commissioner for South Africa in 1897, a realist who had early regarded the conflict as something to be got over, brought to the daunting problem the incisive abilities of late-Victorian Balliol.[19] He endeavoured to reconcile British and Dutch, and

[19] Alfred Milner, Viscount Milner (1845–1925), came on his father's side from a Lancashire family, on his mother's side of military background. His paternal grandfather had been in business in Germany, where he had married Sophie von Ruppard; his father, Charles Milner, became a London doctor but 'found a rabbit more inviting than a patient, and a pheasant than a fee', so he had to teach English literature at the University of Tübingen. Milner was early educated in Germany, where he developed a passion for swimming and boating for which his defective eyesight was no handicap. On his father's death he lived in some poverty in London when he attended King's College, whence in 1872 he won the top scholarship to Balliol, though he thought he had 'gone to the dogs' in the examination, in part by a brilliant essay on whether wars were likely to diminish as nations became more civilized. Milner then won the Hertford, Craven, Eldon and Derby scholarships, became President of the Union, took a first in Greats and was elected a

cope with the even more intricate problem of the Bantu, essential to the economy but alien to it. 'Anglo-Dutch friction,' he wrote, 'is bad enough but it is child's play compared with the antagonism of Black and White.' Nor had he illusions about the future. 'People think the war decided that South Africa should remain for good and all part of the British Empire,' he wrote in 1905, 'I never took that view ... it only makes that result possible, at most probable. To make it certain requires years of patient policy.'

Now also Governor of the Transvaal and Orange Free State colonies, Milner and his famous *kindergarten* (a term at first of derision not of respect) of able young Oxford men, set about rehabilitating the country.[20] The Boers had to be resettled, the British compensated, the municipal government of Johannesburg reformed; its water supply improved, its slums cleared, its boundaries defined, and the railways had to be reconstructed. The British gave the country £5,500,555 outright and, without extra taxation, Milner raised £30,000,000. An indemnity, secured on the mines, was remitted— a sequel to the conflict often forgotten. To restore the mines, shut down for two years at a loss of £35,000,000 to full production, Milner

---

Fellow of New College. In 1889 he was appointed Under-Secretary to the Egyptian Ministry of Finance, and in 1892–7 Chairman of the Board of Inland Revenue. But he had found 'the sober satisfactions of a well rendered estimate are tame compared with Empire making', and in 1897 accepted the High Commissionership of South Africa, along with the Governorship of Cape Colony. After leaving South Africa in 1905 Milner went into business in the City, devoted himself to the Rhodes Trust and to promoting the ideas of the founders of the *Round Table*, and took up the cause of Ulster. In 1916 Lloyd George made him a member of the War Cabinet, and his most important work, greater than that in South Africa, was to bring about the unity of the Allied Command under Foch. In that year he became briefly Secretary of State for War, then for the Colonies. In 1921 he retired and married, but died of sleeping sickness after a final visit to South Africa. In 1902 he was created Baron Milner, in 1902 a Viscount and in 1921 K.G. For the fullest account of his work in South Africa, see *The Milner Papers*, ed. Cecil Headlam, 'South Africa 1897–1899 and 1899–1905', London, 2 vols, 1931.

[20] These Liberal Imperialists long had great influence. R. H. Brand, Lionel Curtis, Geoffrey Robinson (afterwards Dawson), Editor of *The Times*, and Dougal Malcolm, private secretary to Lord Selborne, Milner's successor, all became fellows of All Souls: Philip Kerr, of New College, later Marquess of Lothian, was Ambassador to the United States, in the early stages of the Second World War, and Patrick Duncan, Governor-General of South Africa. Kerr and Curtis successfully edited the *Round Table*, which propagated liberal imperialism, if their associates, L. S. Amery, afterwards Colonial Secretary, held a more conservative view. T. E. Lawrence, who wanted to create a 'Brown' Dominion in the Middle East, was associated with the group.

imported fifty-one thousand indentured Chinese: an expedient that roused the British Liberals to a fit of moral indignation very useful in the election of 1905.[21] By that year the mines were again in full operation; and, with the economy in better shape, Campbell-Bannerman's Liberal government decided to grant responsible government to the Boer territories: 'the right thing to do', wrote Lionel Curtis, but risking another collision with the Cape Colony and another war. So the only way to avoid the catastrophe was to unite all four colonies under one government. 'We decided to start a movement for South African Union.'[22]

Early in 1907 the Selborne Memorandum based on the draft of Curtis and his collaborators, proved decisive.[23] Briefly, it argued in the idiom of the day, that since the British and Dutch were both 'Teutonic' they were bound to merge; that geographical barriers between the colonies were negligible; that buffer states as on the Northwest Frontier in India were impracticable; and that now that Rhodes had 'saved the hinterland of South Africa', there should be a Union, as in the United States, to assimilate it. Only a Union government, too, could deal with the 'native' problem—and establish a 'self-contained and self-governing society on the basis of a race wholly removed from them in descent, habits and civilization'. Moreover, since 'any attempt to manage the domestic affairs of a white population by a constant exercise of the direct authority of the Imperial Parliament in which the people concerned are not represented is, save under very special circumstances, doomed to failure',[24] it was imperative to create institutions reflecting the 'natural unity of the country'. The example of Canada with its close confederation was invoked. Only a Union Parliament could create a South African rather than a provincial public opinion.

[21] It was objected that Milner wanted to bring them in to prevent the settlement of British small farmers who would make South Africa democratic, though such settlement was obviously impracticable. The public, as in Australia, also became concerned about the morals of the Chinese, who were well able to look after themselves and had never been imported to settle.

[22] Lionel Curtis, *With Milner in South Africa*, Oxford, 1951, p. 345. This memoir is very illuminating.

[23] *A Review of the Present Mutual Relations of the British South African Colonies*: a memorandum prepared by the Earl of Selborne at the request of the Government of Cape Colony; in A. P. Newton's *The Unification of South Africa*, London, 1924, Vol. II, pp. 54–175. See also *The Selborne Memorandum on the Union of South Africa*, ed. Basil Williams, Oxford, 1925. Selborne, a son-in-law of Lord Salisbury and a Liberal Unionist had been First Lord of the Admiralty, when he founded Osborne and Dartmouth, appointed Fisher as First Sea Lord and created the R.N.V.R.

[24] Selborne, *op. cit.* p. 58.

Milner was sceptical. He had left South Africa convinced of failure; only massive British immigration—not forthcoming—could prevent the Afrikaaners dominating a Union, a thought not lost on the Boer generals, Botha and Smuts. Indeed, the latter, who thought the Union would develop as in Canada, played the most decisive tactical part in achieving it, so that 'more than any other national constitution within the Commonwealth, that of the Union of South Africa bears the imprint of one man's mind'.[25] In 1910 Botha, formerly Prime Minister of the Transvaal, became the first Prime Minister of the Union. Smuts, who had organized *Het Volk* to reconcile *bittereinders* with *hensoppers*, and persuaded Campbell-Bannerman to grant responsible government to the Afrikaaner states, became his Minister of Mines, Defence, and the Interior.

Ou Baas and *Klein Baas* now supplemented each other. Botha farmed 11,000 acres and embodied traditional Afrikaaner qualities in a magnanimous way; Smuts, the Cambridge-trained philosopher and lawyer turned commando leader, was known, like William of Orange in compliment, as 'Slim'; only Gandhi, adept in the higher humbug, could go one better and present him with a pair of sandals he had made when Smuts had him gaoled.

But the hagiography that Botha and Smuts have commanded should not obscure their good sense. They wanted a United South Africa as a Dominion of the British Empire, internally as free as Canada or Australia; and Smuts with his world horizons, came to regard the Commonwealth as a pilot project for a League of Nations. Like the Liberal Imperialists of the *Round Table*, who thought it 'an anomaly if there should be no means of marshalling the whole strength and resources of the Empire effectively behind its will, when its mind is made up',[26] Smuts understood that without British protection South Africa could be highly vulnerable. Hence, along with his belief in self-government and the rule of law, his support of Empire and Commonwealth in the First World War, when Botha campaigned in German Southwest Africa and Smuts in German East.

But in South Africa Boer nationalism led by Hertzog proved stronger than either the Liberal Imperialists or Smuts expected. When in 1926 Hertzog's government tried to disenfranchise the natives in the Cape and Smuts and Hofmeyr opposed the Bill, Hofmeyr resigned but Smuts had to compromise. It was the price of

[25] W. K. Hancock, *Smuts: The Sanguine Years 1870–1919*, Cambridge, 1962, p. 268; with its sequel, *Smuts: The Field of Force 1919–1950*, Cambridge, 1968: this work is a classic biography.
[26] Editorial manifesto in the first number of the *Round Table*, 1910.

the power which enabled him to bring South Africa into the Second World War, and worth it, for as his biographer has well written. 'If Hitler's image was not to be stamped on this planet, his country was geopolitically necessary and he was politically necessary.'[27] And if the world citizen was repudiated by his parochial constituency and apartheid and secession would follow, the Union of South Africa had already achieved what its architects, British and Afrikaaner, had meant it to do in the world conflicts many of them foresaw.

IV

In 1889 when Rhodes got his charter, the northern hinterland lay open for settlement. It was believed that beyond Bechuanaland there might be territories as rich as the Transvaal, and the Chartered Company set out to forestall the Germans and the Boers. North of the Limpopo from his 'Buck' Kraal, Kwa Bulawayo—the place of Him who Kills with Affliction—beyond the granite Matoppos and commanding the road to the north, Lobengula, paramount chief of the Matabele, was lord of a vast area. Known, macabrely and respectfully, as 'Stabber of the Sun', and 'Eater of Men', and surrounded by his official praisers or *M'Bongos* and with sixty wives, he was nearly six feet tall, weighed about 300 lb and measured 55–60 inches across the chest. 'He treads the ground,' wrote an observer, 'in a manner that shows he is conscious of absolute power.' He was a rainmaker and smeller out of witchcraft, and habitually devoured great masses of unevenly roasted meat 'like the pieces we give to the lions in the Zoo'.[28] He looked at once worried, good-natured and cruel, and he had a pleasant smile. In 1868 he had succeeded his father, Mzilikazi, who had led a forced migration north-west over the *veldt* until he had put the Matoppos between them and the *Voortrekkers*. From their military *kraals*, they had since tormented the Mashonas, the Barotse and the Bechuana.

But this sometimes amiable savage was now fated for destruction. Large, copper-coloured and dangerous, he depended like Cetshwayo, on the warriors he held in leash. At first he had welcomed missionaries, hunters and concessionaires, particularly if the latter brought him cases of champagne; and he had already sealed an agreement with Kruger's government. So by 1888 Rhodes persuaded the ailing and elderly Sir Hercules Robinson, then High Commissioner of South Africa, to instruct Moffat, the missionary who translated the

[27] Hancock, *op. cit.* Vol. II, p. 413.
[28] See Ian Colvin, *The Life of Jameson*, 2 vols, London, 1922, Vol. I, p. 97.

New Testament into modern English, to make him promise not to alienate territory without British consent. All the stops were pulled out, more cases of champagne brought up by oxwagon, and next year Lobengula, persuaded by Rhodes' emissaries, Rudd and James Rochfort Maguire, a roving Fellow of All Souls, signed away the entire mineral wealth of his territories in return for £1,200 a year, some obsolescent rifles and an armed river steamer. Suspecting this deal, Lobengula then executed the counsellor who had recommended it, and sent two *Indunas* to solicit the protection of Queen Victoria. They returned much impressed; and the British sent back some Lifeguards in full fig, with a letter of reassurance. And Rhodes sent him Dr Jameson, his most brilliant fixer, who at once charmed him. Even so, in 1890 Lobengula only reluctantly accorded Jameson's white *Impi* 'the road to the north'.

But the white *Impi*, of two hundred young settlers and five hundred of the Chartered Company's mounted police and including Selous, the most famous big-game hunter of the day, penetrated to the high *veldt* of Mashonaland and founded the frontier town of Salisbury. It was called after the Prime Minister and it commanded the headwaters of the Zambesi and a potential route to the sea.

Already by 1893, when the Matabele resumed their usual raids and massacred the Mashonas, the Company found itself at war. Two columns, one of 258 Europeans, 118 Bantu, 3 guns and 2 'galloping Maxims', a screw gun and a Hotchkiss, with wagons that could contract into *laager* like a porcupine, advanced against the Matabele. In the Imbembesi Valley five or six thousand warriors, their leaders in ostrich feather capes, and oxtail garters, fiercely attacked the British *laager*. But Lobengula's obsolete rifles were their undoing. Instead of stealing up and charging at night, with oval shields and stabbing assegais, they attacked with rifle fire in daylight and, since they thought the more elevated the sights the greater the impact, they fired too high. Eight hundred of their crack Umbezi regiment were mown down for four European killed and five wounded. 'Fancy the Umbezi,' said a warrior brought dying to the *laager*, 'being beaten by a lot of boys.' 'No civilized troops,' said the British, 'could have stood the terrible fire so long.' Lobengula fled, to perish, probably from smallpox; but not before the British hunting him down had been surrounded and, after singing 'God save the Queen', speared to a man. He was entombed in a walled-up cave, an assegai through his belly to keep him upright.

When in 1896, while Dr Jameson was on trial in London after his Raid, the Matabele rose again and the Mashona as well, both maddened by drought and an eclipse of the moon, they were rounded up by a column under Lieutenant-Colonel Plumer, afterwards Lord Plumer of Messines. And when they retreated to their fastness in the Matoppos, Rhodes himself went to meet them unarmed. With only six companions, he waited until 'twenty or thirty warriors emerged from the surrounding scenery', and wisely let them orate for hours. And, when, at the second *indaba*, the *Mjakas*—the young warriors—came armed and threatened him, Rhodes commanded them to 'go back', rode in among them and 'argued imperiously',[29] to the great satisfaction of the older *indunas*. So they called Rhodes *Lamula M'Kunzi*—Separator of the Fighting Bulls—and made peace. And here he found the 'View of the World', on the Matoppos where he would be interred.

Such were the beginnings of Rhodesia, nearly as much mythologized as those of the American Far West. Until 1923 the Chartered Company would rule it—'smelling slightly of the blood of the Matabele'.[30] The beginnings had been hard: there were drought and *rinderpest*. Rhodes was informed by one settler who had given up, that the enterprise was a 'bloody fyasco'; and by a Scot who carried on, that he 'didna come here for posterity': but when Rhodes observed the site of a synagogue he said, 'Ah, if the Jews come here, the country's all right.'

Rhodesia thus developed under a Chartered Company, not as a Crown Colony; and settlers early resented decisions from Whitehall—as when, in 1894, Lord Ripon, Secretary of State for the Colonies in Gladstone's last administration, and his advisers, innocent of the facts of local life, decreed that the defeated Matabele should keep their weapons to deal with the baboons,[31] arms that would come in handy in 1896.

Though Rhodesia became viable, even prosperous, south of the Zambesi the Company itself made a loss. But it recouped itself from the copper-mines to the north. It had two Dukes on its board, one of them royal; but in the twenty-five years of its Charter, which expired in 1914, it paid no dividends. When it claimed seven million pounds compensation for running the country, it obtained only three and a quarter, and even after selling its mineral rights to the Southern Rhodesian government, it did not break even. Worse, in 1918, Lord Sumner, on the Judicial Committee of the Privy Council, literally cut much of the ground from under the settlers' feet: for he ruled, with impeccable legal rectitude, that the defeat of Lobengula had invalidated the latter's dubious concessions. The settlers' victory had

[29] Lockhart and Woodhouse, *op. cit.* p. 353.
[30] For a vivid evocation, see James Morris, *Pax Britannica*, pp. 83–103.
[31] Morris, *op. cit.* p. 89.

been their legal undoing and all the land not under private title came under the crown. The metropolitan government could thus have its say in 'native' policy. Even so, when in 1923 the Southern Rhodesian settlers had to choose between joining the South African Union and self-government under the Crown, they chose the British connection.

In Northern Rhodesia, which was far more sparsely settled, the Company, relieved of its political and administrative obligations, began to prosper; though they never acquired Katanga, they acquired the copper and zinc of Broken Hill. The Colonial Office, now in charge, favoured the Bantu interests: the Barotse, for example, with whose leader Rhodes had made a treaty, practised indirect rule in their reserved territories. Nyasaland, originally colonized by Scottish missionaries from Blantyre, and defended from slavers by Lugard in the service of the African Lakes Company, had been declared the British Central African Protectorate in 1889. Sir Harry Johnston, the British consul at Mozambique and afterwards administrator of the territory, resisted the attempts of Rhodes' Chartered Company to break through to the coast, and assuaged the resulting friction with the Portuguese. In 1893, Rhodes negotiated but failed to buy up the African Lakes Company. The country in 1907 called Nyasaland remained separate from Northern Rhodesia, the settlers subsisting mainly by tobacco and tea plantations.

Such, contrary to Rhodes' ambition that the country called after him would form part of a United South Africa, was the sequel to the original settlement. It is not surprising to an historian, that, given their pioneering traditions and their early relations with the Bantu and British governments, the White Rhodesians, only two generations later, would make their Unilateral Declaration of Independence. Whatever the shifts of power in Africa and the doubtful long-term expediency of the decision, like the Americans in the eighteenth century, they had merely refused to obey a parliament in which they were not represented.

CHAPTER 23

East Africa; Egypt; the Sudan

Northward beyond the Rhodesias and Nyasaland, the East African coast extended from Kilwa, the Rufiji and Dar-es-Salaam, past the clove-rich island of Zanzibar, up to Mombasa and Malindi and so to Somaliland. The narrow coastal belt was rich and luxuriant, with a soft tropical climate; but, once inland, there generally extended a forbidding strip of thorn and scrub until the country rose to the vast plateau of East Africa at around 3,000 feet, from which rose magnificent mountain ranges, the highest peaks at Kilimanjaro and Mount Kenya; and where, in the miniature grand canyon at Olduvai, are the most ancient traces of the ancestors of mankind. This area extended to the great lakes: Tanganyika, Victoria and on to Lake Albert, while, to the north, Lake Rudolf extended from what would become northern Kenya into Ethiopia.

In this immense and diverse country there were far more animals than humans: gigantic herds of zebra, wildebeeste, antelope and their predators possessed the land, and elephants and rhinoceros ranged the forest and savannah.

For the outer world this country of Masai and Nandi warriors, and Kikuyu and Luo cultivators, of Chagga and Arusha, and of fierce Somali tribesmen to the northeast, held little attraction; and it was not until the 'eighties when the scramble for Africa set in that there was competition for it. The only area which was lush and fertile, with an easy climate and heavy population, was Uganda, bordering on the northern shores of Lake Victoria and extending northwest to Lakes Kioga and Albert and the headwaters of the Nile. It would be mainly the strategic importance of Uganda, which bordered the Southern Sudan, that would lead to the building of the Uganda railway, to the foundation of Nairobi and to white immigration into the highlands of Kenya. The country that today contains some of the finest game reserves in the world—the Selous National Park in the latitude of Kilwa, the Serengeti in Tanganyika, the Tsavo in Kenya and the Murchison Falls National Park in Uganda, was long left to itself by Europeans.

Strategically—and it was strategy alone that interested British governments in East Africa, then of little economic importance compared with West—the paramountcy in Zanzibar established in the mid-Victorian times was considered sufficient. The British fleet commanded the Indian Ocean, and it was only now that it appeared urgent to keep other Europeans out. Indeed, the British had encouraged the German takeover of German East Africa in return for German support against the French in Egypt and the Russians at Constantinople.

The British had established themselves in Zanzibar ostensibly to suppress the slave-trade, and they undermined the authority of Sultans, who were their allies, in pursuit of this objective. For apart from the cultivation of cloves in the rich tropical island, and they were tended by slaves, the Sultanate had few resources; particularly after, under British pressure, it had been separated from Muscat in Southern Arabia. By 1870 Sultan Barghash, alarmed at the erosion of his wealth and authority by the suppression of the slave-trade, was proving recalcitrant; and in 1873 Sir John Kirk, Livingstone's companion on the Zambesi,[1] was appointed Consul-General and, three years later, political agent by the British government, posts he held until 1887.[2] Like others in the outposts of Empire, Kirk suffered greatly at the hands of Gladstone, who had no interest in areas of East Africa with 'unpronounceable names', and who often refused to take account of the reports of those on the spot. And once the British occupied Egypt, even Lord Salisbury was ready to sacrifice East African interests in return for a free hand elsewhere. By 1885 the Germans had obtained Kilwa and Dar-es-Salaam, and were already occupying great areas of Tanganyika. As Salisbury wrote, 'I have been using the credit I have got with Bismarck in the Caroline Islands and Zanzibar to get help in Russia, Turkey and Egypt. He is rather a Jew, but on the whole I have got my money's worth.'[3] And

[1] See Sir R. Coupland, *Kirk on the Zambesi*, London, 1928, for an interesting account, written with the author's usual skill.

[2] Born in 1832, in a Scots manse, Kirk had served as a doctor in the Crimean War; but he was more interested in botany than medicine and his life work was on *The Flora of Tropical Africa* (1868–1917). He was also an administrator and diplomat, who played a difficult hand with great skill, and managed to preserve the British standing in Zanzibar, the base of later expansion. He was made K.C.B. in 1870 and died in 1922.

[3] Cited in Robinson and Gallagher, *op. cit.* p. 196.

in the Anglo-German agreement of the following year the British retained their paramountcy over Mombasa as well as Zanzibar.

The usual expedient of extending a sphere of influence through a chartered company was still to hand. But it was not adopted until 1888, and then in part because of French moves in Madagascar. The objective of the Imperial British East Africa Company was Uganda, but Salisbury was much more interested in using it to enhance the political hold on the coast and Zanzibar. Though the company was chartered in that year, it had neither the resources nor the government backing to make it formidable. It was only after 1895 when an East African protectorate was proclaimed that commitment in Uganda, with its command of the sources of the White Nile, became inescapable and the strategic necessity for a Mombasa, Nairobi, Kiguma railroad ensured that Kenya would be developed by Europeans.

The railway, opened in 1903, put Kenya on the map; so much so that part of the highlands was offered to the Jews as a National Home, to be rejected, it was alleged, after their representatives had witnessed a Masai war-dance. Sir Charles Eliot,[4] the Commissioner, wrote *The East African Protectorate*, the first comprehensive survey; and another very different, though almost equally versatile character had settled in Kenya. In 1897 Lord Delamere, a landowner who found country life in Cheshire tedious, had arrived at Berbera in Somaliland to shoot big game.[5] In 1903 he took up a ninety-nine-year lease of 100,000 acres in Kenya; by 1915 perpetual leases became available, and after the First World War wealthy British settlers took up huge estates. Here, by 1926, in country hitherto the hunting grounds and pastures of the Masai, about twelve thousand Europeans had settled in about 10 per cent of the whole country. Nairobi, originally a mere railhead, became a hectic metropolis, and the goings-on in the 'Happy Valley' among the richer expatriates became legendary. More advantageously, merino sheep were acclimatized, and large areas developed for cereal crops, cattle and coffee

[4] Scholar of Balliol, Fellow of Trinity, Oxford, winner of the Hertford, Craven, Ireland and Derby scholarships and the master of an astonishing range of languages, ancient and modern. Diplomat and Vice-Chancellor of Sheffield and Hong Kong universities, and ambassador to Japan, he wrote on Hinduism and Buddhism as well as marine biology, and retired to Japan.

[5] Sir Hugh Cholmondely, third baron, 1870–1931. He became the representative and leader of the settlers, and a member of the legislative council who often represented the settler interest in London. For an account of this splendid eccentric, who should have been an Elizabethan, see Elspeth Huxley, *Lord Delamere and the Making of Kenya*, 2 vols, London, 1935.

plantations. With the development of the country Indian *banyas* and coolies arrived—more of them than the Europeans—and the Colonial Office was confronted with the claims of settlers, Indians and Africans. In the early 'twenties Delamere's vision of a white man's country, linking up with the Rhodesias and the Cape, had been accepted by some Conservatives; although, in 1929, a Labour government was at pains to declare that the interests of the Africans must be paramount, a policy first adumbrated by the Duke of Devonshire in 1923.

In 1922, besides the already vast Kenya and Uganda protectorates, the erstwhile 'German East Africa' also came under British control as a mandated territory under the League of Nations. Tanganyika, as it was now known, was ably ruled by Sir Donald Cameron, a Creole from Demerara, who applied the principles of indirect rule he had assimilated in Nigeria.[6] He opposed the creation of a Union of Kenya, Uganda and Tanganyika, envisaged by Delamere as a potential white-run dominion; and with the world economic depression of the 'thirties, the palmiest days of European settlement were over, though most settlers continued to set standards of production and livestock hitherto unknown to Africans.

II

Beyond the Kenya highlands and northern Tanganyika lay Uganda, unknown to Europeans until the arrival of Speke and Grant. Here an originally pastoral people, probably from the Ethiopian highlands, had long ruled a predominantly negro peasantry. Although they were literate, they had not invented the wheel or the plough, and their history is alleged to have been 'a crime to which there had been no eye-witnesses', they were the most elaborately organized society in tropical Africa. The richest area was Buganda on the northern shores of Lake Victoria-Nyanza, and its Baganda inhabitants, who spoke Luganda, were more sophisticated than the Bunyoro on Lake Albert or the Lango beyond Lake Kioga. As the scramble for Africa developed, the strategic importance of Uganda, commanding the headwaters of the White Nile, became inescapable to British governments, though not yet to the public, still chary of expensive commitments in Equatorial Africa. But the Imperial East Africa Company was now becoming insolvent, and following Stanley's incursion in 1875, three years later Catholic and Protestant missionaries had penetrated the country, hitherto pagan, save for a veneer of Muslim conversions at the court. Though both in competition with the Muslims, the two kinds of Christians soon

[6] See his *My Tanganyika Service and some Nigeria*, London, 1939.

denounced each other, and Mutesa, the able but sanguinary Kabaka who had welcomed Speke, was shrewd enough to play the three parties off against each other.

In Buganda, a country of lush vegetation, heavy rainfall, banana groves and red earth, the Kabaka was absolute, as Speke had found when Mutesa had told a page to try out a carbine on one of his subjects, with fatal effect. Now in 1884 a new Kabaka, Mwanga, aged eighteen, was as bewildered as his councillors by the claims of Muslims, Protestants and Catholics. Moreover, he was addicted to *bang*, which produces sudden anger, and also to sodomy.[7] In 1886 he became frantic when thirty of his pages, converts to Christianity, refused to submit to a fate that they now thought literally worse than death. Rather than accept their Kabaka's embraces, they chose to be trussed and roasted in slow fires, reckoning it better, like the English Protestants during the Marian persecutions, to suffer a brief torment than the hell-fire that the missionaries had taught them to expect. And the year before, on the orders of the Kabaka's subordinates, an Anglican bishop, James Hannington, arriving to take over the immense diocese of Eastern Equatorial Africa, had been summarily executed.[8]

By 1888, while the Catholic *Wa-Fransa* were fighting it out with the Protestant *Wa-Inglesa*, the Muslims had set about converting and circumcising the Baganda with new zeal. The Kabaka and his advisers were now even more distracted: 'they eat my land', said Mwanga, not unnaturally—for he was the incarnation of its spirit, or, as Lugard's biographer puts it, their 'Queen Bee'. Nor was he without cunning, though there was 'nothing sensitive at all about Mwanga, his features [were] dark and coarse and there [was] something about him—a certain air of swashbuckling authority and passions—which indeed makes one think of the Roman Emperors at their worst'.[9]

So 'Arabs, Catholics and Protestants then enjoyed a brief span of

[7] Perham, *op. cit.* Vol. I, pp. 215–16, q.v., for an account of him.

[8] This adventurous prelate, the son of a warehouseman at Hurstpierpoint, had started life in the family business and been a major in the Sussex Artillery Volunteers. After study at Oxford, and an initial failure in his examination in the diocese of Exeter, he had been ordained in 1874. Invalided home from his first mission to East Africa, he returned to Mombasa in 1885 and proceeded through the healthier Masai country, walking a hundred and seventy miles in a week. But by choosing this unusual route he roused the suspicions of the Baganda, who had enough Christians on their hands already, and was killed after eight days' confinement and privation in a dark and noisome hut.

[9] Alan Moorehead, *The White Nile*, New York, 1962, pp. 316–17, q.v., for a vivid account.

bloody supremacy', and when in 1891 Lugard arrived in the employment of the Imperial East Africa Company, he described Uganda as a hornet's nest. Undeterred, he entered Mwanga's great thatched hut, with its forest of tree trunks floored with dried grass, to confront a packed and armed assembly. He obtained recognition of the privileges of the Company; then, with a tiny force of Sudanese and Somalis and one elderly maxim gun that was likely to jam[10] but could shoot at long range through the clearings in the banana groves, he defeated the Muslims and pacified the Christians. In 1892 a final settlement was achieved. The Kabaka, who now vacillated between Catholic and Protestant beliefs or reverted to a more congenial paganism, and who annoyed Lugard by 'giggling and caressing' his 'courtiers' in public, recognized the suzerainty of the now near bankrupt Company, admitted a Resident and agreed to put down slavery and the import of firearms. Even the rival Christians were officially reconciled.

This success, which won Lugard the C.B. and the execration of most Liberals, made him the lion of a London season, a publicity he knew how to handle, with access to Hatfield and to Chamberlain's mansion at Highbury in Birmingham. But it had been achieved in the knowledge that the Company would have to evacuate Uganda. The Church Missionary and Anti-Slavery Societies, with plenty of material for propaganda, won a reprieve, and Rosebery, now the Liberal Foreign Secretary, who understood as well as Salisbury the strategic importance of the country, imposed a compromise on Gladstone's last cabinet. Sir Gerald Portal, a skilled diplomat, who had been *Chargé d'Affaires* in Cairo under Baring, was now Consul-General at Zanzibar and who died of fever after making his report, was appointed Commissioner for Uganda, to take over from the Company. In 1893 against a background of a Franco-Russian threat to Egypt and in Asia, he advised the government that it was 'hardly possible that Uganda, the natural key to the whole of the Nile Valley ... should be left unprotected and unnoticed by other powers because an English Company has been unable to hold it and because Her Majesty's Government has been unwilling to interfere'. Though public opinion was moved by the campaign to put down slavery and to spread Anglican Christianity, the 'preoccupations of Portal and his masters were much more those of the strategist than the evangelist'.[11] So in March 1894, when Gladstone had retired and Rosebery became Prime Minister, the Company was bought out

[10] 'He had very little confidence in his veteran Maxim gun.' Perham, *op. cit.* p. 223.

[11] Robinson and Gallagher, *op. cit.* p. 328.

on highly unfavourable terms and a Protectorate was declared over Uganda. Mwanga, who had now turned Muslim, fled to the camp of his former enemy, the redoubtable Kabarega of the Bunyoro of northern Uganda: by 1899 both were apprehended and deported to the Seychelles, where four years later Mwanga died.

By 1903, the long-planned strategic railway from Mombasa to Kisumu on Lake Victoria, which alone could give easy access to Uganda, but of which the cost had hitherto seemed prohibitive, had at last been constructed. Many of those working on it had been devoured by lions, who, presented with an unwonted opportunity, had become man-eaters, for *l'appétit vient en mangeant*.

In 1899–1901 Sir Harry Johnston became special commissioner. An artist, explorer and naturalist—he had discovered the okapi and the five-horned variety of giraffe—and he could illustrate his own books, as in his *The Uganda Protectorate*, still an illuminating work.[12] Within a framework of modern law and administration the Baganda social order remained feudal,[13] but the customary cruelties of the past were put down. A boy Kabaka, Daudi Chwa, who would later attend the coronation of George v, made a more docile monarch than Mwanga. But he retained the picturesque trappings, if not the arbitrary power, of his ancestors—the elaborate court etiquette, the drums and harps and horns, the great vermilion royal canoes like Viking ships that, propelled by twenty-four boatmen, swept past the papyrus and water-lilies of the shores of Lake Victoria-Nyanza.

III

The strategic importance of Uganda, commanding the head-waters of the Nile, was shared by the Sudan. But it was Egypt that was vital: and here the first moves had been made to protect the British communications with India and the Far East. The British occupation of Egypt, more than Leopold's adventures in the Congo,

[12] Of substantial Scots business background, Johnston had early travelled and painted in Tunisia, Angola and the Congo, and ascended Kilimanjaro. In 1885 he had entered the Consular Service in West Africa, when his handling of King Ja-Ja of Opobo in the Niger delta brought him credit. Appointed Cosul at Mozambique he at first collaborated with Cecil Rhodes, but, as commissioner of Nyasaland, resisted his designs. Johnston wrote books on Liberia, on the *Negro in the New World* and an elaborate treatise on *The Comparative Study of the Bantu and semi-Bantu languages*.

[13] They had provided the great anthropologist Frazer with many examples of superstition. They greatly feared the ghosts of buffaloes they had killed, and put the skulls in special huts when they propitiated the ghosts, and would 'make a sick man in clay and bury it, so that any who steps over it would carry off the disease: Sir James Frazer, *The Golden Bough*, abridged edition, 1925, pp. 145 and 523.

had set off the scramble for Africa. Palmerston's and Disraeli's policy in the Levant had been to sustain the ramshackle Turkish Empire: Constantinople, it was thought, not Egypt, was the best barrier to Russian designs. Hence, in 1879, the occupation of Cyprus, and an understanding with the French over Egypt.

For, since Napoleon's incursion in 1798, the French had been culturally and economically the predominant European influence in the country. When Napoleon had arrived, with scholars, experts and a printing press as well as an army, Egypt had been a decayed area of the Ottoman Empire, with, at most, two and a half million inhabitants, untouched by modernity. Then, after the eviction of the French, an illiterate Macedonian officer of the Turkish Army had become the Ataturk of Egypt. Muhammad Ali (1805–48) had imported French officers and engineers, doctors and economists; brought in cotton plants from India and restored the irrigation; and in 1818 he had massacred the Mamlūks who, with their harems, eunuchs and the slave-boys of their *Ghilman*, had misgoverned Egypt for centuries. For he invited them to a coffee party, and as they left, filing out down a narrow passage one by one, they were decapitated as they emerged. He had also conquered the eastern Sudan (Nubia), and when the Turks denied him his reward for his support in the disastrous campaign against the Greeks that ended at Navarino, he had conquered Syria. Egypt was thus dragged by an adventurer of genius into the nineteenth century, and although the Alids soon lapsed from the ability of their founder, this Macedonian dynasty tried to rule Egypt until the mid-twentieth century. Ali's eldest son, Ibrahim, had massacred the Wahabis in Arabia, but he had succumbed in 1848 through drinking two bottles of iced champagne in one glorious draught. Abbas I (1848–54) had tried, in vain, to reverse his grandfather's policies, and Said (1854–63) had allowed de Lesseps to make the Suez Canal, with European capital and Egyptian forced labour, and the monopoly of controlling it for ninety-nine years. Ismail (1836–79), a more sympathetic character, with expanding revenues from the cotton exports which flourished during the American Civil War, was more positively deleterious. Fascinated by French civilization and avid for quick results, he had a fine run for his creditors' and his people's money, culminating in 1869 in the visit of the Empress Eugénie on the Imperial yacht for the opening of the Suez Canal, and in the première of Verdi's *Aïda* in 1871, when the Khedive's 'harem put in an appearance *en bloc* and occupied three boxes in the first tier'.[14] These junketings and vast expenditure on well-intentioned projects in Egypt and the Sudan, were Ismail's

[14] George Martin, *Verdi: His Life and Times*, London, 1965, p. 387.

ruin. By 1876 he owed £68,110,000 of funded debt and £26,000,000 of floating debt to foreign creditors. And the British as well as the French were now involved. In the following year Disraeli, to keep the French out, bought the Khedive's 44 per cent of the shares of the Canal Company: 'a coup worthy of Sidonia. "It is just settled," he wrote to the Queen, "you will have it, Madam ... Four millions sterling and almost immediately. There was only one firm that could do it —Rothschilds. They behaved admirably." '[15] The four million had not gone far towards settling Ismail's debt. In 1877 a *Caisse de la Dette* was set up and Egypt declared bankrupt. And Sir Evelyn Baring, afterwards Earl of Cromer, and from 1877 to 1880 one of the ablest of the British pro-consuls of the late-Victorian and Edwardian Empire, was appointed a Commissioner. After an interval as financial member of the Viceregal Council in India, he would return in 1883 as Consul-General and plenipotentiary in Egypt, and rule it indirectly until 1906.[16] Under his regime the country became solvent and its ruling classes, if not its peasants, prospered. But, by 1880, before this appointment, the Egyptian kettle boiled over. In 1879 Ismail, packed off to an agreeable life in Italy, had been succeeded as Khedive by his son Tewfiq (1879–91) who appeared to the Egyptians as a mere debt-collector for the infidels. Landowners, Muslim conservatives, Westernized intellectuals, *fellaheen* conscripted to forced labour and heavily taxed, and, most decisively, the mainly Circassian officers, all detested the regime. And next year Ahmad Arabi Pasha, the first Egyptian nationalist colonel, made a *coup d'état*. The British and French were confronted with their first Suez crisis.

In 1882 a Franco-British fleet proceeded to Alexandria; but in fear of Germany and engaged in more than usually hectic political strife at home, the French withdrew. What Gladstone thought a trap, in fact, became an opportunity. For Gladstone's hand was now

[15] Robert Blake, *Disraeli*, London, 1966, pp. 585–6. The investment was a good one. The shares cost £4,000,000: by 1898 they were worth £24,000,000 and in 1913 more than £40,000,000.

[16] He was born in 1841, the son of Henry Baring, M.P., and Cecilia, eldest daughter of Vice-Admiral William Lukin Windham of Felbrigg Hall, Norfolk, who, as heir to William Windham, Pitt's Secretary of State at War, had assumed the Windham name. Baring's father came of the great banking family which had emigrated to England from Bremen and begun as cloth manufacturers near Exeter. Sir Francis Baring had become a London financier and died worth £7,000,000 in 1810. Commissioned in the Royal Artillery, Baring had served in the Ionian Isles and in Greece; in Malta and Jamaica. He then became private secretary to Lord Northbrook, Viceroy of India, whence he was seconded to Egypt. In 1892 he was created Baron Cromer, and Earl of Cromer in 1901.

forced. The Egyptians were building forts which could make the anchorage indefensible, and when they refused to dismantle them, the British had either to withdraw or bombard. They bombarded: for ten and a half hours. And since Gladstone characteristically forbade them to land for four days, the Egyptians naturally killed about fifty Europeans and looted foreign property.

Sir Garnet Wolseley then advanced on Cairo, and routed Arabi's army at Tel-el-Kebir. But the brisk intervention and withdrawal envisaged by the cabinet was, of course, impracticable. And there was nothing for it, if control of the canal and the strategically placed country were to be maintained, but a permanent occupation.

Baring, on his return the following year, had no illusions about the new commitment: 'I have never been,' he wrote, 'neither am I now in favour of a British occupation of Egypt, but we must leave a government which should act in conformity with the commonplace requirements of modern civilization.'[17] Level-headed and tenacious, 'a good man', said Lord Rosebery, 'to go tiger shooting with', Baring was coldly determined to rehabilitate Egypt on Western lines. In Ismail's flamboyant regime he could see nothing but 'the ignorance, dishonesty, waste and extravagance of the East', along with a 'hasty and inconsiderate endeavour to Westernize'. And the British, he wrote, an alien people, had had to 'control and guide a second alien race, the Turks, by whom they are disliked, in the government of a third race, the Egyptians'.[18] Ismail had employed disreputable adventurers and suffered from *hubris*; his government had dispensed venal justice and was indifferent to sanitation; the Egyptians wrote the wrong way round, omitting the short vowels; their books on love made the *Decameron* a model of refinement, and polygamy degraded the women and enervated the men. Business was in the hands of 'Levantine nondescripts whose ethnological status defied definition', and accuracy and common sense were abhorrent to the oriental mind. 'A European,' Baring wrote, 'would think that, where a road and a paved walk existed, it required no great effort of the reasoning faculty to keep the human beings on the sidewalk and the animals on the road. Not so the Egyptians.'[19] And although the exploited *fellaheen*, on whom the whole society was based, were 'kindly and jovial', they were unstable and ungrateful. No wonder that *al Lord* or 'Overbearing' was feared but not loved.

The first way to rehabilitate Egypt was by perennial irrigation: Baring brought in engineers from India, the scene of the greatest

[17] *Modern Egypt,* Vol. II, pp. 564–5.
[18] *op. cit.* Vol. I, p. 5.
[19] *op. cit.* Vol. II, p. 152.

British achievements in this field, and they set about a restoration which included the Aswan Dam, then one of the biggest in the world, and, incidentally, the restoration of Karnak. The raising of cotton —already the main export—sugar cane, tobacco and cereals all increased, even if the profits still went to the Khedives, the great landowners and the foreign investors. Bilharzia, conveyed by water-snails in the extended irrigation, infected the peasantry, but, with the control of cholera and plague, the population vastly increased, so that by the mid-twentieth century it would be about twenty-five million.

By 1885 the great European powers had lent £9,000,000 to pay off foreign creditors, and £1,000,000 remained to rehabilitate the country. Railways were built, Port Said and Ismailia developed to serve the Canal. But there were few factories: the country produced raw materials for a world market, and all but 10 per cent of the companies were financed by foreigners. The investors, the Pashas and the infidel high administrators prospered, and by 1904 British predominance was officially recognized by the French. But there was growing resentment at British control. The poet Cavafy, a clerk in the Irrigation office in Alexandria from 1892 to 1922, 'a Greek gentleman', as E. M. Forster described him, 'in a straw hat standing ... at a slight angle to the universe ...' had other things to think of; but the Egyptian intellectuals felt a European-style nationalism. Pan-Islamic ideas were getting about. The officers, the main source of educated leadership in the mainly peasant country, resented British control. The young Abbas Hilmi himself insulted Kitchener, Sirdar of the Army, on parade.

Then, in 1914, when the Turks joined the central powers, the British declared a Protectorate and sent Abbas Hilmi packing, to be succeeded by his uncles Husayn and Fuad, the latter Khedive in 1917 and King in 1922. Egypt now swarmed with troops as it became the headquarters of Middle Eastern Command, the base of Allenby's campaigns and Lawrence's guerrilla warfare; Egyptian troops were raised, labour requisitioned. There were more industries; there was more prosperity; but inflation in the cities and the villages caused wider discontent. Then in 1922, following the trend of the times, Egypt was proclaimed independent. A constitution was devised, with Islam as the established religion, the language Arabic. But the nationalists still campaigned against the powers the British had reserved—defence, foreign policy, the protection of foreigners and foreign interests and the control of the Sudan. Zaghlul Pasha, the leader of the nationalist *Wafd* (delegation), attempting to go to Paris to put his case at the Peace Conference had been deported to

Malta, thus becoming a popular hero. A militant Muslim brother-
hood arose, hostile to the West. In 1924 Sir Lee Stack, Governor-
General of the Sudan, was assassinated in Cairo. But with their
commitment in Palestine, Trans-Jordan and Iraq, Egypt became
all the more vital to the British. By the Anglo-Egyptian treaty of
1936 a compromise would be reached: their troops withdrawn to the
Canal zone, the British would retain the use of ports, aerodromes
and railroads, but the right to protect foreigners and their interests
was abandoned.

The British thus held to their original purpose, the control of the
Canal, the strategic base. It was for that, not for the interests of
cosmopolitan bond-holders, that they had occupied Egypt. In the
second German war that policy was vindicated, to the benefit of most
Egyptians and of the world.

IV

Since they had occupied Egypt, the British had inevitably been
involved in the *Bilad-al-Sudan*—'the country of the blacks'. Here
from 1899 to 1953 they would establish an Anglo-Egyptian Condominium. The huge area contains very different environments and
peoples: the Danakil camel nomads range over the torrid deserts of
the north: south of Khartoum in the grasslands of Kordofan and
Darfur live the pastoral Baqqara, among whom the Mahdi found his
most formidable followers. Both are Muslims. To the southwest, in
the Bar-al-Ghazel and in Equatoria the people are pagan, an extrapolation of the forest cultures of tropical Africa. And in the southeast the cattle-obsessed Nuer and Dinka who inhabit the country
east and south of the Sudd, where the White Nile works its way
through fever-stricken papyrus swamps, matted vegetation and proliferating water hyacinth, contrast with the Shilluk agriculturalists
around Malakal. The change was total between the blazing deserts of
the north and the lush savannah and tropical swamps of the Ugan-
dan borders; and the people of north and south detested each other
only less than they hated the Turks and Egyptians.

This vast and often forbidding area had been subdued by order
of Muhammad Ali, whose Macedonians, Albanians, Circassians and
Turks had crushed an uncoordinated resistance. Khartoum had been
founded and an administration set up, relatively so efficient that
Muhammad Ali had its organizer poisoned as a rival. But under
Abbas and Said this detested *Turkiya* fell into lethargy and corruption: elephant hunters poached on the government's monopoly of
ivory; slavers rounded up their victims, even from Uganda. Ismail,
full of grandiose and often humanitarian ambitions and determined

on reform, appointed the explorer, Sir Samuel Baker, Governor of Equatoria; then, in 1874, the already famous 'Chinese' Gordon was appointed. Three years later, Gordon was made Governor-General of the entire Sudan, replacing the Turkish one from whose hospitable orgy—'a mixed ballet of soldiers and completely naked young women who danced in a circle, beat time with their feet and accompanied their gestures with a curious sound of clacking in which the guests were expected to participate'[20]—Gordon walked out.

Fanaticism, for once, was on the Christian side. Gordon's first government in the Sudan is no part of the history of the Empire: suffice it that when, following Ismail's fall in 1879, the infidel Gordon resigned, he left the *Turkiya* even more detested than before; and two years later Muhammad Ahmed, the Mahdi (the Guide), the son of a boatman of Dongola in the north, launched an unlimited *Jihad*. His Baqqara horsemen captured El Obeid, the capital of Kordofan, and in 1883 massacred an ill-found Turko-Egyptian army under the English Colonel Hicks Pasha at Shaykun south of it. The British, now in control of Egypt, refused to sanction further expensive and doubtless disastrous expeditions: but they had to protect the withdrawal of the Egyptians from the Sudan. Gladstone's cabinet, in face of popular clamour, now turned again to Gordon, of all people, to 'report' on this difficult task. They can hardly all have been so inept as to think him the best man to evacuate a country he had once ruled; probably some influential people hoped that, once on the spot, Gordon would force the Prime Minister's hand.

The rest of the tragedy is familiar; one of the set pieces of late-Victorian history. The blue-eyed Christian hero, betrayed by devious politicians (Gladstone thought the Mahdi's followers 'a people rightly struggling to be free') was cut down on the steps of the palace of Khartoum, 'by dervishes, yelling *Malaoun el yom yomek* —"accursed one, your time has come!"'. As even Baring testified, 'The Nile expedition was sanctioned too late, and the reason why it was sanctioned too late was that Mr Gladstone would not accept simple evidence of a plain fact.'[21] When, at the 'frightful' news, the Queen telegraphed *en clair* that 'all this might have been prevented and many precious lives saved by earlier action', she expressed, as usual, the prevalent feelings of the country. The Grand Old Man

[20] Lytton Strachey, *Eminent Victorians*, London, 1922 edition, p. 224. This evocation, though falsely alleging that Gordon drank, remains highly readable.

[21] Quoted in Sir Philip Magnus' *Gladstone: A Biography*, London, 1954, p. 321, q.v., for a masterly account of Gladstone's part in the affair, a classic example of an eloquent and tortuous politician's self-deception.

became the Murderer of Gordon and his reputation never recovered from the reproach.[22]

As Gladstone remarked, Gordon—the Lawrence of Arabia of the day and more, and almost as neurotic—had, of course, 'turned upside down every idea and intention with which he had left England'. Perhaps he had tried to put a fast one over Mr Gladstone; if so, he paid with his life. For Baring, concerned only with making Egypt solvent, Gordon had become simply a nuisance—a 'flighty eccentric—unfit for work requiring a steady head, who had thought more of his personal opinion than of the interest of the state'.

The Mahdi, like many of his magnetic kind—and his charm was hypnotic—had soon lapsed from his original asceticism, and he died soon after his triumph; but by 1892 his Khalifa, Abd Allahu Ibn Muhammad, out of a nightmare of famine, internal strife and frantic expansion, had created a tolerable order. Based on Omdurman, and still employing literate bureaucrats of the Turkish regime, it gave the central Sudan what it wanted—a firm authority. And in the outer territories it managed to delegate power without breaking up. 'For many years the commonly held conception of the Khalifa's rule had been one of unbridled and savage barbarism. Recent scholarship has demonstrated that this clearly was not the case, as a most cursory examination of the Khalifa's administration will make apparent.'[23] The Sudanese had struggled to be free only of foreigners; internally they needed and desired an autocratic rule. It was not, then, simply to avenge Gordon or in reaction to Sudanese attacks, which had been scotched in the relatively brief phase of aggression, that the British decided to conquer the Sudan; it was because of the European scramble for Africa.

When, in 1896, the Khalifa's armies defeated and slew the Abyssinian Negus John, the Italians had taken a hand and mounted the expedition so cut up at Adowa. Now the British launched a supposed diversion in the northern Sudan; not to pull Italian chestnuts out of the fire, but to forestall the French, then advancing from the western Sudan towards the Upper Nile. As Kitchener, Sirdar of an Anglo-Egyptian army, began his inexorable advance with a railway, supply depots and gunboats that would conquer the entire Sudan, a Captain Marchand, with a token force, was marching across the breadth of central Africa to Fashoda. For the British there now appeared no choice: an imperial strategy had dictated the occupation of Egypt. It now dictated the occupation of the Sudan. The

[22] Magnus, *op. cit.* p. 326.
[23] R. O. Collins and R. L. Tignor, *Egypt and the Sudan*, London 1967, p. 111.

Khalifa's regime must be ironed out, and, incidentally, Gordon avenged. For the war was 'deliberately started by England, after careful planning and preparation, as a calculated act of policy. It did not, like most of English wars, break out of its own accord.'[24]

By June 1896 Kitchener's army had routed the Sudanese at Firket, proving that the British-trained Egyptians 'could fight'; by September they were at Meroe; a railroad by-passed the loop of the Nile across the Nubian desert, constructed to take locomotives loaned by Cecil Rhodes. That August, the British had concentrated their force at Atbara, at the confluence of that river and the Nile. As he was meant to do, and fortunately for Kitchener whose plans were being sabotaged by political and military enemies, the Khalifa responded to the challenge. Kitchener's army stormed the Sudanese *Zariba* and, after a grim interview with the Sirdar, the Emir was paraded in chains. The campaign culminated in the battle of Omdurman, when 8,200 British and 17,600 Egyptian and Sudanese routed some 60,000 of the Khalifa's horde who flung themselves with superb courage against Kitchener's line, to be mown down by machine-guns, rifles and artillery. The young Winston Churchill, who wrote a vivid account, here charged with the 1st Lancers. By 11.30 a.m. Kitchener handed his binoculars to an A.D.C., remarked that the enemy had had a 'thorough dusting' and ordered the advance on Omdurman and Khartoum. The victory had cost the invaders 48 killed, including three British officers and 25 other ranks, and 434 wounded, as against over 11,000 'dervish' dead and about 16,000 wounded and prisoners. Gordon had been more than avenged: the British and Egyptian flags again floated over Khartoum, and when, at the service of thanksgiving the troops sang 'Abide with me', Gordon's favourite hymn, even Kitchener was seen to weep. Next year the Khalifa was hunted down and shot: Kitchener was raised to the peerage as Baron Kitchener of Khartoum and given a grant of money and the thanks of Parliament.

He had lost no time in dealing with Captain Marchand, who had now arrived at Fashoda. Proceeding upriver with a substantial force, Kitchener, fluent in French, and acting with an unwonted diplomatic skill, persuaded the Captain of the impropriety of flying the French flag in the dominion of the Khedive. The Fashoda crisis, never as bad as it looked, for the French had neither the naval power nor the political solidarity to withstand a major war, subsided. Next year, the Anglo-Egyptian Condominium was arranged —a characteristically subtle device of Baring's—and Kitchener became briefly the first Governor-General of the Sudan.

[24] Magnus, *Kitchener,* p. 98.

The British had taken over a daunting task. The country was an economic liability and at first needed military government. Under Sir Reginald Wingate, who had accounted for the Khalifa, a small administration was built up on the lines of the Indian Civil Service; and following the assassination of Sir Lee Stack, manned entirely by the British. This Sudan Political Service, recruited by methods less exacting than the I.C.S. and manned by the more athletic and forceful products of the public schools, brought the huge country into order and relative prosperity.[25] Cotton and cereal crops were developed in Gezira between the Blue and White Niles, and the Gordon Memorial College, founded in 1902 at Khartoum, gave a mainly technical education to a few Sudanese.

When Sudanese nationalism revived, the inspiration came from Egypt. Hence, in 1924, Allenby's brisk removal of all Egyptian troops and most Egyptian officials, to be replaced by Sudanese. Political interests at Gordon College had never been encouraged and indirect rule was developed to oust the few Westernized 'intellectuals'. Since most Sudanese detested the Egyptians and respected authority if sufficiently strong, there were no further significant upheavals.

Meanwhile, on the southeastern maritime flank of Abyssinia, the British, who had taken over Aden in 1839, extended their sphere of influence inland into what in 1934 would become the Aden Protectorate. By the 'eighties they had also brought the Sultanate of Socotra under 'protection', and they took over a slice of northern Somaliland as well, a barren enough territory, to keep the French and Italians out of it. Here, until 1920, they encountered a brisk and prolonged resistance from Sheikh Muhammad Hassan, whom they termed the 'Mad Mullah' but whose tactical dispositions in difficult country showed formidable method, defeated Richard Corfield's camelry in 1913, and exacted a rueful respect from his opponents.

V

During the scramble for Africa, north of the Ruvuma, Nyasaland and the Rhodesias, the British had thus reluctantly created a vast new colonial empire, extending by 1922 into the mandated territory of Tanganyika as well as over Kenya and Uganda, then over occupied Egypt and the Anglo-Egyptian Sudan. It now extended from the Cape to the Mediterranean, and was rounded off by British Somaliland commanding the southern exit from the Red Sea. But

[25] Under the rule, it was said, of Blacks by Blues.

the aim of this 'colonialism', as has been stressed, was strategic, not economic, since few of the territories were then valuable. For British imperial strategy was now global and defensive; indeed the aims of all the powers in the scramble for Africa must be seen as such. But as their manoeuvres did not avert two World Wars, Africa would soon be unscrambled again.

CHAPTER 24

The Commonwealth of Australia; New Zealand Democracy

The intractable problems of South Africa, shelved but not solved, were not paralleled in Australasia. In Australia the palaeolithic aborigines had been few and ineffective; in New Zealand the well-established Maori had proved numerous and formidable: but finally outclassed by European weapons, diminished by European disease and then gradually reconciled—for here there was no racial discrimination—the survivors would adapt themselves to Western civilization and even, in time, increase.

Neither of these colonies of settlement contained the equivalents of *Afrikaaners* or French-Canadians; and racial and cultural origins, geographical isolation, economic interest and the needs of defence still made them look to the home country. In spite of social prejudice against the 'languid captain Vernon de Vere', or the 'rosy-cheeked darling of the English rectory',[1] both unfavourably compared with the leather-cheeked and muscular Australians of the outback; and in spite of resentment against some aristocratic or quasi-aristocratic governors, good apparently for little else but to smile approval at the races, the vast majority of Australians took the ties with the Empire for granted, and were united in demanding a white Australia, free of 'niggers', Chinese, Lascars or *Kanakas*. If radicals resented the arrogance of 'rum- or wool-begotten' wealth, and intellectuals deplored what they considered an egalitarian mediocrity, there was little of the sheer class warfare endemic in Europe; the country was united in a cult of cricket, race-meetings and open-air life, in an environment of vast prospects and brilliant light. Hence a consensus of political opinion and a state '*socialisme sans doctrines* in an English society ... in the antipodes but with two important innovations—labour legislation and full democracy'.

[1] Bell and Morrell, *Select Documents, op. cit.* p. 198.

By the early twentieth century, moreover, with the rise of Japan as a first-class power following the defeat of Russia in the Far East, and with European and American power politics invading the Pacific, the Australian States, in spite of a natural disunity of temperament, of short-term economic interests and geography—since the easiest communication was still by sea, railways were tardily developed—brought themselves, after negotiations lasting a decade, to a loose federation, mainly for foreign and fiscal policy and defence, when, in 1901, the Commonwealth of Australia came into being. The New Zealanders, meanwhile, who would reject union with Australia, had already by 1876 made their own provinces into a Union.

The population of Australia remained very small for the enormous area: only about four million at the turn of the century, and in spite of prosperity and expansion in the decade before the Great War, only five million by the end of it. The current and dramatic expansion of the economy into an 'Australia Unlimited', with American affinities, did not fully set in until the mid-twentieth century, when a population of seven million in 1945 would become twelve by the end of the 'sixties. In New Zealand the population in 1914 was still only about a million, though doubled by 1956. Yet both countries made a disproportionate contribution to the war of 1914–18, when the Australians lost 60,000 dead out of an army of 329,000; and the New Zealanders' casualties amounted to one in seven of their population. Like the response of Canada, this reaction shows up the extraordinary miscalculation of the rulers of Germany, deceived by the situation in Ireland and convinced that before their onslaught the British Empire would disintegrate.

II

The political domination of the great sheep-masters, which had transformed the Australian economy from the original fringe settlement and created the 'pastoral ascendancy', had been challenged by the radical democracy of the Diggers and the failed Diggers after the 'fifties; but the demand to 'unlock the pasture lands' only made sense in the areas suited for large-scale mechanized farming. In Australia, as in South Africa, a democracy of smallholding farmers was economically impracticable; and here already the main centres of population were the big cities. By 1900 two-thirds of the population were urban. The belated and massive construction of railways, which brought the mileage of 1,000 miles in 1870 to 10,800 twenty years later, would now promote exports. The recession of the 'seventies had hit most of these, including wool, increasing political conflict. The radicals had long demanded protection for nascent industries, which the free-trading sheep-masters and merchants would not adopt; and during the 'nineties major strikes made colonial politics more than usually acrimonious. Moreover, though in 1861 in New South Wales a 'Selection' Act had limited the great pastoral leases, and allowed 'selectors' who could pay 5s. an acre to purchase up to 320, the ranch-owners themselves bought up the land through nominees, and in 1882 less than a hundred big sheep-masters still controlled eight million acres.

Some Australians now took to 'bush-ranging', like the original escaped convicts; and as late as 1880 the notorious Ned Kelly, endowed, because he wore home-made iron armour, with a spurious glamour, had a brief if exciting career. The sons of an Ulster convict, Kelly and two brothers had taken to stealing horses; and when in 1878 the police came after her sons, their redoubtable mother felled one policeman with a shovel; Kelly wounded another, and vanished into the bush. With other desperadoes, the 'Kelly Gang' then terrorized the borders of Victoria and New South Wales. They were particularly clever and enterprising at raiding banks. Run to earth in a wooden hut, they were all shot up, save Kelly, who was wounded, taken and hanged; to the grief of many admirers who were always against police authority as such. Australian folk-lore was thus enriched with a more ruffianly equivalent of Buffalo Bill.

In spite of the conflict between pastoral and manufacturing interests, Australia stood up better than many countries to the depression, and during the 'eighties considerable British capital was invested in the country. Gold was discovered in Queensland and silver at Broken Hill, South Australia; and in the 'nineties gold-fields at Coolgardie opened up better prospects in Western Australia. In Queensland big cotton and sugar plantations were worked, mainly by *Kanakas* from the south-western Pacific. And when, following the agitation for a 'white Australia', the Polynesians were removed, the white labourers combined with the dockers of Brisbane in a powerful Queensland labour movement, which in 1899 had briefly brought about the first Labour state government in Australia, or, indeed, anywhere.

But it took a Federal Government to create the basis of Australian social democracy. Since 1890 determined reformers had been at work, and by July 1900—though only 59·37 per cent of an electorate of 983,486 bothered to vote—a Commonwealth Bill was sanc-

tioned by plebiscite.[2] The Constitution was more like that of the
United States than that of Canada. The Americans had invoked the
Creator, and the Australians also invoked the Almighty. 'Whereas,'
runs the preamble of 1899, 'the people of New South Wales, Victoria,
South Australia, Queensland and Tasmania [Western Australia ad-
hered the year after], relying on the blessing of Almighty God,
have agreed to unite in one indissoluble Federal Commonwealth
under the Crown ... be it enacted, etc.' And so it was. Chamberlain,
still involved in the Boer War, welcomed 'the great work of Australian Federation ... prepared with so much ability in the Australian
colonies', and contributing, as many imperialists hoped, to a federation of the Empire.

The powers of the Federal government were strictly limited. There
were two houses, a Senate and a House of Representatives: the former composed of six senators from each state, voting as one electorate; the latter elected by adult suffrage. Votes for women, already
established in South Australia, had been adopted in all the States by
1909. Both Houses were thus democratically elected; and since most
Australians had, or expected to get, a stake in the country, there
was less real conflict between oligarchs and radicals than the idiom
of colonial politics suggests. The division came rather over protection or free-trade, and the protectionists won.

The first Federal Government was sited at Melbourne; but by
1909, after much controversy, a Federal capital was laid out in a
spacious setting at Canberra in its own territory, made available by
New South Wales. As usual among the British, no general principles
had been proclaimed: here was a pragmatic settlement and it succeeded.

There had been much state rivalry to be overcome: New South
Wales, the senior colony, looked down on Victoria as 'a cabbage
garden', and feared the economic predominance of South Australia.
Sydney clung to free-trade: they would be 'voluntarily placing a bar
across Sydney harbour' by accepting the same restrictions as Melbourne. And what, it was demanded, would happen when new territories were opened up? But the overwhelming argument to Federation was strategic. At present, it was pointed out, if an enemy
landed in Western Australia or at Port Darwin, no one could get
at them—for the 'break in railway gauge would be fatal to celerity
of movement'. It was essential to have common communications

[2] In New South Wales with its free-trading interests, the majority was fairly
narrow: 100,742 to 82,741, and in Queensland 44,800 to 19,691. But in Victoria
it was overwhelming: 152,653 to 9,805; in South Australia and the Northern
Territories 66,990 to 17,053, and in Tasmania 13,437 to 7,910.

over the vast area. There had to be a Federal Military College.
Strategic and economic facts combined to create an Australian
Commonwealth.

Within this framework, the class conflicts then mounting in Europe
were less severe. Since 1824–5 Trade Unions had been legal; and
during the 'seventies and 'eighties they had strengthened their position. But the demands were constitutional. The powerful Australian
Labour Federation formed in 1890, had demanded an eight-hour
day and a statutory minimum wage 'to prevent Australians to be
degraded by competition to the level of Chinese and *Europeans*'.[3]
The Australian Workers Union also demanded social justice, education, equal opportunities. In 1894 they had prefaced their constitution by declaring that men should be 'co-operators—mates—
instead of antagonists'[4]—a 'mateship' in the tradition of Robert
Owen, not of Karl Marx. Organized labour looked to constitutional
reform, not revolution, to 'secure and maintain a fair rate of re-
muneration for shearing and other classes of labour', and to obtain
equitable agreements between employer and employees. Far from
wanting to overthrow capitalism, they wanted to 'improve the relations between capital and labour' and 'settle disputes by means of
conciliation and arbitration'. Save in extreme crises, they were not
to strike without a majority by plebiscite. They were militant, but
militant social-democrats. In this hopeful atmosphere, which would
worsen during and after the Great War, Federal measures of reform
had much scope; and 'the vigorous quality of colonial democracy
was never more confidently in control than in the years that followed
the formation of the Commonwealth'.[5] Under the Liberal leader,
Alfred Deakin,[6] the most ardent advocate of Federation, and

---

[3] Bell and Morrell, *Select Documents, op. cit.* p. 752 (my italics).

[4] Bell and Morrell, *op. cit.* p. 743.

[5] R. M. Crawford, *Australia*, revised edition, London, 1970, p. 143.

[6] Alfred Deakin (1856–1919) was the son of a Melbourne accountant, and
through his mother of Shropshire descent. He made his way as a lawyer and
journalist, and in 1886, as Minister of Water Supply and Public Works in the
state government, put through an Irrigation Act for Victoria. He visited the
United States, India and Egypt and wrote books on irrigation; but his overriding interest was in Federation, and in 1900 he visited London to promote the passage of the Bill to secure it. He became Attorney-General in
the first Federal administration, then, as Prime Minister, again visited
London to advocate the independent Australian Navy, agreed in principle in
1910. Deakin was not long in office; but his brisk flair for political manoeuvres
and compromise was decisive for Federation and for playing in the new
Commonwealth government. He was a versatile and talented writer. His book
on India, *Temple and Tomb,* is still worth reading. See W. Murdoch, *Alfred
Deakin*, London, 1923.

Prime Minister of Australia briefly in 1903–4, then in collaboration with Labour in 1905–8, again in 1910 and also under the Labour Prime Minister, Andrew Fisher[7] (1908–9 and 1910–15), the foundation of social welfare was secured. In 1904 a Commonwealth Court of Conciliation was set up with compulsory powers in disputes which cut across state boundaries, within which arbitration had already been accepted. And in 1907 its President, Justice H. B. Higgins, made his memorable 'harvester' judgment, so-called because the subject had been the wages paid by the protected manufacturers of agricultural machinery. Assuming, as he later put it in a wry phrase, that 'marriage was the usual fate of adult men', he laid down a basic living wage calculated on the 'normal needs of the average employee ... in a civilized community, with a family to support'. By 1908 comprehensive protection, with a preference for British goods, was also imposed; and the Labour government brought in old age and disability pensions and maternity benefits. It was Fisher who, in 1914, at once declared that Australia was at war 'to the last man and the last shilling', and who, following Deakin's policy, had already organized military training for a citizen army within Australia.

The war brought inflation and social conflict, but it also brought prosperity; and more power to the Federal government. The British bought up the entire wool clip and vast amounts of wheat were paid for, if not, for lack of shipping, always transported. Meat and butter were in insatiable demand, and financial and administrative arrangements gave new experience to Australians. Heavy industry developed: production of pig-iron rose from 47,000 tons in 1913 to 332,000 in 1919. German concerns exploiting zinc and copper were taken over, and the steel industry would hold its own after the war. Textiles also further developed, and the country emerged with its economy on a new scale.

In the Labour leader William Morris Hughes, who succeeded Fisher in 1915, Australia found a dynamic Prime Minister, her first to have world influence. Born in 1862, this son of a North Welsh carpenter had emigrated to Queensland in 1884, then settled in

[7] Andrew Fisher (1862–1928) was the son of an Ayrshire coal miner, and his maternal grandfather had been a blacksmith. He went down the mine, but read Emerson and Carlyle and made his mark as a radical. In 1885 he emigrated to Queensland when he worked as a miner and engine driver. He soon became a member of the State parliament, and founded a radical newspaper. Elected to the Federal parliament, Fisher became Leader of the Labour party in 1907, and after 1908 alternated with Deakin as Prime Minister. Fisher was a steady dependable Scot who launched the Federal Labour Party into power and put through much welfare and semi-socialist legislation.

poverty in the dockside area of Sydney. He soon made his way as a Trade Unionist, entered the New South Wales Parliament and in 1901 the Federal House of Representatives. Like his compatriot, Lloyd George, he was a brilliant demagogue: a small man with an 'engagingly ugly face' and 'big ears' who, though slightly deaf, soon learned to 'use his deaf aid as a weapon'.[8] In 1910 he became Attorney-General in Fisher's government, and as Prime Minister he came to England in 1916 to deal ably with problems of finance and shipping. But, again like Lloyd George, he split his party: for in 1916 he failed to carry conscription for service overseas and roused the hatred of many Australian-born Irish, infuriated by the incidents of the Dublin Rebellion. So Hughes and twenty-four followers merged with a relatively conservative Country party to make a Nationalist coalition which held office until 1923. At the Peace Conference, Hughes, who preferred Clemenceau to President Wilson, played a realistic hand, obtained a mandate under the League of Nations for part of New Guinea and enhanced Australian standing and power in the southwest Pacific.

But in 1916 the Labour Party, as after MacDonald's defection in 1931 in Great Britain, had been thrown into confusion. When, in 1923, Hughes' coalition broke up, the phase of Scots and Welsh leadership ended;[9] a Nationalist–Country party government came in until 1929, under Stanley Melbourne Bruce, afterwards Viscount Bruce of Melbourne. Pledged to an expansive policy of 'men, money and markets' and to a 'white Australia', Bruce came to power on the post-war boom; but by 1926 recession was setting in, and after a phase of apparent prosperity Australia was hard hit by the world depression of 1929–31.

The country was now in debt, the trade balance adverse, unemployment rife. In 1929 a Labour government under J. A. Scullin did its best; but the deflationary measures it had to take and the increased taxation it had to impose alienated its own supporters. The currency was heavily devalued, and following an attempt to take control of the Commonwealth Bank, Scullin's administration was swept aside by a more conservative United Australia Party led by J. A. Lyons, a Tasmanian of Catholic Irish origins who had broken with the Labour Party over its economic policies. This financially orthodox government would last until 1937 and coincide with better times.

[8] *D.N.B.*

[9] After the break up of his Coalition, Hughes retained his political following; was in and out of important office until 1944, and kept his parliamentary seat until his death in 1952. He was a fluent writer and a forceful and adaptable politician.

For in spite of the current economic crisis when, in 1931, the Statute of Westminster had recognized the sovereignty of the Australian Commonwealth, the Continent was basically in good shape to seize the chances of economic revival, which in fact came sooner to Australia than to most countries. The natural economic and psychological resilience of the country and people again became taken for granted, and the promise of 'Australia Unlimited' which would open after the Second World War was already on the horizon. In a century and a half the tiny penal settlement on the fringe of a vast unexplored continent had become a nation to be reckoned with.

III

The relatively small population of New Zealand was far from conceding Australia's superiority. Often of Scots descent, the settlers went their own way and created their own version of British civilization and welfare in the Antipodes. The loose federation of provinces inaugurated in 1865 was adaptable to autonomous change, and in 1876, after much controversy, it became a Union. Towards the end of the second bout of Maori wars in the North Island, a government led by William Fox[10] (1869–73), the most effective advocate of full responsible government, set about rehabilitating the country. The colony was £7,000,000 in debt; but Fox appointed a brilliant Jewish financier, Julius Vogel,[11] as colonial treasurer, and this proto-Keynesian economist decided to spend New Zealand out of its depression. Determined to develop both islands, he raised big public loans, encouraged immigration, founded a shipping line to San Francisco and initiated government-sponsored life insurance. He succeeded Fox as Prime Minister and, abandoning his previous defence of the provinces, put through the Union, in spite of the passionate opposition of the veteran Governor Sir George Grey. After

[10] Born in 1812 at Westoe, County Durham, and educated at Wadham College, Oxford, Fox became a barrister and in 1842 emigrated to New Zealand, where he became agent for the New Zealand Company and a prominent politician. He had already been Prime Minister in 1856, 1861 and 1863–4. He was particularly able in negotiating with the Maori, but as an ardent tee-totaller, he advocated restrictive laws, so that it is still hard to get a drink in New Zealand after six o'clock. He wrote *The War in New Zealand, 1860*, a vivid account, which reflects upon the conventional tactics of the imperial troops. He was knighted in 1879 and died at Auckland in 1893.

[11] Vogel (1835–99), a Londoner educated at University College School and the School of Mines, had joined the Gold Rush in Victoria, whence he removed to Otago when gold was struck there. At Dunedin he founded the *Otago Daily Times* and by 1866 he was head of the provincial administration, and had already entered the Federal Parliament in 1863.

this achievement in the interest of the richer provinces of the South Island, he left the country, to become its agent-general in London.

Like many enterprising financiers, Vogel had been over sanguine: the world recession and fall in wool prices now hit New Zealand as it did Australia; and when in 1884 Vogel returned to New Zealand and again took office in coalition with the Radicals, the ministry failed to make ends meet and was ousted in 1887. And, the year before, Vogel's attempt to take over Samoa had been prevented by the imperial government which wanted no more responsibility in the Pacific. So the financier now quitted New Zealand for good.[12] But the work of this promoter had been decisive for the infrastructure of the economy and for settlement; and with the economic revival during the early twentieth century it brought in its returns. Even during the depression in the 'eighties refrigerated ships had begun to take New Zealand lamb and butter to British markets.

But the depression had promoted a much more radical Liberal party led by Richard J. Seddon, Prime Minister by 1893. He came of Lancashire and Scots origin, began life as an engineer, then became a storekeeper and political boss. With revived prosperity, a measure of social democracy was put through: known as 'King Dick', this astute demagogue and party manager presided over the foundation of a pioneer welfare state. For by 1879 manhood suffrage had been adopted; now Seddon introduced votes for women, non-contributory old-age pensions and the beginning of a national health service. In 1894 compulsory arbitration was accepted on industrial disputes, and hours and conditions of work in factories better regulated. Seddon was a zealous imperialist, who at once sent a contingent of volunteers to the South African war, and who wanted Imperial Federation; a bluff and genial figure at the Diamond Jubilee and at the coronation of Edward VII, though Beatrice Webb found him 'incurably rough in manner ... a gross, illiterate but forceful man'; able and courageous, but 'incurably vulgar'.[13]

This statesman's long regime marked the political decline of the 'early colonial gentry, with their public school or university background, their Latin tags and cultivated English speech, their sheep-runs and their clubs ... Rarely since that time has any member of

[12] See Vogel's *Great Britain and Her Colonies*, 1865, and *New Zealand in the South Seas* for his optimistic imperialism. In 1875 he was knighted, but after his second return to England fell into illness and poverty, though he retained his resilience enough to write a novel, *Anno Domini 2000 or Women's Destiny*. One of his sons, by the daughter of a New Zealand architect, perished in the massacre of Wilson's Commando, cut off in pursuit of Lobengula.

[13] Quoted by Keith Sinclair, *A History of New Zealand*, Harmondsworth, 1959, pp. 186–7.

the former oligarchy held high political office'.[14] This decline encouraged the settlement of small leasehold farmers on Crown lands; they were here better placed than in Australia, and they would prosper as refrigeration led to an export of cheese and butter, by the 'twenties far surpassing that of wool or meat. This agricultural interest was social-democratic and the votes of these 'Cow Cockies' (cockatoos since some had arrived from Australia), along with those of the majority of Trade Unionists, outweighed those of the extremist urban Federation of Labour or 'Red Feds' created in 1912, for there was relatively little large-scale industry. Hence a consensus of social-democratic opinion which sanctioned experiments in state control, but was not Marxist. Hence, too, the legislation which, rare at the time, made New Zealand, by 1907 a Dominion, a pioneer Welfare State.

This trend continued when, in 1912, William Massey[15]—known as 'Farmer Bill'—became Prime Minister as leader of the more conservative Reform Party, and after making a coalition with the Liberals in 1915, held office until his death in 1925. His predominance coincided with that of the North Island, with its expanding agriculture and dairy farming, and his political support came from the lesser farmers for whom he secured freeholds instead of leases. With their backing, he was able to break a violent miners' strike in 1911 and halt a dockers' strike and an attempted general one in 1913. Like his contemporary Hughes in Australia, he was a strong imperialist, and just as sceptical of Wilson's aspirations to found an effective League of Nations, preferring the protection of the British Navy in the southwestern Pacific. Massey disliked Dominion Status as a sham; even in 1931 New Zealanders did not welcome the Statute of Westminster. They knew on which side their bread was buttered and preferred the reality of strategic protection to a nominal independence. But Massey did accept a League mandate for western Samoa, though the New Zealanders proved unsuccessful in handling the inhabitants, whom they provoked to resistance.

New Zealand thus came through the war and its aftermath under firm leadership; but the slump of 1929–31 underlined its dependence

[14] Sinclair, *op. cit.* p. 168.

[15] Born in Ulster of strict Presbyterian stock, Massey had come out to New Zealand in 1870 and farmed near Canterbury and at Mangere near Auckland. He received his first invitation to stand for parliament when working on top of a haystack, and had little sympathy with urban interests. He took his grim Presbyterian faith very seriously and his Ulster obstinacy made up for a lack of finesse, even at the Paris Peace Conference.

on markets overseas. Yet, in spite of recession, the country was set on a promising course. Within less than a century both islands had been explored and mastered: if the Maoris had been warred down and dispossessed, they had kept more than most indigenous peoples and would enter the modern world without losing their identity.

And already a New Zealander was having a decisive influence on the world. Born in 1871, the fourth of the twelve children of a Scots wheelwright from Perth, who raised and milled flax near Nelson, and on his mother's side of Essex stock, Ernest Rutherford, later Lord Rutherford of Nelson, had been brought up to farm. He studied at Canterbury College, Christchurch, where he won a scholarship to Trinity College, Cambridge. Here, at the Cavendish laboratory, under the direction of another genius, Sir J. J. Thomson, he began the research which, founded on his experiments at McGill University, Montreal, proved that radio-activity derived from the disintegration of one kind of matter into another. Then at Manchester in 1906 Rutherford proved that atoms contain colossal pent-up force, and pointed the way towards its release. He was aware of the possibilities of destruction as well as mastery latent in his discovery, but he died in 1937 before the invention of the atomic and hydrogen bombs.

For good and ill a New Zealand physicist had decisively contributed to the most epoch-making discovery of the twentieth century, while his compatriots in a country of superb scenery and fine climate were building up in miniature the most healthy and sensibly organized of the British colonies of settlement.

IV

The egalitarian mateship of a *Socialisme sans doctrines* and the democratic structure of the Federal and State constitutions, the power of the Trade Unions and the absence of the kind of hierarchy in Church and State still prevalent in Great Britain, did not prevent the antipodean British from remaining predominantly conservative and insular. In Australia the social ascendancy of the pastoral landowners, with huge estates and flocks of over twenty thousand sheep, persisted when their political power had been eroded; their aloofness was encouraged by the influence of elite schools. And here, as in Great Britain, the prevalent political party would be of the Right. Lord Bruce of Melbourne had accepted a Viscountcy; Sir Robert Menzies, the successor of Lyons and the founder of the Liberal Party which derived from the United Australia and Country Parties in 1944, proved from 1949 until 1966 the dominant politician in Australia; he would be knighted while in office, retain his following and become Lord Warden of the Cinque Ports. Far from taking a free and easy view of Edward VIII's making a morganatic marriage, both Dominions would come down heavily against it.

This Conservative interest would repeatedly out-manoeuvre a Labour Party, handicapped with the electorate by its supposed tolerance towards Communism; and with a Macmillan-style policy of promoting prosperity and a Nationalist policy of keeping Australia 'white', it reflected the wishes of an increasingly affluent people. Australia would cease to be a pioneer country in state-organized welfare and become more Americanized, more socially competitive, while the traditional British indifference to 'intellectuals', in Australia would render the mass media singularly banal. A vigorous life would go on in the universities, but it would not have much impact on the vast majority, whose cult of the beach, the sea, the racecourse and the cricket pitch would be more representative of the broad middle stratum of Australian society, between the more cosmopolitan rich and the depressed immigrant labourers and outcast remnant of the aborigines.

The vision of a free, democratic and egalitarian society, so strong in the nineteenth century, would thus become less attractive, as the prospects of competitive affluence in a managerial society increased. And fear and resentment of alien revolutionary ideas were intensified by the cold war and the rise of a revolutionary regime in China.

Yet the hope of maintaining a European-descended and exclusive society, with a population comparable to that of a Scandinavian state, in a sub-continent capable, with modern techniques, of supporting one vastly larger, would seem unrealistic. Impending over 'white' Australia are the vast populations of Asia. In view of the strategic and demographical facts, the security of both Australia and New Zealand would increasingly depend on the power of the United States, as they would come more into the economic orbit of North America and Japan.

The pattern of immigration was also to change. Between 1947 and 1961 only 32·4 per cent of immigrants would come from Great Britain and the Dominions; 16·7 per cent from Italy, 20·3 per cent from Eastern Europe; the Dutch and the Germans would contribute 8·8 per cent and 8·2 per cent and the Greeks 6·4 per cent. The cumulative effect of this immigration was bound to change the traditional Australian way of life, so that the insularity of the British and Irish Australians is being modified within the country at the same time as the difficulties of almost entirely excluding Asians are becoming plain. These problems are more urgent in Australia than in New

Zealand, but basically the same prospects confront both these ex-trapolations of Europe on the other side of the world. Yet both countries make up in vigour what they lack in numbers, and both are determined to keep their own character.

CHAPTER 25

The Far East: Malaya and the Pacific

When with brilliant strategic insight Raffles had founded Singapore, which by 1832 had become the capital of the British Straits Settlements, the Malay peninsula north of it was dominated by autocratic Muslim Sultans of varying and competing power. Johore, Singapore's closest neighbour, was bordered on the west coast by Malacca, and by the nine small sultanates combined in the late nineteenth century into Negri Sembilan. Northward beyond Malacca lay Selangor; then Perak; and, extending to the border, the Sultanate of Kedah, which formed the hinterland of Penang. Beyond Johore, in the centre and east of the peninsula, were Pahang; then Kelantan in the interior and Trengganu on the coast, both subject to claims of Siamese overlordship, and economically less developed than the Sultanates bordering the Straits of Malacca. These states were politically archaic: surrounded with elaborate ritual and display, their Sultans wielded absolute power, but their authority much depended on the local chiefs, themselves autonomous in their own districts. Below the fierce, colourful and proud rulers who competed with one another and fought within their families over their rights of succession, were the easy-going Malay villagers, their settlements strung out along the rivers that were the natural focus of commerce and communication. They relied mainly on rice; they had fowls and goats and the ubiquitous water buffaloes. The wealth of the 'Golden Chersonese' was still relatively undeveloped; though already the Chinese were working the opencast tin-mines. With more scientific technology in the early twentieth century, they would produce half the world's supply.

The British, since 1786 in possession of Penang, had taken over Malacca from the Dutch during the Napoleonic Wars, and from Penang founded Singapore. In 1826 the three territories had been grouped together as the Straits Settlements under the East India

Company, and when in 1867 the Colonial Office took over, the economic potential of the area was becoming obvious, while the opening of the Suez Canal enhanced the importance of Singapore. The increasing strife between the states of the peninsula, their internecine vendettas and endemic piracy, accorded ill with these prospects, and from 1874 to 1888 the British improvised a form of indirect rule which was the foundation of modern Malaya.

Naturally the Sultans resented this rule. And the Chinese, engaged in exciting feuds between their own secret societies—Ghe Hin against Hai San—were reluctant to end them. Modern administrators, intent on making a rich area safe from exploitation, were confronted with the aftermath of decades of neglect by the East India Company and by the picturesque and medieval confusions of the East.

In 1873–5, Sir Andrew Clarke, a Sapper colonel with wide experience in Australia and on the Gold Coast, who had also supervised the adaptation of the docks at Chatham, Portsmouth, Malta and Bermuda for ironclads, surveyed the newly opened Suez Canal and recommended its purchase by a British Company, became Governor of the Straits Settlements. He had been instructed by Gladstone's government to persuade the rulers to rescue 'their fertile and productive countries from the ruin that must befall them if the present disorders continue unchecked'.[1] And he interpreted his instructions in a broad way. First he tackled the disorders in Penang and Perak where the Ghe Hin and Hai San were at their most belligerent (they fought it out in war boats as well as on land), where piracy was rampant and where there was a disputed succession. Under the Pangkor Engagement of 1874 he induced the chiefs to recognize the legitimate, and soon puppet, Sultan Abdullah, and—most to the point—admit a British Resident.

The next centre of piracy down the coast was in Selangor, and here with the backing of the small British China Fleet, the next Resident was installed. His assistant, Frank Swettenham, would become the main architect of British Malaya and already had the reputation among the Malays as 'very clever at gaining the hearts of rajahs by soft words'.[2] A born diplomat with a tact and subtlety

---

[1] D. G. E. Hall, *A History of South East Asia*, London, 1961, p. 475.

[2] Sir Frank Swettenham (1850–1946) was the son of a Derbyshire attorney and educated at St Peter's School, York. Appointed a cadet in the Straits Settlements Administration in 1871, he soon became fluent in Malay. In 1882 he became Resident in Selangor; in 1889–95 in Perak; in 1895 Resident-General of the first Federation, and in 1901–4, High Commissioner for the Malay States and Governor of the Straits Settlements. He was knighted in

not always apparent among British administrators, Swettenham was able to persuade rather than compel; being a good shot and a *bon viveur* into the bargain, he won influence in the small ruling circle of late-Victorian and Edwardian England itself.

His task was tricky: in 1875 he narrowly escaped assassination, when his senior colleague, James Birch, a brisk and earnest reformer, unable to speak Malay, and fresh from the efficient administrations of the Straits Settlements and Ceylon, was speared at Pasit Salak through the palm-leaf lattice of his riverside bathhouse near his moored sampan. Swettenham, more adroit, escaped downriver by night.

The murder had been abetted by the apparently reconciled Abdullah, who after a spirit *séance* in which Birch's death had been forecast,[3] had sent a *Kris* to the local rajah who was to do the deed. It was the Sultan's protest against the consequences of the Pangkor engagement which, as he now realized, deprived him of his prized traditional rights of exacting forced labour and arbitrary taxes.

The outrage brought the conflict with the British to a head. Troops arrived from India; the chiefs immediately implicated were hanged; Sultan Abdullah was exiled. By the late 'seventies British Residents were in *de facto* control of the more promising parts of Malaya. Slavery and debt slavery were abolished; police and law courts organized. The rulers were won over with posts in the administration and a substantial fixed share of the revenues; the Sultans presided over the State Councils, attended by the Resident, by the principal chiefs and by representative Chinese. Malay headmen kept order in the villages, but courts of justice were conducted by British magistrates. Since before the Japanese invasion the Malays were the most unpolitically minded people in Southeast Asia, 'though that blissful state of mind was not to survive',[4] political resentment was swamped in a new prosperity.

The stage was now set for major economic expansion. In 1896 the Federated Malay Straits came into being, the federal capital at Kuala Lumpur in Selangor. Northward from Johore, which remained independent until 1914, when it became a protectorate, the states were Negri Sembilan, Selangor and Perak, and the large but sparsely populated Pahang east of them and bordering the China Sea. By 1909 there was a Federal Council, to which the

---

1897. On retirement he was influential in the City as director of various rubber companies. He wrote *Malay Sketches*, 1895, *The Real Malay*, 1899 and *Footprints in Malaya*, 1942.

[3] J. Kennedy, *A History of Malaya*, 2nd edition, 1970, p. 174.

[4] Hall, *op. cit.* p. 667.

Resident-General became Chief Secretary. The whole peninsula was thus divided into the Federated Malay States; the 'unfederated' States of Kedah and Perlis on the west, and Kelantan and Trengganu on the east, hitherto under Siamese suzerainty, but ceded to the British in that year; and the Sultanate of Johore. The Straits Settlements remained politically under the Colonial Office, but were economically an integral part of the peninsula.

The takeover in Malaya had been stimulated and conditioned by the French advance in Indo-China, when in 1904 the clever Siamese, who alone among the peoples of the area modernized their administration enough to survive as an independent power, and played the Europeans off against each other, obtained a Franco-British guarantee of their territorial integrity, and the British obtained Western Siam as their sphere of influence—a major economic advantage. Thus the French in Indo-China, the British in Malaya and the Dutch in Indonesia came to dominate Southeast Asia until the Japanese attack.

The first concern of the British after imposing peace, was to build roads and railways. The state-controlled railways, built mainly by Indian and Chinese labour, were completed in 1908, when the Federated Malay Railways extended from the vicinity of Penang to Johore; twelve years later they were linked to Singapore by a causeway, and by 1931 with the Siamese railways to Bangkok. Meanwhile a road network was constructed, often through matted jungle and high ground, so that by the 'twenties Malaya would have the best roads in mainland Asia.

Concurrently, and providing most of the revenue for this expansion, came first a boom in tin, then in rubber. Tin-mining, until the early twentieth century mainly a Chinese undertaking, by 1912 was being greatly developed by European technology and more massive investment. Apart from the intrinsic value of the metal, the mass production of tinned food now stepped up demand. But this long established mining and smelting industry was now surpassed. By 1920 Malaya was producing 53 per cent of the world's supply of rubber and it still produces over a third. As cheap automobiles poured from the production lines in Europe and America, the demand became insatiable; rubber plantations would extend over two-thirds of all the cultivated land in the country and employ a fifth of the male population. When in the 'seventies, as already recorded, Wickham had smuggled the seeds of Para rubber out of Brazil, and the seedlings had been reared in Kew Gardens and acclimatized in Ceylon, he had also transformed the prospects of Malaya. In 1888 Henry Ridley, a stout, ebullient little man, known with ironic respect as 'Rubber Ridley', who lived to be a hundred, arrived in Singapore as Director of the Botanical Gardens. This fortunate enthusiast travelled in Borneo, Sarawak and Indonesia; in India, Burma and the West Indies, and he held the appointment until 1911.[5] Gradually he persuaded the planters to go in for rubber. In 1897 only 345 acres were under cultivation; but by 1905 there were 50,000; and by 1910–12, when Brazilian wild rubber had been overpriced, Malayan plantation rubber began to undersell it. Indians and Chinese swarmed into Malaya to work on the plantations, for the individualist and leisurely Malays, who trained monkeys to run up palm-trees to throw down the coconuts, thus sparing human effort, long preferred to do their own subsistence farming in their own time—though as rubber proved profitable they would cultivate smallholdings of it. Such was the influx of Chinese and Indians that, although in 1922 immigration was restricted, by 1931 the Malays formed slightly less than half the population of their own land—1,962,000 to 1,709,000 Chinese and 624,000 Indians— and the country came to depend on imported rice.

The rubber boom, at its peak in 1910–12, lasted on and off—with fluctuations that gave many shareholders a ride—until the post-war depression in 1922. It then suffered a real collapse in the world slump. But an International Regulation Committee managed to rationalize and limit world production, and what with the armaments race and the expansion of the automobile and electrical and pharmaceutical industries, by the 'thirties rubber recovered and would even survive the wreckage created by the Japanese occupation.

At first supplementary to rubber, the oil-palm from West Africa was also acclimatized, and though beyond the resources of all but major companies, it proved another source of profit, employment and revenue. Along with increased production of fruit, vegetables, pepper and sugar, the wealth of Malaya was thus developed mainly by British, American and Chinese capital—the British investment in 1931 was 70 per cent. And the resulting revenues paid for a major campaign against tropical disease—particularly beri-beri and malaria.

In 1881 Ronald Ross, knighted in 1911, had entered the Indian Medical Service and been posted to Madras: he had then served in Burma and in the Andamans.[6] Influenced by the ideas of Sir Patrick

[5] He was a Norfolk man, appropriately a descendant of George III's first de facto Prime Minister, the third Earl of Bute, who had inspired the foundation of Kew Gardens. He wrote Spices, 1912, and the Flora of the Malay Peninsula, 5 vols, 1922–5, and the Dispersal of Plants throughout the World, 1930. He became a Fellow of the Royal Society.

[6] Born in 1857, son of General Sir Campbell Ross of the Indian Army, and

Manson, Ross now tackled the problem of malaria, and in 1897–8 discovered that the parasite of this disease was conveyed to its victims by the anopheles mosquito, not, as hitherto assumed, by 'bad air'. Appointed to the Liverpool School of Tropical Medicine, Ross set himself to eradicate the illness; in 1910 he wrote *The Prevention of Malaria*, and in 1926 became the first Director of the Ross Institute for Tropical Diseases.

The consequences of his epoch-making discovery, one of the greatest by-products of the British Empire, were decisive for Malaya. Already by 1910 on the European-owned plantations the deaths from the disease had fallen from 62·9 in a thousand to 18·57. And the medical services already established in Malaya served to promote the campaign far into Southeast Asia. With better health, better communications, basic education and a measure of indirect rule, political tensions were still unimportant; though the Chinese always had a divided loyalty since their way of life conformed to their own civilizations. But its condition was not then such that they were able, or desired, to promote its political expansion, feeling themselves politically well out of it.

Still separate from the Federation, as the capital of the Straits Settlements, Singapore had now become a great cosmopolitan centre of banking, commerce, shipping and communications. While the Federation had tariffs, Singapore throve by free-trade, and a population of 80,500 in 1860 had become well over a quarter of a million by 1901, and by 1950 a million, of whom 800,000 were Chinese. The island also became a base for the Royal Navy, now converted to steam, and so able to overtake the nimble pirate galleys which had often outmanoeuvred their pursuers in the age of sail. The big P & O's going to the Far East and Australia also needed a deep-water harbour and docks, and by the 'seventies, Singapore was well equipped. By 1905 the government in the Straits Settlements bought up the leading dock company, and by 1913 the Singapore Harbour Board were controlling one of the major centres of shipping and cables in the world, the natural focus of the whole rich area of Sarawak and North Borneo, Indonesia, the Gulf of Siam and the South China Sea.

Besides smelting tin and processing and storing rubber, Singa-

---

by temperament an artist and man of letters, Ross had no great enthusiasm for routine medicine, and had failed his examinations at St Bartholomew's Hospital in London. He was a versatile linguist and writer, and his *Memoirs*, 1923, are highly readable and entertaining. See also R. L. Megroz, *Sir Ronald Ross, Discoverer and Creator*, 1931. He was made F.R.S. in 1901 and awarded a Nobel Prize in the following year. He died in 1932.

pore exported sago, that detested standby of Victorian and Edwardian nurseries, and pineapples, no longer in their natural form an
exotic luxury, were now tinned and mass-marketed in 'chunks'.
Orchids, too, so much prized in the 'nineties by Edwardian and
American plutocrats, were now exported, and hybrid varieties produced, as in South and Central America, while coconut oil and
copra—the dried kernel of the palm fruit—as well as opium, met a
steady demand, the duty on the last (an exception to the general
free-trade), greatly contributing to the revenues. All this expansion
was financed by merchant bankers, very knowledgeable about
Southeast Asia and the Far East, whose offices, like those of the
shipping lines and export houses, had transformed the tiny settlement pioneered by Raffles into one of the most wealthy cities in
Asia.

In Singapore, as in Malaya, the British residents were few, if
affluent. The city was mainly run by the Chinese, and its strategic
naval base, elaborately fortified in the 'thirties, secured by the fleet.
Long considered impregnable, it would prove hopelessly vulnerable
to air power and assault by land, particularly as there were no
proper defences on the landward side.

In Sarawak the Brooke rajahs had maintained their benevolent
autocracy. The second rajah, Sir Charles Brooke, who had succeeded his uncle in 1868 and reigned until 1916, proved an able
ruler; and when in 1888 the British made the country a protectorate, it retained complete internal autonomy. With new communications and port facilities, the country prospered from a growing
trade with Singapore; oil resources, mineral and timber wealth
were developed. In the same year the Sultanate of Brunei accepted
a British Protectorate. Next year, further up the coast, North Borneo
and Sabah on the Sula Sea, long exploited by a British Company,
also became a British Protectorate, administered by the now Chartered Company. The island of Labuan, off the coast, a Crown Colony, and coaling station since 1848, was transferred in 1907 to the
Straits Settlements, as in 1886 had been the Cocos or Keeling Islands, atolls way out in the Indian Ocean, early settled by a Scots
eccentric, Clunies Ross, and annexed by the British in 1857. The
islands now became important as a cable station, and off them the
German raider *Emden* was sunk by an Australian cruiser in 1914,
as the Falklands had occasioned the end of the German squadron in
the Pacific and South Atlantic.

Thus was improvised, out of the casually administered Straits
Settlements of the East India Company, an extraordinary but viable
patchwork of Federated and Unfederated States, protected Sul-

tanates, strategic coaling bases and cable stations; all brought into a surprising coherence and apparently protected by the big naval base at Singapore. British commercial imperialism had brought this area of Southeast Asia into a world-wide economy.

Nor was it a one-sided exploitation. 'The imperial powers provided a vast amount of capital and technical skill, without which the development of the "colonial" territories in their present economic importance could never have taken place. They revolutionized health conditions and delivered great masses of people from the decimating or enfeebling dominion of frightful diseases. Their research in tropical agriculture and their scientific investigation ... laid the sure foundation on which prosperity and higher standards of life could be built up. Investigation of their fabulous profits, as far as it has gone, has tended to show that, as in all fables, imagination considerably outstripped reality, that the critics of "colonialism" have not taken account of the heavy losses that have occurred ... And in most cases foreign investors contributed the major part of the state revenues. On the facts as they are at present available, the sober historian dare not commit himself to the sweeping generalizations that are the weapons in political warfare.'[7] The British, in fact, were relatively humane exponents of a modernity which was bound to come.

II

Northeast from Malaya and strategically and commercially bound up with it, lay the ancient kingdom of Siam; while, impending over it and all Indo-China, extended the vast territories of China, now under the declining Manchu Empire but still the dominant fact of life in the Far East. Save for the Crown Colony of Hong Kong, now augmented by a slice of its hinterland at Kowloon, and for a naval base at Wei-Hai-Wei, the British had no possessions in this vast area; but their commercial and strategic interests were far-flung, and they took their full share in the exploitation of China, now in full political decadence under the *de facto* rule of the Empress Regent Tzu-Hsi (1875–1908) one of the more peculiar and sinister characters in world history.

In this context, peripheral but very important to the Empire, two personalities greatly contributed to the British influence in the Far East: Sir John Bowring, Governor of Hong Kong 1854–9, who fostered the modernization of Siam, officially admitted to be a British sphere of influence; and Sir Robert Hart, Inspector-General of the

[7] Hall, *op. cit.* pp. 670–1.

Imperial Chinese Maritime Customs Service from 1864 to 1906, who became the most influential foreigner in China.

Bowring was one of the most versatile mid-Victorian philologists and writers. Coming from a family of long-established wool merchants in Devon, he had early learnt many European languages including Russian, and became proficient in Chinese.[8] Bentham had appointed him editor of the *Westminster Review*, and, though unsuccessful in his own business, he was regarded by governments as an authority on economics. In 1847 he had been appointed Consul at Canton and proved just the man to negotiate with the highly intelligent, if arbitrary, King Monkut Rama IV of Siam, a philologist in the Pali scriptures, who was determined, unlike the contemptuous Manchu rulers of China, to adapt his country to the modern world. In 1855 Bowring went to Bangkok and concluded a Treaty of Friendship and Commerce, which conceded extra-territorial rights and commercial advantages to the British, for Monkut thought the best way of preserving his kingdom was to insure with the British against the French in Indo-China. And his policy paid off: in the event, Siam, with truncated territories, would survive.

British influence continued under King Chulalongkorn (1868–1910) who abolished the *Kow-Tow*, put down slavery and improved the economy and administration; indeed, his successor Maha Vajivarudh (1910–25), who had been educated in England, overdid the British influence, for he greatly admired the English public schools and had a passion for Boy Scouts. But when he founded the White Tiger Scout Corps for his grown-up officials (supplemented by Tiger's Whelps in the schools) dangerous resentment was aroused among his numerous princely relatives, who thought Scouts undignified and wanted appointments for themselves. But he founded a university and, surviving threats of assassination and a military coup, wisely came to the aid of the Allies in the First World War, a move which brought his country membership of the League of Nations.

Thus in an area long within the sphere of the East India Company's ambitions and of obvious strategic importance for the Gulf of Siam and the South China Sea, the peripheral influence of the British Empire was enhanced.

In China there was more at stake. A vast and ramified European trade was being conducted from the Treaty Ports with the interior of China, and it could continue only if, *faute de mieux*, the tottering

[8] He translated Russian, Finnish, Polish and Magyar poetry, as well as producing a *Batavian Anthology*. He also wrote *The Kingdom and People of Siam*, 1857, as well as *Autobiographical Recollections*, 1877.

Manchu government was kept in being. It was kept relatively solvent; and the coasts, rivers and posts viable mainly by a cosmopolitan Chinese Maritime Customs Service administered by Sir Robert Hart. The eldest of the twelve children of a Methodist minister in Belfast, Hart had chosen a more colourful setting for his career. Coming out to the East as a cadet in the consular service, he had early mastered fluent and idiomatic Chinese; he was appointed Inspector-General at the age of twenty-eight, and his charm and hospitality ingratiated him both with the foreign community and the Chinese establishment. For forty-two years he managed an enormous concern, and although suddenly dismissed in 1906 by the Empress Dowager in the final paroxysm of the regime, which culminated when she had her son, the Emperor Kwang-hsu, assassinated the day before her own death, he was given more Chinese honours than any other European.[9] So through all vicissitudes the Chinese Customs carried on, to the benefit of many Chinese, if not without benefit to the foreigners, who in 1916 still 'enjoyed a state far grander than the British in India ... and it was abundantly clear why so many had come to China to make a career. They made it, and a good deal more besides.'[10]

But the British position, like that of other European powers, was being undermined. In 1894–5 the modernized armies of Japan totally defeated the Chinese and mastered Korea; in 1900 the Boxer Rising against the foreigners—so-called since its leaders called themselves 'Fists of Patriotic Harmony'—was put down by a joint European expedition to Peking; in 1904–5 Japan defeated the Russians and became a great power; but the Customs Service, handed over to the Chinese in 1931, carried on until the final Japanese invasion before the Second World War. It set unwonted standards of efficiency and stability, if it emphasized the semi-colonial status of China. With foreign capital and expertise, much of it British, Chinese mineral resources began to be developed, and communications to be improved: but by the early nineteenth century European manufactures and Asian rice and opium were pouring into China in such quantity that an adverse trade balance worsened; the value of the *Tael* diminished, and foreign-induced inflation increased the hardships of the peasantry, already subject to plundering armies, periodic floods and famines. In the vast interior of China xenophobia naturally increased: railway lines were torn up; missionaries and other foreign devils lynched. The masses were beginning to stir; the quasi-

[9] Hart wrote *These from the Land of Sinim*, 1901: see Juliet Bredin, *Sir Robert Hart: The Romance of a Great Career*, 1909.

[10] Sir Maurice Bowra, *Memories, 1899–1939*, London, 1966, p. 55.

colonialist supremacy to be challenged. In the shipping, insurance and merchant offices along the great *Bund* at Shanghai—the most massively wealthy of the cosmopolitan Treaty Ports—and in the crowded prosperity of the British Colony of Hong Kong, a cosmopolitan affluence seemed secure, part of a world finance capitalism at its climax; and not least because it appeared protected by the British Navy, the long arm of the Empire, based on Singapore. But since the Russo-Japanese War a typhoon had been brewing up. The First World War proved Japan's opportunity to seize and exploit great areas of China: the prelude to a massive assault on the European empires in the East. More permanent, after 1911 a series of republican regimes emerged in China itself, the prelude to the massive reassertion of Chinese power and solidarity under Mao Tse-tung. Only Hong Kong would remain to the Commonwealth because it paid the Chinese to accept the status.

III

The strategic importance of the islands of the Pacific Ocean, little appreciated by mid-Victorian governments, became apparent during the scramble for colonies and naval and cable bases which set in during the 'eighties. By 1906 large spheres of influence had been defined. In the northeastern Pacific the United States first annexed Midway Island, then in 1898 the Hawaian group, including Honolulu—much the largest and most populous in Polynesia. In the central Pacific the French extended their influence round Tahiti over the Marquesas, Society Islands and the Tuamatus, and westwards annexed New Caledonia opposite Brisbane. The Germans in the western Pacific seized northeastern New Guinea, the Carolines, the Marshalls, Nauru, and Guam, and bought the Ladrones north and northeast of it from Spain. In the southwestern Pacific they also tried to take Samoa, with its small harbour at Apia, but were prevented in 1888–9 by the Americans and British—an occasion when all the ships but the British cruiser *Calliope* were driven ashore by a hurricane. Then, while the British were preoccupied with the war in South Africa, the Germans partitioned the islands with the Americans who took over Pango Pango with its magnificent harbour, while the Germans now succeeded in taking Apia.

The British, whose language remained predominant over all the Pacific, and who had already under Disraeli's government accepted Fiji from King Thakombau in 1874, in 1901 made Tonga a Protectorate, and in the 'nineties took over the Solomon and Gilbert and Ellice Islands north of it. In 1914 the New Zealanders promptly captured German Samoa, and in 1920 obtained a mandate for it, while the British took Nauru, to be assigned under mandate to a British–Australian administration. In the eastern Pacific the British held Pitcairn, populated by the descendants of the mutineers of the *Bounty*.

In Fiji they created one of their better colonial administrations: a form of indirect rule designed to preserve and adapt Fijian institutions. Its principal architect (1874–80) was a Scots aristocrat, Sir Arthur Gordon, the youngest son of the fourth Earl of Aberdeen, the mid-Victorian Prime Minister.[11] After his term in Fiji, he became Governor of New Zealand, then of Ceylon. In 1893 he was created Lord Stanmore. He was a high Anglican who thought that his work was 'what God meant him to do', determined and able to promote the interests of the peoples he was set to rule. Opinionated, on occasion brusque, careless of comforts and immensely energetic, he was an individualist in the old Whig tradition. He was too independent and didactic for the Colonial Office, but he was a good linguist and a good diplomat, and he set himself to prevent the Fijian way of life being destroyed. There were, of course, aspects of it that had to go: when, for example, a big war canoe was launched, girls had been used as rollers to give it luck; and, as in neolithic Britain, the main framework of a chief's house had been driven home over victims who were buried alive. And cannibalism, as in New Zealand, was a hallowed Fijian custom—although the term had originated in the West Indies, Fiji became in popular view the location of the 'Cannibal Islands'. In spite, or perhaps in part because of these barbarities and this diet, the Polynesian strain in the strongly Melanesian population produced an aristocracy of superb courage and physique, sophisticated manners and subtle mind. They kept their distance by elaborate ritual and a *mana* so strong that the touch of a chief could produce the equivalent of an electric shock, and the existence of a complex etiquette puzzled early missionaries, who 'found it difficult to understand the courtesy, the formality, the dignity of a people who were capable of performing acts of hideous cruelty'.[12]

Gordon enjoyed and observed the elaborate ritual of being a chief among chiefs in Fiji, and won *mana* by wearing the scarlet gown of

---

[11] Arthur Charles Hamilton-Gordon (1829–1912), a Douglas on his mother's side, was educated at Trinity, Cambridge, and after a short spell in Parliament as a Liberal, had become Lieutenant-Governor of New Brunswick, in 1866 Governor of Trinidad, and in 1871–4 of Mauritius. He wrote a short biography of his father, and four volumes of *Fiji: Records of Private and of Public Life 1875–80*, 1897.

[12] J. D. Legge, *Britain in Fiji 1858–1880*, London, 1958, p. 7, q.v., for a classic account of this experiment in indirect rule with a full bibliography.

a Doctor of Laws of Oxford University over the already resplendent uniform of a Victorian Governor.

The essence of the problem, which he went far to solve, was how to reconcile the interests of the European planters with those of the Fijians, and how to make the colony pay its way without swamping the islands with imported and now mainly Indian labour. He was concerned, as well he might be, by the impact of European settlement and land-grabbing; and, as an admirer of Sir Henry Maine (whose *Ancient Law*, 1861, had been amplified by his *Lectures on the Early History of Institutions* in 1874), he devised 'principles of native administration [which] approximated closely to those developed by Lord Lugard in Nigeria, and by Cameron in Tanganyika—the principles of Indirect Rule'.[13] In following these general lines Gordon's experiment in Fiji anticipated 'the more influential work later to be done in Africa'.

No one could prevent a measles epidemic that in 1875 diminished the Fijian population of about 200,000 by a quarter, and the other diseases and maladjustments that brought it to 84,475 by 1921—a figure which would rise again only by 1948 to 123,995[14]—but Gordon did much to preserve the patterns of social and economic life natural to the Fijians. Being born orators, the chiefs took kindly to the parliamentary form of government, already set up by Thakombau in 1871 before the British takeover.

During the 'sixties the American War between the States had set off a boom in Fijian or 'Sea Island' cotton; but by the 'seventies there was a slump and the planters turned to sugar. It was to prevent the Fijians from being proletarianized that Gordon sanctioned the importation of Indians, as in the Caribbean after the abolition of slavery; they found Fijian conditions better than those in India and by 1948 there would be 129,761 of them, more than the Fijians themselves.

On a shoe-string budget, which left most medical services and education to the missionaries, Gordon preserved the old hierarchy; a mixture of feudal and communal obligations, and in 1952 Ratu Sir Lala Sukuna, a descendant of Thakombau *Rex*, whose war club, first presented to Queen Victoria and embellished with doves and ferns, now served as the Mace of the Fijian Parliament, would become its Speaker.

In Tonga, the nearest important area to Viti Levu with its modern capital at Suva and its future airport at Nandi, and to Vanua Leru northeast across Bligh Water, Taugu'ahau Tupou, the ablest of the

[13] Legge, *op. cit.* pp. 165–7.
[14] Legge, *op. cit.* p. 3.

Tongan Chiefs, had early become a Wesleyan, and had shrewdly advised Thakombau to follow his example in Fiji. He had changed his name to George and his Queen's to Charlotte—Salote in Tongan —and he died in 1893, aged ninety-six. It was in Tonga, first of all of the Pacific islands, that cricket was introduced, and the 'craze became so extravagant that in order to avert famine as a result of the neglect of the plantations, it had to be prohibited on six days of the week'.[15] Under the influence of a power-hungry missionary, Shirley Baker, Prime Minister from 1880 to 1890 until removed by the British for his chaotic and insolvent administration, George I Tupou sponsored a schism in the fold, and to this day there is a separate Free Wesleyan Church in Tonga. In 1901 a Treaty of Friendship and Protection was concluded with the British and renewed in 1951. The monarch's ample and genial descendant, Queen Salote, undaunted by the British climate, would win more acclaim than any other colonial visitor at the coronation of Elizabeth II.

So, if the European impact on the peoples of the Pacific was sometimes fatal, it was often mitigated by British colonial rule, and potentially self-governing institutions were grafted on to existing traditions. From big volcanic tropical islands to tiny coral atolls a coherent administration was established, to be reinforced by better medical and educational services in the twentieth century. The incongruous Puritanism imposed by missionaries, who insisted on clothing their converts in unhealthy and hideous European clothes and cut down their natural sexual and ritual enjoyments, was the price paid for the abolition of cannibalism, infanticide and endemic war; and if some South Sea Islanders died from sheer boredom and despair, as well as drink and European disease, today the humanists and anthropologists have a better understanding of their societies, now re-emerging in a more natural, if modernized form. The provincial Puritanism of the missionaries had never appealed to 'the heathen', and Europeans have since learnt a thing or two from them. *Coming of Age in Samoa* is now cited as an example of a sane upbringing.

The environment, though, as Robert Louis Stevenson on Samoa and Gauguin on Tahiti discovered, humanly never such a paradise as believed, remained attractive. The matted and still malarial jungles of parts of Melanesia would form a horrible setting to some of the most ferocious battles of the Second World War; but vegetation was lush and the light brilliant, and the tropical rainfall was seldom either sparse or overwhelming. Rare and colourful birds ranged through varied foliage, brilliant fish through clear waters; taros, yams,

[15] G. H. Scholfield, *The Pacific, Its Past and Future*, London, 1919, p. 199.

breadfruit and sweet potatoes provided a staple diet; bananas and delicious paw-paws grew wild; pineapples and citrus fruits flourished under cultivation. The ubiquitous coconut-palm provided food and drink as well as a vast export of copra; sugar cane had been easily acclimatized, rice flourished. Modern aircraft have now abolished the isolation of the major islands, but apart from some mining and phosphate industries—the latter among the nastiest anywhere—the blight of modern industry and pollution has seldom descended on this vast and oceanic world: the scene, after initial private exploitation and outrage, of some of the British Empire and Commonwealth's more successful achievements.

Victoria RI, Queen of Great Britain and Ireland and Empress of India

On Chilkoot Pass during the Klondike gold-rush, May 1898

Gold-miners' rest hotel, New Zealand

Australian gold-diggers, early 1850s

Mission house in the South Seas

Massacre of John Williams at Erromanga in the New Hebrides, 1839

Mr Punch's Victorian Era: 'Justice'

2nd Afghan War: the Amir Yakub Khan and Major Cavagnari signing the Treaty of Gundamuk

The Burma Expedition: departure of King Thibaw from Mandalay

Delhi Durbar, in the presence of King George V and Queen Mary, 1911

Camp of Exercise, India 1885–6: Commander-in-Chief's luncheon party

BOOK V

From Empire to Independence: the
New Commonwealth

CHAPTER 26

The Variety of Empire

On 18th November 1918, after the Armistice that concluded the Great War, Lord Curzon moved in the House of Lords to present a 'humble address of congratulation to His Majesty upon the surrender of all his enemies'. 'The British flag,' he stated grandiloquently, 'has never flown over a more powerful and united empire ... Never did our voice count more in the councils of nations; or in determining the future destinies of mankind.'[1] Indeed, as Curzon's biographer observes, 'no victory has ever been so wide, so overwhelming, so unquestioned. We possessed physical supremacy such as had never been known since the days of Hadrian or Alexander. We seemed the masters of the World.'[2]

In Great Britain and throughout the Empire the old order seemed re-established. And even with the rise of aggressive dictatorships in Germany and Italy and the mounting ambitions of Japan, the shift in its foundation would be masked. With appeasement of class conflict at home—Baldwin's main objective—and of the dictators abroad —Chamberlain's obstinate purpose—it was still hoped that somehow the vast accumulated and vulnerable heritage of three centuries could be adapted and preserved. A gradual extension of responsible self-government within a British Commonwealth might retain those huge territories with their colossal investments in a common allegiance to the Crown; the worldwide commercial and financial interests would be defended, and the whole concern still exercise a powerful, pacific and, on critical occasions, united influence on world affairs.

In the event, when, after the German surrender in 1945, Churchill broadcast to the nation in a more homely and concise idiom, he spoke in a much more sombre tone. 'I wish,' he said, 'I could tell you

---

[1] Quoted in Harold Nicolson's *Curzon: the Last Phase 1919–25, A Study in Post War Diplomacy*, London, 1934, p. 2.

[2] Nicolson, *op. cit.*

tonight that our toils and troubles were over ... and if you thought that I ought to be put out to grass I would take it with the best of grace. But, on the contrary, I must warn you ... that there is still a lot to do ... if you are not to fall back into the rut of inertia, the confusion of aim, and the craven fear of being great.' The country, he said, should remain 'unflinching ... till the whole task is done and the whole world is safe and clean'.[3]

The war with Japan was swiftly concluded; but the world would not become either safe or clean. Cumulatively two World Wars had created a new polarization of belligerent power, this time outside Europe and outside the Commonwealth; and Great Britain, overstrained by the second and economically more ruinous effort, would cease to be an imperial power, reverse the policy of seven centuries and, from being the centre of the greatest oceanic and economic empire in history, merge an already diminished sovereignty into a European organization; while the nations of the Commonwealth, down to tiny Caribbean islands, attained complete independence.

Thus, within little more than half a century, the near suicide and eclipse of Europe in two bouts of appalling and global conflict exacted its price from victors as well as vanquished: the two German hammer-blows for *Weltmacht*, though they failed to win it, first cracked, then shattered the might of the British Empire. Further, the First War let loose an attempt at world revolution when a Marxist–Leninist government seized power in Russia after the collapse of the Tsarist regime. Hence a radiating attack on capital and on 'bourgeois' civilization itself, which in Lenin's realistic interpretation and Trotsky's fanatical vision was interpreted in terms of a revolt, not merely of the masses in the advanced countries led by Marxist elites, but also of colonial peoples against the capitalist West and the United States. This movement would combine with the spread of nationalist doctrines emanating from Europe to undermine the self-confidence and prestige of even liberal imperialism in Great Britain itself and in the Commonwealth. It was the two World Wars and their consequences that turned the foreseen, gradual and guarded policies of a confident liberal imperialism towards the swift transformation of the Old Commonwealth into a New Commonwealth of independent states, in a sudden and almost desperate dismantling of what had been the greatest of all the European maritime hegemonies.

For Great Britain, as for other European colonial powers, there is thus, contrary to much received opinion, little mystery about the causes of metropolitan decline, with its repercussions over the Empire

[3] Winston S. Churchill, *The Second World War*, abridged edition, London, 1959, p. 929.

and Commonwealth. It followed, as did the decline of the other major European hegemonies—French and Dutch, and the disruption of the Tsarist, Austro-Hungarian and Turkish Empires, the partition of Germany and rise of American and Russian super-powers—from an obvious and brutal political cause implicit in the clash of national sovereignties in 1914. Other and more subtle reasons will be considered, but the immediate cause is plain and overwhelming. And its sequel would be a strategic revolution caused by air power, intercontinental ballistic missiles and the thrust into outer space: all adverse to a small island dependent on sea power and imported supplies.

II

It is no part of this narrative, concerned much more with the achievements of the British Empire and with the emergence of an independent new Commonwealth in the light of world history, than with the swift political recession, to retrace the familiar events which mark the descent from the apparent apex of power signalized by Curzon's address, or to summarize in a chapter the colossal and crucial effort of Great Britain and the British Commonwealth in their 'finest hour'. It will be more pertinent, looking back over it all, to observe the long-term world influences that emanated and still emanate from the period of British imperial power, which have changed the patterns of civilizations old and new as no other empire has done and which can hardly be eradicated. But before reflecting upon them, it is worth recalling the extraordinary geographical and social variety of the achievement.

The British Empire and Commonwealth, at its territorial climax on entering the Second World War, contained the largest, if the least populated area of North America, the huge continent of Australia and the beautiful and fertile islands of New Zealand, and it still included the Union of South Africa, then as now by far the wealthiest and most industrialized state in all that continent. These Dominions of settlement were still sparsely populated for their size and with vast social and economic potential, the first three of mainly European stock right through and practising the constitutional self-government and rule of law originally worked out in Great Britain. Here alone, apart from the rule of India and in the West Indies and the huge brief hegemony in tropical Africa, in Egypt and the Sudan, in Malaya, the Far East and the Pacific and over the chain of strategic naval and cable bases around the world, new nations with great prospects had already been launched. And if they were already being drawn into the orbit of the United States, the greatest Anglo-Saxon power, that mighty civilization had itself derived its constitution, laws and language mainly from British colonial America.

The Dominions' outlook and way of life reflected their contrasting environments. The huge continental hinterland of Canada, including the Canadian Arctic, had an American sweep of forest, prairie, tundra and mountains, and an extreme climate. Southern Ontario could grow vines; but the rigours of the sub-Arctic and Arctic were quasi-Siberian; and if Vancouver and Charlotte Sound had the mild winters of the Pacific, the St Lawrence was iced up for half the year. But mineral wealth, fisheries, cereal crops and pastures had all fulfilled the expectations of the Durham Report; and the long passenger and freight trains of the Canadian Pacific which had first integrated the economy and 'left the Indians of the Six Nations dazed among the conifers as its coaches swept by with a wail of the steam whistle to the Pacific',[4] were now being supplemented, and would be in part superseded, by the automobiles and aircraft that would better abolish distance by the mid-twentieth century. Here Scots, English and Irish had got out of their islands; more enterprising and versatile than most of the conservative agrarian French-Canadians, they were exploiting immense, if arduous, continental opportunities.

In Australia, too, the insular close-knit and class-ridden British society was being transformed and opened out by sheer scale. As in Canada, old social divisions were altered; and though the arid outback made most Australians urban, they lived more spaciously than in the huddled European towns. With better physique and more *élan* than most of the metropolitan British, these Australian individualists were often as rough as the Canadians of the backwoods and as intolerant. And to metropolitan ears their idioms and accents were equally strident. Philistine materialists, it was said, with a cult of sport, beer and betting; but a remarkable and hardy people who were mastering an alien continent and with formidable intellectual and cultural potential. Here again, climatic contrasts dwarfed anything in Great Britain: from the apple orchards and temperate hills of Tasmania and the near-Mediterranean climate of Sydney, to the Sahara-style desolation of the red-earthed interior, the tropical plantations of Queensland and the fantastic shapes and colouring of the coral of the Great Barrier Reef, where the Pacific rollers broke in thunder as in the time of Cook. Indeed, compared with that of Canada, the Australian environment was even more un-European; with its thin-leaved eucalyptus trees and sparse undergrowth set

[4] James Morris, *Pax Britannica*, p. 376. This chapter on the imperial railways is one of the best in a brilliant book.

against pale translucent distances; its peculiar, atavistic animals and brilliant birds. As in North America, much good colonial architecture had survived; and beneath a brash modernity this civilization retained its character, while continental European immigrants would bring it diversity. Here, even more than in Canada, so close to the powerhouse of the United States, the British had created a more egalitarian society, with its cult of 'mateship' and physical well-being, though equality did not extend to wealth.

In New Zealand, in the equivalent latitudes of France and Spain, the settlers had exchanged one insularity for another; and the predominantly Scots tradition made for a more conventional self-sufficiency. But the mountains and fjords of the South Island were on a Scandinavian scale, and the genial climate of the North Island had a touch of the sub-tropical. The life was still mainly agricultural and pastoral, and the population was still only around two million as against over fifty million in the comparable area of the British Isles. Here the British, at home urbanized and industrialized, had regained the kind of life of their country-bred ancestors, but with better techniques and a more flexible social order. So long as the United States strategically dominated the Pacific, even isolation had its advantages; and the people of a miniature welfare state in a setting of mountains, pastures and pervading sea could be counted fortunate in a world of war, megalopolitan industry, over-population and pollution.

Although both the antipodean Dominions were mainly and inevitably concerned with Southeast Asia and the Far East and increasingly drawn to the United States, they also had a strange and potentially important commitment to the far south. Here they were responsible for the largest areas of the high Antarctic continent. In 1775 Cook wrote of the Antarctic, 'The risque one runs in exploring a coast in these unknown icy seas is so very great, that I can be bold to say that no man will ever venture further south than I have done; and that the lands that lie to the South will never be explored. Thick fogs, snow storms, intense cold and every other thing that can render navigation dangerous must be encountered.' History has disproved his pessimism; and if modern technology and communications have not yet tamed, still less exploited, the huge ice-bound continent, one need not expect in an age that is conquering space that the Antarctic will much longer defy current ingenuity and enterprise. The problem will be how not to ruin it.

The price of this expansion of the colonies of settlement into great Dominions had been a tragic confrontation between a technologically advanced civilization and neolithic barbarism or palaeolithic savagery. In Canada, as in the United States, the Amerindian societies had been swamped and coralled; in Australia nomadic aborigines had been driven from their hunting grounds, dispossessed and degraded. Only in New Zealand had the Maori been able to recover. But these had been normal consequences of exploration and conquest; and they were on a much smaller scale than the massacres and deportations of the totalitarian regimes of the twentieth century which, in this regard, of all centuries has the least right to censure its predecessors.

The component states of the Union of South Africa had not, like the other dominions, been true colonies of settlement. Both the British and long-established Dutch remained a small minority in a country already inhabited by the Bantu and 'Coloured', without whose labour it could never have prospered. And since, in spite of their victory in 1899–1902, the British could not run South Africa without the collaboration of the Afrikaaners, the latter in the event came to dominate the country. Well knowing the fate of South Africa if Hitler defeated the British Commonwealth, Smuts and his collaborators just kept their colleagues in line; but the sequel would be *apartheid*; and despite the hopes of liberal imperialists, the Union would quit the Commonwealth. In the end the Afrikaaners won.

The decision reflected the environment. Most of South Africa was unfit for the kind of democratic settlement realized in Canada, Australia and New Zealand: the rich farming of the Cape and Natal demanded big estates and capital; the mines vast investment. And since a huge and cheap labour force was both available and ineradicable, there was room only for skilled and highly paid Europeans, managers and technicians. Hence a more plutocratic and privileged society, with a gulf fixed between the ruling minority and the Bantu millions, and a great but precarious concentration of wealth. Yet the windswept sunburnt solitudes of the *veldt*, the sub-tropical luxuriance of coastal Natal and the vineyards, orchards and fisheries of the Cape more than offset the urban agglomeration of Johannesburg, and the more representative white South African, with his clipped precise speech, remained, as Botha and Smuts, a countryman, not a speculator in cosmopolitan finance.

III

In contrast to the Dominions, the Empire in India had been imposed on a civilization older, much larger and in some aspects more sophisticated than that of the British Isles. The architecture of both Muslim and Hindu India, from the marble Persian austerity of the

Taj Mahal and the more Indian elaborations of Fatehpur Sikri, to the Mauryan pillars of Sarnath, the elephants carved on the gateways at Sanchi and the Dravidian *stupas* of the south, had been superb. The Muslim artists, as Mansur, Bichitr and Abu Hasan, who had depicted the court of Jahangir with such economy, detail and harmonious colour, had nothing in their idiom to learn from the West, and their art was debased when their successors tried to do so. The Hindu paintings in the Ajanta caves can compare with the masterpieces of Europe and China; and the poets of the Muslim court could compare with their Persian models, Hafiz and Firdausi; while no contemporary European rulers left such perceptive autobiographies as the *Babur-nama* or the *Tuzuk i-Jahangiri*.

As for the Hindus, the great Sanskrit epics are earlier than Homer; the dramas and poems of Kalidaṣa had been written when the Anglo-Saxons were illiterate barbarians, and from Persian translations of the tales and romances of Dandin and Bana much European fiction derives. Indian mathematicians had invented the symbols which through the Arabs came to supersede the clumsy Roman methods of calculation in the West and so in the modern world. Moreover, this Indian civilization had spread Buddhism to China and the Far East, and brought the first elaborate culture and art to Indonesia. The British were ruling not a country but a civilization—a sub-continent with complex patterns of cultures and languages—at once fiercely military, as among the Mughals and Rajputs, the Sikhs and the Pathans; and pacifist, ascetic and unworldly, as among the Yogis and holy men of the pre-Aryan civilization. The country was still half-medieval; some arrogant princes as fierce as their own tigers, with their jewels and elephants, like fifteenth-century European lords writ large. The temples and religious orders were still in a similar relation to the mass of the peasantry as had been the monks and friars of Catholic Christendom, and the new Westernized intelligentsia and politicians were more incongruous to their own countrymen than the hierarchy and *panache* of the British Army in India. Hence, to this day, it is in India that the old military pomp and ceremonial of the Empire are still most conspicuously preserved; nor is it surprising that the pacifist tradition of Gandhi, now repudiated by many Indians as humbug, though its tactical advantages are admitted, has since given way to one more historically representative.

Administratively part of the *Raj*, but contrasting with Muslim and Hindu India, Burma was a predominantly Buddhist civilization with affinities with Siàm. It was rich in rice and timber, and its gold-sheathed pagodas and fantastic temples and palaces shimmered in tropical heat or were deluged by monsoon rains. Its peoples were varied and colourful: predominantly of Tibeto-Burman stock, but including the Shans of the eastern plateau who were related to the Thais, the dark Mons of the south, and the primitive hillmen of Kachin and Patkai. In this teeming population, augmented by immigrant Indians and Chinese, the British numbered at most twelve thousand. Here their influence proved relatively ephemeral.

The Crown Colony of Ceylon presented as rich a variety of scenery and climate. The high country to the south, with its mountains rising to seven and eight thousand feet, catches both the southwest and southeast monsoons, while the dry lowlands of desiccated forest, savannah and scrub are more akin to parts of southern India. It was still a predominantly peasant country, engaged in subsistence farming of rice, and since it had no resources in coal or oil, dependent on hydro-electric power for modern development. By contrast with the primitive agriculture, the planters on tea and rubber estates and in pineapple orchards had long built up a prosperous export trade, while Colombo had become a major port for world shipping. The Buddhist Sinhalese were far the greatest part of the population; next came Hindu Indian Tamils, indigenous or immigrant; then Muslim Arabs and Malays. There was also a considerable Christian community, mainly Catholic.

The stage was thus set for a rich permutation of political conflict; particularly when Western-educated intellectuals introduced nationalist and communist ideas, already influential during the 'thirties. It was a country of great social as well as geographical contrasts, where cosmopolitan hotels and luxurious clubs existed within range of primitive jungle which harboured elephant, leopard and bear. Though contrary to general belief spices were rare, monkeys and tropical birds were ubiquitous. The urban minorities but not the peasantry were more aware of Western ideas and the world economy than the generally inward-looking Burmese.

IV

Africa presented as great a variety of peoples and environments as India; but often a variety of barbarisms. The elaborate, wealthy and often advanced cultures of West Africa were riven with ancient tribal animosities: Ashanti against Fanti, Yoruba against Ibo. Indirect rule only postponed these conflicts; and the huge and apparently successful colony of Nigeria contained a fundamental division between the Muslim peoples of the north, of the sub-Saharan savannah and uplands, and the negroes of the rain-forest, mango-swamps and estuaries of the coast. In East Africa, again, the variety of peoples and places was fantastic. On the coast the clove-scented tropical island of Zanzibar and the ancient ports of Kilwa, Dar-es-Salaam and Mombasa and, northward, the blazing heat and semi-desert of Somaliland, contrasted with the highlands of Kenya and Tanganyika, and the magnificent interior around the great Lakes; while Uganda with its banana-groves, sugar canes and lush vegetation, belonged more to the catchment area of the White Nile than to the potentially rich farming and pastoral country between the great lakes and the Indian Ocean. But unlike West Africa, the plateaux of Kenya and Tanganyika invited European settlement; always, as in Rhodesia, a minority culture, dependent on African labour and goodwill, and so precarious.

The tropical West Indies were very different. The native Amerindians had long been swamped by Europeans, Africans and Asians. After the doldrums of the mid-nineteenth century, following the abolition of slavery and free-trade, the economies had precariously revived. Jamaica now had a population of nearly two million, eighty per cent African. Roughly 150 miles long and, at widest, 50 miles across, the island had a mountainous interior and luxuriant plateaux, soaked with the trade-wind rains, and temperatures ranging from the heat of the plains round Kingston to the cool air of the Blue Mountains which rose to 7,000 feet. There was a rich variety of timber, with ebony and giant cotton trees, and Jamaica had the largest deposits of bauxite for aluminium in the world. Bananas had replaced sugar as the main export, and tourism had developed; but overpopulation and unemployment drove many Jamaicans to claim their right, as citizens of the Commonwealth, to migrate to the metropolitan country, thus creating a new 'colour' problem for Great Britain and themselves.

In Central America, British Honduras had become a Crown Colony in 1884. Its population was under 100,000, but the country was rich in mahogany and tropical timber; most of it was low-lying, the coast fringed with mangrove swamps and bordered by reefs. British Guiana, by 1966 Guyana, bought from the Dutch in 1814, was very large but with less than three-quarters of a million inhabitants, of whom ninety per cent lived on the fertile coastal plain originally reclaimed by the Dutch. Its magnificent tropical forests, still not much exploited, harboured sloths, tapirs, ocelots, iguanas and the giant anaconda. In and around the Essequibo and Demerara lurked cayman crocodiles; macaws and toucans flashed through lush vegetation. Here, too, there was bauxite, but the main crops were sugar, coconuts and rice. The people were mainly Asian and African, and only one per cent was European. Hence, racial and political conflict between Asians and Africans, and an instability alarming to the neighbouring and oil-rich state of Venezuela. By 1970 Guyana would be independent within the Commonwealth.

Neither in Egypt, accorded internal self-government in 1922 but alight with nationalist feeling, nor in the Sudan could the British be anything but a garrison and an administration. The former contained the most majestic and, next to Sumeria, the most ancient of old civilizations; the latter covered vast areas of desert, savannah and swamp, containing, like Nigeria, many contrasting peoples. It would be held for less than a century. The other commitments in the Near and Middle East would be even briefer, though the strategic grip on Aden was already long established, and the domination of the Persian Gulf and the coastal sheikdoms of Southern Arabia, one of Curzon's essential aims, would be relinquished only when the hold on India, the strategic base of Middle Eastern power, had been abdicated.

The Mandate for Palestine, accepted in 1921 and perforce relinquished in 1948, had proved a burden for the British, if decisive for the Near East. It led to the establishment of a militant Jewish national state; nor did the Mandate over Transjordan of 1921 or the Mandate over Iraq, agreed in 1922, confirmed in 1924 and relinquished in 1932, realize the hopes of a Semitic Federation or even a Dominion reconciling Jews and Arabs within the Empire. The attempt to mix the twentieth century with a still semi-medieval society in Palestine naturally failed; Samuel, Storrs and Plumer, all liberal imperialists, failed to tame the passions of the Near East by a paternalism resented even by those whom it could benefit. The decision to accept the Mandates and the deeper involvement outside an already restive Egypt would be justified by its strategic results in the Second World War; but as a long term commitment it would prove impracticable.

V

These projects of an oil-rich 'brown' Federal Dominion, strategically placed between Egypt and India and including a 'national home' for the Jews, were typical of the false optimism of the 'twenties. The colonial Empire in the East, on the other hand, had solid foundations. It would survive even the Japanese assault and the communist infiltration, and prove to be the foundation of modern Malaysia. In Malaya, in a latitude equivalent to Uganda, the Congo and Venezuela, a tropical ocean bounded the serried ranks of rubber and oil-palm plantations and in the laboriously cleared enclaves in the jungle the tin-mines were being exploited with modern techniques. Some of this prosperity spilled over through public services into the lives of the Malays; less into those of immigrant Indians; most of it was mopped up by European, American and Chinese shareholders or sustained the privileged world of business in Singapore.

VI

This unprecedented variety of Empire in the Dominions, India and the tropical colonies, was held together by strategic naval and cable bases strung out across the world.

Nearest the island itself, with its great naval dockyards and arsenals, lay Gibraltar—the 'Rock' with elaborate tunnels and emplacements and its prospect south to Africa. It commanded the western entrance to the Mediterranean. Then came Malta, with the massive fortification of the Grand Harbour whence the Knights had beaten off the Ottoman Turks; with its elaborate neolithic temples, its wealth of baroque architecture clustered around the steep streets of Valetta and culminating in the martial memorials of the Knights under the round vaulting of the great cathedral.

In the eastern Mediterranean lay Cyprus: it had been 'leased' from the Turks until annexed in 1914. Of all these bases it had the most rich and ancient history; here pre-Hellenic peoples had traded and fought and an elaborate Graeco-Roman civilization had flourished, to be succeeded by a blend of Byzantine, French and Venetian influences, then by the levelling of Turkish conquerors which never destroyed a Greek tradition rooted in prehistoric times. Not that the British were much aware of this colourful history: they did not bother to found so much as a university college, let alone a university, in one of the most culturally interesting islands of the Levant.

Such were the Mediterranean strongholds, linking Great Britain with Egypt and commanding the Straits of Gibraltar, the Sicilian Channel and the exit from the Dardanelles.

South from Port Said and Suez at the north and south entrances to the Canal, down past Jidda and Massawa to the mouth of the Red Sea, lay Aden, the most repellent of the imperial strong-points and coaling stations, sweltering in its amphitheatre of jagged hills. It was a centre both of nefarious and legitimate trade with Abyssinia and, together with the equally barren island of Socotra and the arid coast of British Somaliland, it commanded the routes to the Persian Gulf, India and East Africa. It was also part of the network of British influence, based strategically on India, over the Yemen, Muscat and

Oman, and the Trucial sheikdoms on the straits of Hormuz which commanded Quatar, Bahrein and the Iraqi coast.

Southward, far out in the Indian Ocean, lay the Seychelles and Mauritius, both acquired during the Napoleonic Wars. Here a French way of life provided amenities unusual in the Empire; and superb scenery and fertile soil remained largely inaccessible to the outer world until the coming of modern aircraft. They also made relatively agreeable places of exile for recalcitrant African rulers or Levantine politicians.

East of the major bases at Trincomalee and Singapore, the island of Lebuan, off Brunei, now served as a cable station to Hong Kong, the only Crown Colony on the fringes of the China coast. But like the Treaty Ports and the vast European trade network in the interior, it was strategically indefensible in the face of any major resurgence of China, or of the mounting threat of Japanese attack. All this vast wealth in the Far East was a European and American hostage to fortune, dependent on Anglo-American control of the Pacific and the China Seas; in the last resort, on naval supremacy on the other side of the world. Meanwhile Hong Kong was the centre of far-flung commercial and financial interests, and a Crown Colony where a crowded, swarming, Chinese life was most closely juxtaposed with a spacious, luxurious and precarious European prosperity.

Out in the enormous spaces of the Pacific the formerly German base in Samoa had become a mandated territory under New Zealand; and Fiji, the administrative centre of the High Commissioners for the southwest Pacific, was now strategically more important through a direct all-British cable link with London. Supplementing cables, wireless stations had now become a major imperial interest; though, because of the delays over the Marconi Scandal in 1911, that company, the only one that could successfully set up the necessary stations, had only been accorded a final contract in 1913: the Empire had gone into the First World War with its wireless stations in England and Egypt unready and in Aden and India not even begun. But by 1934 all this strategic network had been completed when the companies involved had been merged in Cables and Wireless Ltd, over which the British government had effective control.

In spite of the variety and political success of the British administration in the southwest Pacific, the area remained, to the concern of the Australians and New Zealanders, the least defensible part of the Empire; and when under the Treaty of Washington in 1922 the British accepted parity with the United States and exchanged their alliance with Japan for a sixty per cent limitation of Japanese tonnage and a four-power pact for the supposed security of the Pacific, they had tried to meet accomplished facts. Predominance in the area had passed to the United States, merely supplemented by the over-estimated British base on Singapore. Here, as elsewhere, the Washington Treaty had been a turning point, marking the beginning of imperial recession, though the colonies and spheres of influence in the tropical Pacific remained a picturesque asset.

On the North American continent on the Canadian Pacific coast, the naval base at Esquimault, long linked by rail with the St Lawrence and the maritime provinces on the Atlantic, was now, like Singapore, subordinate to American strategy. But it was still in the north and south Atlantic that, as always, the most vital areas of British strategic defence remained. In the First World War the submarine had brought the British nearest to defeat, and the control of the western approaches was still as essential as in 1588. Hence, in the north Atlantic, the importance of Halifax, Nova Scotia and of Placentia Bay and Gandar, Newfoundland; and on the other side of the ocean, of the naval bases in Northern Ireland and Eire.

VII

Such in a broad view is the overall picture of the Empire and Commonwealth in the 'thirties at its greatest expansion. It contained a greater variety of peoples and places than any previous or contemporary domination, and it was much more vulnerable than it looked.

It was, in fact, in important aspects neither one thing nor the other. It was not a close-knit political union organized for war; nor was it an effective customs union. It thus contrasted with the much smaller but more compact German Empire, by the early twentieth century its chief rival, or the close-knit military and naval power of Japan. Nor was it united, as had been the Spanish Empire in South America or the medieval Arab hegemonies in North Africa and the East, by an official religion spread wide and deep among the subject peoples. The British, unlike the Spaniards in Mexico or the Portuguese in Brazil, had seldom intermarried with the indigenous populations. In spite of the extraordinary range and variety of the Empire, they had not become cosmopolitan, as had the Romans. They remained insular, sometimes provincial; aloof alike from their subjects in Asia and Africa and from their allies or enemies on the continent of Europe. Like the even more provincial Dutch, with whom they were racially akin, they were officially Protestant, and they had not, like the French and the Iberians, inherited the cosmopolitan and relatively tolerant outlook of the Roman Empire and

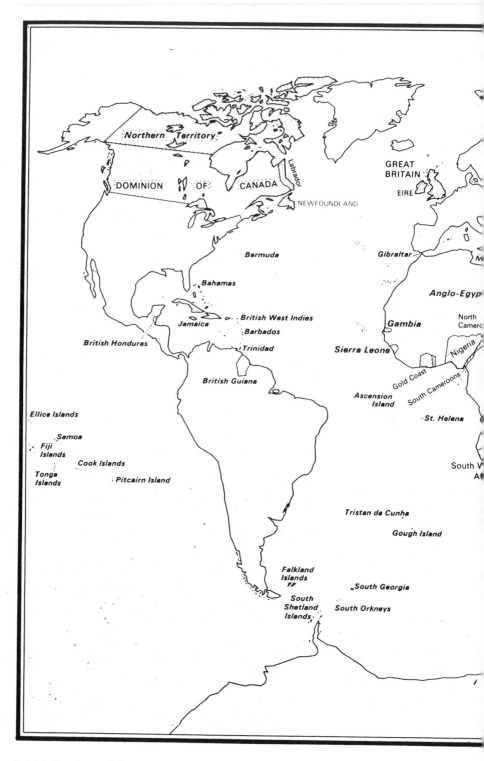

British Empire and Commonweath in 1939

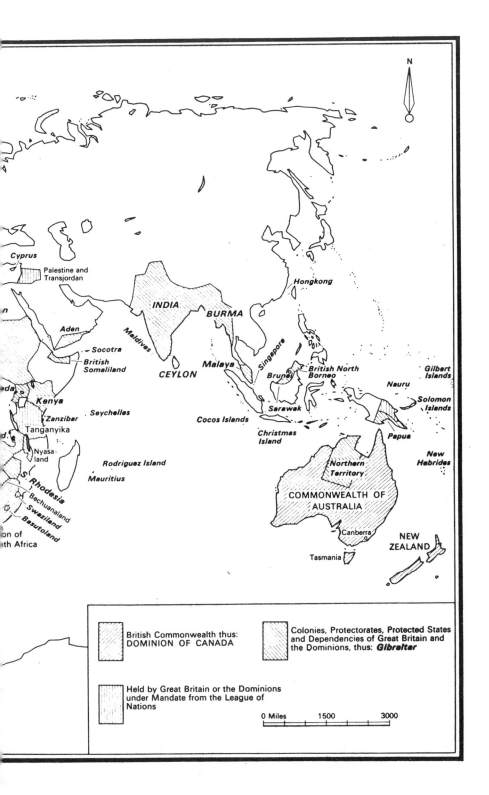

Cyprus

Palestine and
Transjordan

Hongkong

INDIA   BURMA

Aden

Maldives

Socotra
British
Somaliland   CEYLON   Malaya   British North
                                    Singapore   Borneo   Gilbert
                                              Brunei   Islands

Kenya   Nauru

Zanzibar   Seychelles   Sarawak   Solomon
Tanganyika   Cocos Islands   Islands

Nyasa-   Christmas   Papua
land   Island

S. Rhodesia   Rodriguez Island   New
                                              Northern   Hebrides
Bechuanaland   Mauritius   Territory
Swaziland
Basutoland   COMMONWEALTH OF
on of   AUSTRALIA
th Africa

                                          Canberra   NEW
                                                          ZEALAND

                              Tasmania

N

British Commonwealth thus:
DOMINION OF CANADA

Colonies, Protectorates, Protected States
and Dependencies of Great Britain and
the Dominions, thus: *Gibraltar*

Held by Great Britain or the Dominions
under Mandate from the League of
Nations

0 Miles   1500   3000

the Catholic Church. Roads, railways and canals, vast irrigation projects, the massive infrastructure of a modern economy and administration, had been built on a scale that surpassed any previous construction outside the United States; but the British in India and the colonial Empire had created them as the agents of an external power. In the imperial capital they had always retained their own traditional ways of life, modified only by their economic and social affinities with the other great 'Anglo-Saxon' power in North America. The Conservative Prime Minister, Bonar Law, might be a Canadian from New Brunswick, and Sir Winston Churchill and Harold Macmillan be half-American; Lloyd George was Welsh and MacDonald a Scot, but there was no question, save for the *tour de force* of Disraeli who came of a Jewish family long assimilated, of Great Britain being ruled, as Rome had been, by natives of Asia or Africa. Moreover, in Asia and the tropical colonies, as in Malta or Cyprus, the British had long remained self-consciously alien; following their own conventions, observing their own peculiar hierarchies, playing their own team-games and even demanding their own often unsuitable cuisine—for, whatever its other achievements, the British Empire has hardly been a gastronomic blessing to mankind. Imposing as their Empire appeared even in the 'thirties, and although it still commanded immense strategic advantages, the mental horizons of the British had seldom been really global, unlike the horizons of Hadrian or Marcus Aurelius which had encompassed their own geographically smaller but culturally ecumenical world.

Further, they had never been the strongest power in their own continent. They had survived by a diplomacy aiming to maintain a balance of power under which no rival would be strong enough to unite the Continent against them. After the First World War it had already become clear that power was passing to super-states outside Europe; that the old strategy was not enough. In spite of their final and greatest exploit, after the Second World War the British would begin to realize that they were after all, by descent, mentality and physique, simply Northern Europeans.

VIII

As a liner or aircraft heads south from Great Britain towards Gibraltar, the first link in the old imperial chain of defence, the relatively pale colours of the British seas change to the sapphire and indigo of the mid-Atlantic, and then, east of Gibraltar, into the glitter of the Mediterranean. Far the greater areas of the Empire and the Commonwealth were in the sun. But the island base, the strategic and economic focus of the whole worldwide domination, was in the rain-swept British Isles, with the bitter olive-green breakers of the North Sea on the one hand and the grey north Atlantic on the other. The discrepancies in scale and climate have always been extraordinary. Though distances have been mastered by modern aircraft, the contrasts remain, underlining the size and variety and dispersion of the islanders' achievement.

Thus, spread out around the globe, the British Empire and Commonwealth, at its greatest extent between the wars, contained a fantastic variety of countries and peoples, protected by British naval power and by bluff, wealth and the kind of credit and prestige enjoyed by a conservative, long-established business house. For, in spite of its naval and military might, it remained essentially civilian: founded not by state enterprise but mainly by the spontaneous initiative of a mercantile and industrial people, who had got a start over all rivals during the first Industrial Revolution. Like any great established business, its scale and wealth made it cautious; and its policies had long been increasingly defensive—the British government having reached out only when it had to acquire new protectorates and mandates to preserve older interests, strategic and economic. It was apt, too, to take the soft option: selling traditional goods in easy markets rather than moving into the fields of new technology in more competitive ones; concentrating on the secondary business of banking, insurance and finance abroad, rather than on primary productive industries at home; and reluctantly turning, after the collapse of the gold standard and of free-trade in the great Depression, to half-hearted protectionism which restricted the world trade on which Great Britain itself was bound to depend.

The whole vast but casually organized and vulnerable hegemony thus presented a tempting prospect to those German rulers who in 1914 had wanted war and plunder in the traditional way; it would, again, to the demagogue dictators of 1939, riding the tigers of their own nationalistic peoples, or vowed, following Marxist–Leninist dogma, to destroy the capitalist and social-democratic regimes within the Empire and Commonwealth and spread world revolution, even by colour war.

Apparently secure, rich and varied as was the immense area surveyed at the time of Curzon's 'humble address', by the 'twenties and the 'thirties the British Empire and Commonwealth was entering an increasingly hostile world. Its final and greatest victory would be won in an age when the Empire was already becoming an anachronism. Yet, in spite of the consequent political recession and swift dismantling, the Empire over the centuries has become one of the greatest facts in world history, and its influence is still persuasive and probably permanent. The stages and the metropolitan causes for the post-war collapse and the nature of this world-historic influence now demand consideration.

CHAPTER 27

Metropolitan Decline

All empires depend on the metropolitan power which has created and sustained them. It was decisive that just when the responsibilities of empire were most onerous and over-extended, a shift of political power and attention occurred within the island base itself. The British establishment had for centuries avoided the extremities of revolution and reaction by coming to terms with new men and new classes as they attained social and economic weight; and now the apparently most imposing imperial expansion coincided with the rise to political power of the classes least interested in the Empire. The influence of those most aware of the importance and range of the Empire-Commonwealth was now being eroded.

The Dominions of settlement had been created mainly by 'working-class' emigration, voluntary or forced, but there had never been a deep-rooted popular feeling for political ties with them. And the *Raj* in India, like the government of the colonial Empire, had long appeared the affair of the monarch, the ruling establishment and the fighting services. Patriotism in 1914 had been militant; but by 1919 it was widely thought 'not enough' until the mortal danger of the Second World War revived it in full force. Protected from invasion by their fleets, most of the British had for centuries been a mainly civilian people; and with the advent of full social democracy they would become more indifferent to an Empire which they identified with the ruling classes and the rich. Most of the people, after severe unemployment and poverty between the wars, became even more insular, preoccupied with raising their own living standards, with social security and 'safety first'.

And governments now depended more than ever on the mass electorate; since 1911 the major powers of the House of Lords had been abolished, the monarchy had long been relegated to a symbolic and advisory role and the old balance of King, Lords and

Commons superseded. Lloyd George in the crisis of the First World War had introduced a more autocratic and personal style of government, and the scope and power of administration had been greatly extended. This style of government, modified between the wars, would be enhanced under Churchill's wartime coalition, and its powers continued by the Attlee administration to create a social democratic welfare state. The British then submitted to a bureaucracy and taxation unheard of in their history; and the resilience, the initiative and the compulsions which had created the Empire and Commonwealth were undermined.

The Baldwin/Chamberlain governments had been thoroughly representative of the will of an insular and apathetic electorate, anxious even to evade the responsibilities which the Empire and Commonwealth implied, and uninterested in the doings of the political gangsters who were plotting their destruction. In a world overshadowed by the appalling danger, the warnings of Churchill were constantly disregarded. If the National government of the 'thirties succeeded in assuaging class conflict within the island and smothering the extremists of both the Right and the Left, they proved representatively incapable of the realistic conduct of foreign policy in a world which they no better understood than did the voters who had elected them. Nor were they any better at organizing the defence of the richest and most vulnerable empire in the world, already in the 'thirties increasingly hard to manage with the spread of European-style nationalism beyond Europe and, in particular, in the Commonwealth, and the doctrines of Marxist–Leninist world revolution emanating from Moscow.

Such were the main political aspects of metropolitan decline. In the life and death struggle of the Second World War, the British would rally under a traditional kind of leadership in their finest hour; but after it, all the symptoms would recur even more decisively in a politically overstrained and economically crippled country. Hence the hasty political dismantling and abdication in India, Burma and Ceylon, by the first Labour government with a massive majority, when, both by necessity and by conviction, Clement Attlee presided with a dowdy and precise ability over the first phase of the political dissolution of the British Empire, already implicit in the principles of nationalism endorsed by the British in the Treaty of Versailles.

II

By the mid-twentieth century strategic, economic and intellectual changes had also confirmed political decline. The British Empire and Commonwealth had always been based on sea power. Even during the Marlborough and Napoleonic Wars no great armies had been committed to the Continent: subsidies and blockade from an invulnerable island base had been the consistent strategy. But in the First World War massive conscript armies had been sent to the Continent. The British could no longer take as much or as little as occasion served; and instead of the limited Peninsular War or the campaign of Waterloo, the British and imperial armies had experienced the massacres of Ypres, the Somme and Passchendaele. Indeed, the war had transformed the British, who invented the tank and attained air mastery, into one of the greatest military powers in Europe. In such a traditionally civilian society a profound disgust for war had set in, as in the 'twenties all over Europe, and the Empire was identified with militarism. Thus the necessary abandonment of the old strategy for unlimited commitment had its political sequel.

Even more seriously—although in spite of tactical reverses Jellicoe at Jutland had not 'lost the war in an afternoon', the island base had been defended, and the blockade maintained—the coal- and oil-burning battleships and battle-cruisers, with fifteen-inch guns, had now been challenged by the submarine. In 1917 the island itself had come within measurable distance of famine; and it was only when Lloyd George's government forced the Admiralty to organize convoys that the threat had been overcome. No such strategic danger of starvation had ever occurred before; the over-populated island was now far more vulnerable. And, even more menacing, the development of air power had already poised the most deadly strategic threat. Though the Zeppelin raids had been only a nuisance, they had been without precedent; and in the Second World War the Battle of Britain would be even more crucial than the Battle of the Atlantic. The island would suffer unheard of destruction and civilian casualties. The House of Commons itself would be destroyed and the major ports and industrial cities knew flame and ruin as the sirens howled their warnings and the searchlights traced their apparently ineffectual patterns on the sky. The whole people had to 'take it' as never before; civilians, as elsewhere, were no longer exempt from the horrors of modern barbarism.

Nor was this all. With the invention of atomic and hydrogen

bombs and intercontinental ballistic missiles, ultimate strategic power, for what it was now worth, passed to huge continental states: to the United States in collaboration with Canada; to the U.S.S.R.; potentially to the Chinese. First had come the obscene stutter of the flying bomb, then the unheralded and thunderous explosion of great rockets; and if the rocket sites in the Pas de Calais had not been mopped up following the invasion of France, there would have been much greater devastation; as frightful perhaps as that inflicted by the allied bombers on Köln, Dresden, Hamburg and Berlin; while the sinking of the *Prince of Wales* battleship and the battle-cruiser *Repulse* by Japanese warplanes had led to the fall of Singapore and the surrender of eighty-five thousand men, the greatest military disaster in British imperial history. And now when a few hydrogen bombs could blot out all life in the country, the strategic position of the island base has become, to say the least of it, eroded; the counteracting British contribution to the deterrent had to be based on atomic-powered submarines that lurked in the oceans, on Canada and the rocket ranges in Australia, as had the training of aircrews on Canada and South Africa in the Second World War. Of all the major components of the Commonwealth the metropolitan power was now the most crucially vulnerable; a fact that was bound to diminish its authority.

In 1956 this vulnerability put paid to the last Franco-British attempt to assert a strategically desirable but politically ill-conceived 'colonialist' authority at Suez, when a *volte face* of American disapproval and a rumble of strategic menace from the Kremlin led to hasty and ignominious withdrawal, leaving exactly the power vacuum in the Near East that the rulers of the Empire in the 'twenties had managed to avoid.

So, like the other Europeans, the British in their island had not really recovered from the consequences of the First World War and were knocked out as a first-rate world power by the Second, while their colonial Empire, like the French, the only one of comparable scale, had to be rapidly transformed. Oddly enough, only the oldest and least liberal of the European maritime colonial dominations, the Portuguese, would stagger on: an anomaly in the world in which the tide of European domination had receded.

The British Empire-Commonwealth and their allies had thus twice defeated the German attempt at *Weltmacht*, launched as it had been from an inadequate, because only European, base; but now the British had to settle for what they could and preserve the economic interests which had always been their main preoccupation as a trading and industrial nation. The British had long in-

tended gradually to emancipate the Empire; now the habit of compromise and of sacrificing appearances for essentials made them do
so more rapidly, with more success than any other colonial power.
Indeed, with a characteristic realism, they would retain a good deal
more than was apparent.

III

Not that trade within the Empire and Commonwealth had ever
exceeded that with the rest of the world. Since the mid-nineteenth
century the British had lived by world trade, and were economically worse hit by the collapse of the international monetary system
in 1929–31 than they had been by the First World War. The catastrophe was hardly offset by the Ottawa Conference of 1932. A ten
per cent tariff imposed on general imports, and limited 'preferences'
and 'quotas', arranged with the dominions and colonies within a
'sterling area' not even coincident with the Empire, proved a poor
substitute for cosmopolitan free-trade. Imperial Federation, that
'political arabesque', had already faded before the nationalism of
the Dominions. Now their economic nationalism had become
plain.

As already stressed, the causes of the economic malaise that now
haunted the former workshop of the world go far back into the late
nineteenth century. But for all this loss of competitiveness and new
enterprise, the City of London remained the greatest mercantile and
financial capital in Europe and its network spread over vast areas
of the world; yet at home the country was now an even more 'terrible
hive' of population and the most proletarianized and urban of all
the economically advanced states. Hence a clash between the restrictive demands of financial orthodoxy to maintain the credit on
which the country had to depend and the need for full employment
for the people. The debts incurred in the Great War had contributed
to this crisis. Huge loans to Russia had been repudiated; vast American loans had to be repaid; the reparations exacted from the Germans had merely made them bankrupt, or if paid in kind, competitors. The return to the gold standard in 1925 had been a desperate
attempt to maintain the international medium of exchange, but in
1931 it had to be abandoned. A runaway devaluation was only prevented at the price of wrecking the Labour Party, by the formation
of a 'National' government and by Snowden's rigidly orthodox
finance.

An apparent economic clash of interest between the City and the
majority of the people had thus been reflected in politics. The price

of containing devaluation and inflation had been massive unemployment. There had always been a gulf between the ruling classes
and the workpeople—between 'them' and 'us'. Now it had widened,
and bitter memories of hunger marches in the rain and of ex-
soldiers making pathetic music in the streets went deep. This social
resentment would last: hence the vote, which in 1945 astonished
the world, not against Churchill, but against the Conservative
Party; and also the resentment against 'imperialism' and 'colonialism', felt as part of a capitalistic establishment.

The Labour government that in 1945 came to power with a big
majority was committed to creating a welfare state; but it had inherited a worse financial and economic predicament than the governments of the 'twenties. The country was now in debt to the tune of
over £4,000 million, of which only about a quarter had been paid off
by the sale of the enormous British investments and assets abroad,
with consequent loss of interest payments; while exports were run
down to less than half their pre-war volume. Eighteen million tons
of shipping had been lost, and unprecedented damage inflicted on
factories, housing and communications. 'Austerity' still had to be
endured; and the country was now the pensioner, almost the mendi-
cant, of the United States. When in 1945 'Lend-Lease' arrangements
were abruptly cancelled, only the generous improvisation of Marshall Aid saved Great Britain and the rest of western Europe from
collapse. And although a further loan of $3,750,000 tided over the
worst crisis, the attempt to develop an insolvent welfare state led
in 1949 to a major devaluation of the pound to $2.80. Even stricter
exchange controls had to be imposed; and the British who by fighting on alone had made the liberation of the Continent possible,
became the poor and often despised relations of the beneficiaries of
the Anglo-American victory in western Europe.

These obvious facts, too familiar to be dwelt upon, are often
forgotten in relation to the dismantling of Empire, and the hasty
launching of the New Commonwealth; but they contributed greatly
to rapid and sometimes disastrous improvisations, and to the failure
to give a lead to a more united western Europe. It is not often that
the British establishment loses control of events; but in the anti-
climax of the country's finest hour they came near to doing so,
overcome by the penalties of their timid and provincial policies in
the 'thirties and by worldwide events on a scale that now dwarfed
the island, overstrained by the greatest war effort of any of the
powers concerned in relation to population and resources, and riven
by the 'alienations' and class resentments that had long been building up; though, in face of the waning of European power, the rise

of extra-European nationalisms and a precarious economy, such hostility was a luxury.

IV

Since the 'twenties these political and economic causes of metropolitan decline had interacted with a mounting criticism and hostility to the old order and outlook which had somehow survived the First World War, but which the Second World War and its sequel would largely destroy.. The mass of the people had still been imperialist, even Jingo, in 1914, but after 1918 this certainty had waned. The views of the anti-imperialists began to count more. These influences were not decisive, for the decision was being made by the rise of nationalism within the Empire following the First World War, but they hastened the abdication.

For what they were worth politically, most of the fashionable writers—Lytton Strachey, Aldous Huxley, Osbert Sitwell, E. M. Forster, D. H. Lawrence—were hostile to the Empire, which was thought militarist, and to the Commonwealth, which was thought boring. H. G. Wells, with a much wider public, had long abandoned his liberal imperialism for a campaign for world management, even world government. The followers of G. E. Moore, the Cambridge philosopher who had dispersed much metaphysical fog, were sceptical of political action and concerned with intense personal relationships, while Bertrand Russell (to whom his Sovereign is said to have remarked, rightly, when he conferred upon him the Order of Merit, 'You have often behaved in a way that would not do', if generally practised) was pacifist and anti-imperialist. And Bernard Shaw had long conducted a scintillating attack on the old order and most of its works. Among intellectuals it had for some time been unfashionable to read Kipling; Proust was now *de rigueur*, while W. H. Auden, the young poet who already commanded most influence among his contemporaries, detested the public face of empire, as indeed of most government. The bias was unrepresentative, but influential circles were now pacifist, cosmopolitan and neo-pagan; and those neo-pagans who might have been interested in the Empire, considering the great variety of behaviour current within it, preferred their paganism in the Mediterranean style, especially those brought up on Greek and Roman literature.

The splendid range and variety of the Empire and Commonwealth, with its openings not only for soldiers and administrators but for geographers, archaeologists, anthropologists, sociologists and historians, were strangely disregarded. So, while highly competent administrators, doctors, anthropologists and soldiers were doing admirable work in the Empire and Commonwealth, and devoted missionaries were persuading their flocks to abandon witchcraft and human sacrifice for a milder alternative, and while the most popular Anglo-Saxon social contribution to world civilization—the cult of team games—was being successfully propagated, again providing a salutary substitute for more damaging forms of violence, the main intellectual fashion in the island itself set strongly against the Empire and Commonwealth, of which the scale and fascination was now little understood.

This new erosion of confidence and solidarity in the island base had also drawn on older tradition. There had always been strong currents of opinion running against the Empire: 'Little Englanders' were nothing new, and the old Nonconformist anti-imperialism of Bright and even of Gladstone had deep roots and was shared by the young Lloyd George, who had been nearly lynched as a pacifist during the Boer War. Ramsay MacDonald, afterwards Prime Minister, had suffered much obloquy for his opposition to the declaration of war in 1914. It was not only the Quakers who demanded disarmament: the majority of the electorate in the 'thirties who only wanted a quiet life, and thought that a 'fair' deal could be made with homicidal maniacs, could see no reason why, when Hitler reoccupied the strategic Rhineland and broke the Treaty of Versailles, he should not have 'gone into his own back garden'. The complicated class resentments so characteristic of the British were extrapolated into the Empire. The intellectuals of the Left were for once united with a good many of the work people in a common resentment of the establishment and its assumptions, including 'imperialism'.

And here was the opportunity of the real revolutionaries: the Marxists, Leninists and Trotskyites, set on global subversion. So, across a wide political spectrum an anti-imperialist body of opinion built up, including dedicated Marxist–Leninists who believed that the Empire was the final phase of a degenerate capitalism, inevitably doomed before the oncoming world revolution.

Moreover, although the official ceremonial and established Anglican religion which enveloped the Empire and Commonwealth seemed unimpaired, even the classes, who ran it no longer had the shared convictions and solidarity of their forebears who had, mainly on their own private initiative, created both the Old Colonial and nineteenth-century Empire. The steady will to power had become debilitated at the centre just when the danger and almost uncontrollable complexity of events demanded unremitting self-confidence determination and realism. As Gaetano Mosca and James Burnham have pointed out, in the general circulation of changing elites which is one of the few constant patterns in history, rulers may often become cynical, frivolous or bored; but it is unusual that the heirs of Empire turn so much against their own traditions, cease to believe in themselves and so risk being replaced by those who do.

In contrast, among the indigenous leaders and sometimes the masses in the countries of the Empire and Commonwealth, there was militant self-assertion. Just when in the island base itself the Empire and even the Commonwealth were losing their appeal, a rampant centrifugal nationalism was emerging in them. The British themselves had assiduously created political nation states where there had been none before and trained up whole new literate classes, often impatient of their own inherited cultures, avid for Western ideas of liberty and equality, and susceptible to anti-imperialist ideas, often emanating from Great Britain. The people naturally wanted positions and salaries that only 'Africanization' or 'Asianization' could bring them. These 'clerks of Empire' formed the cadres of nationalist movements for independence. The British had generally admitted that such movements must come; but the two World Wars greatly accelerated the pace.

V

Between the wars the critics within the island base itself by no means had it all their own way. A conservative and plutocratic establishment still commanded a ramified and massive influence. The Monarchy, the Court, the old political families and the country gentry, the high officials and the leaders of the armed services, the judges, the eminent lawyers, most of the bishops, the heads of Oxbridge colleges and of the great schools, the officials of the B.B.C. under the regime of Reith, still held predominant power—enough to put the brake upon radical change. And the politicians, as MacDonald found out in a capitalist world, had to toe the line to the interests of cosmopolitan finance and the City of London, with which the whole economic viability of the country was bound up. Inflation had not yet eroded fixed but substantial independent incomes; death duties were not crippling; there was no capital gains tax. Ordinary middle-class households included domestic servants and most of the writers and academics hostile to the establishment lived in comfort, if not in luxury. Travel was cheap, as yet untrammelled by exchange restrictions. But the structure was brittle. One more upheaval—and the Second World War provided it—and the foundations would shift; with the spreading seismic tremors the

Empire and Commonwealth would enter their final transformation.

Gradually, after the Second World War, a minority began to realize that only through closer ties with the continent of Europe could Great Britain regain prosperity and influence. In spite of official discouragement and popular indifference, the movement spread. Under the Macmillan government of 1956–64 the British began to edge towards a closer, a novel commitment. A more viable and politically powerful Great Britain would become a better asset to the Commonwealth. But the new move reversed the policy of centuries, and it disconcerted much Commonwealth opinion. For it was made in terms of a European Common Market and it might in time be made in terms of a political confederation. For the island base itself had ceased to be primarily the centre of an extra-European oceanic Empire or even of a New Commonwealth of equals. The British had reverted, like the French, the Dutch, the Belgians and the Italians, to a European role, though, like the rest of western Europe, economically and politically part of an Atlantic civilization and strategically and economically dependent on American support.

CHAPTER 28

The Empire-Commonwealth in World History

The shifts of political power, economic necessity and public opinion within the island base thus contributed to the transformation of the old British Empire and Commonwealth into a New Commonwealth of Nations and to a reversal of traditional policy towards western Europe. The swift transformation was in tune with the times; alien rule over unwilling peoples now had little point and imperialist grandeur looked tarnished after the flash of the hydrogen bomb. The British speeded up a policy long accepted, and hastily emancipated their subject peoples to maintain what mutually advantageous strategic, economic and cultural contacts they could. To relinquish the politically untenable was plain common sense.

The causes of this abdication have already been considered; but it is interesting to survey the positive side of these transactions the launching of new independent states in Asia and Africa and the kind of countries they are. Chequered as has been the immediate sequel, their emergence will be looked back upon as changing the pattern of world history.

The British, like all imperial powers, had exploited their dependents; but, following the American secession, they had early accorded responsible government to their colonies of settlement, the 'Dominions', and had held out the prospect of 'Dominion Status' for India and the colonial Empire. Parliamentary democracy, the structure of the Liberal experiment in their own country, had been gradually acclimatized in societies that were quite non-European. Indeed, their Liberal imperialism had accumulated considerable goodwill; and in the Second World War most Asians and Africans preferred the British to the racialist tyrannies of Hitler or Mussolini or to co-prosperity under the Japanese. And they are now independent because the Axis powers suffered defeat.

To the British war effort—the greatest of any in relation to population and territory—the Canadians contributed nearly three-quarters of a million men and the Australians and New Zealanders no less than two hundred thousand each. Armies of two and a half million were raised in India, and four hundred thousand troops came from the colonial Empire. Save for the nationalists of the Indian Congress, who wanted the British to leave their country to the Japanese, most of the leaders and peoples of the British Commonwealth, including a majority of white South Africans, knew a mortal threat when they saw one.

The post-war transformation took not much more than a quarter of a century. With their usual indifference to legalistic form, the British pragmatically adapted the Commonwealth, even assimilating republics into an institution hitherto united in allegiance to the Crown. They did not, as some Dominion statesmen would have preferred, withdraw into a racially homogeneous and still British Commonwealth of originally constituent members; they managed to keep vast Asian and African majorities within a sort of club, that time-honoured British invention, of which the rules like the British Constitution itself, remained conveniently unwritten. At the cost of the secession of South Africa and the defiance of Rhodesia, an always rather casual imperialism became even more tenuous, but still tenacious. It combined some of the most highly developed countries in the world, as the United Kingdom and Canada, with countries of ancient civilization but relatively limited technology, as well as with undeveloped states in tropical Africa. And in spite of the sheer loss of power and will, of popular apathy at the centre and of the hangover of resentment from colonialist times, the New Commonwealth has often assuaged the more violent forms of nationalism, the discrepancies of wealth and the tensions of colour, and helped its member states to resist exploitation by powers intent on a world conflict which would benefit none of them.

The New Commonwealth is often written off as so riven with distrust between the British and their former dependents and between the often incongruous members themselves that it cannot be taken seriously. Yet, as with all great empires, the British influence remains pervasive. In face of political tyranny and bureaucratic corruption and the rush of cosmopolitan managerial exploitation, the tradition of the rule of law, of parliamentary democracy, of the responsibility of governments to the governed, of tolerably just administration and respect for human rights, may still diminish the more flagrant abuses, humanize governments and protect basic liberties. Liberal social-democracy has not played its last card; and if the emancipated masses tend to follow charismatic leaders, and revert to more indigenous forms of government, since, in the absence of experienced elites, military and tribal rule has set in, the inherited apparatus of administration has remained, and the weakness is rather in lack of entrepreneurial talent following the anti-commercial 'administrative' bias of the former rulers. With experience, the new elites may well be able to revert to more flexible forms of government and to more sophisticated forms of power. If British direct influence has receded, it remains potentially important.

II

But before one considers further the quality of this influence, the stages of the transformation from Empire to independence and the prospects of the New Commonwealth demand attention.

Naturally it was in Ireland that the prelude was played out. Following the rebellion of 1916 and its variously ghastly sequels, Lloyd George had shelved the problem by partition. It appeared an ingenious solution, since a federal self-governing Dominion was impracticable. But it had proved in fact to be a failure: in 1921, only three years after the conclusion of the First World War, and at the metropolitan heart of the Empire, a spreading fissure had begun. If the British could not control Ireland, what could they control? The lesson was not lost on the Indian Congress Party, and on other dissidents throughout the Empire. The Anglo-Irish Treaty had been no more advantageous to the British than the Treaty of Vereeniging.

But it took the Second World War to set off the final and massive transformation. Significantly, in 1947 when India, Pakistan, Burma and Ceylon were emancipated, the Secretary of State for Dominion Affairs had become Secretary of State for Commonwealth Relations. And when in 1949 a Conference of Commonwealth Prime Ministers accepted the Republic of India into the Commonwealth they took a radical decision. 'Once the principle of republican membership of the Commonwealth had been conceded, the time had arrived for pronouncing obsequies over the doctrine of common allegiance.'[1] In 1953 the Queen became officially 'Head' of the Commonwealth. She remained Queen of the United Kingdom, Canada, Australia, New Zealand, even of South Africa; but for the Commonwealth, as such, the Crown had become entirely symbolic.[2]

Strategically and politically the transfer of power in the Indian

[1] S. A. de Smith, *The New Commonwealth and its Constitutions*, London, 1964, p. 13.

[2] *op. cit.* p. 17.

sub-continent was the most massive and epoch-making abdication. India had long been the most important area of the Empire, the military base of British domination in the East. Now it was abandoned, and with it British paramountcy of the Persian Gulf and southern Arabia. The power to protect East Africa, Malaya and Australasia was now greatly diminished: once India had gone, the rest would follow.

After this crucial decision, there followed an interval of mounting, diverse and prolonged crises: in Palestine, in Malaya, in Kenya, in Cyprus, and culminating in 1956, after Nasser had nationalized the Canal, in the resounding fiasco at Suez. Then after Ghana had become independent in 1957 and by 1960 a republic of equal status with the former Dominions—a portent paralleled by the departure of South Africa from the organization in the following year—there followed the swift emancipation of all the British colonies in Africa and, concurrently, of the major West Indies. In the Far East, Malaya, independent by 1957, became by 1963 part of a Malaysian Federation including Sarawak and Sabah. The British kept their military bases in Gibraltar, Malta and Cyprus, but they withdrew from Aden. By the 'seventies there would be, constitutionally speaking, hardly anything significant left, save in theory the rebellious Crown Colony of Rhodesia, which in 1965 had declared unilateral independence. The transformation from the British Commonwealth to the Commonwealth of Nations was complete.

III

What kind of countries were these equal members of the New Commonwealth? They presented an immense variety of environment, scale and tradition; and they were potential contributors to the world civilization already, following the advances of science and technology, on the horizon of the late twentieth century. Most of them would lapse into styles of government more indigenous and less exacting than the Western parliamentary model the British had imposed upon them; but they would retain much of its structure and a Western type of administration. Their charismatic leaders, like those of the late Roman Empire who had astutely placed themselves at the head of movements of mass emotion and discarded the exacting Stoic rationalism of the pagan elites, would be saviours and architects of prosperity: *Euergetoi*, with modern technology behind them. There would be *coups* and counter-*coups*, military takeovers, civil wars; but the new states would gradually become viable: new blends of civilization would emerge.

In Ireland the future had no such promise. Here, as in so much of the Empire and Commonwealth, Federation would have made sense : but Irish history made political compromise unlikely. Indeed, the Irish would lose their point if they succumbed to it. It had been no one's fault that the First World War had stalled Asquith's Home Rule Bill in 1914; but the Rebellion and its consequences had reflected centuries of conflict. The archaic vendettas of Protestant and Catholic Christians had been made more virulent by partition : in 1937 the Irish Free State had become the Republic of Eire, and by 1949 it had left the Commonwealth. Even then, the Southern Irish were racked with the sense of alien oppression; the millennial resistance of the only Celtic-Iberian people never politically subjugated by the Roman Empire went on, with the added fervour of modern nationalism. Northern Ireland, still an organic part of the United Kingdom, remained intransigent. The Treaty of 1921 had set off a civil war between the Southern Irish themselves; the very existence of Northern Ireland remained the symbol of 'Saxon' domination. The Irish, who had so greatly contributed to the creating of the British Empire, remained obstinately backward-looking and introspective within their island, though extremely enterprising outside it. Short of total abdication and throwing the island into internecine conflict, the British were still confronted with a problem that appeared insoluble. In the 'seventies the tragic insular conflict would flare up again, its motives incongruous in the twentieth century, but destined perhaps to be diluted in the island's membership of a European Common Market.

It had been the fate of the British, renowned in the nineteenth century, though not before it, for their 'phlegm', to rule Asian peoples as temperamental as the Southern Irish, and divided not merely by sectarian strife but by different religions and ways of life. In the subcontinent of India—like Europe a geographical rather than a political expression—a Federal Dominion had long been envisaged. Hatred between Muslims and Hindus had prevented it. The Hindu Congress Party were getting their own back on the Mughal Empire; the Muslim League remembered centuries of proud Muslim domination. In 1947 the *Pax Britannica*, the greatest British benefit to the sub-continent, had dissolved into mutual massacres : about half a million people were killed; six million Hindus and Sikhs had left Pakistan; six and a half million Muslims had left India in mass migrations unprecedented even in the history of Asia. There emerged out of the British *Rāj* the Indian Democratic Republic and Union of States—in Hindi *Bharat*—its capital at New Delhi, its emblem the lions on the Mauryan pillars at Sanarth, its population by 1967 over

511 million. Pakistan, by 1956 an Islamic Republic, had been improvised from territories eleven hundred miles apart, its western population nearly 54 million, its eastern about 59 million. Both India and Pakistan were peasant countries: India 82 per cent rural, Pakistan 90 per cent. The former had far greater resources and potential; the latter produced wheat and rice essential to the Indian economy. The partition had also cut across a mutual dependence on irrigation from the Indus: political and religious obsessions had exacted their price. Both states remained within the Commonwealth, though in 1948, 1966 and 1971 they would go to war.

The Indian prospect was the more hopeful. The Republic had inherited the British administration, most of it already run by Indians. A Council of States or *Rajya Sabha*, and a *Lok Sabha* or House of the Peoples, formed the legislature; a President was chosen by an elected College; the Prime Minister and Cabinet were responsible to the *Lok Sabha*. Though the vast majority of the people were illiterate, there was universal suffrage. A federal union combined a contrasting variety of states and the princely states were brought into it. Hyderabad by force. In Kashmir a Hindu Rajah ruled a population who were three-quarters Muslim, and in 1948, at the cost of war with Pakistan, India occupied most of the country; in Kerala a Communist regime was put down; in 1961 the Indians occupied Portuguese Goa. There was not much *Satyagraha* now.

But through all these vicissitudes the Congress Party retained control. The assassination of Gandhi had given the Republic a grim start, but Jawaharlal Nehru, who came of a wealthy Brahmin political family, originally from Kashmir, and who had been educated at Harrow and Cambridge and studied in the Middle Temple in London, proved a wary and successful statesman, faced by colossal problems within the country and following a policy of non-alignment outside it. Prime Minister until his death in 1964, his position remained unassailable and in 1967 his daughter Mrs Indira Gandhi followed him in the same office.

There were considerable assets. The British had left one of the largest state-owned railway systems in the world, which, unlike most of them, paid its way; the Second World War had left India with large sterling balances. Although the partition had dislocated transport and trade, the potential for tea and jute exports was vast. There was a wealth of timber, from the oaks and pines and deodars of the foothills of the colossal Himalayan mountain barrier that, with an average crest of 19,000 feet, protected northern India from the extremities of the central Asia climate, to the palms and mangroves of the

Bengal estuary and the teak forests of the south. There was, too, a potential wealth of coal and iron.

On the other hand, the difficulties and drawbacks were immense. The population was officially 83 per cent Hindu, only 10·7 per cent Muslim, 1·8 per cent Sikh; but there were profound linguistic divisions between the north, where the people spoke Punjabi, Hindi and Bengali—all Indo-Aryan speech—and the Dravidian-speaking south. The martial Rajputs of the north, the Brahmins of Uttar Pradesh, the highly educated Bengalis, the Banyas of Gujerat, contrasted with the Maratha farmers of Maharashtra and the Tamils of the south. When, according to schedule, Hindi became the official language, the Hindus were forced to retain English as well. The governing elites, like the British, were still a tiny minority in a sea of peasant illiteracy and a welter of languages and religions.

As all over Asia, farming was primitive, livestock of poor quality —the Constitution itself protected the sacred and dilapidated cows; nor, save for tamed elephants, are the Indian fauna often tangible assets—the bears in the Himalayas, the black buck, sambur and antelopes, or their diminishing predators, tiger and panther, jackals and wild dogs, and the maccaque and langur monkeys, the crocodiles and the ubiquitous kites.

Since 1952 a succession of five-year plans have made some headway in increasing agricultural and industrial production, but India remains dependent on the monsoons, on an elaborate and costly irrigation, on peasant farming, on huge loans from the United States and the British and the Soviet Union—an economic liability, its trade balance now adverse, its population far too big. In a civilization that has always made a cult of fertility, government has had to spend £20,000,000 on propaganda for birth control. The potential and grandeur of Indian civilization remains: it has acclimatized parliamentary government, and its strategic position and size make it a major fact in world politics, perhaps a potential leader of the neutralist states.

In Pakistan the British legacy was less lasting. It was an Islamic state, its population 88 per cent Muslim and 90 per cent rural. Sovereignty over the universe, proclaims its constitution, belongs to Allah, and even democracy is limited by the teachings of Islam. West Pakistan included the mountainous areas of Baluchistan and the Northwest Frontier, the deserts and irrigations of Sind; the Punjab, with its wheat and barley, its cool sunny winters and fierce summer heat. It included the big cities of Karachi and Lahore. East Pakistan, its capital at Dacca and centred on the Brahmaputra delta, was a flat rice-growing country, of mangrove swamps and floods and teeming population. The people were just as different. In the west, Punjabis who spoke Urdu, Baluchis, and Pushtu-speaking Pathans, the fiercest warrior tribesmen of the sub-continent. In the east, Bengali-speaking agriculturalists, a Hindu minority of nearly nine and a half millions, and a miscellany of primitive Moghs, Murungs, Parkoors and Kyangs of Mongoloid affinities.

Governments faced even more daunting problems than they did in India. Muhammad Ali Jinnah, the Quaid-i-Azam, great leader and main architect of Pakistan, had died in 1948, in the same year as Gandhi; three years later Liaquat Ali Khan, the Prime Minister, had been assassinated. By 1958 Ayub Khan, the Commander-in-Chief, proclaimed martial law. His presidential regime, by 1962 supported by a revised constitution, had considerable success. The peasant majority was brought through local councils into a drive for better production. By the mid-'sixties the country was self-supporting in cereals, if not in rice. Jute and cotton, hides, sugar and tobacco were exported, timber and fisheries developed. But the regime was basically conservative, the main assets of the country in the hands of a few great capitalists; there was widespread discontent and, when in 1969 Ayub Khan resigned, the Army under Yahya Khan again took control. More radical reforms were attempted, a massive campaign against illiteracy and corruption in the educational system launched, the constitution made more democratic. But when in 1971 nationalists in East Pakistan broke into revolt and India again attacked, Bangladesh—the land of Bengal—would hive off as a separate state. Like the initial massacres, it was a predictable outcome of a desperate remedy. In fear of India, Pakistan has established close links with the Communist powers, but its affinities are more with Iran and Turkey, Muslim powers which were modernized by methods other than parliamentary democracy. Still in dire need of capital investment and foreign loans to develop its industries, Pakistan now looks more to them than to the West, while in 1971 India made a 'Treaty of Friendship' with the U.S.S.R.

The sovereign republic of Burma or Myanma, with a population of over twenty-five million, and independent by January 1948, had at once left the Commonwealth. By 1962 it had reverted to a military dictatorship more consistent with its past than the parliamentary democracy devised after the eviction of the Japanese. Here the British influence had proved ephemeral: indeed 'if the idea of the rule of law ever took root in Burma at all it was but a tender plant and has now totally died out, except perhaps in the inner recesses of the minds of a few of Burma's distinguished lawyers trained in the West'.[3]

[3] F. S. V. Donnison, *Burma*, London, 1970, p. 244.

The omens had always been adverse. Three months before Independence, Aung San, who with astute timing had helped to evict the Japanese and become its main architect, had been shot down along with seven colleagues by political gunmen. The Burmese Union had always been artificial, it now threatened to break up. Besides the predominant Burmese with their agglutinative monosyllabic language akin to Chinese, though written in characters derived from Pali, Karens in the Irrawaddy delta, Shans in the east, Cachins in the north, all spoke different languages. There were regional revolts, infiltration by the Chinese, a communist rebellion, with difficulty put down.

The country was overwhelmingly rural. Oil and coal resources were considerable, silver and lead were mined, jade exported to China. But the essential exports were rice, timber and cotton. The rich alluvial soils of the Irrawaddy, Chindwin and Sittang produced an enormous rice crop, as well as sugar cane, cotton and tobacco, much in demand for the ubiquitous Burmese cheroots.

Intent on developing these resources, Premier U Nu had set about nationalizing as much of the economy as he could and avoiding commitment to either great power bloc. He wanted Burma for the Burmese. The British had preserved and developed the forests that covered half Burma—in particular the monsoon teak forest and tidal forests of the south. The rice export had been the foundation of the economy. Soon both assets had been run down: by 1967 Burma, which had left the sterling area the year before, would hardly be self-sufficient even in rice. When in 1962 the Sino-Burmese General Ne Win made his *coup* and imprisoned the Prime Minister for six years, the political and economic situations had both greatly deteriorated.

Many Burmese did not mind: they wanted to opt out of the twentieth century and turn inwards on their own tradition, content with life in villages of bamboo and thatch, with Buddhist *pongyis* living on the alms of those anxious to acquire merit, with building even more pagodas, with their ancient theatre, their gongs and festivals. But the general was a Marxist, claiming to represent the vanguard of peasants and workers, and determined to clean up the corruption of an inefficient social democracy. So when in 1968, baffled by the immense difficulties, Ne Win released U Nu and other politicians to advise on 'Internal Unity', he promptly turned down their disarming suggestion that the former Prime Minister should be restored to office. The Burmese thus reverted to a regime more akin to their old monarchy. After all, like the Maoris, they had always distinguished between themselves, as *Lu* 'true men', fully human, and peoples of other races: even the Chinese were *Tayok*; as for anyone else, they were just *Kala*—foreign barbarians.[4]

The people of Ceylon, independent with Dominion status by 1948, had wider horizons. The island had always been a centre of oceanic commerce and communications and much longer subjected to Europeans. Here, in miniature, elaborate conflicts would occur between Buddhist Sinhalese and Hindu Tamils, spiced with the latest Marxist–Leninist and Trotskyite doctrines of Westernized politicians. But the constitution remained conservative; it included a Governor-General, representing the Crown, and it would not be until 1972 that the island would become the republic of *Sri (Blessed) Lanka*. At first the richer European and Sinhalese planters and the Muslim merchants of Colombo—the population was more than half a million—had retained their political power; but the mainly agricultural country was basically poor, and post-war recession and inflation went along with a rise of population to ten and a half million by 1963. Over seven million were Sinhalese and two million indigenous or immigrant Tamils.

Here was the chance for militant nationalists and communists, and parliamentary government had a rough ride. In 1952 the able Prime Minister D. S. Senanayake, leader of the moderate United National Party, had been killed in a riding accident, and then S. W. R. D. Bandaranaike, whose Sinhalese and Buddhist Freedom Party had attained power by 1956, had been shot in 1959 by an infuriated Buddhist monk, disappointed of academic promotion. Next year Mrs Sivima Bandaranaike had made history by becoming the first woman to become a Prime Minister anywhere; but her regime, like those of Mrs Meir in Israel and Mrs Gandhi in India, could not afford to be mild. Her government nationalized key industries and banks; too much dependent on the world price of tea, the economy deteriorated —there were strikes and a state of emergency. But after a conservative interval under Senanayake's son, in 1970, Mrs Bandaranaike, in coalition with communist groups returned to power, to be confronted in the following year by attempted revolution reflecting widespread unemployment and poverty, and only put down by armed force. This turbulence was due to the poverty of the masses, the communal hatreds between Tamils and Sinhalese, and the very success of Ceylonese medicine and education which had produced a population explosion and an intellectual proletariat.

No government could have satisfied the popular demands, and all governments had to contend with strikes and riots: but the structure of British administration had survived, military dictatorship had

[4] Donniston, *op. cit.* p. 231.

been avoided, and the island, whose Prime Minister, in 1950, had devised the Colombo plan to help underdeveloped areas of Asia, had remained within the Commonwealth. Dependent as was their island on overseas trade, the Sinhalese had asserted and traded a Buddhist Asian personality against both power blocs; but they had not, like the Burmese, turned their backs on the modern world.

Such were the four Asian states launched into independence by the British in 1947–8. All had reverted to their pre-colonialist traditions. In every state major political leaders had been assassinated: Gandhi, Liaquat Ali Khan, Aung San, Bandaranaike. All had reacted to the twentieth century after their kind. But, save in Burma, the British legacy had proved decisive, and most decisive in India, not just a state but a civilization. All have been overshadowed by the struggle between the super-powers, first polarized between the West and the U.S.S.R., then triangulated by the rise of China and the rift between the Russian and Chinese communists. All had done their best to avoid commitment in the imbecile competition, though willing to exploit it. All are basically peasant countries, with relatively underdeveloped industries and inadequate capital investment—their rulers faced with the colossal responsibilities of reconciling contrasting races and religions, and delivering the goods to increasingly demanding peoples. In a world of increasing uniformity and drabness all, as the British had intended, have remained themselves.

IV

The swift abdication in India had deprived the British of the broad strategic base of their power in the East. In the Middle East the mandate in Palestine became untenable, and broke down after the British withdrawal into the Arab–Israeli war of 1948 and the emergence of the state of Israel. In the same year, following the rise to power of Mao Tse-tung in China, communist guerrillas began to penetrate Malaya, where for twelve years the British had to fight a jungle war; in Kenya the Mau-Mau rising among the Kikuyu, with its atavistic rituals and atrocities, created another long state of emergency; and in Cyprus nationalist rebellion flared up. In 1956, following the failure at Suez, the Anglo-Egyptian condominium over the Sudan was dissolved; and the Sudan with a population of about fifteen million, one of the least educated in Africa, with 171 languages, became an independent state. It would be ruled and exploited from Khartoum in the north, though, oddly, its emblem was a rhinoceros between palm-trees, a beast of the equatorial south. Predictably, by 1958 a military regime had taken over; indeed, as more African states gained independence, the road to power would lie more often through Sandhurst than by way of a university.

By 1957 the British had had enough. The Macmillan government decided to speed up an accepted policy and climb down before being pushed out. Following the emancipation of Ghana in that year, all the African colonies except Rhodesia were launched into independence. They were as colourful and various as the former Asian dependencies, but in a different way. In West Africa they were rooted in ancient cultures; but in East and south Central Africa modernity had often been imposed on barbarism. It is interesting to consider the results.

Of the forty states which emerged out of colonial Africa only Ethiopia and Liberia had not been colonized by Europeans, and boundaries were generally artificial. The imposition of the Western structure of nation-states was incongruous in tribal societies, and the first problem of the new governments was to hold them together. They had to assess their resources, develop the communications and transport left by the colonial governments, adapt and acclimatize their rural and illiterate people to urban life and modern agriculture. Even in colonial times capital investment had been inadequate and production had been low; it was now apt to deteriorate. And most of the economies were too dependent on a single crop. On the other hand, in contrast to the Asian states, the African nations were under-populated for their size; and save for Nigeria, with a population of nearly fifty-eight million, none of the former British colonies in Africa had more than ten and a half million inhabitants (the population of Ceylon), and many much less. The task before the governments was thus herculean; but the tiny elites were seldom weighed down by the burdens of tradition, religious hatreds and over-population as in the old countries of Asia, though tribal feuds could be disruptive.

The first and most sensational experiment was launched in West Africa. Here, in 1960 the Republic of Ghana, its flag three equal horizontal stripes in red, white and green with an evocative black star on the white stripe, had emerged from the Gold Coast Colony and mandated Togoland. Its capital was at Accra and its population by 1970 about eight and a half million. Its President, Kwame Nkrumah, was a militant prophet of Pan-African union and his National Party 'the vanguard of the people in the struggle to build a socialist society'. He was the most charismatic of African leaders, playing out his part on a world stage.

Here in a climate that averaged more than 80° and where the moist monsoon air from the mid-Atlantic met the dry Harmattan from the Sahara in crashing thunderstorms and torrential rain, half the world's supply of cocoa was raised, mainly by small farmers cultivating a couple of acres. It was a predominantly flat country, its most fertile area the great estuary of the Volta, harnessed in the 'sixties for electric power by the Volta dam. Oil-palms, bananas, cassava and sorghum, maize and ground-nuts flourished. There was a wealth of tropical fauna: as the brilliantly striped Bongo forest antelopes, hartebeests, bushbuck and *duiker*[5] (or 'diver') in the savannah, as well as a noxious variety of giant ants, green mambas, scorpions and kites. There were plenty of pigs and poultry; the coast and estuaries swarmed with fish.

In this relatively prosperous setting, where a literate middle class had been long established, the populace were 42 per cent Christian; the rest, save for a few Muslims, animist pagan. Their paramount chiefs·with their stools and umbrellas retained much prestige, while the ancient feuds of Fanti and Ashanti had been assuaged. And the colonialist legacy had been substantial. Prospects were good; and although the talented Nkrumah, who had imposed single-party rule by 1960, soon became corrupted by power, developed delusions of grandeur, even, it was said, of divinity, and by 1966 had to go, the military junta who took over have restored a more democratic form of government.

The Federation of Nigeria had been the model colony of British tropical Africa; with its large area and population, rich oil and timber resources, its standing army of 300,000 men, it looked the most promising and powerful of the new states. It even had a favourable trade balance. But, in fact, when Nigeria, with part of the British Cameroons included, and already independent by 1960, had become a republic in 1963, it proved politically brittle. Its very prosperity set off competition for its oil-wells, and the basic contrast between the Muslim Fulani and Hausa, pastoral people of the savannah, and the Christian or pagan negroes of the rain-forest proved disruptive. There were four major languages, Fulani and Hausa in the northern plateau, Ibo and Yoruba in the negrolands; in the north nearly half the people were Muslim; in the south a third were Christian. The ancient hierarchic city-states, the semi-divine kings, the cult associations and secret societies, the tribal loyalties, all made for disruption. By 1966 a mutiny of the Ibos, who murdered the Federal Prime Minister, was put down by Hausa regiments under General Yakobo Gowon; next year Colonel Ozukwa proclaimed an independent Biafra in eastern Nigeria and took Benin. After severe casual-

---

[5] So-called from 'the animals habit of leaping high out of long grass and plunging into it from aloft head first'. E. G. Boulenger, *World Natural History*, with an introduction by H. G. Wells, London, 1937, p. 90.

ties, famine and devastation, Biafra was suppressed, and the new Federal Constitution of twelve states given a chance to prove itself.

In spite of these disasters, the economy of the country remained sound. Apart from the vast oil-fields, the palm-oil for soap and margarine, the mahogany and ebony, the kapok and the iron-ore, the peasant economy has proved resilient, though literacy is among the lowest in the continent. The most populous country in all Africa retains its economic and political potential.

No such promise had illuminated the prospects of Sierra Leone when in 1961 it, too, became independent. Here an unhealthy coastal plain was backed by high wooded hills and the Mende and Temne tribesmen had been among the more primitive Africans. The population was under three million, the capital Freetown. The main crop was rice diversified by cocoa, pepper and pimentos. There were diamonds, often irregularly marketed and so causing concern in the world diamond industry. The fauna were diverse: including bush pigs and civet cats; in the estuaries hippopotami and manatees; tarpon and barracuda in the ocean. But the economy had been improved by Creole negroes from the West Indies who had returned to the land of their ancestors and the Christians were catered for by a Roman Catholic Archbishop of Freetown and Bo, and by an Anglican bishop of West Africa.

By 1967, following the death three years earlier of the able civilian, Sir Milton Margai, and consequent conflicts, the Army took control. The next year, its N.C.O.s overthrew their officers and restored a civilian form of government. A republic by 1971, Sierra Leone faces a predictably uncertain future.

Gambia, the old British colony in West Africa, was economically even less viable, its main asset the deep Gambia River navigable far into the interior, but whose headwaters were in the former French colony of Senegal. Here Mandingo tribesmen raised rice in paddy fields reclaimed from mangrove swamps, and the main export was oil-seeds. There are Nile crocodiles in the Gambia, though how they got there is hard to say, and crops suffer the depredations of baboons. Independent in 1965 and by 1970 a republic within the Commonwealth, Gambia is a typically artificial creation of the partition of Africa. Only, it would seem, within a wider economic context can it be more viable.

On the other side of Africa another clutch of independent states had been loosed, with great variety of environment and potential. How did these often synthetic nations shape?

On balance, the account is favourable, for here there was often a relatively clean canvas. Somalia, devised in 1960 out of British Somaliland and the mandated territory formerly colonized by the Italians, known to the ancient Egyptians as the land of Punt, whence had come frankincense and ostrich feathers, was the most heavily handicapped. North it faces southern Arabia across the Gulf of Aden, and here temperatures can average 108°, with a rainfall of three inches a year. It is a country of scrub and sand, better for camels and ostriches than mankind. South, below the Horn of Africa, tropical agriculture and banana groves supported a more settled population—the Sab—despised by the nomadic Muslim Cushites who fight over the wells in the north. It is a land of zebra and wild asses, of koodoo and dik-dik antelopes, of warthogs and baboons. There are even some surviving lions with their attendant hyenas. There are no railways. Save for an export of bananas to Italy, here is a subsistence economy, pastoral or crudely agricultural. Here about two and three-quarter million people, their birth rate the highest and their literacy the lowest in Africa, have been grouped under a democratic Muslim republic, its capital at Mogadishu, the supporters of its heraldic shield two leopards rampant. By 1969 it had become a military dictatorship. The 'mad Mullah' had not fought in vain.

The neighbouring state of Kenya, independent in 1963, with a population of about nine and a half million, 97 per cent African, had emerged from severe vicissitudes. The settlement of Europeans on vast estates in the Kenya highlands at the expense both of the Masai and of the Kikuyu, whom they had formerly raided, had created fierce resentment; and although the colonialist regime had tentatively collaborated with Africans, the resistance had culminated in the long Mau-Mau rising, which had subjected its adherents to hideous rituals to destroy their tribal loyalty and induce ruthless commitment. After independence, Jomo Kenyatta, who, after reading anthropology at the London School of Economics and writing a study of the Kikuyu, had been imprisoned for years for complicity with the Mau-Mau rebellion, had become, first, Prime Minister, then President of the independent state. But the hatred of other tribes for the dominant Kikuyu and Luo still raised tensions, which demanded all Kenyatta's formidable powers. In spite of this background, here constitutional government has survived, and conciliation has often succeeded.

This fine country is one of great contrast, from snow-capped Mt Kenya, over 17,000 feet, to the palm-fringed coast at Mombasa. Its famous and relatively undiminished wild life includes antelope, gazelle, impala, zebra and giraffe; lion and cheetah; huge flocks of flamingos and pelicans. The Tsavo game park is only one of the reserves created by policies more enlightened than those now common in black Africa.

West of Kenya across the northern part of Lake Victoria lies the ancient kingdom of Uganda, independent by 1962. The most elaborate in tropical East Africa and long the most remote, it is the most prosperous of the new states, with big exports of cotton and coffee; it has copper-mines in the Ruwenzori mountains, and the peasants work a rich tropical agriculture. Hydro-electric power has been developed at the Owen and Murchison Falls, and light industries process coffee, cotton, sugar and tobacco. Large herds of humped zebu cattle are pastured on the savannah and European strains have been acclimatized. There are elephant, buffalo, eland, kudu. The lakes swarm with fish. The population of about eight and a half million in 1958 is largely self-supporting and there is a favourable balance of trade.

Politically Uganda has been less successful. Even as a protectorate it had been artificial, and the predominant Baganda around Lake Victoria resented federation with the outlying Bunyora, Toro, Ankole and Busoga. In 1953–5 the Kabaka Mutesa II had been deported by the British for refusing to collaborate. With independence he consented to be a constitutional President, but by 1966 Milton Obote, the Prime Minister and leader of the People's Party, drove him from the country, and the descendant of semi-divine kings died in penury and exile. In turn, Obote was himself ousted by General Amin who dissolved the Parliament and established a military dictatorship, intolerant, to put it mildly, of foreigners.

The economy has remained sound: Makerere University College, by 1970 a University, was the most flourishing in East Africa, and Kampala, the natural centre of communication and commerce, has over three hundred thousand inhabitants. The problems of Uganda have been more tribal than racial or economic.

Neighbouring Kenya and Uganda to the south, lies Tanzania, its capital Dar-es-Salaam, which gained its independence in 1964. The President Julius Nyerere has managed to reconcile about eleven million variegated tribesmen of the high interior of Tanganyika with three-quarters of a million urban Zanzibaris and Pembans, some of whose ancestors lived very well off the tribesmen through the slave-trade. Here, even more than in Kenya, geographical contrasts are extraordinary. Kilimanjaro at 19,340 feet has perpetual snow and ice and its slopes harbour mountain gorillas; the immense plateau with its brisk dry air and sunshine contains the headwaters of the Nile, the Congo and the Zambesi, and swarms with big game; Zanzibar and Pemba on the India Ocean, humid and tropical, are rich in cloves, citrus orchards, mangos, palms, *bêches-de-mer* and fisheries.

Life in the highlands, long terrorized by slavers, is still primitive and pagan, dependent on a sparse uncertain rainfall. The tsetse fly limits livestock; and locusts are a menace, both combatted by government. But the western forests above Lake Tanganyika contain valuable timber, as well as chimpanzees, and conservation, developed over the last decade, is a priority. Eighty per cent of the people are agriculturalists, but there is considerable mineral wealth, and hydro-electric power has been developed.

Nyerere, a former graduate of Makerere and Edinburgh Universities, and a Catholic, came to power as leader of the Tanganyika African National Union, and while in principle non-aligned in the world-power struggle, he has got help from both sides, including China. After all, in the early fifteenth century great Chinese fleets had dominated the Indian Ocean before anyone had heard of the Portuguese.

Such have been the beginnings of the three independent states launched by the British in East Africa; and the East African community set up in 1967, with a common market, economic and social councils, and headquarters at Arusha in Tanzania, has considerably offset political divisions.

In East Africa the Africans so completely outnumbered anyone else, that African rule was inevitable. But in British Central Africa substantial European settlement and investment created an acute political problem. By 1962 the economically viable federation of Northern and Southern Rhodesia and Nyasaland devised in 1953 had broken up. Two years later Northern Rhodesia, its copper-belt second only to that in the United States, had hived off in the Republic of Zambia, its capital Lusaka, its motto 'One Zambia, one Nation', its President Kenneth Kaunda. The three and a half million Bantu on the Lundi uplands and the Barotse plains cultivated maize and tobacco and there was good timber; but copper provided 90 per cent of exports, dependent on transport in Rhodesia, now again a Crown Colony, though with a kind of dominion status.

Here the British faced an acute dilemma : whether to alienate all black Africa—in particular the new states within the Commonwealth —by acquiescing in European domination in a colony, at least in theory, under metropolitan control, or to alienate the settlers who had transformed the economy and were determined to maintain political supremacy. Economic sanctions, applied after the colony had declared unilateral independence, would in fact hit Zambia more than Rhodesia. Nyasaland, now independent as Malawi, though in

economic terms poor, was more self-sufficient; it possessed a relatively prosperous agriculture, and its President, Dr Hastings Banda,
proved authoritarian, capable and astute.

Southwest of Rhodesia, the large area of Bechuanaland, including
the Kalahari Desert and the Okarango swamps, had much potential
mineral wealth. With a population of about 600,000 it became independent as Botswana, while Basutoland became Lesotho, its inhabitants just under a million. The Kingdom of Swaziland, founded in
1846 by Mswazi who had fought off the Zulus, had been accorded
internal self-government in 1883. Here about 374,000 people raised
cotton, cereals, sugar and livestock: there was good irrigation and
extensive forest. Independent by 1968, its capital at Mbabane, and
subsidized by the Colonial Development Fund, the country has
proved viable.

So, by the end of the 'sixties, in a broad and hasty sweep, the
British launched all their colonies in Africa, save Rhodesia, into
independence; and Rhodesia, as might be expected from its history,
had proclaimed its own.

V

The relatively small populations, huge areas and undeveloped
economies of Africa contrasted with the ancient, complicated and
wealthy pattern of the main British possessions in Southeast Asia.
Here, following the eviction of the Japanese, the Federation of
Malaya had been reconstituted. Independent by 1957, it lay on the
periphery of communist China, and the guerrilla infiltration, though
mastered, had not been eradicated. Then, in 1963, on Malayan
initiative and backed by the British, a more ambitious Federation
of Malaysia was devised, including Sarawak and Sabah across 1,600
miles of sea. Its capital was at Kuala Lumpur and at first it included
Singapore. But since the latter depended on free-trade and Malaya on
customs revenues, two years later the island set up its own polyglot
republic, the official languages being Malay, English, Tamil and
Mandarin. In Malaysia, as in Singapore, constitutional government
had survived.

Hardly had the Chinese communist infiltration been scotched,
than a new threat developed from the southeast. The British now
had to defend Malaysia against Indonesian attack and Philippino
hostility. By 1964 British, Australian, Malayan and Gurkha forces
were fighting in the matted jungles of North Borneo; Indonesian
commandos attacked Malaya itself. With the decline of Sukarno's
power, peace was patched up, and the dispute taken to the United

Nations for a less exacting confrontation. The rich and strategically important area had been kept within the Commonwealth. But here, again, the British had had enough. They would gradually withdraw from military commitments in Southeast Asia.

In the Pacific, meanwhile, by 1962 Western Samoa, formerly in trust to New Zealand, had left the Commonwealth; but in 1970, Fiji, always a more successful administration, became autonomous within it, its able Prime Minister, Sir Kamisase Mara. But the security of the Pacific, like that of Southeast Asia and Australia, now depended on American strategic power.

In the Caribbean, as in central Africa, though not in Malaysia, the stock remedy of Federation failed. In 1962 Jamaica left the Federation of 1958, and this broke up. The variety of islands and population, the contrasts in economic development, the self-interest of local politicians, had wrecked it. During the 'sixties Jamaica, Barbados, Trinidad and Tobago and British Guiana were all launched into independence within the Commonwealth, the last in 1969, as the Republic of Guyana.

VI

In the strategic bases that had linked the Empire the British long held on to all they could. Cyprus had proved the worst problem. The Christian Greek-Cypriots wanted *enosis*—union with Greece; the Muslim Turkish minority was irreconcilable to it. A conflict older than that in Ireland or India, going back into classical antiquity when the Greeks had fought Persians, Europeans against Asians, was here often complicated by the resentment of the Cypriots at being treated by the British as if they were a 'colonial' and primitive people, instead of the heirs of a civilization ancient when the British were barbarians.

After the war, the demand for *enosis*, already militant in the 'thirties, had become more strident. The British had tried military repression, and in 1956 had deported Archbishop Makarios to the Seychelles. But he had been moderate compared to Colonel Grivas, the guerrilla leader of E.O.K.A. (the National Organization for Cypriot Struggle). So the political archbishop was brought back and proved willing to settle, not for union with Greece but for an independent Cypriot state. In 1960 after the Greek- and Turkish-Cypriots had met in neutral Zürich, Cyprus became an independent republic outside the Commonwealth, subsidized by the British to the tune of £12,000,000. The imposing and wily Makarios became its first President; the Vice-President, Dr Kutchuk, represented the Turks. In the following year it looked as if conciliation had succeeded: the new republic rejoined the Commonwealth.

In the event the constitutionally elaborate compromise failed to work: nationalist, racial and religious passions were too strong and, although the British managed to retain enclaves for their military bases on the island, they were reduced, as at Suez, to handing over to a United Nations peace-keeping force.

In Malta, following the Second World War, enthusiasm for union with Italy had naturally diminished, and here again the British had tried conciliation. Since 1921 the Crown Colony had been accorded internal self-government; restored in 1947, it was limited only by British control of external affairs. But when in 1955 the nationalist Dom Mintoff proposed that Malta should become part of metropolitan Great Britain, and be represented in the British Parliament, the Catholic hierarchy within the island would have none of it. In 1964 Malta became an independent state within the Commonwealth, heavily dependent on British subsidies and the obsolescent British dockyards, while the British maintained their bases on the island. Political autonomy and strategic importance were here complicated by the presence of N.A.T.O. headquarters in Valetta. If the strategic importance was now negative, the communist power had still to be kept out. So Mintoff astutely put the island up for auction, and got away with increased subsidies, not just from Great Britain but from the N.A.T.O. powers.

In Aden, the British held on tenaciously. Since 1937 a Crown Colony, it had been merged in 1963 into the Federation of South Arabia. But here again, Federation failed: the economic and social discrepancies broke it up. A National Liberation Front began to shoot it out with the Yemenis, and in 1967, following attacks on them fomented by the Egyptians, the British pulled out. They handed over to the prevalent National Liberation Front, and Aden became an independent republic, part of the Republic of South Yemen, which included Perim, Kamarin and Socotra. With the closing of the Suez Canal, Aden's strategic importance has diminished, and it has reverted to a Southern Arabian orbit.

Gibraltar, the oldest strategic base, remained a Crown Colony. Here about twenty-six thousand people in the huddled town under the Rock depended entirely on imported supplies. Even the Spanish workers in the docks had to trek daily across the causeway joining the fortress to Spain. With the closing of the Suez Canal, port traffic had diminished; moreover Madrid demanded 'decolonization' and hampered communications by land and sea.

This move commanded little support from Gibraltarians. In

1967 they voted to remain a British Colony by 12,138 to 44. Two years later the British gave complete self-government to an elected Assembly, reserving only defence, security and external affairs. They also subsidized the precarious economy. Since the Rock retains some strategic value and the people have no mind for union with Spain, the British seem likely to stay there. The Maltese and Cypriots, on the other hand, with deep-rooted civilizations behind them, are reverting to their natural Mediterranean ways of life, with the often incongruous British veneer diminished.

So, across the enormous area, by premeditated intention speeded up by two World Wars, the peoples of the New Commonwealth of Nations have been launched from Empire into independence. By 1946 the oldest dominion, Canada, had asserted separate citizenship and soon the Australians and New Zealanders had followed. By 1948 the metropolitan British themselves had to assert their own identity: a British subject is now a citizen of the United Kingdom and Colonies, and there are not many of them.

VII

The remaining ties look tenuous and diminishing: visits of the Monarch, as Head of the Commonwealth, and of the Royal Family; or by the current Prime Minister or his colleagues; conferences of Prime Ministers held outside Great Britain, as at Lagos in 1966 and Singapore in 1971, and then hardly a success. The economic ties are considerable: aid of £420,000,000 from 1951 to 1967; British investment, still three times as much as American; the waning attractions of the sterling area discredited by successive devaluations. Since 1965, of course, a Commonwealth Secretariat in London, its Secretary-General a Canadian, has provided information and furthered contacts. The network of ecclesiastical hierarchies and missionary organizations continues intact. An association of Commonwealth Universities promotes academic intercourse; a pervasive influence is the growing circulation of British books and the increasing speed and cheapness of air travel. But the British hold on administration and technology is challenged by the Americans, Continental Europeans, Russians and Chinese; many students from the Commonwealth now go to universities outside it. As the world becomes more cosmopolitan the exclusively British influence is bound to wane. Only so long as all concerned think them worth while can the ties of the Commonwealth continue. At present most governments of the countries concerned seem to think they are.

VIII

In 1922 the American philosopher, George Santayana, wrote enthusiastically of the British Empire, 'Never since the days of heroic Greece has the world had such a sweet, just, boyish master. It will be a black day for the human race when scientific blackguards, churls and fanatics manage to supplant him.' If he wildly romanticized both the Ancient Greeks and the British, perhaps, after half a century, many people would, in principle, agree with his conclusion.

For the world into which the states of the New Commonwealth have been launched is extremely dangerous: riven with ideological conflicts, nationalist passions, economic maladjustment and the mutual animosities of colour; seething with the revolution of rising expectations. Civilization exists under a balance of terror maintained by the mutual nuclear blackmail of the super-powers, and nuclear weapons may well proliferate to lesser states. The countries of the New Commonwealth are subjected to fanatical nineteenth-century doctrines seeking to pull them into a global class conflict irrelevant to their needs. The United Nations may give them a forum; it cannot give them security. And behind the immediate political dangers and in both the Western and the communist societies, a worldwide managerial elite are extending their control over the peoples and their environments, and technology is pervading and dictating the patterns of life. The threats to liberty are many and urgent: and perhaps, in so-called undeveloped areas with strong indigenous traditions, more open societies may better survive.

Meanwhile, no sensible historian would confuse the immediate waning of the British Empire with its long-term legacy: the last and greatest of the European sea-borne Empires, and the one dismantled and transformed with the least friction, is unlikely to be an ephemeral influence. And its peoples have certainly been better equipped to face the current dangers.

The most obvious and pervasive legacy is the language. The United States emerged from the British Empire, and English in various idioms and intonations is now the most widespread world language, and with it goes a world literature. English is essential in politics, administration and business, in science and medicine, in universities and schools and mass communication. As the Romance tongues of Europe descend from Latin, so English, in changing and various forms, will obviously have as lasting an influence. Already some Asians and Africans now speak it better than many of the British. In the perspective of world history a whole new English-speaking culture is in the offing, which will reflect the rich contrasts in traditions and environment of the Commonwealth peoples. If the island base itself subsides into a suburban egalitarianism while its elites become cosmopolitan Europeans, other power-houses of energy and civilization may take over.

The political legacy is also decisive. The rule of law, parliamentary government and the institutions and routine of relatively efficient administration, are the best answer so far evolved to the problems of combining liberty and order. They are of all forms of public power the least oppressive and the most flexible; the most likely to adapt societies to the changing facts of power and the demands of their people without the damaging interludes of revolution and counter-revolution and the consequent abuses of arbitrary power.

In the Dominions of Settlement now within the Commonwealth this legacy is secure. It has survived in India, far the largest of the former dependencies; and if this exacting model, exported to more primitive societies, has often been supplanted by more primitive and authoritarian regimes consistent with their pre-colonial past, here is nothing surprising. History does not proceed by leaps; it takes decades and even centuries for peoples to adapt, and in public as in private life the dead generally rule the living. If the Liberal Experiment even in the countries that invented it is becoming precarious, it can hardly be expected to take on at once in countries where it is alien, and where the urgent social needs are stark and rudimentary. Moreover, though authoritarian governments may have taken over, the structure of administration, of law-courts, of local government have remained: standards have been set. Contacts with politically more mature societies have been maintained, both through the Commonwealth and the United Nations—itself a form, if as yet an ineffective one, of constitutionalism.

In spite of appearances—a nightmare of archaic-style political conflict—the most important facts of the late twentieth century are the rise of science and technology. Both are global; both are dragging mankind and its old institutions into new ways of life, government and administration. And here the British legacy has been of cardinal importance. The Romans brought law; the British brought steam as well. The infra-structure of the Indian administration and economy was created by the British in railways and irrigation; the medical advances they pioneered have led to the doubtful benefit of a population explosion and also to its potential control. Better farming can bring far more benefits to undernourished peoples than any amount of political wizardry. Add to this that British explorers and missionaries often first revealed huge countries to their own inhabitants, and brought peoples confined to tribal areas into contact with the modern world. The Empire after all, was not, as its enemies allege, ever a mere instrument of exploitation; in its own interests it brought huge areas into the orbit of the most advanced civilization on the planet. And this legacy has remained in fields fundamental to any modern society.

Equally important is the structure of education left by the British, which still best maintains the Commonwealth as a credible institution. Technology and administration are useless without the people to run them, and the most pressing problem in the new states is how to produce elites who can. Nor is it possible to conduct a modern economy if the bulk of the peoples is illiterate. So here from the elementary school to the university is a most important legacy and one which, under all the political conflicts, is still being continuously developed.

Other British influences are patently apparent. The British, after all, invented modern organized games. Apart from blood-sports and horse-racing, constant in all aristocracies, the British founded the cult of football and cricket, so that Maoris excel at the former and West Indians at the latter, and the annual fixtures command vast popular interest, when not bedevilled by political agitation. These bloodless circuses have greatly improved on popular entertainments current in the Roman Empire; among like-minded peoples they can even diminish the prejudices of colour. For this cult of sport has now become worldwide, culminating in the Olympic events which are increasingly cosmopolitan.

The Commonwealth and Great Britain itself cannot resist the tides of cosmopolitan change which are blending local cultures together as nation states and even regional self-sufficiency become more plainly obsolescent. For the overwhelming fact of our time is the rise of a global civilization, and if and when world order is achieved the central problem may well be how to preserve the old variety of cultures within it. Whatever the event, this global civilization will be a blend of cultures which will no longer be dominated by Europeans. It will probably make much of the old British tradition look provincial and puritanical, but if it is to be truly civilized and creative it will need the British tradition of the rule of law, self-government and toleration. Civilization, after all, is a state of mind.

So now that the British Empire and Commonwealth are receding into history, and as those who have been part of them come to sort out the surviving benefits from the disadvantages with calmer minds, we may conclude that its swift political collapse and transformation need not deeply offset its long-term and, on balance, salutary achievement.

As previously emphasized, it has not gone down in ruin; it has not been overrun. The sheer size of this last of the European maritime dominations always made it more fragile than it looked: most of the mid-Victorians never expected it to last. It was only the liberal imperialists of the defensive climax who tried to make it endure by a gradual devolution of power and the grant of 'Dominion status' as the dependent peoples came to political maturity. And in some sense, though Imperial Federation proved a dream, not least because the British themselves, following the experience of the Irish in the Commons, would never have accepted a representatively imperial Parliament, these liberal hopes have in part been realized, in that the Commonwealth has been deeply influenced by British ideas: of compromise, of relative tolerance, of pragmatic commonsense which discards ideologies.

In the Preface to this work it was remarked that the British would 'hardly achieve a clearer sense of confidence and purpose within the European Community on a basis of collective amnesia', that Continental Europeans 'naturally want to know what the islanders are like', and that those outside Europe who have been part of the British Empire may now, following its transformation, want to take an objective view of it. It is hoped that the preceding pages may have furthered these aims. In retrospect, three conclusions at least seem plain: the vigour and enterprise which went into the creation of the Empire, the good sense that set about its transformation, and the promise to which that transformation has given rise. For the British Empire and Commonwealth have been and still are a lasting influence, going far beyond the fortunes of the island base—in the Americas, in Asia and Africa, in Australasia and the Pacific. The English-speaking peoples and those influenced by British civilization will doubtless give it new interpretations in different settings, according to temperament, resources and surroundings, and carry on this creativeness in new ways. Nor does it seem likely that the people who originated it all will cease to show, in a new and European context, the enterprise deployed over four centuries.

Thus, not without honour, the last of the European sea-borne Empires has concluded the phase of world history inaugurated by the Portuguese, when at the end of the fifteenth century they outflanked the mighty land Empires of Asia by rounding the Cape, and by the Spaniards, who, following Columbus, discovered and subdued Central and South America. Today the super-powers are continental and civilization, if they do not destroy it, is becoming global.

As the nations move into its next phase, symbolized by man's first view of his own planet, turning in homely colours in the blackness of outer space, the memory of this final European *tour de force* will record one of the greater achievements of world history.

INDEX